D0202595

Sixth Edition

International Accounting and Multinational Enterprises

LEE H. RADEBAUGH
Brigham Young University

SIDNEY J. GRAY
University of Sydney

ERVIN L. BLACK
Brigham Young University

WILEY

JOHN WILEY & SONS, INC.

Publisher	Susan Elbe
Executive Editor	Christopher DeJohn
Acquisitions Editor	Mark Bonadeo
Production Editor	Nicole Repasky
Project Editor	Ed Brislin
Senior Marketing Manager	Amy Yarnevich
Designer	Hope Miller
Senior Media Editor	Allie K. Morris
Editorial Assistant	Alison Stanley
Production Services Management	Hermitage Publishing Services
Cover Photo Credit	© Corbis Images

This book was set in 10/12 pt. ITC New Baskerville x 30 picas by Hermitage Publishing Services and printed and bound by Hamilton Printing. The cover was printed by Lehigh Press.

This book is printed on acid-free paper. ∞

To order books or for customer service please, call 1-800-CALL WILEY (225-5945).

Library of Congress Cataloging in Publication Data:

ISBN-13 978-0-471-65269-4

Printed in the United States of America.

10 9 8 7 6 5 4 3

ABOUT THE AUTHORS

Lee H. Radebaugh, MBA, DBA (Indiana University)

Professor Radebaugh is the KPMG Professor in the School of Accountancy at Brigham Young University and Editor of *Journal of International Accounting Research*. He is also the Associate Director of the MBA program. He previously served as the Associate Dean of the Marriott School at BYU and Director of the School of Accountancy. In addition, he was the Director of the BYU Center for International Business Education and Research (CIBER). He received his MBA and Doctorate from Indiana University. He previously taught at Penn State University from 1972 to 1980. In 1975 he was a visiting professor at Escuela de Administración de Negocios para Graduados (ESAN), a graduate business school in Lima, Peru. In 1985, he was the James Cusator Wards visiting professor at Glasgow University in Scotland.

Lee Radebaugh is the author of *International Business: Environments and Operations* (Pearson Prentice Hall, eleventh edition) with John D. Daniels and Daniel L. Sullivan, *Globalization and Business* (Pearson Prentice Hall), *Global Accounting and Control* (John Wiley & Sons) with Sidney J. Gray and Stephen Salter, and several other books. He has also published several other monographs and articles on international business and international accounting in journals such as the *Journal of Accounting Research*, the *Journal of International Business Studies*, the *Journal of International Financial Management and Accounting*, and the *International Journal of Accounting*.

His primary teaching interests are international business and international accounting. He is an active member of the American Accounting Association, the European Accounting Association, and the Academy of International Business, having served on several committees, and as the President of the International Section of the AAA and the Secretary-Treasurer of the AIB. He is also active with the local business community as former President of the World Trade Association of Utah and member of the District Export Council. In 1998, he was named the "Outstanding International Accounting Educator" of the International Section of the American Accounting Association and "International Person of the Year" by the World Trade Association of Utah.

Sidney J. Gray, BEc (Sydney), Ph.D. (Lancaster), FCCA, CPA, ACIS, MCMI

Professor Gray received his economics degree from the University of Sydney and his Ph.D. in international accounting from the University of Lancaster. He teaches and researches international business strategy, cross-cultural management, and international accounting at the University of Sydney, Australia, where he is a Professor and Head of the School of Business. He was formerly a Professor at the University of New South Wales in Australia, at the University of Warwick in England, and the University of Glasgow in Scotland.

Sid Gray has published in many leading journals around the world including *Journal of Accounting Research, Abacus, Journal of International Business Studies, Journal of International Financial Management and Accounting, Accounting and Business Research, European Accounting Review, International Journal of Accounting*, and the *Journal of Business Finance and Accounting*. He is the author/co-author of more than 20 books and monographs and 150 articles. His books include *Global Accounting & Control* (John Wiley & Sons) with Stephen Salter and Lee H. Radebaugh and *Financial Accounting: A Global Approach* (Houghton Mifflin) with Belverd E. Needles, Jr.

He is active in many academic and professional organizations. He has served as President of the International Association for Accounting Education and Research (IAAER), Chairman of the British Accounting Association, and Secretary General of the European Accounting Association. He has served as a member of the Accounting Standards Committee for the U.K. and Ireland and as a member of the Consultative Group to the International Accounting Standards Committee. In 1994, he received from the American Accounting Association's International Section the award of "Outstanding International Accounting Educator." Most recently, he was President of the Australia–New Zealand International Business Academy.

Ervin L. Black, MBA, Ph.D.

Professor Black is an Associate Professor at Brigham Young University where he specializes in financial and international accounting. Professor Black has authored or coauthored numerous articles in business research journals, including *The Journal of Accounting and Economics, Accounting Horizons, The Journal of Business Finance and Accounting, Venture Capital, Business Process Management Journal* and *The Journal of the American Taxation Association*. Professor Black received his Ph.D. from the University of Washington and holds an MBA and Bachelor of Arts degrees from Brigham Young University. He taught at the University of Washington, University of Wyoming, and the University of Arkansas prior to coming to BYU in 2000. His primary teaching interests are international accounting, accounting research, and financial accounting. He is a member of the American Accounting Association, European Accounting Association, British Accounting Association, and the International Association for Accounting Education and Research. He is also on the Board of Directors for the Foundation for International Law and Management which publishes the *International Law and Management Review*.

PREFACE

The global challenges of doing business in the twenty-first century require account-ants and managers who are more aware of the international financial complexities involved and who have knowledge and understanding relevant to solving problems arising from the ever-increasing pace of international business, finance, and invest-ment. This is especially true in light of the trend toward convergence of account-ing standards for publicly listed companies worldwide.

TARGET AUDIENCE

Our aim in writing this book is to contribute to the development of internationally competent people in accounting and business. The target audience for the book at the senior undergraduate level includes both accounting and business students. At the Master's level those students looking to broaden their horizons. In addition, this book should be helpful to practicing accountants, managers, and consultants who wish to become more involved in the international aspects of accounting.

A STRATEGIC APPROACH

This book presents international accounting within the context of managing multi-national enterprises (MNEs). We focus on the business strategies of MNEs and how accounting applies to these strategies. This unique approach gives students the opportunity to learn about international accounting from a perspective similar to what they will experience in the business world. The book also discusses accounting issues in the context of different countries. We discuss the key factors that influence accounting standards and practices in different countries, and how those factors impact the harmonization of standards worldwide. In particular, we have tried to concentrate on culture and its unique contribution to accounting standards and practices. Our emphasis is on the needs of users of financial and accounting infor-mation across borders with the aim of enhancing their understanding of how to use information and therefore make more informed decisions in an increasingly com-plex and dynamic international business environment.

CONTENTS OF THE BOOK

This book emphasizes the international business context of international account-ing and financial decision-making. In this latest edition of the book we have restruc-

tured the text to provide a better flow of material and also to present it more suc-
cinctly. At the same time, an in-depth and balanced coverage is provided of key
issues relevant to users at both the internal and external levels of international
business activity.

- Chapter 1 examines international accounting issues in the context of
  international business.

- Chapter 2 looks at international patterns of accounting development and
  the impact of culture on accounting.

- Chapters 3 and 4 provide a comparative international analysis of financial
  accounting especially from a cultural perspective. Chapter 3 deals more
  with developed countries, whereas Chapter 4 deals more with developing
  countries.

- Chapter 5 focuses on the use of financial statements across borders by
  managers and investors and the problems of understanding the meaning
  of financial information in different national contexts.

- Chapter 6 examines issues associated with corporate transparency and disclosure in an international context and the pressures for both traditional
  as well as more market-oriented approaches to disclosure.

- Chapter 7 focuses on the participants and factors involved in the global
  convergence of accounting and reporting including the emergence of the
  International Accounting Standards Board as a major player in the development of International Financial Reporting Standards that can be used
  by publicly listed companies worldwide.

- Chapter 8 analyzes the concepts, issues, and practices involved with the
  often controversial areas of international business combinations, goodwill,
  and intangibles.

- Chapter 9 provides an analysis and review of issues and developments
  relating to international segment reporting.

- Chapter 10 deals in some detail with the problems and impact of foreign
  currency transactions and the translation of foreign currency financial
  statements.

- Chapter 11 analyzes the problems of accounting for price changes internationally and provides a comparative analysis of practices around the
  world.

- Chapter 12 deals with corporate governance issues and techniques that
  companies use in the area of accounting and managerial control.

- Chapter 13 examines the area of foreign exchange risk management and
  the role that accountants play in helping to minimize foreign exchange risk.

- Chapter 14 examines some of the special problems of budgeting and performance evaluation in the multinational enterprise with particular reference to the complexities of foreign exchange and transfer pricing.

- Chapter 15 provides an examination of auditing issues relevant to the multinational enterprise, a review of audit standards internationally, and an update on efforts to harmonize auditing internationally.

- Chapter 16 concludes the book with a discussion of the challenges of coping with the complexities of taxation across borders and the need for effective tax planning.

CHAPTER MATERIALS

Each chapter provides objectives and concludes with a summary of the main points of the chapter. A major change in the book is the addition of more discussion questions, exercises, and cases. Each chapter has 15 discussion questions, 15 exercises, and 2 cases. The cases can be found on the book companion website: www.wiley.com/college/radebaugh. This will be a big help to faculty members who like to assign written assignments and encourage class discussion. Throughout the book, reference is made in the text to relevant research, and items of special interest are highlighted either in tables or exhibits.

Another major addition to the text is a Practice Set prepared by Professor Teresa Conover of the University of North Texas. The Practice Set is designed to provide scenarios for business transactions and then give students a chance to provide financial information according to U.S. GAAP and IFRS to compare the impact of different accounting standards on financial reporting. The student portion of the book companion website contains the materials that make up the Practice Set. Each new copy of the textbook contains a registration code that allows a student to access these materials, which are password protected. . The Practice Set is for Global Corp., a new U.S.-based company, which is interested in financial reporting under international accounting standards (IFRS). They have decided to account for their transactions under both U.S. GAAP and IFRS for a one-year period. At the end of the one-year period, they will prepare their financial statements and notes under each of the methods. Students are responsible for journalizing the transactions and preparing any necessary adjusting entries, ledgers, trial balances, financial statements, footnotes, etc.

INSTRUCTORS' MATERIALS

This book is accompanied by an Instructor Manual that includes chapter outlines, a chapter overview, teaching suggestions, lecture notes, and solutions for the discussion questions, exercises, and cases. Also available is a Test Bank containing multiple-choice and true/false questions and PowerPoint Presentations for each chapter. These are all accessible at the book companion web site.

ACKNOWLEDGMENTS

We would like to thank our many colleagues from around the world for their contributions to the international business and accounting literature. Their research has been of great benefit to us and has helped to ensure the relevance and reliability of the subject matter. Many individuals have been helpful in the process of producing the book. We would like to thank the following reviews of the fifth edition for providing valuable feedback. Orapin Duangploy at University of Houston, Samir B. Fahmy at St. John's University, Adnan Abdeen at California State University at Los Angeles, Uwe Rudolf at Luther College, and David Durkee at Weber State University. We would especially like to thank Exequiel Hernandez, Dirk Black, and Julie Hales at Brigham Young University, Teresa Conover at the University of North Texas, and Mark Bonadeo and his team at John Wiley & Sons for their assistance.

LEE H. RADEBAUGH
SIDNEY J. GRAY
ERVIN L. BLACK

CONTENTS

CHAPTER ONE

INTERNATIONAL ACCOUNTING AND INTERNATIONAL BUSINESS

Chapter Objectives

- Identify the key trends in the development of accounting through history
- Highlight the evolution of business to modern times
- Identify the key environmental influences on business and accounting
- Discuss the major factors influencing the development of accounting and information disclosure in the global economy
- Discuss the important accounting dimensions of global business and the major topics that comprise the field of international accounting
- Introduce the chapters in the book

INTRODUCTION

What an exciting time to study international accounting as we enter the new millennium! We are closer than ever to having a uniform set of international accounting standards that firms can use as they list on stock exchanges all over the world. International business activity is increasing dramatically through traditional exporting and importing of goods and services as well as foreign direct investment. Capital markets are opening up and becoming more transparent, and capital flows freely around the world at a quicker pace. Stock markets are linking up with each other just as firms are increasing their global competitiveness, and accounting will be one of the key areas that will help determine how successful cross-border stock market linkages become. Companies are finding that they need to move quickly outside of their home country capital market if they want to be a truly multinational

1

Strategic Decision Point

DaimlerChrysler is one of the world's leading automotive companies, with passenger car brands that include Mercedes-Benz, Chrysler, Jeep®, and Dodge. It was formed in 1998 by the merger of the German company, Daimler-Benz AG and the American company, Chrysler Corporation. DaimlerChrysler has manufacturing, assembly, and sale operations worldwide and a global workforce of 387,000 employees. In addition to sales and manufacturing operations worldwide, DaimlerChrysler has a global shareholder base, issuing shares not only in its headquarters country, Germany, but also the United States, France, Switzerland, and Japan. DaimlerChrysler is affected by global events. As noted in its Q1 2005 Interim Report, "DaimlrCrysler assumes that the global economy will continue its present development in the coming months, thus expanding in line with its long-term growth trend. However, if raw-material prices, particularly for oil, remain at the current high levels for a longer period or rise even further, global economic development is expected to be negatively affected. Rising interest rates could also have a negative effect on consumer spending. For the further course of the year, the growth of worldwide demand for automobiles is likely to be slower than in 2004. Whereas further expansion of truck markets is expected in the NAFTA region, there are indications of decreasing market expansion in Europe. In general, we expect the highly competitive situation across the entire automotive industry to continue, due to further reductions in product lifecycles and ongoing over-capacity." DaimlerChrysler is a good example of a global company that must deal with all of the complexities of different national environments as well as global trends and provide a return to shareholders worldwide.

---

corporation, and the U.S. stock market has emerged as the location for new issues of foreign corporations. A new currency, the euro, was introduced in Europe in 1999, changing forever the notion of foreign exchange risk in Europe and changing the way European companies keep their accounts. And now the euro is even turning out to be a competitor for the U.S. dollar in global currency markets. To embark on our journey into the new millennium of international accounting, we will first trace the international development of accounting, highlight some of the critical factors that determine national differences in accounting systems, provide an initial perspective on these differences and their importance for accountants in the modern world, and outline the focus of the book. In addition, we will examine some of the key elements of international business and how they affect company strategy and the accounting function within that strategy.

THE INTERNATIONAL DEVELOPMENT
OF THE ACCOUNTING DISCIPLINE

Many books have been written on the origin of accounting, but no one has been able to establish when it really began. Clearly, accounting is a function of the business environment in which it operates, and it originated in order to record business transactions. The origin of accounting and its subsequent changes are therefore best studied in the context of the history of commercial transactions. Although the recording of transactions is probably as old as the history of record keeping, we tend to think of the establishment of double-entry accounting, the basis for modern accounting, as the key event. In 1994, the seventeenth annual congress of the European Accounting Association (EAA) was held in Venice to celebrate the 500-year anniversary of the publication of the first printed book on double-entry accounting by Luca Pacioli. Why were the Italians so influential in the development of double-entry accounting, and could it have developed elsewhere?

Early Italian Influence

Record keeping, the foundation of accounting, has been traced back as far as 3600 B.C., and historians know that mathematical concepts were understood in various ancient civilizations from China, India, and Mesopotamia—often referred to as the "Cradle of Civilization"—to some of the ancient native cultures of Central and South America. Business transactions in different areas around the world, including the city-states of central and northern Europe, probably gave rise to the recording of business transactions.

Double-entry accounting was probably developed in the Italian city-states between the thirteenth and fifteenth centuries. The most significant influences on accounting took place in Genoa, Florence, and Venice. There is no defining moment when double-entry accounting was born, but it seems to have evolved independently in different places, responding to the changing nature of business transactions and the need to record them properly. The Genoese system was probably a development of the ancient Roman system. Commercial activity had been flourishing in Genoa for a long time, and Genoa was at the height of its wealth and power during the fourteenth century. The Genoese system assumed the concept of a business entity. Because it recorded items in terms of money, it was the first to imply that dissimilar items could be compared in terms of a common monetary unit. The system also implied some understanding of the distinction between capital and income in that it included both expenses and equity accounts. The oldest double-entry books were the Massari (treasury officials) ledgers of the Commune of Genoa, dating from 1340. Given that they were written in perfect double-entry form, it stands to reason that the concepts must have originated and evolved earlier than that. In fact, the government of the Commune of Genoa decreed in 1327 that government accounts had to be kept in the same way that the banks kept their accounts. It would therefore seem natural that double-entry accounting existed with Genoese banks prior to 1327, even though we have no records of Genoese banks prior to 1408.

Florentine commerce also flourished in the thirteenth and fourteenth centuries, giving rise to double-entry accounting there as well. In 1252, Florence coined the gold florin, which was soon accepted as the standard gold piece all over Europe. A major achievement in Florence was the development of large associations and compagnie (partnerships) that pooled capital, initially within family groups and then from outside the family groups. Given the nature of Florence as an artistic center, it is easier to find manuscripts relating to the development of bookkeeping. The account books of the fourteenth century reflect the partnership contracts of the compagnie, which identified the capital of the separate partners, made provisions for the division of profits and losses, clearly defined the duties of each partner, and provided for the dissolution of the compagnie. Records were often kept in great detail, almost in narrative form. Until the influence of the Venetians, Florentine accounts listed debits above credits rather than on separate pages. Separate columns for transactions were needed to record which monetary value was used.

However, Venice was key in the spread of double-entry accounting. Venice was the key commercial city of the Renaissance because of its commercial empire and advantages as a port. The Venetians may not have developed double-entry accounting before the Genoese and Florentines, but Venice "developed it, perfected it, and made it her own, and it was under the name of the Venetian method that it became known the world over" (Peragallo, 1938).

Luca Pacioli

Luca Pacioli, who was born in San Sepolcro in the Tuscany region of Italy in 1447, was not an accountant but was educated as a mathematician by Franciscans and actually became a Franciscan monk himself. In 1464, he became the tutor of the three sons of a Venetian merchant, then left Venice to study mathematics. After becoming a Franciscan monk, he accepted a teaching position at the University of Perugia, then traveled extensively and taught at the universities of Florence, Rome, Naples, Padua, and Bologna. In 1494, in Venice, he published the first significant work on accounting up to that point, *Summa de Arithmetica, Geometria, Proportioni et Proportionalita,* more commonly known as *Summa de Arithmetica.* His discussion of accounting comprises one of the chapters in the *Summa de Arithmetica.* Given the extreme detail included in the book and the fact that Pacioli was not a merchant or bookkeeper, many historians believe he got his information from somewhere else. In fact, Pacioli did not claim that his ideas were original, just that he was the one who was trying to organize and publish them. His objective was to publish a popular book that everyone could use, following the influence of the Venetian businessmen rather than the bankers. Wherever his ideas originated, the Venetian method became the standard for not only the Italians but also the Dutch, German, and English authors on accounting.

Pacioli introduced three important books of record: the memorandum book, the journal, and the ledger. The memorandum book included all information on a transaction. From the memorandum book, a journal entry was made into the journal. Information was then posted to the ledger, the center of the accounting system. Pacioli felt that all transactions required both a debit and credit in order for the transaction to remain in equilibrium.

Subsequent Developments

The growing literature on accounting represented an attempt to describe good practices rather than challenge underlying assumptions or develop a general theory of accounting. The literature began to change during the 1550s to reflect new commercial and political realities. The rise of nation-states and the need to manage public finances increased the importance of good accounting practice. However, a major change was the decline of Italy as a world commercial power. As commercial traffic shifted from the ports of Venice to the Atlantic shipping routes, Italy slipped in importance, and relatively few new developments took place in accounting. It is true that changing business forms that emphasized large-scale business enterprises caused a change in focus, but accounting authors still clung to the old forms of accounting, and no new theories developed.

The French Revolution in the late 1700s marked the beginning of a great social upheaval that affected governments, finances, laws, and customs. Italy came under the influence of the French and then the Austrians, and their system of double-entry accounting was also influenced. It is interesting to note that Napoleon was surprised at how efficient the Italian system of accounting was. The serious study of accounting and development of accounting theory also began in this period and has continued to the present day. However, the influence of the Arabs, Genoese, Florentines, and Venetians continues to be felt in the double-entry system we use today. Even the British, who acquired their knowledge of double-entry accounting soon after Pacioli's *Summa de Arithmetica* was published, did not begin adopting double-entry accounting quickly until the Industrial Revolution of the period 1760–1830. At that point, the importance of accounting grew substantially.

As the scale of enterprises increased following technological breakthroughs such as mass production, and as fixed assets grew in importance, it became necessary to account for depreciation, the allocation of overhead, and inventory. In addition, the basic form of business organization shifted from proprietorships and partnerships to limited liability and stock companies and ultimately to stock exchange listed corporations. Accounting had to adapt to satisfy these new needs. Increased government regulation of business made new demands on firms, which also generated new accounting systems. Most notable was the increased taxation of business and individuals, which brought with it new tax accounting systems and procedures.

Since the early 1900s, the rapidity of change and the increasing complexity of the world's industrial economies necessitated still more changes in accounting. Mergers, acquisitions, and the growth of multinational corporations fostered new internal and external reporting and control systems. With widespread ownership of modern corporations came new audit and reporting procedures, and new agencies became involved in promulgating accounting standards: namely, stock exchanges, securities regulation commissions, internal revenue agencies, and so on. Finally, with the dramatic increase in foreign investment and world trade and the formation of regional economic groups such as the European Union, problems arose concerning the international activities of business. This phenomenon remains particularly complex, for it involves reconciling the accounting practices of different nations in which each multinational operates, as well as dealing with accounting problems unique to international business.

NATIONAL DIFFERENCES IN ACCOUNTING SYSTEMS

One might infer that these historical developments had a uniform effect on accounting systems throughout the world, yet nothing could be further from the truth. Despite some similarities, there are at least as many accounting systems as there are countries, and no two systems are exactly alike. The underlying reasons for these differences are essentially environmental: accounting systems evolve from and reflect the environments they serve, just as in Genoa, Florence, and Venice in the 1400s. The reality of the world is that environments have not evolved uniformly or simultaneously. Countries today are at stages of economic development ranging from subsistence, barter economies to highly complex industrial societies.

While accounting practices were evolving, there were, for example, differences in the amount of private ownership, the degree of industrialization, the rate of inflation, and the level of economic growth. Given these differences in economic conditions, differences in accounting practices should not be surprising. Just as the accounting needs of a small proprietorship are different from those of a multinational corporation, so are the accounting needs of an underdeveloped, agrarian country different from those of a highly developed industrial country. Economic factors, however, are not the only influences. Educational systems, legal systems, political systems, and sociocultural characteristics also influence the need for accounting and the direction and speed of its development.

At the present time, the most important reason for understanding different national accounting systems lies in the increasing globalization of business. Before examining in greater detail the environmental influences on accounting and the unique accounting problems of multinational enterprises, let's take a brief look at the evolution and significance of international business.

THE EVOLUTION AND SIGNIFICANCE OF INTERNATIONAL BUSINESS

International business can be traced back to several centuries B.C. As far as anyone can tell, the reasons and motives were the same then as they are today: people wanted something they did not have in their own country, and they found someone in another country able to provide them with what they wanted. But trade on a major and planned scale did not really begin until the Greeks started exporting inexpensive, mass-produced goods around the fifth century B.C. By the end of the Greek period, there was sufficient trade to have permitted not only full-time professional traders but even some traders who specialized by area of the world or by commodities.

During the Roman period, traders roamed freely through the empire, and with better transportation, political stability, and few tariffs and trade restrictions, trade flourished. In fact, the Roman Empire established the feasibility and desirability of what is now known as the European Union.

During the Middle Ages, international business flourished in some areas of the world. For example, it flourished in Byzantium (present-day Istanbul) until the Crusades, facilitated by the development of banking and insurance and by the first large-scale international trade fairs. However, international trade did not fare as well in Europe until much later. Wars, plagues, and a generally anticommercial religious doctrine hindered commerce both domestically and internationally. It was not until the twelfth century that commercial activity and trade broke out of their undeveloped state. With their resurgence came laws and regulations regarding commerce and trade. Initially developed by guilds, then by city-states, and then much later by nation-states, international commercial regulations have continued to proliferate to the present day.

The Preindustrial Period

As Europe emerged from the Dark Ages, merchants sought ways to increase international business. By that time, however, the right to trade had become a privilege granted by the state, a phenomenon that has persisted to modern times. The privilege was based on what was to be known as mercantilism, a concept by which each state sought to become more pervasive and powerful militarily, economically, and politically than its rivals. During this period of mercantilism, the state was the driving and controlling force behind domestic and international economic activity.

The sixteenth and seventeenth centuries saw the first major foreign investments, under the rubric of colonialism. Governments invested directly in colonies, or gave individuals the right to do so, with the express purpose of obtaining raw materials first, then products, in a near-monopolistic control of trade. Finally, during this period of mercantilism the center of commercial and financial activity shifted steadily westward, from Byzantium to Italy, to the Netherlands and Belgium, and ultimately to Britain. This dominating influence of Western Europe was to last until the twentieth century.

The Industrialization Period

The Industrial Revolution, which began in the latter half of the eighteenth century, continued to have a major impact on international business throughout the nineteenth and twentieth centuries. The Industrial Revolution and its accompanying technologies gave rise to mass production and standardization of products and required sizable capital investments on an unparalleled scale. The emergence of large-scale, limited-liability companies combined with large-scale infrastructure projects such as railroads, canals, and power-generating systems often necessitated obtaining capital from other countries—a major form of international business that has continued to the present. To exploit scale economies of production fully, the exporting of mass-produced goods became a necessity for many firms located in countries with small domestic markets. Simultaneously, industrialization often required an increase in the importation of raw materials and capital goods in many countries that did not possess them in sufficient quantity or quality. The multinational firm as it is known today emerged in this period, with early overseas expansion by firms such as Singer, Ford, Dunlop, and Lever Brothers.

The industrialization process also brought with it growing trade restrictions as many nations sought to protect their "infant industries." Although there was relatively little U.S. government interference or involvement with international trade or investment during this period, there was growing foreign government involvement, particularly in trade. This prompted many firms to begin replacing exports with direct investments in the more protectionist countries in order to keep their established markets. Despite the continued increase in both trade and investments, a trend was established: foreign investments were becoming much more influential.

The Post–World War II Period

The Great Depression and World War II stunted the growth of international business. The reasons are fairly obvious: drastic reductions in income; the bankruptcy of individuals, companies, and governments; then war, the destruction of property, and an end to the stability of money. Throughout this period, trade protectionism and the regulation of capital flows were on the rise, which, when combined with the other factors just mentioned, slowed the growth of international business activity.

At the end of World War II, there was a tremendous pent-up demand for products and services. With some semblance of order restored to international politics and the international monetary system, both trade and investment increased sharply.

The remnants of 1930s and early 1940s protectionism conspired to emphasize investment. The formation of the European Economic Community in the late 1950s (now the European Union), with its strong economy and the elimination of its internal trade restrictions, resulted in significant growth of U.S. manufacturing investment abroad. During the 1970s and 1980s, this trend had slowed considerably, but it was followed by an equally significant increase of foreign investment in the United States. However, the move to a more unified European Union resulted in significant interest in Europe once again.

The Multinational Era

The proliferation of multinational enterprises and their activities has constituted perhaps the most significant development in international business. Their wealth and influence are significant, yet the impressive role that they now play is far from the whole story of the growth in international business. For virtually all of the world's economies, international trade and foreign investment have increased in importance as a percentage of total economic activity.

Reasons for International Involvement

International business includes all business transactions that involve two or more countries. These transactions can be conducted exclusively in the private sector, or they can also involve the public sector. Companies get involved in international business for a variety of reasons. The major reason is to expand sales, perhaps because a firm has excess capacity and does not have additional sales opportunities at home. Thus, it needs to sell products abroad to utilize its capacity more efficiently. International sales can also be profitable.

A second reason to get involved in international business is to gain access to raw materials or other factors of production. Mining and agricultural companies operate in countries where natural resources or climate allow them to pursue their activities. On the other hand, manufacturing companies have found many developing countries in Eastern Europe, Asia, and Latin America to be ideal for doing business because of cheap labor and overhead-type expenses. Thus, they have expanded abroad to gain production efficiencies.

A third incentive for international activity is to gain access to knowledge. Learning about new technology quickly can make a big difference in a company's ability to compete in global markets. New technology is being developed worldwide, so companies cannot rely on their domestic market to keep abreast of new developments.

FORMS OF INTERNATIONAL INVOLVEMENT

When companies, and especially the market seekers, first begin to expand beyond domestic markets, they usually get involved in exports and imports. Merchandise exports are goods sent out of a country, and merchandise imports are goods brought into a country. Exports and imports can also involve services as well as goods. Service exports refer to the receipt of earnings from the performance of services abroad. For example, if KPMG sent auditors to different countries to perform an audit and received a fee for those services, that work would be considered a service export. The country where the work was performed would experience a service import, which would result in an outflow of cash to the exporting country. Other examples of services are travel, tourism, and transportation.

In addition to exporting and importing, companies can expand abroad through one of several types of strategic alliances. A strategic alliance is used to describe a wide variety of collaborations, which are of strategic importance to one or more of the parties involved. Strategic alliances include licensing agreements, franchising, management contracts, custom contracts, and shared ownership of foreign companies. The choice of the type of strategic alliance depends on legal factors, cost, experience, competition, risk, control, and product complexity.

Two similar strategic alliances involve a licensing agreement and a franchise agreement. A licensing agreement exists when one company grants rights to intangible property to another company for a specified period of time in return for a royalty. The intangible property might involve a production process, formula, design, pattern, patent, or invention. Companies enter into licensing agreements to earn a return on their intellectual property without having to undertake the risk of expanding abroad using their own capital. A franchise, such as those of Holiday Inn or McDonald's, involves the use of a trademark that is an essential asset but also provision of assistance on a continual basis in running the business. Holiday Inn, for example, provides a reservation service for franchisees and continual audits on quality, and so on. Sometimes companies will cooperate in the development of new technology or in producing goods and services.

Companies can also invest abroad. A direct investment occurs when a company assumes some degree of control over a foreign corporation in order to influence management decisions. The decision can occur in the form of an acquisition of existing stock in a local firm or in the establishment of a "greenfield investment," which is the establishment of a new firm in a foreign location. If the investor owns 100 percent of the stock in the local firm, that firm becomes a wholly owned subsidiary. If two or more firms are involved in establishing a venture, the operation is known as a joint venture, another form of strategic alliance. Joint ventures often occur because the investor lacks financial or managerial expertise or because the investor needs to rely on the local knowledge of the partner in the venture.

Multinational Enterprises

A variety of terms describe companies involved in international business. The most frequently used term is multinational enterprise (MNE), which refers to companies that have a worldwide view of production, the sourcing of raw materials and components, and final markets. There is no consensus as to how much of a company's sales, assets, earnings, and employees must be abroad for the firm to be considered an MNE, but anything less than 10 percent of these indicators would probably disqualify a company from the elite group of MNEs. More than 10 percent implies that the companies are operating in at least two countries, and most MNEs have significant geographical spread. The lack of a global vision is another indicator that a company is not yet an MNE. Another indicator of multinational involvement is the degree of international experience of key executives. In Chapter 12, we will discuss how MNEs adopt different strategies to operate internationally, including transnational, global, and multidomestic strategies. However, we will continue to use the term *MNE* to refer to companies that are operating in many different countries, regardless of the specific strategic approach they use to sell products and source production.

Large MNEs

It is difficult to identify precisely the largest MNEs in the world because there are different definitions of size. The two most commonly used measures for size are market value and sales. In addition, other measures, such as profits and return on shareholders' equity, are often used to compare companies worldwide. Exhibit 1.1 identifies the top 50 companies in the world by market value and by sales. Although U.S. companies dominate the list, there are companies from other countries in the world. In the *Business Week* Global 1000 companies, 423 are from the United States. Japan has the second largest number of companies with 137, and Britain is third with 73 companies. There are companies from seven developing countries, primarily from Asia and Latin America, with India having the largest number of companies at 8, closely followed by China and Mexico with 6 companies each. It is interesting to note that Wal-Mart de Mexico is the third largest company in Mexico, while its parent, Wal-Mart Stores of the United States is the fifth largest company in the world in market value and #1 in sales. Gazprom of Russia is the 47th largest company in the world in market value, the highest-ranking company from a developing country. Most of the companies in the top 50 would also qualify as MNEs because of the importance of global markets to sales. It is interesting to note that the firms on the list are from a variety of industries. Even though the large MNEs are the ones most noticed and discussed, a company does not have to be large to be engaged in international business. The probability that a firm will engage in international transactions increases with firm size and as the firm begins to saturate the domestic environment. However, even small companies can export or import, manufacture products abroad or source production to independent manufacturers abroad, or get involved in licensing agreements. This is especially true of high-tech start-up companies that often get involved in international business immediately. In addition, some companies such as Nike design products in the domestic market but

Exhibit 1.1   Top 50 Companies by Market Value and Sales

| \multicolumn{5}{Top 50 Companies by Market Value in 2004} |

<table>
<tr><td colspan="5" align="center">Top 50 Companies by Market Value in 2004</td></tr>
<tr><td colspan="2" align="center">Rank</td><td rowspan="2"></td><td rowspan="2"></td><td align="center">Market Value</td></tr>
<tr><td>2004</td><td>2003</td><td align="center">Name</td><td>Country</td><td align="center">($ Billions)</td></tr>
</table>

2004	2003	Name	Country	Market Value ($ Billions)
1	1	General Electric	U.S.	328.11
2	2	Microsoft	U.S.	284.43
3	3	Exxon Mobil	U.S.	283.61
4	4	Pfizer	U.S.	269.66
5	5	Wal-Mart Stores	U.S.	241.19
6	6	Citigroup	U.S.	239.43
7	9	BP	Britain	193.05
8	10	American International Group	U.S.	191.18
9	13	Intel	U.S.	184.66
10	8	Royal Dutch Petroleum	Netherlands	174.83
11	21	Bank of America	U.S.	169.84
12	7	Johnson & Johnson	U.S.	165.32
13	14	HSBC Holdings	Britain	163.09
14	12	Vodafone Group	Britain	159.15
15	18	Cisco Systems	U.S.	152.23
16	11	International Business Machines	U.S.	150.55
17	17	Procter & Gamble	U.S.	139.35
18	22	Berkshire Hathaway	U.S.	136.86
19	26	Toyota Motor	Japan	130.65
20	20	Coca-Cola	U.S.	125.56
21	19	Novartis	Switzerland	125.51
22	16	GlaxoSmithKline	Britain	124.05
23	24	Total	France	122.94
24	15	Merck	U.S.	105.21
25	31	Nestle	Switzerland	104.87
26	32	Wells Fargo	U.S.	99.85
27	28	Altria Group	U.S.	98.20
28	36	ChevronTexaco	U.S.	96.70
29	40	Roche Holding	Switzerland	95.93
30	25	Verizon Communications	U.S.	95.77
31	38	Royal Bank of ScotlandGroup	Britain	94.37
32	23	NTT DoCoMo	Japan	92.17
33	35	Pepsico	U.S.	91.28
34	33	Dell	U.S.	90.08
35	46	UBS	Switzerland	84.79
36	48	Eli Lilly	U.S.	83.21
37	50	ENI	Italy	82.07
38	37	Home Depot	U.S.	81.73
39	41	United Parcel Service	U.S.	80.69
40	60	Nippon Telegraph & Telephone	Japan	79.02
41	29	SBC Communications	U.S.	78.41
42	42	AstraZeneca	Britain	78.36
43	44	Time Warner	U.S.	77.64

(continues)

Exhibit 1.1   (*continued*)

Top 50 Companies by Market Value in 2004

Rank 2004	Rank 2003	Name	Country	Market Value ($ Billions)
44	49	J.P. Morgan Chase	U.S.	75.25
45	58	Telefonica	Spain	72.08
46	NR	Samsung Electronics	Korea	71.07
47	NR	Gazprom	Russia	70.78
48	51	Deutsche Telekom	Germany	70.53
49	30	Amgem	U.S.	70.02
50	27	Nokia	Finland	66.95

Source: *Business Week* Global 1000

Top 10 Companies by Sales in 2004

Rank 2004	Rank 2003	Name	Country	Sales ($ Billions)
1	1	Wal-Mart Stores	U.S.	263.00
2	5	BP	Britain	232.57
3	3	Exxon Mobil	U.S.	222.88
4	4	Royal/Dutch Shell Group	Britain/Neth.	201.73
5	2	General Motors	U.S.	195.32
6	6	Ford Motor	U.S.	164.51
7	7	DaimlerChrysler	Germany	156.60
8	8	Toyota Motor	Japan	153.11
9	9	General Electric	U.S.	134.18
10	14	Total	France	118.44
11	12	Allianz	Germany	114.95
12	15	ChevronTexaco	U.S.	112.94
13	31	Axa	France	111.91
14	36	ConocoPhillips	U.S.	99.47
15	20	Volkswagen	Germany	98.94
16	16	Nippon Telegraph & Telephone	Japan	98.23
17	17	ING Group	Netherlands	95.89
18	13	Citigroup	U.S.	94.71
19	19	International Business Machines	U.S.	89.13
20	25	American International Group	U.S.	81.30
21	21	Siemens	Germany	80.50
22	29	Carrefour	France	79.77
23	26	Hitachi	Japan	76.42
24	40	Hewlett-Packard	U.S.	73.06
25	28	Honda Motor	Japan	72.26
26	39	McKesson	U.S.	69.51
27	27	U.S. Postal Service	U.S.	68.53
28	24	Verizon Communications	U.S.	67.75
29	44	Assicurazioni Generali	Italy	66.75
30	32	Sony	Japan	66.37
31	34	Matsushita Electric Industrial	Japan	66.22

Top 10 Companies by Sales in 2004

Rank		Name	Country	Sales ($ Billions)
2004	2003			
32	41	Nissan Motor	Japan	65.77
33	38	Nestle	Switzerland	65.41
34	37	Home Depot	U.S.	64.82
35	78	Berkshire Hathaway	U.S.	63.86
36	33	Nippon Life Insurance	Japan	63.84
37	35	Royal Ahold	Netherlands	63.46
38	55	Deutsche Telekom	Germany	63.20
39	52	Peugeot	France	61.38
40	30	Altria Group	U.S.	60.70
41	58	Metro	Germany	60.66
42	57	Aviva	Britain	59.72
43	63	Eni	Italy	59.30
44	59	Munich RE Group	Germany	59.08
45	48	Credit Suisse	Switzerland	58.96
46	NR	State Grid	China	58.35
47	89	HSBC Holdings	Britain	57.61
48	54	BNP Paribas	France	57.27
49	60	Vodafone	Britain	56.84
50	53	Cardinal Health	U.S.	56.83

Source: Fortune Global 500

manufacture all of their products offshore through independent manufacturers—in countries outside their home country.

The Decision to Become Global

The decision to become global depends on how effectively management assesses two different but interactive dimensions: the external environment and the internal capabilities of the firm.

Environmental Constraints   Environmental constraints strongly influence the elements of the management process, which in turn affect management and managerial effectiveness, which determines firm efficiency (Farmer and Richman, 1965). Figure 1.1 identifies the major international and local constraints that affect the MNE. The environmental constraints are grouped into four categories: educational, sociological (or sociocultural), political and legal, and economic. The educational characteristics include the level of literacy, the availability of specialized and higher education, the attitude toward education, and the match of education with skill requirements in the economy. Sociocultural characteristics include the attitude toward managers and authority, interorganizational cooperation, attitude toward achievement and work, class structure and individual mobility, and attitudes toward wealth, rationality, risk taking, and change.

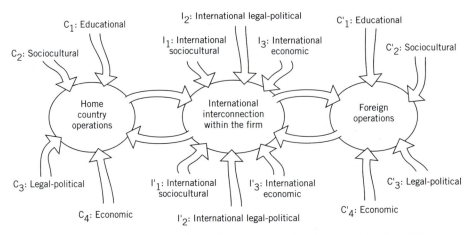

Figure 1.1   International and Local Constraints Affecting a Multinational Firm

Among the major political and legal characteristics are the relevant legal rules of the game and flexibility in their application, defense and foreign policy, political stability, and political organization. Key economic characteristics are the general economic framework, fiscal and monetary policy, economic stability, capital markets, factor endowments, and market size.

These constraints are labeled C1 (educational), C2 (sociocultural), C3 (legal-political), and C4 (economic). The basic idea behind Figure 1.1 is that management operating in the home country is influenced in its operating decisions by the environmental constraints in that country. Any company, domestic or foreign, needs to be aware of those constraints. When operations are set up in a foreign country, the constraints change. There are economic constraints in both the home and foreign country, but those constraints may be different.

As Figure 1.1 shows, there is also a list of international environmental constraints, and each country has its own unique set. Firms that cross national boundaries must adjust to the new set of environmental constraints in the host country. However, the mere crossing of boundaries introduces a different set of international environmental constraints. The sociological constraints (I1) include national ideology, the attitude toward foreigners, and the nature and extent of nationalism. The attitude toward investments by U.S. MNEs, for example, may be very different in the United Kingdom than it is in Iran. Important legal-political constraints (I2) are relevant legal rules for foreign business—such as import-export restrictions, foreign investment restrictions, profit remission restrictions, and exchange control restrictions. Economic constraints (I3) include the general balance-of-payments position, international trade patterns, and membership and obligations in international financial organizations.

Environmental constraints can rarely be changed by the MNE, so management has to decide whether or not those constraints would permit successful foreign investment. Sometimes management becomes overwhelmed with the differences and takes a polycentric attitude, which implies that all operating policies and procedures must be adjusted to the local environment. This is especially true of

MNEs from the Western Hemisphere investing in Asia. In other cases, management takes an ethnocentric attitude, which means that everything the MNE does in the home country can be transferred to the foreign country, in spite of the environmental differences. Although the MNE can act as an agent of change in many circumstances, the ethnocentric attitude is usually a little extreme.

An important dimension of the environmental constraints is that some countries might have country-specific advantages, also known as location-specific advantages, that might strongly influence foreign investment. For example, the existence of a key natural resource; the availability of a plentiful, cheap labor supply; or the presence of a large market are country-specific advantages and are reasons why an MNE might want to invest in a particular location. These country-specific advantages would exist as incentives, rather than barriers, to investment.

Firm-Specific Advantages   The firm-specific advantages, also called ownership-specific advantages, relate primarily to the intangible assets that the firm possesses. In many cases, MNEs are basically in oligopolistic industries. However, smaller firms may have a firm-specific advantage because of a market niche or unique product capability. Typically, these firm-specific advantages are not easily duplicated by competitors, except in the long run or at very high costs. Thus, "The core skill of the MNE can be some element of its management structure, marketing techniques, or overall strategic planning that leads to a firm-specific advantage. These firm-specific advantages are modeled as endogenous to the MNEs, since their internal markets permit the MNEs to control them" (Rugman, Lecraw, and Booth, 1985).

A firm with a set of firm-specific advantages has a variety of options available for their productive use. As we mentioned earlier, the firm could exploit this advantage through exports. However, barriers to exports then lead the firm to explore other options. Selling the firm-specific advantage to another firm is a possibility, but the gains from the sale would not be as high as they would if the firm were to use the firm-specific advantage internally. A firm that decides to use the firm-specific advantages rather than sell them to other firms internalizes the firm-specific advantages.

ENVIRONMENTAL INFLUENCES ON ACCOUNTING

Now that we have examined the origins of accounting and international business, let's focus more specifically on factors in the domestic and international environment that influence accounting. To a large extent, corporate accounting and information disclosure practices are influenced by a variety of economic, social, and political factors. A model of the environmental influences is presented in Figure 1.2. These include the nature of enterprise ownership, the business activities of the enterprise, sources of finance and the stage of development of capital markets, the nature of the taxation system, the existence and significance of the accounting profession, the state of accounting education and research, the nature of the political system, the social climate, the stage of economic growth and development, the rate of inflation, the nature of the legal system, and the nature of accounting regulation. The nature of accounting systems at the country level will vary according to the relative influence of these environmental factors; such systems will, in turn, tend to reinforce established patterns of behavior.

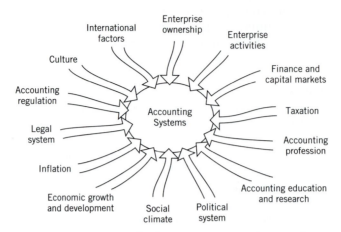

Figure 1.2 Environmental Influences on Accounting Development

With respect to **enterprise ownership,** the need for public accountability and disclosure will be greater where there is a broad ownership of shares compared to family ownership. Where there is state ownership, the influence of centralized control on accounting systems will tend to override the serving of microeconomic objectives. The activities of enterprises will also influence the nature of the accounting system depending on whether the business is agricultural, extractive, or manufacturing; whether it is diversified; whether it is multinational; and whether it is a large group of companies or a small business.

The **sources of finance** are another important influence. Clearly, there will be more pressure for public accountability and information disclosure when finance is raised from external shareholders via stock exchanges rather than banks or family sources, where information will be available more directly.

Taxation is a very important factor in situations where accounting systems are strongly influenced by state objectives; that is, in countries like France and Germany, public accounting reports are used as a basis for determining tax liabilities. In the United States and the United Kingdom, on the other hand, the published accounts are adjusted for tax purposes and submitted separately from the reports to shareholders.

Where there is a more developed **accounting profession** there are likely to be more developed, judgmentally based public accounting systems rather than more centralized and uniform systems. Furthermore, the development of professional accounting will depend on the existence of a sound infrastructure of **accounting education and research,** which is often lacking in developing countries.

The **political system** is obviously a very important influence on accounting in that the nature of the accounting system will reflect political philosophies and objectives (e.g., central planning versus private enterprise). The **social climate,** that is, attitudes toward informing and consulting employees and toward environmental concerns, will also be influential. In Europe, for example, there is a much more positive approach to the disclosure of information relating to such matters than in the United States.

The nature and extent of **economic growth and development** will also be influential insofar as a change from an agricultural to a manufacturing economy will pose new accounting problems, such as the depreciation of machinery, leasing, and so on. In many countries, services are now becoming more important, and thus problems related to how to account for intangible assets such as brand names, goodwill, and human resources have become significant. **Inflation** is often associated with economic growth and is a major influence on accounting where hyperinflation has been rife (e.g., in South America) to the extent that alternative systems to the traditional historical cost approach are often used.

The **legal system** is also important in determining the extent to which company law governs the **regulation of accounting.** In countries such as France and Germany, with a tradition of codified Roman law (or civil codes)—versus common law as in the United Kingdom and the United States—accounting regulations tend to be detailed and comprehensive. Furthermore, the accounting profession tends to have much less influence in setting accounting standards in such countries compared to countries such as the United Kingdom and the United States, where company law is supplemented by professional regulation.

In addition, the influence of **culture** (i.e., societal or national values) on accounting traditions and practices needs to be taken into account. **International factors** are also bringing about changes in the environment that are creating harmonization in international accounting in contrast to the constraining influences operating at national levels. One important international factor is colonial influence. Countries that are former colonies of the United Kingdom tend to use the British approach to accounting, whereas former French colonies tend to use the French system. In addition, membership in regional trade blocs, such as the European Union, often results in a convergence of accounting standards for countries within the bloc. Finally, the International Accounting Standards Board, an international organization dedicated to the convergence of accounting standards worldwide, is working hard to bridge the differences in accounting standards worldwide so that investors can make decisions based on common accounting standards and practices worldwide.

Naturally, the influence of these factors is dynamic and will vary both between and within countries over time. Moreover, an evolutionary process of some complexity appears to be at work that is reflected in a growing number of international and regional influences. These include the activities of MNEs and intergovernmental organizations such as the United Nations (UN), the Organization of Economic Cooperation and Development (OECD), and the European Union. In the European context, the European Union is an especially significant influence in that any agreement on the harmonization of accounting and information disclosure eventually becomes legally enforceable through a process of implementation in the national laws of the member countries.

Although there are many differences in national environments, with correspondingly varying effects on accounting systems, there are also many similarities. Attempts to classify countries and identify patterns or groupings are still very much in the early stages. However, such efforts appear to be a useful way to gain a better understanding of the key factors influencing the development of accounting systems and thus help us predict likely changes and their impact.

Accounting systems in socialist economies tend to be quite different from those in developed market economies such as the United States, Japan, and the EU countries. In the former socialist economies of Russia and Eastern Europe, for example, accounting is making a transition to a market approach. As far as public accounting and reporting in the market economies are concerned, however, a number of distinct models of accounting appear to be identifiable, including, at the very least, the British-American and continental European traditions. But given the factors of change at work, making accurate assessments or predictions about the future evolution of accounting is difficult. Because of the activities of many national and international organizations and the changing nature of business and especially multinational operations, accounting today is in a state of flux. It may well be that new models or patterns of accounting and reporting are being formed. The British and continental European traditions, for example, are now being coordinated and to some extent fused through EU efforts to harmonize accounting.

We will now discuss in greater detail some of the factors that have greatest influence on the development of accounting and information disclosure by corporations.

MAJOR DEVELOPMENT FACTORS

Corporations as Legal Entities

The emergence of corporations, the separation of ownership and control, and the development of securities markets have been particularly important for accountability and disclosure. There is little doubt that a highly influential factor in the United States, the United Kingdom, and other market economies was the recognition of corporations as legal entities with the public ownership of shares and the legal right of limited liability.

The characteristics of these early corporations necessitated disclosure to protect two groups in particular. First, as a consequence of limited liability, the resources available to creditors if the corporation were liquidated were limited to those of the corporation itself. Given that the liability of the shareholders was limited to their investment, disclosure was seen as a necessary means of regulation. Information disclosure, or "transparency," would help creditors determine the extent to which they were prepared to commit resources to the corporation as well as the use of resources they had already committed.

The second major reason for the close relationship between limited liability and disclosure was the protection of shareholders. The emerging entrepreneurs often came from backgrounds that did not give them easy access to the capital necessary to launch and expand individual projects. The introduction of limited liability removed a major disability. Those who owned capital often were unwilling to become involved in what frequently were risky projects because they stood to lose not only their investment but the rest of their personal wealth as well. Limited liability restricted the potential loss to the investment in the corporation. Since many of these investors were not directly involved in the running of the business, it was considered essential for their protection that they should have access to information on a regular basis.

Accountability to those with a direct financial relationship with corporations has been strongly influenced by two other developments—the growth of professional management and the emergence of securities markets.

Professional Management

The separation of ownership and control of corporations appears to have resulted from the emergence of professional management composed of individuals whose positions of power within corporations stemmed from their possession of administrative and/or technical skills rather than ownership of the corporation's capital. The growth in size and the increasing complexity of business are the basis for the growth in the importance of management. At the same time, in many countries (e.g., Italy, Greece, Switzerland) most businesses are still family owned and financed, and, even where they are listed, control is retained by family holdings.

Whether, and to what extent, the separation of ownership from management and the division of the corporation into two essentially distinct groups result in behavior different from that of a corporation owned and controlled by the same persons is a matter of considerable controversy. Concern over the possibility of a conflict of interest when owners and management were different people and the bad experience of individual cases were further reasons for maintaining and expanding accounting and information disclosure. Owners could now be reassured that management was not behaving in a manner detrimental to the owners' interests.

Securities Markets

Corresponding to the growth in the number, size, and complexity of corporations was the demand for finance in the form of shares, or what is termed *equity investment,* as well as loans. This gave rise to the development of capital markets where the raising of finance could be facilitated. A major factor influencing accounting was the emergence of stock exchanges or securities markets, which have their origins in the desire of shareholders to trade their investments without liquidating the company, and the need for a mechanism to raise new finance in an efficient manner. The former reason, the exchangeability of shares, occupies the major portion of the market's time and energy, especially in countries such as the United States, the United Kingdom, and Japan. The relative market capitalization of the world's major developed securities markets is shown in Figure 1.3, from which it can be seen that the United States is dominant with a 43 percent share followed by Japan at 7 percent, to the United Kingdom at 20 percent, and France at 4 percent. The top five exchanges are the New York Stock Exchange, the London Stock Exchange, NASDAQ, the Tokyo Stock Exchange, and the Paris Stock Exchange.

There are also a growing number of securities markets that have been termed "emerging" markets (e.g., in China, Eastern Europe, Latin America, and the developing countries of Africa). Indeed, securities markets are seen to be fundamental elements of the transition to a market economy, which necessarily involves the privatization of state-owned enterprises and the need to attract foreign investment.

The growth of securities markets necessitated the expansion of information availability to a wider audience: in particular, potential investors interested in buying and selling shares. As most private shareholders were not capable of comprehensively analyzing the financial disclosures of corporations, they tended to rely on

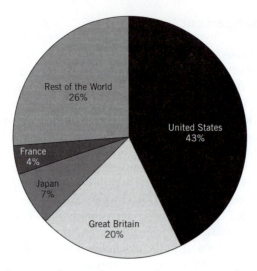

Figure 1.3   Market Capitalization by National Securities Market (Top 4 Countries)

specialist advisers and financial analysts. These analysts now act as interpreters of corporate reports for many investors, current and potential. In this way the information needs of investors, and financial analysts in particular, have acted as a constant pressure on corporations to increase both the quality and the quantity of their disclosures. Furthermore, it has often been in the interests of corporations and their managers, who are concerned to raise capital at favorable rates and to maximize the value of their corporation, to respond to such pressures. Thus, the emergence of securities markets has served to both deepen and broaden disclosure.

The importance of the information used by potential investors and the recommendations of financial analysts has meant that the financial disclosures of public corporations whose shares are traded have become publicly accessible. Corporate reports are available to groups other than investors and creditors not because of any pressure directly exerted by these groups but because of the necessity of available corporate information for unidentifiable potential investors. Indeed, many companies issue their reports on the Internet so that information is instantaneously available.

The predominant influence of securities markets and their regulatory bodies in determining the quality and quantity of publicly available information in corporate reports is reflected in the strong correlation between well-developed markets and the degree of financial disclosure in corporate reports. Countries with active and well-developed markets (e.g., the United States and United Kingdom) generally have a greater degree of public financial disclosure than those with relatively less developed markets.

Why is it that securities markets and the interests of shareholders/investors have apparently been the predominant force behind the emergence of public corporate disclosure? We have already argued that the existence of an active market necessitates the publication of financial information for share-trading decisions by shareholders and potential investors. What distinguishes shareholders from other finance providers is that most shareholders are "outsiders." Despite being nominal owners of the corporation, they have perhaps the least access to private information and arguably the least control unless they are institutional investors with significant shareholdings. The bargaining power of other finance providers (e.g., bankers) is such that these participants do not have to rely on published reports exclusively, if at all. In France and Germany, for example, the public ownership of shares in corporations is much less widespread than in the United States and the United Kingdom. In France, the government has played a major role in the supply of finance to corporations. In Germany, the banks are a significant source of loan finance and are often major equity investors in their own right.

These "other" finance providers generally have, as a result of their power, the ability to obtain considerably more detailed and up-to-date information than "outsiders." Therefore, disclosure to finance providers can be seen as a spectrum: at one end, that of least disclosure, are shareholders and investors (with the exception of those who are directly involved with the company). Toward the other end, information disclosure is less restricted and varies in its nature depending on the purpose for which it is required and the power of the finance provider.

The myth that shareholders control public corporations still persists. Although this may be the case for small private corporations where the number of investors is limited, it does not apply, in the normal course of events, to large public corporations. Private investors in public corporations, where there is usually a widespread dispersion of share ownership, tend to exert little direct influence on the running of a corporation. These shareholders are usually passive, exercising their "power" on the advice and initiative of management (i.e., the board of directors).

The possibility of adverse changes in share prices may exert some indirect discipline on management, on account of their effect on financing potential and the possibility of takeover. But this is unlikely to be significant in countries where there are few shareholders and where securities markets are of relatively less importance as sources of finance (e.g., in many continental European countries).

Taking the place of the relative lack of influence of shareholders in many countries has been the influence of governments, as in France and Sweden, in the development and use of accounting systems that facilitate the provision of information for national economic planning and control. In France, for example, a uniform national accounting system was developed over the years as a basis for macroeconomic planning and corporate taxation. For many governments, including France, Germany, Italy, and Japan, the collection of taxes is closely linked to information disclosed by companies in their published accounts. Hence, the tax rules have had a major influence on the accounting methods used. This is an entirely different orientation from the United States and the United Kingdom, where professional accountants have played a preeminent role in the development of accounting systems and forms of corporate reporting directed primarily to shareholders.

Trends in Securities Markets

There has been a strong move among securities markets to attract companies from abroad to list on their exchanges. In 2004, for example, the trading volume of non-U.S. firms listed on the New York Stock Exchange was 10.5 percent of the Exchange's total trading volume. Although that is a relatively small percentage, that trading volume on its own would make trading in non-U.S. listed companies the second largest market in the world (http://www.nyse.com/international/ 1088623922129.html). However, the new Sarbanes–Oxley law on corporate governance and internal controls must be applied to foreign listers on any U.S. exchange, and the law is proving to be a barrier to attracting new business and even holding on to existing business.

Another trend in securities trading in Europe has to do with the consolidation of European stock exchanges. Prior to the 1999 introduction of the euro, the common currency used in Europe, there were 32 different stock exchanges in Europe. Three stock exchanges dominate trading in Europe—the Frankfurt Stock Exchange, the London Stock Exchange, and Euronext NV, which includes the French, Dutch, Belgian, and Portuguese stock and futures markets and the London International Financial Futures & Options Exchange, known as Liffe (http://www.euronext.com/home/0,3766,1732,00.html). Consolidation of other exchanges has taken place as well, such as the creation of Eurex, the joining together of the German and Swiss futures and options exchanges, which created the world's biggest derivatives exchange. The Finnish and Swedish exchanges also combined into one exchange called OMX AB. The move to consolidate derives from the increase in competition to offer the lowest fees for listing and trading securities (Ascarelli and McKay, 2005).

Markets in developing countries are growing as well. One reason is the overall growth in business and the desire of companies to access capital markets instead of relying on banks and family wealth. Another reason is the privatization of national companies as countries try to reduce budget deficits and get their economies under control. Also lurking on the horizon is China, which is opening up its borders to foreign direct investments and is increasingly changing its business model to that of a market economy. Even though the overall market capitalization of the developing countries is relatively small compared to that of the industrial countries, it is clearly increasing.

A Wider Audience

Accountability and information disclosure by corporations has developed historically in response to those with direct financial investment. In recent years, however, there has been an increasing acknowledgment that since finance providers, such as shareholders, bankers, lenders, and creditors, are not the only group affected by the actions of a corporation, there is an obligation to report to a wider audience, which includes employees, trade unions, consumers, government agencies, and the general public. There are a variety of reasons for this widespread belief that companies should explicitly disclose information to groups other than finance providers. One of the most significant reasons is the development and growth of the influence of trade unions and employees in most developed countries. They have been instrumental in voicing the view that those who are significantly affected by decisions made by institutions in general must be given the opportunity to influence those decisions. Furthermore, there is growing public concern about the impact of corporations on externalities (e.g., pollution of the environment and the influence of large corporations on national economic and social policies).

These developments, among others, have expanded the concept of "account-ability" and the desire of various groups in society to monitor and influence the behavior of business corporations. Wider corporate accountability thus has become an issue of major interest in recent years. To what extent has it affected corporate reports? The development of accounting by corporations has been constrained by restrictions on both the supply and demand sides.

On the supply side, explicit acknowledgment of the "rights" of nonfinance providers, such as trade unions, to information may, for some corporations, mean that they would be committed to pursue goals other than those they have tradi-tionally followed. From a managerial perspective, this could endanger the growth or survival of the corporation. The extent to which corporations' behavior has been influenced in the goals of nonfinance providers is another matter. But many cor-porations, regardless of what they actually do, have been reluctant to formally acknowledge the influence of other "stakeholders."

Corporate reports may be used as a source of information helpful for making decisions and reporting on management's stewardship to finance providers. Increasing information disclosure to nonfinance providers may be seen as increas-ing the power of the recipients to influence the behavior of the corporation as well as providing material for criticism of the corporation's performance.

A further constraint is that many of the expectations of nonfinance providers are not clearly defined, and the techniques to measure them do not exist. Although the information requests of finance providers relate to the periodic financial resources and position of a corporation and the results of its operations, many of the information requirements of nonfinance providers appear to relate to a corpo-ration's social as well as economic performance. Not only are measurement tech-niques often unavailable or underdeveloped but often there is not even general agreement on the broad elements of accountability involved.

On the demand side, information already made available to the public may satisfy the demands of the nonfinance providers, making additional information unnecessary. The disclosure of additional information may not be that helpful.

The ability of nonfinance providers to influence corporate behavior varies considerably. Those with limited or no influence can exert little direct pressure for increased disclosure, whereas those with some power may be able to bypass the pub-lished corporate report and obtain information directly, and in greater detail, in special reports. In many European countries, especially Germany and France, trade unions or employee representatives have, through various forms of "codetermina-tion" or collective bargaining, obtained access to information. In Germany, for example, this right to disclosure is established in law, with works councils given access to a wide range of financial and nonfinancial information. The philosophy behind this is that such access will promote mutual trust between employers and employees. The availability of information for bargaining with corporations can be double-edged, however, in the sense that the information may not substantiate opinions previously held and could therefore reduce rather than enhance the influence of the user group concerned.

An acknowledgment of a right of access to information implies certain politi-cal values—essentially those of liberal democracies, like those established in West-ern Europe. In countries where democracy is not as well established (e.g., in some African countries), the conditions necessary for increased accountability and dis-closure are considerably less well developed.

An Evolutionary Process

Public accounting and disclosure in corporate reports has been a spinoff from the evolution, over a considerable period of time, of accountability and disclosure to finance providers. The major impetus has been provided by the growth of active and well-developed securities markets. In many countries, such markets are not well developed, and while their limited maturity in this respect may not ultimately prevent wider disclosure, it would necessitate measures significantly different from those experienced in many of the developed countries.

ACCOUNTABILITY AND MULTINATIONAL ENTERPRISES

We have considered the evolution of information disclosure by enterprises, but we have not yet distinguished between those whose ownership and operations remain essentially in one country (i.e., domestic enterprises) and those that operate simultaneously in a number of countries (i.e., MNEs). What differentiates MNEs from domestic firms, and how do, or should, these factors affect the accountability and reports of MNEs?

Foreign direct investment (FDI) by MNEs entails certain benefits and costs for host countries. In this context, the demand for greater disclosure from MNEs may be viewed as part of a bargaining process—an effort by host countries, and developing countries in particular, to improve their bargaining powers. The fact that MNEs operate in a number of different nation-states has given them an opportunity to take actions in their own best interest that are not available to others. This is the basis for a conflict of perspectives between that of a national view of various groups within the nation-state and the multinational view of the MNEs. While business activities in a single country are for many MNEs just a part of their global operation, this is the part that is of primary concern for most of those affected in the host country.

The multinationality, size, and complexity of MNEs have enabled some of them to undertake actions detrimental to a host country. Cases of tax avoidance bordering on evasion, political interference, discriminatory practices, and so on are well documented. Whether these are exceptions or whether they represent more general practice is a matter of debate. The known cases, however, have been sufficient when combined with other factors to increase the pressure for greater accountability and disclosure.

Accountability by MNEs thus may be differentiated from accountability by domestic corporations, though both are business organizations with many features in common. A domestic corporation's primary operations are in one country, and its cross-frontier relationships are with unrelated parties. On the other hand, MNEs operate in a number of countries with different laws and currencies, and there is usually a significant volume of transactions between units located in different countries. The common control of these globally dispersed operations provides the opportunity to coordinate pricing, sourcing, and location decisions in a manner that, while increasing the net return of the group, may be detrimental or, alternatively, advantageous to individual nation-states. This special impact of MNEs appears to have given rise to pressure for more accountability and information disclosure.

ACCOUNTING ASPECTS OF INTERNATIONAL BUSINESS

A firm's first exposure to international accounting usually occurs as a result of an import or export opportunity. In the case of exports, a domestic company may receive an unsolicited inquiry or purchase order from a foreign buyer. Assuming the domestic company desires to make the sale, it needs to investigate the foreign buyer, particularly when the buyer asks for the extension of credit. This procedure is often not as easy as it appears.

First, the buyer may not be listed in any of the international credit rating directories, such as Standard & Poor's. If not, the seller may need to ask its bank to have its foreign affiliates check on the buyer's creditability. Alternatively, it may ask the buyer to supply financial information. The buyer may be willing to supply financial statements, but these statements may be difficult for the domestic company to interpret. The statements may be in a foreign language and may be based on accounting assumptions and procedures unfamiliar to the company's accountants. Most companies new to international business must then get help, either from a bank or from an accounting firm with international expertise. If the foreign buyer pays in its own currency, the selling company must become familiar with the potential gains and losses from changes in the exchange rate that may occur between the time the order is booked and the time the payment is received.

The selling company must also deal with a host of other international details—special international shipping and insurance documents, customs declaration forms, international legal documents, and so on. Once again, the services of lawyers, shippers, bankers, and accountants with international expertise are needed.

In the case of a potential import, the international accounting aspects are not as involved because most of the details are the responsibility of the foreign seller. However, if the foreign seller requires payments in his or her currency or if the domestic buyer wants information about the reliability of the foreign supplier, the buyer may need to consult an international bank, lawyer, or accounting firm.

Establishing an Internal International Accounting Capability

As the firm becomes increasingly involved in trade, the international accounting activity increases, and so do the costs of using outside expertise. At some point it becomes feasible for the company to develop the international capabilities of its own staff, including its own accountants.

The next major development that is likely to necessitate increased international accounting skills is the creation of a separate organization within the company to handle international trade. This may be an export department. Special accounting systems and procedures must be established in control, reporting, and taxation areas.

Typically, the next evolutionary step is the establishment of a foreign operation of some kind. In the minimal case, the company may decide to license a foreign manufacturer to produce its product or some part of its product. This involves selecting a potential licensee, analyzing its reliability and capability, and drawing up a contract. It also involves developing an accounting system to monitor contract performance and royalty and technical payments and to handle the foreign money flows into the company's tax and financial statements.

At the other end of the spectrum, the company may establish a wholly owned subsidiary in a foreign country. Accounting for the foreign subsidiary would include (1) meeting the requirements of the foreign government, which would be based on procedures and practices different from those in the parent company's country; (2) establishing a management information system to monitor, control, and evaluate the foreign subsidiary; and (3) developing a system to consolidate the foreign subsidiary's operating results with those of the parent for financial and tax-reporting purposes.

Between these extremes are a host of alternatives: opening up a sales office, setting up a warehouse, forming a joint venture with another company, and buying into an existing company. Each brings with it new international dimensions and requirements for management and, more specifically, for the company's accountants. It should also be pointed out that, before any of this takes place, a thorough study of market conditions—legal, economic, political, and sociocultural—should be made, including detailed feasibility studies and risk analysis. All of these steps require the collection and appropriate analysis of information in both quantitative financial terms and qualitative terms.

During a first venture into any of these more advanced areas, the international expertise of outside groups can be indispensable because of the money and risks involved in international trade. However, using outside international experts in no way lessens the need to develop in-house international capabilities, not only in accounting but in other functional areas as well.

Finally, some knowledge of international accounting may be necessary even if a firm is not involved in international business per se—for example, if the firm wishes to borrow money or to buy or sell stocks or bonds outside its home country. In some cases, it may be cheaper to borrow money or issue stocks or bonds abroad because interest rates are lower or exchange rate movements are favorable. In order to take advantage of these situations, the firm needs to know not only the relevant foreign laws, regulations, and customs but also the domestic legal, tax, and accounting treatments of any of these transactions. Alternatively, there may be better investment opportunities abroad for short-term liquid funds because of higher returns, predicted exchange rate movements, or both.

From an investment standpoint, the firm must know exactly what it is doing as well as know all the attendant risks. This entails an understanding of the financial statements, the terms of the foreign offer, and foreign currency movements. And as was the case with raising capital abroad, the investing firm must understand both the foreign and domestic laws and the tax and accounting treatments of the transaction being considered.

THE FIELD OF INTERNATIONAL ACCOUNTING

The study of international accounting involves two major areas: descriptive/comparative accounting and the accounting dimensions of international transactions/multinational enterprises.

The first area is fascinating because it is fundamental to an understanding of the nature and uses of accounting. However, it would be impossible to study accounting for each country in the world in the same depth that one does for one's own country. Although some description is necessary when studying accounting in different countries, the important issues are the forces and conditions that create international differences. Some countries, such as the United States, the United Kingdom, Germany, and France, are key countries to study because of their strong influence on the rest of the world. Colonial ties and direct investment require a basic understanding of those countries and their accounting systems. Even though it is important to understand the differences and unique aspects of accounting in different countries, the trend is toward convergence of accounting standards and practices internationally, especially for companies raising capital on national and foreign capital markets. Thus, the field of descriptive/comparative accounting is important as it relates to the convergence process.

Earlier we described the issues relating to international transactions and multinational enterprises. Obviously, firms that are not considered multinational enterprises are involved in import/export transactions and require special attention. However, multinational enterprises have these problems and a host of others. Financial reporting problems, translation of foreign currency financial statements, information systems, budgets and performance evaluation, audits, and taxes are some of the major problems faced by these firms.

Overview of the Text

International accounting should be studied in the context of MNEs from a strategic perspective. Thus, we focus on the strategies of MNEs and how accounting is relevant to those strategies. However, this focus on the strategic context of the MNE does not imply that we are ignoring other important international accounting perspectives. The book is divided into two parts. The first part focuses on financial accounting issues central to the financial reporting process and the convergence of standards and practices. The second half focuses on managerial, auditing, and taxation issues.

Chapter 1 not only sets up the logic for the book, but it also provides the general background on MNEs for students who have never taken an international business class. In addition, this chapter identifies the major environmental influences on accounting development.

In Chapter 2, we discuss different ways to classify accounting regimes in different countries, and we show how culture influences accounting systems. This chapter is important in understanding accounting systems and practices in different countries as outlined in Chapters 3 and 4.

Chapters 3 and 4 show why companies need to be aware of the different accounting systems and accounting traditions they face in different parts of the world. We concentrate on some important studies that have attempted to explain why accounting systems differ from one country to another. This chapter emphasizes the importance of understanding similarities and differences in accounting systems, particularly in the context of multinational strategy. We conclude with a discussion of some of the unique accounting traditions and underlying roots of practice in a number of important countries of the world with different cultural backgrounds. Chapter 3 focuses on accounting in a sample of developed countries, and Chapter 4 focuses on accounting in a sample of developing countries.

Chapter 5 introduces techniques for comparing the financial statements of companies from different countries. We examine the extent to which international differences in accounting principles have an impact on measures of earnings and assets. Foreign companies that list their securities on a U.S. stock exchange must provide a reconciliation of their earnings and stockholders' equity to U.S. GAAP earnings and stockholders' equity, an important point of discussion in this chapter.

Chapter 6 deals with a number of important international transparency and disclosure and reporting issues, some of which are discussed in more detail later (e.g., segment reporting).

Chapter 7 examines the key international convergence issues at work in the world today. In particular, the International Accounting Standards Board is stepping forward to establish international reporting standards that can be adopted worldwide. It is working with, rather than competing with, the major national standards setters, including the Financial Accounting Standards Board in the United States.

Chapter 8 is the first of several chapters that examine important financial reporting issues. In particular, we discuss different consolidation methods that are used around the world, the importance of the equity versus the cost method, and the issue of whether or not companies should consolidate operations, especially foreign operations. In addition, we deal with some of the current issues arising in cross-border mergers and acquisitions. Issues involved in accounting for goodwill and intangible assets are also discussed, especially the advantages and disadvantages of alternative accounting methods relating to goodwill, brands and trademarks, and research and development costs.

Chapter 9, which discusses segment reporting, concentrates on the reasons companies are required to provide line-of-business and geographic segment information. New standards worldwide have caused this area to change dramatically in recent years.

Chapter 10 initially deals with accounting for foreign currency transactions and then examine how MNEs translate the results of their foreign operations and consolidate those results with domestic operations.

Chapter 11 concludes the discussion of key accounting concepts by looking at accounting for price changes and inflation. This is especially relevant in the context of foreign operations and foreign exchange accounting. Although inflation in general has fallen in recent years, it is never far away and must be addressed.

Chapter 12 begins a series of chapters discussing special managerial issues. Chapter 12, on corporate governance and control of operations, begins with a discussion of global strategy and structure and then moves on to corporate governance and control systems. Particular emphasis is placed on emerging research in the area of corporate governance internationally.

Chapter 13 builds on Chapters 10 and 11 by discussing foreign exchange risk management and the role of accounting in providing information to corporate treasury so that proper hedging strategies can be undertaken.

Chapter 14 focuses on international budgeting and performance evaluation issues and trends and on how companies coordinate these issues in a multinational environment.

Chapter 15 deals with the international auditing of foreign operations and concentrates on three key issues that relate to auditing: the nature of the accounting and auditing profession worldwide, the organization of international public accounting firms, and the harmonization of auditing standards and practices.

In Chapter 16, the final chapter, we focus on the multinational enterprise as it attempts to satisfy the tax codes in its own country and to operate in different tax environments around the world. We discuss some key issues relating to the taxation of exports and imports as well as the earnings of foreign operations. The chapter ends with a discussion of how firms can plan their operations in a complex international taxation environment.

SUMMARY

1.   Although the recording of transactions is probably as old as the history of record keeping, we tend to think of the establishment of double-entry accounting, the basis for modern accounting, as the key event. Modern accounting originated in Genoa, Florence, and Venice and spread to the rest of the world thanks to the work of Luca Pacioli, the first person to document the double-entry accounting system.

2.   The development of increasingly complex business practices constantly transforms and presents new challenges to the accounting profession.

3.   One of the major developments shaping the accounting profession is the increasing globalization of business. The period after World War II, known as the multinational era, showed a strong increase in international trade and marked the appearance of very large multinational enterprises. This globalization presents new challenges for the accounting profession.

4.   Accounting is influenced by a variety of environmental factors. These factors shape, reflect, and reinforce accounting characteristics unique to each national environment.

5.   Major factors promoting the development of corporate reporting internationally include the ownership of stocks (shares) by the public, the growth of professional management, and the emergence of securities markets.

6.   At the same time, major factors constraining public reporting and disclosure include the financing of business by banks and government agencies, the design of accounting information systems for government planning and control, and the influence of tax rules.

7.   In recent years, a wider audience for corporate reports has been recognized, including employees, trade unions, consumers, government agencies, and the general public.

8.   Accountability and disclosure pressures on MNEs are different from those on domestic corporations because of the global reach, size, and complexity of MNE operations.

9.   As companies become more international, they face the challenges of developing internal expertise in international accounting practices to deal with currency fluctuations, different tax laws, legal systems, and the like.

10.   The study of international accounting involves two major areas: descriptive/comparative accounting and the accounting dimensions of international transactions/multinational enterprises.

Discussion Questions

1. In your opinion, when did the practice of accounting begin? Justify your answer.
2. What conditions came together to make Italy, and specifically Venice, the birthplace of modern accounting?
3. Based on the brief history of accounting and business provided in this chapter, list some of the key historical events that have shaped the accounting profession so far. For each event, briefly explain how that event affected the practice of accounting.
4. Identify the most important business, cultural, and political forces at work in your own country. In your opinion, how will those developments affect the accounting profession?
5. What international pressures for change in accounting do you think are going to be most important during the early years of the twenty-first century?
6. How important a constraint on change are national cultural differences likely to be? Are cultures themselves changing? in what way?
7. The International Accounting Standards Board (IASB), based in London, England, was established with the goal of developing a set of international accounting standards to increase the comparability of financial reporting worldwide. Do you think this is a worthwhile goal? Why or why not?
8. Given the increased globalization of the last few decades, can small domestic business survive? What advantages and disadvantages do they have compared to MNEs? (*Hint:* look at Figure 1.1.)
9. One of the environmental influences on accounting is the existence of a sound infra-structure of accounting education and research. Evaluate accounting education and research in your own country. How could it be improved to prepare you to compete in an increasingly global economy?
10. Evaluate the political and legal systems in your country. Do they support or hinder the establishment of MNEs? Why?
11. How important is the stock market in your country? Is it getting more important? If so, how and why?
12. The chapter states that securities markets are crucial in promoting the development of external reporting systems. What role does accounting information play in securities markets?
13. Do companies have a responsibility to disclose information to nonfinance providers (the "wider audience" mentioned in the text)? If they do, what kinds of extra information should companies disclose to nonfinance providers?
14. What extra accountability obligations emerge when a company decides to grow outside of its home country?
15. Chances are you will someday work for a MNE. What accounting skills do you think you will need to succeed in an international environment?

Exercises

1. Based on the brief history of accounting and business provided in this chapter, list the key historical events that have shaped the accounting profession so far. For each event, briefly explain how that event affected the practice of accounting.
2. Make a list of the most important business, cultural, and political forces at work in your own country. For each item you listed, answer the following questions:
   a. How will this development affect the accounting profession in this country?
   b. How will this development affect the accounting profession in other countries?
3. In Chapter 7, you will learn more about the IASB. To familiarize yourself with this organization, do the following:

    a.   Go to the IASB's website at www.iasb.org, find the purpose of the IASB, and summarize it in one paragraph.

    b.   Consider the economic, political, and cultural realities the world is facing today. Based on these considerations, do you think the IASB will accomplish its mission? What are the major threats this organization faces?

4.   As the text mentions, more and more companies are conducting business in foreign countries. A distinguishing characteristic of MNEs is that they are listed on foreign stock exchanges. Go to the website of the New York Stock Exchange (NYSE) at www.nyse.com and find a list of all the foreign (non-U.S.) companies listed on the exchange. Answer the following questions:

    a.   Which foreign country has the most companies listed on the NYSE?

    b.   Which regions/continents are the most strongly represented on the NYSE? Which are the least represented?

    c.   Why are some regions of the world less represented on the NYSE?

5.   Now that you have found foreign companies listed on a U.S. stock exchange, pick a stock exchange in a different country and find a list of the foreign companies listed on that country's exchange. You can find a list of world stock exchanges at www.fibv.com. Once you have done so, answer the following questions:

    a.   Which foreign country has the most companies listed on the exchange?

    b.   Which regions/continents are the most strongly represented on the exchange?

    c.   Why are some regions of the world less represented on the exchange?

6.   Find out what listing requirements must be met by foreign companies wishing to be listed on your country's stock exchange. If your country does not have an exchange, you can choose another country's exchange. You can find a list of world stock exchanges at www.fibv.com.

7.   Choose one of the MNEs from Exhibit 1.1. Find that company's most recent annual report on the web and answer the following questions:

    a.   What percentage of total revenues comes from foreign operations?

    b.   In what countries does the company operate? Why do you think it chose to expand into those countries?

    c.   To gather and summarize all the data required to create its annual report, the company you chose had to integrate financial information from various countries. What challenges do you think the firm faced in trying to integrate information from so many different origins?

8.   The following statement is taken directly from the text:

    There are also a growing number of securities markets that have been termed "emerging" markets (e.g., in China, Eastern Europe, Latin America, and the developing countries of Africa). Indeed, securities markets are seen to be fundamental elements of the transition to a market economy, which necessarily involves the privatization of state-owned enterprises and the need to attract foreign investment.

    a.   Do you agree with this statement?

    b.   Why is the existence of a securities market fundamental in a market economy?

9.   As mentioned in the text, the influence of culture (i.e., societal or national values) is an important environmental influence on accounting traditions and practices. Religion has a strong influence on culture in some nations. For example, the laws and organizations of Islamic nations are based on the Muslim faith. The International Islamic University Malaysia has an Islamic accounting website found at http://www.iiu.edu.my/iaw/. Take some time to learn about Islamic accounting. How has the Islamic culture and religion shaped accounting in predominantly Muslim nations?

10. Toyota is a well-known Japanese automaker with operations in several parts of the world. At the end of the chapter is a case on *Toyota's Global Expansion*. Understanding the Japanese accounting environment will greatly aid you in preparing for this case.

Visit http://marriottschool.byu.edu/teacher/Acc645/account/Japan.htm and read the article on Japanese accounting.

11. Ahold is a food products MNE based in the Netherlands. On the website is a case on *Ahold and the Challenges of Going Global*. Understanding the Dutch accounting environment will greatly aid you in preparing for this case. Go to the web and learn about accounting practices in the The Netherlands. Answer the following questions:

   a. How do the legal system and culture influence accounting?
   b. How does membership in the EU affect accounting practices?
   c. How are accounting standards set?
   d. What are some of the key accounting practices?

12. Consider the following statement:

   Globalization refers to the deepening relationships and broadening interdependence among people from different countries. ... The growth of globalization creates both opportunities and threats for individuals, companies, and countries.

   a. What are some of the opportunities created by globalization?
   b. What are some of the threats posed by globalization?

13. Schering is a German company in the medical industry. In its 2003 annual report, the company disclosed the following information:

   We have spent substantial amounts on environmental protection and safety measures up to now, and anticipate having to spend similar amounts in 2004 and subsequent years. In 2003, our operating and maintenance costs in the field of environmental protection and safety totaled €76m (2002: €74m). Our capital expenditure on environmental protection projects and other ecologically beneficial projects totaled €15m (2002: €15m). We estimate that operating and maintenance costs for safety and environmental measures will rise to between €76m and €80m annually by 2008. We expect capital expenditure on environmental projects and other ecologically beneficial projects to be between €5m and €15m annually over the same period. (Schering 2003 Annual Report)

   a. Who would be most interested in this type of financial information?
   b. Would this kind of information be valuable in determining the future financial performance of the company?
   c. Why would Schering be interested in reporting about its environmental protection and safety efforts?

14. StoraEnso is a multinational Swedish company in the paper, packaging, and forest products industry. Along with its traditional annual report, the company publishes a Sustainability report for shareholders and the public. Visit www.storaenso.com and find the latest Sustainability report. Answer the following questions:

   a. What is disclosed in the Sustainability report?
   b. Why do you think StoraEnso spends so much time and energy on disclosing that kind of information?
   c. Do you think disclosing that kind of information helps StoraEnso be more profitable? Why?

15. A new trend in investing is to look for companies that are not only profitable but also show a high degree of what is called corporate sustainability. Sustainability is a relatively new concept, but one that is increasing in popularity among investors and the general public. In response to this, Dow Jones created the Dow Jones Sustainability Indexes (DJSI). Visit www.sustainability-index.com and answer the following questions:

   a. What is corporate sustainability?
   b. How does the concept of sustainability create a demand for nontraditional financial information? How will this affect international accounting practices?
   c. What does the DJSI measure? Why would corporations want to be a part of this index?
   d. Find a list of current DJSI members. Do you recognize any of the companies?
   e. Do you think firms will benefit from establishing sustainability strategies? How?

Case: Toyota's Global Expansion
Case: Ahold and the Challenges of Going Global

These cases can be found on the following website: www.wiley.com/college/radebaugh

Selected References

Alexander, John R. "History of Accounting," http://www.acaus.org/acc_his.html, December 14, 2004.

Ascarelli, Silvia, and Peter A. McKay, "European Exchanges Gobble Up Each Other," The *Wall Street Journal*, January 20, 2005, p. C1.

Baydoun, N. and R. Willett. 1995. "Cultural Relevance of Western Accounting Systems to Developing Countries." *Abacus* (March): 67–92.

Berle, A., Jr., and G. C. Means. 1932. *The Modern Corporation and Private Property*. New York: Macmillan.

Chatfield, Michael. 1977. *A History of Accounting Thought*. New York:

Choi, Frederick D. S. 1974. "European Disclosure: The Competitive Disclosure Hypothesis." *Journal of International Business Studies* (Fall).

Daniels, John D., Lee H. Radebaugh, and Daniel L. Sullivan. 2004. *International Business Environments and Operations*. 10th ed. Upper Saddle River, NJ: Prentice Hall.

Edwards, J. R. 1989. *A History of Financial Accounting*. London: Routledge.

Farmer, Richard N., and Barry M. Richman. 1965. *Comparative Management and Economic Progress*. Homewood, IL: Irwin.

Galbraith, John K. 1967. *The New Industrial State*. Boston: Houghton Mifflin.

Gray, S. J. 1980. "The Impact of International Accounting Differences from a Security Analysis Perspective: Some European Evidence." *Journal of Accounting Research* (Spring).

Gray, S. J. 1989. "International Accounting Research: The Global Challenge," *International Journal of Accounting* 23(4).

Gray, S. J. 1998. "Towards a Theory of Cultural Influence on the Development of Accounting Systems Internationally." *Abacus* (March).

Gray, S. J., and C. B. Roberts. 1997. "Foreign Company Listings on the London Stock Exchange," In T. E. Cooke and C. W. Nobes, eds., *The Development of Accounting in an International Context*. London: Routledge.

Hill, C. W. 2000. *International Business*. New York: McGraw-Hill.

ICAEW. "Accounting History." http://www.icaew.co.uk/library/index.cfm?AUB=TB2I_7258, December 14, 2004.

Kreiger, Lee T. A., and R. H. Parker, 1979. *The Evolution of Corporate Financial Reporting*. London: Nelson.

McMickle, Peter L., and Richard G. Vangermeersch. 1987. *The Origins of a Great Profession*. Memphis, TN: Academy of Accounting Historians.

Parker, R. H. 1989. "Importing and Exporting Accounting: The British Experience." In A. G. Hopwood, ed., *International Pressures for Accounting Change*. Englewood Cliffs, NJ: Prentice Hall.

Peragallo, Edward. 1938. *Origin and Evolution of Double Entry Bookkeeping*. New York: American Institute.

Rugman, Alan M., Donald J. Lecraw, and Laurence D. Booth. 1985. *International Business: Firm and Environment*. New York: McGraw-Hill.

Seidler, Lee J. 1967. "International Accounting—The Ultimate Theory Course." *Accounting Review* 41(4): 775–81.

Ten Have, O. 1976. *The History of Accountancy*. Trans. A. van Seventer. Palo Alto, CA: Bay Books.

United Nations. 1997. *World Investment Report 1997: Transnational Corporations, Market Structure and Competition Policy*. New York: UN.

CHAPTER TWO

INTERNATIONAL ACCOUNTING PATTERNS, CULTURE, AND DEVELOPMENT

Chapter Objectives

- Discuss different ways to identify and classify accounting systems internationally
- Examine the key dimensions of national culture and how they influence behavior in work situations
- Identify accounting values that influence comparative accounting practice
- Show how cultural values and accounting values relate to each other in the development of accounting standards and practices worldwide

INTRODUCTION

Although there is a growing awareness of the varying influences of environmental factors on accounting development in a global context, many experts also realize that there may be systematically different patterns of accounting behavior applicable to various groups of countries. In this chapter we will examine the extent to which we can identify and classify accounting systems internationally. To assess whether there are systematic similarities or differences in accounting systems that may enable certain countries to be classified together, it is necessary to determine an appropriate scheme of classification. In essence, the classification of accounting and reporting systems, as in the case of political, economic, and legal systems, should sharpen our ability to describe, analyze, and predict the development of accounting systems. Such information is likely to provide useful input for making

---

Strategic Decision Point

Different accounting patterns of behavior can be identified which are the out-comes of many years of development influenced by factors such as cultural values, legal systems, political orientations, and economic development. The challenge now is to adapt what has served well in the past to the new global imperatives of transparency and credibility of accounting in order to facilitate efficient flows of capital to the world's financial markets. To do this requires recognition that tradition and culture shape accounting thought in a country and that change is more likely achieved when it is truly informed by an under-standing of that country's heritage. In Germany and Japan, for example, the accounting profession's role in standard setting has been relatively minor compared to that of the United States and United Kingdom. Thus, new insti-tutions have only recently been established which incorporate significant pro-fessional input to standard setting in a way that harmonizes with IASB gover-nance structures.

---

strategic planning and control decisions and for formulating policies to harmonize international accounting systems.

PURPOSES OF INTERNATIONAL CLASSIFICATION

The classification process should help us describe and compare international accounting systems in a way that will promote improved understanding of the com-plex realities of accounting practice. The classification scheme should contribute to an improved understanding of (1) the extent to which national systems are similar to or different from each other, (2) the pattern of development of individual national systems with respect to each other and their potential for change, and (3) the reasons some national systems have a dominant influence whereas others do not. Classifica-tion should also help policymakers assess the prospects and problems of international harmonization. Policymakers at the national level will thus be in a better position to predict likely problems and identify solutions that may be feasible given knowledge of the experience of countries with similar development patterns. Developing coun-tries seeking to choose an appropriate accounting system will also be better informed about the relevance for them of the systems used by other countries. The education of accountants and auditors who operate internationally would also be facilitated by an appropriate classification system. Similarly, such a system would promote a better understanding of and solution to problems involving the establishment of appropri-ate accounting and control systems for multinational enterprises (MNEs).

CLASSIFICATION OF ACCOUNTING AND REPORTING SYSTEMS

Research into the international classification of accounting systems has taken two main forms. In the deductive or judgmental approach, relevant environmental factors are identified, and, by linking these to national accounting practices, international groupings or development patterns are proposed. In the inductive or empirical approach, individual accounting practices are analyzed, development patterns or groupings are then identified, and finally explanations keyed to a variety of economic, social, political, and cultural factors are proposed.

The Deductive Approach

The environmental analysis performed by Gerhard Mueller in his book *International Accounting* (1967) provides a pioneering starting point for discussing the deductive approach to accounting classification. Mueller identified four distinct approaches to accounting development.

1. In the macroeconomic pattern, business accounting correlates closely with national economic policies. The goals of the corporation usually follow rather than lead national economic policies. Here, accounting income might be smoothed to promote economic and business stability, depreciation rates adjusted to stimulate growth, special reserves created to promote investment, and social responsibility accounting developed to meet macroeconomic concerns. Mueller gave Sweden, France, and Germany as examples of this approach.

2. In the microeconomic pattern, accounting is viewed as a branch of business economics. In this pattern, a fundamental orientation exists toward individual economic entities. Here, accounting concepts are derived from economic analysis. A fundamental concept is concerned with the maintenance in real terms of the monetary capital invested in the corporation. Replacement-value accounting as used by some companies in the Netherlands is often assumed to fit the microeconomic approach, together with developments in segmental reporting and the disclosure of employee costs, pensions, long-term commitments, and so on.

3. In the independent discipline pattern, accounting is viewed as a service function and is derived from business practice. A deep-seated respect for pragmatism and judgment exists here. Accounting is considered to be capable of developing its own conceptual framework, derived on a piecemeal basis from its own successful business practices. Income is a pragmatic measure that seems useful in practice, and full and fair disclosure is a "generally accepted accounting principle" that has evolved over the years. Mueller cited the United States and the United Kingdom as comprehensive examples of this approach.

4. In the uniform accounting pattern, accounting is viewed as an efficient means of administration and control. Here, a more scientific approach to accounting is adopted whereby a uniform approach to measurement, disclosure, and presentation will promote ease of use and a means of control for all types of businesses by all kinds of users, including managers, governments, and tax authorities. Centrally planned economies, as well as other countries with a strong government involvement in economic

planning, such as France, Germany, Sweden, and Switzerland, are given as typical examples.

Although Mueller perceived all these judgmentally assessed patterns or approaches as closely linked to economic or business factors, he recognized a wider set of influences, such as legal system, political system, and social climate, as relevant to accounting development, though without offering precise specification. Mueller gave no explicit recognition to cultural factors, which were presumably subsumed within the set of environmental factors he identified.

Mueller's further contribution to the research on classifying international accounting was his categorization of business environments, which he then linked to different types of accounting systems. Using assessments of economic development, business complexity, political and social climates, and legal systems, Mueller identified 10 country groupings. Although Mueller pointed out that different business environments need different accounting systems, he did not empirically assess accounting differences in practice.

Mueller's environmental analysis was adapted and extended by Nobes (1983), who based his hypothetical classification on an evolutionary approach to the identification of measurement practices in developed Western nations. Nobes adopted a hierarchical scheme of classification (see Figure 2.1) to lend more subtlety and discrimination to the assessment of country differences. However, like Mueller, he made no explicit mention of cultural factors. Nobes made a basic distinction between microeconomic and macroeconomic systems, and a further disaggregation between business economics and business practice orientations under the micro-based classification. Under the macro-uniform based classification, he made a disaggregation between a government/tax/legal orientation and a government/economics orientation. He then hypothesized further disaggregations between U.K. and U.S. influences under the business practices orientation and between tax-based and law-based systems under the government/tax/legal orientation. The increased discrimination permitted by this analysis, however, is balanced by the problems of allocating countries to categories—for example, to tax-based or law-based families when both aspects are influential, as with France versus Germany. Japan is also difficult to categorize given the macro-based continental European influences of taxes, as well as the micro-based U.S. influence on the securities laws.

Nobes then tested this classification system by means of a judgmental analysis of measurement and valuation reporting practices in 14 developed countries. He used a structural approach to accounting practices whereby he assessed major features such as the importance of tax rules, the use of prudent/conservative valuation procedures, and the making of replacement cost adjustments. Nine factors were identified as those likely to predict which countries would be grouped together, and Nobes then scored these factors based on questionnaires and personal judgment.

His statistical analysis did indeed provide strong support for the classification of countries as either micro-based or macro-based, but it went little beyond this. Nevertheless, empirical research by Doupnik and Salter (1993) on a larger number of countries also provided broad support for Nobes's classifications. In a study of 50 countries, communist as well as capitalist, the macro/micro classification was clearly supported by both measurement and disclosure practices.

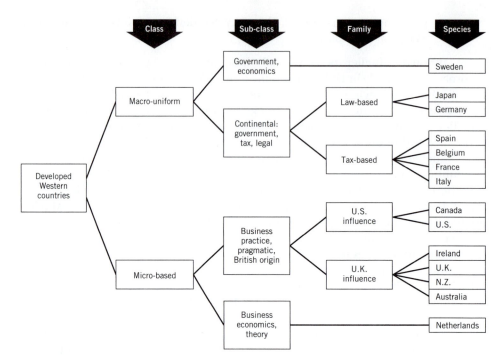

Figure 2.1   A Hypothetical Classification of Financial Reporting Measurement Practices in Developed Western Countries

More recently, Nobes (1998) has updated his classification scheme to distinguish between strong and weak equity market and shareholder orientations (see Figure 2.2). This incorporates changes that are taking place internationally whereby some companies in countries such as Germany and Japan are accounting on a basis consistent with U.S. generally accepted accounting principles (U.S. GAAP) or International Accounting Standards (IASs).

The Inductive Approach

By way of contrast to the studies discussed in the previous section, the inductive approach to identifying accounting patterns begins with an analysis of individual accounting practices. Perhaps the most important contribution of this type was by Nair and Frank (1980), who carried out a statistical analysis of international accounting practices using the Price Waterhouse surveys of 1973 and 1975. They made an empirical distinction between measurement and disclosure practices because these were considered to have different patterns of development.

The empirical results, using factor analysis applied to individual practices, showed that with respect to the Price Waterhouse (1973) data it was possible to identify four measurement groupings characterized broadly as the British Commonwealth, Latin American, continental European, and U.S. models. This result seems plausible and fits quite well with prior research on national accounting sys-

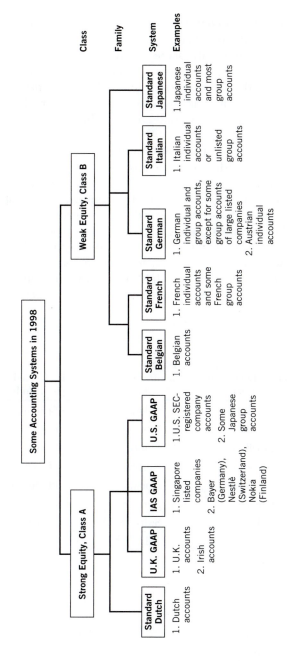

Figure 2.2 Reasons for International Differences in Financial Reporting

39

tems. Regarding disclosure, however, seven groupings were identified that could not be plausibly described, nor could any explanation be offered for the differences between them and the measurement groupings.

With respect to the Price Waterhouse (1975) data, it was possible to identify five measurement groupings of countries, with Chile as a single-country "group" (see Exhibit 2.1). However, the number of groupings increased to seven when disclosure practices were considered, the same number as in the results of the 1973 data analysis. The measurement groupings were characterized broadly, in this case, as the British Commonwealth, Latin American/south European, northern and central European, and U.S. models. The disclosure groupings, on the other hand, could not be similarly described, nor could any plausible description or explanation be offered.

Subsequent to the identification of country groupings, Nair and Frank attempted to assess the relationships of these groupings with a number of explanatory variables. Although relationships were established with respect to some of the variables—which included language (as a proxy for culture), various aspects of economic structure, and trading ties—it was clear that there were differences between the measurement and disclosure groupings. Moreover, the hypotheses that cultural and economic variables might be more closely associated with disclosure practices and trading variables with measurement practices were not supported.

One problem with this type of research is the lack of reliability and relevance in the data for the research problem under investigation. Problems arose in the

Exhibit 2.1   Measurement Groupings (1975 Survey)

I. British Commonwealth Model	II. Latin American/ South European Model	III. Northern and Central European Model	IV. United States Model	V
Australia	Argentina	Belgium	Bermuda	Chile
Bahamas	Bolivia	Denmark	Canada	
Fiji	Brazil	France	Japan	
Iran	Colombia	Germany	Mexico	
Ireland	Ethiopia	Norway	Philippines	
Jamaica	Greece	Sweden	United States	
Malaysia	India	Switzerland	Venezuela	
Netherlands	Italy	Zaire		
New Zealand	Pakistan			
Nicaragua	Panama			
Rhodesia	Paraguay			
Singapore	Peru			
South Africa	Spain			
Trinidad	Uruguay			
United Kingdom				

Source: R. D. Nair and W. G. Frank, "The Impact of Disclosure and Measurement Practices on International Accounting Classifications," *Accounting Review* (July 1980): 433.

Price Waterhouse surveys with respect to data errors, misleading answers, swamping of important questions by trivial ones, and exaggeration of differences between the United States and the United Kingdom. Perhaps the fundamental weakness of the surveys was that some confusion existed between the rules (mandatory and nonmandatory) and actual practices, which are often different.

From this review of some of the major studies in international classification it seems clear that research in this area is still in a relatively early stage with only very broad country groupings or accounting patterns so far identified. Furthermore, only very general relationships between environmental factors and accounting systems have been established.

Also noteworthy is the fact that in all this classification research, little explicit attention has been given to the influence of culture as a possibly more fundamental factor underlying differences in international accounting systems.

CULTURAL INFLUENCES ON ACCOUNTING SYSTEMS

In accounting, the importance of culture and its historical roots is now increasingly being recognized. Although there has been a lack of attention to this dimension in the past in the international classification literature, Harrison and McKinnon (1986) proposed a methodological framework incorporating culture for analyzing changes in corporate financial reporting regulation at the nation-specific level. The use of this framework to assess the impact of culture on the form and functioning of accounting was demonstrated through an analysis of Japan's accounting system. Culture is considered an essential element in the framework for understanding how social systems change because culture influences norms and values and group behavior within and across systems.

Complementing this approach is the proposal by Gray (1988) that a theoretical framework incorporating culture could be used to explain and predict international differences in accounting systems and to identify patterns of accounting development internationally.

Gray argued that culture, or societal values, at the national level may be expected to permeate organizational and occupational subcultures as well, though with varying degrees of integration. Accounting systems and practices can influence and reinforce societal values. With this in mind, we can perhaps obtain more fundamental insights than we hitherto have into why there are differences between national systems of accounting and reporting, both internal and external.

Figure 2.3 shows a model of the process whereby societal values influence the accounting subculture. The figure shows the influence of societal values on the institutional framework for the development of accounting, for example, the legal system, professional associations, and so on. Accordingly, the value system or attitudes of accountants are shown as being related to and derived from societal values and particularly work-related values. Accounting "values" or attitudes, for example, conservatism, will, in turn, have an impact on the development of accounting systems in the individual country. This is particularly true for measurement and disclosure practices and the approach to regulation, that is, statutory versus professional or self-regulation.

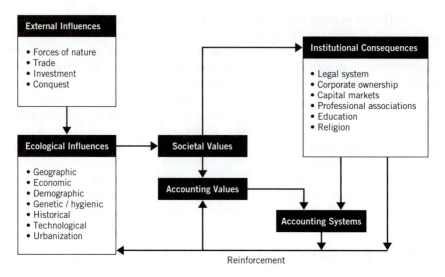

Figure 2.3   Culture, Societal Values, and the Accounting Subculture

Source: S. J.Gray, "Towards a Theory of Cultural Influence on the Development of Accounting Systems Internationally," *Abacus* (March 1988): 7.

More specifically, Gray explored the extent to which the cultural values identified by Hofstede (1980) from his cross-cultural research into work-related values could be helpful in this task.

CULTURE, SOCIETAL VALUES, AND ACCOUNTING

Structural Elements of Culture that Affect Business

Hofstede's pioneering research in the 1970s was aimed at detecting the structural elements of culture, particularly those that most strongly affect known behavior in the work situations of organizations and institutions. In perhaps one of the most extensive cross-cultural surveys ever conducted, psychologists collected data about "values" from the employees of an MNE located in more than 50 countries. Hofstede's statistical analysis and reasoning revealed four underlying societal value dimensions—that is, collective values at the national level along which countries could be positioned. These dimensions, with substantial support from prior work in the field, were labeled Individualism, Power Distance, Uncertainty Avoidance, and Masculinity. Subsequent research by Hofstede and Bond (1988) into Chinese values revealed a fifth dimension: a short-term versus long-term orientation, or what was termed Confucian Dynamism. Such dimensions, which we will discuss shortly, were perceived to represent elements of a common structure in cultural systems. It was also shown how countries could be grouped into culture areas, on the basis of their scores on the four value dimensions, using cluster analysis and taking into account geographical and historical factors. Exhibit 2.2 shows the countries within each of the identified culture areas and any identifiable subgroups of countries within each group.

Exhibit 2.2   Culture Areas

More developed Latin	Less developed Latin	More developed Asian
Belgium	Colombia	Japan
France	Ecuador	
Argentina	Mexico	
Brazil	Venezuela	
Spain	Costa Rica	
Italy	Chile	
	Guatemala	
Less developed Asian	Panama	**African**
Indonesia	Peru	East Africa
Pakistan	Portugal	West Africa
Thailand	Salvador	
Taiwan	Uruguay	
India	**Near Eastern**	**Asian colonial**
Malaysia	Arab countries	Hong Kong
Philippines	Greece	Singapore
	Iran	
	Turkey	
	Yugoslavia	
Germanic	**Anglo**	**Nordic**
Austria	Australia	Denmark
Israel	Canada	Finland
Germany	Ireland	Netherlands
Switzerland	New Zealand	Norway
	United Kingdom	Sweden
	United States	
	South Africa	

Source: G. Hofstede, *Culture's Consequences* (Beverly Hills: Sage, 1980), p. 336.

In a recent update, Hofstede (2001) summarizes the many studies that have replicated his research or extended it to many countries not covered by his original study. Given the limitations of any attempts to measure culture, most of these studies tend to confirm his findings, thus demonstrating the overall usefulness of his framework in giving insight into cultural values at the national or societal level. At the same time, Hofstede does recognize that cultural values are likely to change over time and that further research is required to assess the extent and reasons for change.

If societal value orientations are related to the development of accounting systems, given that such values permeate a nation's social system, then—as Gray suggests—there should be a close match between culture areas and patterns of accounting systems internationally.

Furthermore, assuming that Hofstede has correctly identified Individualism, Power Distance, Uncertainty Avoidance, Masculinity, and Confucian Dynamism as significant cultural value dimensions, it can then be argued that it should be possible to establish their relationship to "accounting values." If such a relationship exists, then a link between societal values and accounting systems can be established and the influence of culture assessed.

Before an attempt can be made to identify significant accounting values that may be related to societal values, it is important to understand the meaning of the four value dimensions initially identified by Hofstede (1984).

> **Individualism versus Collectivism** Individualism stands for the preference for a loosely knit social framework in society wherein individuals are supposed to take care of themselves and their immediate families only. Its opposite, collectivism, stands for the preference for a tightly knit social framework in which individuals expect their relatives, clan, or other in-group to look after them in exchange for unquestioning loyalty (the word "collectivism" is not used here to describe any particular political system). The fundamental issue addressed by this dimension is the degree of interdependence a society maintains among individuals. It relates to people's self-concept: "I" or "we."
>
> **Large versus Small Power Distance** Power Distance is the extent to which the members of a society accept the idea that power in institutions and organizations is distributed unequally. This affects the behavior of the less powerful as well as the more powerful members of society. People in Large Power Distance societies accept a hierarchical order in which everybody has a place that needs no further justification. People in Small Power Distance societies strive for power equalization and demand justification for power inequalities. The fundamental issue addressed by this dimension is how a society handles inequalities among people when they occur. This has obvious consequences for the way people build their institutions and organizations.
>
> **Strong versus Weak Uncertainty Avoidance** Uncertainty Avoidance is the degree to which the members of a society feel uncomfortable with uncertainty and ambiguity. This feeling leads them to hold beliefs promising certainty and to maintain institutions protecting conformity. Strong Uncertainty Avoidance societies maintain rigid codes of belief and behavior and are intolerant of deviant persons and ideas. Weak Uncertainty Avoidance societies maintain a more relaxed atmosphere in which practice counts more than principles and deviance is more easily tolerated. The fundamental issue addressed by this dimension is how a society reacts to the fact that time only runs one way and that the future is unknown, and whether it tries to control the future or just lets it happen. Like Power Distance, Uncertainty Avoidance has consequences for the way people build their institutions and organizations.
>
> **Masculinity versus Femininity** Masculinity stands for the preference in society for achievement, heroism, assertiveness, and material success. Its opposite, Femininity, stands for the preference for relationships, modesty, caring for the weak, and the quality of life. The fundamental issue addressed by this dimension is the way in which a society allocates social (as opposed to biological) roles to the sexes.

The fifth dimension, labeled Confucian Dynamism, refers to a **short-term versus long-term orientation.** This dimension is described as Confucian because the values involved seem to be identifiable with the teachings of Confucius, a legendary Chinese intellectual of the sixth century B.C. The short-term orientation emphasizes respect for tradition; respect for social and status obligations regardless of cost; social pressure to "keep up with the Joneses," even if it means overspending; small savings levels and so little money for investment; a concern to get quick results; a concern for appearances; and a concern for truth rather than virtue. The long-term orientation, on the other hand, emphasizes the adaptation of traditions to meet modern needs; a respect for social and status obligations within limits; a thrifty and sparing approach to resources; large savings levels and funds available for investment; perseverance toward achieving gradual results; a willingness to subordinate personal interests to achieve purpose; and a concern for a virtuous approach to life.

Accounting Values

Having identified societal values, is it possible to identify significantly related accounting values at the subcultural level of the accountant and accounting practice? Gray (1988) proposed the identification of four accounting values, derived from a review of accounting literature and practice, as follows:

1. *Professionalism versus statutory control:* This value reflects a preference for the exercise of individual professional judgment and the maintenance of professional self-regulation as opposed to compliance with prescriptive legal requirements and statutory control.

2. *Uniformity versus flexibility:* This value reflects a preference for the enforcement of uniform accounting practices between companies and for the consistent use of such practices over time, as opposed to flexibility in accordance with the perceived circumstances of individual companies.

3. *Conservatism versus optimism:* This value reflects a preference for a cautious approach to measurement that enables one to cope with the uncertainty of future events as opposed to a more optimistic, laissez-faire, risk-taking approach.

4. *Secrecy versus transparency:* This value reflects a preference for confidentiality and the disclosure of information about the business only to those who are most closely involved with its management and financing as opposed to a more transparent, open, and publicly accountable approach.

What arguments are there to support these accounting value dimensions? How do they relate to societal values? What impact are they likely to have on the development of national accounting systems?

Professionalism versus Statutory Control   Gray proposed this value as a significant accounting value dimension because accountants are perceived to adopt independent attitudes and to exercise their individual professional judgments, to a greater or lesser extent, throughout the world.

A major controversy in many Western countries, for example, surrounds the issue of the extent to which the accounting profession should be subject to public regulation or statutory control or should be permitted to retain control over accounting standards as a matter of private self-regulation.

The development of professional associations has a long history, but associations are much more firmly established in the Anglo-American countries, such as the United States and the United Kingdom than in some of the continental European countries (e.g., France, Germany, and Switzerland) and in many of the less developed countries.

In the United Kingdom, for example, the concept of presenting "a true and fair view" of a company's financial position and results depends heavily on the judgment of the accountant as an independent professional. This is so to the extent that accounting information disclosures beyond, and sometimes contrary to, what is specifically required by law may be necessary. This contrasts with the traditional position in France and Germany, where the professional accountant's role has been concerned primarily with the implementation of relatively prescriptive and detailed legal requirements. With the implementation of the European Union (EU) directives in the 1980s, this situation was changed to the extent that there is some movement, if not convergence, toward a more statutory approach.

To what extent then can professionalism be linked to the societal values of Individualism, Power Distance, Uncertainty Avoidance, Masculinity, and Long-Term Orientation? Professionalism can perhaps be linked most closely with the individualism and uncertainty-avoidance dimensions. A preference for independent professional judgment is consistent with a preference for a loosely knit social framework where there is more emphasis on independence, a belief in individual decisions, and respect for individual endeavor. This is also consistent with weak uncertainty avoidance where practice is all-important, where there is a belief in fair play and as few rules as possible, and where a variety of professional judgments tend to be more easily tolerated. There also appears to be a link, if less strong, between professionalism and power distance in that professionalism is more likely to be accepted in a small power distance society where there is more concern for equal rights, where people at various power levels feel less threatened and more prepared to trust each other, and where there is a belief in the need to justify the imposition of laws and codes. Professionalism would also seem to be linked with masculinity and short-term orientation to the extent that this implies a concern with individual assertiveness and social status.

Uniformity versus Flexibility   This is a significant accounting value dimension because attitudes about uniformity, consistency, or comparability are a fundamental feature of accounting principles worldwide. This value is open to different interpretations, ranging from a relatively strict intercompany and intertemporal uniformity, to consistency within companies over time and some concern for comparability between companies, to relative flexibility of accounting practices to suit the circumstances of individual companies.

In countries such as France and Spain, for example, a uniform accounting plan as well as the imposition of tax rules for measurement purposes have long been in operation because there has been a concern to facilitate national planning and the pursuit of macroeconomic goals. In contrast, the United Kingdom and the United States have demonstrated more concern with intertemporal consistency and some degree of intercompany comparability because of a perceived need for flexibility.

To what extent can uniformity be linked to societal value dimensions? Uniformity can perhaps be linked most closely with the uncertainty-avoidance and individualism dimensions. A preference for uniformity is consistent with preference for strong uncertainty avoidance, which leads in turn to concern for law and order and rigid codes of behavior, need for written rules and regulations, respect for conformity, and search for ultimate, absolute truths and values. This value dimension is also consistent with a preference for collectivism, as opposed to individualism, with its tightly knit social framework, belief in organization and order, and respect for group norms. There also seems to be a link, if less strong, between uniformity and power distance: uniformity is more easily facilitated in a large power distance society in that the imposition of laws and codes promoting uniformity are more likely to be accepted.

Conservatism versus Optimism   This is a significant accounting value dimension because "conservatism" is arguably "the most ancient and probably the most pervasive principle of accounting valuation" (Sterling, 1967).

Conservatism or prudence in asset measurement and the reporting of profits is seen as a fundamental attitude of accountants the world over. Moreover, conservatism varies according to country, ranging from a strongly conservative approach in Japan and some continental European countries (such as France, Germany, and Switzerland) to the much less conservative, risk-taking attitudes of accountants in the United States, the United Kingdom, and, to some extent, the Netherlands.

The varying impact of conservatism on accounting measurement practices internationally has also been demonstrated empirically. Such differences appear to be reinforced by the relative development of capital markets, the differing pressures of user interests, and the influence of tax laws on accounting practice in the countries concerned.

To what extent, then, can conservatism be linked to societal value dimensions? Conservatism can perhaps be linked most closely with the uncertainty-avoidance dimension and the short-term versus long-term orientations. A preference for more conservative measures of profits and assets is consistent with strong uncertainty avoidance that stems from a concern with security and a perceived need to adopt a cautious approach to cope with the uncertainty of future events. A less conservative approach to measurement is also consistent with a short-term orientation where quick results are expected and hence a more optimistic approach is adopted relative to conserving resources and investing for long-term results. There also seems to be a link, if less strong, between high levels of individualism and masculinity, on the one hand, and weak uncertainty avoidance on the other, to the extent that an emphasis on individual achievement and performance is likely to foster a less conservative approach to measurement.

Secrecy versus Transparency   This is a significant accounting value dimension that stems as much from management as it does from the accountant because of the influence of management on the quality and quantity of information disclosed to outsiders. Secrecy, or confidentiality, in business relationships is nevertheless a fundamental accounting attitude.

Secrecy also appears to be closely related to conservatism. Both values imply a cautious approach to corporate financial reporting in general, but secrecy relates to the disclosure dimension and conservatism relates to the measurement dimension. The extent of secrecy appears to vary across countries, with lower levels of disclosure—including instances of secret reserves—evident in Japan and continental European countries such as France, Germany, and Switzerland than in the United States and United Kingdom. These differences also seem to be reinforced by the differential development of capital markets and the public ownership of shares, which often provide incentives for the voluntary disclosure of information.

To what extent then can secrecy be linked to societal value dimensions? A preference for secrecy is consistent with strong uncertainty avoidance because the latter stems from the need to restrict the disclosure of information to outsiders to avoid conflict and competition and to preserve security. A close relationship between secrecy and power distance also seems likely in that high power distance societies are likely to be characterized by the restriction of information to preserve power inequalities. Secrecy is also consistent with a preference for collectivism, as opposed to individualism, in that its concern is for the interests of those most closely involved with the firm rather than external parties. A long-term orientation also suggests a preference for secrecy that is consistent with the need to conserve resources within the firm and to ensure that funds are available for investment relative to the demands of shareholders and employees for higher payments. A significant but possibly less important link with masculinity also seems likely to the extent that societies that place more emphasis on achievement and material success will have a greater tendency to publicize such achievements and success.

A matrix showing the nature of the relationships of accounting values with societal values is shown in Exhibit 2.3.

Accounting Values and International Classification

Having related societal values to international accounting values, it is possible, as Gray argues, to make a useful distinction between the authority for accounting systems on the one hand—that is, the extent to which such systems are determined and enforced by statutory control or professional means—and the measurement and disclosure characteristics of accounting systems, on the other. In this way, accounting values can be linked to specific accounting system characteristics (see Figure 2.4).

The accounting values most relevant to the professional or statutory authority for accounting systems as well as their enforcement appear to be professionalism and uniformity. Both are concerned with regulation and the degree of enforcement or conformity. Accordingly, these can be combined and the classification of culture areas hypothesized on a judgmental basis, as shown in Figure 2.5. In making these judgments, we will refer to the relevant correlations between value dimensions and the clusters of countries identified from the statistical analyses carried out by Hofstede. From this classification it seems clear that the Anglo and Nordic culture areas can be contrasted with the Germanic and more developed Latin culture areas as well as the Japanese, Near Eastern, less developed Latin, less developed Asian, and African culture areas. The former colonial Asian countries are separately classified because they represent a mixture of influences.

The accounting values most relevant to the measurement practices used and the extent of information disclosed are the conservatism and secrecy dimensions,

Exhibit 2.3 Matrix of Relationship of Accounting Values with Societal Values

Basic Value System \ Accounting Values	Professionalism	Statutory Control	Uniformity	Flexibility	Conservatism	Optimism	Secrecy	Transparency
Individualism	Positive	Negative	Negative	Positive	Negative	Positive	Negative	Positive
Collectivism	Negative	Positive	Positive	Negative	Positive	Negative	Positive	Negative
Large Power Distance	Negative	Positive	Positive	Negative	n/a	n/a	Positive	Negative
Small Power Distance	Positive	Negative	Negative	Positive	n/a	n/a	Negative	Positive
Strong Uncertainty Avoidance	Negative	Positive	Positive	Negative	Positive	Negative	Positive	Negative
Weak Uncertainty Avoidance	Positive	Negative	Negative	Positive	Negative	Positive	Negative	Positive
Masculinity	Positive	n/a	n/a	n/a	Negative	Positive	Negative	Positive
Femininity	Negative	n/a	n/a	n/a	Positive	Negative	Positive	Negative
Short term	Positive	Negative	n/a	n/a	Negative	Positive	Negative	Positive
Long term	Negative	Positive	n/a	n/a	Positive	Negative	Positive	Negative

Note: n/a = not applicable.

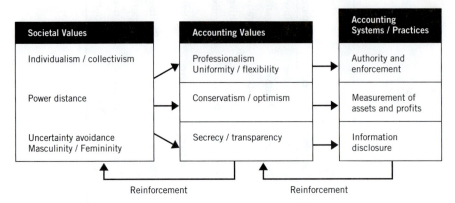

Figure 2.4   Culture and Accounting Systems in Practice

respectively. These can therefore be combined and the classification of culture areas hypothesized on a judgmental basis, as shown in Figure 2.6. As before, in making judgments about these classifications, we have again referred to the relevant correlations between value dimensions and the resultant clusters of countries identified from the statistical analysis carried out by Hofstede. Here again, there appears to be a sharp division of culture area groupings with the former

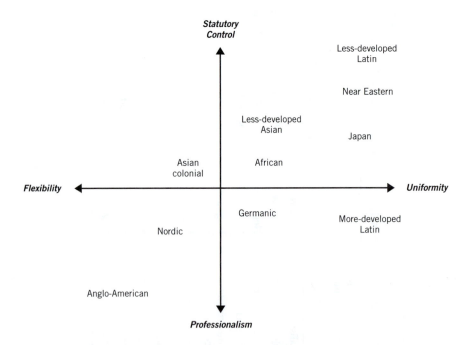

Figure 2.5   Accounting Systems: Authority and Enforcement

Source: S.J. Gray, "Towards a Theory of Cultural Influence on the Development of Accounting Systems Internationally," *Abacus* (March 1988): 12.

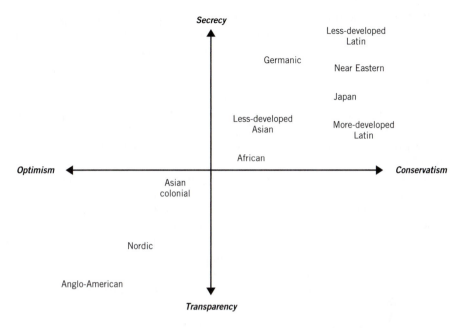

Figure 2.6   Accounting Systems: Measurement and Disclosure

Source: S. J. Gray, "Towards a Theory of Cultural Influence on the Development of Accounting Systems Internationally," *Abacus* (March 1988): 13.

Asian colonial group relating more closely with the Anglo and Nordic groupings. This can be contrasted with the Germanic and more developed Latin groupings, which are related to the Japanese, less developed Asian, African, less developed Latin, and Near Eastern-area groupings. In broad terms, countries can be grouped as either relatively optimistic and transparent or relatively conservative and secretive.

This classification of country groupings by culture area can be used as a basis for further assessing the relationship between culture and accounting systems. This classification is particularly relevant for understanding systems authority and enforcement characteristics, on the one hand, and measurement and disclosure characteristics, on the other.

In the wake of Gray's analysis, further research is needed to test the extent to which culture influences the development of international accounting practices and whether the hypothesized country groupings can be empirically supported. The research findings to date do tend to support the significance of culture as an influential factor in the development of accounting. Salter and Niswander (1995, p. 390) concluded from an empirical study of 29 countries that Gray's model "provided a workable theory to explain cross-national differences in accounting structure and practice which is particularly strong in explaining different financial reporting practices." To explain professional and regulatory structures, however, Salter and Niswander suggested that the inclusion of variables such as the development of financial markets and levels of taxation enhances the explanatory power of the model.

With respect to the conservatism dimension, empirical studies of profit measurement practices in France, Germany, the Netherlands, Sweden, the United Kingdom, and the United States indicate the existence of significant differences that support the importance of this dimension internationally. These findings are elaborated in Chapter 5.

The significance of the secrecy/transparency dimension has also received some support from recent research findings on information disclosure practices in some major countries, including Canada, France, Germany, Japan, the Netherlands, Switzerland, the United Kingdom, and the United States (see Chapter 6 for more information).

In a recent critical review of tests of Gray's theory of cultural relevance, Doupnik and Tsakumis (2005) argue that substantial opportunities for research continue to exist as many of the relationships proposed in Gray's framework have yet to be adequately tested. Furthermore, they suggest that alternatives to Hofstede's dimensions might be explored such as those developed more recently by Schwartz (1994), which are based arguably on more generalizable samples, with a view to exploring the links between accounting and culture further. A greater use of the experimental method is also proposed as a way to more closely investigate the cause/effect relationship between culture and the accountant's application of financial reporting rules.

INTERNATIONAL PRESSURES FOR ACCOUNTING CHANGE

It is also important to appreciate the potential impact of forces for change that arise from international factors. Accordingly, the model developed by Gray (1988) to elaborate the process of accounting change is shown in Figure 2.7, which identifies a number of important international pressures affecting accounting change, including growing international economic/political interdependence, new trends in foreign direct investments (FDI), changes in multinational corporate strategy, the impact of new technology, the rapid growth of international financial markets, the expansion in business services, and the activities of international regulatory organizations.

Let us consider briefly some of the pressures for change that arise from growing international interdependencies and from concerns to harmonize the regulatory framework of international economic and financial relationships. Although basic distinctions have been made and may to some extent still be made between East and West (i.e., socialist countries and Western capitalist countries) and North and South (i.e., developed and developing countries), dramatic changes are occurring at the political level, which in turn are causing economic changes that are restructuring the landscape of international business and accounting. Most notably, the hitherto centrally planned economies of the former Soviet Union and Eastern Europe are embracing a more Western market-oriented approach to economic development, as is the People's Republic of China. Furthermore, the growing worldwide trend toward the deregulation of markets and the privatization of public sector corporations in many developing as well as developed countries has opened up new opportunities for international investment and international joint ventures and alliances.

Economic groupings, such as the EU, have been a major influence in promoting economic integration through the free movement of goods, people, and

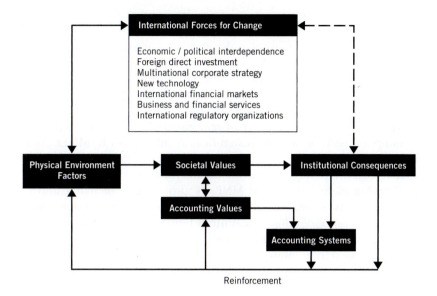

Figure 2.7   Change and Development of Accounting Values and Systems Internationally

Source: S. J. Gray, "International Accounting Research: The Global Challenge," *International Journal of Accounting 23,* no. 4 (Winter 1989): 294.

capital between countries. To achieve its goals, the EU has embarked on a major program of harmonization, including measures to coordinate the company law, accounting, taxation, capital market, and monetary systems in the EU countries. While the goal of removing all nontariff barriers has proved elusive, the EU has emerged as a major economic and, to some extent, political force in recent years. In addition, the EU is committed to helping the process of economic integration on a broader European-wide scale following the events and reforms that have taken place in Eastern Europe.

International organizations, such as the United Nations (UN) and the Organization for Economic Cooperation and Development (OECD), are also deeply involved in the development of international business on a global scale. The UN is responsible for the emergence of organizations such as the World Bank, the International Monetary Fund (IMF), the UN Conference on Trade and Development (UNCTAD), and the World Trade Organization (WTO). UNCTAD includes the work of the former Commission on Transnational Corporations, which was designed to promote an effective international framework for the operations of transnational corporations and to monitor the nature and effects of their activities. In particular, the UNCTAD and its Intergovernmental Working Group of Experts on International Standards of Accounting and Reporting (ISAR) has been involved, among other things, in initiatives to develop international standards of accounting and reporting and to promote accounting education in Russia and Africa.

The OECD, in contrast to the UN, is focused mainly on the development of the industrialized countries of the world. The major objectives of the OECD are to foster international economic and social development, and to this end a Code of Conduct, including information disclosure guidelines, has been issued relating to the operations of multinationals in order to encourage them to develop positive relationships with host countries.

Although the relationships between MNEs and host countries have become less antagonistic and more pragmatic and businesslike in recent years, a number of areas of continuing concern remain. There is little doubt that MNEs exert a significant impact on the culture and social development of host countries. Employment and consumption patterns are often significantly influenced by MNEs. As a result, there is pressure for more accountability to employees and consumers and for some consultation with the parties affected by the decisions of MNEs.

The environmental impact of MNEs is also an area of major and growing importance in terms of accountability. Whereas developed countries have a growing array of regulations, developing countries tend to have lower standards and are more concerned with improving economic conditions. At the same time, many MNEs have increased their awareness of pollution, safety procedures, and the need for stronger community relations. In this context, both the UN and OECD have been concerned with providing guidelines to MNEs, including the disclosure of relevant information, to encourage positive relationships with host countries.

At the level of international financial markets, there has been an interest in harmonizing differences in tax regimes, exchange controls, restrictions on foreign investments, and accounting and disclosure requirements, which still provide obstacles to the globalization of securities markets. The OECD and especially the EU have been influential in efforts to harmonize the minimum requirements for the admission of securities to the listing and content of prospectuses. In addition, the International Co-ordinating Committee of Financial Analysts Societies and the International Organization of Securities Commissions (IOSCO), both private organizations, are seeking to promote the internationalization and integration of securities markets on a global basis.

As to the internationalization of accounting and auditing standards, the International Accounting Standards Board (IASB) and the International Federation of Accountants (IFAC) are both involved in the harmonization effort and provide a professional counterpoint to the activities of intergovernmental organizations such as the UN, OECD, and the EU.

The brief discussion of some of the international pressures for change highlights the dynamic nature of accounting and accountability globally. National cultures, traditions, and practices will be increasingly challenged in the years ahead as the pressures for global convergence increasingly impact accountants and accounting practices.

SUMMARY

1. Patterns of international accounting development can be identified using a classification scheme to assess similarities and differences.

2. International accounting classification helps to describe and compare accounting systems in a way that will promote improved understanding of the nature and problems of accounting practice.

3.   International classification research has been both deductive, whereby relevant environmental factors are identified and linked to accounting practices, and inductive, whereby accounting practices are analyzed and development patterns identified.

4.   Although international classification research is still at a relatively early stage, it is possible to identify some broad country groupings and patterns of accounting development. At the very least, a macro/micro or strong/weak equity market pattern can be observed. Within that framework, U.S., U.K., and continental European models can be identified.

5.   Cultural influences on accounting development are now increasingly being recognized. Their importance in explaining fundamental accounting differences internationally seems clear, and some support has been received from recent empirical research.

6.   It is possible to identify key accounting values derived from societal cultural influences: professionalism, uniformity, conservatism, and secrecy. An international classification of accounting systems can be made on the basis of the link between accounting values, on the one hand, and accounting system characteristics, on the other.

7.   The accounting values of professionalism and uniformity are linked to the authority and enforcement characteristics of accounting systems.

8.   The value of conservatism is linked to the measurement of assets and profits, while secrecy is linked to the nature and extent of information disclosure or transparency.

9.   A comparative analysis of accounting systems reveals not only distinctive patterns of accounting but also unique features that are applicable to each country, depending on history and culture.

10.   Major international forces for accounting change are at work in the global environment, including a growing international economic/political interdependence, new trends in FDI, changes in multinational corporate strategy, the impact of new technology, the rapid growth of international financial markets, the expansion in business services, and the activities of international regulatory organizations.

Discussion Questions

1.   Why is the classification of accounting systems likely to be useful?

2.   What would be an example of a "deductive approach" to classifying a country's accounting system?

3.   What would be an example of an inductive approach to classifying a country's accounting system?

4.   To what extent is the strong/weak equity market distinction a useful way to identify different patterns of accounting development?

5.   Are cultural influences likely to have a larger impact on accounting measurement or disclosure practices?

6.   To what extent do you think culture explains the relative importance of stock exchanges and professional accounting associations around the world?

7.   Where does your country fit in terms of professionalism/statutory control and uniformity/flexibility?

8. Compare your country with a country that has a different professionalism and uniformity profile.

9. Where does your country fit in terms of conservatism/optimism and secrecy/transparency?

10. Compare your country with a country that has a different conservatism and secrecy profile.

11. To what extent are countries changing with respect to national cultures and accounting values? Are they converging or diverging?

12. How important a constraint on change are national cultural differences likely to be? Are cultures themselves changing? In what way?

13. What other factors are likely to be important constraints on accounting change?

14. Which countries have the greatest potential for accounting change? What are your reasons for thinking this?

15. What international pressures for change in accounting do you think are going to be most important during the early years of the twenty-first century?

Exercises

1. Form into small groups and have each group select two countries from different culture areas (as defined by Hofstede). Identify and compare each country's societal and accounting values.

2. Locate each country in Gray's Authority and Enforcement and Measurement and Disclosure frameworks. How do the countries compare? Comment on the relevance and reliability of your findings.

3. List six cultural traits that you think have impacted the accounting system in the United States and your country.
   a. Independence
   b. Competition
   c. Excellence
   d. Quality vs. Quantity
   e. Progress
   f. Short-term Relationships

4. Give an example of professionalism vs. statutory control within your country. How does this example relate to the five societal values? Give concrete examples.

5. Give an example of uniformity vs. flexibility within your country. How does this example relate to the five societal values? Give concrete examples.

6. Give an example of conservatism vs. optimism within your country. How does this example relate to the five societal values? Give concrete examples.

7. Give an example of secrecy vs. transparency within your country. How does this example relate to the five societal values? Give concrete examples.

8. Consider Parmalat's accounting problems in 2003. What societal values and accounting values most contributed to Parmalat's falsified statements?

9. Consider Enron's accounting problems. What societal values and accounting values most contributed to Enron's collapse?

10. Because of the accounting scandals of the early twenty-first century, new laws like Sarbanes-Oxley have been enacted. What societal and accounting values do the laws attempt to change?

11. How has globalization impacted the viability of cultural accounting analysis? In other words, has globalization increased the common development of accounting values and decreased the importance of national societal values?

12. Using the accounting and societal values discussed in the chapter, construct a basic ideal accounting system. Is there a country that uses your system? Is there a country that closely approximates your system?

13. The chapter discusses how cultural and governmental influences impact accounting and financial reporting standards. Do accounting and financial reporting standards influence governmental or cultural standards? Consider Argentina and Russia. Support your answer.

14. Discuss the benefits and difficulties experienced by both a MNE and a host country when the MNE enters the country.

15. How have the social values, accounting values, and accounting system traits in the United States been impacted by recent globalization? What is a good measure of a country's accounting system inertia (the amount that a country's accounting system affects more than is affected by globalization of accounting systems and standards)?

Case: General Motors and Japanese Convergence vs. Chinese Convergence

Case: Inductive Methods and Deductive Methods Relating Reporting Standards to Cultural Values

These cases can be found on the following website: www.wiley.com/college/radebaugh

Selected References

Baydoun, N., and R. Willett. 1995." Cultural Relevance of Western Accounting Systems to Developing Countries." *Abacus* (March): 67–92.

Chanchani, S., and R. Willett. 2004. "An Empirical Assessment of Gray's Accounting Value Constructs." *International Journal of Accounting* 39(2): 15–24.

Choi, Frederick D. S. 1974."European Disclosure: The Competitive Disclosure Hypothesis." *Journal of International Business Studies* (Fall): 15–24.

Doupnik, T. S., and S. B. Salter. 1993. "An Empirical Test of a Judgmental International Classification of Financial Reporting Practices." *Journal of International Business Studies* (first quarter): 41–60.

Doupnik. T. S., and S. B. Salter. 1995. "External Environment, Culture, and Accounting Practice: A Preliminary Test of a General Model of International Accounting Development." *International Journal of Accounting* 30(3): 189–207.

Doupnik, Timothy S., and George T. Tsakumis. 2005. " A Critical Review of Tests of Gray's Theory of Cultural Relevance and Suggestions for Future Research." *Journal of Accounting Literature,* forthcoming.

Gray, S. J. 1980. "The Impact of International Accounting Differences from a Security Analysis Perspective: Some European Evidence." *Journal of Accounting Research* (Spring): 64–76.

Gray, S. J. 1985. "Cultural Influences and the International Classification of Accounting Systems." Paper presented at the European Institute for Advanced Studies in Management Workshop on "Accounting and Culture," Amsterdam (June).

Gray, S. J. 1988. "Towards a Theory of Cultural Influence on the Development of Accounting Systems Internationally." *Abacus* (March): 1–15.

Gray, S. J. 1989. "International Accounting Research: The Global Challenge." *International Journal of Accounting* 23(4): 291–307.

Gray, S. J., and H. M. Vint. 1995. "The Impact of Culture on Accounting Disclosures: Some International Evidence." *Asia-Pacific Journal of Accounting* 2: 33–43.

Harrison, G. L., and J. L. McKinnon. 1986. "Culture and Accounting Change: A New Perspective on Corporate Reporting Regulation and Accounting Policy Formulation." *Accounting, Organisations and Society* 11(3): 233–252.

Hofstede, Geert. 1980. *Culture's Consequences: International Differences in Work-Related Values.* Beverly Hills, CA: Sage.

Hoftstede, Geert. 1984. "Cultural Dimensions in Management and Planning." *Asia Pacific Journal of Management* (January): 81–90.

Hofstede, Geert. 1991. *Cultures and Organizations.* Maidenhead, England: McGraw-Hill.

Hofstede, Geert. 2001. *Culture's Consequences: Comparing Values, Behaviours, Institutions and Organizations Across Nations.* 2nd ed. Thousand Oaks, CA: Sage.

Hofstede, Geert, and Michael H. Bond. 1988. "The Confucius Connection: From Cultural Roots to Economic Growth." *Organizational Dynamics* 16(4): 5–21.

International Accounting Standards Board. www.iasb.org.uk.

International Association for Accounting Education and Research. www.iaaer.org.

Jaggi, B. C. 1973. "The Impact of the Cultural Environment on Financial Disclosures." *International Journal of Accounting* (Spring): 75–84.

McKinnon, J. L. 1986. *The Historical Development and Operational Form of Corporate Reporting Regulation in Japan.* New York: Garland.

Mueller, Gerhard G. 1967. *International Accounting.* New York: Macmillan.

Mueller, Gerhard G. 1968. "Accounting Principles Generally Accepted in the U.S. versus Those Generally Accepted Elsewhere." *International Journal of Accounting* (Spring).

Nair, R. D., and Werner G. Frank. 1980. "The Impact of Disclosure and Measurement Practices on International Accounting Classifications." *Accounting Review* (July): 426–451.

Nobes, C. W. 1983. "A Judgmental International Classification of Financial Reporting Practices." *Journal of Business Finance and Accounting* (Spring): 1–19.

Nobes, C. W. 1984. *International Classification of Financial Reporting.* London: Croom Helm.

Nobes, C. W. 1998. "Towards a General Model of the Reasons for International Differences in Financial Reporting." *Abacus* (September): 162–187.

Nobes, C. W., and R. H. Parker, eds. 2000. *Comparative International Accounting.* 6th ed. Englewood Cliffs, NJ: Prentice-Hall.

Parker, R. H. 1989. "Importing and Exporting Accounting: The British Experience." In *International Pressures for Accounting Change,* edited by A. G. Hopwood. Englewood Cliffs, NJ: Prentice-Hall: 7–29.

Perera, H. 1994. "Culture and International Accounting: Some Thoughts on Research Issues and Prospects." *Advances in International Accounting* 7: 267–285.

Pourjalali, G., and G. K. Meek. 1995. "Accounting and Culture: The Case of Iran." *Research in Accounting in Emerging Economies* 3: 3–17.

Salter, Stephen, and Frederick Niswander. 1995. "Cultural Influence on the Development of Accounting Systems Internationally: A Test of Gray's (1988) Theory." *Journal of International Business Studies* 26(2): 379–397.

Saudagaran, Shahrokh, and Gary Biddle. 1992. "Financial Disclosure Levels and Foreign Stock Exchange Listing Decisions." *Journal of International Financial Management and Accounting* (Summer): 106–148.

Schwartz, S. H. 1994. *Individualism and Collectivism: Theory, Method and Applications.* Thousand Oaks, CA: Sage.

Sterling, Robert R. 1967. "Conservatism: The Fundamental Principle of Valuation in Traditional Accounting." *Abacus* (December): 109–132.

United Nations. 1977. *International Standards of Accounting and Reporting.* New York: UN.

United Nations. 1988. *Conclusions on Accounting and Reporting by Transnational Corporations.* New York: UN, revised.

Weetman, P., and S. J. Gray. 1990. "International Financial Analysis and Comparative Corporate Performance: The Impact of U.K. versus U.S. Accounting Principles on Earnings." *Journal of International Financial Management and Accounting* (Summer/Autumn): 111–130.

Weetman, P., and S. J. Gray. 1991. "A Comparative Analysis of the Impact of Accounting Principles on Profits: The U.S.A. versus the U.K., Sweden, and the Netherlands." *Accounting and Business Research* (Autumn): 363–379.

Zeff, S. A. 1972. *Forging Accounting Principles in Five Countries.* New York: Stipes.

CHAPTER THREE

COMPARATIVE INTERNATIONAL FINANCIAL ACCOUNTING I

Chapter Objectives

- Compare accounting systems in developed Anglo-American countries, namely, the United States, the United Kingdom, and Australia
- Compare accounting systems in developed Nordic countries, namely, the Netherlands and Sweden
- Compare accounting systems in developed Germanic countries, namely, Germany and Switzerland
- Compare accounting systems in developed Latin countries, namely, France and Italy
- Compare accounting systems in developed Asian countries, namely, Japan

INTRODUCTION

In this chapter, we will outline the accounting systems of selected developed countries using the cultural classification identified in previous chapters as the basis for discussion. Accordingly, we will review the accounting systems of the United States, the United Kingdom, and Australia as representatives of the Anglo-American culture area; the Netherlands and Sweden as representatives of the Nordic countries; Germany and Switzerland as representatives of the Germanic countries; France, Italy, and Spain as representatives of the Latin countries; and Japan as a representative of the Asian countries. The developing countries of Brazil, Mexico, China, India, Indonesia, Malaysia, Russia, and Thailand will be discussed in Chapter 4.

Comparative economic data on the countries covered in this chapter are presented in Exhibit 3.1. These countries dominate the world capital markets. In addi-

Strategic Decision Point

In the business world, many uncertainties exist. As such, assigning probabilities to uncertainties is necessary to apply some accounting standards. Accounting standards reflect this requirement through verbal probability expressions, such as that of IAS 18, which states that revenue should be recognized when "it is probable that the economic benefit associated with the transaction will flow to the enterprise." Accountants are required to measure the probabilities of future events and to determine whether the probability meets the requirement of being "probable" or "remote." A recent study conducted by Doupnik and Richter (2004) analyzed the impact of culture on the interpretation of verbal probability expressions. Their research found that German accountants were generally more conservative in applying these probability expressions. Furthermore, the study concludes that national culture can affect the way accountants measure probability as described through the expressions used in the standards. Differences in the way people apply the criteria may result in differences in the application of recognition criteria.

The IASB was created to increase comparability across nations. However, this goal may be negatively affected if cultural differences impinge on the interpretations made by accountants. Even if the world adopts a common set of standards, will they be applied consistently across cultures? What can the IASB do to mitigate this issue?

Exhibit 3.1   Economic Data for Developed Countries

	GDP PPP (in billions)	GDP Per Capita	Population (in millions)	Unem- ployment	Infla- tion	Area per sq km (in thousands)	Imports (in billions)	Exports (in billions)
U.S	$10,990.0	$37,800	293.0	6.0%	2.3%	9,631.4	$1,260.0	$714.5
U.K.	$1,666.0	$27,700	60.3	5.0%	1.4%	244.8	$363.6	$304.5
Australia	$571.4	$29,000	19.9	6.0%	2.8%	7,686.9	$82.9	$68.7
Netherlands	$461.4	$28,600	16.3	5.3%	2.1%	41.5	$217.7	$253.2
Sweden	$238.3	$26,800	9.0	4.9%	1.9%	450.0	$83.3	$102.8
Germany	$2,271.0	$27,600	82.4	10.5%	1.1%	357.0	$585.0	$696.9
Switzerland	$239.3	$32,700	7.4	3.7%	0.6%	41.3	$102.2	$110.0
France	$1,661.0	$27,600	60.4	9.7%	2.1%	547.0	$339.9	$346.5
Italy	$1,550.0	$26,700	58.1	8.6%	2.7%	301.2	$271.1	$278.1
Spain	$885.5	$22,000	40.3	11.3%	3.0%	504.8	$197.1	$159.4
Japan	$3,582.0	$28,200	127.3	5.3%	−0.3%	337.8	$346.6	$447.1

Source: Compiled from *The World Bank* www.worldbank.com/data/countrydata/countrydata.html and *The World Factbook* www.cia.gov/cia/publications/factbook/, December 2004.

tion, they are leading the development of international accounting standards. Six of these countries are among the founding members of the International Accounting Standards Committee, now known as the International Accounting Standards Board (IASB): France, Germany, Japan, the Netherlands, United Kingdom, and the United States.

ANGLO-AMERICAN ACCOUNTING

There is no doubt that Anglo-American accounting can be distinguished from accounting in continental Europe, Asia, Latin America, and many other parts of the world. It is practiced not only in the United States and United Kingdom but also to an important extent in countries and regions where, for example, the United Kingdom has had a major colonial influence, such as in Australia, Canada, Hong Kong, India, Ireland, Kenya, Malaysia, New Zealand, Nigeria, Singapore, and South Africa. Anglo-American accounting tends to be relatively less conservative and more transparent than that of the Germanic and Latin countries and Japan.

United States

Accounting in the United States is very similar to that in the United Kingdom, as might be expected given the historical and investment connections between the two countries. Just as the language and legal system of the United States were exported from the United Kingdom, so, too, were the founding fathers of U.S. accounting, including pioneers such as Arthur Young (a Glasgow University graduate of the 1880s). Nevertheless, the United States has adapted rather than adopted the United Kingdom's accounting tradition. Indeed, recent historical and environmental circumstances of the United States have given rise to some significant distinguishing features.

In the United States, accounting focuses on large corporations and the interests of investors, though the needs of creditors and other users are recognized. The relevance of information to business decisions is paramount subject to the constraint of reliability.

The securities markets are the dominant influence on accounting regulation in the United States. Dealings in securities and investor protection are regulated and enforced at the federal government level under the Securities Act of 1933 and the Securities Exchange Act of 1934, which were passed in response to the stock market crash of 1929 and subsequent financial crises.

The Securities and Exchange Commission (SEC) was established with the legal authority to enforce the securities laws and to formulate as well as enforce accounting standards. However, the SEC recognizes as authoritative the generally accepted accounting principles (GAAP) embodied in standards issued by an independent Financial Accounting Standards Board (FASB), which was established in 1973 following criticism of the standard-setting procedures of the American Institute of Certified Public Accountants. Thus, the standard-setting role has been delegated to the FASB, with the SEC acting in a supervisory capacity only if it deems it necessary to intervene, which it has done only on rare occasions (e.g., with respect to oil and gas accounting). Corporations are required to follow FASB standards; otherwise the SEC will refuse registration and hence trading in their securities. Only listed corporations (a minority of U.S. corporations) are required to comply with the very detailed regulations imposed by the SEC for investor protection purposes.

The FASB has a very open approach to standard-setting known as operating "in the sunshine." All meetings are open to the public, and a variety of opinions are sought in an elaborate "due process" to ensure that the public interest is properly served. To help formulate new standards and improve existing ones, the FASB has developed an explicit conceptual framework of objectives and qualitative characteristics for financial reporting in its series of statements on financial accounting concepts. The FASB's pronouncements on accounting practice are issued as Statements of Financial Accounting Standards (SFAS). More than 150 of these had been issued by 2004. Taken together, the FASB standards are quite detailed and voluminous compared to, for example, U.K. standards. This suggests that while the United States is similar in many ways to the United Kingdom, it is unique in having perhaps the most comprehensive system of accounting regulations in the world, at least as far as securities markets are concerned.

United Kingdom

In the United Kingdom, as in the United States, primacy of place is given to the information needs of investors. It is expected, however, that most of the needs of other groups will be similar to those of investors and will thus be satisfied in any event. The special needs of other groups are usually met privately or on a voluntary basis (e.g., a value-added statement for employees).

Like the United States, the securities markets of the United Kingdom have a significant influence on accounting practice. However, they do not dominate the process of accounting regulation. Company law in the United Kingdom has a much wider remit than the U.S. securities laws as far as the provision of accounting information is concerned. The U.K. Companies Act of 1985, which consolidated all previous extant companies acts and was amended by the companies act passed in 1989, includes accounting requirements for all limited liability companies, not just large companies or those listed on stock exchanges. In addition, the accountancy profession and, to a lesser extent, the stock exchange, are involved in the accounting regulatory process.

There have been a number of substantial revisions to U.K. company law in recent years, primarily to implement the European Union (EU) Fourth Directive on company accounts and the Seventh Directive on consolidated accounts, in 1981 and 1989, respectively. Prior to the 1980s, company law was perceived as providing little more than a framework for accounting regulation within which the accounting profession could set more detailed accounting rules or standards as appropriate. While company law did in fact incorporate specific requirements, these were mainly concerned with disclosure, thus leaving matters of accounting treatment to the judgment of the profession. This flexible approach is still enshrined in the legal requirement that company accounts must present "a true and fair view" of a company's results and financial position. This principle overrides the detailed requirements of the law, and accounting standards for that matter, to the extent that additional or, in exceptional circumstances, alternative information should be provided. The principle that accounts should present a true and fair view has also been adopted by the EU in its accounting directives.

The accounting profession in the United Kingdom has enjoyed a substantial amount of independence since professional associations were first formed in the 1850s. Accounting was largely an "independent discipline" derived from the needs of individual businesses. Accountants were independent professionals making judgments, either as company accountants or as auditors, on the appropriate method to be used in individual accounts. This accounting tradition has now evolved to a much more regulated state as a result of criticisms concerning the flexibility of professional accounting standards used in the preparation of company accounts as well as governmental pressures and developments in EU harmonization.

In 1970, to stave off government intervention and the creation of a U.S.-style SEC, the profession set up its own self-regulatory organization, the Accounting Standards Steering Committee (ASSC), which was subsequently renamed the Accounting Standards Committee (ASC). The aim of the ASC was to develop Statements of Standard Accounting Practice (SSAPs) with adoption and enforcement being the responsibility of the six professional bodies involved. A total of 25 SSAPs were issued by the ASC under this system until 1990 when, following sustained criticism of its effectiveness in curbing "creative accounting," a new standard-setting framework was established. An independent Accounting Standards Board (ASB), similar to the FASB in the United States, was set up, guided by a Financial Reporting Council (FRC), which represented a wide constituency of interests.

The new ASB has the power to issue Financial Reporting Standards (FRSs) on its own authority. There is also a legal sanction for companies that do not comply with FRSs in that any departures from accounting standards must be explained and the financial effects disclosed. The FRC's Financial Reporting Review Panel and the Department of Trade and Industry are also empowered to investigate complaints about departures from accounting standards that do not appear to result in a true and fair view and to go to the courts, if necessary, to require a company to revise its accounts. The ASB recognizes that the requirement to give a true and fair view may justify a departure from accounting standards, but it is imposing a stricter regime than in the past that is consistent with the statement that "because accounting standards are formulated with the objective of ensuring that the information resulting from their application faithfully represents the underlying commercial activity, the Board envisages that only in exceptional circumstances will departure from the requirements of an accounting standard be necessary in order for financial statements to give a true and fair view" (Foreword to Accounting Standards, June 1993, paragraph 18).

In 2002, the EU adopted a regulation to endorse and require International Financial Reporting Standards (IFRS) with the exception of IAS 32 and 39, which are currently in the process of being revised by the IASB. As such, the ASB is preparing for convergence with IFRS for consolidated statements in 2005, as required by the EU regulation. This requirement marks another substantial revision to U.K. company law. The ASB hoped to incorporate IFRS before 2005, but the process has been difficult with the IASB's slow progress, and they continue to issue new standards to help them comply with IFRS.

Australia

Although Australia's accounting history is young, the English influence can be seen in Australia's accounting structure. Much like the United States, Australia grew as a result of British migration in the 1800s. As such, Australia's accounting practices focus more on the information needs of investors than on the tax needs of the country. In 1991, the Australian Securities & Investments Commission was created to help regulate and enforce company law to protect consumers, investors, and creditors.

Accounting standards are created by the Australian Accounting Standards Board (AASB). Originally, the AASB worked jointly with the Public Sector Accounting Standards Board to create Australian standards. The Urgent Issues Group (UIG) was established in 1994 to help address urgent issues in the accounting field, much like the Emergency Issues Task Force (EITF) in the United States.

In 1999, Australia's standard-setting process was reorganized through the Corporate Law Economic Reform Program Act. This reorganization created the Financial Reporting Council (FRC) to oversee the actions of the AASB. The FRC can give the AASB direction but will not be able to influence the content of particular standards. The AASB now has the responsibility of creating standards for both the public and private sector and has its own research team and staff. The UIG continues to provide timely guidance on urgent accounting issues. Australia adopted IFRS in 2005 at the some time as the EU.

NORDIC ACCOUNTING

Accounting in the Nordic countries is in some respects similar to that of the Anglo-American countries, but there are some important Germanic influences, especially regarding the significance of taxation. This group includes the Netherlands, Denmark, Sweden, and Finland (all members of the EU) as well as Norway. Nordic accounting tends to be less conservative and more transparent than that in the Germanic and Latin countries, but not as much as that in the Anglo-American group of countries.

The Netherlands

The Netherlands is famous for its business economics approach to accounting. Whereas investors have pride of place as users of accounts, the information needs of other users and especially employees are recognized on a voluntary basis. The practice of social reporting has been established since the 1970s and involves disclosures mainly about employment and personnel policies in both annual reports and special reports.

Accounting in the Netherlands is similar in many ways to that of the United Kingdom and the Anglo-American approach as a whole. Company law and the accounting profession are the major influences, and although the number of companies listed on the stock exchange is relatively small, there is more of a tradition of public ownership of shares and an international business outlook than in many other continental European countries.

Company law in the Netherlands is incorporated in the Civil Code, which is based on Roman law. It is similar to most continental European countries except that the Civil Code traditionally has not provided a detailed framework. Governments have had a somewhat laissez-faire attitude toward commercial matters, much as in the United Kingdom. However, the influence of company law has grown steadily since 1970 through the Act on the Annual Accounts of Enterprises and the implementation of the EU Fourth and Seventh Directives, in 1983 and 1988, respectively. Before 1970 there was a virtual absence of legislation on accounting, a gap that was filled by the influential Dutch accounting profession now known as the Royal Nederlands Institut van Register accountants (NIVRA).

Despite the currently detailed provisions of the Civil Code, the overriding criterion is the application of "generally acceptable accounting principles," which is more or less the Dutch equivalent of the United Kingdom's "true and fair view." Guidelines as to what are "acceptable"—as opposed to the U.S. "accepted"—principles are provided by the Council for Annual Reporting, which consists of representatives of the employers, users, employees, and the accounting profession (NIVRA). Although these guidelines, which complement and supplement the law just as the accounting standards in the United Kingdom do, are not mandatory, they are followed by most companies.

A novel feature of regulation in the Netherlands is the Civil Code provision that interested parties, including shareholders, employees, works councils, and trade unions, may complain to the Enterprise Chamber (Ondernemingskamer) of the Court of Justice in Amsterdam if they believe that the accounts do not comply with the law. Hence, through this means the company law is being supplemented by a body of interpretative case law. This is perhaps another example of the unique Dutch compromise between the continental European and Anglo-American legal traditions and culture. As part of the EU, the Netherlands adopted IFRS for listed companies beginning in 2005.

Sweden

The accounting tradition in Sweden gives preference to the information needs of creditors, government, and the tax authorities. However, this situation has been changing quite rapidly because of the growing involvement of major Swedish companies in international mergers and acquisitions and their need to seek financing in international financial markets. The Swedish stock market has also grown in importance and is a potential focal point for the Nordic countries. Recent developments suggest the emergence of a two-tier approach to corporate reporting, with the accounts of individual companies prepared on a traditional basis in contrast to the consolidated accounts of major groups, which may be focused more on shareholder information needs and the standards applicable in an international capital market context.

Although the development of accounting in Sweden, as in France and Germany, has been strongly influenced by legal and taxation requirements, there is also a tradition in Sweden of involvement by the accounting profession in the standard-setting process. The influence of the stock exchange is also important with respect to accounting and disclosure by large corporations. Many of these corporations are multinationals and are thus exposed to international capital market pressures. But in contrast to the Netherlands, the overriding influence in Sweden has been the state, which has been committed, in general, to the use of accounting information for the purpose of macroeconomic planning and policy making. In this regard, the Swedish tax system has been used aggressively to promote macroeconomic objectives and as such has encouraged a more conservative approach to income measurement.

Company law governing accounting is embodied in the 1975 Companies Act, the 1976 Accounting Act, and the 1981 Act on the Annual Accounts in Certain Forms of Business Enterprise. Although the Accounting Act required that generally accepted accounting principles be followed, these principles were not defined. However, this situation changed somewhat following the New Accounting Act of 1995, which implemented the EU Accounting Directives. Over the years, the law has tended to provide a framework rather than detailed requirements. This flexibility has enabled the Swedish accounting profession, the Foreningen Auktoriserade Revisorer (FAR), founded in 1923, to play an influential role by making recommendations on accounting matters. However, in 1976, the government established the Bokforingsnamnden (BFN), or Accounting Standards Board, to make recommendations on accounting matters within the framework of company law.

More recently, in 1991, an Accounting Council (Redovisningsradet) was established to take over the standard-setting role of the FAR but in the form of a body that is representative of a broader constituency (i.e., industry, government, and the profession) and also independent of the accounting profession, like the FASB in the United States. The stock exchange supports both the new Accounting Council and BFN and, in addition, encourages listed companies to disclose additional information about their performance, prospects, financial goals and strategies, and the company's business environment. The recommendations issued by the Accounting Standards Board and the Accounting Council are not mandatory but advisory in the context of company law. In practice, therefore, the approach to accounting standard-setting in Sweden seems to be very much consensus oriented and somewhat flexible despite the legal and taxation influences at work. As part of the EU, Sweden was also required to use IFRS for listed companies beginning in 2005.

GERMANIC ACCOUNTING

In many respects, the Germanic group of countries differs significantly from the Anglo-American and Nordic groups. The influences of company law and taxation are paramount. The Germanic group includes Germany and Austria (members of the EU) as well as Israel and Switzerland. Germanic accounting has also had some influence in France, Japan, and a number of former European colonies in Africa. Germanic accounting tends to be relatively conservative and secretive compared to Anglo-American accounting.

Germany

The accounting tradition in Germany gives preference to the information needs of creditors and the tax authorities. In a recent study, Black and White (2003) provide evidence that balance sheet items such as book value of equity is more value relevant than earnings in Germany. In the more investor-oriented United States, earnings is more value relevant than is book value of equity. However, large listed corporations and especially MNEs are now aiming to present more shareholder-oriented corporate reports.

Company law seems to be the predominant influence on accounting in Germany. The legal system in Germany is highly codified and prescriptive because it is based on the Roman law system as opposed to the Anglo-American common law system. The laws on accounting in Germany amend the Commercial Code (Handelsgesetzbuch). A tradition of uniformity in accounting has dominated Germany and has led to the development of uniform accounting in France. The German tax laws are also a strong influence to the extent that the annual accounts form the basis for the tax accounts. This principle is known in Germany as the Massgeblichkeitsprinzip. Thus, any allowance or deduction claimed for tax purposes must be charged in the annual accounts.

The accounting profession is relatively small, and professional pronouncements have much less status than do those, for example, in the United States, the United Kingdom, and the Netherlands. The German stock market is still relatively small, reflecting the fact that the major sources of finance have been the banks along with the government and family interests. Those corporations that are listed tend to be quite closely held by these interested parties. Nevertheless, the stock market is becoming more important in Germany, and many German multinational enterprises (MNEs) are listed in other European countries, with a growing number also listed in the United States. This is influencing corporate reporting behavior and encouraging some voluntary disclosure of information.

The Commercial Code sets out the detailed accounting requirements governing limited liability corporations. This was revised by the Accounting Directives Law of 1985, which implemented the EU Fourth and Seventh Directives. While the concept of "a true and fair view" was incorporated in the EU directives, this seems to have been interpreted for German purposes as a requirement to present transparent and reliable financial statements in accordance with the legal provisions. In practice, the tax rules tend to dominate legal decisions on accounting issues, and hence the development of accounting principles within the legal framework can be traced to this source rather than to the accounting profession, which consists of the Institut der Wirtschaftsprüfer in Deutschland (IDW) and the Wirtschaftsprüferkammer. A German Accounting Standards Board was established similar to the FASB in the United States, and the Commercial Code was revised to permit consolidated accounts to be prepared on the basis of U.S. GAAP or International Accounting Standards. However, Germany adopted IFRS for listed companies beginning in 2005 as part of the EU regulation. Furthermore, the German Federal Ministry of Justice created the Financial Reporting Enforcement Panel (FREP) to discover infringements in financial reporting for listed companies, including compliance with IFRS, and to take appropriate enforcement action.

Switzerland

Much like Germany, the accounting tradition in Switzerland gives preference to the information needs of creditors and the authorities. However, the importance of the

Swiss securities market is growing, and many large Swiss companies are seeking capital in international financial markets. As a result, a growing number of large companies are making extensive voluntary disclosures of information consistent with internationally accepted practice.

The secrecy of the Swiss is world renowned; indeed, Swiss accounting is among the most conservative and secretive in Europe and the world today. As in Germany, Swiss accounting practice is dominated by company law and the tax regulations governing the accounting profession, which is small and still in the early stages of setting accounting standards. However, in contrast to Germany, the legal requirements relating to accounting are modest and still permit the creation of secret reserves. Furthermore, only listed companies, banks, insurance companies, and railways are required to file or publish annual accounts. This is not surprising given that most companies are small and family owned and managed.

Nevertheless, times are changing, albeit rather slowly, and Swiss corporations face increasing competition in international business and financial markets. Company law has been revised with changes inspired by the EU Fourth and Seventh Directives. An accounting standards board has also been established to make accounting and reporting recommendations for Swiss companies.

The existing Swiss Commercial Law (Code of Obligations) provides the general principles of bookkeeping practice to be followed by all enterprises as well as other rules specifically on accounting for limited liability companies. However, these accounting rules are very conservative and focus primarily on the interests of creditors. In effect, they institutionalize the practice of secret reserves by permitting assets to be undervalued. The essential feature of the law is a concern with the maintenance of share capital in nominal terms (i.e., historical costs). Accordingly, historical costs form the upper limit of valuations, while at the same time there is no prescribed lower limit. Moreover, there is only minimal disclosure of information to shareholders.

Recognition of this unsatisfactory state of affairs gave rise to the 1983 proposals for company law reform but within a philosophy that the law should provide only general principles and that a liberal approach to financial reporting should be preserved. Given the very strong Swiss tradition of democracy and the innate conservatism of the Swiss, it is not surprising that the proposed reforms have taken so long to be implemented. The objectives of the new law, approved in 1992, included improving the disclosure of information to investors and strengthening the protection of shareholder interests. The specific reforms designed to achieve this involved requiring all public and large private companies to publish annual accounts, improving the layout of the annual accounts, incorporating generally accepted accounting principles into the law, allowing the revaluation of investments in land and buildings, requiring disclosures in the notes to the accounts, and, perhaps most important, making the presentation of consolidated accounts compulsory for listed and large corporations. However, proposals to restrict the formation of secret reserves were not accepted.

Along with company law reform, the accounting profession has embarked on the development of its accounting standard-setting process, inspired greatly by the model of the FASB in the United States. In 1984, following an initiative by the Swiss Institute of Certified Accountants, the Foundation for Accounting and Reporting Recommendations was established. The foundation supervises an independent Accounting Standards Board, with a broadly based membership that makes recommendations on financial accounting and reporting. These recommendations are intended to improve the quality of accounting in Switzerland by elaborating on and supplementing the company law. IFRS become mandatory for listed companies in Switzerland beginning in 2005.

LATIN ACCOUNTING

The Latin group of countries is similar to the Germanic group with regard to company law and taxation but they have a unique flavor in many respects. The Latin group can be divided into the more developed group, which includes Argentina, Belgium, France, Portugal, Spain, and Italy; and the less developed group, which includes such countries as Brazil, Chile, Colombia, Mexico, Peru, and Uruguay. The colonial influences of France and Belgium, on the one hand, and Spain and Portugal, on the other, are also visible in a number of African (e.g., Zaire, Senegal) and South American (e.g., Argentina, Brazil, Mexico, Peru) countries, respectively. Latin accounting tends to be relatively more conservative and secretive compared to the Anglo-American countries.

France

The accounting tradition in France gives preference to the information needs of creditors and the tax authorities, as in Germany. This emphasis is changing, however, at least to some extent, with respect to large listed corporations and especially MNEs. International market pressures would seem to be encouraging a much more shareholder-oriented approach, especially with respect to the consolidated accounts. Indeed, French law has been amended recently to permit consolidated accounts to be prepared using U.S. GAAP or International Accounting Standards.

As in the Germanic countries, company law seems to be the predominant influence on accounting in France. The laws relating to accounting can be traced back to the original Code de Commerce of the early 1800s. French law reflects the classic position, dating from the French Revolution and the Code Napoléon, that engagement in commerce creates obligations to keep accounts and prepare financial statements. Related to this is the uniquely French emphasis on uniformity and its application through the standardized national code of accounting, the Plan Comptable Général.

This code, which was based on German ideas and developed during the German occupation of 1940–1945, was first implemented in 1947. The aim, which is still an underlying objective, was to promote more effective national economic planning. The code is the responsibility of the Conseil Nationale de la Comptabilité, the French National Accounting Council (with a broadly based membership), and is implemented through company law. The contents of the Plan Comptable Général are extensive and include a detailed Chart of Accounts, with numeric coding for all the accounts, rules relating to valuation and profit measurement, models for financial statement presentation, consolidation requirements, and so on. The influence of the code is all pervasive and promotes a much more legalistic approach to accounting than the more judgmental Anglo-American approach. A new accounting law, passed in 1983, implemented the revised (1982) version of the Plan Comptable Général, which was prepared in response to the EU Fourth Directive. Further laws were passed in 1985 and 1986 to implement the EU Seventh Directive on consolidated accounts.

Apart from company law and the Plan Comptable Général, taxation is a major influence on French accounting. The tax laws tend to override the accounting rules to the extent that charges deductible for tax purposes must be recorded in the accounts if the tax benefit is to be claimed. However, under the 1982 Plan Comptable Général, the rules permit a distinction to be made between economic depreciation and exceptional depreciation, the latter being the excess of tax deductible over economic depreciation.

The accounting profession in France is relatively small and lacks the status of its counterparts in the Anglo-American countries. Interestingly, the roles of public accounting and auditing are carried out by separate institutions established by law (i.e., the Ordre des Experts Comptables et des Comptables Agrées [OECCA] and the Compagnie Nationale des Commissaires aux Comptes [CNCC]).

The stock market is also still relatively small in France, as in Germany, which reflects the fact that the major sources of finance are banks, the government, and family interests. However, more emphasis on investor interests has been given in recent years following the establishments in 1967 of the Commission des Opérations de Bourse (COB). This is the French equivalent of the U.S. Securities and Exchange Commission (SEC), but in practice it has promoted developments in financial reporting, such as consolidations and disclosure, by seeking the cooperation of corporations rather than through the enforcing of regulations. As part of the EU, the French adopted IFRS for listed companies beginning in 2005.

Italy

As in France, the interests of the government and tax authorities take precedence over those of shareholders, although the balance is now changing somewhat as major Italian companies become more involved in international financial markets.

In Italy, the influences of company law (the Civil Code) and the taxation regulations on accounting are similar to those in a number of other continental European countries and especially France, Belgium, and Spain. Italian accounting in practice is in many respects comparable with that of its European neighbors despite the fact that the EU Fourth and Seventh Directives were only implemented, somewhat belatedly, in 1991. This is especially true for listed companies, which are subject to additional legal and stock exchange regulations. Furthermore, a number of major MNEs make voluntary disclosures of information in response to international capital market pressures.

While the origins of double-entry bookkeeping can be traced to Italy in the thirteenth century, the filing of annual accounts by limited liability companies has been required by law only since 1882. Following amendments to the Civil Code in 1942 and 1974, an increasingly stricter regime was imposed, which in 1991 was updated by the implementation of the EU Directives.

Given that the accounts are used as the basis for taxation, as in most continental European countries, there has been a tradition of conservatism to minimize taxable profits and distributions to shareholders. It is also not uncommon for Italian companies to present different sets of accounts for management, the taxation authorities, and shareholders, but the scope for this has been reduced in recent years. In this regard, listed companies have been subject to additional regulation primarily by the Commissione Nazionale per le Società e la Borsa (CONSOB), which is more or less the equivalent of the U.S. SEC. The CONSOB was established in 1974 and has been responsible for a number of important developments including the requirement that, in addition to the statutory audit, listed companies have a more extensive audit by an approved auditing firm. The CONSOB also had the authority to require the filing of consolidated accounts by groups of companies, but in practice companies were encouraged rather than required to do so.

Implementation of the Fourth and Seventh EU Directives has brought about a change of emphasis in Italian accounts with the introduction of the true and fair view concept and the requirement that consolidated accounts be presented. Italy has been slow to adopt the EU directives because the interests of external users of accounts and the protection of shareholders have not been considered as important as the need to support and develop the interests of major family or state-owned industrial enterprises. This has been reinforced by the legal heritage of the nineteenth century, which has tended, like the Swiss, to protect the right of companies to keep the secrets of their business from competitors and outsiders, including until recently external shareholders.

The professional accounting bodies in Italy, the Consiglio Nazionale dei Dottori Commercialisti and the Consiglio Nazionali dei Ragioneri, are essentially advisory. There is a joint body that issues recommendations on accounting principles. The accounting bodies have recommended the use of IASB standards for matters not covered by them. It is also noteworthy that the CONSOB has recommended that listed companies adopt the profession's statements on accounting principles. However, listed companies were required to use IFRS starting in 2005.

ASIAN ACCOUNTING

The Asian group of countries have cultures quite distinct from the Anglo-American, Nordic, Germanic, and Latin groupings. However, as far as accounting is concerned, many have a colonial history, such as Indonesia (Netherlands); India, Pakistan, Hong Kong, Singapore, and Malaysia (United Kingdom); and the Philippines (Spain/United States). China has been influenced by both Western ideas and the socialist uniformity of the former Soviet Union. Even in Japan, with its unique culture, it appears that both German and U.S. influences have been important in establishing the Japanese accounting tradition. Asian accounting tends to be relatively more conservative and secretive compared to the Anglo-American countries.

Japan

Despite the significance of the stock market, the accounting tradition in Japan gives preference to the information needs and priorities of creditors and the tax authorities.

The government has been a major influence on all aspects of accounting in Japan. The Commercial Code, modeled after the German commercial code of the nineteenth century, was introduced in 1890 with the objective of protecting creditors. After World War II, the Commercial Code was revised to protect the interests of investors as well, following U.S. practice. Furthermore, in 1948, a new securities and exchange law was introduced, modeled on the U.S. securities laws of 1933 and 1934, to protect investors in public corporations listed on stock exchanges or with stocks (shares) traded on the over-the-counter market.

The corporation tax law is another major, if not overriding, influence on income measurement practices in that corporate tax returns must be based on the annual accounts approved by shareholders. Much like France and Germany, tax-deductible expenses including depreciation cannot be claimed for tax purposes unless they are charged in the individual company accounts. Thus, there is a tendency toward very conservative accounting in Japan.

Government institutions are directly involved in accounting standard setting. The Business Accounting Deliberation Council (BADC), which establishes Financial Accounting Standards for Business Enterprises, is an advisory body within the Ministry of Finance (MOF). The MOF is responsible for the securities and exchange law and its related accounting regulations. On the other hand, the Ministry of Justice is responsible for the application of the Commercial Code. With accounting systems under the jurisdiction of two government institutions, there is no unified approach to regulation. In fact, a number of large listed corporations are obliged to prepare two sets of financial statements, one required by the Commercial Code and the other by the Securities and Exchange Law, though it is the form of presentation rather than the substance that must be different. The Commercial Code also requires only nonconsolidated financial statements. The Securities and Exchange Law, on the other hand, requires consolidated financial statements and an independent audit, but such statements have been regarded as supplementary information to the parent company accounts.

Accounting for business combinations has been a source of concern in Japan due to the unique nature of business. Keiretsu conglomerate groups are a form of business combination in which there are systems of interlocking directorates of related businesses formed to work together. In a keiretsu are found banks, manufacturers, suppliers, and so on. There are interlocking shareholders who are not necessarily majority owners, but who in effect control the companies in the keiretsu. As Japan's economy has struggled in recent years, the keiretsu has been more open to doing business with other business entities.

The accounting profession in Japan is small and has lacked influence in the accounting standard-setting process, but it provides recommendations on the practical application of the legal accounting regulations. The Japanese Institute of Certified Public Accountants was established by law in 1948, although an earlier body had been in existence since 1927. In 1991, a new body, the Corporation Finance Research Institute (COFRI), was also established with the purpose of providing authoritative advice to the BADC in the MOF. A special interest in the international aspects of accounting regulation appears to be an important motivation for this new development.

Although the traditional sources of finance in Japan were the banks, which dominated the Zaibatsu industrial groups up until the end of World War II, there was a substantial broadening of share ownership and development of the securities market following the subsequent breakup of the Zaibatsu by the American postwar administration. However, since then, new keiretsu groupings have emerged, involving a number of listed companies. These are supported by a member bank that acts as a principal source of funds. They also maintain cross-holdings in each other to ensure control and employ a variety of other mutually beneficial informal relationships. In general, there tends to be a secretive approach in Japan, with a lack of public information disclosure.

There is also an interesting international dimension to accounting in Japan. Many Japanese companies prepare an additional set of financial statements in English for the foreign readers of accounts, which are often referred to as "convenience translations." Furthermore, approximately 30 Japanese companies listed in the United States prepare their consolidated financial statements in accordance with U.S. GAAP rather than reconcile Japanese GAAP income and shareholders' equity with U.S. GAAP as permitted under the Form 20F filing required by the SEC. The main reason for this appears to be that when Japanese corporations were first listed in the United States, there were no Japanese consolidation requirements, and hence it was considered appropriate to adopt U.S. GAAP. Indeed, these major MNEs often go beyond U.S. requirements in response to competitive pressures in the international capital marketplace. Most recently, an accounting standards board has been established in Japan (ASBJ) similar to the FASB in the United States. Japan now appears poised to participate more fully in the international standard-setting process than it has done in the past. In June 2004, a study group appointed by Japan's Ministry of Finance conducted research that compared Japanese accounting standards to IFRS. Their report recommends that the European Commission consider Japanese accounting standards as equivalent to IFRS, as non-European companies listed on the European exchange will be required to use IFRS by 2007.

SUMMARY

1.   Anglo-American accounting is clearly distinguishable from other country groups, especially with respect to the emphasis on investor interests and disclosure to the stock market.

2.   The United Kingdom has had a major colonial influence on the accounting systems of many developing countries.

3.   Nordic accounting has many features that are comparable with Anglo-American accounting, but it also has some similarities to Germanic accounting.

4.   In the Germanic countries (Germany, Austria, and Switzerland), the influences of company law and taxation are paramount.

5.   Germanic and Latin accounting have many similar features, particularly with respect to the influences of company law and taxation, but they are also distinguishable in a number of respects, especially in the emphasis given to uniform accounting.

6.   Japanese accounting is unique despite being influenced by both the Anglo-American and Germanic traditions.

7.   Accounting for business combinations has been a source of concern in Japan due to the unique nature of business, in which keiretsu conglomerate groups have dominated the economy. These, however, are becoming less powerful.

8.   The major factors of government, the stock markets, company law, the accounting profession, the taxation authorities, and accounting conservatism and secrecy, tend to influence the development of accounting to a greater or lesser degree depending on the history and culture of the country concerned.

9.   The growing internationalization of business and securities markets is bringing about some convergence of accounting practice at the level of consolidated accounts prepared by MNEs that are listed on stock exchanges—and especially those competing for capital in the international context.

10.   Accounting practices are converging worldwide, especially in the developing countries. The EU has agreed to adopt IFRS beginning in 2005, and the United States is working to converge its accounting practices with IFRS.

Discussion Questions

1.   To what extent are countries changing with respect to national cultures and accounting values?

2.   How does culture impact the development of accounting?

3.   What is the purpose of classifying accounting systems?

4.   What are the prospects for the global convergence of accounting systems?

5.   Which countries have the greatest potential for accounting change? What are your reasons for thinking this to be the case?

6.   Describe some of the most significant differences between the countries noted above.

7.   Many of Japan's companies listed in the United States create financial statements based on U.S. GAAP rather than just providing a reconciliation. Discuss the pros and cons of this practice for the Japanese companies.

8.   How does the Keiretsu form of business organization affect accounting in Japan?

9.   Countries such as Germany and France are "code law" countries in which portions of their financial accounting and reporting practices derive from law and other portions come from professional standards. Explain the pros and cons of formal legal requirements in terms of the quality of financial reporting.

10.   What accounting issues are raised when companies list on multiple country stock exchanges?

11.   In France, the roles of public accounting and auditing are carried out by separate institutions established by law. What is the impact of this practice on the usefulness of accounting in France?

12.   To which country can the origins of double-entry bookkeeping be traced? What is the usefulness of double-entry bookkeeping?

13.   Compare Latin accounting to Germanic and Anglo-American accounting.

14.   Compare Japanese accounting to Anglo-American accounting.

15.   List the major accounting models in the world and their distinguishing features.

Exercises

Exercises 1–3: Form into small groups and have each group select two countries from different culture areas (as defined by Hofstede).

1. Identify and compare each country's societal and accounting values.
2. Locate each country in Gray's "Authority and Enforcement" and "Measurement and Disclosure" frameworks. How do the countries compare?
3. Comment on the relevance and reliability of your findings.

Exercises 4–5: It may seem natural to think that your home country's accounting standards are better than those of other countries.

4. Discuss the differences that exist and some of the explanations for those differences.
5. Are these differences actually weaknesses in the other country's system, or are they justified?

Exercises 6–8: Consider the four value dimensions identified by Hofstede and the four accounting values identified by Gray.

6. What mix of accounting values would you argue produces an ideal accounting system?
7. How do those accounting values relate back to the four value dimensions? In other words, which value dimensions lead to the ideal accounting values?
8. What countries seem to fit those values identified as ideal?
9. Many of the countries discussed in this chapter have their own standard-setting bodies. Why should (or shouldn't) a country have its own standard-setting organization?

Exercises 10–11: IFAC (the International Federation of Accountants) is a worldwide organization of professional accounting bodies.

10. Visit IFAC's website (www.ifac.org) and look up two of the accounting organizations discussed in this chapter.
11. What is the purpose of IFAC? What educational and auditing resources are available on the IFAC website?
12. Go to the website of one of the stock exchanges and find two companies that are listed from another country. Find these companies' annual reports and determine which accounting principles are used by each of these companies. Websites are: the New York Stock Exchange (www.nyse.com), NASDAQ (www.nasdaq.com), or the London Stock Exchange (www.londonstockexchange.com).
13. The U.S., U.K., and Australian accounting systems are very similar. What other developed countries have Anglo-American accounting systems? Find the accounting standard-setting body for one of these countries and determine at least one difference in accounting principle as compared to the Anglo-American countries studied in this chapter.
14. If an accounting system is concerned primarily with collecting taxes, how will it differ from an accounting system concerned with providing relevant and reliable information to investors? Which countries covered in this chapter have traditionally had a focus on tax?
15. If the primary source of capital for a company is from banks and other lenders, how will that affect the type of accounting information provided? Compare this to companies that get capital from shareholders.

Case: Reporting Standards vs. Tax Standards
Case: EU Conversion

These cases can be found on the following website: www.wiley.com/college/radebaugh

Selected References

Achleitner, Ann-Kristin. 1995. "Latest Developments in Swiss Regulation of Financial Reporting." *European Accounting Review* 4(1): 141–154.

Bailey, D. 1995. "Accounting in Transition in the Transitional Economy." *European Accounting Review* 4(4): 595–623. (Entire issue devoted to accounting in Eastern Europe and the former U.S.S.R.)

Barrett, M. Edgar. 1976. "Financial Reporting Practices: Disclosure and Comprehensiveness in an International Setting." *Journal of Accounting Research* 14(1): 10–26.

Black, E. L., and J. J. White. 2003. "An International Comparison of Income Statement and Balance Sheet Information: Germany, Japan and the U.S." *European Accounting Review* 12(1): 29–46.

Choi, F. D. S., and K. Hiramatsu, eds. 1987. *Accounting and Financial Reporting in Japan*. Princeton, NJ: Van Nostrand Reinhold.

Cooke, T. E. 1988. *European Financial Reporting: Sweden*. London: Institute of Chartered Accountants in England and Wales.

Cooke, T. E., and M. Kikuya. 1992. *Financial Reporting in Japan: Regulation, Practice, and Environment*. Oxford: Basil Blackwell.

Cooke, T. E., and R. H. Parker, eds. 1994. *Financial Reporting in the West Pacific Rim*. London: Routledge.

Doupnik, Timothy S., and Martin Richter. 2004. "The Impact of Culture on the Interpretation of "In Context" Verbal Probability Expressions." *Journal of International Accounting Research* 3(1): 1–20.

Doupnick, T. S., and S. B. Salter. 1993. "An Empirical Test of a Judgmental International Classification of Financial Reporting Practices." *Journal of International Business Studies* 24(1): 41–60.

Doupnik, T. S., and S. B. Salter. 1995. "External Environment, Culture, and Accounting Practice: A Preliminary Test of a General Model of International Accounting Development." *International Journal of Accounting* 30(3): 189–207.

Fortune Global 500. www.fortune.com/fortune/global500/

Frost, C. A., and G. Pownall. 1994. "Accounting Disclosure Practices in the United States and the United Kingdom." *Journal of Accounting Research* 32(1): 75–102.

Gordon, P. D., and S. J. Gray. 1994. *European Financial Reporting: United Kingdom*. London: Routledge.

Gray, S. J. 1980. "The Impact of International Accounting Differences from a Security Analysis Perspective: Some European Evidence." *Journal of Accounting Research* 18(1): 64–76.

Gray, S. J., A. G. Coenenberg, and P. D. Gordon. 1993. *International Group Accounting: Issues in European Harmonization*. London: Routledge.

Gray, S. J., and H. M. Vint. 1995. "The Impact of Culture on Accounting Disclosures: Some International Evidence." *Asia-Pacific Journal of Accounting* 2: 33–43.

International Association for Accounting Education and Research. www.iaaer.org

International Accounting Standards Board www.iasb.org.uk

Nair, R. D., and Werner G. Frank. 1980. "The Impact of Disclosure and Measurement Practices on International Accounting Classifications." *Accounting Review* 55(3): 426–450.

Ordelheide, D., and D. Pfaff. 1994. *European Financial Reporting: Germany*. London: Routledge.

Parker, R. H. 1989. "Importing and Exporting Accounting: The British Experience." In *International Pressures for Accounting Change,* edited by A. G. Hopwood. Englewood Cliffs, NJ: Prentice-Hall.

Puxty, A. G., H. C. Willmott, D. J. Cooper, and A. Lowe. 1987. "Modes of Regulation in Advanced Capitalism: Locating Accountancy in Four Countries." *Accounting, Organizations, and Society* 12(3): 273–291.

Riccaboni, A., and R. Ghirri. 1994. *European Financial Reporting: Italy.* London: Routledge.

Rivera, J. M., and A. S. Salva. 1995. "On the Regional Approach to Accounting Principles Harmonization: A Time for Latin American Integration?" *Journal of International Accounting Auditing & Taxation* 4(1): 87–100.

Saudagaran, Shahrokh, and Gary Biddle. 1992. "Financial Disclosure Levels and Foreign Stock Exchange Listing Decisions." *Journal of International Financial Management and Accounting* 4(2): 106–148.

Saudagaran, S. M., and J. G. Diga. 2000. "The Institutional Environment of Financial Reporting Regulation in ASEAN." *International Journal of Accounting* 35(1): 1–26.

Scheid, J.-C., and P. Walton. 1992. *European Financial Reporting: France.* London: Routledge.

Street, D. L., N. B. Nichols, and S. J. Gray. 2000. "Assessing the Acceptability of International Accounting Standards in the US: An Empirical Study of the Materiality of US GAAP Reconciliations by Non-US Companies Complying with IASC Standards." *International Journal of Accounting* 35(1): 27–64.

Taylor, Peter, and Stuart Turley. 1986. *The Regulation of Accounting.* London: Basil Blackwell.

Walton, P., ed. 1995. *European Financial Reporting: A History.* London: Academic Press.

Walton, P., ed. 1996. *Country Studies in International Accounting—Europe.* Cheltenham, U.K.: Edward Elgar.

Weetman, P., and S. J. Gray. 1990. "International Financial Analysis and Comparative Corporate Performance: The Impact of U.K. versus U.S. Accounting Principles on Earnings." *Journal of International Financial Management and Accounting* (Summer/Autumn).

Weetman, P., and S. J. Gray. 1991. "A Comparative Analysis of the Impact of Accounting Principles on Profits: The U.S.A. versus the U.K., Sweden, and the Netherlands." *Accounting and Business Research* 21(84): 363–379.

Zeff, S. A. 1972. *Forging Accounting Principles in Five Countries.* New York: Stipes.

Zeff, S. A. 1995. "A Perspective on the U. S. Public/Private-Sector Approach to the Regulation of Financial Reporting." *Accounting Horizons* 9(1): 52–70.

Zeff, S. A., F. Van der Wel, and K. Camfferman. 1992. *Company Financial Reporting: A Historical and Comparative Study of the Dutch Regulatory Process.* Amsterdam: North-Holland.

Zeff, S. A., F. Van der Wel, and K. Camfferman. 1997. *Company Financial Reporting: A Historical and Comparative Study of the Dutch Regulatory Process.* Amsterdam: North-Holland.

CHAPTER FOUR

COMPARATIVE INTERNATIONAL FINANCIAL ACCOUNTING II

Chapter Objectives

- Compare accounting systems in developing Anglo-American countries, namely, India and Malaysia
- Compare accounting systems in developing Latin countries, namely, Brazil, Argentina, and Mexico
- Compare accounting systems in developing Asian countries, namely China, Indonesia, and Thailand
- Compare accounting systems in developing Eastern European countries, namely, Poland, Russia, and the Czech Republic

INTRODUCTION

In this chapter, we outline the accounting systems of selected developing countries using the cultural classification identified earlier in previous chapters as the basis for discussion. Accordingly, we review the accounting systems of India and Malaysia as representatives from the Anglo-American culture area; Brazil, Argentina, and Mexico as representatives of Latin countries; China, Indonesia, and Thailand as representatives of Asian countries; and Poland, Russia, and the Czech Republic as Eastern European countries.

Before comparing countries, it is important to gain a background understanding of each country's overall economic situation. Comparative economic data on the stated countries is listed in Exhibit 4.1. This exhibit illustrates that developing countries tend to have lower GDP per capita than developed countries, as compared to Exhibit 3.1. In addition, it shows that developing economies are less stable, as illustrated by the varying inflation rates and unemployment rates. Exhibit 4.2 provides data on individual country preferences toward certain stock exchanges. As

> ## Strategic Decision Point
>
> Obstacles faced in emerging markets are extensive. Because many of these countries are just beginning to set up their accounting standards, the integrity and transparency of their financial reports are subject to question. Even though the World Bank and the International Federation of Accountants do their best to facilitate development in these countries, emerging markets are being left behind in the creation of international accounting standards.
>
> In the meantime, these countries face obstacles in obtaining international capital and in reaching their full potential. Furthermore, they run the risk of financial crisis. These countries do not have the means to establish accounting standards themselves as their countries face more pressing needs—thus, they look to the creation of IFRS. However, most IFRS are only applicable to the largest firms in developing countries. They need standards that are adapted to small- and medium-sized entities in order to reap the full benefit of the global standards. Furthermore, each country needs to understand the meaning of each standard and have a way to enforce correct application. What can the accounting profession do to aid these developing countries? What can be done to ensure proper compliance in these countries? The IASB is currently discussing different options to determine whether they should create a set of financial standards for small multinational enterprises.

Exhibit 4.1   Economic Data for Developing Countries

	GDP PPP (in billions)	GDP Per Capita	Population (in millions)	Unemployment	Inflation	Area per sq km (in thousands)	Imports (in billions)	Exports (in billions)
India	$3,033.0	$2,900	1,065.1	9.5%	3.8%	3,287.6	$74.2	$57.2
Malaysia	$207.8	$9,000	23.5	3.6%	1.1%	329.8	$74.4	$98.4
Brazil	$1,375.0	$7,600	184.1	12.3%	14.7%	8,512.0	$48.3	$73.4
Argentina	$435.5	$11,200	39.1	17.3%	13.4%	2,767.0	$13.3	$29.6
Mexico	$941.2	$9,000	105.0	3.3%	4.5%	1,972.6	$168.9	$164.8
China	$6,449.0	$5,000	1,298.8	10.1%	1.2%	9,597.0	$397.4	$436.1
Indonesia	$758.8	$3,200	238.5	8.7%	6.6%	1,919.4	$40.22	$63.89
Thailand	$477.5	$7,400	64.9	2.2%	1.8%	514.0	$65.3	$76.0
Poland	$427.1	$11,100	38.6	20%	0.7%	312.7	$63.7	$57.6
Russia	$1,282.0	$8,900	143.8	8.5%	13.7%	17.075.2	$74.8	$134.4
Czech Republic	$161.1	$15,700	10.2	9.9%	0.1%	78.9	$50.4	46.8%

Source: Compiled from *The World Bank* www.worldbank.com/data/countrydata/countrydata.html and *The World Factbook* www.cia.gov/cia/publications/factbook/, December 2004.

Exhibit 4.2   Number of Companies in Developing Countries Listed on Foreign Exchanges

	NYSE	NASDAQ	London Stock Exchange
India	8	3	17
Malaysia	0	0	3
Brazil	37	1	0
Argentina	10	3	1
Mexico	22	3	0
China	17	0	5
Indonesia	2	0	2
Thailand	0	0	0
Poland	0	0	8
Russia	6	0	4
Czech Republic	0	0	3

Source: Compiled from *New York Stock Exchange* www.nyse.com, NASDAQ www.nasdaq.com, and *London Stock Exchange* www.londonstockexchange.com

noted in the exhibit, some countries, such as Brazil, prefer to have all their companies listed in the United States. Other countries, such as India, tend to have stocks listed on all three exchanges. Exhibit 4.3 provides information on each country's preference toward International Financial Reporting Standards (IFRS). Lastly, Exhibit 4.4 provides other useful information about each country. The legal origin helps us understand where the country's accounting standards originated from.

Exhibit 4.3   IFRS Acceptance

	Not Permitted for Domestic Listed Companies	Permitted for Domestic Listed Companies	Required for Some Domestic Companies	Required for All Domestic Listed Companies
India	X			
Malaysia	X			
Brazil	X			
Argentina	X			
Mexico	X			
China			X	
Indonesia	X			
Thailand	X			
Poland				X
Russia			X	
Czech Republic				X

Source: Deloitte IAS Plus www.iasplus.com.

Exhibit 4.4   Other Country Data

	Legal Origin	Income Group	Rating on Accounting Standards[a]
India	English	Low	45
Malaysia	English	Upper Middle	76
Brazil	French	Lower Middle	54
Argentina	French	Upper Middle	45
Mexico	French	Upper Middle	60
China	German	Lower Middle	52
Indonesia	French	Low	65
Thailand	English	Lower Middle	64
Poland	German	Upper Middle	36
Russia	Socialist	Lower Middle	32
Czech Republic	German	Upper Middle	38

[a] Higher scores indicate higher rating on accounting standards.

ANGLO-AMERICAN ACCOUNTING

Anglo-American accounting can be found in countries where the United Kingdom has had a major colonial influence, such as in Australia, Canada, Hong Kong, India, Ireland, Kenya, Malaysia, New Zealand, Nigeria, Singapore, and South Africa. These countries tend to favor the needs of investors and to be relatively less conservative and more transparent than the Germanic and Latin countries.

India

In the 1950s, more than 50 percent of India was in real poverty. However, India has significantly improved its economy over the past decade. Not only has the poverty level fallen, but economic growth has risen and various social indicators have improved, such as life expectancy and literacy.

Because of India's English legal origin, its accounting standards focus on the information needs of investors. In 1949, the Institute of Chartered Accountants in India (ICAI) was created as the national organization of registered accountants in India. Subsequently, the Accounting Standards Board (ASB) was established to formulate accounting standards in order to assist the Council of the ICAI in creating and modifying accounting standards in India. The ICAI is a full member of the International Federation of Accountants (IFAC) and is expected to promote IFRS in order to achieve international harmonization. As such, the ASB gives consideration to International Accounting Standards (IAS) and IFRS issued by the International Accounting Standards Board (IASB) and tries to implement them into their standards to the extent possible, considering the circumstances in India.

The prime minister of India recently announced that financial reforms should continue to be made at a rapid pace. In response, Sunil Goyal, president of the ICAI, said, "This is good news for us simply because financial sector reforms necessarily imply a greater bias on accountability and transparency. As a community of accounting professionals, it is our duty and our particular skill to help bring about accountability and transparency. These two items require a greater stress on the application of standards and a greater degree of ethicality."[1] As financial reforms in India continue, we should see these values being promulgated through Indian Accounting Standards.

MALAYSIA

Although Malaysia has struggled historically, the country has sustained rapid growth over the last 30 years. Furthermore, Malaysia's poverty level has decreased, and income inequalities have diminished. Prospects over the next few years are promising, with anticipated growth in GDP, private consumption, and private investment.

Like Indonesia, Malaysia's legal system originated from the United Kingdom. As would be expected, its accounting system also aims to meet the information needs of investors. The Malaysian Institute of Accountants (MIA) was established in 1967 under the Accountants Act as the regulatory authority of the accounting profession. However, Malaysia restructured its accounting system in 1997 with the Financial Reporting Act, which created the Financial Reporting Foundation (FRF) and the Malaysian Accounting Standards Board (MASB). The FRF oversees the work of the MASB but is not involved in the standard-setting process. The MASB is an independent body created to develop and issue accounting standards in Malaysia. This new framework creates an independent standard-setting process representative of all relevant parties, including preparers, users, regulators, and accountants.

The MASB is a strong supporter of international harmonization and has thus adopted 26 of their 32 standards from their corresponding IFRS prior to revisions made by the IASB in 2003 and 2004. Because its policy is conversion with IFRS, the MASB works to strictly maintain the wording of the original IFRS standards. Any changes are made only to enhance the quality of reporting and not to alter the principles behind the original standard. As such, the MASB takes care to preserve the structure of the original standard and clearly state any additions.

LATIN ACCOUNTING

The unique flavor of Latin accounting can be found in a number of developing countries, specifically, Brazil, Chile, Colombia, Mexico, Peru, and Uruguay. Latin accounting tends to be relatively more conservative and secretive compared to the Anglo-American countries.

BRAZIL

As in France and Italy, the accounting tradition in Brazil gives preference to the information needs of creditors and the tax authorities. Although the interest of

---

[1] http://www.icai.org/institute/m_journal.html, President's Message, October 4, 2004.

domestic and foreign investors in Brazilian companies listed on the stock exchange has grown, this is still of minor significance as far as attitudes to accounting and disclosure are concerned.

As in other Latin countries, the influences of government, company law, and taxation regulations on accounting are of fundamental importance. In this, Brazil's cultural heritage of Portuguese colonization is a significant underlying factor. Although the basic commercial code was established in 1850, the corporation law of 1976 contains the basic requirements governing the preparation of financial statements and disclosures for public companies. In addition, the Commissâo de Valores Mobiliarios (CVM), the SEC, prescribes accounting standards for listed companies. The stock market, through small relative to those in the United States and the United Kingdom, is one of the major markets in Latin America and is growing in importance. Indeed, a number of Brazilian companies are now listed on U.S. stock markets.

The accounting profession in Brazil is not as well developed as in the Anglo-Saxon countries, but the institute for Brazilian accountants, the Instituto Brasileiro de Contadores (IBRACON), and the Conselho Federal de Contabilidade, or Federal Accounting Council, issue accounting standards that form the basis of generally accepted accounting principles. If the CVM approves such standards, they become obligatory for listed companies, and in general it appears that the CVM tends to rely on the accounting profession to develop accounting standards.

Argentina

Historically, Argentina's accounting has focused on meeting the needs of creditors and tax authorities. The Argentine commercial code requires all companies to provide annual reports, and public companies also have to issue quarterly statements.

Argentina's accounting system, however, is unique to Latin America. Accounting standards are set by the Argentine Federation of Expert Councils on Economies (FACPCE), but the structure of the FACPCE differs from that of other Latin countries. The FACPCE consists of 24 separate councils or *consejos* that come together to approve Technical Resolutions (TR), which relate approved accounting norms on specific subjects. Each council represents a different jurisdiction of Argentina. After the TR is approved by the FACPCE, the individual councils determine whether to ratify the TR as is or with amendments for their specific region. As a result, harmonization across the country can be achieved only if each jurisdiction adopts the standard without modification. Because of the individualist nature of each region, this ratification treatment has the potential to result in very divergent practices countrywide. Fortunately, most of the TRs have been adopted without modification.

Argentina also has shown confusion over who can issue laws regarding accounting standards. Consider the following: Because Argentina's inflation rate has been high in the past, the concept of general price level (GPL) has been of central consideration in formulating accounting standards. Specifically, GPL accounting allows Argentines to adjust balance amounts on their financial statements to reflect purchasing power. However, the national government issued a decree to the Argentine regulatory institutions, such as the CNV and the Central Bank, that they should no longer accept GPL adjusted financials. Although FACPCE felt that the decree was contrary to law, it modified GPL accounting so that the use is optional if inflation is lower than 8 percent. Should inflation rates increase above 8 percent, Argentines will be confused as to which law to follow.

The FACPCE is working toward harmonization with IFRS. Although many amendments have been made to eliminate differences, Argentina believes some differences should still exist because they address issues not covered under IFRS.

Mexico

Like Brazil, Mexico gives preferences to the information needs of creditors and tax authorities. The French origin of Mexico's legal system is a significant factor in this preference.

Since the creation of the North American Free Trade Agreement (NAFTA), Mexico's economic development has been improving. However, with other international countries becoming more prominent in the global arena, it is important for Mexico to access funding. Mexico needs increased transparency among its corporations in order for its economic development to continue.

Historically, Mexican accounting has been influenced by the United States' generally accepted accounting principles (GAAP) and auditing standards (GAAS). This strong influence can be attributed to Mexico's need for foreign investment from the United States. Furthermore, many Mexican companies seek to be listed on the world's largest exchanges. Their tendency to look to the United States' accounting standards has increased since the inception of NAFTA. However, Mexico frequently looks toward IFRS when U.S standards do not meet Mexico's needs.

The Mexican Constitution establishes professional associations to regulate their respective fields of activity. Societies of accountants throughout the country delegate their regulatory capacity to the IMCP, Mexico's self-regulated institution overseeing the accounting profession. The IMCP issues accounting and auditing standards, as well as a code of ethics for accountants. Much like the AICPA in America, the IMCP establishes continuing education requirements, conducts investigations, and oversees professional conduct. More recently in 2001, the IMCP formed the Mexican Council for Research and Development of Financial Reporting Standards (CINIF). This institution is responsible for creating accounting standards in line with IFRS. Actual GAAP will remain effective until modified or replaced, but rights to analyze, evaluate, modify, and issue GAAP have been transferred to the CINIF. On May 1 2004, the standards issued by the IMCP were passed to CINIF, which currently is the new institution in charge of reviewing and issuing the new Mexican GAAP. As of the beginning of 2005, Mexican GAAP was approximately 70 percent in line with international standards.

ASIAN ACCOUNTING

Many of the developing Asian countries have a colonial history, these countries include Indonesia (Netherlands); India, Pakistan, Hong Kong, Singapore, and Malaysia (United Kingdom); and the Philippines (Spain/United States). China has been influenced by both Western ideas and the socialist uniformity of the former Soviet Union. In 1997, many of the developing countries in Asia experienced declining confidence in their financial markets, which resulted in the Asian financial crisis. One of the cures for this "Asian flu" was to increase accounting quality and transparency by adopting higher quality accounting standards.

China

A major shift of emphasis is under way in China from a primary focus on the information needs of government, that is, needs involving national planning and taxation, to a broader view of user needs that includes those of investors, creditors, and enterprise management. A more micro-oriented decision-making approach is thus being encouraged that retains a measure of macroeconomic control—a difficult balance to strike given China's tradition of uniformity and detailed regulation. Moreover, this tradition appears to be consistent with established Chinese cultural values and hence will be difficult to change.

The People's Republic of China (PRC) is a communist country. Hence, government, through laws passed by the National People's Congress, is the major influence on accounting and auditing. Although the history of accounting in China can be traced back 2000 years or so, it was only in the early 1900s that double-entry bookkeeping was introduced. By the 1940s, Western-oriented accounting systems were established in large corporations, and teaching in the universities was increasingly influenced by ideas from the United Kingdom and the United States. However, the founding of the PRC in 1949 led to a dramatic change of approach with the introduction of Soviet Union-style accounting and an emphasis on uniformity and centralized control for national planning purposes. Since 1978, this approach has been increasingly modified following China's new "open door" policy to the outside world and its ambitious program for modernization. Once again, ideas and information from Western countries and indeed all over the world were sought to help China promote its concept of a socialist market economy based on public ownership and central planning, but with the market now playing an increasingly important role.

With economic reform and moves to a more market-oriented economy have come a series of accounting reforms. The Accounting Law of the People's Republic of China, adopted in 1985 and revised in 1993 and again in 1999, established general principles concerning the nature and role of accounting and empowered the Ministry of Finance (MOF) to issue accounting standards.

In 1992, the Basic Accounting Standard for Business Enterprises, the conceptual framework of PRC accounting, was issued. Beginning in 1993, specific accounting standards were developed on a variety of topics, with 10 final standards issued to date. In 1998, the old rules applicable to joint stock companies were replaced by the issuance of the Accounting System for Joint Stock Limited Enterprises. Following the revision of the accounting law in 1999, the PRC State Council also issued Financial Accounting and Reporting Rules (FARR) for Enterprises, which updates the definitions of assets, liabilities, owners' equity, revenues, and expenses that were previously set out in the Basic Standard. The FARR also specifies the components of the financial statements, including a cash flow statement as well as a balance sheet and income statement.

The new accounting standards, structured as a basic standard and a series of specific standards, represent a major change of approach in Chinese accounting in that all enterprises are now required to comply with a unified set of accounting principles. However, what is most significant is the content of the new accounting standards. It represents a new era in Chinese accounting, one based on a Western market-oriented approach rather than the old Soviet Union style. Fund accounting, based on the equality of fund sources with fund applications, has been abolished and replaced by the accounting equation, where assets equal liabilities plus capital or owners' equity. In making this change, the interests of a wider group of users beyond government have been recognized, namely, investors, creditors, and enterprise management. Accounting information must now meet much more than the requirements of national macroeconomic control. So that an enterprise's financial position and operating results can be understood and financial practices and administration strengthened, accounting information must also now meet the needs of external users and management.

Although the government, through the MOF and its official accounting agency, the Department of Administration of Accounting Affairs (DAAA), has been decisive in reforming accounting, it is fair to say that accounting organizations, notably the Accounting Society of China, a body that fosters research on accounting theory, practice, and education, have played an important advisory role. The society, established in 1980, set up a research group in 1987 on accounting theory and standards with the majority of its members comprised of university professors. International accounting firms, notably Deloitte Touche Tohmatsu, have also been influential.

With respect to the practicing side of the profession, the auditing function, having been abolished after the founding of the PRC, was resumed only in 1983 with the establishment of the government's Audit Administration. Similarly, the Chinese Institute of Certified Public Accountants was reestablished by the government only in 1988. With the rapid pace of accounting reform, China currently has a serious shortage of accountants.

Indonesia

Historically, Indonesia's accounting system was based on the Netherlands' accounting system as a result of the Dutch influence on the country. However, when the ties between the two countries were broken in the mid-1900s, Indonesia turned to U.S. accounting practices. The Indonesian Institute of Accountants (IAI) was created in 1959 to guide accountants throughout Indonesia. In the 1970s, the IAI created a code of conduct and adopted accounting principles and standards based on U.S. GAAP at the time. As such, Indonesia's accounting system focuses on the information needs of investors over the needs of government. In 1974, IAI created the Financial Accounting Standards Committee to set accounting standards.

Indonesia has had remarkable economic development over the past decade. However, the Asian financial crisis caused the country to return to its previous poverty levels. Since the crisis, Indonesia has instituted several political and social reforms, which resulted in substantial changes and returned poverty levels to their pre-crisis levels.

In 1994, the Financial Accounting Standards Committee was reconstituted as the more independent Financial Accounting Standards Board (DSAK) of the Indonesian Institute of Accountants. Currently, the DSAK is working to harmonize Indonesian accounting standards with IFRS.

Thailand

Thailand is the only country in Southeast Asia that avoided colonial rule. However, its accounting system values transparency and the information needs of investors, much as in the Anglo-American countries. After the financial crisis in 1997, Thailand implemented reforms to increase corporate governance and boost incentives for competition. The Thai economy recovered quickly and has since sustained growth. Poverty levels have also decreased as a result of the strengthening economy.

Accounting standards are issued by the Institute of Certified Accountants and Auditors of Thailand (ICAAT), established in 1948. However, Thai accounting standards must be approved by the Ministry of Commerce and placed into law before the companies are required to adopt them. To date, the ICAAT has adopted 21 of the IAS standards.

The Thai Securities Exchange Commission requires all companies listed on the Stock Exchange of Thailand (SET) to be reviewed by independent, external auditors. Furthermore, companies listed on the SET must comply with a rigorous set of disclosure requirements. These requirements illustrate Thailand's focus on meeting the information needs of investors. In addition, it was recently decided that supervision of listed companies will be transferred from the Ministry of Commerce to the Thai SEC, which will result in one organization regulating and enforcing the law for listed companies.

EASTERN EUROPEAN ACCOUNTING

Eastern European accounting has historically been based on the socialist concept of a planned economy. As such, their accounting is geared toward the needs of tax authorities and focuses little on reflecting the profit of the company. However, in recent years, countries in Eastern Europe have been attempting to transition from centrally planned socialist countries to the Western-style market economy. This section discusses how Russia, Poland, and the Czech Republic are changing their accounting systems as they move toward market economies.

Poland

Poland began its transition to a market economy in 1990 using what is now called the shock therapy model, meaning that all reforms were made concurrently. In fact, Poland's goal was to set up the basis for a market economy in just one year by creating the legal, institutional, and economic institutions necessary to help privatize the economy. Although their transition began under difficult conditions, such as high inflation, their country emerged as one of the leaders among the transition countries. Poverty and unemployment are still high in Poland, but the country is continuing to make progress. Perhaps most notable is Poland's admission to the European Union (EU) in 2004.

Under the communist regime, accounting existed to regulate the use of state resources and prevent theft of public assets. The Ministry of Finance created accounting to control the actions of individual enterprises. The Soviet accounting plan was introduced in 1953–1954, which allocated surpluses to fund state activities. As such, accounting existed not to measure profit or efficiency but to help the government allocate excess funds to various state activities. Performance measures were used only to determine how well enterprises reached state targets for surpluses. Although there were no penalties for failures, enterprises still ran the risk of receiving disfavor from the Communist Party.

Poland's accounting system underwent transitions in three stages: 1991, 1994, and 2000. Accounting decree 1991 was issued by the Ministry of Finance to provide some intermediate rules to facilitate the economy's transition to a market economy. However, this decree was made without consulting the different users of financial information and was highly criticized as being unhelpful, for there were many inconsistencies between the Act and the commercial code. However, it did redefine the auditor's role from one of tax compliance to one of measuring the true economic value of the entity. This reflects a shift away from their heavy tax orientation.

The Accounting Act of 1994 was issued to bring Polish accounting closer to EU standards. Poland adopted the idea of the "true and fair view" and issued standards to fill in missing gaps in its system. The Act discarded the requirement to use a chart of accounts and required companies to develop their own accounting plans. In addition, it authorized the securities exchange to create rules for listed companies, specifically in the area of disclosure. The Accounting Act of 2002 was issued to make Polish accounting standards more in line with IFRS. Furthermore, it created rules in areas that previously had only guidance under tax law.

Poland's entrance into the EU marks a huge step for the country because of the rigorous set of admission requirements. In order to become a member of the EU, countries must harmonize their financial requirements with EU requirements and IFRS. Once a member, the country is required to follow EU rules immediately with no transition periods. Poland's membership in the EU illustrates the country's efforts to become a market economy. Although local companies face the challenge of adopting many new amendments, the structure is in place to help Poland succeed in its newly created market economy. As part of the EU, Poland adopted IFRS in 2005.

Russia

Although the economic situation in Russia has improved, it differs from other transitioning economies in the following ways. First, the share of new enterprises is low compared to other economies. Second, many Soviet-style production units still exist that are operating at losses. The country's ability to sustain growth is constrained by its dependence on natural resources, specifically oil and gas. Furthermore, they continue to be dominated by unreformed monopolies.

In the Russian Federation, the government has sole control over the accounting system as a result of its socialist background. Accounting standards in Russia were formulated to keep track of inputs and outputs. Thus, the standards reflect little about value and profit. Companies in Russia are more likely to understate revenues to reduce their tax burden then they are to overstate revenues to appear more profitable. Generally, the Russian Ministry of Finance creates accounting regulations. However, the Central Bank of the Russian Federation (CBRF) is responsible for creating accounting and auditing standards for banks and credit institutions. In addition, the CBRF monitors their activity and sets minimum capital requirements.

In 2002, the Russian prime minister announced that Russian companies and banks would be required to prepare financial statements in accordance with IFRS beginning in 2004. Specifically, all consolidated statements by companies and banks should be prepared with IFRS. Individual bank financial statements should also be prepared with IFRS, but individual company financial statements should continue to be prepared with Russian GAAP. Although most listed companies in Russia already prepare statements based on U.S. GAAP or IFRS, many still use outdated Russian accounting standards (RAS) that are based on a planned economy. The Russian conversion to IFRS is an attempt to attract more investment at the recommendation of economists. Even though the prime minister's efforts are commendable, many believe that Russian companies will be unable to make the deadline as a result of the magnitude of the change as well as the expense involved. Furthermore, it is unclear whether Russia will be required to continue using RAS to prepare statements for tax authorities.

Czech Republic

The Czech Republic gained its independence in 1993 and subsequently followed the lead of Poland and implemented the shock therapy model in an effort to convert to a market economy. Though highly successful for the first few years, the Czech Republic ran into problems with its currency in 1996, which required it to make tight monetary policy decisions. The economy is still suffering with a large fiscal deficit and rising inflation. However, many feel that the Czech Republic's transition to a market economy is complete, signified by its entrance into the EU in 2004.

The Czech Republic introduced a new tax and accounting system in 1993. Like Poland, this marked a shift away from a heavy tax orientation. Standards are still created by the Ministry of Finance, but they now focus more on standards for a market-driven economy. The Czech Republic is currently working toward eliminating differences between Czech accounting rules and IFRS. The Accounting Act of 2002 allows Czech companies to opt for using IFRS over Czech rules.

Like Poland, the Czech Republic's admission to the EU marks a huge step for the country because of the rigorous set of accession requirements. In addition, it illustrates the country's success in becoming a market economy, even though economic struggles may still exist. As part of the EU, the Czech Republic adopted IFRS in 2005. The Czech Republic's challenge now is to continue with its rapid pace of change without senior management disregarding the changes as a nuisance. Conversion to IFRS will require the efforts of the whole company in order to embed the new system in the company's measurement processes.

The current tax system still depends on accounting rules. As such, changes in current accounting regulations affect income before tax purposes for tax calculations. Should the government fail to amend the tax act before IFRS becomes the country's required standards, it will lose its power to amend rules to adjust the tax base.

SUMMARY

1.   Anglo-American accounting can be seen in countries influenced by the United Kingdom. These countries emphasize the needs of investors and work toward providing more transparency.

2.   Nordic and Germanic accounting has had little influence on developing countries.

3.   Latin accounting has influenced the systems in Brazil and Mexico, resulting in systems with a heavy tax orientation.

4.   Argentine accounting is unique to Latin America because accounting regulations vary from region to region.

5.   One outcome of the Asian financial crisis of 1997 was that many Asian countries are seeking to increase accounting quality and transparency by adopting higher quality accounting standards.

6.   In Asia, Chinese accounting strongly reflects its communist heritage but is becoming increasingly open to Anglo-American influences.

7.   Indonesia and Thailand have both independently made efforts to harmonize their standards with IFRS.

8.   Eastern European countries have made substantial efforts to develop market economies. As such, their accounting systems have moved away from their heavy tax orientation to meet the needs of investors.

9.   Poland and the Czech Republic, as well as other former Soviet-bloc countries are entering the European Union, which requires all publicly owned companies to use IFRS beginning in 2005.

10.   Russian accounting is focused on the taxation needs of the country, and it highly reflects the result of a planned economy. With the planned conversion to IFRS, the country is hoping to increase transparency and encourage investment.

Discussion Questions

1.   Which developing countries have the greatest potential for change?

2.   What infrastructure is needed to encourage higher quality accounting in developing countries?

3.   What differences did you note between developing and developed countries?

4.   Why should we expect differences in the accounting systems of developing and developed countries?

5.   It seems that a common trend among developing countries is to base their standards on IFRS. What are some of the advantages and disadvantages of this treatment?

6.   As countries such as Russia, China, and the Czech Republic restructure their economies from central planning to a market-oriented economy, what changes are necessary in their accounting systems?

7. Explain some challenges faced by developing countries as they work to build their accounting systems.

8. What role does tax legislation play as countries develop their financial accounting practices for developing countries?

9. What role does education play as countries develop their financial accounting practices?

10. What is the role of CINIF in the development of Mexican accounting standards?

11. What are the costs and benefits of listing on foreign stock exchanges for companies from developing countries?

12. Compare and contrast accounting in Brazil, Argentina, and Mexico.

13. Compare and contrast accounting in India and Malaysia.

14. Compare and contrast accounting in China, Indonesia, and Thailand.

15. Compare and contrast accounting in Poland, Russia, and the Czech Republic.

Exercises

1. Consider the differences between developing countries and developed countries:
    a. How are the accounting systems going to be different?
    b. Why might these differences be justified?

2. As a potential investor in one of the developing countries, list some requirements in financial reporting you would want before investing in their stock market.

3. Imagine you are a developing country working to build up your accounting system.
    a. Explain your standard setting process—what regulatory bodies should be involved and what should their role be?
    b. What would you do before you started creating standards (consider IFRS, create a principle framework, etc...)?
    c. What are some of the challenges you might face (speed of issuance vs. quality of standards issued)?

4. In Exhibit 4.2, several companies from each of the countries discussed in this chapter list on the NYSE, NASDAQ, and/or London Stock Exchange.
    a. Go to the website of each of these stock exchanges and find at least one company from the developing countries on each exchange.
    b. Find out in which year the company was listed on the exchange.

5. Mexico, Brazil, and Argentina have a history of high inflation during periods of their history. How does inflation impact accounting and financial reporting in these countries? Compare this to countries that have not had high inflation.

6. Companies from each of the developing countries discussed in this chapter refer to IFRS in their financial statements. Go to the International Accounting Standards Board website (www.iasb.org) and identify five companies that refer to IFRS.

7. IFAC (the International Federation of Accounants) is a worldwide organization of professional accounting bodies. Visit IFAC's website (www.ifac.org). Find out if the accounting organizations discussed in this chapter are members of IFAC.

8. If an accounting system is primarily concerned with collecting taxes how will it differ from an accounting system concerned with providing relevant and reliable information to investors? Which countries covered in this chapter have traditionally had a focus on tax?

Exercises 9–10: Form into small groups and have each group select two countries from different culture areas (as defined by Hofstede).

9. Identify and compare each country's societal and accounting values.

10. Locate each country in Gray's "Authority and Enforcement" and "Measurement and Disclosure" frameworks. How do the countries compare? Comment on the relevance and reliability of your findings.

11. Compare the strengths and weaknesses of accounting in the Eastern European countries to those from Latin America.

12. Exhibit 4.2 provides the number of companies from the developing countries covered in this chapter that are listed on each of the three major worldwide stock exchanges: NYSE, NASDAQ, and London Stock Exchange. Do you notice any patterns in the listing behavior by country? What factors might explain the listing patterns observed in the table?

13. Refer to Exhibit 4.3 and discuss the factors that might explain the acceptance of IFRS or not in the developing countries covered in this chapter.

14. Exhibit 4.4 provides information on the legal origin, income group, and accounting rating. Do you notice any patterns? What is the correlation between these factors?

15. Which of the countries covered in this chapter have private financial accounting standard-setting boards? What are the costs and benefits of a private vs. governmental standard setting board?

Case: Small GAAP vs. Large GAAP
Case: Developing Countries

These cases can be found on the following website: www.wiley.com/college/radebaugh

Selected References

Bailey, D. 1995. "Accounting in Transition in the Transitional Economy." *European Accounting Review* 4(4): 595–623. (Entire issue devoted to accounting in Eastern Europe and the former U.S.S.R.)

Banerjee, B. 2000. "Regulation of Accounting in India: Issues and a Suggested Framework." *Indian Accounting Review* 4(2): 21–35.

Chen, Y., P. Jubb, and A. Tran. 1997. "Problems of Accounting Reform in the People's Republic of China." *The International Journal of Accounting* 32(2): 139–153.

Chow, Lynne Min-Ying, Gerald Kun-Kwai Chau, and Sidney J. Gray. 1995. "Accounting Reforms in China: Cultural Constraints on Implementation and Development." *Accounting and Business Research* 26(1): 29–49.

Cooke, T. E., and R. H. Parker, eds. 1994. *Financial Reporting in the West Pacific Rim.* London: Routledge.

Enthoven, A. J. H., Y. V. Sokolov, S. M. Bychkova, V. V. Kovalev, and M. V. Semenova. 1998. *Accounting, Auditing, and Taxation in the Russian Federation.* Montvale, NJ and University of Texas at Dallas (Richardson: TX), Institute of Management Accountants.

Foreman-Peck, Alex. 2003. "Glasnost in the Boardroom." *The Banker,* (London). 153(937): 65.

Goyal, Sunil 2004. "President's Message." Institute of Chartered Accountants in India, New Delhi. (http://icai.org/institute/m_journal.html).

Hove, M. R. 1986. "Accounting Practices in Developing Countries: Colonialism's Legacy of Inappropriate Technologies." *International Journal of Accounting* 21(1): 81–100.

http://asianbondsonline.adb.org/

http://www.masb.org.my

http://www.worldbank.org

International Monetary Fund. 1999. "Experimental Report on Transparency Practices: Argentina," as accessed on http://www.imf.org/external/np/rose/arg/index/htm

Jermakowicz, E., and D. F. Rinke. 1996. "The New Accounting Standards in the Czech Republic, Hungary, and Poland vis-à-vis International Accounting Standards and European Union Directives." *Journal of International Accounting, Auditing & Taxation* 5(1): 73–87.

Kříž, Petr, and Tomáš Bašta. 2003. "Financial Reporting Standards Are Marching In." PricewaterhouseCoopers, American Chamber of Commerce EU Report.

Lefebvre, C., and Liang-vi Lin. 1990. "Internationalization of Financial Accounting Standards in the People's Republic of China." *International Journal of Accounting* 25(3): 170–183.

MacLullich, Katarzyna Kosmala, and Calin Gurau. 2004. "The Relationship Between Economic Performance and Accounting Systems Reform in the CEE Region: The Cases of Poland and Romania." Centre for Economic Reform and Transformation, School of Management and Languages, Heriot-Watt University.

Marangos, John. 2002. "A Political Economy Approach to the Neoclassical Model of Transition—New Perspectives on Transition Economies: Europe." *American Journal of Economics and Sociology* 61(1): 259–276.

Quinn, Lawrence R. 2004. "Emerging Pains." *CA Magazine* 137(3): 30–37.

Rivera, J. M., and A. S. Salva. 1995. "On the Regional Approach to Accounting Principles Harmonization: A Time for Latin American Integration?" *Journal of International Accounting Auditing & Taxation* 4(1): 87–100.

Saudagaran, S. M., and J. G. Diga. 1997a. "Financial Reporting in Emerging Capital Markets: Characteristics and Policy Issues." *Accounting Horizons* 11(2): 41–64.

Saudagaran, S. M., and J. G. Diga. 1997b. "The Impact of Capital Market Developments on Accounting Regulatory Policy in Emerging Markets: A Study of ASEAN." *Research in Accounting Regulation* (Supplement 1): 3–48.

Saudagaran, S. M., and J. G. Diga. 2000. "The Institutional Environment of Financial Reporting Regulation in ASEAN." *The International Journal of Accounting* 35(1): 1–26.

Steff, Steven A. 1998. "Normas Contables Argentinas (Argentine Accounting Norms)." *Issues in Accounting Education, Sarasota* 13(3): 779–783.

Tang, Y., W. L. Chow, and B. J. Cooper. 1994. *Accounting and Finance in China.* Hong Kong: Longman.

Tas-Anvaripour, Neside, and Barry Reed, 2003. "Diagnostic Study of Accounting and Auditing Practices (Private Sector): Republic of Indonesia." Asian Development Bank.

Whalen, Jeanne. 2002. "Russia Mandates All Firms' Books Meet Global Rules," *Wall Street Journal* (Europe), Brussels, July 25, 2002, p. A1.

Xiao, Z., and A. Pan. 1997. "Developing Accounting Standards on the Basis of a Conceptual Framework by the Chinese Government." *The International Journal of Accounting* 32(3): 279–299.

CHAPTER FIVE

INTERNATIONAL FINANCIAL STATEMENT ANALYSIS

Chapter Objectives

- Assess the importance of international accounting differences from the perspective of financial analysts and other users of financial statements
- Identify major differences in accounting principles around the world that affect financial results
- Provide a quantitative analysis of how differences in accounting principles can impact the reported earnings of U.S. and U.K. firms and the analysis of comparative performance
- Show how reported earnings are affected by differences in accounting principles in other parts of the world, with special reference to continental Europe and Japan
- Review developments in the effort to achieve global accounting convergence

INTRODUCTION

This chapter examines the importance of differences in international accounting from the perspective of financial statement analysis. We will also assess the extent to which there are systematic differences across countries as a result of the differential impact of accounting principles on measures of earnings and assets. For the purposes of financial analysis, it is necessary not only to be aware of international differences in accounting but also to be able to assess their impact on earnings and assets and the key indicators and ratios involved, for example, earnings per share, return on equity, leverage (gearing), and so on. In doing so, we will look at the impact of differences in accounting principles around the world, with special ref-

---

Strategic Decision Point

Recently, the Financial Accounting Standards Board (FASB) in the United States and the International Accounting Standards Board (IASB) have sponsored research in conjunction with the International Association for Accounting Education and Research (IAAER) on the reporting of financial performance. This project intends to expand the information available to investors, creditors, and other financial statement users. The financial performance project focuses on form and content, classification and aggregation, and display of specified items in interim and annual financial statements. Significant financial reporting concerns have been raised by constituents, including the proliferation of pro forma earnings measures, the lack of a common definition of financial performance, and the need for a better understanding of the use of key financial measures and ratios derived from financial statements.

Some of the questions that may be answered during the research related to the financial performance measurement project include:

- Should a performance statement, of which the current income statement is one example, be the primary focus of financial reporting?
- How should a performance statement complement the other primary financial statements in providing information to financial statement users?
- How should the performance statement be articulated with and supplemented by the other existing basic financial statements? For example, not all countries currently require a cash flow statement. How should the cash flow statement be used? Is the direct or indirect method preferable?
- What information should be presented in the performance statement? In light of the wide range of business models and cultural differences, will one approach to defining the components of the statement be applicable to all entities?

---

erence to a selection of major countries. We will also attempt to assess the differential impact of "conservatism" on measurement practices, as discussed earlier, in the context of cultural influences on accounting.

INTERNATIONAL ACCOUNTING DIFFERENCES AND FINANCIAL STATEMENT ANALYSIS

Just as business and financial markets have become increasingly internationalized, so has the significance of differences in international accounting become more important from the perspective of international financial statement analysis. The key question concerns the extent to which international accounting differences impact assessments of earnings and future cash flows and their associated risks and uncertainties.

These assessments are important to portfolio investors making their stock (share) valuations. They are also important to corporations concerned with foreign direct investment (FDI), which involves the valuation of potential acquisitions and participating interests/joint ventures or the raising of capital or the listing/trading of stocks (shares) on foreign stock exchanges. A growing number of corporations are listed internationally (see Figure 5.1), with London being recently overtaken by New York as the most popular stock exchange, and many more are seeking to become so. In addition, there has been a dramatic increase in emerging stock markets and competition for international investment.

International accounting differences pose a number of problems from a financial analysis perspective. First, in attempting to value a foreign corporation, there is a tendency to look at earnings and other financial data from a home country perspective, and hence there is a danger of overlooking the effects of accounting differences. Unless significant differences are taken into account, possibly with some restatement involved, this could have very serious consequences. Second, an awareness of international differences suggests the need to become familiar with foreign accounting principles in order to better understand earnings data in the context in which such measures are derived. Third, issues of international comparability and accounting harmonization become highlighted in the context of considering alternative investment opportunities. In this regard, Choi and Levich (1991) provide a useful framework for analyzing the impact and relevance of accounting diversity in similar or dis-

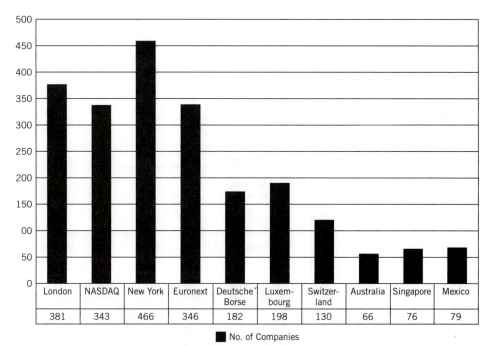

	London	NASDAQ	New York	Euronext	Deutsche Borse	Luxem-bourg	Switzer-land	Australia	Singapore	Mexico
	381	343	466	346	182	198	130	66	76	79

■ No. of Companies

Figure 5.1   International Stock Market Comparisons of International Company Listings on Foreign Exchanges (2003)

Source: FIBV, 2004.

similar economic environments (see Exhibit 5.1). In similar economic environments or situations, accounting diversity is illogical and leads to noncomparable results (box C). Logical practice suggests similar accounting treatments (box A). Where economic environments are dissimilar, however, as is likely in the case of international investment (boxes B and D), accounting diversity may well be justified, especially where the sources of such dissimilarity are in the company laws, tax regulations, sources of finance, business customs, accounting culture, and so on (box D). On the other hand, similar accounting treatments may be justifiable where such factors are of similar significance (box B). The importance of understanding environmental and cultural factors is thus emphasized.

In a survey to explore how capital market participants respond to accounting diversity, Choi and Levich sampled the opinions of institutional investors, multinational enterprises (MNEs) issuing securities, banks underwriting international securities, and regulatory bodies. Only 48 percent of those interviewed were apparently affected by international accounting diversity (see Exhibit 5.2), but it seems that the 52 percent of respondents claiming to be unaffected were in fact coping by various means, including (1) restating accounts to their own GAAP, (2) developing foreign GAAP capabilities, (3) using other sources of information, and (4) using different investment approaches, for example, a "top-down" macroeconomic approach to country selection coupled with stock diversification within a country. Similar approaches were used by those respondents whose investment decisions were apparently affected by accounting diversity. For the investor group, Exhibit 5.3 shows the wide-ranging nature of the effects arising both from GAAP differences and from disclosure differences. The results of this study suggest that the problems and costs arising from international accounting diversity are very real and need to be investigated further to assess whether and how they might be resolved. At the least, there is a clear need to assess the extent of such diversity and its impact on measures of earnings and performance.

Exhibit 5.1   Accounting Diversity and Economic Environments

| | | Economic Situation of Two Firms | |
		Similar	Dissimilar
	Similar	Logical Practice Results Comparable (A)	May or May Not Be Logical Results May or May Not Be Comparable (B)
Accounting Treatment	Dissimilar	Illogical Practice Results Not Comparable (C)	Logical Practice Results May or May Not Be Comparable (D)

Source: F. D. S. Choi and R. M. Levich, "International Accounting Diversity and Capital Market Decisions," in *Handbook of International Accounting,* edited by F. D. S. Choi (New York: John Wiley, 1991), p. 7.4.

Exhibit 5.2   Capital Market Effects of Accounting Diversity: Summary Findings for Investors, Issuers, Underwriters, Regulators, and Others

Key Questions
Does accounting diversity affect your capital market decisions?

	Yes	No	N.A.	Total
Investors	9	7	1	17
Issuers	6	9		15
Underwriters	7	1		8
Regulators	0	8		8
Raters and others	2	1		3
Total	24	26	1	51[a]

[a] The International Accounting Standards Committee was interviewed, but their answers are not included here.

Source: F. D. S. Choi and R. M. Levich "International Accounting Diversity and Capital Market Decisions," in *Handbook of International Accounting,* edited by F. D. S. Choi (New York: John Wiley, 1991), p. 7.16.

MAJOR DIFFERENCES IN ACCOUNTING PRINCIPLES AROUND THE WORLD

The extent of accounting diversity around the world is undoubtedly significant enough to make the job of the financial analyst a very difficult one in terms of making international comparisons.

If we now focus on some key measurement issues in a selection of major countries, that is, the United States, the European Union (EU) (including the United Kingdom, the Netherlands, France, and Germany), Brazil, Switzerland, China, and Japan, we can gain some insight into the variety of accounting principles in use that can impact earnings and assets differentially.

For these countries, some of which are representative of the culture classifications identified earlier and whose accounting systems have been discussed in Chapters 3 and 4, the accounting principles relating to a selection of key measure-

Exhibit 5.3   Capital Market Effects of Accounting Diversity: Investors

	From GAAP Differences	From Disclosure Differences
Geographic spread of investments	3	3
Types of companies/securities selected	6	7
Information processing costs	5[a]	2[b]
Assessment of security returns or valuation	8	8

[a] Two reported these costs were significant.
[b] Both feel this cost is significant.

Source: F.D.S. Choi and R. M. Levich, "International Accounting Diversity and Capital Market Decisions," in *Handbook of International Accounting,* edited by F.D.S. Choi (New York: John Wiley, 1991), p. 7.18.

ment issues are presented on a comparative basis in Exhibit 5.4. From this summary, it can be seen that there are some important differences across countries.

With respect to the measurement basis used, the conservative application of historical cost is generally required in the United States, Brazil, Switzerland, China, and Japan. However, in the EU countries, there tends to be a more flexible approach, especially in the United Kingdom and the Netherlands. In those two countries, historical cost is frequently modified by revaluations to market value or replacement cost, especially in the case of land and buildings and to a lesser extent, plant and equipment.

Depreciation accounting in the United States and the EU, especially the United Kingdom, tends to be based on the concept of useful economic life, whereas in France, Germany, Switzerland, and Japan, the tax rules generally encourage more accelerated methods.

Inventory measurement is generally based on the principle of "lower of cost and market" but with some variation as to the meaning of market, that is, net realizable value or replacement cost. LIFO (last-in, first-out) is sometimes permitted for tax purposes (for example, in the United States and Japan), but more often it is not (for example, in the EU). Construction contracts are generally accounted for using the percentage-of-completion method, but the more conservative completed contract method may be used in Switzerland, China, and Japan.

Research and development (R&D) costs are usually expensed immediately in the Anglo-American and Germanic countries, though in Brazil a more flexible approach is generally adopted. A permissive approach is also generally adopted toward capitalizing the borrowing costs of assets.

The treatment of retirement benefits is generally accounted for on the basis of accrued and/or projected benefits likely to be payable to employees, in contrast to the more pay-as-you-go approach of Brazil and China.

The treatment of taxation is a major area of differentiation with the measurement of accounting income strongly influenced by the tax rules in France, Germany, Brazil, and Switzerland.

The treatment of business combinations around the world varies to the extent that the pooling-of-interests method is required or permitted in certain specified circumstances. Generally, however, the purchase method is required. But with the purchase method comes a major area of differentiation and controversy between countries, that is, the treatment of goodwill. In Brazil, China, and Japan, the amortization method is required in contrast to the United States and the United Kingdom, where the amortization method is not required but valuations are subject to impairment tests.

Related to goodwill is the issue of intangibles, such as brands, publishing rights, and patents, which are generally capitalized, except in Switzerland, but subject usually to amortization or if not, to impairment tests.

Finally, the issue of foreign currency translation is important in that earnings measures are impacted by the choice between average or closing rates. Here, there would seem to be some flexibility in general, with either actual or average rates permitted.

Although there is a growing awareness of this diversity of measurement principles and practices internationally, much less is known about the overall impact of accounting differences on earnings and shareholders' equity. After all, differences

Exhibit 5.4   International Differences in Accounting Principles: Some Key
Measurement Issues

U.S./E.U. Accounting Issues	United States	European Union
Measurement Basis		
• Property	Historical cost required	Periodic revaluations (IAS 16)
• Plant and Equipment	Historical cost required	Revaluations permitted (IAS 16)
• Inventories	• Lower of cost and market (Net realizable value) • LIFO permitted	• Lower of cost and market (Net realizable value) • FIFO; LIFO not Permitted (IAS 2)
Depreciation Accounting	Usually straight line—based on useful economic life	Usually straight line—based on useful economic life (IAS 16)
Construction Contracts	Percentage-of-completion method	Percentage-of-completion (IAS 11) method
Research and Development Costs	Expensed immediately	Expensed immediately (IAS 38)
Borrowing Costs of Assets	Treated as cost of the asset	Usually expensed Immediately (IAS 23)
Exchange Rates for Income Statement Translation	Actual or average rates	Closing rate (IAS 21)
Retirement Benefits	Costs based on accrued benefits	Costs based on accrued or projected benefits (IAS 26/ FRS 17)
Deferred Taxation	Full deferral	Full deferral (IAS 12)
Business Combinations	Pooling not permitted	Pooling not permitted (IFRS 3)
Goodwill (Positive)	Nonamortization method required—subject to impairment tests	Nonamortization method required—subject to impair- ment tests (IAS 36/FRS 11) Is not so currently, but is expected to be soon, as the U.K. has declared intent to converge with IAS.
Intangibles (brands, publishing rights, patents)	Amortized according to usage trend-some assets subject to impairment tests	Carried at cost, amortized, can be revalued (IAS 38)

Brazil/Switzerland Accounting Issues	Brazil	Switzerland
Measurement Basis		
• Property	Historical cost plus inflation adjustments	Usually historical cost but lower valuations permitted
• Plant and Equipment	Historical cost plus inflation adjustments	Usually historical cost
• Inventories	• Lowest of cost and market (net realizable value) • Weighted average or FIFO; LIFO not permitted	• Lower of cost and net market • Various methods permitted
Depreciation Accounting	Usually straight-line	Accelerated methods permitted
Construction Contracts	Percentage-of-completion permitted	Completed contract method permitted

(continues)

Exhibit 5.4   (*Continued*)

Brazil/Switzerland Accounting Issues	Brazil	Switzerland
Research and Development Costs	Capitalization permitted	Usually expensed immediately
Borrowing Costs of Assets	Treatment as cost of the asset permitted	Treatment as cost of the asset permitted
Exchange Rates for Income Statement Translation	Average or closing rate	Usually average rates
Retirement Benefits	Costs expensed as paid	Costs based on accrued or projected benefits
Deferred Taxation	Accounting income strongly influenced by tax rules	Accounting income strongly influenced by tax rules
Business Combinations	Purchase method normally required	Pooling permitted in specified circumstances
Goodwill (positive)	Amortization method required	Immediate write-off permitted
Intangibles (brands, publishing rights, patents)	Capitalization permitted subject to amortization	Capitalization permitted subject to amortization

Asian Accounting Accounting Issues	China	Japan
Measurement basis • Property	Historical cost required	Historical cost normally required but land can be revalued
• Plant and Equipment	Historical cost required	Historical cost required
• Inventories	• Provisions for losses permitted • Various methods permitted including LIFO	• Normally at cost; Lower of cost and market permitted • Various methods permitted including LIFO
Depreciation Accounting	Usually straight-line	Accelerated methods permitted
Construction Contracts	Completed contract and percentage-of-completion methods permitted	Completed contract and percentage-of-completion methods permitted
Research and Development Costs	All expensed except legal costs and patent registration	Generally expensed as incurred
Borrowing Costs of Assets	Treatment as cost of the asset permitted	Treatment as cost of the asset permitted
Exchange Rates for Income Statement Translation	Average rates	Average or closing rates
Retirement Benefits	Costs expensed as paid	Present Value of projected benefits
Deferred Taxation	Recognized to the extent of taxable profit in the next three years	Temporary differences less nonrecoverable amount
Business Combinations	Purchase method normally used; no requirement	Some pooling permitted
Goodwill (positive)	Amortization method required, contract 10 years	Amortized, no more than 20 years
Intangibles (brands, publishing rights, patents)	Amortized over estimated useful life, max of 10 years	Amortized over useful life

with respect to various aspects of measurement may well compensate for each other to the extent that their overall impact may not be significant. The important question is whether accounting differences systematically impact measures of income. In other words, do these differences really matter?

Although there has been a relatively limited amount of research into the quantitative impact of international accounting differences, there is growing evidence concerning relationships between U.S. accounting principles and those in the United Kingdom, a number of EU countries, and Japan.

THE IMPACT OF U.S.-U.K. ACCOUNTING DIFFERENCES: A QUANTITATIVE ANALYSIS

Let us first examine the question of whether there is an overall quantitative impact on earnings arising from differences between U.S. and U.K. accounting principles. Using U.S. GAAP as the yardstick, we can make an assessment of the relationship between U.K. earnings reported under U.K. GAAP and U.K. earnings adjusted in accordance with U.S. GAAP. Given that "conservatism" is a major influence on measurement practices, then this relationship can be described in terms of relative conservatism.

Accordingly, an index of conservatism can be calculated, as shown by Gray (1980), using the following formula:

$$1 - \left(\frac{RA - RD}{|RA|} \right)$$

where
RA = adjusted earnings (or returns)
RD = disclosed earnings

In the case of U.S. versus U.K. accounting principles, this becomes

$$1 - \left(\frac{\text{U.S. GAAP Earnings} - \text{U.K. GAAP Earnings}}{|\text{U.S. GAAP Earnings}|} \right)$$

An index value greater than 1 means that U.K. GAAP earnings are less conservative than the U.S. GAAP measure would have been. An index value less than one means that U.K. earnings are *more* conservative than the U.S. measure would have been. An index value exactly *equal* to 1 indicates neutrality between the two systems with respect to the effect of accounting principles. The denominator has been taken as U.S. GAAP earnings to provide a benchmark against which U.K. GAAP earnings can be compared.

To illustrate the effect of the index, take two examples:

Example 1: U.K. GAAP earnings £110 million   Example 2: U.K. GAAP earnings £90 million
          U.S. GAAP earnings £100 million   U.S. GAAP earnings £100 million

Index $1 - \left(\dfrac{100 - 110}{100} \right)$ $1 - \left(\dfrac{100 - 90}{100} \right)$

          $= 1.1$ $= 0.9$

Note: The data can also be restated in $ terms as required.

Having established an overall index of conservatism, it is then possible to establish the relative effect of the various individual adjustments by constructing partial indices of adjustment using the formula:

$$\text{Partial index of ``conservatism''} = 1 - \left(\frac{\text{partial adjustment}}{|\text{ U.S. GAAP Earnings }|} \right)$$

For example:

	Millions of Pounds
U.K. GAAP earnings	120
Adjustments for U.S. GAAP:	
Deferred taxation	(15)
Goodwill amortization	(5)
Adjusted earnings per U.S. GAAP	100
Overall index of "conservatism"	1.2
Partial index for deferred taxation	$1 - \left(\dfrac{-15}{100} \right) = 1.15$
Partial index for goodwill	$1 - \left(\dfrac{-5}{100} \right) = 1.05$

An opportunity to compare earnings resulting from U.K. accounting principles with those that would have resulted under U.S. accounting principles is given by those U.K. corporations obliged to report to the SEC in the United States. The Form 20-F report to the SEC contains a reconciliation of U.K. earnings with the earnings that would have been reported under U.S. GAAP. The effect of each accounting policy, which differs between the two countries, is quantified separately. In addition to the quantified difference, the accounting policies as they affect the corporation are explained by way of note, which occasionally gives further insight into the differences between U.K. and U.S. accounting practice. British Telecom is an example of a U.K. corporation reporting under 20-F.

The reconciliations disclosed in Form 20-F can be used to test whether U.K. GAAP earnings before extraordinary items are systematically less conservative than they would be if U.S. GAAP were applied or, conversely, whether U.S. reporting practices are more conservative than U.K. reporting practices. This data is, of course, much more reliable than any independent attempt to adjust company accounts for international differences because it is provided by the company itself and is subject to audit.

The SEC requires a report on Form 20-F where the corporation sponsors an American Depositary Receipt (ADR), which is traded on one of the national stock exchanges such as the New York Stock Exchange (NYSE), the American Stock Exchange (AMEX), or the National Association of Securities Dealers Automated Quotations (NASDAQ).

Based on the analysis of 37 U.K. corporations providing reconciliations on Form 20-F, Weetman and Gray (1990) found that statistically significant differences existed and that U.S. GAAP measures of earnings for the period 1985–1987 were much more conservative than U.K. GAAP earnings. More specifically, it was evident that U.K. earnings were, on average, between 9 and 25 percent higher than U.S. earnings as a result of differences in accounting principles.

The most frequently occurring adjustments were found to be those dealing with amortization of goodwill and deferred taxation. Of the two, the amortization of goodwill was the dominant effect when measured as a percentage of U.S. reported earnings. In fact, up to 18 percent of the difference between U.S. and U.K.-based earnings, on average, was taken up by goodwill amortization, which was generally not found in U.K. profit and loss accounts at that time. In a follow-up study, Weetman, Jones, Adams, and Gray (1998) discovered that the tendency for U.K. GAAP to result in higher earnings had continued. In 1988, U.K. earnings were, on average, 17 percent higher than U.S. earnings, and the gap had widened to 25 percent by 1994 (see Exhibits 5.5 and 5.6).

In summary, the differences between U.S. and U.K. accounting principles show that in practice, U.K. GAAP is significantly less conservative, or the U.S. more conservative, as far as the quantitative impact on earnings is concerned. Although this is contrary to what might be expected from two major Anglo-American countries with similar accounting traditions, an important question still to be addressed

Exhibit 5.5   Number of Companies Making Each Category of Adjustment to Profit, Together with Mean and Median Index of Comparability for 1988 and 1994

Nature of Adjustment to Profit	1988 Count	1988 Mean	1998 Median	1994 Count	1994 Mean	1994 Median
Overall	25	1.17	1.10	25	1.25	1.18
Goodwill	24	1.13	1.06	23	1.21	1.15
Deferred tax	22	1.06	1.01	23	1.00	1.00
Pensions/post-retirement benefits/insurance	10	1.01	1.01	19	1.02	1.02
Asset/expense	14	0.98	0.99	14	1.12	1.01
Historic cost/revalued asset	13	0.95	0.98	18	0.98	0.99
Intangibles	3	1.08	1.07	5	1.34	1.06
Restructuring	—	—	—	5	0.80	0.88
Foreign currency translation	5	1.00	1.01	4	0.94	0.99
Financial instruments	2	1.26	1.26	4	0.98	1.04
Leasing	2	1.05	1.05	4	1.16	1.15
Revenue recognition	3	1.02	1.00	3	0.95	0.99
Extraordinary items	12	0.95	1.05	—	—	—
Miscellaneous	5	1.01	1.03	13	0.98	1.01

The following outliers were excluded from calculation of the mean values of profit in respect of the 1994 data:

1. ICI Group plc (overall index of comparability and partial index of comparability for pension costs and retirement benefits)

2. WPP Group plc (overall index of comparability and partial index of comparability for amortization of goodwill)

Source: P. Weetman et al., *Accounting and Business Research* (Summer 1998): 196.

Exhibit 5.6   Frequency Table of Distribution of Values of Index of Comparability for Profit

Level of Materiality	Index Values	1988	1994
Adjustment to U.K. profit is – 10% or more of the amount of U.S. profit	≤0.90	5	4
Adjustment to U.K. profit between – 5% and – 10% of the amount of U.S. profit	0.91–0.94	1	1
Adjustment to U.K. profit within +/– 5% of U.S. profit	0.95–1.04	3	2
Adjustment to U.K. profit is between +5% and +10% of the amount of U.S. profit	1.05–1.09	3	1
Adjustment to U.K. profit is +10% or more of the amount of the U.S. profit	≥ 1.10	13	17
Total		25	25
Range (excluding outliers): lowest value		0.65	0.75
highest value		1.79	2.76

The following outlying index values were eliminated before calculating the t-statistic

Name:	Index value eliminated	Year	Cause
ICI Group plc	3.36	1994	Large pension expense adjustment
WPP Group plc	10.77	1994	Low U.S. profit figure

Source: P. Weetman et al., *Accounting and Business Research* (Summer 1998): 197.

is this: how different are the United States and United Kingdom from other countries with quite different accounting traditions?

A GLOBAL PERSPECTIVE ON EARNINGS MEASUREMENT

The available evidence suggests that earnings measured under U.K. accounting principles tend to be systematically higher or less conservative than earnings measured under U.S. accounting principles. But what do we know about the relative impact of Anglo-American accounting principles on earnings compared to those of continental Europe and Japan?

Continental Europe

The importance of understanding how accounting differences can affect the interpretation of company accounts in Europe has been emphasized again recently. It is not so clear, however, how the net effect of such differences has an impact on earnings. An early attempt to quantify, in practice, the impact of French and German accounting principles compared to U.K. accounting principles was made by Gray (1980) in an empirical study of 15 French, 28 German, and 29 U.K. companies for

Exhibit 5.7   A Comparative Analysis of Profits-Measurement Behavior in France, Germany, and the United Kingdom, 1972–1975

Reported Profits Classified Using an Index of Conservatism		France	Germany	United Kingdom	Total Disclosures
I.	0.50	12	12	2	26
II.	0.50–0.74	20	35	10	65
III.	0.75–0.94	14	37	5	56
Pessimistic (<0.95)		46 (77%)	84 (75%)	17 (14%)	147
IV.	0.95–0.99	4	4	11	19
V.	1.00	1	1	4	6
VI.	1.01–1.05	0	4	17	21
Neutral (0.95–1.05)		5 (8%)	9 (8%)	32 (28%)	46
VII.	1.06–1.25	3	6	37	46
VIII.	1.26–1.50	2	6	20	28
IX.	1.50	4	7	10	21
Optimistic (>1.05)		9 (15%)	19 (17%)	67 (58%)	95
Total Disclosures		60 (100%)	112 (100%)	116 (100%)	288

Source: S. J. Gray, "International Accounting Differences from a Security Analysis Perspective: Some European Evidence," *Journal of Accounting Research* (Spring 1980): 68.

the period 1972–1975. The database for this study was provided by DAFSA Analyse of Paris with its data bank of European company accounts adjusted according to the "European Method" used by financial analysts. Using this adjusted basis of earnings as the yardstick for comparison, we calculated a "conservatism" index for each company as in the U.S.-U.K. comparative analysis, and the summarized results are shown in Exhibit 5.7.

From this it appears that earnings tend to be more conservative or understated in France and Germany than in the United Kingdom. The statistical significance of this hypothesis was supported by the results of a series of statistical (chi-square) tests as shown in Exhibit 5.8. It should be noted in this regard that there were no significant differences between France and Germany.

Exhibit 5.8   Comparative Analysis of Profits-Measurement Behavior: Chi-Square Test Statistics 1972–1975 (2×2 Analysis, One-Tailed Test)

Comparative Analysis	1972	1973	1974	1975
France/United Kingdom	6.67[a]	10.40[b]	16.30[b]	11.54[b]
Germany/United Kingdom	9.27[b]	19.36[b]	16.97[b]	9.53[b]
France/Germany	0.05	0.003	0.30	0.67

[a] Significant at the 0.01 level.
[b] Significant at the 0.001 level.

Source: S. J. Gray, "International Accounting Differences from a Security Analysis Perspective: Some European Evidence," *Journal of Accounting Research* (Spring 1980): 69.

Weetman and Gray (1991), using more recent data disclosed to the SEC under Form 20-F, examined the impact of accounting differences on earnings in practice in the Netherlands, Sweden, and the United Kingdom. The research results tended to suggest that the Netherlands is at the less conservative end of the spectrum, similar to, but not as extreme as, the United Kingdom, while in Sweden the tendency was to be more conservative than U.S. GAAP.

Japan

We suggested in Chapter 3 that accounting in Japan is the subject of many influences with a unique outcome. Despite the growing internationalization of Japanese accounting standards, the influence of taxation, creditor interests, and a conservative culture have ensured that measures of earnings are relatively understated compared to the United States. A study by Aron (1991) concluded that Japanese earnings in 1990 were understated by 33.9 percent, on average, compared to earnings measured under U.S. GAAP. This estimate was calculated for stock market listed companies taken as a whole by making adjustments, on a judgmental basis, for the impact of tax-deductible reserves, consolidation practices, and depreciation. After making further adjustments for cross-holdings and differences in capitalization, it was suggested that the average Japanese price-earnings ratio becomes 12.51 and not 34.30 as reported by Morgan Stanley Capital International Perspective. Thus, the mystery of relatively high Japanese price-earning ratios was resolved to some degree. However, it should be noted that differences in financial ratios such as corporate liquidity and gearing (leverage) are not just the result of accounting differences but also differences in the financial systems and norms of countries. In Japan, for example, higher levels of gearing and short-term payables are considered normal relative to the United States because of longer-term relationships with bankers and suppliers. Similarly, a longer-term view tends to be taken of profitability, with much more emphasis placed on achieving growth in sales and market share.

Data at the corporate level on the impact of Japanese/U.S. GAAP differences is not readily obtainable because most Japanese companies listed in the United States report in accordance with U.S. GAAP. However, a study by Cooke (1993) provided some interesting case evidence to suggest a relatively "conservative" Japanese approach to earnings measurement.

A COMPARATIVE GLOBAL ANALYSIS

Although there is a pressing need for further research in this area, the research to date provides a global perspective that indicates that U.S. accounting principles are significantly more conservative than the United Kingdom but significantly less conservative than Japan and many continental European countries in terms of their impact on earnings. If the United States is taken as the yardstick with an index number of 100, then its relationship, on average, with the United Kingdom, Belgium, France, Germany, the Netherlands, Spain, and Japan can be shown as it is in Figure 5.2. Of course, this is a very judgmental impression based on the limited evidence available.

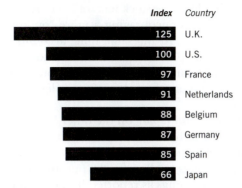

Index	Country
125	U.K.
100	U.S.
97	France
91	Netherlands
88	Belgium
87	Germany
85	Spain
66	Japan

Figure 5.2   The Comparative Impact of International Accounting Differences on Earnings: Earnings Adjustment Index Based on U.S. GAAP

Overall, the United Kingdom is significantly less conservative than other countries, with Japan at the other end of the spectrum. The continental European countries, on the other hand, are largely bunched together in a more conservative group compared to the United States. This suggests that significantly different approaches to accounting measurement are likely to persist despite the continued international harmonization efforts to achieve global comparability.

INTERNATIONAL ACCOUNTING DIFFERENCES AND THE STOCK MARKET

While the persistence of significant international measurement differences poses problems for financial analysts and those concerned with international harmonization, there is an important question concerning how stock prices react to earnings calculated under different GAAPs. The evidence on this issue is thus far limited, though some early research by Meek (1983) indicated that U.S. stock prices react to foreign GAAP earnings. More recently, research by Pope and Rees (1992) suggests that in the case of U.K. corporations listed in the United States and also reporting under U.S. GAAP, there is significant incremental explanatory power given by the U.S. GAAP earnings adjustment information. Furthermore, research by Amir, Harris, and Venuti (1993) of Form 20-F reconciliations for companies in 20 countries supports the value relevance of the U.S. GAAP information. However, more recent research by Rees (1995, 1996), Barth and Clinch (1996), and Fulkerson and Meek (1998) is less clear, with mixed results.

FACTORS INFLUENCING MEASUREMENT DIFFERENCES

The reasons for measurement differences can be found in the environmental and cultural factors influencing accounting principles in these countries. In the United

States and the United Kingdom, the stock market is a dominant influence, with the information needs of investors encouraging a more "optimistic" view of earnings and hence higher share prices. At the same time, accounting principles are relatively flexible, the accounting profession is relatively independent of government, and the tax rules have only a limited influence on accounting practice. Underlying cultural values tend to both motivate and reinforce a less conservative approach to measurement taken overall.

In continental Europe and Japan, on the other hand, taxation and sources of finance are relatively major influences compared to the stock market. These countries, have a tradition of commercial codes and accounting plans. Moreover, it is common for the tax authorities to allow for tax purposes only those items charged in the accounts and to tax earnings as reported in the accounts. This tends to lead to a more conservative application of accounting principles in order to report lower earnings for tax purposes. In addition, the significance of creditors and loan finance relative to equity provides a further conservative influence in that lower earnings will tend to better meet the interests of creditors and lenders vis-à-vis shareholders. Thus, the users of financial statements in these countries may be more concerned with balance sheet data than the more conservative income statement. Black and White (2003) find that balance sheet information is more value relevant than income statement information in Germany and Japan. In contrast, they find that income statement information is more informative in the United States. The legal requirements relating to accounting are also usually more detailed, with the result that professional influence is relatively low and is limited mainly to the audit function. Finally, underlying cultural values tend to both motivate and reinforce a more conservative approach to measurement.

GLOBAL ACCOUNTING CONVERGENCE

Although a number of organizations around the world, including the United Nations and the EU, have been concerned with harmonizing international differences in accounting and reporting, the most important body in recent years has been the International Accounting Standards Board (IASB), formerly the International Accounting Standards Committee (IASC) established in 1973, which sets International Financial Reporting Standards (IFRSs).

The main reason for developing international standards has been to achieve a degree of comparability that will help investors make their decisions while reducing the costs of MNEs in preparing multiple sets of accounts and reports. It is also fair to say that the IASB sees itself as playing a major role in coordinating and harmonizing the activities of the many agencies involved in setting accounting and reporting standards. IASB standards are also intended to provide a useful model for developing countries wishing to establish accounting standards for the first time.

In the early days, international standards were developed allowing substantial flexibility to accommodate different national interests, but since the late 1980s, there has been growing pressure to develop more uniform standards to facilitate cross-border capital raisings and stock exchange listings. A core standards program to promote the development of more uniform and high-quality standards was initiated in cooperation with the International Organization of Securities Commissions

(IOSCO) and was completed in 1998. As of May 2000, IOSCO recommended acceptance of international standards subject to supplemental treatments where necessary. The IASB is hoping that IOSCO's endorsement will lead to a greater recognition of International Financial Reporting Standards and the promotion of global convergence. A growing number of companies are also electing to follow international standards, though compliance is not always as comprehensive in practice as claimed (Street, Gray, and Bryant, 1999; Street and Gray, 2001). Most recently, effective 2005, the EU countries have decided to adopt approved international standards for financial reports by all listed companies.

A key question now is whether all IOSCO members, and especially the United States, will accept the IASB's standards in practice as "global" standards with equal, if not greater, status compared to domestic standards. Further analysis of global accounting convergence issues is provided in Chapter 7.

SUMMARY

1.   The significance of international accounting diversity for the global investment community and the problems of international financial statement analysis have received increasing recognition.

2.   There are many significant differences in accounting principles around the world that impact reported earnings and financial position.

3.   Research into the quantitative impact of U.S.-U.K. accounting differences reveals that such differences are systematic and that they do matter. U.K. earnings are significantly higher or less conservative than U.S. earnings on the basis of GAAP differences.

4.   The impact of U.K. GAAP on earnings also seems to be significantly less conservative compared to France, Germany, the Netherlands, Sweden, and a number of other continental European countries.

5.   Accounting principles in Japan are significantly more conservative than those in the United States and the United Kingdom with respect to their impact on earnings and assets.

6.   When making comparisons between the United States and the United Kingdom, on the one hand, and continental Europe and Japan, on the other, it is clear that while accounting measurement practices in the United States are significantly more conservative than the United Kingdom, they are significantly less conservative than Japan and many continental European countries.

7.   The impact of differences in accounting principles tends to reflect the dominant stock market focus of the United States and United Kingdom versus the taxation/creditor emphasis still important in continental Europe and Japan. At the same time, these differences seem to be motivated and reinforced by underlying differences in cultural attitudes toward conservatism or prudence in accounting measurement.

8.   Although research on the reaction of stock prices to international accounting differences is still somewhat limited, findings tend to support the value relevance of such differences to investors.

9.   Efforts to achieve global accounting harmonization have been made since the early 1970s, notably by the International Accounting Standards Commit-

tee (IASC), recently renamed the International Accounting Standards Board (IASB).

   10.   Endorsement of International Financial Reporting Standards by IOSCO is a promising step forward toward acceptance of a global set of accounting standards.

Discussion Questions

1. What are the following groups concerned about when looking at foreign financial statements?

    - Banks/Creditors
    - Investors
    - Industry Analysts
    - Managers

2. Should internal management of international companies be concerned about the international differences in accounting methods? Why or why not? If yes, which differences are especially important to management?

3. How do international accounting standards help financial statement analysis? Do the standards hinder the analysis?

4. You are considering diversifying your personal investment portfolio by investing in domestic or foreign banks. Discuss the process for comparing a public U.S. bank (e.g., Bank of America) with a Japanese bank. What are your main concerns? Which areas are of least risk in this comparative analysis?

5. Name three hindrances to simple, quality international financial statement analysis. What can be done/is being done to mitigate those problems?

6. Why does the European Union want to standardize the accounting practices of its member countries?

7. How will the European Union's standardized use of IFRS impact the conservatism index and the differences between earnings reported by different European nations?

8. What is the advantage of seeking funding in the international market?

9. How do international accounting standards reduce the cost of obtaining capital?

10. If accounting principles around the world are harmonized, will this necessarily eliminate the diversity of earnings measurements practices?

11. Do you think it inevitable that pressure for the globalization of measurement principles and practices will overcome local environmental and cultural influences? If so, when?

12. To what extent is it possible for investors to cope with international accounting differences without making any adjustments or reconciliations to their home country GAAP?

13. How desirable are reconciliations such as those required under the SEC's Form 20-F regulations for foreign corporations?

14. How does the conservatism index relate to risk? In other words, does a more conservative country inherently have less risk?

15. Do you think that complete global convergence in accounting practices is possible? What types of countries and companies will have the hardest time converging?

Exercises

Volkswagen and GM (exercises 1–7)

1. If you were to make a tender offer for Volkswagen, how much would you offer? Why?
2. If Volkswagen were to sell bonds on the U.S. market, do you think its interest rate would be greater or lesser than GM? Why?
3. Compute the following ratios for both companies in 2003. What do the results mean? What are some possible reasons for the differences in ratios?
   - Current Ratio
   - Asset Turnover
   - Times Interest Earned
   - Debt-to-Equity Ratio
   - Earnings per Share
4. Which of the statements do you prefer? Why? Which of the statements is more transparent?
5. What differences should you look for when adjusting Volkswagen's results to GAAP reporting standards? In other words, what are some of the major accounting differences between Germany and the United States that are relevant to this industry?
6. If you were a bank, to whom would you rather lend money? Why?
7. If you were an equity investor, in whom would you rather invest? Why?

GENERAL MOTORS CORPORATION AND SUBSIDIARIES
Consolidated Statements of Income

GENERAL MOTORS CORPORATION AND SUBSIDIARIES	Years Ended December 31,		
	2003	2002	2001
	(dollars in millions except per share amounts)		
Total net sales and revenues (Notes 1 and 24)	$185,524	$177,324	$169,051
Cost of sales and other expenses (Note 5)	152,071	146,793	138,847
Selling, general, and administrative expenses	21,008	20,690	19,433
Interest expense (Note 16)	9,464	7,503	8,317
Total costs and expenses	182,543	174,986	166,597
Income from continuing operations before income taxes, equity income and minority interests	2,981	2,338	2,454
Income tax expense (Note 11)	731	644	1,094
Equity income (loss) and minority interests	612	281	(138)

(continues)

Income from continuing operations	2,862	1,975	1,222
Loss from discontinued operations (Note 2)	(219)	(239)	(621)
Gain on sale of discontinued operations	1,179	—	—
Net income	3,822	1,736	601
Dividends on preference stocks	—	(46)	(99)
Earnings attributable to common stocks (Note 20)	$3,822	$1,690	$502
Basic earnings (loss) per share attributable to common stocks $1–2/3 par value			
Continuing operations	$5.10	$3.53	$2.21
Discontinued operations	$2.14	$(0.16)	$(0.42)
Earnings per share attributable to $1–2/3 par value	$7.24	$3.37	$1.79
Losses per share from discontinued operations attributable to Class H	$(0.22)	$(0.21)	$(0.55)

Earnings (loss) per share attributable to common stocks assuming dilution $1–2/3 par value

Continuing operations	$5.03	$3.51	$2.20
Discontinued operations	$2.11	$(0.16)	$(0.43)
Earnings per share attributable to $1–2/3 par value	$7.14	$3.35	$1.77
Losses per share from discontinued operations attributable to Class H	$(0.22)	$(0.21)	$(0.55)

Reference should be made to the notes to consolidated financial statements.

GENERAL MOTORS CORPORATION AND SUBSIDIARIES
CONSOLIDATED BALANCE SHEETS

	December 31,	
ASSETS (dollars in millions)	2003	2002
Cash and cash equivalents (Note 1)	$32,554	$20,320
Other marketable securities (Note 6)	22,215	16,825
Total cash and marketable securities	54,769	37,145
Finance receivables – net (Note 8)	173,137	134,643
Loans held for sale	19,609	15,720
Accounts and notes receivable (less allowances)	20,532	16,337
Inventories (less allowances) (Note 9)	10,960	9,737
Assets of discontinued operations	—	18,653
Deferred income taxes (Note 11)	27,190	39,767

Net equipment on operating leases (less accumulated depreciation) (Note 10)	34,383	31,026
Equity in net assets of nonconsolidated affiliates	6,032	5,097
Property – net (Note 12)	38,211	35,956
Intangible assets – net (Notes 1 and 13)	4,760	10,796
Other assets (Note 14)	58,924	14,176
Total assets	$448,507	$369,053

LIABILITIES AND STOCKHOLDERS' EQUITY

Accounts payable (principally trade)	$25,422	$21,138
Notes and loans payable (Note 16)	271,756	200,168
Liabilities of discontinued operations	—	7,956
Postretirement benefits other than pensions (Note 17)	36,292	38,152
Pensions (Note 17)	8,024	22,679
Deferred income taxes (Notes 11 and 15)	7,508	6,523
Accrued expenses and other liabilities (Note 15)	73,930	65,344
Total liabilities	422,932	361,960
Minority interests	307	279
Stockholders' equity (Note 19)		
$1–2/3 par value common stock (outstanding, 561,997,725 and 560,447,797 shares)	937	936
Class H common stock (outstanding, 958,284,272 shares in 2002)	—	96
Capital surplus (principally additional paid-in capital)	15,185	21,583
Retained earnings	12,752	10,031
Subtotal	28,874	32,646
Accumulated foreign currency translation adjustments	(1,815)	(2,784)
Net unrealized gains (losses) on derivatives	51	(205)
Net unrealized gains on securities	618	372
Minimum pension liability adjustment	(2,460)	(23,215)
Accumulated other comprehensive loss	(3,606)	(25,832)
Total stockholders' equity	25,268	6,814
Total liabilities and stockholders' equity	$448,507	$369,053

Reference should be made to the notes to consolidated financial statements.

Volkswagen AG

Million €	Note	2003	2002
Sales revenue	1	**87,153**	**86,948**
Cost of sales		77,754	74,188
Gross profit Automotive Division[a]		**+9,399**	**+12,760**
Gross profit Financial Services Division[a]	2	**+1,261**	**+1,238**
Distribution costs		7,846	7,560
Administrative expenses		2,274	2,155
Other operating income	3	4,403	4,137
Other operating expenses	4	3,163	3,659
Operating profit		**+1,780**	**+4,761**
Share of profits and losses of Group companies accounted for using the equity method	5a	+511	+534
Other income from investments	5b	−32	+12
Interest result	6a	+125	−478
Other financial result	6b	−855	−843
Financial result		**−251**	**−775**
Profit before tax		**+1,529**	**+3,986**
Income tax expense	7	411	1,389
current		623	1,369
deferred		−212	20
Profit after tax	8	**+1,118**	**+2,597**
Minority interests	9	−23	−13
Net profit attributable to shareholders of Volkswagen AG		**+1,095**	**+2,584**
Earnings per ordinary share €	10	**+2.84**	**+6.72**
Diluted earnings per ordinary share €	10	**+2.84**	**+6.72**
Earnings per preferred share €	10	**+2.90**	**+6.78**
Diluted earnings per preferred share €	10	**+2.90**	**+6.78**

[a] The result from the operating loose and rental business is indicated in the grass profit of the Automotive Division. ©VOLKSWAGEN AG Annual Report 2003

Volkswagen AG

Million €	Note	Dec 31, 2003	Dec 31, 2002
Assets			
Non-current assets			
Intangible assets	11	8,202	7,736
Tangible assets	12	23,852	22,842
Investments in Group companies accounted for using the equity method	13	3,360	3,397

Million €	Note	Dec 31, 2003	Dec 31, 2002
Other financial assets	13	607	588
		36,021	**34,563**
Leasing and rental assets	14	**8,906**	**8,445**
Current assets			
Inventories	15	11,670	10,677
Financial services receivables	16	39,365	37,512
Trade receivables	17	5,497	5,747
Other receivables and assets	18	5,201	4,055
Securities	19	3,148	3,192
Cash and cash equivalents	20	7,536	2,987
		72,417	**64,170**
Deferred tax assets	21	**1,515**	**1,445**
Prepayments and deferred charges	22	**277**	**273**
Total assets		**119,136**	**108,896**
Equity and Liabilities			
Capital and reserves	23		
Subscribed capital		1,089	1,089
Capital reserve		**4,451**	**4,451**
Revenue reserves		14,171	13,905
Accumulated profits		4,719	5,189
		24,430	**24,634**
Minority interests	24	**104**	**57**
Provisions	25	**22,810**	**22,349**
Deferred tax liabilities		**2,472**	**2,558**
Liabilities			
Non-current borrowings	26	25,936	19,488
Current borrowings	26	28,922	26,113
Trade payables	27	7,822	7,236
Other payables	28	6,318	6,128
		68,998	**58,965**
Deferred income	29	**322**	**333**
Total equity and liabilities		**119,136**	**108,896**

©VOLKSWAGEN AG Annual Report 2003

DaimlerBenz (exercises 8–11) (See the following information to answer the questions)

8.   Discuss the arguments for and against DaimlerBenz listing its shares in the United States.

9.   Identify and discuss the major differences between U.S. and German accounting principles.

10.   Calculate the "conservatism" index and returns on equity for 1992 and 1993 under both German and U.S. GAAP.

11.   Does it appear that German GAAP are more or less conservative than U.S. GAAP? How can you explain your findings?

Daimler-Benz (Germany)

Valuation in Consolidated Financial Statements Adjusted to U.S. Accounting Principles

We began to conform our balance sheet accounting and valuation methods to international conventions with the 1989 consolidated financial statements, in order to simplify comparison with other companies as well as to improve our method of reporting. We were the first German company to list its stock on the New York Stock Exchange, and therefore reconciled net income and stockholders' equity to generally accepted accounting principles in the United States (U.S. GAAP). It became apparent that there were still substantial differences between our accounting principles and the U.S. accounting principles, which have a decisive influence on financial reporting.

In the 1993 consolidated financial statements, we have therefore adapted our methods of accounting and valuation as closely as possible to U.S. GAAP. These measures, which at the same time achieve substantial alignment between the German commercial balance sheet and the German tax balance sheet, have generated a one-time income before tax of DM 2.6 billion in the German consolidated financial statements. This amount is classified as extraordinary income. The balance of the differences are from rules and regulations regarding obligatory accounting and valuation procedures.

Our annual report includes a reconciliation of the net income and stockholders' equity determined according to the principles of the German "Handelsgesetzbuch" (Commercial Code) to those amounts reported under U.S. GAAP.

Additional Information in Accordance with the "U.S. Generally Accepted Accounting Principles" (U.S. GAAP)

With the introduction of DaimlerBenz stock on the New York Stock Exchange, we are filling an annual report as Form 20-F with the Securities and Exchange Commission (SEC). Much of the content of this filing is information taken from our annual report; however, additional data and financial information is provided determined on the basis of U.S. accounting principles. In the following section we have set forth what we consider to be the most important information from the Form 20-F. Since there are substantial differences, especially in the annual net income and stockholders' equity, the reconciliations are required to convert certain financial data from the German consolidated financial statements to the values calculated by using U.S. generally accepted accounting principles.

Differences in Accruals as a Result of the Change in the Treatment of Provisions and Valuation Methods

U.S. accounting principles do not allow the formation of the extensive loss provisions as permitted by German law. The excess German loss provisions have to be dissolved which has an effect on the net income as well as stockholders' equity. According to U.S. GAAP, the stockholders' equity increased by DM 5.8 billion during 1995 as a result of the dissolution of certain loss provisions which also changed the inventory and receivables value. We use the term *Appropriated Retained Earnings* to disclose to the American investors that such retained earnings are not available for distribution as dividends. This term also establishes a bridge between the two different accounting cultures.

Long-Term Manufacturing

Customer deposits and manufacturing costs are reported under German law in accordance with the completed contract method, whereas U.S. principles generally require that the percentage-of completion method be used. The majority of contracts within the group require partial prepayment as well as partial recognition of profits based upon payments received. Contracts of this nature are also customary in the United states and are recognized under its accounting regulations. The resulting differences therefore are not material.

Goodwill and Acquisition of Investments in Businesses

Under German accounting regulations goodwill can be allocated to stockholders' equity, or capitalized and amortized generally over the expected useful life which in Germany ranges between 5 to 15 years. Under U.S. GAAP the difference between acquisition costs and market value must be capitalized and amortized over a period not exceeding 40 years.

Disposal of Investment in Businesses

Under German accounting principles sales of subsidiaries and shareholdings in businesses must be allocated to the period in which the contract is signed. According to U.S. GAAP, the gain or loss on investment cannot be recognized until after the actual monetary exchange of the investment.

Pension Provisions

According to U.S. accounting principles, the determination of provisions for old-age pensions requires, among other things, a determination for anticipated increases in wages and salaries. The calculation is not based on the discount rate of 6 percent for unaccrued interest, which is applicable under German tax law but incorporates the respective actual interest rates. Another difference is a result of the requirement that health care costs for retirees be actuarily calculated and accrued for in the United States.

Currency Translation and Financial Instruments

Unrealized exchange profits and losses on financial instruments are treated differently in the two accounting systems. Under German law, according to the imparity principle, only unrealized losses are to be recorded, whereas under U.S. GAAP unrealized profits as well as losses must be recorded.

Other Differences in Valuation

Additional differences between German and American accounting methods may occur with respect to inventories, minority interests, and leasing activities.

Deferred Taxes

Under German accounting regulations, deferred tax assets are established only for the elimination processes in consolidation. Under U.S. accounting principles deferred tax assets can also be recorded for valuation adjustments and existing tax loss carryforwards.

Reconciliation of Consolidated Net income and Stockholders' Equity to U.S. GAAP

		1993	1992
		in millions of DM	
Consolidated Net Income in Accordance with German			
Commercial Code		**615**	1,451
%	Minority interest	(**13)**	(33)
Adjusted net income under German regulations		**602**	1,418
+/−	Changes in appropriated retained earnings: provisions, reserves, and valuation		
	differences	(**4,262)**	774
		(**3,660)**	2,192
Additional adjustments			
+/−	Long-term contracts	**78**	(57)
	Goodwill and business acquisitions	(**287)**	(76)
	Business dispositions	—	337
	Pensions and other postretirement benefits	(**624)**	96
	Foreign currency translation	(**40)**	(94)
	Financial instruments	(**225)**	(438)
	Other valuation differences	**292**	88
	Deferred taxes	**2,627**	(646)
Consolidated net income (loss) in accordance with U.S. GAAP before cumulative effect of changes in accounting principles in accordance with U.S. GAAP		(**1,839)**	1,402
Cumulative effect of changes in accounting in accordance with U.S. GAAP for postretirement benefits other than pensions (net of tax of 33 million DM)		—	(52)
Consolidated Net Profit in Accordance with U.S. GAAP		(**1,839)**	1,350
Earnings (loss) per share in accordance with U.S. GAAP		**DM (39.47)**	DM 29.00[1]
Earnings (loss) per American Depositary Share[2] in accordance with U.S. GAAP		**DM (3.95)**	DM 2.90
Stockholders' Equity in Accordance with German			
Commercial Code		**18,145**	19,719
%	Minority interest	(**561)**	(1,228)
Adjusted stockholders' equity under German regulations		**17,584**	18,491
+/−	Appropriated retained earnings/ (provisions, reserves, and valuation		
	differences)	**5,770**	9,931

	23,354	28,422
Additional adjustments		
+/− Long-term contracts	**207**	131
Goodwill and business acquisitions	**2,284**	1,871
Pensions and other postretirement benefits	**(1,821)**	(1,212)
Foreign currency translation	**85**	(342)
Financial instruments	**381**	580
Other valuation differences	**(698)**	(1,708)
Deferred taxes	**2,489**	(138)
Stockholders' Equity in Accordance with U.S. GAAP	**26,281**	27,604

[1] Includes the negative effect of the change in accounting for postretirement benefits other than pensions of 1.12 DM per share (0.11 DM per American Depositary Share).
[2] Corresponds to one-tenth of a share of stock of 50 DM per value.
Source: Daimler-Benz, 1993 Annual Report.

Matterhorn (exercises 12–15)

Jack Stone is in a real quandary. He has only two weeks in which to make a final recommendation on the acquisition of Matterhorn, a Swiss manufacturer of high-quality mountain climbing equipment. Matterhorn is a Swiss corporation, with a large percentage of the stock owned by Hans Groberg and his family. Hans started the business 30 years ago and is anxious to sell so he can retire. He has two sons and a daughter who manage various Matterhorn subsidiaries, but none of them is anxious to take over the business. Since beginning the business, some of the stock has been sold to nonfamily members, so Hans's personal holdings are less than 15 percent. However, his control over Matterhorn has never been questioned by other shareholders. The banks have provided substantial financing for Matterhorn and control most of the proxy votes of other shareholders at the annual meetings.

Part of Jack's dilemma is that he has no idea what to offer Matterhorn shareholders for their stock. The Swiss company law requires that financial statements be prepared, but the information disclosed is rather limited. Jack computed a price-earnings ratio for Matterhorn and discovered that it was four times that of a similar company in the United States, and he suspects that Matterhorn's earnings were understated in comparison with U.S. GAAP. On the balance sheet, he noticed that certain fixed assets were carried at a value of Swiss franc, even though their insured value was several million Swiss francs. In talking with a CPA who had experience in Switzerland, Jack found out that hidden reserves, which tend to understate the value of assets and overstate expenses, were allowed. Jack tried to understate the value of assets and overstate expenses, were allowed. Jack tried to get Matterhorn's accountant to show him how the hidden reserves really affected the books, but the accountant was hesitant to do so.

Another problem is trying to get a picture of the whole corporation. Matterhorn's financial statements—such as they are—contain the results of only the parent. Jack knows that at least 10 subsidiaries controlled by Han's children were not consolidated with Matterhorn's operations. Jack has tried to get copies of the financial statements of the subsidiaries and a summary of intercompany transactions but still has not received a response.

12. What are the major problems Jack faces in trying to evaluate this investment opportunity?

13. Why is the consolidation issue so tricky here?

14. What are some major differences in disclosure between Switzerland and the United States as brought out in this case?

15. Why are the Swiss so conservative and secretive in their accounting?

Case: Alcatel and Lucent
Case: Hanson and ICI

These cases can be found on the following website: www.wiley.com/college/radebaugh

Selected References

Adams, C. A., P. Weetman, E. A. E. Jones, and S. J. Gray. 1999. "Reducing the Burden of U.S. GAAP Reconciliations by Foreign Companies Listed in the United States: The Key Question of Materiality." *The European Accounting Review* 8(1): 1–22.

Amir E., T. S. Harris, and E. K. Venuti. 1993. "A Comparison of the Value-Relevance of U.S. versus non-U.S. GAAP Accounting Measures Using Form 20-F Reconciliations." *Journal of Accounting Research* 31, supplement: 230–264.

Aron, Paul H. 1991. "Japanese P/E Ratios in an Environment of Increasing Uncertainty." In *Handbook of International Accounting*, edited by F. D. S. Choi. New York: John Wiley.

Barth, M., and G. Clinch. 1996. "International Accounting Differences and Their Relation to Share Prices: Evidence from U.K., Australian and Canadian Firms." *Contemporary Accounting Research* (Spring): 134–170.

Bhushan, R., and D. R. Lessard. 1992. "Coping with International Accounting Diversity: Managers' Views on Disclosure, Reconciliation and Harmonization." *Journal of International Financial Management and Accounting* 4(2): 149–164.

Black, E. L., and J. J. White. 2003. "An International Comparison of Income Statement and Balance Sheet Information: Germany, Japan and the US." *European Accounting Review.* 12(1): 29–46.

Brown, R. R., V. E. Soybel, and C. P. Stickney. 1997. "Achieving Comparability of U.S. and Japanese Price Earnings Ratios." In *International Accounting and Finance Handbook,* edited by F. D. S. Choi. 2nd ed. New York: John Wiley, pp. 7.1–7.18.

Choi, F. D. S., and K. Hiramatsu. 1987. *Accounting and Financial Reporting in Japan.* New York: Van Nostrand Reinhold.

Choi, F. D. S., and R. M. Levich. 1990. *The Capital Market Effects of International Accounting Diversity.* Homewood, IL: Dow Jones-Irwin.

Choi, F. D. S., S. K. Min, S. O. Nam, H. Hino, J. Ujiie, and A. I. Stonehill. 1983. "Analyzing Foreign Financial Statements: The Use and Misuse of International Ratio Analysis." *Journal of International Business Studies* (Spring–Summer): 113–131.

Cooke, T. E. 1989. "Voluntary Corporate Disclosure by Swedish Companies." *Journal of International Financial Management and Accounting* (Summer): 171–195.

Cooke, T. E. 1993. "The Impact of Accounting Principles on Profits: The US versus Japan." *Accounting and Business Research* (Autumn): 460–476.

Fortune Global 500. www.fortune.com/fortune/global500/

Frost, C. A., and G. Pownall. 1996. "Interdependencies in the Global Markets for Capital and Information: The Case of SmithKline Beecham plc." *Accounting Horizons* (March): 38–57.

Fulkerson, C. L., and G. K. Meek. 1998. "Analysts Earnings Forecasts and the Value Relevance of 20F Reconciliations from Non-US to US GAAP." *Journal of International Financial Management and Accounting* (9): 1–15.

Gray, S. J. 1980. "International Accounting Differences from a Security Analysis Perspective: Some European Evidence." *Journal of Accounting Research* (Spring): 64–76.

Harris, T. S., M. Lang, and H. P. Möller. 1994. "The Value Relevance of German Accounting Measures—An Empirical Analysis." *Journal of Accounting Research* (Autumn) 32(2): 187–209.

International Accounting Standards Board. www.iasb.org.uk

International Organization of Securities Commission. www.iosco.org

Meek, G. 1983. "U.S. Securities Markets Responses to Alternative Earnings Disclosures of Non-US International Corporations." *The Accounting Review* (April): 394–402.

Norton, J. 1995. "The Impact of Financial Accounting Practices on the Measurement of Profit and Equity: Australia versus the United States." *Abacus* 31(2): 178–200.

Pope, P. F., and W. P. Rees. 1992. "International Differences in GAAP and the Pricing of Earnings." *Journal of International Financial Management and Accounting* (Autumn): 190–210.

Radebaugh, L. H., G. Gebhardt, and S. J. Gray. 1995. "Foreign Stock Exchange Listings: A Case Study of Daimler-Benz." *Journal of International Financial Management & Accounting* 6(2): 158–192.

Rees, L. L. 1995. "The Information Contained in Reconciliations to Earnings Based on U.S. Accounting Principles by Non-U.S. Companies." *Accounting and Business Research* (25): 301–310.

Rees, L. L. 1996. "A Comparison of Investors' Abilities to Assimilate U.S. GAAP Disclosures." *Journal of Accounting and Public Policy* (15): 271–287.

Street, D. L., and S. J. Gray. 2001. *Observance of International Accounting Standards: Factors Explaining Non-Compliance*. ACCA Research Report No. 74, Association of Chartered Certified Accountants.

Street, D. L., S. J. Gray, and S. M. Bryant. 1999. "Acceptance and Observance of International Accounting Standards." *The International Journal of Accounting* 34(1): 11–48.

Weetman, Pauline, and S. J. Gray. 1990. "International Financial Analysis and Comparative Corporate Performance: The Impact of U.K. versus U.S. Accounting Principles on Earnings." *Journal of International Financial Management and Accounting* (Summer–Autumn): 111–130.

Weetman, Pauline, and S. J. Gray. 1991. "A Comparative International Analysis of the Impact of Accounting Principles on Profits: The USA versus the UK, Sweden and the Netherlands." *Accounting and Business Research* (Autumn): 363–379.

Weetman, P., E. A. E. Jones, C. A. Adams, and S. J. Gray. 1998. "Profit Measurement and UK Accounting Standards: A Case of Increasing Disharmony in Relation to US GAAP and IASs." *Accounting and Business Research* (Summer): 189–208.

CHAPTER SIX

INTERNATIONAL TRANSPARENCY AND DISCLOSURE

Chapter Objectives

- Explain the importance of corporate transparency and information disclosure
- Discuss the meaning of corporate transparency
- Show how corporate disclosures are an important way of communicating to stakeholders in the company
- Evaluate the incentives to disclose information and the costs involved
- Review international disclosure regulation and reporting trends
- Highlight important issues found in corporate reports, such as the chairperson's statement, the review of corporate strategy and results, external and unusual events, acquisitions and disposals, human resources, social responsibility, R&D, capital investment, and future prospects
- Describe other types of corporate disclosures, such as the review of operations, including segmental information and the review of financial position and results
- Review issues relating to the frequency and timeliness of corporate reporting internationally

INTRODUCTION

In this chapter we examine differences in transparency and disclosure practices by multinational enterprises (MNEs) and across countries. The lack of "transparency"

Strategic Decision Point

A lack of financial reporting transparency was a key contributor to the Asian financial crists. For example, Arthur Levitt, Chairman of the U.S. Securities and Exchange Commission (Levitt, 1998) stated:

> "The significance of transparent, timely and reliable financial statements and its importance to investor protection has never been more apparent. The current financial situations in Asia ... are stark examples of this new reality. These markets are learning a painful lesson taught many times before: investors panic as a result of unexpected or unquantifiable bad news."

Alan Greenspan (1998, p.6.), Chairman of the U.S. Federal Reserve, said of the crisis: "a major improvement in transparency, including both accounting and public disclosure, is essential". Similarly, the President of the World Bank (Wolfensohn, 1998) noted: "The culture of the region has not been one of disclosure."

Since the crisis, the global challenge is how to respond to the growing pressures for transparency as a means to promote confidence that the information provided by companies is both comprehensive and reliable.

---

of company accounts and reports is a major issue and concern in many countries around the world consistent with the growing need to attract and retain foreign capital and facilitate capital raisings internationally.

As Susilowati, Morris, and Gray (2004) explain, corporate transparency has become a more widely discussed issue in the financial press and academic literature in response to growing accountability concerns. Some key factors have been the Asian financial crisis of 1997/1998 and recent major corporate failures around the world, such as those of Enron and WorldCom in the United States, HIH in Australia, and Parmalat in Italy. Achieving higher levels of transparency of corporate operations is now a goal of regulators and standard setters around the world.

Corporate transparency matters to firms in order to help stock market investors distinguish good quality firms from bad quality firms; otherwise they will tend to treat all firms as being of "average" quality which punishes good quality but rewards bad quality firms. Thus, financial reporting transparency can have signaling properties for good quality firms. Corporate transparency matters to regulators for macroeconomic reasons—to restore confidence in and expand capital markets, and to encourage investment in the economy.

THE MEANING OF TRANSPARENCY

Bushman and Smith (2003, p. 76) defined corporate transparency as "the widespread availability of relevant, reliable information about the period performance, financial position, investment opportunities, governance, value, and risk of publicly traded firms." Corporate transparency has been measured as a combination of many firm-specific and country-specific factors. Bushman and Smith's measure of corporate transparency includes financial reporting, governance disclosures, availability of annual reports in English, the penetration and ownership of the media in a particular country, and the ease with which private information about firms can be collected and disseminated. Similarly, PricewaterhouseCoopers Opacity Index (2001, p. 4) measures opacity (the converse of transparency) at the country level as a function of five dimensions: corruption levels, legal and judicial opacity, economic/policy opacity, accounting/corporate governance opacity, and the impact of regulatory opacity and uncertainty/arbitrariness. At the country level, Bushman, Piotroski, and Smith (2004) identify two kinds of corporate transparency: financial transparency and governance transparency. Country-level financial transparency is made up primarily of corporate disclosure intensity, timeliness of disclosures, the number of analysts, and media development.

In the above measurements of corporate transparency, disclosure of financial information in company annual reports, either voluntarily or in accordance with accounting standards, plays a central role. Indeed, it appears to be a necessary but not sufficient component of corporate transparency.

DISCLOSURE IN CORPORATE REPORTS

The amount of information disclosed by MNEs in corporate reports has expanded considerably in recent years. The major source of pressure for increased disclosures has been the financial and investment community. Both MNEs and standard-setting bodies in countries with well-developed securities markets, such as the United States, the United Kingdom, France, Germany, and Japan, have been concerned primarily with responding to pressures from this direction. There has also been something of an explosion in the demand for information by a wide range of other participant groups including governments, trade unions, employees, and the general public.

The Pressures for Information Disclosure

Not surprisingly, MNEs are concerned about the manner in which apparently ever-increasing requirements for information disclosure are determined by regulatory bodies and standard-setting agencies at both governmental and professional levels. The pace at which regulation has accelerated since the early 1970s is such that it is sometimes suggested that only a time lag separates a request from its eventual declaration as a required disclosure. Such a view may vastly oversimplify the technical and political process through which standards are established—a process in which many companies directly or indirectly participate. But the ultimate result, albeit at times postponed or slowed down, has been increasing accounting and disclosure requirements.

The acceleration in the demand for information for investment purposes appears to be unsustainable and hence must eventually decline. However, the increasing internationalization of financial markets and share ownership, combined with a concurrent growth in awareness of the considerable diversity of accounting principles and practices in different countries, has fueled the demand for additional information disclosures to increase both the quality and comparability of MNE reports.

Apart from the investor group, there is a growing belief among other groups—such as governments and trade unions—that both an increased availability and an improved quality of information are essential. It can be argued that many of these demands are general, vague, and imprecise. However, as the demand has grown, so too has its precision at both the national and international levels. International organizations such as the UN, OECD, European Union, and IASB are now issuing more detailed requirements and recommendations.

At a time when some may have thought that for MNEs headquartered in countries with well-developed securities markets, the demand for information might have eased, there has been a growing and articulated demand from a range of non-traditional information users for more information, some of it already available to and directed at investors—others demanded by emerging user groups. This demand has been spurred, of course, by key factors such as the Asian financial crisis and major corporate failures and scandals around the world.

Users with the ability or power to obtain "tailor-made" reports, such as trade unions at national levels with adequate bargaining power and organizational ability, are apparently learning the limitations of corporate annual reports. They are increasingly concentrating their energies on obtaining special-purpose reports more in line with their specific information needs. While this has the effect of reducing the demands on the annual publication of the general-purpose corporate report, it increases the pressures on corporations to improve the availability of more comprehensive information through other channels.

Thus, the increased supply of information appears in some respects to have actually increased, rather than reduced, the demand for additional information. If the demand for information was fixed, corporations could include this as one of the benefits to be matched against the costs of information disclosure. However, this is clearly not possible in the current dynamic context of information demand. But to what extent is the information demanded likely to be used and understood—and by whom?

Communicating to Users

The decisions of corporations and/or regulatory bodies as to which groups have a right to or should be provided with information are a major determinant of the content of corporate reports—and influence in particular the range of information. Equally important is the decision about to whom the information is aimed; this determines its depth. Despite the long history of information disclosure by corporations, only recently have systematic efforts been made to assess the ability of supposed users actually to use corporate annual reports. There is growing evidence that these reports are neither read nor understood by a considerable percentage of those whom they are supposed to inform, especially the layperson investor.

The direct users are apparently the relatively small number of experts who have the necessary ability and experience to analyze financial information. No group is without its information analysts. Many investors and shareholders do not make invest-ment decisions alone but rely on the advice of experts. They may do this by buying advice or by consulting the financial press or other sources of interpretation.

Why do only a minority directly use corporate reports? The fact is that corpo-rations, of even moderate size, are complex organizations. A comprehensive cor-porate analysis necessitates not only the use of financial information but additional data as well as to assess current and future trends. In the main, MNEs are especially complex, and so too are their corporate reports. Not only do MNEs produce a vari-ety of products, but they operate in a number of countries and therefore in differ-ent operating environments with a variety of risks, opportunities, and pressures. Accordingly, MNE corporate reports have some characteristics that are rarely, and sometimes never, found in those of domestic corporations. Their worldwide con-solidated financial statements are usually drawn up according to the accounting standards and practices of one country only, usually that of the MNE's headquar-ters. Few users are familiar with the accounting practices of more than one coun-try, and there is an inevitable tendency by many users to interpret MNE corporate reports as if they were drawn up according to the practices of their own rather than the source country.

Limiting or reducing (by simplifying) the information in annual accounts may make them superficially more intelligible to a wider audience. But it may well result in the omission of essential information useful to the direct users—the experts. To suggest otherwise is to confuse corporate annual reports with the underlying reality they attempt to portray. This is not to say that the clarity of such reports cannot be improved, or that some information provided may not be super-fluous. However, if corporate reports were to be pitched at the level of the layper-son, they would have to be reduced substantially in size. This would mean forego-ing important elements in the accounting and information message and lowering the standard of analysis of those who actually, rather than ideally or hypothetically, use them.

Just as the majority of information providers consider questions regarding the comprehensiveness of information to be within the ambit of conventional wisdom, "information for all with a legitimate interest," so too on the demand side there is a failure to appreciate the difference between actual users of information and those on whose behalf the information is used. The OECD, for example, refers to infor-mation that should "improve public understanding." Such a distinction is unneces-sary, however, because what ultimately matters, from the user's perspective, is the expanded availability of relevant information. Ironically, what might appear elit-ist—aiming information at the experts—is likely to be the most democratic. In this way, the information needs of the many groups affected by the operations of MNEs are perhaps best served in practice. At the same time, there is presumably some limit to the quantity of information that can be conveniently analyzed even by experts.

The view that does not differentiate between different levels of interpretive abilities within groups, but sees them as homogeneous, has tended to dominate the disclosure debate. A major objective of corporate reports is, or perhaps should be, to serve primarily those users who have limited authority, ability, or resources to obtain information and who rely on financial statements as their principal source of information. As we have suggested, however, this is probably best achieved through the medium of expert users, in that they are likely to be able to make the most effective use of the information disclosed.

The Importance of Information Disclosures

Although there is no doubt about the continuing significance of accounting measurement issues, the importance of information disclosed in financial statements and accompanying reports is being increasingly recognized by multinational corporations. This information provides an important input to the financial analysis process of evaluating the quality of earnings and financial position, both current and prospective. A particularly important motivation for voluntary information disclosures by MNEs is that corporate reports provide the opportunity to communicate more policy and future-oriented information about the corporation. This may better inform or influence investors in the increasingly globalized securities markets. It is interesting, for example, that most of the fortune Global 500 firms now provide financial and other corporate information on the Internet. This trend is likely to have an increasing impact on the disclosure practices of stock exchange-listed companies around the world.

It is generally accepted that the costs of providing information should not exceed the benefits derived by the users of the information. In particular, the need for MNEs to maintain business confidentiality in sensitive areas and to avoid jeopardizing their competitive position should be taken into account. At the same time, this need must be weighed against the interests of analysts, investors, and the public in the transparency of multinational business operations. In practice, it appears that the more specific and the more future oriented—and especially the more quantitative—the information proposed for disclosure, the more sensitive becomes the attitude of MNEs toward its provision.

Managerial Incentives to Disclose Information

Management provides information both voluntarily and in response to regulation. There may be incentives for the management of an MNE to disclose information voluntarily if it perceives it to be in its own interests and those of the corporation to respond to the information demands of users and participant groups. Research by Meek and Gray (1989) and others has shown, for example, that voluntary disclosures are forthcoming when corporations are competing for finance from investors, especially in a cross-border context. Where governments and trade unions exert an influence over the environment in which the MNE operates, there will also be strong influences on the MNE to disclose information to compete with other MNEs for investment opportunities or to exchange it to maintain existing rights or avoid potential constraints on their operations.

On the other hand, if management decides that the information demands are unreasonable or inimical to their interests or those of the MNE (e.g., when the information is unfavorable or contains "bad news"), they must either achieve some compromise or accept the consequences, if any, of nondisclosure. Thus, a diverse and complex set of factors influence corporate disclosures (see Figure 6.1).

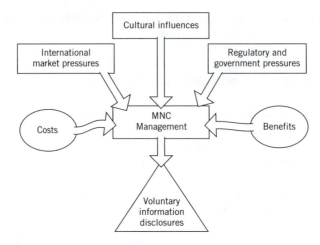

Figure 6.1   The Costs and Benefits of Voluntary Disclosures by MNCs

Costs of Information Production

The disclosure of information has a direct monetary cost. MNEs are understandably unwilling to incur increased costs through expanded disclosures unless they are required to do so or the potential benefits exceed the estimated costs. The direct cost of information disclosure to a corporation is the value of the resources used in gathering and processing the information as well as in its audit and communication.

The direct costs of such disclosures will preeminently depend on the internal structure of the MNE and information generated in order to manage this structure. The closer existing information is to the disclosure requested, the lower will be the actual direct cost of producing the information. Because the information needs of management are not always identical with those of other groups, the absence of complete harmony between internal and external information needs is inevitable.

Apart from the direct costs of disclosure there are the indirect costs relating to competitive disadvantage, with its associated disincentives to innovate or invest, as well as the costs resulting from interference or regulation by governments.

Competitive Disadvantage of Disclosure

The most frequently cited objection to increased disclosure requirements is that of competitive disadvantage (i.e., the use of the additional information by competitors to the detriment of the corporation disclosing the information). It is a major basis for the resistance to expanded disclosures.

In some circumstances, disclosure of information could be damaging to MNEs. As a general rule, the more specific or future oriented a disclosure is, the greater the potential competitive disadvantage for the disclosing corporation. What of the relatively small percentage of possible disclosures that hypothetically could cause damage to the discloser? Should this danger definitively rule out their release? Information that allows competitors to increase their well-being at the expense of the discloser is damaging for the discloser but profitable for the competitor.

Exhibit 6.1   Cost Factors Constraining Voluntary Information Disclosure as Perceived by U.K. and U.S. Financial Executives

	Rank	
	U.K.	U.S.
Cost of competitive disadvantage	1	1
Cost of data collection and processing	2	2
Cost of auditing	3	3
Possibility of claims from employees or trade unions	4	9
Threat of takeover or merger	5	6
Cost of publication	6	5
Technical processing problems	7	3
Possibility of intervention by government agencies	8	8
Possibility of claims from political or consumer groups	9	10
Possibility of intervention by taxation authorities	10	7

Note: Items with higher ranks have greater constraints
Source: S. J. Gray, L. H. Radebaugh, and C. B. Roberts, "International Perceptions of Cost Constraints on Voluntary Information Disclosures," *Journal of International Business Studies* (Winter 1990): 602.

The dilemma is to distinguish between disclosures, which, for the economy as a whole, result in aggregate competitive advantages exceeding aggregate competitive disadvantages from those that do not. What is detrimental or beneficial to the economy in the short term may, in some circumstances, have the opposite effect in the longer term. Increased competition through disclosure could lead to greater vigor in the economy. It could also lead to a decline in business incentives as a result of the appropriation of rewards by competitors facilitated by expanded disclosures.

The relative importance of various possible costs of disclosure was explored, for example, in a study by Gray, Radebaugh, and Roberts (1990). The study found general agreement by both U.S. and U.K. financial executives (see Exhibit 6.1) that the indirect cost of competitive disadvantage was the most important cost factor constraining voluntary disclosures. However, the results of the tests showed that, overall, there were significantly different perceptions in the responses concerning the impact of several of the types of costs involved, including the possibility of claims from employees or trade unions and technical processing problems.

Managerial Attitudes to Voluntary Disclosures

Demands for additional information disclosures have come from both international organizations (in particular the UN, OECD, EU, and IASB) and the host governments and societies in which MNEs operate. However, the growing globalization of capital markets indicates the presence of significant market pressures for additional information about MNE operations as well as the existence of prospects for and concern about the international coordination of capital market regulations. It is against this background that MNE management must weigh the costs and benefits of voluntary information disclosures.

Exhibit 6.2   The Net Costs or Benefits of Disclosure of Specific Items Perceived by U.K. and U.S. Financial Executives—Items with Highest Net Costs

	Rank	
	U.K.	U.S.
LoB profits; narrow definition	1	2
Describe major legal proceedings	2	9
Quantitative forecasts; sales and profits	3	7
LoB sales; narrow definition	4	4
Geographical profits; narrow definition	5	3
Inflation-adjusted profits	6	5
LoB segment transfers	7	12
Geographical segment transfers	8	13
Describe major patents and expiry dates	9	8
Foreign assets by country	10	10
Geographical sales data; narrow definition	11	6
Employment information	23	2
Value-added statements	24	1

Source: S. J. Gray, L. H. Radebaugh, and C. B. Roberts, "International Perceptions of Cost Constraints on Voluntary Information Disclosures," *Journal of International Business Studies* (Winter 1990): 602.

Gray, Radebaugh, and Roberts (1990) also examined the extent to which there are perceived net costs or benefits for disclosing specific items of information voluntarily, the types of costs involved, and the significance of cost constraints with respect to specific disclosures. The results of the study showed that, on average, the respondents tended to perceive most voluntary or discretionary disclosure items as giving rise to a net cost (see Exhibit 6.2). At the same time, there was a wide range of views depending on the specific item of information concerned. However, items perceived as giving rise to major net costs in both the United States and the United Kingdom were inflation-adjusted profits, quantified forecasts, and narrowly defined segment information.

Corporate Disclosure Practices

In terms of voluntary disclosure practices by MNEs, a study by Meek, Roberts, and Gray (1995) examined the factors influencing the voluntary disclosures of 226 MNEs from the United States, the United Kingdom, and continental Europe. A wide range of information disclosures were examined and categorized into three types: strategic, nonfinancial, and financial. A common benchmark of voluntary disclosures was established that would apply to all countries, and a disclosure score was calculated for each company. The means and standard deviations for all companies and for the United States, the United Kingdom, and the continental European groupings are shown in Exhibit 6.3. Scores for these groupings are also given for the inter-

Exhibit 6.3 Voluntary Disclosure Scores by Multinationals

	Strategic Information		Nonfinancial Information		Financial Information		Overall Disclosures	
	Mean	Standard Deviation	Mean	Standard Deviation	Mean	Standard Deviation	Mean	Standard Deviation
All Companies	21.03	13.81	18.06	11.01	16.62	8.89	18.23	7.49
U.S. All Companies	17.22	10.52	11.89	7.10	16.54	6.81	15.20	5.40
U.S. International	20.03	10.98	14.50	7.41	17.27	7.12	17.09	5.55
U.S. Domestic	14.41	9.32	9.27	5.73	15.81	6.46	13.32	4.56
U.K. All Companies	16.83	8.52	25.70	9.15	14.58	9.30	18.73	6.78
U.K. International	17.41	9.70	25.71	10.28	16.92	10.44	19.87	7.95
U.K. Domestic	16.24	7.27	25.69	8.03	12.24	7.44	17.60	5.24
Cont. Euro. All Companies	36.52	16.56	23.01	12.41	19.67	11.83	25.16	8.30
Cont. Euro. International	36.51	17.54	21.87	13.28	23.19	9.34	26.23	8.36
Cont. Euro. Domestic	36.53	15.05	24.16	11.65	16.15	13.16	24.09	8.29

Source: G. K. Meek, C. B. Roberts, and S. J. Gray, "Factors Influencing Voluntary Annual Report Disclosures by U.S., U.K., and Continental European Multinational Corporations," *Journal of International Business Studies* (third quarter, 1995): 564.

nationally listed and domestically listed samples; from these it can be seen that the internationally listed MNEs tend to disclose more information voluntarily.

Taken overall, the results of the study showed that all MNEs regardless of size or home country provide more information in their annual reports than the regulations require. With respect to the factors influencing voluntary disclosure, statistical support was found for size, international listing status, country or region of origin, and industry. A relatively weak multinational effect was also detected. The results also indicate that the factors explaining voluntary annual report disclosures differ by information type.

The largest MNEs are those that set the trends in providing voluntary disclosures of nonfinancial and financial information. There are also industry patterns to these two types of disclosures, suggesting that MNEs pay attention to what their closest competitors disclose when making decisions about such disclosures. Nonfinancial information is also a European phenomenon. Finally, strategic information disclosures are a special feature of continental European MNEs and, generally speaking, are also significant for internationally listed MNEs.

As suggested by Gray (1988), cultural values are also likely to influence the values of managers, which in turn may affect their attitudes, behavior, and decision making relating to corporate disclosures. Archambault and Archambault (2003), for example, developed a "model of cultural, national, and corporate factors that influence the financial disclosure of corporations" (p. 173). The empirical evidence from 33 countries showed that disclosure is a complex process that is affected by a broad range of social systems, including culture, national, political, economic system, and corporate financial and operating systems. Companies were found to disclose more information if they were in common law countries, consistent with Gray (1988) and Doupnik and Salter (1995). Hofstede's four cultural dimensions were also shown to be associated with disclosure. In addition, disclosure was found to decrease in association with adult illiteracy. Religion was also reported to be a significant factor influencing disclosure. There was a significant negative association between disclosure and inflation, possibly owing to the higher inflation levels in emerging markets. At the same time, disclosure was significantly positively associated with market capitalization, number of foreign listings, dividends, and the use of a large multinational auditor. In examining corporate financial and operating systems, they nevertheless found that individual company differences still strongly influenced disclosure practices.

Disclosure behavior may also be explained by different attitudes and practices relating to corruption. If corruption hinders economic development, then it may also hinder financial reporting transparency due to the secretive nature of the corrupt activity itself. Attempts may be made to ensure that any corrupt activities a corporation has engaged in are not discovered by the public or by government authorities. In short, corruption could act as a hindrance to the enforcement of accounting standards and to the suppression of information dissemination generally.

La Porta et al. (1998) include corruption as one of their (negative) enforcement variables. They demonstrate a negative relationship between corruption and accounting standards: the higher the level of corruption in a country, the poorer the quality of its accounting. The PricewaterhouseCoopers Opacity Index (2001) also includes corruption as one of the five factors making up the index. Levels of corruption tend to be higher in developing countries than in developed countries and corruption is positively correlated with the opacity of accounting standards, a finding consistent with La Porta. Salter (1998) also found that the average levels of actual disclosure practices in developing nations were significantly lower than those in developed countries. Overall, these findings suggest that higher corruption levels are associated with poorer disclosure practices, though this does not necessarily establish a causal link.

INTERNATIONAL DISCLOSURE REGULATION

As indicated earlier, management's disclosure pattern may be set not only by its own preferences and cultural tendencies but also by regulation. International information disclosure requirements concerned specifically with the form and content of the directors' report in the EU center primarily on the Fourth (1978) and Seventh (1983) Directives on company annual accounts and consolidated accounts, respectively. In the case of MNEs, the EU Seventh Directive, which has been implemented in all member countries, is especially relevant. Under Article 36 of the Directive, the annual report of the Board of Directors must include a "fair review of the development of the business", together with an indication of any important events that have taken place since the end of the year and any "likely future development." An indication must also be given of activities in the field of Research and Development. As far as individual companies, as opposed to groups of companies, are concerned, the Fourth Directive incorporates similar requirements.

Also relevant here are the information disclosure requirements in the United States. The SEC requires a "management discussion and analysis" of the financial statements to be provided in annual reports. This is expected to include discussion of the results of operations, liquidity, and capital resources, and preferably, the impact of inflation. In addition, the disclosure of future-oriented information is desirable. The discussion of these topics on a segmental basis for each business segment is also encouraged. The purpose of the SEC requirements is to provide a framework for discussion that allows management some flexibility to comment on the specific features of the corporation and its industry and that encourages innovation in presentation (e.g., the mixing of narrative commentary and quantitative date) to promote effective communication. The aim is to provide users with an understanding of management's own insights into strategy and performance. This example has been followed in the United Kingdom with the nonmandatory statement by the Accounting Standards Board (ASB) recommending the provision of an "Operating and Financial Review."

The relative strength of disclosure regulation internationally was estimated in a study by Adhikari and Tondkar (see Exhibit 6.4). This study revealed significant variations in the overall quantity and level of detail of disclosure (both financial and nonfinancial) that are required as part of the listing and filing requirements of stock exchanges around the world. Disclosure scores were calculated on a weighted as well as unweighted basis for a total of 35 stock exchanges. The weighted scores were based on the relative importance of the disclosures to stock market analysts. The New York Exchange was clearly the leader in terms of disclosure requirements, with London not far behind.

Exhibit 6.4 Accounting Disclosure Requirements of Global Stock Exchanges

	Weighted and Unweighted Disclosure Scores	
	Disclosure Scores	
Stock Exchange (Country)	Weighted	Unweighted
1. Sydney (Australia)	74.60	74.64
2. Vienna (Austria)	54.17	53.52
3. Rio de Janeiro (Brazil)	67.28	68.75
4. Toronto (Canada)	79.00	78.64
5. Bogotá (Colombia)	54.58	54.48
6. Copenhagen (Denmark)	67.20	66.86
7. Cairo (Egypt)	49.02	48.02
8. Helsinki (Finland)	70.54	71.05
9. Paris (France)	76.20	76.16
10. Frankfurt (Germany)	67.20	66.86
11. Athens (Greece)	60.00	59.41
12. Hong Kong (Hong Kong)	77.04	75.77
13. Bombay (India)	58.23	58.84
14. Milan (Italy)	68.46	68.39
15. Tokyo (Japan)	77.68	77.68
16. Seoul (Korea)	71.43	72.00
17. Luxembourg (Luxembourg)	66.62	66.64
18. Kuala Lumpur (Malaysia)	75.69	75.41
19. Mexico (Mexico)	70.55	70.68
20. Amsterdam (Netherlands)	73.19	72.84
21. Wellington (New Zealand)	67.13	65.91
22. Oslo (Norway)	60.63	60.59
23. Karachi (Pakistan)	55.71	55.82
24. Lisbon (Portgula)	65.68	65.50
25. Singapore (Singapore)	80.89	80.32
26. Johannesburg (South Africa)	74.50	73.48
27. Madrid (Spain)	68.84	68.36
28. Stockholm (Sweden)	60.54	60.05
29. Zurich (Switzerland)	52.24	52.39
30. Taipei (Taiwan)	72.19	71.70
31. Bangkok (Thailand)	74.78	75.41
32. Istanbul (Turkey)	50.68	50.68
33. London (United Kingdom)	86.21	84.86
34. New York (United States)	90.31	90.75
35. Caracas (Venezuela)	73.67	73.32

Source: A. Adhikari and R. H. Tondkar, "Environmental Factors Influencing Accounting Disclosure Requirements of Global Stock Exchanges, *"Journal of International Financial Management and Accounting"* (Summer 1992): 105.

The study also found that the size of the equity market was significant in determining the level of disclosure. Clearly, those countries with more developed stock markets tend to have higher levels of disclosure regulation compared to those in some of the emerging economies (e.g., India and Pakistan), although Switzerland has one of the lowest levels of disclosure consistent with its reputation for "secrecy." However, no significant relationships were found for the other variables examined—that is, degree of economic development, type of economy, activity on the equity market, and dispersion of stock ownership.

A further study of disclosure levels by Saudagaran and Biddle (1995) provided information on the relative rankings of eight major stock markets according to the judgments of a wide range of interested parties such as corporate managers, investment bankers, public accountants, stock exchange officials, attorneys, and academics. The survey included an assessment of capital market expectations as well as statutory and stock exchange reporting requirements. As Exhibit 6.5 shows, the United States ranked highest, with Canada and the United Kingdom not far behind. Switzerland is clearly perceived to have the lowest disclosure level, which is consistent with its reputation for "secrecy."

More recently, disclosure levels in Asian developing countries have begun to be examined. Morris, Ho, Pham, and Gray (2004), for example, investigated whether there was any improvement in the financial reporting transparency of Indonesian firms' financial reports following the Asian financial crisis. They also identified major economic factors associated with transparency. Financial reporting transparency was measured by indices comprising items from seven major accounting issues covered by Indonesian accounting standards (PSAK) and items in IASs and U.S. GAAP not already included in the local Indonesian standards.

Exhibit 6.5 Disclosure Level Survey Results[a] (based on 142 responses)

	Mean Ranks				
	Statutory Reporting Requirements	Exchange Reporting Requirements	Capital Market Requirements	Overall Disclosure Levels	Disclosure Level Rank (DLR)
United States	7.27	7.29	7.17	7.28	8
Canada	6.48	6.38	5.91	6.41	7
United Kingdom	5.84	5.87	6.09	6.02	6
Netherlands	4.68	4.80	4.50	4.75	5
France	4.11	4.50	4.13	4.17	4
Japan	3.82	4.04	4.22	3.83	3
Germany	3.96	3.90	4.04	3.81	2
Switzerland	2.70	2.78	3.17	2.60	1

Spearman Rank Correlation between Overall Disclosure Levels and:

Statutory Reporting Requirements	**.976**
Exchange Reporting Requirements	**1.000**
Capital Market Expectations	**.952**

[a] Ranks are in descending order with '8' ('1') indicating highest (lowest) disclosure level.
Source: S. M. Saudagaran and G. C. Biddle, "Foreign Listing Location: A Study of MNCs and Stock Exchanges in Eight Countries," *Journal of International Business Studies* (Second Quarter, 1995): 331.

Because low levels of transparency were alleged to have helped cause the crisis, it was expected that the financial reporting transparency of Indonesian companies' financial reports would have increased after the crisis. A significant increase in the level of financial reporting transparency, in all mandatory and voluntary indices, was observed between 1996 and 2000 (see Exhibit 6.6). However, levels of transparency in 2000 remained low overall. The increase is not only because of change in Indonesian standards (PSAK), but also because of a significant increase in compliance with the standards that were operative in both years. The mandatory indices exceeded the voluntary indices each year, suggesting, not surprisingly, that compliance with the PSAK is more important for Indonesian companies than voluntary adoption of IASs and U.S. GAAP items not already covered by PSAK. Voluntary disclosure did not appear to have been influenced by the crisis, once other factors were controlled for. Overall, the influence of the crisis was not very strong in terms of compliance with mandatory disclosures, suggesting weak enforcement in practice by regulators and auditors.

The modest levels of transparency found by Morris et al., (2004) were also consistent with La Porta et al. (1998), who reported that, across 49 countries, the quality of accounting information was inversely related to share ownership concentration and protection of minority stakeholders from expropriations by insiders. In Indonesia, concentrated share ownership by families or other insiders is common. The country has a civil law legal system, which does not protect minority stakeholders as much as do other legal systems. However, it is difficult to determine

Exhibit 6.6 Changes in Transparency in Indonesia After the Asian Financial Crisis

Dependent Variable		Min	Max	Mean	Standard Deviation	Paired t-test Probability	Paired Wilcoxon Probability
TRANSP1	1996	0.0500	0.4500	0.2465	0.0954		
	2000	0.0500	0.5500	0.2848	0.1039	(0.000)**	(0.000)**
TRANSP2	1996	0.0313	0.4063	0.1708	0.0741		
	2000	0.0313	0.4063	0.1979	0.0809	(0.005)**	(0.004)**
TRANSP3	1996	0.0588	0.2941	0.1468	0.0534		
	2000	0.0588	0.3529	0.1705	0.0685	(0.000)**	(0.000)**
TRANSP4	1996	0.0000	0.3333	0.0404	0.0682		
	2000	0.0000	0.3333	0.0685	0.0865	(0.001)**	(0.001)**
TRANSP5	1996	0.1429	0.4286	0.2929	0.0851		
	2000	0.1429	0.5714	0.3189	0.0862	(0.000)**	(0.001)**

Notes:

TRANSP1: Indonesian Standards (PSAK) as at 1996 and 2000 (excluding new standards)
TRANSP2: Indonesian Standards as at 2000
TRANSP3: IASs and U.S. GAAP disclosures
TRANSP4: U.S. GAAP only disclosures
TRANSP5: IAS only disclosures
**   Significantly different from zero at a 1% level (two-tailed test)
*   Significantly different from zero at a 5% level (two-tailed test)

the direction of causality in these relationships: family or insider control may be the result of weak shareholder protection laws or vice versa.

CORPORATE REPORTING TRENDS

In the following review of reporting trends, we will discuss the information disclosures in directors' reports in the context of three fairly well-accepted categories of disclosure: the corporate review, the operations review, and the financial review.

The *corporate review* includes information disclosures relevant to the overall performance of a corporation. This group of items includes:

1. The chairperson's statement
2. The review of corporate strategy and result
3. External and unusual events information
4. Acquisitions and disposals information
5. Human resources information (including information about management and organizational structure and labor employment information)
6. Social responsibility information
7. Research and development information
8. Investment program information
9. Future prospects information.

The *operations review,* on the other hand, includes:

1. A more detailed discussion and analysis of operations
2. Disaggregated analysis by business and geographical segment

The *financial review* includes the discussion and analysis of

1. Results
2. Liquidity and capital resources
3. Asset valuations and inflation

CORPORATE REVIEW INFORMATION

The corporate review is a review of the business activities of the corporation as a whole and is consistent with the scope of the requirements of the EU's Fourth (1978) and Seventh (1983) Directives. The content of the corporate review typically includes:

1. **The Chairperson's Statement** This statement provides a platform for insights from the chairperson or chief executive in his or her leadership role about the overall performance and prospects of the corporation.

2. **A Review of Corporate Strategy and Results** (including also a Mission Statement) MNEs invariably provide some narrative commentary and data that are relevant to a review of corporate strategy and results. A mission statement or statement of objectives is increasingly included (see, for example, the statement by Unilever in Exhibit 6.7).

Exhibit 6.7   Unilever's Corporate Purpose

Our purpose in Unilever is to meet the everyday needs of people everywhere—to anticipate the aspirations of our consumers and customers and to respond creatively and competitively with branded products and services which raise the quality of life.

Our deep roots in local cultures and markets around the world are our unparalleled inheritance and the foundation for our future growth. We will bring our wealth of knowledge and international expertise to the service of local consumers—a truly multi-local multinational.

Our long-term success requires a total commitment to exceptional standards of performance and productivity, to working together effectively and to a willingness to embrace new ideas and learn continuously.

We believe that to succeed requires the highest standards of corporate behavior toward our employees, consumers, and the societies and world in which we live.

This is Unilever's road to sustainable, profitable growth for our business and long-term value creation for our shareholders and employees.

More information tends to be disclosed in this review of corporate strategy and results when stock market pressures exert themselves (e.g., when corporations are changing their strategy or are subject to the threat of a takeover bid). The merger of Daimler with Chrysler, for example, in 1998 prompted substantial discussion in the Daimler-Chrysler annual report about the strategy of the new company and gave rise to a new mission statement (see Exhibit 6.8).

3. **Comments on External and Unusual Events** MNEs also tend to provide some commentary on the impact of external events such as exchange rates, interest rates, government policy, market conditions, and foreign competition. Many corporations also report unusual events affecting the corporation, such as factory explosions, fraud, and litigation.

4. **Acquisitions and Disposals Information** Discussion and analysis of acquisitions and disposals are not widespread. While disclosure levels are relatively high in the United States and United Kingdom, information on acquisitions and disposals is rarely comprehensive or well presented elsewhere.

5. **Human Resources Information** Many MNEs provide information that is relevant to an assessment of human resources. This area of disclosure

Exhibit 6.8   DaimlerChrysler

OUR PURPOSE *is to be a global provider of automotive and transportation products and services, generating superior value for our customers, our employees, and our shareholders.*

OUR MISSION *is to integrate two great companies to become a world enterprise that by 2001 is the most successful and respected automotive and transportation products and services provider.*

We will accomplish this by constantly delighting our customers with the quality and innovation of our products and services, resulting from the excellence of our processes, our people and our unique portfolio of strong brands.

often includes information about management and organizational structure as well as labor and employment. Information about senior management (e.g., names, experiences, responsibilities, but excluding the directors) and organizational structure tends to be provided by only a minority of MNEs. However, disclosure levels for these areas are relatively high in Australia and New Zealand, France, Sweden, and the United States.

Disclosures about labor and employment are made by a majority of MNEs, with disclosure levels relatively high in France, Germany, the Netherlands, Sweden, Switzerland, and the United Kingdom. The nature and extent of narrative commentary and data vary considerably and include such topics as labor relations, training, welfare benefits, and safety. It is interesting to note that France requires a separate *bilan social* (social balance sheet or social report) containing details of pay structure, health and safety conditions, hours worked, absenteeism, strikes, industrial relations, and so on. This encourages some French MNEs to include employment information in their annual reports.

6. **Value-Added Information** Although U.S. companies regard value-added information as a costly disclosure, value-added information often proves quite interesting and useful reading. Value-added statements show, in financial terms, the contribution of all stakeholders, and especially employees, to business performance. A minority of MNEs—primarily European firms—provides this information. An example of a value-added statement is given by BMW (Germany) (see Exhibit 6.9).

The purpose of the value-added statement, which shows the value added to materials and services purchased externally, is to present the results of a corporation's operations that are attributable to the efforts of a more broadly defined group of participants, rather than just the investor group, and to show the distribution of wealth created to all stakeholders.

7. **Social Responsibility Information** The term *social responsibility* refers to accountability to society as a whole with respect to matters of public interest such as community welfare, public safety, and the environment. A growing number of MNEs disclose social responsibility information such as environmental protection and cleanup information. Increasingly, many MNEs provide statements affirming their commitment to conduct business responsibly (see GlaxoSmithKline in Exhibit 6.10).

8. **Research and Development Information** It is generally accepted that R&D is a critical element of corporate success in the longer term. Information about R&D activities is disclosed by only a small majority of MNEs. While the nature and extent of the information, both narrative commentary and data, vary substantially, disclosure levels are relatively high in Germany, Japan, the Netherlands, Switzerland, the United Kingdom, and the United States.

9. **Investment Program Information** It is generally accepted that the quality of a corporation's capital expenditures, as opposed to acquisitions of ongoing businesses from other corporations, is a critical factor in cor-

Exhibit 6.9 BMW Group Value-added Statement

in euro million	2003	2003 in %	2002 reclassified	2002 in %	Change in %
Work performed					
Revenues	41,525	97.1	42,411	96.6	
Financial income	148	0.3	409	0.9	
Other income	1,111	2.6	1,077	2.5	
Total Group output	**42,784**	**100.0**	**43,897**	**100.0**	**−2.5**
Cost of materials	20,905	48.9	21,955	50.0	
Other expenses	7,074	16.5	7,335	16.7	
Bought-in costs	**27,979**	**65.4**	**29,290**	**66.7**	**−4.5**
Gross added value	**14,805**	**34.6**	**14,607**	**33.3**	**1.4**
Depreciation and amortisation	3,255	7.6	2,902	6.6	
Net added value	**11,550**	**27.0**	**11,705**	**26.7**	**−1.3**
Applied to:					
Employees	7,066	61.2	6,588	56.3	7.3
Providers of finance	1,077	9.3	1,629	13.9	−33.9
Government/public sector	1,460	12.6	1,468	12.5	−0.5
Shareholders	392	3.4	351	3.0	11.7
Group	1,555	13.5	1,669	14.3	−6.8
Net added value	**11,550**	**100.0**	**11,705**	**100.0**	**−1.3**

BMW Group value added 2003
in %

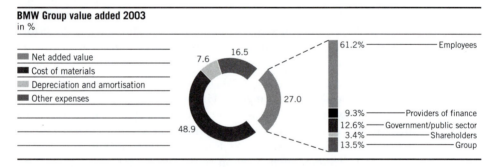

Net added value
Cost of materials
Depreciation and amortisation
Other expenses

16.5
7.6
27.0
48.9

61.2% —————— Employees
9.3% ———— Providers of finance
12.6% ——— Government/public sector
3.4% ————— Shareholders
13.5% —————— Group

porate success in the longer term. However, information about the corporation's investment program, including the nature, location, and significance of capital expenditure tends to be provided by only a small majority of MNEs. Disclosure levels are relatively high in Australia, New Zealand, the Netherlands, Switzerland, and the United Kingdom.

10. **Future Prospects Information** Users are interested in improving their understanding of the current and past activities of MNEs, but they are also, often primarily, interested in the corporation's future prospects. Information about future business prospects is disclosed by a majority of MNEs. However, this information is usually provided in the form of narrative commentary—as might be expected given the sensitive nature from

Exhibit 6.10   GlaxoSmithKline

Corporate Responsibility

GlaxoSmithKline is one of the world's leading pharmaceutical companies. We develop medicines and vaccines to treat and prevent dozens of diseases. The very nature of our business is to improve human life by helping people to do more, feel better, and live longer. This is the mission that drives us to seek new treatments and to bring them to patients who need them. But clearly we must do this in a way that ensures a profitable and sustainable future for our business.

Solid financial performance is closely connected to responsible business practice. We believe that companies that understand and address the impact of business on society and the environment will be the leaders of the future. This is why GlaxoSmithKline is committed to connecting business decisions to ethical, social and environmental concerns.

We aim to provide information that gives reassurance about the way we do business. If you have any feedback or questions on corporate responsibility or this section of our website, please write to.

---

a competitive disadvantage perspective of quantitative, future-oriented information. The nature and extent of the information provided vary substantially and are often general and very limited. Disclosure levels, however, are relatively high in Germany, Hong Kong, the Netherlands, the United Kingdom, and the United States.

OPERATIONS REVIEW

The operations review relates to the activities of the various segments of the corporation's operations. This is where a more detailed review of business activities is provided on a disaggregated basis. Segmental reporting is now a well-established practice in information disclosures by MNEs, but the focus of attention has been on quantitative rather than qualitative information. In practice, the majority of MNEs provide additional narrative commentary, and sometimes quantitative data, on a segmental basis in their operations review.

1. **Review of Business Segments** It is common practice for MNEs to provide a review of operations categorized by business segment, and a substantial majority of them do so. These reviews are often extensive, containing both narrative commentary and quantitative data. In countries where requirements governing the disclosure of quantitative segmental data have only recently been introduced or do not exist (e.g., Italy, Japan, Switzerland), this data often has been incorporated voluntarily into the operations review. The United States and Canada have recently provided for segmental disclosure on a management basis, with disclosure being provided along the lines of the corporate organizational structure.

   In countries where quantitative disclosure requirements are effective, the business segments reviewed tend to be consistent with the quantitative data disclosed, and in some cases, the operations review provides even more disaggregated and extensive information.

2. **Review of International Operations and Geographical Segments** In contrast to business segments, a review of operations categorized by geographical segment is less common in practice. However, a discussion of activities on a geographical basis is frequently incorporated into the analysis of business segments. Some MNEs provide a review of international or geographical segment operations in addition to a review of business segment operations. Whether or not this information is provided seems to depend on the organizational structure of the corporation or the directors' aim of emphasizing international operations, which, for example, seems quite common in the case of Japan.

The discussion and analysis of international operations are an important area of information because the business activities of MNEs are becoming increasingly complex and geographically diversified.

FINANCIAL REVIEW

The financial review relates to the discussion and analysis of the financial results and position of the corporation as a whole. The topics discussed include results, liquidity and capital resources, and asset valuations and inflation. The scope of this review is broadly consistent with the requirements in the United States to provide a "management discussion and analysis" of matters relevant to an improved understanding of the factors influencing a corporation's performance. Items included are:

1. **An Analysis of Results** U.S. MNEs, consistent with SEC requirements, generally provide a more extensive discussion of events with a potential impact on earnings. Also included are the correlation of past trends with current sales and earnings, the reconciliation of underlying causes and economic influences with any changes in sales in the current year, and the disclosure of any matters that are expected to impact future operations.

2. **An Analysis of Liquidity and Capital Resources** Disclosure levels are relatively high in France, Germany, Italy, the Netherlands, the United Kingdom, and the United States. Notably, U.S. MNEs generally provide a more extensive discussion, consistent with SEC requirements, and deal with funding obligations under existing contracts and expectations regarding future contracts, including the funding of projected business expansions. Plans to remedy liquidity problems are also discussed by some corporations.

3. **An Analysis of Asset Values and Inflation** Apart from South America, requirements in the area of asset values and inflation are limited, despite some experience of inflation accounting in a number of countries. A discussion of asset valuations and the impact of inflation is provided in practice by only a small minority of MNEs. It is noteworthy, however, that disclosure, in terms of both narrative commentary and data, is especially evident in the Netherlands, Sweden, Switzerland, and the United Kingdom.

FREQUENCY AND TIMELINESS OF REPORTING

A further major disclosure issue concerns the timeliness and frequency of corporate reporting by MNEs. The need for information to be updated more frequently is becoming increasingly important to investors in the dynamic context of international securities markets. In practice, the development from reporting annually to a more frequent half-yearly and even quarterly basis has been somewhat slow.

In the United States and Canada, quarterly reports are required, though listed foreign companies are exempt if their local requirements specify only biannual reports. In Europe, the EU Directive on Interim Reports requires listed companies to provide half-yearly reports, but this is limited to abridged statements of income together with some brief commentary on operations. Many MNEs go beyond this to provide a full income statement and balance sheet. A number of MNEs also voluntarily provide unaudited quarterly reports in response to stock market and investor pressures (e.g., Volvo, ICI, Sony, Unilever).

The IASB also has a standard on Interim Financial Reporting, IAS34 (effective 1999), but this does not prescribe the frequency of reports, referring only to the minimum content of interim reports.

The timeliness of reporting, whether it be annual, half-yearly, or quarterly, is a related issue, and here requirements and practices vary, though the norm for the publication of annual reports is usually set at a limit of six months from the financial year-end.

GROWING PRESSURES FOR TRANSPARENCY

There is growing pressure around the world to promote greater "transparency" and disclosure consistent with the importance of cross-border capital raisings and the growth of world trade and investment. Disclosure regulation varies internationally, and there is often a lack of transparency, especially in the emerging economies.

Although many MNEs are unwilling to disclose additional information, a growing number of major MNEs are more enlightened and often perceive it to be in their own interests to make voluntary disclosures likely to be relevant to external stakeholders, particularly investors. However, the nature of the disclosures would seem to depend not only on international capital market factors but also on local national concerns and traditions. The IASB is endeavoring to raise the standard of disclosure globally. One of the most important areas concerns segmental disclosures where the latest standards endeavor to reveal the returns and risks of MNE operations on a more strategic and hence more insightful basis.

SUMMARY

1. Transparency and disclosure in MNE annual reports is an important complement to the financial statements. Additional information helps users gain a better understanding of the nature and effects of the activities of MNEs and to better analyze and assess the quality of earnings and financial position.

2.   At the same time, MNEs need to consider the costs involved, maintain business confidentiality in sensitive areas, and avoid jeopardizing their competitive position. In practice, the more specific and future-oriented the item of information disclosure, the less likely are MNEs to want to make disclosures.

3.   There are significant variations in the overall quantity and level of detail of disclosure required by stock exchanges around the world.

4.   Mandatory requirements are often not adequately enforced, for example, in Asian developing countries.

5.   In practice, MNEs voluntarily disclose a wide range of additional narrative and quantitative information, though this tends to vary in volume, type, and quality according to the size of the MNE, its international stock exchange listing status, the geographical location of its headquarters, and the nature of its business operations.

6.   The largest MNEs tend to be the trendsetters in providing voluntary disclosures of nonfinancial and financial information. There are also industry patterns to these two types of disclosure. Nonfinancial information disclosure is also a European phenomenon. Strategic information disclosures are a special feature of continental European MNEs and are also significant for internationally listed MNEs in general.

7.   Additional voluntary information disclosures by MNEs in their annual reports relate to a wide range of information disclosed in the corporate review. The kind of information disclosed by MNEs includes information relevant to the overall performance and prospects of a corporation, corporate strategy and results, external and unusual events, acquisitions and disposals, human resources, social responsibility, R&D, investment programs, and future prospects.

8.   Information disclosed by MNEs in the operations review often includes a discussion and analysis of operations disaggregated by business and geographical segment.

9.   Information disclosed in the financial review often includes a discussion and analysis of results, liquidity and capital resources, and asset valuations and inflation.

10.   The frequency and timeliness of reporting varies around the world with quarterly reports required in North America and half-yearly reports required in Europe.

Discussion Questions

1.   Why has corporate transparency and disclosure become such a major issue around the world?

2.   What is meant by corporate transparency? Is it sufficient to disclose financial information?

3.   What are the benefits of disclosing detailed financial reports to users as compared to providing simplified reports?

4.   To what extent are information disclosures in directors' annual reports, as opposed to the financial statements, likely to be useful to financial analysts and investors?

5.   Explain the incentives that might encourage management to disclose information.

6. What are the likely costs to MNEs of making additional voluntary disclosures?

7. How real is the claim by management that more transparency can give rise to competitive disadvantage?

8. What are the likely benefits to MNEs of making additional voluntary disclosures?

9. Are MNEs always likely to have a competitive advantage relative to smaller domestic companies with respect to information disclosures about their business activities?

10. In which countries are stock exchange disclosure regulations most stringent? less stringent? What are the reasons for this?

11. Why is there weak enforcement of accounting regulations in some developing countries (e.g., Indonesia)?

12. Discuss the kinds of information you would like to see in the corporate review, the operations review, and the financial review sections of an MNEs directors' report.

13. Discuss the relevance to financial analysts and investors of additional disclosures by MNEs with regard to corporate strategy and related issues.

14. Why is information relevant to future prospects likely to be of interest to financial analysts and investors? What are the constraints on MNEs providing such voluntary disclosures in practice?

15. Why is a requirement for quarterly reporting only found in a few countries? What are the likely benefits and costs of quarterly reporting?

Exercises

In groups of three or four students, select three major companies, listed on U.S. exchanges, from different countries with operations in oil and gas or pharmaceuticals. Using information from annual reports, websites, and other public sources, prepare a comparative and critical analysis of their corporate disclosures. Each person should choose one of the companies. Read the company's latest annual report or 10-K (www.edgar.sec.gov) and do exercises 1–4.

1. Identify which groups (government, trade unions, lay investors, analysts, competitors, etc.) are most likely to use each of the items listed in the report's table of contents.

2. Do any of the items seem to be completely superfluous? Is there any information that you think should be included that is not included in the annual report?

3. What information do you think is the most valuable to competitors? What information is most valuable to investors?

4. Is the company an MNE? What disclosures does the report include to help foreign investors? How much of the foreign disclosures is government mandated?

Compare your company's latest annual report with the annual report from 1998 and do exercises 5–8.

5. What has been added to the annual report? What has been deleted from the disclosures?

6. Which of the two reports appears to have more future-focused, quantitative data? Would you expect the more recent report to be more or less quantitative? Why?

7. From a disclosure point of view, discuss the advantages and disadvantages of seeking international financing.

8. Read IAS 14 (www.iasb.org). Compare and contrast the U.S. and IASB approaches to segmental disclosure.

Use Electrolux's 2003 Annual Report to do exercises 9–11. (http://electrolux.com/node648.asp)

9. Read the environmental disclosures. What indications are there that Electrolux is doing well from an environmental standpoint? What indications are there that Electrolux is doing poorly from an environmental standpoint?

10. Does the information provided in the environmental disclosures impact your desire to invest in the company? Should it?

11. Read the disclosures on liquidity and capital resources. What do each of these disclosures tell you about the current position and likely future position of the company?

Refer to the excerpt below from the 2004 Annual Report of Schering AG concerning the 2005 forecast from the annual report of Schering AG (www.Schering.de) to do exercises 12–15.

12. List the items forecasted, the forecast horizon of each item, and the amount forecasted.

13. How might an analyst or investor use this information?

14. Compare and contrast Schering's forecast disclosure with Electrolux's 2004 outlook.

15. Overall, how useful is the forecast statement? Why?

Excerpt from 2004 Annual Report of Schering AG.

Outlook 2005

For fiscal year 2005, we expect a currency adjusted net sales increase in the mid-single digit range and a further increase in our profitability.

We expect a continuous strong double-digit growth of Yasmin®. In addition, we forecast that net sales of Betaferon®, for which we expect promising new study results, will continue to increase in local currencies.

Our U.S. business should increase in the double-digit range in local currency.

In 2005, we expect that the operating margin of 15.5% reached in 2004 will further increase and that we will achieve our operating profit margin goal of 18% (based on a U.S. dollar/euro exchange rate of 1.20) in 2006.

Case: Infosys Technologies (India)
Case: Stora Enso and the Versel Vision—A Model of Sustainability

These cases can be found on the following website: www.wiley.com/college/radebaugh

Selected References

Accounting Standards Board. ASB Statement. 1993. *Operating and Financial Review.* London: ASB (revised January 2003).

Adams, C. A., W. Y. Hill, and C. B. Roberts. 1998. "Corporate Social Reporting Practices in Western Europe: Legitimating Corporate Behaviour." *British Accounting Review* (30): 1–21.

Adhikari, A., and R. H. Tondkar. 1992. "Environmental Factors Influencing Accounting Disclosure Requirements of Global Stock Exchanges." *Journal of International Financial Management and Accounting* 4(2): 75–105.

Archambault, J. J., and M. E. Archambault. 2003. "A Multinational Test of Determinants of Corporate Disclosure." *The International Journal of Accounting* 38: 173–194.

Beets, S. D., and C. C. Souther. 1999. "Corporate Environmental Reports: The Need for Standards and an Environmental Assurance Service." *Accounting Horizons* (June): 129–145.

Bushman, R. M., and A. J. Smith. 2003. "Transparency, Financial Accounting Information and Corporate Governance." *FBRNY Economic Policy Review* (April): 65–87.

Bushman, R. M., J. Piotroski, and A. J. Smith. 2004. "What Determines Corporate Transparency?" *Journal of Accounting Research* 42(2): 207–252.

Buzby, S. L. 1975. "Company Size, Listed vs. Unlisted Stocks, and Extent of Financial Disclosure." *Journal of Accounting Research* (Spring): 16–37.

Choi, F. D. S. 1998. "Financial Reporting Dimensions of Asia's Financial Crisis." *Indian Accounting Review* 2(2): 1–11.

Chow, C. W., and A. Wong-Boren. 1987. "Voluntary Financial Disclosure by Mexican Corporations." *The Accounting Review* 62(3) (July): 533–541.

Cooke, T. E. 1989. "Voluntary Corporate Disclosure by Swedish Companies." *Journal of International Financial Management and Accounting* (Summer): 171–195.

Cooke, T. E. 1991. "An Assessment of Voluntary Disclosure in the Annual Reports of Japanese Corporations." *The International Journal of Accounting* 26(3): 174–189.

Craig, R., and J. Diga. 1998. "Corporate Accounting Disclosure in ASEAN." *Journal of International Financial Management & Accounting* 9(3): 246–274.

Doupnik, T. S., and S. B. Salter. 1993. "An Empirical Test of a Judgemental International Classification of Accounting Practices." *Journal of International Business Studies* 24: 41–60.

European Union. 1978. Fourth Directive for the Co-ordination of National Legislation Regarding the Annual Accounts of Limited Liability Companies. Brussels: EC.

European Union. 1983. Seventh Council Directive on Consolidated Accounts. Brussels: EC.

Firth, M. A. 1979. "The Impact of Size, Stock Market Listing, and Auditors on Voluntary Disclosure in Corporate Annual Reports." *Accounting and Business Research* (Autumn): 237–249.

Fortune Global 500. www.fortune.com/fortune/global500/

Frost, C. A., and K. P. Ramin. 1997. "Corporate Financial Disclosure: A Global Assessment." In *International Accounting and Finance Handbook,* edited by F. D. S. Choi. 2nd ed. New York: John Wiley: 18.1–18.33.

Gray, S. J. 1988. "Towards a Theory of Cultural Influence on the Development of Accounting Systems Internationally." *Abacus* (March): 1–15.

Gray, S. J., and C. B. Roberts. 1989. "Voluntary Information Disclosure and the British Multinationals: Corporate Perceptions of Costs and Benefits." In *International Pressures for Accounting Change,* edited by A. G. Hopwood. Englewood Cliffs, NJ: Prentice-Hall: 116–139.

Gray, S. J., L. H. Radebaugh, and C. B. Roberts. 1990. "International Perceptions of Cost Constraints on Voluntary Information Disclosures: A Comparative Study of U.K. and U.S. Multinationals." *Journal of International Business Studies* (Winter) 21(4): 597–622.

Greenspan, A. 1998. "Testimony before the Committee on Banking and Financial Services of the US House of representatives." *BIS Review* 6: 1–8.

Healy, P. M., and K. G. Palepu. 1993. "The Effect of Firms' Financial Disclosure Strategies on Stock Prices." *Accounting Horizons* 7 (March): 1–11.

International Accounting Standards Board. www.iasb.org.uk

International Accounting Standards Committee. 2000. International Accounting Standards Committee, Objectives and Procedures. London: IASC.

International Organization of Securities Commissions. www.iosco.org

La Porta, R., Lopez-de-Silanes, F., Shleifer, A., and Vishny, R.W. 1998. "Law and Finance." *Journal of Political Economy* 106(6): 1113–1155.

Levitt, A. 1998. "The Numbers Game." Presentation at the New York University Center for Law and Business. New York, September 28, as cited by Rahman (1998).

McLeay, S. J. 1983. "Value Added: A Comparative Study." *Accounting Organizations and Society* 8(1): 31–56.

McNally, G., L. Eng, and C. Hasseldine. 1982. "Corporate Financial Reporting in New Zealand: An Analysis of User Preferences, Corporate Characteristics, and Disclosure Practices for Discretionary Information." *Accounting and Business Research* (Winter): 11–20.

Meek, G. K., and S. J. Gray. 1988. "The Value Added Statement: An Innovation for U.S. Companies?" *Accounting Horizons* (June): 73–81.

Meek, G. K., and S. J. Gray. 1989. "Globalization of Stock Markets and Foreign Listing Requirements: Voluntary Disclosures by Continental European Companies Listed on the London Stock Exchange." *Journal of International Business Studies* (Summer) 20(2): 315–336.

Meek, G. K., C. B. Roberts, and S. J. Gray. 1995. "Factors Influencing Voluntary Annual Report Disclosures by U.S., U.K. and Continental European Multinational Corporations." *Journal of International Business Studies* (Third Quarter), 26(3): 555–572.

Morris, R. D., Ho, B. U. S., Pham, T. and S. J. Gray, 2004. "Financial Reporting Practices of Indonesian Companies before and after the Asian Financial Crisis." *Asia Pacific Journal of Accounting and Economics* 11(2): 193–221.

Nobes, C. W., and R. H. Parker, eds. 2000. *Comparative International Accounting*. Englewood Cliffs, NJ: Prentice-Hall.

Organization for Economic Cooperation and Development. 1976. *International Investment and Multinational Enterprises*. Paris.

PricewaterhouseCoopers. 2001. The Opacity Index.

Rahman, M. Z. 1998. "The Role of Accounting Disclosure in the East Asian Financial Crisis. Lessons Learned?" UNCTAD Study: Accounting and Asian Financial Crisis.

Roberts, C. B., and S. J. Gray. 1997. "Corporate Social and Environmental Disclosures." In *International Accounting and Finance Handbook,* edited by F. D. S. Choi. New York: John Wiley.

Salter S. B. 1998. "Corporate Financial Disclosure in Emerging Markets: Does Economic Development Matter?" *The international Journal of Accounting* 33(2): 221–234.

Salter, S. B., and F. Niswander. 1995. "Cultural Influence on the Development of Accounting Systems Internationally: A Test of Gray's (1988) Theory." *Journal of International Business Studies* 26(2): 379–397.

Saudagaran, S. M., and G. C. Biddle. 1995. "Foreign Listing Location: A Study of MNCs and Stock Exchanges in Eight Countries." *Journal of International Business Studies* (second quarter): 319–342.

Susilowati, I., R. D. Morris, and S. J. Gray. 2004. "Corporate Transparency in an International Accounting Context." *Indian Accounting Review* 8(1): 1–24.

United Nations, 1988. *Conclusions on Accounting and Reporting by Transnational Corporations.* New York: UN (revised 1994).

United Nations. 1993. *Transnational Corporations in World Development.* New York: UN.

Wallace, R., and K. Naser. 1995. "Firm-specific Determinants of the Comprehensiveness of Mandatory Disclosure in the Corporate Annual Reports of Firms Listed on the Stock Exchange of Hong Kong." *Journal of Accounting and Public Policy* (14): 311–368.

Willard Report. 1998. *Report of the Working Group on Transparency and Accountability.* G22 Working Group. October.

Wolfensohn, J. D. 1998. Address to the Overseas Development Council on Asia's Coming Explosion, Washington, DC, March 19, as cited in Rahman (1998).

Zarzeski, M. T. 1996. "Spontaneous Harmonization Effects of Culture and Market Forces on Accounting Disclosure Practices." *Accounting Horizons* (March): 18–37.

CHAPTER SEVEN

INTERNATIONAL ACCOUNTING STANDARDS AND GLOBAL CONVERGENCE

Chapter Objectives

- Identify the impact on multinational enterprises (MNEs) of the different pressures leading to accounting harmonization and disclosure
- Show how governments get involved in the harmonization of accounting directly or indirectly through groups such as the UN, the Organization for Economic Cooperation and Development (OECD), and the European Union
- Discuss how trade unions and employees are interested in harmonizing accounting to get information that will help them formulate policy concerning MNEs
- Describe how the International Organization of Securities Commissions (IOSCO) is representing investors in pushing for harmonization of accounting to facilitate cross-border comparisons of financial statements
- Examine how accountants, through the International Accounting Standards Board (IASB), are pushing for harmonization

INTRODUCTION

The previous chapters have explored the significance of differences in international accounting and the factors giving rise to them. We will now look at the pressures for the global harmonization of accounting and reporting, with special reference to the impact on MNEs.

Strategic Decision Point

In an effort to achieve international harmonization of accounting standards, the IASB faces the challenge of determining what type of standards—rules-based or principles-based—will lead to greater convergence.

Historically, rules-based accounting led to detailed and complex accounting standards, which resulted in somewhat arbitrary rules that allow companies to structure transactions in their favor, thus potentially exacerbating the principle-agent problem between managers and owners. As such, many believe that principles-based standards will encourage reporting that reflects the "true" underlying economic substance. Rather than forming transactions to meet various criteria, companies would be required to analyze the substance of their transaction to determine the appropriate accounting treatment and resulting financial statements. Furthermore, principles-based accounting is viewed as providing increased protection for companies. In the event of a lawsuit, companies can defend their treatment as using their best judgment.

Although international regulators favor principles-based standards, they worry about the U.S. tendency toward litigation. Another concern of the IASB is how to ensure consistent application of the principles-based standards around the world. Even if principles-based standards better reflect economic substance, they may make comparability across companies virtually impossible.

International pressures for improvement in the comparability of accounting and information disclosure by corporations, especially MNEs, arise from the diverse interests and concerns of a wide range of participant groups and organizations. Underlying these pressures is the fundamental belief that improvements in comparability will facilitate more informed international comparisons of corporate performance and prospects, with consequent economic benefits. The role and impact of MNEs will be revealed more clearly and will thus assist in monitoring and, if necessary, in controlling MNE behavior. Furthermore, national and international policy-making is expected to be enhanced by more comprehensive accountability for large and complex organizations.

MNE corporate reports are clearly an important current and potential source of information and are required for a wide range of purposes.

Pressures for the harmonization of international accounting as a means of achieving comparability are growing, but the term *harmonization* is often used rather loosely and sometimes interchangeably with standardization. To clarify these concepts, it is helpful to think of a spectrum ranging from total flexibility and diversity to total uniformity. Harmonization implies a more flexible approach compared to standardization, which in turn suggests a more strict approach that results ultimately in a state of uniformity. As we will see, different organizations have different approaches to the achievement of international comparability.

Which groups of users and organizations are interested in the affairs of MNEs and the harmonization or standardization of international accounting? The power and global reach of MNEs is such that most nations and many people are affected, directly or indirectly, by their operations. It is possible, however, to distinguish a number of groups that, while having some common concerns, have other unique

Figure 7.1   Multinational Corporations: Participants and Pressures for
International Hamonization

concerns. Why is it that they want information relating to MNEs? What is the nature
of the information that they desire or need to satisfy their decision requirements?
Why do they wish to influence the behavior of MNEs with respect to accounting and
information disclosure? The major participant groups are as follows:

- governments
- trade unions and employees
- investors (including financial analysts)
- bankers and lenders
- accountants and auditors

Here we will be concerned, in particular, with the activities and influences of
international intergovernmental, trade union, professional accounting, and invest-
ment/banking organizations involved in the setting of international standards for
accounting and reporting. A simplified model of the participants and pressures
involved in the demand for information disclosure by MNEs is set out in Figure 7.1.
National and international participant groups are distinguished, though clearly
there is likely to be considerable interaction between these two levels as well as
between and within groups at all levels.

Although the focus of our discussion will be on major participant groups, it is
also recognized that there will be differences in information needs not only between
groups but to some extent within them as well.

GOVERNMENTS

Both the role of government in determining the content and nature of corporate
reports and especially the extent of government involvement in the process have
been widely studied. The extent of government involvement is comprehensive in

some countries, especially those with a tradition of detailed prescriptive legislation (e.g., France and Germany), in contrast to the Anglo-American countries where the emphasis is on delegation to autonomous or quasi-autonomous private professional bodies. The literature on the role of government as an actual or potential user of corporate reports, however, is very sparse. Much of the discussion contains little more than assertions that governments are users of such reports. The report of the United Nations' Group of Experts, for example, specifies governments, together with a long list of other users, including investors, lenders, and suppliers, but provides little further elaboration other than to mention the needs of home and host countries and especially developing countries.

The information governments require of corporations varies and is influenced by, for example, the extent of government planning and regulation. However, such information is often vast and far too extensive to be included in a corporate annual report, which if it contained all such information, would become totally unwieldy. Moreover, in addition to the question of quantity, much of the information is mutually regarded by both supplier and receiver as confidential and is thus limited to restricted special-purpose reports. Although the relative power of corporations (and MNEs in particular) and governments is a matter of controversy, it is evident that governments usually have the authority to demand and receive whatever information they need from MNEs. The extensive and mainly confidential information needs of governments, both home and host, combined with their power to obtain such information, would thus seem to support the view that governments are not important users of published corporate reports. Yet a great deal of the pressure for increasing the amount of information disclosure by MNEs has come from governments (e.g., through their participation in and support of the UN's activities). This apparent paradox may be explained by identifying certain specific, rather than general, circumstances wherein governments may in fact be users. These circumstances reflect the transnational nature of MNEs, the role of intergovernmental bodies, the heterogeneous nature of governments, the limited expertise of some governments, and the relative power distribution between MNE and host country.

First, information relevant to an MNE subsidiary's operations may not be available from the subsidiary but only from outside the country, for example, from the parent corporation or elsewhere within the MNE group. In such circumstances, a government may have limited authority to obtain the information. Although some MNEs may supply information where and when requested, there may be others that do not or do so only to a limited extent. Where such information is not provided, governments may be unable or unwilling to press for it. Accordingly, they may, in some circumstances, use the MNE's worldwide consolidated annual financial statements together with segmental information to provide an insight, albeit limited, into the performance of subsidiaries at the country level.

Second, the important role of MNEs in world trade and development has meant that many governments wish to evaluate and monitor directly, or through international intergovernmental organizations, the strategy, performance, behavior, and consequences of MNE operations as a whole. A major source of such global information is the MNEs' corporate financial reports. Information that is not drawn up on a similar basis, as with MNEs based in many different countries, cannot be adequately aggregated. Thus, the governmental need for evaluation is reflected in demands not only for increased availability of information but also for greater comparability of the information so that it can be aggregated.

Third, unlike investors but to some extent like trade unions, governments are neither single individuals nor organizations. The varying roles of governments are performed by a large range of departments or agencies. Special reports supplied to one unit (e.g., taxation authorities) are usually not available to other sections of government. The existence of discrete governmental units requires that some of them rely on corporate reports rather than on the more detailed information available only to other units. In some circumstances, what is available in corporate reports may be adequately comprehensive for the analytical purposes in question.

Finally, although governments are often characterized as having adequate power to require whatever information is needed from MNEs, this power is not unlimited and is often overstated. There is no doubt that it is extensive in many countries. However, in some host developing countries, which are especially dependent on MNEs, requests for some types of information (e.g., social and environmental) may receive a negative response from the MNE. Increased availability of information in MNE corporate reports would mean that governments would have direct access to the information without having to bargain for it and thus possibly offend each MNE. Uniform disclosure requirements would also prevent MNEs from playing one potential host country against another in the competition for investment, thereby pressuring them to reduce their information disclosure requirements.

Governments would, therefore, seem to have an interest in gaining access to more information disclosure concerning extranational operations—that is, for accountability and predictive purposes, their concern is to place the operations of the MNE subsidiary into the context of MNE operations as a whole. Accordingly, both worldwide aggregated and geographically disaggregated financial information is likely to be useful for this purpose. Moreover, the demand for greater international comparability of MNE information disclosure seems to be motivated by the desire of governments at the national level, especially in host countries, or through intergovernmental organizations such as the UN, OECD, and the EU, to monitor the activities of MNEs in general as a basis for policy formulation.

Many governments believe that their bargaining power to obtain sufficient comparable information from MNEs is likely to be enhanced by involvement in intergovernmental organizations.

United Nations

The UN first became involved in the information disclosure debate in 1976 when a group of experts were appointed through the activities of the Commission on Transnational Corporations (now included in the work of the UNCTAD) to formulate proposals following a study of the impact of MNEs on development and international relations. Not only did this study identify a problem in international comparability with respect to the information provided by MNEs, but it also revealed an apparently serious lack of information, both financial and nonfinancial. As a result, the Group of Experts concentrated on the development of lists of minimum items of financial and nonfinancial information to be disclosed by MNEs in their general-purpose corporate reports, both at the level of the MNE group as a whole and through its individual member corporations. The outcome of those deliberations was a comprehensive and detailed set of proposals incorporating, most importantly, worldwide consolidated financial statements, segmental or disaggregated information, and a wide range of nonfinancial and "social" information. These proposals were meant to be used as the basis for developing a set of international standards in the context of a code of conduct for MNEs. In 1979, this process was taken a step further with the establishment of an ad hoc intergovernmental "working group of experts" from 34 countries, including 22 countries from Africa, Asia, and Latin America. It is the UN's comprehensive spread of membership that ensured such strong representation from the developing countries compared to those of the industrialized West and Eastern Europe. This emphasis on developing countries tended also to suggest a prime concern to monitor and, if necessary, control MNE activities. From a political standpoint, they also represented quite different interests from those of the OECD, which is composed of developed countries, and the IASB, which represents professional accounting interests.

Working Group of Experts (ISAR)   A major aim of this group would have been to recommend international standards that member countries would agree to support and, if necessary, to enforce by law. But progress in reaching agreement was slow and in some cases, particularly regarding nonfinancial information, impossible. In October 1982, the majority of countries recommended that the group continue its work in a more permanent form. There was general consensus that any group established

> should serve as an international body for the consideration of issues of accounting and reporting falling within the scope of the work of the Commission on Transnational Corporations in order to improve the availability and comparability of information disclosed by transnational corporations; the Group should review developments in this field including the work of standard setting bodies; the Group should concentrate on establishing priorities, taking into account the needs of home and host countries, particularly those of developing countries.

This proposal was accepted by the UN, and the Intergovernmental Working Group of Experts on International Standards of Accounting and Reporting (ISAR) held its first session in 1983. Since then, sessions have been held every year on a variety of issues, including accounting for inflation, pension accounting, intangible assets, joint ventures, privatizations, environmental reporting, and social responsibility. In 1988, the Group of Experts published its agreed-upon *Conclusions on Accounting and Reporting by Transnational Corporations* (revised in 1994), and in 1989 the Group's contribution to the conceptual framework debate was published as *Objectives and Concepts Underlying Financial Statements*.

With the recent deterioration in investor confidence resulting from accounting scandals and corporate failures, many countries have expressed a need for practical guidance on corporate governance. Recent sessions with the ISAR have focused primarily on transparency and disclosure in corporate governance in order to help meet this need. The group deliberated issues such as financial disclosures, ownership and control structures, the role and function of the board of directors, the background and qualifications of the board of directors, performance evaluation mechanisms, compensation and succession plans, risk management and internal controls, auditor independence, and environmental and social stewardship. The results of their deliberations were published as their agreed conclusions regarding *Transparency and Disclosure Requirements for Corporate Governance.*

The group does not appear to have had much direct influence on the development of international accounting standards, either at the professional or at the MNE level. Yet it seems to have had a useful monitoring role in officially endorsing, where appropriate, desirable international standards. At the same time, there have been some useful contributions to the debate on a number of important questions (e.g., intangible assets, environmental reporting, etc.). A noteworthy recent development is the UN's involvement in accounting education and development, with special reference to Russia and the developing countries of Africa. Specifically, the IASB requested that UNCTAD lead the work of translating IFRS into Russian. In addition, a member of UNCTAD was recently invited to become a member of the Standards Advisory Council for the IASB. This places UNCTAD in a good position to bring the views of developing countries to the deliberations of the SAC. UNCTAD is also represented in the Advisory Panel on Small and Medium-sized Entities of the IASB.

Organization for Economic Cooperation and Development

The OECD has a much more limited membership of countries than the UN. With only 30 member countries, as opposed to the UN's more than 190, the OECD represents the interests of an industrialized and substantially Western group of nations, including Australia, Canada, France, Germany, Japan, the Netherlands, the United Kingdom, and the United States. These countries are home for most of the world's MNEs. In 1976, following consultations with business and trade union interests, a set of Guidelines for Multinational Enterprises was approved with the aim of strengthening confidence between MNEs and governments and to meet criticisms about MNE activities. The guidelines are described as a "set of principles or recommendations covering a broad range of issues in business ethics ... designed to prevent misunderstandings and build an atmosphere of confidence and predictability" (OECD, Policy Brief, June 2003). The intention was to encourage the positive contributions of MNEs to economic growth and social progress while minimizing or resolving problems. Governments agreed to recommend these guidelines, which related to financing, taxation, competition, and industrial relations, as well as information disclosure, to MNEs. In practice, however, only a handful of MNEs appear to have taken serious notice of the guidelines. The recommendations relating to information disclosure are outlined in Exhibit 7.1. Compared to the UN's Conclusions, the OECD's Guidelines are very brief and general and are concerned with information disclosure by the MNE as a group entity.

Although the information recommendations were left essentially unchanged in the 1979 revision of the Guidelines, it was decided that the OECD should continue its efforts in this area by establishing a working group as a basis for contributing to and participating in the international standard-setting process. The OECD did not, however, attempt to establish itself as a standard-setting body in its own right. In this regard, a survey of accounting standards in OECD member countries was carried out in 1980 to assess the diversity of practice and the potential for

Exhibit 7.1   OECD Guidelines for Multinational Enterprises: Disclosure of Information

1. Enterprises should ensure that timely, regular, reliable and relevant information is disclosed regarding their activities, structure, financial situation and performance. This information should be disclosed for the enterprise as a whole and, where appropriate, along business lines and geographic areas. Disclosure policies of enterprises should be tailored to the nature, size and location of the enterprise, with due regard taken of costs, business confidentiality and other competitive concerns.

2. Enterprises should apply high quality standards for disclosure, accounting, and audit. Enterprises are also encouraged to apply high quality standards for non-financial information, including environmental and social reporting where they exist. The standards or policies under which both financial and non-financial information are compiled and published should be reported.

3. Enterprises should disclose basic information showing their name, location and structure, the name, address and telephone number of the parent enterprise and its main affiliates, its percentage ownership, direct and indirect in these affiliates, including shareholdings between them.

4. Enterprises should also disclose material information on:

   a. The financial and operating results of the company.

   b. Company objectives.

   c. Major share ownership and voting rights.

   d. Members of the board and key executives, and their remuneration.

   e. Material foreseeable risk factors.

   f. Material issues regarding employees and other stakeholders.

   g. Governance structures and policies.

5. Enterprises are encouraged to communicate additional information that could include:

   a. Value statements of statements of business conduct intended for public disclosure, including information on the social, ethical, and environmental policies of the enterprise and other codes of conduct to which the company subscribes. In addition, the date of adoption, the countries and entities to which such statements apply, and its performance in relation to these statements may be communicated.

   b. Information on systems for managing risks and complying with laws, and on statements of codes of business conduct.

   c. Information on relationships with employees and other stakeholders.

Source: Organization for Economic Cooperation and Development, *The OECD Guidelines for Multinational Enterprises* (OECD, 2000).

harmonization. Further studies have been made on topics such as consolidations, segmental disclosures, and intangible assets. In general terms, it seems that the OECD aims to work toward promoting international understanding and agreement on a variety of issues as a basis for improving the comparability and harmonization of accounting and reporting standards.

The guidelines were revised again in 2000 in order to respond to additional concerns relating to the impact of MNEs on home and host countries. Today there is growing evidence that the guidelines are becoming more of an international benchmark. A study by the OECD claims that companies cite the guidelines as often as they cite other major corporate responsibility initiatives. In addition, the 37 adhering governments and the European Commission have worked to further promote the guidelines through conferences, mailings, and concrete measures. The guidelines continue to be nonbinding, but many governments have committed to promote their observance and implementation. The OECD is currently working with different organizational bodies, such as the UN, to determine whether they can collaborate on these initiatives to enhance organizations.

European Union

As of 2004, the EU consisted of 25 nations (Austria, Belgium, Cyprus, Czech Republic, Denmark, Estonia, Finland, France, Germany, Greece, Hungary, Ireland, Italy, Latvia, Lithuania, Luxembourg, Malta, the Netherlands, Poland, Portugal, Slovakia, Slovenia, Spain, Sweden, and the United Kingdom). The EU has been involved in the international harmonization of accounting and reporting standards since the middle 1960s as part of its program of company law harmonization, which was undertaken after the Treaty of Rome (1957). The activities of the EU have taken place in the context of promoting the goal of European economic integration and development whereby corporations, including MNEs, should have the freedom to become more international by being able to do business and compete within a common framework of law, taxation, and financial resources.

As far as company law is concerned, the basic principle is that no corporation should be at a competitive disadvantage as a result of legal differences between countries. An important part of the company law harmonization process is the public disclosure of comparable and reliable financial information to protect the interests of shareholders, lenders, suppliers, and other interested parties. The harmonization of accounting and reporting in the EU is especially significant for MNEs because, in contrast to the UN and OECD, any agreement that takes the form of a directive has the force of law and each member country has the obligation to incorporate such directives into its respective national law. Regulations, on the other hand, become law throughout the EU without having to go through the national legislative process. The major position with respect to EU directives and regulations relevant to accounting and information disclosure as of 2004 is shown in Exhibit 7.2.

We will now briefly outline those directives that have special relevance, paying particular attention to the Fourth and Seventh Directives, which are arguably fundamental to EU accounting harmonization. The First and Second Directives were approved in 1968 and 1976, respectively, and were concerned with basic issues such as the publication of accounts and minimum capital.

Fourth Directive   The Fourth Directive was approved in 1978, adding detailed requirements relating to information disclosure, classification and presentation of information, and methods of valuation. Implementation has taken some time, however, with Italy finally amending its company law only in 1991.

Agreement on the Fourth Directive involved a long and difficult period of consultation and negotiation, especially in view of the fact that the United Kingdom and Ireland, along with Denmark, joined the EU (which was then composed of Belgium, France, Germany, Italy, Luxembourg, and the Netherlands) only in 1973 and

Exhibit 7.2   EU Directives and Regulations Relevant to Corporate Accounting and Disclosure

Directives on Company Law	Date Adopted	Subject
First	1968	Publication of accounts, ultra vires rules
Second	1976	Separation of private from public companies, minimum capital, limitation on distribution
Third	1978	Mergers/fusions
Fourth	1978	Annual accounts, content, valuation, presentation rules
Fifth	Withdrawn because of political deadlock	Structure, management, and audit of companies
Sixth	1982	Demergers/spinoffs
Seventh	1983	Consolidated accounts, including associated companies
Eighth	1984	Qualifications and work of auditors
Ninth	(Predraft stage??)	Links between public company groups
Tenth	Withdrawn because of political deadlock	International mergers of public companies
Eleventh	1989	Disclosure relating to branches
Twelfth	1989	Single-member companies
Thirteenth	1989	Mergers
—	(Drafts 1980, 1983)	Employee information and consultation
—	1979	Admission of securities to listing
—	1980, 1982, 1987	Listing particulars
—	1982	Interim reporting by listed companies
—	1986	Accounts of banks
—	1991	Accounts of insurance companies
—	1999	Valuation Rules (amends Fourth and Seventh Directives and "Accounts of banks")
—	2003	Modernization and updating of accounting rules (amends Fourth and Seventh Directives, "Accounts of banks," and Accounts of insurance companies)
—	2003	Amounts expressed in Euro
Regulations		
European company statute	(Drafts 1970, 1975, 1989)	Proposals for a European company subject to EU laws
European economic interest grouping	1985	Proposals for a business form facilitating joint ventures
European Commission Regulation	2002	Listed companies to use IAS by 2005
European Commission Regulation	2003, 2004	Adoption of certain international accounting standards

with quite different traditions of accounting and information disclosure policy. The result was a compromise between the continental European and Anglo-American systems, with perhaps more emphasis placed on disclosing the nature and effect of differences between countries than on removing them.

The intention of the Fourth Directive was not necessarily to produce uniformity but rather to bring about a coordination or harmonization of existing legal requirements. Nevertheless, the Fourth Directive does provide a broadly uniform structure for the classification and presentation of information, albeit with different layouts permitted for the balance sheet and profit and loss account, incorporating some choice of presentation. Of particular interest is the scope allowed for a more analytical approach in the balance sheet (see Exhibit 7.3) and in the choice between analyzing costs on an operational basis or by type of expenditure in the profit and loss account (see Exhibits 7.4 and 7.5). A modified balance sheet (showing account headings only) is also permitted, provided that the detailed information required is given in the notes.

A significant feature of the Fourth Directive is its detailed requirements concerning the principles and application of conventional historical cost accounting. There is substantial flexibility, however, concerning inventory valuation, depreciation, and the treatment of goodwill. At the same time, alternative valuation approaches such as current replacement cost, revaluations to market value, and price-level adjustments are permitted either in the main accounts or in supplementary statements.

The directive also incorporates disclosure requirements that have significantly increased the level of information disclosed in many of the EU countries. The impact of the directive has been felt most sharply in countries like Italy and in some relatively new EU member states (e.g., Finland, Greece, Portugal, and Spain) where information disclosures have been relatively less developed than in France, Germany, and the United Kingdom.

Another important feature of the Fourth Directive is the adoption of the U.K. concept of a "true and fair view." However, whether or not this has had any major impact in other EU countries is not clear. The application of this concept would have an overriding effect in that it might require the disclosure of additional, or in exceptional circumstances, different information from that required specifically by the Fourth Directive. It seems, however, that continental European countries have not yet been much affected in practice by this strictly British philosophy.

Taken overall, the Fourth Directive seems to have been a significant starting point in the harmonization process. Its inherent flexibility concerning measurement and valuation principles and its lack of comprehensiveness with respect to issues such as foreign currency translation, leases and funds, or cash flow statements leaves much to be desired. On the other hand, the directive has done much to raise the level of information disclosure and transparency throughout the EU countries.

Seventh Directive   In 1983, the Seventh Directive on consolidated accounts was adopted. This raised issues of special relevance to MNE operations and was the subject of some controversy. Of particular importance were issues concerning the definition of a "group." Here, the U.K. approach, based on share ownership and legal rights to control other corporations, was contrasted with the German approach,

Exhibit 7.3   EU Fourth Directive

Balance Sheet: (Analytical Layout)			
A. Called-up Share Capital Not Paid			X
B. Fixed Assets			
I. Intangible Assets			
1. Development costs	X		
2. Concessions, patents, licenses, trade marks, and similar rights and assets	X		
3. Goodwill	X		
4. Payments on account	<u>X</u>		
		X	
II. Tangible Assets			
1. Land and buildings	X		
2. Plant and machinery	X		
3. Fixtures, fittings, tools, and equipment	X		
4. Payments on account and assets in course of construction	<u>X</u>		
		X	
III. Investments			
1. Shares in group companies	X		
2. Loans to group companies	X		
3. Shares in related companies	X		
4. Loans to related parties	X		
5. Other investments other than loans	X		
6. Other loans	X		
7. Own shares	<u>X</u>		
		<u>X</u>	
(total of B)			X
C. Current Assets			
I. Stocks			
1. Raw materials and consumables	X		
2. Work-in-progress	X		
3. Finished goods and goods for resale	X		
4. Payments on account	<u>X</u>		
		X	
II. Debtors			
1. Trade debtors	X		
2. Amounts owed by group companies	X		
3. Amounts owed by related companies	X		
4. Other debtors	X		
5. Called-up share capital not paid	X		
6. Prepayments and accrued income	<u>X</u>		
		X	
III. Investments			
1. Shares in group companies	X		
2. Own shares	X		
3. Other investments	<u>X</u>		
		X	

IV. Cash at Bank and in Hand   X

(total of C)   X

D. Prepayments and Accrued Income (Total of C and D)   X

E. Creditors: Amounts Falling Due Within One Year

1. Debenture loans	(X)
2. Bank loans and overdrafts	(X)
3. Payments received on account	(X)
4. Trade creditors	(X)
5. Bills of exchange payable	(X)
6. Amounts owed to group companies	(X)
7. Amounts owed to related companies	(X)
8. Other creditors including taxation and social security	(X)
9. Accruals and deferred income	(X)

(total of E)   (X)

F. Net Current Assets (Liabilities) (C+D–E)   X

G. Total Assets Less current Liabilities (A+B+F)   X

H. Creditors: Amounts Falling Due after More Than One Year

1. Debenture loans	(X)
2. Bank loans and overdrafts	(X)
3. Payments received on account	(X)
4. Trade creditors	(X)
5. Bills of exchange payable	(X)
6. Amounts owed to group companies	(X)
7. Amounts owed to related companies	(X)
8. Other creditors including taxation and social security	(X)
9. Accruals and deferred income	(X)

X

I. Provisions for Liabilities and Charges

1. Pensions and similar obligations	(X)
2. Taxation, including deferred taxation	(X)
3. Other provisions	(X)

X

J. Accruals and Deferred Income   X

K. Capital and Reserves

I. Called-up Share Capital   X

II. Share Premium Account   X

III. Revaluation Reserve   X

IV. Other Reserves   X

1. Capital redemption reserve	X
2. Reserve for own shares	X
3. Reserves provided for by the articles of association	X
4. Other reserves	X

X

V. Profit and Loss Account   X

X

Exhibit 7.4 EU Fourth Directive

Profit and Loss Account (Operational Basis)		
1. Turnover		X
2. Cost of sales		(X)
3. Gross profit or loss		X
4. Distribution costs		(X)
5. Administrative expenses		(X)
6. Other operating income		X
7. Income from shares in group companies		X
8. Income from shares in related companies		X
9. Income from other fixed asset investments		X
10. Other interest receivable and similar income		X
11. Amounts written off investments		(X)
12. Interest payable and similar charges		(X)
13. Tax on profit or loss on ordinary activities		(X)
14. Profit or loss on ordinary activities after taxation		X
15. Extraordinary income	X	
16. Extraordinary charges	(X)	
17. Extraordinary profit or loss		X
18. Tax on extraordinary profit or loss		(X)
19. Other taxes not shown under the above items		(X)
20. Profit or loss for the financial year		X

which was based on effective management control as well as share ownership criteria. This issue was resolved by a compromise whereby control criteria other than ownership could be applied by member countries on an optional basis. There were also issues relating to the measurement of performance and financial position of the MNE group. Further questions included the extent to which consolidation requirements should be applied to MNEs that were based outside the EU but had groups of subsidiaries in one or more EU countries.

The first proposal was issued in 1976 and revised in 1979, but it was only in 1983 that agreement was reached, following substantial further revisions. These revisions allowed for some flexibility of interpretation and the availability of options, which could be adopted by the decision of individual member countries. While this provision would seem to undermine somewhat the objectives of comparability, the Seventh Directive is a major development. It requires worldwide consolidations, the use of a "fair value" approach when accounting for assets purchased through acquisitions, the equity treatment of associated corporations, and segmental disclosures of turnover by line of business and geographical area. It appears likely that the extent of information disclosure throughout the EU has been substantially enhanced as a result of this directive. The United Kingdom and, to a significant extent, the Netherlands are the exceptions given that the Seventh Directive has essentially adopted Anglo-American consolidation principles. Although this

Exhibit 7.5   EU Fourth Directive

Profit and Loss Account (Type of Expenditure Basis)		
1. Turnover		X
2. Change in stocks of finished goods and in work-in-progress		(X)
3. Own work capitalized		X
4. Other operating income		X
5. a. Raw materials and consumables	(X)	
b. Other external charges	(X)	(X)
6. Staff costs:		
a. Wages and salaries	(X)	
b. Social security costs	(X)	
c. Other pension costs	(X)	(X)
7. a. Depreciation and other amounts written of tangible and intangible fixed assets	(X)	
b. Exceptional amounts written off current assets	(X)	(X)
8. Other operating charges		(X)
9. Income from shares in related companies		X
10. Income from other fixed asset investments		X
11. Other interest receivable and similar income		X
12. Amounts written of investments		(X)
13. Interest payable and similar charges		(X)
14. Tax on profit or loss on ordinary activities		(X)
15. Profit or loss on ordinary activities after taxation		X
16. Extraordinary income	X	
17. Extraordinary charges	(X)	
18. Extraordinary profit or loss		X
19. Tax on extraordinary profit or loss		(X)
20. Other taxes not shown under the above items		(X)
21. Profit or loss for the financial year		X

directive has now been adopted in all EU member countries, some countries have been slower than others to implement it (e.g., Italy adopted the directive only in 1991).

Additional Directives   The Eighth Directive, adopted in 1984, is another important directive in that it deals with the qualification and work of auditors across the EU member countries, including the setting of minimum educational requirements, to encourage the mobility of professional auditors.

A further important and highly controversial proposed directive, which was issued in 1980 and subsequently shelved, concerned employee information and consultation with special reference to MNEs. This proposed directive, usually referred to as the Vredeling Proposals, called for the regular provision of information to employees in subsidiary corporations about the activities of the MNE at group level as well as at the level of the individual subsidiary. The information disclosures proposed covered areas such as organization structure; employment; the economic and financial situation; probable development in production, sales, and employment; rationalization plans; and plans for new working methods or other methods that could have "a substantial effect" on employee interests. Furthermore, under the proposed directive, employees would need to be consulted when decisions proposed by management were likely to affect their interests (e.g., in the case of a factory closure or any change in the activities of the subsidiary corporation). This proposed directive met with considerable opposition from MNEs and some governments, but the issues involved have been raised again in the context of implementing the EU's Charter of Fundamental Social Rights, which was approved in 1990.

Related to developments in accounting harmonization are those concerned with the harmonization of stock exchange regulations and securities laws. These were designed to ensure that both existing and potential investors have access to sufficient information in the context of promoting the development of a "European" capital market with active and well-developed stock exchanges in all the EU countries. A number of relevant directives have been approved, including the minimum conditions for listing and the disclosure of information (listing particulars) for the admission of shares to official stock exchange listings. These directives were adopted in 1979 and 1980, respectively. Furthermore, a directive on interim reports, adopted in 1982, required listed corporations to publish half-yearly reports of financial results together with information on trends and likely future developments in the current year of operations.

As far as future EU accounting harmonization efforts are concerned, it seems that, consistent with the deregulation fervor of the 1992 initiative to remove nontariff barriers, there are no plans to issue any new accounting directives. In fact, rather than attempt to achieve further harmonization, it is now considered more effective to adopt a "mutual recognition" approach to accounting and disclosure requirements. This is a process whereby the regulations in one country are accepted as equivalent in another, subject to the minimum standards set in the Fourth and Seventh Directives. In 1990, the EU Commission established a European Accounting Advisory Forum to encourage consultation between professional and governmental standard-setting agencies as well as other interested parties. The forum's purpose was to deal with new or unresolved issues in the context of promoting international harmonization in the EU and the world at large. Although the forum did not set accounting standards, it was hoped that any consensus on such matters as foreign currency translation, for example, would serve as guidelines for adoption by national standard-setting agencies throughout the EU countries.

Adoption of IFRS   In 2000, however, the European Commission signaled a major change of stance on international harmonization by announcing a proposal to require all listed companies in the EU to publish consolidated financial statements in accordance with International Financial Reporting Standards (IFRS) beginning in 2005.[1] This proposal was adopted as regulation by the European Parliament and

---

[1] Only nonpublicly traded companies will continue to use individual country GAAP.

Council in 2002. The EU's endorsement of IFRS includes all existing IASs and SICs with the exception of IAS 32 and 39 and their related SICs. These two IASs, which deal with the measurement and disclosure of financial statements, are not included because they are currently under revision by the IASB due to controversy. The EU had planned to impose the two standards in 2005 but in February 2004 threatened to change that plan unless an agreement could be reached between the IASB and the European Commission. Without revisions, French banks and insurers find the standards unsuitable because of the potential negative side effects of implementation. This potential action by the EU is argued to undermine the goal of global convergence. Although this is a very important vote of support for the IASB, there is some concern that this development may lead to a European version of IFRS. The IASB was organized as an independent body so that it could avoid political interference and lobbying for watered-down standards. Exposure Drafts have been written for both IAS 32 and IAS 39.

This brief review of the activities and influence of international intergovernmental organizations such as the UN, OECD, and EU in accounting and information disclosure demonstrates an international concern not only to harmonize accounting measurement and presentation practices but also to ensure the disclosure of sufficient comparable information internationally. This process is perceived to be essential as a basis for promoting fair competition and a degree of protection for investors and other parties and for ensuring that policy making is informed and that control, where necessary, is exercised. Intergovernmental involvement is seen to be influential in this process. Such a process is not necessarily detrimental to the interests of MNEs in that there is clearly an intergovernmental concern to promote international business and the growth of MNEs as much as to regulate their activities. However, there are likely to be differences in emphasis and approach according to the membership and objectives of the intergovernmental organization concerned.

TRADE UNIONS AND EMPLOYEES

The term *trade union* encompasses a number of different but related organizations. The trade union organizations that participate at intergovernmental levels are the international trade union confederations (ITUCs)—for example, European Trade Unions Confederation (ETUC), the International Confederation of Free Trade Unions (ICFTU), and the World Confederation of Labor (WCL). These represent the national central trade union organizations. In addition, there are international trade union secretariats, each of which concentrates on a specific industry and represents internationally those trade unions involved with the relevant industrial category. Their direct contact with MNEs, albeit limited, is with individual MNEs rather than intergovernmental organizations. In the national context, trade union attempts to influence the behavior of MNEs may take place at a variety of levels ranging from activities at shop-floor level to influencing national government policy. The relationships of trade unions with MNEs are considerably more complex and varied than, for example, those of investors in the context of stock markets. The perceived information needs of trade unions will depend on the specific point of contact with MNEs and the purpose for which information is required.

Trade unions are primarily grounded in the national territory within which they operate. It is within national states that trade unions have developed and where their power exists. Whereas MNEs have grown beyond the limits of national territories, trade unions have done so only to a very limited extent. The growing gap between the location of international business and national trade unions is in the eyes of the national trade unions a potential, and in some instances actual, disability for them.

Trade Union Proposals   In 1977, the ICFTU, WCL, and ETUC issued their own set of accounting and information disclosure requirements. The focus of this document was on MNEs and the need for international harmonization, with recommendations on taking a more uniform approach to accounting as well as comprehensive and detailed disclosures of financial and nonfinancial information. The ICFTU had also issued an earlier "multinational charter" in 1975, which emphasized the need for MNEs to be more publicly accountable and called for legal regulation to require the disclosure of more information, including a report about matters of a social nature and information about future prospects, investment, and employment.

Their purpose in these proposals, however, was not to facilitate interfirm comparisons—although this may be of some limited interest—but rather to provide a reliable basis for the formulation of policy concerning MNEs. Such policy development is inhibited not only by gaps in the availability of information for obtaining an accurate aggregate picture of their activities and impact but also by the variation in the methods of measurement used and a lack of what is considered necessary information.

Main Concern   The main national trade union concern, shared by international trade union organizations as well, centers on an increase in information disclosure relating to the operations of MNE subsidiaries. Of particular concern to trade unions in relation to MNE information disclosures are the consequences of the transfer pricing policies of each MNE's subsidiaries.

The relationship between an MNE subsidiary and other units of the MNE, especially those outside that subsidiary's country of location, may affect the relevance and reliability of the financial position and performance reported by the MNE subsidiary. Although the impact of MNE intragroup transactions is of concern to a range of interested groups, many of them (e.g., revenue and taxation authorities) do not rely on corporate reports for their information because they have access to greater amounts of information directly from the corporation concerned. For those who are interested in the affairs of MNE subsidiaries but who have to rely wholly or mainly on corporate reports for financial information (e.g., trade unions), the impact of such subsidiaries' transactions with related parties is of crucial interest. Because the primary concern of most regulatory bodies and accounting commentators is with the information needs of investors, MNE subsidiary transactions have received little attention to date.

Although trade unions and employees require information about the performance and future prospects of MNEs just as much as other groups do, information regarding the terms, conditions, scale, security, and location of employment are of special concern to them. Their primary interest is with the national situation of each MNE subsidiary and its relationship with other subsidiaries in the MNE group. International trade union organizations are also concerned with obtaining information about related party transactions and transfer pricing practices as a basis for formulating overall policy toward MNEs.

INVESTORS

Investors, including financial analysts, are those who have access to corporate reports and use them and other publicly available information as a basis for making investment decisions. Investors are "outsiders" to the MNE and range from the sophisticated to the layperson, from the active to the passive, and from the diversified to the nondiversified. Primarily, investors own or are potential owners of shares in the MNE parent corporation, though there may also be a limited number of investors in MNE subsidiaries.

The interests of investors in obtaining more information from MNEs are represented by international organizations of financial analysts and to some extent by bodies such as the International Organization of Securities Commissions (IOSCO), which is involved with the regulation of stock exchanges.

Besides additional information disclosure, especially information about the future prospects of MNEs on a worldwide basis, such as up-to-date measurements relating to earnings and asset values, investors and financial analysts are concerned about the lack of comparability of much of the information that is currently provided. At the same time, some observers argue for a shift of emphasis in the stock market toward an information approach. There, the concern would be to ensure the disclosure of a wide range of relevant information relating to earnings prospects as opposed to an emphasis on the calculation and prediction of earnings on a standardized basis. This problem of information asymmetry has become even more important to investors in recent years because of various accounting scandals and the corresponding lack of investor confidence. It is important that different classes of investors are not at a disadvantage because of differential access to accounting information.

Although such a change in emphasis may be desirable, particularly with respect to the needs of expert financial analysts in well-developed and efficient securities markets, international financial analysts, professional accountancy organizations, and governments continue to be concerned in practice with the lack of international comparability of corporate reports for investor purposes. The perceived problem is that even across countries where extensive corporate reporting requirements exist (e.g., the United States and the United Kingdom), the corporate annual reports of corporations may not be comparable—the variety of measurement methods and disclosures thwart effective comparative evaluation of financial position and performance. Even in the EU, the Fourth and Seventh Directives effectively allow corporations a choice of accounting alternatives in many instances, including basic valuation principles.

Why is there such concern with comparability between corporations? The purpose of comparisons is to evaluate alternatives and, therefore, comparisons are especially relevant to those who wish to choose between corporations in an international context. Investor decisions are characterized by a choice between alternative corporations in the process of buying, holding, or selling the shares of different corporations. For the diversified investor holding a portfolio of shares, however, it is a corporation's risk and return relative to the market as a whole and its effect on overall portfolio risks and returns that will be of special concern.

International Organizations   To facilitate the analysis and comparison of MNE reports based on different accounting influences at the national level and to enhance understanding of those from other than the user's country, investors and financial analysts—for example, the International Coordinating Committee of Financial Analysts Associations (ICCFAA)—support progress toward international accounting harmonization.

Another important organization in the context of securities market regulation and the protection of investors is IOSCO. This is the leading organization for securities regulatiors and has as its mission the global coordination of stock exchange rules so as to encourage both multilisting by corporations and international securities trading. The international standardization of accounting regulations, together with sufficiently detailed information disclosures, is an important factor in achieving these objectives. IOSCO has developed a close relationship with the International Accounting Standards Board, as discussed later.

Comparable Information   The evident concern of investor-related groups with comparability does not necessarily indicate uniformity, at least in the short term, but rather a degree of standardization and a minimum of information disclosure concerning accounting differences, enough to enable comparisons to be made. Evidence concerning the operations of well-developed securities markets such as in the United States and the United Kingdom suggests that such markets tend to be "efficient" in the sense that expert or sophisticated investors will ensure that share prices quickly reflect all publicly available information. In setting share prices, it is believed that experts will allow for the effect of differences in accounting methods, to the extent that this is possible with the available information. Of course, even the experts will not be able to allow for differences that are not disclosed or generally known about, nor will they be able to compensate for any absence of relevant information which is not otherwise obtainable from alternative sources. Even if the experts were able to unravel the differences, there may well be a cost savings if corporations were able to adopt a degree of standardization that did not entail any loss of information content.

With regard to the information to be disclosed, it has been suggested that investors are only concerned with overall MNE results, as reported in worldwide consolidated financial statements and thus are not interested in segmental or disaggregated information. However, an analysis of aggregate results often requires an understanding of the profitability, degree of risk, relative performance, and potential for growth of the component parts. As a diversified corporation's performance and future prospects are the sum of its various parts, investors are also likely to be interested in disaggregated, or segmental, information.

Geographical segmentation is of special relevance to MNEs, which are, by definition, diversified across national boundaries. Segmental information on an industrial, line-of-business (LOB), or product-line basis is also relevant to those MNEs active in a number of industries, but it is not exclusive to them in that such a corporation may confine its operations to one country. This interest in segmental information is not to say that aggregate financial information is necessarily of any less importance to investors. On the contrary, knowledge of the total results of operations, including resources and obligations, of the MNE on a worldwide basis is also essential to an overall assessment of risks and returns. Worldwide consolidations are, however, by no means the norm in all countries.

In summary, the kind of disclosure relevant to investors and financial analysts would appear to include information relating to the performance and future prospects of the worldwide operations of the MNE group and, in particular, geographical and line-of-business segmentation. In the absence of a sufficient degree of international accounting harmonization, there is a demand for additional information disclosures that will assist in determining the validity and effect of MNE measurement practices and so facilitate international comparisons.

BANKERS AND LENDERS

Like investors, the information needs of bankers and lenders appear to be focused on corporate information relating to financial position, performance, and future prospects. There is, however, a difference in emphasis in that there is likely to be particular concern with the security of loans advanced (i.e., the risk of default on obligations to pay loan interest and to refund the loans when due). It would seem that in countries where bankers and other lenders are more significant than shareholders as financiers of corporations, as in France, Germany, and Japan, this is likely to have a conservative influence on the measurement of publicly disclosed financial performance and wealth. At the same time, this group of information users is likely to have more direct access to the required information and does not, therefore, have to rely primarily on publicly available corporate reports.

In the context of international accounting harmonization, international banking organizations are apparently involved to the extent that they support the goal of requiring more comparable information from their clients, including governments, financial institutions, and corporations. Of particular importance here are the international development banks (e.g., the Asian Development Bank, the European Investment Bank, the European Bank for Reconstruction and Development, the International Bank for Reconstruction and Development, and the World Bank, with special reference to the International Finance Corporation [IFC]). In addition, a host of banks are involved in international lending in the Eurocurrency markets and newly emerging international markets in Singapore, Hong Kong, Japan, and the Middle East.

International banks often require special financial reports, and the IFC has gone so far as to issue detailed instruction booklets on accounting and reporting standards, which are likely to have an impact on practice in a number of developing countries. MNEs are also often motivated to increase the quantity of information disclosed in their corporate reports voluntarily through the process of competing for funds in the Eurocurrency and other international capital markets.

ACCOUNTANTS AND AUDITORS

The role of accountants as the preparers and users of information in MNEs is an extremely important one with respect to technical skills, influence, and responsibility. This is reinforced by the role of the accountant as the auditor or verifier of corporate reports issued by MNEs to external parties.

Although international firms of accountants, which have grown primarily in response to the growth of MNEs, are active in the international harmonization of accounting and reporting, it is at the level of international professional organizations that most of the developments are taking place, notably the IASB, previously known as the International Accounting Standards Committee (IASC).

International Accounting Standards Board

The IASB, though closely related to the International Federation of Accountants (IFAC), was granted an independent responsibility for the development of international accounting standards. The IFAC, on the other hand, concerned itself primarily with the promulgation of international auditing guidelines or standards.

Formation and Structure   The predecessor of the IASB, the International Accounting Standards Committee (IASC), was established in 1973 by leading professional organizations in Australia, Canada, Germany, Ireland, Japan, Mexico, the Netherlands, the United Kingdom, and the United States. As of 2000, the IASC had a membership comprising 143 organizations from 104 countries, including the founder members, most of whom maintained membership of the governing board and thus retained a significant measure of influence. When compared with the membership of the UN, however, it was clear that the membership of the IASC had been relatively limited and, of course, had been bounded by the need for the existence of a professional accountancy organization—something that has often been outside the experience of socialist and emerging economies. However, in May 2000, the IASC was formally restructured and renamed IASB, and a new constitution was adopted. The IASC felt the need to restructure primarily because pressure had grown for the IASC to become more independent of professional accounting bodies from around the world, with the aim of working more closely with those who actually set local standards (i.e., the national standard setters) to reach agreed solutions. It was also felt that the IASC exists to serve a wider public interest and that greater assurance of that objective should be given. Accordingly, the governance of IASB was vested in a board of trustees, with a new standards board empowered to make decisions on international accounting standards (see Figure 7.2). The 14 board members represent diverse backgrounds with 5 auditors, 3 preparers, 3 users, 1 academic, and 2 others. Details on these board members can be found in Exhibit 7.6. As of March 2004, the IASB had a membership of 158 professional accounting bodies in 118 countries.

The stated objectives of the IASB are "(a) to formulate and publish in the public interest accounting standards to be observed in the presentation of financial statements and to promote their worldwide acceptance and observance, and (b) to work generally for the improvement and harmonization of regulations, accounting standards, and procedures relating to the presentation of financial statements."

In practice, the main aim of international accounting standards is to achieve a degree of comparability that will help investors make their decisions while reduc-

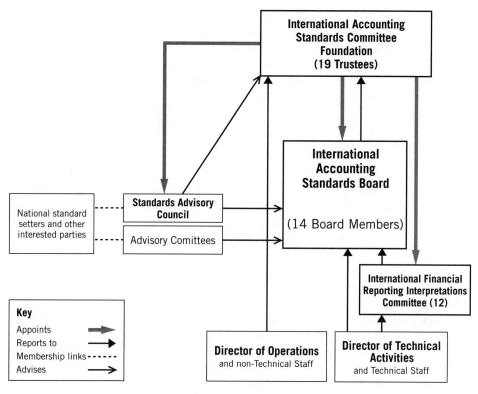

Figure 7.2 The IASB's Governance Structure

Source: IASB website, www.iasb.org.

Exhibit 7.6 IASB Board Members

Name	Title	Native Country	Type
Sir David Tweedie	Chairman	Scotland	Auditor
Thomas E. Jones	Vice Chairman	Britain	Preparer
Mary E. Barth	—	America	Academic
Hans-Georg Bruns	Liaison to Germany	Germany	Preparer
Anthony T. Cope	—	Britain	User
Jan Engström (male)	—	Sweden	Preparer
Robert P. Garnett	—	South America	User
Gilbert Gélard	Liaison to France	France	Auditor
James J. Leisenring	Liaison to U.S.	America	Other
Warren McGregor	Liaison to Australia and New Zealand	Australia	Other
Patricia O'Malley	Liaison to Canada	Canada	Auditor
John T. Smith	—	America	Auditor
Geoffrey Whittington	Liaison to U.K.	England	User
Tatsumi Yamada	Liaison to Japan	Japan	Auditor

ing the costs of MNEs in preparing multiple sets of accounts and reports. It is also fair to say that IASB was itself seen as having a global role to play in coordinating and harmonizing the activities of the many national agencies involved in setting accounting and reporting standards. It has been suggested, too, that the IASB's standards provide a useful model for developing countries wishing to establish accounting standards for the first time.

The position of the IASB (as of September 2004) regarding standards is shown in Exhibit 7.7. IASB adopted the 41 IAS standards with its inception and has since completed 5 entirely new standards and revised 15 existing standards. New standards are designated as International Financial Reporting Standards (IFRS), but the inherited standards still hold their original designation of IAS. These cover a wide range of issues, including the disclosure of accounting policies, consolidated financial statements, funds statements, segment reporting, accounting for changing prices, accounting for leases, accounting for the effects of changes in foreign exchange rates, related party disclosures, and financial instruments. The more recent IFRSs address share-based payment, insurance contracts, and first-time adoption of International Financial Reporting Standards.

Achievements   In retrospect, the IASC made remarkable progress toward its goal of achieving worldwide agreement on accounting standards since its formation in 1973, given the very different national cultures and accounting traditions that have evolved in countries around the world for centuries. As the newly established IASB entered 2001, it embarked on a new era of global standard-setting as a restructured, independent standard setter that has widespread support from governments, standard-setting agencies, securities commissions, and professional accounting associations worldwide.

In May 2000, the IASB also received an endorsement from the International Organization of Securities Commissions (IOSCO), following completion in December 1998 of a core set of standards as agreed on with IOSCO in 1995 (IOSCO, 2000a). The 1995 agreement between IASB and IOSCO followed growing recognition of the need for global accounting standards that could be used for cross-border listings and national listings alike. Business preparers were motivated by the possibility of cost savings and investors by the need for more comparable financial information internationally. The Asian financial crisis also highlighted the problems caused by a lack of confidence in accounting in the countries concerned and created pressure for the adoption of a set of globally recognized standards. As Arthur Levitt, former chairman of the SEC in the United States, said, "The significance of transparent, timely and reliable financial statements and its importance to investor protection has never been more apparent. The current financial situations in Asia and Russia are stark examples of this new reality. These markets are learning a painful lesson taught many times before: investors panic as a result of unexpected or unquantifiable bad news" (Levitt, 1998).

Furthermore, as noted earlier, the European Commission announced in 2002 that it will require all EU-listed companies to prepare consolidated financial statements based on IFRS by 2005. Much of the IASB's efforts this past year have focused on the adoption of these standards by the 25 countries of the EU. Indeed, in some countries, such as Belgium, France, Germany, and Italy, companies are now permitted to use IFRS in their consolidated financial statements. Street, Gray, and

Exhibit 7.7   International Accounting Standards (*Source*: IASB *Website, www.iasb.org*)

In effect as of September 2004:

International Accounting Standards deal with most of the topics that are important in published financial statements of business enterprises. They set out principles that can be applied in consistent ways in different countries. They require like transactions and events to be accounted for in a like manner wherever they take place—and different transactions and events to be accounted for in a different manner.

IAS 1	Presentation of Financial Statements
IAS 2	Inventories
IAS 3	(No longer effective. Superseded by IAS 27 and IAS 28)
IAS 4	(No longer effective. Superseded by IAS 16, IAS 22 and IAS 38)
IAS 5	(No longer effective. Superseded by IAS 1)
IAS 6	(No longer effective. Superseded by IAS 15)
IAS 7	Cash Flow Statements
IAS 8	Net Profit or Loss for the Period, Fundamental Errors and Changes in Accounting Policies
IAS 9	(No longer effective. Superseded by IAS 38)
IAS 10	Events After the Balance Sheet Date
IAS 11	Construction Contracts
IAS 12	Income Taxes
IAS 13	(No longer effective. Superseded by IAS 1)
IAS 14	Segment Reporting
IAS 15	(No longer effective. Superseded by IFRS 5)
IAS 16	Property, Plant and Equipment
IAS 17	Leases
IAS 18	Revenue
IAS 19	Employee Benefits
IAS 20	Accounting for Government Grants and Disclosure of Government Assistance
IAS 21	The Effects of Changes in Foreign Exchange Rates
IAS 22	(No longer effective. Superceded by IFRS 3)
IAS 23	Borrowing Costs
IAS 24	Related Party Disclosures
IAS 25	(No longer effective. Superceded by IAS 39 and IAS 40)
IAS 26	Accounting for Reporting by Retirement Benefit Plans
IAS 27	Consolidated Financial Statements and Accounting for Investments in Subsidiaries
IAS 28	Accounting for Investments in Associates
IAS 29	Financial Reporting in Hyperinflationary Economies
IAS 30	Disclosures in the Financial Statements of Banks and Similar Financial Institutions
IAS 31	Financial Reporting of Interests in Joint Ventures
IAS 32	Financial Instruments: Disclosure and Presentation
IAS 33	Earnings Per Share
IAS 34	Interim Financial Reporting
IAS 35	(No longer effective. Superseded by IFRS 5)
IAS 36	Impairment of Assets
IAS 37	Provisions, Contingent Liabilities and Contingent Assets
IAS 38	Intangible Assets
IAS 39	Financial instruments: Recognition and Measurement
IAS 40	Investment Property
IAS 41	Agriculture
IFRS 1	First Time Adoption of International Financial Reporting standards
IFRS 2	Share-based Payment
IFRS 3	Business Combinations
IFRS 4	Insurance Contracts
IFRS 5	Non-current Assets Held for Sale and Discontinued Operations

Bryant (1999) show that a growing number of companies, including multinationals such as Bayer, Essilor, Nestlé, and Pirelli, have also voluntarily adopted IFRS, though many have done so noting exceptions. As of July 30, 2005, nearly 100 countries in 6 continents were permitting or requiring domestic firms to use IFRS.

Obstacles   Nevertheless, the IASB continues to face major obstacles in achieving its goal of worldwide recognition and acceptance of IFRS and their effective use in practice. In particular, the hard-won IOSCO endorsement announced at its annual meeting in Sydney in May 2000 fell short of expectations. Following an assessment of IFRS (then IAS), IOSCO recommended that its members allow multinational companies to use 30 core IAS for the purposes of cross-border listings and capital raisings. However, IOSCO members were also permitted to require reconciliation of certain items, call for supplementary information, and eliminate some of the options that still exist in IAS (see Exhibit 7.8).

Together with this somewhat limited and modest endorsement of IFRS, IOSCO's Technical Committee published a report summarizing its assessment work and noting numerous outstanding issues that members are expected to address through supplemental treatments (IOSCO, 2000b). Hence, in practice, members of IOSCO, including the Securities and Exchange Commission in the United States, will now individually determine whether or not to endorse IFRS for cross-border listings. In this respect, the SEC has a key role to play as guardian of the world's largest capital market.

IFRS and U.S. GAAP   The SEC currently requires the reconciliation of IFRS financial statements to U.S. GAAP, and it remains to be seen whether this barrier to IFRS recognition will be lifted or at least moderated. However, in a meeting in 2002, the FASB and the IASB agreed to quickly commence deliberating differences identified for a resolution in the short-term project with the objective of achieving compatibility by identifying common, high-quality decisions. The convergence project was created to remove individual differences between IFRS and U.S. GAAP. The areas covered in the project were limited to areas where convergence would be achievable in the short term, generally by choosing between IFRS or U.S. GAAP. After analyzing differences, the FASB will either amend applicable U.S GAAP or express to the IASB their reasons for not electing to change. September 30, 2004 was the target date for issuing final statements covering those differences to help ensure sufficient time for due process and for the adoption of IFRS by the EU in 2005.

Since then, the FASB has issued multiple Exposure Drafts that eliminate differences between U.S. GAAP and IFRS. These Exposure Drafts relate to the following topics: accounting for changes in accounting policies, earnings per share, exchanges for nonmonetary assets, classifying liabilities, and inventory measurement.

The FASB is also conducting research on international convergence. Specifically, the objectives are to (1) identify every substantive difference between U.S. GAAP and IFRS, (2) catalog those differences according to the strategy for resolving them, and (3) recommend further agenda decisions to the Board to further the objective of convergence with the IFRS.

The FASB believes the United States will benefit by convergence in the following ways:

Exhibit 7.8   IOSCO Press Release (Extract) Sydney, Australia—17 May 2000

Resolution Concerning the Use of IASC Standards for the Purpose of Facilitating Multi-national Securities Offerings and Cross-border Listings

The following resolution was approved by the President's Committee of IOSCO:

In order to respond to the significant growth in cross-border capital flows, IOSCO has sought to facilitate cross-border offerings and listings. IOSCO believes that cross-border offerings and listings would be facilitated by high-quality, internationally accepted accounting standards that could be used by incoming multinational issuers in cross-border offerings and listings. Therefore, IOSCO has worked with the International Accounting Standards Committee (IASC) as it sought to develop a reasonably complete set of accounting standards through the IASC core standards work program.

IOSCO has assessed 30 IASC standards, including their related interpretations ("the IASC 2000 standards"), considering their suitability for use in cross-border offerings and listings. IOSCO has identified outstanding substantive issues relating to the IASC 2000 standards in a report that includes an analysis of those issues and specifies supplemental treatments that may be required in a particular jurisdiction to address each of these concerns.

The President's Committee congratulates the IASC for its hard work and contribution to raising the quality of financial reporting worldwide. The IASC's work to date has succeeded in effecting significant improvements in the quality of the IASC's standards. Accordingly, the President's Committee recommends that IOSCO members permit incoming multinational issuers to use the 30 IASC 2000 standards to prepare their financial statements for cross-border offerings and listings, as supplemented in the manner described below (the "supplemental treatments") where necessary to address outstanding substantive issues at a national or regional level.

Those supplemental treatments are:

- **reconciliation:** requiring reconciliation of certain items to show the effect of applying a different accounting method, in contrast with the method applied under IASC standards;

- **disclosure:** requiring additional disclosures, either in the presentation of the financial statements or in the footnotes; and

- **interpretation:** specifying use of a particular alternative provided in an IASC standard, or a particular interpretation in cases where the IASC standard is unclear or silent.

In addition, as part of national or regional specific requirements, waivers may be envisaged of particular aspects of an IASC standard, without requiring that the effect of the accounting method used be reconciled to the effect of applying the IASC method. The use of waivers should be restricted to exceptional circumstances, such as issues identified by a domestic regulator when a specific IASC standard is contrary to domestic or regional regulation.

These concerns are identified and the expected supplemental treatments described in the Assessment Report.

IOSCO notes that a body of accounting standards like the IASC standards must continue to evolve in order to address existing and emerging issues. IOSCO's recommendation assumes that IOSCO will continue to be involved in the IASC work and structure and that the IASC will continue to develop its body of standards. IOSCO strongly urges the IASC in its future work program to address the concerns identified in the Assessment Report, in particular, future projects.

IOSCO expects to survey its membership by the end of 2001 in order to determine the extent to which members have taken steps to permit incoming multinational issuers to use the IASC 2000 standards, subject to the supplemental treatments described above. At the same time, IOSCO expects to continue to work with the IASC and will determine the extent to which IOSCO's outstanding substantive issues, including proposals for future projects, have been addressed appropriately.

- Increasing efficiency of the global capital markets by increasing comparability and transparency from country to country
- Reducing the administrative burden on MNEs that are currently required to prepare financial statements under several different accounting methods and reconcile them across borders
- Enabling U.S. companies to access capital markets outside the United States without needing to reconcile U.S GAAP to International Financial Reporting Standards.

Research by Street, Nichols, and Gray (2000) suggests that the gap between IFRS and U.S. GAAP is narrowing. Major areas of difference appear to be limited to property, plant, and equipment revaluations, deferred taxes (where partial rather than comprehensive allocation has been used), goodwill (where goodwill has been charged to reserves contrary to U.S. requirements or different amortization periods have been used), and capitalized borrowing costs (where borrowing costs are expensed rather than capitalized).

In addition, the changes in IFRS following completion of the core standards work program indicate that these differences have been reduced further as IFRS moves closer to U.S. GAAP. This is so much so that it could be argued that IFRS are now, in practice, sufficiently close to U.S. GAAP to be acceptable to the SEC. Alternatively, the SEC may consider it necessary that additional disclosures be provided where companies utilize certain IFRS alternatives that have historically yielded material and significant deviations from U.S. GAAP, such as the revaluation of property, plant, and equipment. However, the number of IFRS subject to additional disclosures is likely to form an increasingly short list.

In addition to sharing the concerns of IOSCO about some of the "quality" issues raised, the SEC in the United States has argued that a comprehensive infrastructure must be in place so that high-quality global accounting standards can be used, interpreted, and enforced consistently around the world. In this regard, the International Federation of Accountants (IFAC) has stated that companies and auditors are asserting that financial statements comply with IFRS when in fact the accounting policies used footnotes to the financial statements that indicate otherwise.

Rules vs. Principles   One major issue faced by the IASB centers on the debate over principles-based standards. In view of the recent accounting scandals, many believe that accounting standards should be based on principles rather than on detailed rules. Sir David Tweedie, chairman of the IASB, has noted that one of the biggest obstacles the IASB faces with the development of international accounting standards is whether to write specific rules or adopt certain principles.

The United States has recently come to realize the problems with rules-based accounting. With over 150 standards, many feel that accounting guidance is too complex to be meaningful. Those who want to get around the rules can do so by structuring transactions around the details. Furthermore, those who want to comply with the rules may find it difficult to determine the exact guidance from the complex standards. As a result, the Sarbanes-Oxley Act, issued in 2002, requires that the SEC examine the feasibility of a principles-based system.

However, principles-based standards are difficult to implement in practice because little guidance exists on how to apply the standards. The more guidance provided on how to apply the principles, the more the standards appear to be based on rules. As a result, comparability between companies is difficult when reporting is based on principles. Furthermore, many reporters want detailed guidance on how to account for complex transactions.

The dilemma of rules vs. principles is illustrated in the following survey conducted by Mike Ng (2004). When asked if companies could apply and interpret current rules-based standards correctly and still not record the transaction such that it does not reflect the economic substance of the transactions, 93 percent felt it was possible. However, when asked if accounting for financial transactions under more general accounting principles would lead to a better reflection of economic reality, only 7 percent agreed. These results illustrate that neither principles-based nor rules-based accounting will ensure that companies report the economic reality of their transactions.

Noncompliance   Research suggests that noncompliance with IFRS is indeed problematic despite the revision of IASI Presentation of Financial Statements in 1997 (effective for accounting periods beginning on or after July 1, 1998). IASI Revised requires that "Financial Statements should not be described as complying with International Financial Reporting Standards unless they comply with all the requirements of each applicable Standard and each applicable Interpretation of the Standards Interpretation Committee. Inappropriate treatments are not rectified either by disclosure of the accounting policies used or by notes or by explanatory material."

Recent research by Street and Gray (2000) found that of 162 companies referring to IFRS (then IAS) in their 1998 and 1999 accounts, only 124 (77 percent) stated that they were fully in compliance with IAS. Whereas a number of companies had responded to IASI Revised by no longer stating exceptions to IAS, 13 companies had decided to no longer refer to IAS, with 11 companies referring only to national GAAP and 2 companies adopting U.S. GAAP. More troubling for the IASB was that 15 companies violated the revised IASI by referring to the use of IAS with exception in 1999.

All of these companies were audited by the six largest international accounting firms. Six of the audit reports only made reference to national GAAP. The remaining nine audit reports stated that the accounts are "in accordance with IAS," and for seven of these nine, the auditors specified exceptions to IAS in the audit report. Thus, although it appears that the international accounting firms are aware of IAS, they are not consistently supporting the enforcement process. It is important that auditors worldwide take a firm stand and insist on full compliance with IAS for those companies claiming compliance with IAS. In particular, actions should support the vision of the largest auditor firms that global accounting standards should be developed and applied on a consistent worldwide basis.

These findings highlight the importance of ongoing efforts by several organizations, including the IASB, IFAC, and the newly formed International Forum on Accountancy Development (IFAD), to raise the standard of accounting and audit practices worldwide.

The restructuring of the IASB should assist in addressing the noncompliance problems identified since the new IASB board includes 14 members that will also serve as liaisons to national accounting standard-setting boards. The idea is that these members will work to harmonize their national standards with IFRS, thereby making it possible for more companies to accurately state that their financial statements are in compliance with both IFRS and national GAAP. Currently, differences between national GAAP and IFRS often make this impossible.

The U.S. SEC has also noted some situations where a foreign registrant's footnotes assert that financial statements comply in all material respects with IFRS or are consistent with IFRS, yet the company has applied only certain IFRS or omitted information without explaining the reasons for exclusion. The SEC has stated that it will challenge such assertions and where they cannot be sustained will require either changes to the financial statements to conform with IFRS or removal of the assertion of compliance with IFRS.

Other notable efforts in 2000 to address compliance problems facing the IASB included the formation of the IFAD and the restructuring of IFAC.

International Federation of Accountants

As previously mentioned, the IFAC is concerned mainly with promulgating international auditing guidelines or standards. The IFAC works to serve the public interest and strengthen international economies and the accounting profession by establishing and promulgating high-quality standards and by promoting international convergence of those standards. The IFAC board is composed of 21 individuals from 17 countries who have taken an oath to serve the public interest and act with integrity. The board works with 157 organizations from 118 countries to help them meet their goals.

IAASB   The International Auditing and Assurance Standards Board was created as an independent standard-setting body under the direction of the IFAC to create quality auditing standards in order to improve public confidence in the auditing profession. Seventy countries have indicated either that they use International Standards on Auditing (ISA) or that their standards are not significantly different from ISAs. The EU adopted ISAs in 2005.

Reforms   In May 2000, IFAC agreed to a restructuring plan where, as part of the restructuring, IFAC and the large international accounting firms undertook a major new initiative. A key aspect of this effort was the establishment of a new IFAC-sponsored grouping of accounting firms that will work closely with IFAC in developing and encouraging implementation of international accounting and auditing standards.

Even more recently, in 2002, the IFAC began discussing reforms to improve trust in the financial reporting process. In November 2003, the following reforms were made after consulting with member bodies, accounting organizations, firms, and regulators:

- Establishment of the Public Interest Oversight Board (PIOB) to oversee the IFAC's standard-setting activities.
- Increased transparency with regard to IFAC governance and international standard setting

- Public participation in the standard-setting process
- A more formal process of communicating with international regulators

The PIOB will consist of 10 members and will oversee the areas of audit performance, standards, independence, other ethical standards, audit-quality control and assurance standards, and education standards.

International Forum on Accountancy Development

IFAD was established following the Asian financial crisis when the accounting profession was criticized for not doing enough to enhance the accounting capabilities of developing and emerging nations. Following discussions between the World Bank and IFAC, it was agreed to form IFAD, which represents an alliance of accountancy groups and firms across the world. IFAD is intended to be a means by which regulators, international financial institutions, investors, and representatives of the accountancy and auditing profession come together to ensure that economic downturns such as the Asian financial crisis are not repeated.

IFAD has been undertaking country-by-country reviews of accounting standards, ethics and disciplinary procedures, corporate governance, banking, and company law. IFAD has benchmarked information collected through these individual country reviews against international standards and will finance consultants to visit countries to help close the gaps wherever these may be identified. IFAD is firmly committed to encouraging conformity and consistency of national accounting standards with IFRS. Successful implementation of IFAD's vision would go far in addressing the key problem of noncompliance with IFRS.

Since its inception, the IFAD has developed the International Financial Framework to facilitate development and implementation of a plan of action to improve standards within national financial frameworks. The IFAD also conducted a GAAP Convergence Survey in 2002; 90 percent of the countries surveyed intend to convert to IFRS. This indicates that the IASB is viewed as the appropriate body to set international accounting standards. In addition, the majority of the countries surveyed indicated that they intend to converge to IFRS by establishing a governmental regulation or a policy by a standard-setting body. However, there are still disagreements between countries regarding some IFRS. The complicated nature of the standards is seen as a barrier to convergence by about half of the countries. Only time will tell if the combined efforts of the IASB, IFAD, and IFAC can overcome national, cultural, and other barriers and achieve global acceptance and enforcement of IFRS around the world.

International Association for Accounting Education and Research

The International Association for Accounting Education and Research (IAAER) was established to help promote excellence in accounting education and to ensure that academia makes a substantial contribution to the development of high-quality international standards.

THE INTERNATIONAL HARMONIZATION
AND DISCLOSURE DEBATE

To what extent MNEs create net benefits for host countries is still a matter of some controversy. However, many governments perceive that accounting harmonization and disclosure may help redress any competitive imbalance between MNEs and host-country domestic corporations and improve the bargaining position of host governments. Naturally, this will be effective only at a cost to both the MNE and the home country. Thus, it may be expected that governments from the industrialized countries, where a significant number of MNEs are based, will not be totally supportive of increased regulation, as indeed is evidenced by the relatively soft approach of the OECD compared to the UN. Whether regulation is necessary as an alternative or supplement to the pressures of market forces in individual host countries, in the home country, and in international financial markets would, therefore, seem to depend on the extent to which a more competitive international environment is considered an acceptable goal.

As far as economic development in the context of regional integration is concerned, there seems little doubt that the long-term goal is to remove market imperfections and that in a community such as the EU, there is a serious commitment to eliminating regulatory barriers despite the short-term costs likely to be incurred in some member countries.

Moving from a regional to a wider international level is, however, an entirely different matter. It is by no means evident that there is a commitment to worldwide economic integration, with its implications for a more competitive environment in which trade and investment would flow freely—the objective of the EU. On the contrary, many governments appear to be more concerned with protecting the interests of their own business community, including MNEs, at the expense of others.

If this is so, there certainly does not seem to be any broad support for the need to develop worldwide accounting standards for all corporations, as envisioned by the IASB. What is left is a set of arguments that relate more to the self-interest of MNEs, professional accounting firms, and members of the business, financial, and investment community. All tend to subscribe to a more harmonized approach to accounting and financial reporting, largely from the dual perspective of minimizing cost and maximizing shareholder wealth in the context of an international capital market.

Furthermore, evidence suggests that national differences in accounting and financial reporting are, to a considerable extent, a function of differences in priorities concerning domestic needs, which are the product of a variety of environmental factors of an economic, political, and cultural nature. Thus, in the case of domestic corporations with no significant international operations or financing, there is little reason to be concerned that worldwide standards serve international objectives, which may well be irrelevant or, at most, of minor significance when compared with domestic objectives.

International classification research has also shown that distinct patterns of accounting and country groupings have emerged over some considerable time, and hence it seems likely that any natural coordination will be a lengthy process. At the same time, the impact of regional economic groupings such as the EU, and perhaps also international intergovernmental organizations such as the UN and OECD, may well be significant, though their influence has yet to become effective. The IASB also has the potential to become a more important influence in the future, particularly with the support of the IOSCO. The current situation is thus highly dynamic. It may well be that new models or patterns of accounting are in the process of being formed, bringing together disparate traditions and thereby enhancing worldwide accounting harmony.

If it is accepted that MNEs are the most important motivation for international standards and are likely to remain so, future developments seem likely to be concerned with resolving a number of significant accounting and reporting problems specific to MNE operations and their involvement in international securities markets. As far as corporate reporting by MNEs is concerned, limited progress has been made in the conceptual and technical development of such key areas as accounting for intangible assets, foreign currency translation, group accounting, segmental reporting, accounting for related party transactions, and nonfinancial disclosures such as social and environmental reporting. There is substantial scope for innovation here if we are to develop corporate reporting systems that can cope more effectively with the complexity of MNE operations.

While reporting requirements at the national level have become more detailed and complex, particularly in the United States, large corporations and MNEs in particular have also become more complex. It may well be that, contrary to popular belief, in practice there is now less, rather than more, effective information disclosure. This raises the question of whether adequate reporting systems exist to match the growing complexity of MNE operations. Judging from the controversy surrounding issues such as group accounting, accounting for intangibles, accounting for inflation, financial instruments, and foreign currency translation, it seems certain that there is much to be resolved internationally as far as external reporting is concerned, despite the undoubted sophistication of many MNE internal accounting systems.

The disclosure of information on the basis of what is used by management is desirable on the presumption that what is useful for management will be useful to external users. This does not mean, however, that it is necessarily an easy task to adapt internal reporting to a form suitable for external reporting or that the costs, especially those relating to competitive disadvantage, are insignificant. A major problem is that national regulation determines to a greater or lesser extent what is reported externally, possibly resulting in incompatible differences. Moreover, to the extent that information is disclosed voluntarily, there are likely to be differences over the content, classification, measurement, and presentation of information between MNEs.

There is a need, therefore, for further research to help develop more innovative external reporting systems that can cope with the complexity of MNE operations as well as tackle problems concerning the feasibility and extent of global harmonization. Currently, the potential for using alternative forms of reporting is restricted, as is knowledge of the costs and benefits involved.

SUMMARY

1. Regardless of the merits of the various interests and claims of participants in setting international standards for accounting and corporate reporting,

there is a well-articulated demand internationally for both additional and more comparable information by a wide range of organizations and user groups.

2.   Major user groups interested in international standard setting include governments and international intergovernmental organizations, trade unions and employees, investors and financial analysts, bankers, lenders, creditors, and, last but not least, accountants and auditors.

3.   There are some similarities between the information needs of user groups, but there are also a number of significant differences involving the quantity of information that should be disclosed, the basis on which the information should be measured, the degree of uniformity such information should have, and the extent to which information disclosures should be mandatory.

4.   The power to influence international accounting and information disclosure practices varies considerably, from the legal force of EU directives and the EU regulation to adopt IFRS throughout the European Union to the guidelines of the OECD and UN and the recommendations of the IASB.

5.   The international harmonization of accounting is complex and dynamic. For example, international organizations have the potential to strongly influence whether national governments decide to implement any international agreements by incorporating them into national law.

6.   A major objective of accounting and information disclosure as far as international intergovernmental and trade union organizations are concerned is to monitor and, if necessary, control MNE operations. At the very least, international accounting standards may be relevant in improving the competitive bargaining power of those involved in economic and social relationships with MNEs.

7.   From the standpoint of investors, financial analysts, bankers, lenders, and creditors, it appears that the prime objective of international accounting standards is to secure additional and comparable information about the financial position, performance, and prospects of corporations and especially MNEs to be used as a basis for investment and lending decisions and to satisfy accountability objectives.

8.   Accountants and auditors also have a vital role to play as preparers, users, and verifiers of information disclosed by MNEs and are heavily involved in the standard-setting processes through the IASB, IFAC, IFAD, and IAAER, which influence international accounting and reporting behavior.

9.   The development of international accounting and disclosure standards—especially those for MNEs—is essentially a political process, with a variety of organizations, both public and private, involved in setting standards that affect MNEs. All of these organizations have differing objectives, scope, and powers of enforcement.

10.   Recent developments suggest a more consultative approach to international accounting harmonization, and, with the support of IOSCO, the IASB has the potential to be recognized as the global standard-setting authority.

11.   Accountants and accounting organizations are an essential part of the international standard-setting process and provide the innovations, technical development, and implementation skills necessary to introduce desired standards of accounting and information disclosure.

Discussion Questions

1.   Discuss the likely future of the European Union's involvement in accounting standard-setting in a global context.

2.   How can global pressures for international accounting harmonization be reconciled with local pressures for addressing national needs and priorities?

3.   Discuss the advantages and limitations of the IOSCO endorsement.

4.   Why are many MNEs voluntarily adopting IFRS rather than U.S. GAAP?

5.   Discuss the problems and prospects of enforcing IFRS.

6.   What is the role of trade unions in international accounting?

7.   Why did the IASC decide to create the IASB to set out international accounting standards?

8.   What problems do you foresee with the implementation of IFRS by 90 countries by 2005?

9.   What are some ways these countries can prepare for convergence and anticipate these problems?

10. Many critics argue that international convergence will never fully occur. Why then is it still important?

11. Would it be important to work toward International Financial Reporting Standards if there were few international corporations?

12. Which body has been more successful in achieving harmonization, the European Union or the IASB? Explain.

13. What are the arguments against harmonization? Who will harmonization hurt the most? least?

14. What have other bodies done to show their interest in international accounting?

15. Discuss the pros and cons of principles-based standards vs. rules-based standards.

Exercises

Exercises 1–5: Form into groups of three or four students representing the various participants in international accounting standard-setting, including the IASB, the IOSCO, the United States, the European Union, developing countries, and MNEs. In particular, discuss the following questions:

1.   Should international accounting standards be set for the world, or should they be restricted to MNEs interested in raising finance from international investors?

2.   Should international accounting standards be set on the basis of a philosophy of "uniformity" or a philosophy of "mutual recognition," where some differences are tolerated?

3.   If the goal is "uniformity," how can the "right" answers be found?

4.   Should the IASB have the authority to set international financial reporting standards, or should standards be the outcome of a more collaborative/consultative exercise?

5.   How can international financial reporting standards be enforced?

6.   Harry Harrison does not understand why he should care about differences between the international financial reporting standards of various countries because he only works for domestic firms. He feels it is a huge waste of time and does not care about differences from country to country.

   a.   Is there substance to his argument?

   b.   Why might he be wrong? What would you tell him to help him change his attitude?

7. Germany's accounting system is generally used to meet the needs of creditors and tax authorities. In other words, there is little difference between their financial books and their tax books. In 2005, Germany was required to use IFRS for their financial statements.

   a. Discuss the issues faced by companies in Germany as they embrace an accounting system different from their traditional tax-oriented system.

   b. What might they do to ease the transition?

Exercises 8–9: Visit the International Accounting Standards Board website (www.iasb.org).

8. What projects are currently being addressed by the IASB? Give a few examples as well as a description.

9. What news has recently been announced about the IASB?

Exercises 10–12: Visit the Financial Accounting Standards Board website (www.fasb.org). Find information on the "Convergence Project."

10. What has already been accomplished toward convergence?

11. What is on the current agenda?

12. What is the difference between short-term convergence and long-term convergence?

13. What are some of the major differences between U.S. GAAP and IFRS as determined by the FASB and IASB?

14. On the IASB website are biographies of the current IASB board members. Where are the members from? What were their prior affiliations? Is this an international representation?

15. ***Fourth and Seventh Directives*** Your country is a member of the European Union and you are preparing your year-end financial statements. According to the Fourth and Seventh Directives, you have a lot of different options/layouts to consider for the presentation of your balance sheet and your profit/loss statement. The balance sheet can be traditional or can present the information in an analytical layout. The profit/loss statement can be presented by analyzing costs on an operational basis or on a type of expenditure basis. You want to determine what the best option is for your company.

   a. Compare and contrast the different presentation options. Does the best option differ from country to country? Why?

   b. Which presentation option do you think provides the most accurate representation of a company?

Case: European Adoption of IFRS
Case: IAS 39

These cases can be found on the following website: www.wiley.com/college/radebaugh

Selected References

Adhikari, A., and R. H. Tondkar. 1995. "An Examination of the Success of the EC Directives to Harmonize Stock Exchange Disclosure Requirements." *Journal of International Accounting Auditing & Taxation* 4(2): 127–146.

Coenenberg, A. G., and S. J. Gray, eds. 1984. *EEC Accounting Harmonization: Implementation and Impact of the Fourth Directive.* Amsterdam: North-Holland. Commission of the European Community. 1980. "Proposal for a Directive on Procedures for Informing and Consulting the Employees of Undertakings with Complex Structures." In *Particular Transnational Undertakings*. Brussels: EC, revised 1983.

Dumontier, P., and B. Raffournier. 1998. "Why Firms Comply Voluntarily with IAS: An Empirical Analysis with Swiss Data." *Journal of International Financial Management & Accounting* 9(4): 216–245.

Emenyonu, E. N., and S. J. Gray. 1992. "European Community Accounting Harmonisation: An Empirical Study of Measurement Practices in France, Germany, and the United Kingdom." *Accounting and Business Research* 22(89): 49–58.

Emenyonu, E. N., and S. J. Gray. 1996. "International Accounting Harmonization in Major Developed Stock Market Countries: An Empirical Study." *International Journal of Accounting* 31(3): 269–279

European Community. 1978. Fourth Council Directive for Coordination of National Legislation Regarding the Annual Accounts for Limited Liability Companies. Brussels: EC. European Community. 1983. Seventh Council Directive on Consolidated Accounts. Brussels: EC (June).

Goeltz, R. K. 1991. "International Accounting Harmonization: The Impossible (and Unnecessary) Dream." *Accounting Horizons* 5(1): 85–88.

Gray, S. J. (with L. B. McSweeney and J. C. Shaw). 1984. *Information Disclosure and the Multinational Corporation*. New York: John Wiley.

Gray, S. J., A. G. Coenenberg, and P. D. Gordon, eds. 1993. *International Group Accounting: Issues in European Harmonization*. London: Routledge.

Hegarty, J. 1997. "Accounting for the Global Economy: Is National Regulation Doomed to Disappear?" *Accounting Horizons* 11(4): 75–90.

Herrmann, D., and W. Thomas. 1995. "Harmonisation of Accounting Measurement Practices in the European Community." *Accounting and Business Research* 25(100): 253–265.

http://europa.eu.int/

http://r0.unctad.org/isar/

http://www.fasb.org

http://www.iaaer.org

http://www.iasb.org

http://www.ifac.org

http://www.oecd.org

International Accounting Standards Board. www.iasb.org.uk

International Accounting Standards Committee. 1999. International Accounting Standards, Shaping the New Millenmium, Annual Review.

International Accounting Standards Committee. 2000. International Accounting Standards, Annual Review.

International Accounting Standards Committee. 2000. International Accounting Standards 2000. London: IASC.

International Federation of Accountants. www.ifac.net

International Forum on Accountancy Development. www.ifad.net

International Organizations of Securities Commissions. www.iosco.orgIOSCO. 2000a. Resolution Concerning the Use of IASC Standards for the Purpose of Facilitating Multinational Securities Offering and Cross-Border Listings. Sydney, Australia, May 17, 2000.

IOSCO Technical Committee. 2000b. IASC Standards—Assessment Report, Report by the Technical Committee, May 2000.

Levitt, Arthur. 1998. "The Numbers Game." Presentation at the New York University Center for Law and Business, New York (September 28).

McGregor, W. 1999. "An Insider's View of the Current State and Future of International Accounting Standard Setting." *Accounting Horizons* (June): 159–168.

Mueller, G. G. 1967. *International Accounting*. New York: Macmillan.

Mueller, G. G. 1997. "Harmonization Efforts in the European Union." In International Accounting and Finance Handbook, edited by F. D. S. Choi. 2nd ed. New York: John Wiley.

Ng, Mike. 2004. "The Future of Standards Setting," *The CPA Journal* 74(1): 18–20.

Nobes, C. W., and R. H. Parker, eds. 2000. *Comparative International Accounting.* Englewoods Cliffs, NJ: Prentice-Hall.

Organization for Economic Cooperation and Development. 1976a. "International Investment and Multinational Enterprises." Guidelines for Multinational Enterprises. Paris: OECD, revised 1979.

Organization for Economic Cooperation and Development. 1976b. International Investment and Multinational Enterprises. Paris: OECD, revised 1979; International Confederation of Free Trade Unions, European Trade Union Confederation, World Confederation of Labour. 1977. Trade Union Requirements for Accounting and Publication by Undertakings and Groups of Companies. Brussels.

Saudagaran, S. M., and J. G. Diga. 1998. "Accounting Harmonization in ASEAN: Benefits, Models and Policy Issues." *Journal of International Accounting Auditing & Taxation* 7(1): 21–45.

Street, D. L., and S. J. Gray. 2000. "IAS 1 Compliance Survey: Challenging Times." *Accountancy* 126(1288): 104–106.

Street, D. L., S. J. Gray, and S. M. Bryant. 1999. "Acceptance and Observance of International Accounting Standards: An Empirical Study of Companies Claiming to Comply with IASs." *International Journal of Accounting* 34(1): 11–47.

Street, D. L., N. B. Nichols, and S. J. Gray. 2000. "Assessing the Acceptability of International Accounting Standards in the U.S.: An Empirical Study of the Materiality of U.S. GAAP Reconciliations by Non-U.S. Companies Complying with IASC Standards." *The International Journal of Accounting* 35(1): 27–63.

Street, D. L., and K. A. Shaughnessy. 1998. "The Evolution of the G4+1 and Its Impact on International Harmonization of Accounting Standards." *Journal of International Accounting Auditing & Taxation* 7(2): 131–161.

Tay, J. S. W., and R. H. Parker. 1990. "Measuring International Harmonization and Standardization." *Abacus* 26(1): 71–88.

Taylor, Stephen, and Stuart Turley. 1986. *The Regulation of Accounting.* London: Basil Blackwell.

United Nations. 1988. *Conclusions on Accounting and Reporting by Transnational Corporations.* New York: UN, revised 1994.

Van Hulle, K. 1992. "Harmonization of Accounting Standards: A View from the European Community." *European Accounting Review* 1(1): 161–172.

Wallace, R. S. O. 1990. "Survival Strategies of a Global Organization: The Case of the International Accounting Standards Committee." *Accounting Horizons* 4(2): 1–22.

Walton, P. 1999. "European Harmonization." In *International Accounting and Finance Handbook.* 2nd ed., 1999 Supplement, edited by F. D. S. Choi. New York: John Wiley, pp. 11.1–11.14.

CHAPTER EIGHT

INTERNATIONAL BUSINESS COMBINATIONS, GOODWILL, AND INTANGIBLES

Chapter Objectives

- Show how countries aggregate information through the process of consolidating financial statements
- Differentiate between acquisition and merger accounting
- Describe the treatment of nonconsolidated subsidiaries
- Discuss the various efforts to harmonize consolidation practices by the International Accounting Standards Board (IASB) and also in the European Union (EU)
- Compare the different attitudes toward the cash flow statement worldwide
- Identify the issues involved in joint venture accounting worldwide
- Examine the conceptual issues involved in accounting for goodwill and other intangible assets
- Identify the major approaches to accounting for goodwill: asset without amortization, asset subject to annual impairment, asset with systematic amortization, and immediate write-off
- Describe the different national practices of accounting for goodwill and the major international efforts at harmonizing these practices
- Examine the choice of accounting methods, national practices, and harmonization efforts with respect to brands, trademarks, patents, and related intangibles

Strategic Decision Point

Vodafone's operations span 26 countries. However, it does not own 100 percent of all of its operations. This circumstance creates confusion when analyzing Vodafone's financial situation. According to GAAP, only companies it controls should be consolidated in the financial statement. However, Vodafone issues pro forma numbers that consolidate all of its operations based on its proportion ownership. In other words, it includes 3 percent of the revenue from China Mobile, a company in which it has a 3 percent stake. Many investors feel that Vodafone's pro forma or "proportionate" revenue does not accurately reflect Vodafone's true growth potential. Because the pro forma number includes some fast-growing operations, specifically its 45 percent stake in Verizon Wireless, it makes the company appear as though it is growing faster than it really is. With the proportionate figure, it includes revenue from assets that it does not control. On the other hand, many investors prefer the proportionate numbers, arguing that they provide information on the generally nonconsolidated assets and are a more accurate reflection of the company's investments.

The FASB and the IASB are currently working on a project to address the issue of consolidation for these type of situations. Specifically, the boards are considering whether the 50 percent rule is the best indicator for determining control for purposes of consolidation. New guidance may reveal a method more like Vodafone's, where all interests are consolidated based on their proportionate values.

INTRODUCTION

The financial performance and future prospects of the multinational enterprises (MNE) as an economic entity are of interest to a wide range of groups, including investors, bankers, employees, and managers. It is in this context that a corporate report on the group of corporations controlled and coordinated by the MNE parent corporation is relevant. Subsidiary corporations may have been established for strategic purposes by the MNE in the process of organic growth or acquired in the context of merger and takeover activity. In addition, the parent may have interests or investments in associated corporations, joint ventures, and alliances that are not controlling interests but are nevertheless significant to its overall financial performance. In this chapter, we will discuss issues relating to consolidated financial statements, including goodwill and intangibles. We will also examine the accounting treatment of joint ventures. National and international developments will also be reviewed in both a comparative and a harmonization context.

CONSOLIDATED FINANCIAL STATEMENTS

There is a recognized need for information about MNE operations on a worldwide basis, but it is a matter of some controversy how best to report this information.

Consolidation is currently accepted in practice as the best means of accounting for groups and business combinations internationally. Consolidated reports are relevant not only to external users, notably investors, but also to managers as a basis for overall control and evaluation of performance. Consolidation involves aggregating, on a "line-by-line" basis, information about the assets, liabilities, revenues, and expenses of the MNE's many individual legal entities into income, financial position, and funds or cash flow statements relating to a single economic entity.

At the same time, it is increasingly recognized that MNE operations are so complex that consolidations are likely to be less than revealing without some disaggregation of the information accumulated—hence, the corresponding demand for segment (disaggregated) information by lines of business and geographical markets. Consolidated and segment statements are thus complementary forms of reporting: each appears to be necessary to make an informed appraisal of MNE operations. Paradoxically, just as consolidations are now becoming accepted in practice as appropriate for groups operating in the international environment, so too are their limitations becoming apparent; they do not reveal any significant differences in the risks and returns applicable to the various operations of the MNE.

Apart from the United Kingdom and the United States—and, more recently, the EU countries—legal and professional requirements relating to group accounts are perhaps not as comprehensive or widespread as might be expected, though the number of countries with regulations in this area is growing. Japan, which first introduced regulations to publish consolidated financial statements in 1976, provides a case study of the significance of such disclosure requirements. Toshiba is a Japanese firm that reported 1976 earnings of U.S.$130 million on a nonconsolidated basis but a loss of U.S.$13 million when its foreign and other subsidiaries were consolidated. Clearly, nonconsolidation can be highly misleading as to overall financial performance, especially for MNEs with complex foreign operations.

In practice, the quality and quantity of consolidated information vary considerably both between and within countries. In the United Kingdom, a parent company balance sheet is always provided in addition to a consolidated balance sheet and income statement. In contrast, in the United States, only consolidated financial statements are provided. In Germany, it is normal practice for both parent company and worldwide consolidated financial statements to be provided.

Consolidation Methods   As mentioned above, consolidation involves aggregating information about the company on a line-by-line basis. An alternative to full consolidation on a line-by-line basis is proportional consolidation, where only the ownership share of assets and liabilities is consolidated on a pro rata or proportional basis. This is typically considered appropriate for joint ventures.

With respect to associated or affiliated corporations, where there is a significant influence but not controlling interest, the majority of MNEs use the equity method, whereby a share of profits is consolidated on a "one-line" basis according to the equity owned by the MNE. The assets and liabilities of the associate are not consolidated. Instead, the investment amount in the MNE parent's books is adjusted to reflect the MNE's share in equity. The more conservative cost method—whereby only dividends received and receivable are included in the results for the year—is widely used, however, in countries such as Australia and Sweden.

Different consolidation methods impact the balance sheet and income statement differently, as a simplified example of a 50 percent-owned foreign company shows (see Exhibit 8.1). As shown in Exhibit 8.1, the balance sheet under full consolidation eliminates the investment amount for the foreign company and instead includes all the assets of the foreign company, with the 50 percent minority interests in them shown separately under shareholders' equity. Under proportional consolidation, 50 percent of the fixed assets and inventory are brought in, in contrast to the equity method, which merely restates the cost of the investment in the foreign company from $M75 to $M80 to reflect the 50 percent share of equity (including the share of income for 2001). In the income statement, net income is the same under each method but presented differently. Under full consolidation, the minority interest share is deducted from gross income, whereas under proportional consolidation, the share of income is incorporated in the proportionate revenues and expenses included in the income statement. The equity approach, on the other hand, is to subsequently add the share of income of the associated company to the parent company's net income. This example excludes issues relating to foreign currency translation, which are discussed in Chapter 11.

Purchase versus Pooling-of-Interests Accounting There are also considerable differences between countries regarding the methods of full consolidation used for

Exhibit 8.1 MNE Consolidation Alternatives

	MNC Parent ($m)	Foreign Company ($m)	Full Consolidation ($m)	Proportional Consolidation ($m)	Equity Method ($m)
Consolidation Method Balance Sheet as at December 31, 2004					
Fixed assets	250	130	380	315 (250 + 65)	250
Investment in Foreign Company (50 percent)	75	—	—	—	80 (50% × 160)
Inventory	50	30	80	65 (50 + 15)	50
	375	160	460	380	380
Share Capital	350	150	350	350	350
Net Income—1995	25	10	30	30	30
Shareholder's Equity	375	160	380	380	380
Minority Interests	—	—	80	—	—
	375	160	460	380	380
Income Statement for 2004					
Revenues	50	20	70	60 (50 + 10)	50
Expenses	25	10	35	30 (25 + 5)	25
	25	10	35	30	25
Income from Foreign Associate Company	—	—	—	—	5 (50% × 10)
	25	10	35	30	30
Minority Interests	—	—	5	—	—
Net Income	25	10	30	30	30

business combinations resulting from mergers and takeovers. For example, the purchase method of consolidation (termed the *acquisition method* in the United Kingdom) is normally used, whereby assets are generally revalued to "fair value" as of the date of acquisition of the subsidiary, and the difference between the purchase cost and the revalued net assets is described as goodwill on consolidation. However, in some countries, the pooling-of-interests method (termed the *merger method* in the United Kingdom) is also permitted in certain circumstances. In this case, assets are not revalued, no goodwill arises, and there is no distinction between pre- and postacquisition earnings. Under purchase accounting, the acquired company contributes to group profits only after the combination, whereas under pooling-of-interests accounting, all the precombination profits are included. This tends to provide an artificial incentive to use pooling, when permitted, to show enhanced profits.

Furthermore, under purchase accounting, the investment by the holding company is recorded at market value, and the assets and liabilities of the acquired company are generally revalued to fair value, as already mentioned, as of the date of the business combination. Under pooling, however, the investment is recorded at nominal value, and assets and liabilities are not revalued. The effect of this difference is that, under the acquisition approach, profits subsequent to combination may be decreased by increased depreciation charges relating to revalued assets. Profits may also be decreased by the amortization of goodwill. Thus, there is a further incentive to use the pooling-of-interests method where this is a permitted alternative to purchase accounting.

The potential for enhancing reported earnings, however, does not rest entirely with pooling. A pessimistic view of asset valuations, in the context of fair value adjustments, could be taken. Furthermore, provisions for reorganization and anticipated future losses (included in the cost of the purchase) could increase goodwill, and, with the immediate write-off of such goodwill against reserves (permitted in Hong Kong but not the United States), could well encourage a preference for purchase accounting.

In a conventional accounting principles context, the rationale for choosing between these two approaches is not well developed. However, what rationale there is seems to reflect the questionable assumption that the nature of ownership is of paramount importance regardless of the economic substance of the business combination. In this context, where one company purchases another and the shareholders of the acquired company cease to have ownership rights, the purchase method is considered appropriate. On the other hand, if there is a continuity of ownership through an exchange of shares, the pooling-of-interests method is considered appropriate. An assumption underlying merger accounting is that all that has changed is the size of the business to be accounted for, with both constituents of the group continuing as before; in other words, there is a uniting of interests. In contrast, purchase accounting treats the business combination from the viewpoint of the shareholders of the acquired company. The subsidiary is also treated as if its assets, liabilities, and goodwill have been purchased separately and contribute to the business from the date of combination. Thus, assets and liabilities are revalued to reflect their purchase values, or new "historical costs," as at the date of acquisition.

In practice, the pooling-of-interests method is used by only a small minority of countries worldwide (see Exhibit 8.2). The United States used to permit the pooling method but prohibited it with the issuance of FAS 144. The statement argues that differences between the two methods affect competition in markets for merg-

Exhibit 8.2   Accounting for Business Combinations

	Pooling Method if Uniting of Interests	Purchase Method if Uniting of Interests
Australia	Not Permitted	Required
Canada	Not Permitted	Required
France	Not Permitted	Required
Germany	Not Permitted	Required
Hong Kong	Not Permitted	Required
Japan	Permitted	Not Permitted
Netherlands	Not Permitted	Required
Singapore	Required	Not Permitted
Sweden	Not Permitted	Required
Switzerland	Permitted	Permitted
United Kingdom	Not Permitted	Required
United States	Not Permitted	Required

ers because the criteria used to determine which method to use does not distinguish economically different transactions. The IASB followed suit with the issuance of IFRS 3 in March 2004, which requires that all business combinations be accounted for under the purchase method. In the United Kingdom, pooling is permitted with FRS 6, which has the objective of ensuring that pooling, called *merger accounting* in the United Kingdom, is used only for those business combinations that are not, in substance, the acquisition of one entity by another but the formation of a new reporting entity as a substantially equal partnership where no party is dominant. In spite of the ASB's reservations toward requiring the purchase method for all combinations, publicly traded companies in the EU will be required to use the purchase method for their financial statements as of 2005.[1]

The Treatment of Nonconsolidated Subsidiaries   Subsidiaries may be nonconsolidated for various reasons. In this regard, the impact on earnings will depend on whether they are accounted for using the equity method or the cost method. If the equity method is used, then reported earnings will tend to be higher because the MNE's share of earnings rather than dividends is included.

In Japan, the United Kingdom, and the United States, the equity method is required. But this is not the case, for example, in Australia, Sweden, and Switzerland. In both the United States and the United Kingdom, recent changes in regulation require the consolidation of all material subsidiaries. Because it is mainly financial subsidiaries that have been affected by these changes, the latter have had the effect of increasing leverage or gearing.

A major problem in Japan, however, is that it is not easy to identify a subsidiary in the first place. The legal criterion of majority share ownership is misleading. Cor-

---

[1] Only nonpublicly traded companies will continue to use country GAAP instead of IFRS

porate groups in Japan are significantly different from groups in the United Kingdom and the United States. Ownership patterns in U.K.-U.S. groups generally reflect a majority shareholding either directly or indirectly via the parent corporation. In contrast, there is a complex pattern of decentralized cross-holdings in Japanese groups (see Figure 8.1).

These groups are known as Keiretsu (i.e., headless combinations). Legal relationships are not the critical factor here. Relationships concerning the supply of raw materials and technology, market outlets, sources of debt finance, and interlocking directorships are also very important. Group consciousness is the key, built on a system of cooperation based on mutual trust and loyalty. Hence, Japanese consolidated accounts are not necessarily an accurate reflection of group results—both earnings and assets may be seriously understated. Many companies may report compliance with U.S. GAAP for U.S. listing purposes, but they are not strictly comparable with U.S. consolidated accounts.

Fair Value Adjustments   Under acquisition accounting, both the United States and the United Kingdom require the revaluation of the assets acquired to fair value, or updated purchase price, usually based on current values. However, this is not required, for example, in Japan or Switzerland where book values are retained even though they may be in excess of fair value.

The financial impact of not restating assets to fair value is that earnings will be relatively overstated on account of lower depreciation charges, and assets will be understated where fair value exceeds book value. In the case of many acquisitions, however, the fair value of assets may be lower than book value—hence, the reverse will apply in countries not requiring restatement (i.e., earnings will be understated).

Accounting for Goodwill   There are a variety of practices for treating goodwill arising from the consolidation of subsidiaries on a worldwide basis. Majority practice worldwide is to treat goodwill as an asset subject to systematic amortization. However, the United States and the IASB treat goodwill as an asset subject to annual impairment testing. A significant minority adopt the method of immediate write-off against reserves. Only a small minority retain goodwill permanently as an asset.

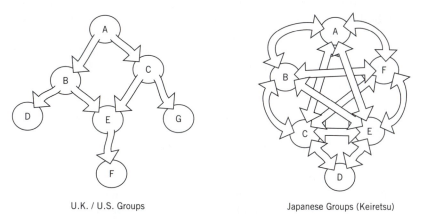

U.K. / U.S. Groups   Japanese Groups (Keiretsu)

Figure 8.1   Corporate Group Share Ownership Patterns

The most restrictive approaches to goodwill can be seen in countries such as Australia, Canada, Japan, Sweden, and the United States, where immediate write-off against reserves is not permitted. Furthermore, maximum amortization periods of between 5 and 40 years are required for some countries, with others requiring annual impairment testing. Some other countries, however, are more flexible, most notably the Netherlands.

International Accounting Standards

In International Accounting Standards 27 (1994) and 28 (1998), the IASB states that worldwide consolidated financial statements should be provided along with information about a group's member corporations, including its associated corporations. Such consolidations should include all subsidiaries, foreign and domestic. Associated corporations, where the investor corporation holds a significant interest, are to be accounted for by the equity method except when the investment is acquired and held exclusively with a view to its disposal. The standards also specify criteria for the exclusion of subsidiaries from the consolidation (i.e., if control is temporary or severe long-term restrictions on the transfer of funds impair control by the parent). Uniform accounting policies for all corporations consolidated are required, or at least any differences in accounting policy must be disclosed.

IFRS 3 on Business Combinations, issued in March 2004, includes requirements relating to the treatment of business combinations and accounting for goodwill. This standard superseded IAS 22, which had been revised in 1993 and 1998 to impose stricter requirements.

Under the original IAS 22, either the purchase method for acquisitions or the pooling-of-interests method for a merging or uniting of interests could be used. But the revised standard (para. 8) tightened up the criteria for pooling as follows: "A uniting of interests is a business combination in which the shareholders of the combining enterprises combine control over the whole, or effectively the whole, of their net assets or operations to achieve a continuing mutual sharing in the risks and benefits attaching to the combined entity such that neither party can be identified as the acquirer." Regarding goodwill, the revised IAS 22 stipulated that goodwill must be recognized as an asset (where goodwill is the excess of the cost of acquisition over the fair value of net identifiable assets acquired) and must be amortized against revenues on a systematic basis over its useful life. The amortization period was not to exceed 20 years unless a longer period could be justified. The method of immediate write-off against reserves was eliminated by the IASB—it was now an unacceptable alternative.

The issuance of IFRS 3 substantially changed the treatment for business combinations. Specifically, the pooling-of-interests method was prohibited. Amortization of goodwill and other intangible assets is also prohibited. Instead, they are subject to annual impairment testing. The project's objective was to improve the quality of, and seek international convergence on, the accounting for business combinations, goodwill, and intangibles.

What chances of success does the IASB have to achieve compliance on a worldwide basis? In practice, a number of countries adopt a flexible approach and permit the immediate write-off of goodwill against shareholders' equity. There are also theoretical arguments to support both the asset-with-amortization and immediate write-off methods. In consequence, enhanced transparency concerning the treatment of goodwill is likely to be more important than the uniformity introduced by the IASB.

Problems and Prospects

While demand for MNE consolidated financial statements has been growing, there has not been a rapid response in practice. Many large MNEs based in countries such as India, Italy, and Switzerland have not provided worldwide consolidated information, although the situation has changed with the relatively recent introduction of new laws. On the other hand, many MNEs have been voluntarily disclosing consolidated information (e.g., Ciba-Geigy in Switzerland and Fiat in Italy). In some countries, such as India and Saudi Arabia, consolidated accounts are still not required. Further developments must be expected with the continuing involvement of the IASB in the setting of international accounting standards, although the European Union has undoubtedly been more influential in the short term in that the Seventh Directive has legal force throughout the EU countries.

Just beneath the surface, however, are many problems to be resolved internationally, especially those relating to determining the appropriate concept of group identification and the relevant techniques of consolidation, including the treatment of associated corporations. Further issues include the disclosure of details of ownership in, and activities of, members of the group. Given the wide variety of participants interested in MNEs, there appears to be pressure to develop disclosure and measurement practices that will provide information to satisfy a number of perspectives. From a governmental and trade union standpoint, for example, additional subgroup consolidated financial statements at the "country" level may be useful, whereas investors who tend to be more concerned with the MNE as a total economic entity may well be satisfied with a group consolidation on a worldwide basis.

A final issue concerns the relevance of the consolidation process itself in the context of MNE operations, with its variety of geographical locations, differential rates of inflation, exchange rates, and political risk. How meaningful is aggregate information of this kind? There seems to be room for experimentation with alternative forms of presentation and disclosure, including the further development of segmental reporting.

Now consider the funds or cash flow statement. This statement may be viewed as one of the required consolidated financial statements, but because it is something of an innovation in many countries, we will discuss it separately.

FUNDS AND CASH FLOW STATEMENTS

The funds statement, or statement of changes in financial position, is becoming increasingly recognized as an important and integral part of the consolidated financial statements. It provides an analysis of the sources and uses of funds accruing to the corporation during the period. The statement shows the inflow of funds from operations and from such items as new loans, equity capital, or the sale of assets together with the outflow of funds for dividends, loan repayments, and new invest-ment. It should be emphasized that the term *funds* does not necessarily imply "cash" flows, though some presentations emphasize the net change in cash/liquid bal-ances as opposed to changes in working capital (i.e., stocks, trade debtors, and creditors).

The purpose of funds and cash flow statements is to provide further insight into the financial performance, stability, and liquidity prospects of the MNE—mat-ters of common concern to all user groups. However, in the context of MNEs, the usefulness of a consolidated funds statement may be extremely limited without additional information on a disaggregated basis. Of special interest from a risk-analysis perspective is the geographical location of the sources and uses of funds—information that is effectively denied by a consolidated statement.

Although there is nothing new about the use of funds and cash flow state-ments, especially by financial analysts and bankers, they appear to be something of an innovation as far as regulation is concerned, despite voluntary disclosures by a significant number of major corporations.

A funds statement is legally required in France, in accordance with the Plan Comptable Général, as well as in Sweden. In other countries, for example, Brazil, Canada, and the Philippines, legal requirements also exist. In addition, a number of economies, including Australia, Hong Kong, New Zealand, and the United States, have professional requirements. Interestingly, in the United States, the funds statement requirement was replaced in 1987 by the pioneering SFAS 95 on cash flow statements. In the United Kingdom, a professional accounting standard on funds statements (SSAP 10) was similarly replaced by a cash flow statement require-ment, Financial Reporting Standard No. 1 (FRS 1), issued by the Accounting Stan-dards Board (ASB) in 1991.

A few countries, including Fiji, Malaysia, Nigeria, and Singapore, have adopted the International Accounting Standard on cash flow statements (IAS 7, revised 1992) in the absence of national requirements. Stock exchange require-ments may also be influential, as in Australia. But in many countries there are no requirements to present a funds or cash flow statement. These include, most notably, Belgium, Germany, India, Italy, Saudi Arabia, and Switzerland (although all publicly owned companies in EU countries will be required to present a state-ment of cash flows as part of their financial statements beginning in 2005).

Despite the relative lack of regulation governing funds and cash flow state-ments, they clearly are increasingly provided in practice and in particular by large corporations, including MNEs, on a voluntary basis.

International Accounting Standard 7 (IAS 7), issued in 1977 and revised in 1992, now requires a cash flow statement. The statement must report cash flows during the period classified by operating, investing, and financing activities. Con-sistent with the U.K and U.S. standards, companies are permitted to use either the direct method, whereby major classes of gross cash receipts and payments are dis-closed, or the indirect method, whereby net profit or loss is adjusted for the effects of transactions of a noncash nature. The direct method is encouraged by IAS 7 on the grounds that this is likely to be more useful in estimating future cash flows. Interestingly, the requirements of IAS 7 have now been endorsed and accepted by the IOSCO and the SEC in the United States.

Problems and Prospects

Although a funds or cash flow statement is a relative newcomer to published corporate reports and is considered to be an innovation in many countries, it is rapidly becoming accepted as an essential and primary financial statement. There is growing pressure from the IASB for the publication of such a statement. Until recently, it was omitted from EU requirements presumably because funds or cash flow statements have not been featured widely in the laws of the member countries, and thus the question of harmonization did not arise from a legal perspective. However, the EU will require the cash flow statement with the adoption of IFRS in 2005. Looking at the world as a whole, we see that accounting regulation in this area is growing but has a tendency to be highly flexible. Many MNEs are voluntarily providing funds or cash flow statements, especially in Germany and Switzerland. However, the presentation of funds or cash flow statements is not well developed in practice, and there is some confusion and doubt about their purpose, effective presentation, and use. With respect to funds statements, there is considerable variation in the definition of funds used, in the items disclosed, in the measurement of funds from operations, and in the form of presentation of the statement. The use of funds statements for comparative purposes is thus likely to be limited. It also seems that the existing forms of the funds statement need to be critically evaluated in light of potential uses. Certainly, the consolidation form is of limited usefulness for understanding the complexity of MNE operations where the geographical location and currency of sources and uses of funds are essential information. There is also the question of whether a cash flow statement could be more useful than a funds statement in an international context, as recently introduced in the United States and United Kingdom and endorsed by the IASB.

JOINT VENTURE ACCOUNTING

Joint venture accounting has become an increasingly important issue with the rapid growth in joint venture arrangements, both between MNEs themselves and between MNEs and host-country corporations or governments. In this regard, there are problems involving the coordination of different cultural and accounting traditions in a way that resolves issues relating to financial control, the measurement of profit, and the valuation of joint venture investments. Relatively little is currently known about either the control processes employed or how best to measure the performance of joint ventures. In the context of joint ventures in Russia, Eastern Europe, and China, major problems have arisen from the fact that the accounting systems used in socialist economies have been very different from those of Western, market-oriented countries. Accounting in a centrally planned context has had primarily a record-keeping function and has not been decision-oriented or concerned with efficiency at the enterprise level. Instead, it has been used as a means of centralized control. At the same time, there has been a tendency to emphasize the receipts and payments approach rather than the accruals approach used in Western accounting systems, with resulting differences in measurements of profit. There have also been differences in terms of asset valuation, depreciation, treatment of liabilities, and use of fund accounting for a variety of purposes, including new investment and social and employee benefits. While changes to a more Western accounting-oriented approach are now taking place, differences in accounting tradition and culture persist and can give rise to problems and misunderstandings.

The recent wave of international joint ventures has also posed a variety of questions concerning financial reporting by the multinational corporation. In this regard, the IASB has attempted to resolve the issues involved from the venturer's perspective in IAS 31 (revised 1998) on Financial Reporting of Interests in Joint Ventures. This can be contrasted with the problems of accounting by joint ventures, which involve decisions about the accounting principles to be used in the joint venture financial statements themselves.

In IAS 31, a joint venture is defined as "a contractual arrangement whereby two or more parties undertake an activity which is subject to joint control." This joint control must involve a contractually agreed sharing of control over an economic activity.

Joint ventures may take many forms, but three broad types are typical: jointly controlled operations, jointly controlled assets, and jointly controlled entities. With respect to joint ventures involving operations and assets rather than entities, IAS 31 requires recognition of the venturer's involvement on the basis of its share in the operations or assets. However, with jointly controlled entities, a choice of two alternatives is provided for preparing consolidated financial statements. The reason for this is that this issue is still a matter of some controversy internationally.

The Benchmark Treatment recommended by the IASB is to use the proportionate consolidation approach by either combining its share of the joint venture's assets, liabilities, income, and expenses on a line-by-line basis with the consolidated group amounts or by including separate line items for its joint ventures in the consolidated financial statements. The Allowed Alternative Treatment is to use the equity method, whereby the share of net income and net assets in joint ventures is brought into the accounts as a single-line item with further information given about the various joint ventures involved in the notes to the accounts.

Whatever method is used, information disclosures are required for contingencies and capital commitments, as are a listing and description of the venturer's interests in significant joint ventures and the proportion of ownership interest it holds in controlled entities. Furthermore, where a venturer uses the line-by-line method of proportionate consolidation or equity method, there must be disclosures of the aggregate amounts of current assets, long-term assets, current liabilities, long-term liabilities, and income and expenses relating to its joint venture interests.

GOODWILL AND INTANGIBLES

The Significance of Intangible Assets

There has been a dramatic growth in the significance of intangible assets relative to the tangible assets of MNEs. A number of major factors are responsible for this growth, including the continuing wave of international mergers, the pursuit of global market leadership often through the development or acquisition of famous brand names, the worldwide expansion of the services sector, the speed and extent of technological change with special reference to the impact of information technology, and the growing sophistication and integration of international financial markets.

As a result, the problems accounting for intangibles including goodwill, brands, patents, and R&D, have been highlighted and have aroused considerable controversy. Many of these problems have yet to be resolved in theory or in practice, and there is currently a variety of accounting treatments that are considered acceptable in the international corporate context.

International Significance   Accounting for intangibles is an issue of major international significance and cannot be dealt with in national isolation. If the arising problems are to be resolved, a substantial effort will be needed in research and experimentation as well as in consultation among all parties concerned internationally. Research and experimentation will likely promote a better understanding of the nature of practice, the reasons underlying the choice of particular valuation methods and disclosures, and the feasibility of new approaches. Wide-ranging consultation and negotiation among standard-setting agencies are also necessary if an international agreement is to be reached on an appropriate regulatory framework for intangible assets.

A statement of the objectives and concepts underlying financial statements—or a conceptual framework—may be useful in providing a basis for evaluating alternative methods of accounting for intangible assets. In this respect, the conclusions of the International Accounting Standards Board (IASB), in Framework for the Preparation and Presentation of Financial Statements (1989), provide some guidance.

In the IASB's framework it is generally accepted that the objective of financial statements is to provide useful information to a wide range of users for decision-making purposes and to keep management accountable for the resources entrusted to them. Such information must be "relevant and reliable." In addition, "accrual accounting" should be used subject to the application of "prudence" when appropriate. Furthermore, the information provided should be "comparable" and "understandable."

Intangible Assets and the Balance Sheet   The purpose of the balance sheet is to provide an indication of the financial strength of a company in a way that should help users to judge the company's ability to meet its obligations. In this context, a key issue is whether the balance sheet should reflect the purchase cost of assets or their value in economic terms, or both. Unfortunately, this question is not resolved by the IASB's conceptual framework—indeed, there appears to have been a conscious attempt to avoid tackling what is undoubtedly a matter of some controversy.

A key concept governing the reporting of assets in the balance sheet is that of "recognition." This requires not only the expectation of future economic benefits but also the measurement of the assets with sufficient reliability, keeping in mind the need to exercise prudence in judging the uncertainty of future outcomes.

Because intangible assets tend to lack physical substance, an important criterion influencing recognition is that intangibles can be identified as resources that indicate the financial strength of a company and its ability to meet its obligations. In this context, the "separability" of the asset would seem likely to weigh heavily in the identification decision in that this would indicate the potential for realization without necessarily threatening the viability of the business as a going concern. At the same time, the criterion of reliable measurement is important but necessarily becomes more judgmental and problematic in the case of intangible assets.

The implementation of objectives and concepts governing financial statements requires considerable interpretation and judgment, especially when concepts conflict. The fundamental unresolved problem is how to decide on an appropriate tradeoff between "relevance" and "reliability" in the provision of useful information to investors and other users. It is therefore difficult to be optimistic that the conceptual framework approach will resolve the problems of intangible assets.

The Stock Market Perspective

Efficient market theory suggests that in highly developed securities markets, such as the United Kingdom and the United States, share prices quickly reflect all publicly available information. The research findings on this issue show that this is in fact the case. The implication of these findings is that it is not the accounting treatment of items such as intangible assets that really matters (i.e., whether they are capitalized or not, how amortized, and so on). More important is the disclosure of relevant information about intangibles and how they have been accounted for. Regardless of accounting treatment, the economic substance of the information disclosed will be incorporated in share prices, provided that there is full disclosure. Following from this, it is important to ensure that sufficiently detailed information is disclosed about the nature and treatment of intangible assets so that users can make their own assessments about the treatment adopted and evaluate the likely effects of using alternative treatments.

On the other hand, not everyone is convinced that markets are efficient and that financial analysts are capable of adjusting for differences in accounting treatments across companies and also countries. This skepticism is increased regarding assessments over time. There is evidence, however, that analysts adjust reported corporate earnings to exclude profits/losses on the sale of property and amortization/valuation adjustments, where these occur, with respect to goodwill. For stock (share) valuation purposes, it would seem the focus is on recurring profits and future cash flow. In addition, there is no doubt that market participants draw on a wide range of information in making their recommendations and decisions. There is also a strong psychological element involved. The securities markets are also significantly affected in general terms by economic and political factors at both the national and international levels.

Regardless of views on market efficiency, it is important for companies to disclose as much information as possible about their affairs, within competitive limits, and to communicate this information effectively in a variety of ways. Such information should not be restricted to accounting information in the financial statements but extended to include qualitative information and quantitative nonfinancial information. In this way, any limitations inherent in financial statements and accounting conventions should be largely overcome and fairer stock (share) prices set.

GOODWILL

The dramatic growth of international mergers and acquisitions together with the major expansion in the service industries, where intangible assets are much more significant, has highlighted the significance of goodwill and the problem of how to account for it. Goodwill, in this context, is the excess of the purchase price for the company as a whole over the fair (current) value of the net assets acquired by the bidding company. This is commonly referred to as *purchased goodwill* and is, in effect, a premium paid to reflect the future earning capacity of the acquisition. Goodwill may, of course, be negative if the purchase price is less than the fair value of the net assets acquired. Another way of looking at goodwill is to define it as the difference between the value of a company or business taken as a whole and the value of its individual assets less liabilities.

With respect to business combinations. it should be noted that goodwill only arises in the context of purchase accounting. Where the pooling-of-interests method is used, the nominal value of the shares issued rather than the market value of the consideration is recognized, with the result that goodwill does not become an issue.

The crux of the problem with goodwill is that it is unlike other assets in that it incorporates the value of future earnings, and it relates to the valuation of the business as a whole. Accordingly, it is currently a matter of considerable controversy as to whether goodwill should be treated as an asset for accounting purposes and, if so, whether or not it should be amortized against future earnings. This is an important issue because profits are used as a significant indicator of business performance. Moreover, if assets are indicators of financial strength, then the question arises whether the "value" of goodwill is relevant in contrast to the traditional emphasis on the existence and cost of tangible assets.

Choice of Accounting Methods

In practice, a variety of approaches is evident in many countries and, depending on the accounting requirements concerned, companies may be able to write off the cost of goodwill directly against reserves (shareholders' equity) or capitalize goodwill as an asset, with or without amortization.

Asset without Amortization   Proponents of this method argue that purchased goodwill should be capitalized on the grounds that future economic benefits are expected for which valuable consideration has been given, and in a successful business, the value of goodwill does not decline because it is being continuously maintained. If goodwill were to be amortized, then this would be double counting (i.e., the cost of maintaining the goodwill plus the amortization cost). Thus, there is no need to amortize goodwill against earnings. Goodwill is also part of the cost of the investment, and to amortize it against the earnings from the investment is to confuse the measurement of earnings with that of the capital invested. It is recognized, however, that periodic revaluations of goodwill may be necessary to recognize any reductions in the value of capital and that in such cases these amounts should be treated as charges against equity or earnings.

Opponents of this method argue that it is inconsistent to treat purchased goodwill as an asset but not internally generated goodwill. Furthermore, purchased goodwill should not be retained indefinitely as an asset because such goodwill is being continuously replaced by new goodwill generated internally since acquisition. It is also argued that the recoverability of purchased goodwill has a high degree of uncertainty in that such goodwill relates to the future of the company as a whole.

Asset with Annual Impairment Testing   Proponents of this method also argue that goodwill should be capitalized on the grounds that future economic benefits are expected for which valuable consideration has been given. Further, they argue that not all goodwill declines in value, and even when it does, it does not decline on a straight-line basis. Therefore, straight-line amortization does not represent economic reality. If it were feasible, goodwill would be divided into its discernible parts and be assessed as finite or infinite and amortized accordingly. However, this method in practice would require numerous subjective judgments and would provide opportunity for manipulation. Instead, proponents of this method argue that goodwill should be tested on an annual basis for impairment. Amortization should not be used because goodwill can have both finite and infinite lives. Furthermore, goodwill cannot be revalued upward, and impairment loss recognized cannot be reversed in future periods. Proponents argue that nonamortization is consistent with how entities manage their business and how investors view goodwill.

Opponents of this method argue that goodwill is a finite asset and that the nonamortization approach essentially allows acquisitive companies to capitalize internally generating goodwill. They argue that this is inconsistent with the general accounting model and gives favor to companies that grow through acquisitions rather than those that grow internally. Most opponents favor amortizing goodwill over 20 years as a below the line item.

Asset with Systematic Amortization   Proponents of this method view purchased goodwill as an asset embodying future economic benefits for which consideration has been given. They believe, however, that goodwill is a cost of resources that will be used up and therefore, should be systematically amortized against earnings. Consistent with the accrual accounting concept, it is argued that costs should be matched against revenues. Goodwill is viewed as similar to other assets that are consumed or used up in the production of future earnings. If goodwill is not amortized, then future earnings would be overstated because there would be a failure to include all the costs incurred to generate such earnings. Furthermore, where any permanent diminution in value occurs, then the effect of any such revaluation should be charged against earnings immediately.

Opponents of this method argue that double counting occurs because expenditures to maintain goodwill are made at the same time as the amortization of purchased goodwill. It is also very difficult to estimate when the goodwill will be exhausted, if at all, and hence the period of amortization will be arbitrary, with a consequently arbitrary and potentially severe impact on earnings. It is argued that amortization, in any event, represents an unrealized loss, not a cash outflow.

Immediate Write-Off   This method is favored by those who argue that purchased goodwill is not an asset for the purposes of financial statements. Goodwill is not separable or independently realizable but exists only by virtue of a valuation of the company or business as a whole. Unlike other productive resources, it is not consumed or used up. Furthermore, the true value of goodwill has no predictive relationship to the costs paid on acquisition in that its value will fluctuate over time according to a variety of economic factors and changes in investor opinion. Comparability between firms is also enhanced in that neither purchased nor internally generated goodwill is recognized as an asset. Accordingly, goodwill is written off against equity (i.e., realized or unrealized reserves including retained earnings) with no charges made against current earnings. Alternatively, the write-off can be shown in a special reserve as a separate negative amount or as a "dangling debit" in the liabilities section of the financial statements, which in effect reduces the equity of the company. A variant of this approach, however, is to write off goodwill immediately against current earnings but usually as an extraordinary or nonrecurring item.

Opponents of this method argue that purchased goodwill is indeed an asset embodying expected future benefits and should be treated as such either with or without amortization. There are likely to be problems with writing off large amounts of goodwill, especially in the case of service companies (with limited tangible assets) and highly acquisitive companies, to the extent that equity may become depleted or even negative and gearing or leverage unduly high. In such situations, the stated financial position would be a misleading indicator of the financial strength of the company.

Comparative National Practices

A variety of approaches to accounting for goodwill is evident in many countries. In a review of countries from different parts of the world, it is clear that the regulations in most countries are fairly flexible, with companies permitted to either treat goodwill as an asset subject to systematic amortization or to write it off immediately against equity (see Exhibit 8.3). Only in a minority of countries (e.g., Switzerland) is goodwill permitted to be capitalized without amortization. However, in recent years, the United States adopted the asset with annual impairment testing method. Other countries and the IASB followed the lead of the United States and also adopted the asset with annual impairment testing method. With the EU's adoption of IFRS in 2005, European countries will also be using impairment testing for their consolidated reporting.

Where the amortization treatment is adopted, a maximum period of amortization is stated in only a minority of cases. Many countries specify only that amortization should be based on the criterion of "useful economic life." In practice, companies adopt a variety of amortization periods to suit their circumstances.

Where an arbitrary period is stated, it is not necessarily the period used in practice. In Japan, the majority of companies immediately write off goodwill on consolidation against current earnings, the incentive being that it is deductible for tax purposes. It should be noted, however, that these amounts are usually small because of the relatively lower number of mergers taking place, compared to the United States and the United Kingdom, and the potential for more nonconsolidated subsidiaries in accordance with the existing regulations. In the United States, it seems that a 5- to 10-year amortization period is common, though most large companies have used up to 40 years, especially those making significant acquisitions. In this context, it is interesting to note a number of MNEs based, for exam-

Exhibit 8.3   Accounting for Purchased Goodwill

	Asset with Amortization	Immediate Write-off against Reserves
Australia	No—subject to impairment tests	No
Brazil	Yes	No
Canada	No—subject to impairment tests	No
France	No—subject to impairment tests	No
Germany	No—subject to impairment tests	No
Greece	No—subject to impairment tests	No
Hong Kong	Yes	Yes
India	Yes—maximum period normally 5 years	No
Italy	No—subject to impairment	No
Japan	Yes—maximum period of 5 years	No
Kenya	No—subject to impairment	No
Philippines	Yes—maximum period 40 years	No
Singapore		Yes
South Africa	No—subject to impairment tests	No
Spain	No—subject to impairment tests	No
Sweden	No—subject to impairment tests	No
Switzerland	Yes	Yes
Thailand	Yes	Yes
United Kingdom	No—subject to impairment tests	No
United States	No—subject to impairment tests	No
IASB	No—subject to impairment tests	No

ple, in France, Germany, Italy, Sweden, and Switzerland adopting a 40-year amortization period consistent with practice in the United States. Electrolux in Sweden, for example, adopted a 40-year period for its American acquisitions, apparently contrary to Swedish law and professional standards, on the grounds that this was in accordance with international practice. However, this was before a new Swedish accounting standard was issued that imposed a 20-year maximum period of amortization and prohibited the immediate write-off method.

In Australia, Canada, France, Japan, the Philippines, Spain, Sweden, and the United States, for example, the method of immediate write-off against equity is not permitted. On the other hand, the majority European practice, along with many other economies, including Brazil, Hong Kong, Kenya, Malaysia, Nigeria, South Africa, and Thailand, tends to be more flexible. Prior to the European Union's Seventh Directive on consolidated accounts, it was common practice in France and Germany for goodwill, arising from consolidation, to be capitalized as an asset without amortization in the balance sheet. With the implementation of the EU Seventh Directive, this practice has been eliminated. The directive gave companies a choice between the systematic amortization of goodwill against earnings over a period not exceeding the useful economic life of the asset or its immediate write-off against equity. Furthermore, EU companies will be required to capitalize goodwill as an asset subject to annual impairment testing starting in 2005, with the adoption of IFRS for consolidated entities.

In the United Kingdom, prior to 1998, the immediate write-off method became the preferred method in practice, mainly because of its favorable effect on reported future earnings. Not only was no amortization of goodwill charged, but the flexible U.K. approach permitted provisions for reorganization costs and anticipated future losses to be offset against the value of net assets acquired, thus enhancing the amount of goodwill to be written off with a further beneficial effect on future earnings. However, these provisions, other adjustments to fair values, and changes in accounting policy must now be disclosed, and any provisions relating to the organization must be treated as part of the postacquisition results of the business combination. The majority of large companies in Germany and the Netherlands followed the U.K. trend toward using the immediate write-off method. On the other hand, the U.K. approach was criticized by U.S. companies on the grounds that U.K. companies had a competitive advantage in making takeover bids internationally because they escaped the burden of goodwill amortization against future earnings hitherto required in the United States. In this regard, the differences between U.K. and U.S. rules were highlighted by Blue Arrow (U.K.) (now Manpower-U.S.) in reporting earnings for 1989 of £65 million under U.K. rules but losses of £686 million under U.S. rules, the main reason being that any goodwill amortization or write-downs in the United States had to be charged against earnings. U.S. concern over this issue has been mitigated recently, however, by the decision to allow goodwill amortization charges to be tax deductible in certain circumstances. Most recently (2001), the FASB has required that amortization of goodwill be dependent on annual impairment tests; that is, if the value of goodwill is less than that capitalized, there would be a charge against income equivalent to the impairment amount concerned.

The problem in the United Kingdom was that with the dramatic growth in merger activity, the amounts written off against equity became so large that many companies became concerned about the effect on the perceived strength of the balance sheet and the degree of gearing of leverage. For example, Saatchi and Saatchi, with negative shareholders' equity, and Hanson, with a negative profit and loss account reserve, both reinstated purchased goodwill in pro forma accounts for the purposes of calculating borrowing limits. This problem has also seemingly motivated some companies, especially in the services sector where the treatment of goodwill has had the most impact, to review their policy toward intangibles and, for example, to treat brands, together with trademarks, patents, licenses, copyrights, publishing rights, and so on, as assets for balance sheet purposes.

In the United Kingdom, the Accounting Standards Board (ASB) has now imposed more restrictive requirements on companies, whereby the amortization method is the only method permitted for the treatment of goodwill. This includes a presumed maximum period of amortization of 20 years, except in special circumstances where purchased goodwill has an indeterminate life believed to be greater than 20 years. In such cases, it can be accounted for as an asset subject to an annual review of its value and assessment of any impairment losses to be charged against income.

International Accounting Standards

The International Accounting Standards Board (IASB) in its revisions of IAS 22 (1993 and 1998), concerning "business combinations," eliminated the immediate write-off method and adopted the asset-with-amortization method. The standard required systematic amortization (usually on a straight-line basis) over a period not exceeding 20 years, unless a longer period could be justified. However, IAS 22 was eliminated with the creation of IFRS 3, which requires that goodwill be tested annually for impairment, much like the treatment required in the United States.

Conclusions

Accounting for goodwill continues to be a major issue of growing significance and controversy, with a variety of treatments in many countries. Although capitalization without amortization is a minority practice, many countries adopt a flexible approach and permit either capitalization with systematic amortization, annual impairment testing, or immediate write-off against equity. In practice, many larger MNEs treat goodwill as an asset subject to systematic amortization. However, only in a small number of countries is a maximum period of amortization specified, the norm being to require amortization over the useful economic life of the asset.

Applying the criterion of "separability," goodwill would not seem to qualify as an asset in the conventional accounting context, given that goodwill is the difference between the value of a business taken as a whole and the sum of its individual assets and liabilities. The problem is that goodwill cannot be unbundled from the business and disposed of as a separate asset. On the other hand, the measurement of purchased goodwill can be carried out with a reasonable degree of certainty, which seems to meet the "reliability" criterion, although this becomes more difficult when deciding on an appropriate period of amortization. Furthermore, because goodwill is a cost incurred with the expectation of future economic benefits, it does appear to meet the "relevance" criterion for asset recognition. Clearly, there is no easy solution to the debate, given the persuasive arguments supporting each of the methods proposed.

At the same time, proposals involving the arbitrary treatment of goodwill do not appear desirable in that there could be negative and unforeseen economic consequences relating to stock market reaction, managerial motivation, takeover activity, and financing policy. Given the controversy involved, we suggest that at the present time a flexible approach to goodwill appears preferable, permitting either immediate write-off against equity or capitalization as an asset, with or without amortization or impairment, depending on the nature of the goodwill concerned. However, such flexibility should be subject to full disclosure of the method used; the reasons for using it; and the assumptions, calculations, and amounts involved to the extent that the data will permit the application of alternative methods. This approach is consistent with the view that from a securities market perspective it is disclosure of the relevant information, not its treatment, that really matters.

Given the growing significance of goodwill, corporations should be permitted to incorporate goodwill as an asset in the balance sheet without amortization where this can be justified—but subject to annual review on a systematic basis and, when necessary, appropriate write-down due to impairment. In other words, a more valuation-oriented approach to the balance sheet could be encouraged. This approach is also consistent with the view that goodwill amortization should not be charged against earnings because the cost of maintaining goodwill is already being accounted for. In any event, financial analysts will eliminate goodwill amortization in making their own valuations of a business. If the value of goodwill is maintained and its life is sufficiently long, it is questionable whether there should be any necessity to amortize it in accordance with the regulations. Clearly, where write-downs or amortization are necessary, such amounts should be identified separately and their details reported.

We also suggest that information disclosures relevant to goodwill and its maintenance, both internally generated and purchased, should be made, within competitive limits. Included here could be information about brands, advertising, market share, innovation, human resources including management, and so on. Consideration could also be given to the presentation of goodwill adjustments, regardless of method, in a separate statement of total gains and losses incorporating other equity adjustments such as asset revaluations and foreign currency translation adjustments.

BRANDS, TRADEMARKS, PATENTS, AND RELATED INTANGIBLES

The pursuit of "globalization" by many MNEs has become associated with the acquisition of famous brand names, as well as trademarks, patents, licenses, franchises, publishing titles, and so on, as a means of rapidly obtaining market share, especially in the service industries. The purchase price of acquired brands is commonly included in the payment of goodwill. Thus, the accounting treatment of brands and related intangibles is closely associated with issues arising in the context of goodwill.

The identification of brand accounting as an issue has arisen from the practice in some countries, notably Australia, France, and the United Kingdom, of putting a separate valuation on acquired brands and including them as assets in the balance sheet. While this is controversial enough, there have also been instances of homegrown as well as acquired brands being capitalized. In some cases, entity as well as product brand names have also been capitalized.

It has been argued that a major reason for capitalizing brands is the result of the controversy over goodwill and, in particular, the practice of immediate write-off, which has the consequence of depleting shareholders' funds. Incorporating brand valuations in balance sheets would restore equity and enhance borrowing capacity. In so doing, it could also, in the U.K. context, facilitate takeovers without consultation with shareholders as required by the London Stock Exchange rules for major transactions, for such transactions are defined in terms of size relative to corporate assets. Another reason for capitalizing brands is that some corporations perceived themselves to have been undervalued by the stock market, and thus vulnerable to takeover, because they did not explicitly recognize the value of their brands. This view was highlighted by the Nestlé (Switzerland) takeover of Rowntree (United Kingdom), where it was claimed that the hostile bid succeeded because of the stock market's lack of appreciation of brand values.

Choice of Accounting Methods

In practice, a wide variety of approaches to accounting for brands and related intangibles is evident, with companies in some countries able to capitalize brands as assets, with or without amortization.

Asset without Amortization   Proponents of this method argue that acquired brands and similar intangibles should be capitalized on the grounds that future economic benefits are expected for which valuable consideration has been given. The value of brands does not decline because it is being continuously maintained through advertising expenditure, sales promotion, and so on. Thus, there is no need to amortize brands against earnings. Brands are considered to be identifiable intangible assets, which can be valued albeit with some judgment involved. It is recognized, however, that there may be instances where either amortization is appropriate or revaluations are necessary with consequent write-downs. The principle of capitalizing brands can also be extended to homegrown brands on the grounds of consistency, comprehensiveness, and comparability.

Opponents argue, however, that while brands are valuable assets, it is impossible to assess the expected future economic benefits with a reasonable degree of certainty. Furthermore, it is very difficult to identify and assess the value of a brand as a separate asset. Although a brand may have legally separable property rights attached, such as trademarks, patents, and designs, they are not themselves the entire brand but only a part of it. There is also a variety of alternative valuation methods that can be used, including historical cost, market valuation, current cost, the allocation of the purchased cost of goodwill, discounted cash flow, and the use of earnings multiples, all of which involve varying degrees of subjective judgment.

Asset with Systematic Amortization   Proponents of this method argue that while acquired brands may be viewed as assets embodying future economic benefits, they are a cost incurred that will be used up in generating future earnings. Such costs should be systematically amortized against earnings consistent with the accrual accounting concept.

On the other hand, opponents argue that if the value of brands is being continually maintained by advertising expenditure and other means, then amortization is inappropriate unless there is evidence to the contrary. If amortization is appropriate, then it should be over the useful economic life of the asset, not an arbitrary period.

Immediate Write-Off   The immediate write-off approach is supported by the argument that brands and related intangibles are not assets for balance sheet purposes because they are not separable from other associated assets, both tangible and human, nor independently realizable. Furthermore, it is not possible to assess the future economic benefits of brands with a reasonable degree of certainty. It is argued, therefore, that "prudence" should govern the "recognition" decision. Accordingly, the cost of brands should be written off immediately against equity or earnings consistent with the treatment of goodwill. This treatment would also enhance comparability between firms.

Opponents of this method, however, argue that brands are indeed assets and should be recognized as such with or without amortization. It is argued that a valuation approach is desirable because it is more relevant to users in providing information about the substance of the business.

Although many countries recognize the cost of acquired trademarks, patents, and similar intangibles as assets, the issue of accounting for "brands" is relatively new and controversial. The controversy has arisen from the recent practice of some large companies, especially in Australia, France, and the United Kingdom, of identifying brands as intangible assets. In Australia, it has been accepted practice for some time now to value licenses, copyrights, and publishing rights, with a similar practice now being followed more recently in the United Kingdom.

Some countries, notably the United States, use a combination of the asset-without-amortization method and the asset-with-systematic-amortization method. If the intangible asset is deemed to have a finite life, it should be amortized over that life, or over the best estimate of that life. However, if the intangible asset is believed to have an infinite life, the asset is not subject to amortization but rather annual impairment testing. Should the classification of an asset change from one with a finite life to one with an infinite life, or vice versa, the accounting treatment should also change and the asset should be tested for impairment. For example, if an intangible asset that is not being amortized is subsequently determined to have a finite life, it should be tested for impairment and should then be amortized over the remaining useful life.

Most companies have valued only acquired brands, usually on the basis of allocating an appropriate proportion of the cost of goodwill, but there have been companies that have valued both homegrown and acquired brands. The valuation approach used here was apparently based on a "current cost" approach and permitted by U.K. company law under the alternative valuation rules introduced following the EU Fourth Directive (1978). Curiously, these rules do not permit a market valuation to be used. Where current cost is the valuation basis, then annual revaluations are necessary. The capitalization of homegrown brands and other intangibles except goodwill is also permitted. This is now common practice among those companies valuing brands. Although a valuation approach seems more relevant, one problem is that the companies concerned have provided very little information about the valuation process involved. This makes the valuations difficult to interpret, with the resulting uncertainty likely to undermine confidence from a securities market perspective.

Although accounting for brands does not yet appear to have become a major issue elsewhere, the international treatment of intangibles such as trademarks, patents, and licenses, tends to be flexible. In continental Europe, for example, the normal practice is for such items to be recognized as assets and then systematically amortized over their useful economic lives. On the other hand, many companies write off intangibles immediately against equity. In the EU, the Fourth Directive states that intangible assets, including internally developed assets, may be recognized in the balance sheet. Under the directive, trademarks, patents, licenses, and similar rights are specifically permitted to be included. But if so, they must be systematically amortized over their useful economic lives or written down to reflect any reductions in value. In some countries, (e.g., France), capitalization without amortization is acceptable if there is no limit to the useful life of the asset concerned.

Under the alternative valuation rules of the Fourth Directive (Article 33), it appears that a current cost valuation of intangible assets is permitted as an alternative to historical cost. The EU countries are required to recognize intangible assets according to IFRS beginning in 2005 for consolidated statements.

In Canada and the United States, identifiable intangible assets such as trademarks, patents, licenses, and copyrights, are recognized as assets and treated similarly to goodwill. Internally developed intangibles, on the other hand, must be written off immediately against earnings.

International Accounting Standards

In 1998, the IASB issued IAS 38 "Intangible Assets," which superseded IAS 4 and IAS 9 on "Depreciation" and "Research and Development Costs," respectively. The standard was subsequently modified in 2004. Intangible assets such as brands, trademarks, and patents are permitted to be recognized only if it is probable that the future economic benefits that are attributable to the asset will flow to the enterprise and that the cost of the asset can be measured reliably. In this regard, internally generated brands, mastheads, publishing titles, customer lists, and similar items should not be recognized as assets (para. 51).

For those assets that are recognized, systematic amortization is required for assets determined to have finite lives, and the assets are amortized over their useful lives. For assets determined to have infinite lives, the asset is not amortized but is tested for impairment at least annually.

Conclusions

Accounting for brands, trademarks, patents, and similar intangible assets is currently a highly controversial issue. These assets are treated in a variety of ways in different countries. Problems associated with the treatment of these kinds of intangibles would seem to be closely linked to the goodwill issue. The capitalization of brand names has become an issue, particularly in countries where there is a more flexible approach to accounting practice in general and the treatment of goodwill has seriously impacted either earnings or equity. So far as the accounting treatment of brands is concerned, the majority practice is to capitalize them as assets without amortization, including homegrown brands in some cases, but subject to revaluation on a periodic basis as appropriate. Trademarks, patents, and similar intangibles tend to be treated as assets subject to systematic amortization but are retained permanently as assets subject to revaluation where they are viewed as having an unlimited life. A minority of companies adopt the method of immediate write-off against equity.

Applying the criterion of "separability," brand names, especially those purchased, may well qualify as assets. Much will depend on the circumstances of each case to determine whether or not brands can be identified separately for valuation purposes. As regards the "reliability" of measurement, there are many problems involved in making an assessment in that the value of goodwill usually includes the value of brands. Although there is an expectation of future economic benefits, there are a number of alternative approaches to the valuation of brands that can be considered acceptable at the present time. Thus, there is considerable debate as to whether brands can be measured with a reasonable degree of certainty. Again, the problem of striking an appropriate balance between "relevance" and "reliability" needs to be resolved.

We suggest that brands, trademarks, patents, and related intangibles, including those developed internally, should be permitted to be capitalized as assets where they can be identified separately. Such valuations would be subject to annual review and, where necessary, appropriate write-down. In some cases, it may be appropriate for brands to be systematically amortized over their useful economic lives. The significance of brands and similar intangibles is such that a valuation-oriented approach could be encouraged, at least in terms of providing supplementary information. Given the variety of valuation methods available (e.g., economic value, net realizable value or market value, and current cost), comprehensive information should be given about the method used, the basis of revaluation, if any, and the basis for the amortization period adopted where applicable. In the case of brands not identified, additional information could be disclosed within competitive limits for balance sheet purposes, including market share, advertising support, and so on.

RESEARCH AND DEVELOPMENT

Technological change, and in particular change in information technology, has been a dramatic feature of recent decades, and MNEs have played a major role in new developments. The significance of R&D expenditures in the overall business context has increased.

R&D expenditures include direct and indirect costs related to the creation and development of new processes, techniques, applications, and products. It has been suggested that three categories of expenditure can be identified.

1. *Pure research*, which is directed primarily toward the advancement of knowledge in general and not toward any specific practical aim or application.

2. *Applied research*, which is directed primarily toward exploiting the knowledge obtained in pure research and to applying it in an area of business interest.

3. *Development*, which is work directed toward the introduction or improvement of specific products or processes.

A variety of expenditures can be classified under the heading of R&D expenditures, including expenditures on tangible fixed assets, which could be subject to the usual requirements relating to such assets, personnel costs, materials and services, software costs, relevant overhead costs, and the amortization of patents and licenses.

Market research and advertising expenditures may also be considered similar to R&D expenditures and treated accordingly.

A variety of approaches to accounting for R&D are evident around the world (see Exhibit 8.4). It is clear, however, that there is a tendency to adopt a relatively

Exhibit 8.4   Comparative National Practices of Accounting for Research and Development

Country or Area	Asset with Amortization	Maximum Amortization Period	Immediate Write-off Against Earnings
Australia	Yes	Not specified	Yes
Brazil	Yes	Not specified	Yes
Canada	Development costs only[a]	Not specified	Yes
France	Yes	Not specified	Yes
Germany	No	Not applicable	Yes
Greece	Yes	5 years	Yes
Hong Kong	Yes	Not specified	Yes
India	Development costs only[a]	Not specified	Yes
Indonesia	Yes	Not specified	Yes
Italy	Yes	5 years	Yes
Japan	Yes	5 years	Yes
Kenya	Yes	Not specified	Yes
Malaysia	Development costs only[a]	Not specified	Yes
Netherlands	Yes[b]	Not specified	Yes
Philippines	Development costs only[a]	Not specified	Yes
South Africa	Development costs only[a]	Not specified	Yes
Spain	Yes	Not specified	Yes
Sweden	Yes	5 years	Yes
Switzerland	Yes	Not specified	Yes
Thailand	Yes	Not specified	Yes
United Kingdom	Development costs only[a]	Not specified	Yes
United States	No[c]	Not specified	Yes
European Union	Yes	5 years	Yes
IASB	Development costs only[a]	Not specified	Yes[d]

[a] Permitted in specified circumstances in the case of development costs only.
[b] A reserve must be established if R&D costs are capitalized.
[c] Exceptions permitted in specified circumstances in the case of computer software development costs.
[d] Unless development costs satisfy asset recognition criteria, in which case they must be capitalized.

prudent approach to asset recognition and the assessment of expected future economic benefits. While the immediate write-off method is widely accepted, there are varying degrees of acceptance of the alternative method of capitalizing and amortizing R&D expenditures.

Expense Research and Development Costs as Incurred   The most prudent approach is found in countries such as Germany and the United States, where all costs are required to be written off against earnings immediately, unless, of course, tangible assets with alternative uses are involved—such assets being amortized against earnings in the usual way. In the United States, there is also an exception permitted in the case of computer software development costs subject to specified criteria concerning recognition.

Capitalize Development Costs   In many other countries, including Canada, India, Malaysia, the Philippines, South Africa, and the United Kingdom, all research costs must be written off immediately, but development costs may be capitalized in certain specified circumstances and amortized to match the future revenues generated by the asset. The usual specified circumstances include the need to have a clearly identifiable project and related expenditures, as well as the satisfaction of criteria concerning the technical feasibility and commercial and financial viability of the project. All the technical, commercial, and financial issues need to be assessed with a reasonable degree of certainty for the development expenditure to be carried as an asset. Such expenditure is also permitted to be carried forward where a company has been contracted to carry out work for which it is to be reimbursed. In practice, only a minority of large MNEs capitalize development costs. This is probably not surprising in view of the difficult judgments involved, which can lead to problems if circumstances change.

Capitalized All R&D Costs   A small number of countries, including Greece, Italy, Japan, and Sweden, permit the capitalization of R&D expenditure, but they require such amounts to be amortized within a maximum period of five years. In the Netherlands, it is necessary to establish a reserve to match the R&D amounts capitalized. It is pertinent to note here that the EU Fourth Directive on company accounts indicates a maximum amortization period of five years, which does not seem to have been observed, at least in terms of national regulation, in most of the member countries. In contrast, in many economies such as Australia, Brazil, Hong Kong, India, Indonesia, Kenya, Spain, Switzerland, and Thailand, there would seem to be a flexible approach to the treatment of R&D expenditures in that there is often a lack of regulation on the issue, and various methods are practiced.

International Accounting Standards

International Accounting Standard 38 (issued in 1998 and revised in 2004) deals with "Intangible Assets," including research and development, and requires the immediate write-off against earnings of research expenditures. In the case of development costs, these should be similarly expensed unless the development project satisfies specified criteria, including the technical feasibility of the product, the separable identification of the costs involved, the existence of a future market or internal usefulness if it is to be used by the enterprise itself, the existence of adequate resources to develop the product, and the expectation that the costs can be recovered from future revenues from the project. If all these criteria are met, the development costs must be recognized as an asset and amortized on a systematic basis over their useful economic life with a rebuttable presumption that this will not exceed 20 years. The same requirements regarding the review of amortization periods and the recognition of impairment losses apply as in the case of all other intangibles.

Conclusions

Accounting for R&D expenditures has become an increasingly important issue, given the rate of technological change and the significance of such expenditures for many companies. A variety of treatments are used in many countries. While the immediate write-off method is widely accepted, there are varying degrees of recognition across countries of the alternative method of capitalizing R&D expenditures subject to systematic amortization. In this context, a significant number of countries permit capitalization with amortization, but only in the case of development costs and where the technical feasibility and commercial and financial viability of the development project can be assessed with a reasonable degree of certainty. A maximum period of amortization is specified in only a small number of countries. In practice, however, only a minority of companies capitalize development costs.

Applying the criterion of separability, R&D expenditure does not appear to qualify as an asset except in cases where development projects are sufficiently advanced to produce assets such as brands, trademarks, patents, or other assets that can be identified separately from their associated tangible assets and the business as a whole. In such cases, the "relevance" criterion is satisfied. Furthermore, at the development stage of a project, it may be possible, regardless of separability, to assess the future economic benefits of the costs incurred with a reasonable degree of certainty, thus meeting the "reliability" criterion.

We suggest that R&D expenditures should be capitalized but only to the extent of development costs. Capitalization should be subject to evidence concerning a project's technical feasibility and commercial and financial viability. In such cases, systematic amortization would be required over the useful economic life of the project together with annual reviews and periodic revaluation according to the circumstances of the company concerned. In addition, full disclosure should be made of the reasons for the capitalization and the assumptions, calculations, and amounts involved. Additional information about the nature of the projects involved also seems desirable, within competitive limits.

SUMMARY

1. Consolidation is the accepted means of accounting for MNE groups and business combinations. The method of full consolidation involves the aggregation, on a line-by-line basis, of information about the assets, liabilities, revenues, and expenses of the MNE's many individual legal entities into income, financial position, and funds or cash flow statements relating to the MNE as a single economic entity.

2. The methods of proportional and equity consolidation may also be used as an alternative to full consolidation, depending on the involvement of the MNE in the investee corporation.

3. While efforts are being made to develop international accounting and disclosure harmonization relating to consolidated financial statements, there is a variety of regulations and practices at national level.

4. Major problem areas include accounting for mergers and acquisitions, criteria for the consolidation of subsidiaries, fair value adjustments, accounting for goodwill, funds or cash flow statements, accounting for associated companies, and joint venture accounting.

5.   A major area of controversy at the international level has been the treatment of goodwill and related intangibles.

6.   While funds statements are increasingly being provided by MNEs, a recent trend is to either emphasize cash flows or to replace funds statements with a cash flow statement.

7.   Joint venture accounting has become a major issue with the growth of strategic alliances and joint ventures by MNEs, including those with governments and corporations in Russia, Eastern Europe, and China. Accounting for the venturer's interest is a controversial issue but usually takes the form of a choice between proportionate consolidation or the equity method, including supplementary disclosures about joint venture interests.

8.   Accounting for intangible assets is an issue of major international significance in the twenty-first century. The continuing wave of international mergers, the pursuit of globalization, the dramatic expansion in services, and the revolution in information technology have all contributed to the realization that there are fundamental problems in this area that need to be addressed.

9.   Much controversy has surrounded the challenge to traditional accounting concepts and practices, which are currently based on the treatment of physical tangible assets.

10.   Theory and practice concerning the treatment of intangible assets is in a state of flux, with a variety of practices evident worldwide. Harmonization efforts are also at an early stage. No easy solutions are available, nor is there any clear consensus on the issues involved.

11.   If company accounts are to reflect the needs of the new millennium, it can be argued that a major change in thinking is required whereby the nature and importance of intangible assets are given much more weight in the theory and practice of accounting and information disclosure.

12.   A more valuation-oriented approach, at least in terms of supplementary information, seems desirable. The balance of argument is thus tipped more in favor of "relevance" in contrast to "prudence" and "reliability." A more positive attitude toward intangibles would result in the recognition of goodwill, brands, and, in certain cases, R&D as assets in the balance sheet. They would be subject to annual review, and write-down or amortization as appropriate, subject to a careful assessment of the current commercial realities.

13.   The competitive pressures of securities markets internationally suggest the need for companies to be much more open in terms of information disclosure about intangible assets and to place more emphasis on effective communications with the investment community.

Discussion Questions

1.   Why are consolidated financial statements useful? What are the drawbacks of consolidated information?

2.   Compare and contrast the different forms of presentation of consolidated financial statements internationally, making reference to the use of full, proportional, and equity methods of consolidation.

3.   Outline the arguments for and against the use of purchase accounting versus pooling-of-interests accounting for business combinations.

4. Explain the difficulties of consolidation in Japan. Why might different treatment of ownership be necessary in Japan?

5. Why has accounting for goodwill become such a significant problem internationally?

6. While the trend among MNEs around the world is to prepare consolidated financial statements, it has been suggested by experts that such statements may hide more than they reveal. Do you agree?

7. Discuss the relevance of funds and cash flow statements, making reference to recent developments in regulation and practice internationally.

8. How important an issue is joint venture accounting? Why is it so difficult to agree on a harmonized approach to this issue?

9. Discuss the reasoning behind the different treatments of joint ventures, noting the two types identified by the IASB. Which one do you feel is the better alternative?

10. What are the arguments for and against the different accounting for goodwill (write-off, amortize, don't amortize)?

11. How do the different views of market efficiency relate to the treatment of intangibles?

12. Why is it so difficult to resolve the debate over the appropriate accounting treatment of goodwill?

13. What kinds of MNEs are concerned about the valuation of intangible assets? Should regulators adopt a more flexible approach to this issue?

14. To what extent are issues concerning intangible assets important in developing countries?

15. Many countries allow different treatment for R&D expenses. Why is this the case? What do you think the best method is?

Exercises

1. **Simple Purchasing Problem:** Mautz Company is considering buying S&H enterprises, which has the following assets and liabilities. Make the journal entry to record the purchase of S&H if the purchase price is $4,620,000.

S&H	Cost	Fair Market Value
Accounts Receivable	540,000	530,000
Inventory	1,420,000	1,500,000
Property, Plant, and Equipment	2,030,000	4,000,000
Accounts Payable	(630,000)	(630,000)
Notes Payable	(1,300,000)	(1,300,000)
Net Assets	**2,060,000**	**4,100,000**

2. **Simple Pooling Problem:** Assume that Mautz Company and S&H want to merge companies and that the companies have the following assets and liabilities. Create the balance sheet of the two newly merged companies under the pooling method.

S&H	Cost	Fair Market Value
Accounts Receivable	540,000	530,000
Inventory	1,420,000	1,500,000
Property, Plant, and Equipment	2,030,000	4,000,000
Accounts Payable	(630,000)	(630,000)
Notes Payable	(1,300,000)	(1,300,000)
Net Assets	**2,060,000**	**4,100,000**

Mautz Co.	Cost	Fair Market Value
Accounts Receivable	780,000	750,000
Inventory	2,750,000	2,600,000
Property, Plant, and Equipment	3,250,000	6,000,000
Accounts Payable	(820,000)	(820,000)
Notes Payable	(2,500,000)	(2,500,000)
Net Assets	**3,460,000**	**6,030,000**

3. **Simple Consolidation Problem:** Walser Co has 80 percent ownership in Marit Inc. The balance sheets and income statements for the two companies are below. Walser Co's ownership in Marit has been accounted for using the equity method. At the end of 2004, Marit owed $5 to Walser Co. Create the consolidated financial statements for Walser Co.

	Walser	80% Marit	Consolidated
ASSETS			
Cash	100	10	_____
Accounts Receivable	350	50	_____
Inventory	250	20	_____
Plant and Equipment	1400	150	_____
Investment in Marit	88	–	_____
Total Assets	**2188**	**230**	_____
LIABILITIES	**1320**	**120**	_____
Minority Interest			
EQUITY	868	110	_____
TOTAL LIABILITIES AND EQUITY	**2188**	**230**	_____
INCOME			
Sales	1500	400	_____
Income from Sub1	64	–	_____
EXPENSES	**750**	**320**	_____
Minority Interest Income	–	–	_____
Net Income	**814**	**80**	_____

4. **Simple Joint Venture Consolidation:** Cardon Co. and Farrell Inc. embarked on a joint venture to bring technology to undeveloped countries. The venture was named

TechCo, and each company had 50 percent ownership. Create the consolidated financial statements for Cardon Company on a proportional basis.

	Cardon	50% TechCo	Consolidated
ASSETS			
Cash	57	16	_____
Accounts Receivable	146	–	_____
Inventory	350	220	_____
Plant and Equipment	875	170	_____
Investment in TechCo	88	–	_____
Total Assets	**1516**	**406**	_____
LIABILITIES	**1190**	**230**	_____
Minority Interest			
EQUITY	**326**	**176**	_____
TOTAL LIABILITIES AND EQUITY	**1516**	**406**	_____
INCOME			
Sales	875	220	_____
Income from Sub1	15	–	_____
EXPENSES	**630**	**190**	_____
Minority Interest Income	–	–	_____
Net Income	**260**	**30**	_____

5. Perform an Internet search to find an article relating to the issues concerning consolidation.
   a. How does the company/country account for the issue?
   b. What are their arguments behind the treatment? Do you feel their argument is valid?

6. Perform an Internet search to find an article relating to issues concerning goodwill.
   a. How does the company/country account for the issue?
   b. What are their arguments behind the treatment? Do you feel their argument is valid?

7. Perform an Internet search to find an article relating to issues concerning joint ventures.
   a. How does the company/country account for the issue?
   b. What are their arguments behind the treatment? Do you feel their argument is valid?

8. Perform an Internet search to find an article relating to issues concerning research and development costs.
   a. How does the company/country account for the issue?
   b. What are their arguments behind the treatment? Do you feel their argument is valid?

9. Bonanza Group acquired the Bargain Company at the beginning of 2004 for a purchase price of $300 million. The book value of the net assets was stated at $200 million, but at "fair value" this was restated at $220 million. Bonanza's policy is to depreciate

assets subject to revaluation on a straight-line basis over a 10-year period. Bonanza Group's earnings before charging for any goodwill amortization or additional depreciation were $50 million. Bonanza's management was wondering whether a change of headquarters might be a good idea from a reported earnings perspective and decided to consider the position in Japan and the Netherlands compared to the United States. Prepare a comparative schedule showing the net earnings after any goodwill or depreciation adjustments in accordance with generally accepted accounting principles in each of the following countries:

    a.   United States (assume goodwill impairment of 25 percent after 3 years and nothing else)

    b.   Japan (assume goodwill amortization over 5 years)

    c.   Netherlands (assume immediate write-off of goodwill against reserves)

10.   Refer to Exercise 9 above. Compare and contrast your findings across the three countries and discuss the significance of the results from the perspective of both Bonanza's management and international financial analysts.

    Exercises 11–13: In Japan, the pooling method is still permitted in business combinations. Unlike the United States and the United Kingdom, whose groups follow a hierarchical structure, Japan's groups are described as "headless combinations" or Keiretsu and are built around trust and loyalty. As such, it is difficult to distinguish a "parent" corporation among the relationships.

11.   What are some of the problems of using the majority shareholder rule to consolidate Japanese financial statements?

12.   What are the reasons behind using a pooling method over a purchase method?

13.   What effect do these different treatments have on the financial statements?

    Exercises 14–15: Hambert Company, located in the United Kingdom, researches different diseases in order to develop medicine to combat them. During the year, Hambert spent over $2.4 million researching various conditions such as cancer, diabetes, and depression. It also spent $1.2 million to determine the effects of different chemicals on improving diabetes. From this information, Hambert spent $500,000 in an effort to introduce a drug for improving diabetes. At the end of the year, Hambert had also spent $3.2 million in an attempt to learn more about a specific aspect of depression, which might be treatable.

14.   Separate the costs into the categories of pure research, applied research, and development. According to U.K. law, which costs should be capitalized, if any, and which should be expensed? What are the arguments behind this treatment?

15.   Now assume your company is located in Germany. How do you treat the various costs? What are the arguments behind this treatment?

Case: Multigroup (Switzerland)
Case: Vodafone's Operations

These cases can be found on the following website: www.wiley.com/college/radebaugh

Selected References

Bailey, D. T., ed. 1988. *Accounting in Socialist Countries.* London: Routledge.

Barwise, P., C. Higson, A. Likierman, and P. Marsh. 1989. *Accounting for Brands.* London: London Business School and Institute of Chartered Accountants in England and Wales.

Choi, F. D. S., and C. Lee. 1991. "Merger Premia and National Differences in Accounting for Goodwill." *Journal of International Financial Management and Accounting* 3(3): 219–240.

Deloitte IAS PLUS website. http://www.iasplus.com

Diggle, G., and C. W. Nobes. 1994. "European Rule Making in Accounting: The Seventh Directive as a Case Study." *Accounting and Business Research* (Autumn) 24(96): 319–333.

Financial Accounting Standards Board. http://www.fasb.org

Egginton, Don A. "Towards Some Principles for Intangible Asset Accounting." *Accounting and Business Research* 20(79): 193–205.

European Community. 1983. *Seventh Council Directive on Consolidated Accounts*. Brussels: EC.

European Union website, http://europa.eu.int/

Geringer, J. N., and L. Hebert. 1989. "Control and Performance of International Joint Ventures." *Journal of International Business Studies* 20(2): 235–254.

Gray, S. J. 1988. "Acquisition and Merger Accounting: A United Approach." *Accountant's Magazine* 92(984): 20–23.

Gray, S. J. 1989. "Accounting for Brands: A Mission Impossible?" *Investment Analyst.* (April): 3–5.

Gray, S. J., A. G. Coenenberg, and P. D. Gordon, eds. 1993. *International Group Accounting: Issues in European Harmonization*. London: Routledge.

International Accounting Standards Board website http://www.iasb.org

International Accounting Standards Committee. 1989. *Framework for the Preparation and Presentation of Financial Statements*. London: IASC.

International Accounting Standards Committee. 1992. IAS 7, *Cash Flow Statements*. London: IASC, revised 1989.

International Accounting Standards Committee. 1994. IAS 27, *Consolidated Financial Statements and Accounting for Investments in Subsidiaries*. London: IASC, reformatted.

International Accounting Standards Committee. IAS 28, *Investments in Associates*. IASB. Revised 2003.

International Accounting Standards Committee. 1998. IAS 22, *Business Combinations*. London: IASC, revised.

International Accounting Standards Committee. 1998. IAS 31, *Financial Reporting of Interests in Joint Ventures*. London: IASC, revised.

International Accounting Standards Committee. 1998. IAS 38, *Intangible Assets*.

Needles, Belverd E., Jr. *Financial Accounting*. 8th ed. Boston: Houghton Mifflin, 2000.

Nobes, C. W., and J. E. Norton. 1996. "International Variations in the Accounting and Tax Treatments of Goodwill, and the Implications for Research." *Journal of International Accounting, Auditing and Taxation* 5(2): 179–196.

Taylor, P. A. 1987. *Consolidated Financial Statements*. New York: Harper & Row.

U.K. Accounting Standards Board. 1991. FRS 1, *Cash Flow Statements*. London: ASB (September).

U.K. Accounting Standards Board. 1994. FRS 6, *Acquisitions and Mergers*. London: Accounting Standards Board (September).

U.S. Financial Accounting Standards Board. 1987. "Statement of Financial Accounting Standards No. 94." *Consolidation of All Majority-Owned Subsidiaries*. Stamford, CT: FASB.

U.S. Financial Accounting Standards Board. 1987. "Statement of Financial Accounting Standards No. 95," *Statement of Cash Flows*. Stamford, CT: IASC.

United Nations. 1988. *Conclusions on Accounting and Reporting by Transnational Corporations*. New York: UN, revised 1994.

CHAPTER NINE

INTERNATIONAL SEGMENT REPORTING

Chapter Objectives

- Identify the major uses and users of segment information
- Discuss the major benefits of segment disclosure from the perspective of predictive ability tests and stock market studies
- Highlight the costs of segment disclosures from the standpoint of preparation and disclosure of information to competitors
- Review the segment reporting requirements of the International Accounting Standards Board (IASB)
- Compare the different regulations for segment disclosures around the world, especially in the United States and the United Kingdom.
- Examine the problems of segment reporting in practice and discuss ways to make segment disclosures more useful

INTRODUCTION

In this chapter we discuss issues relating to segment reporting. Segment reporting is the counterpoint to consolidated information in that it involves the disaggregation of the consolidated financial statements.

To the extent that there is a lack of correspondence between the financial statements of the reporting entity and the nature of the corporation's activities, there appears to be a need for disaggregated information in segment reports. Such information would ensure that overall performance, risks, and prospects can be better evaluated by investors, other users, and management and that a more comprehensive accountability can be achieved. Let's consider the users and uses of seg-

---

Strategic Decision Point

In recent years there has been a continuing trend toward diversification by MNEs, especially with regard to geographical activity. This has raised question as to whether consolidated financial statements are adequate where the corporation's operations consist of a number of activities in a variety of location with different profitability, risk, and growth characteristics. Increasingly, companies such as BMW in Germany are providing disaggregated or segment information in addition to what is required in order to better inform investors.

---

ment information, the benefits and costs involved, the regulatory environment, and the problems of segment reporting in practice.

USERS AND USES OF SEGMENT INFORMATION

Investors are likely to be interested in the future cash flows they may obtain by investing in a company as well as the risk of uncertainty of those cash flows. They are, therefore, interested in the performance of an multinational enterprise (MNE) as a whole rather than in the performance of any specific element of the corporation's activities. However, this does not mean that only consolidated information is valuable to them. Both the size and uncertainty of future cash flows are likely to be affected by many factors, including those related to the industries and countries in which a MNE operates. Different industries and different countries have a variety of profit potentials, degrees and types of risk, and growth opportunities. Different rates of return on investment and different capital needs are also likely to exist throughout the various segments of a business. Because of this diversification of operations, there has been a demand for MNEs to report key items of disaggregated information, especially turnover and profits. Such disaggregated or segment data is typically provided for both geographical areas and lines of business.

Segment information is likely to help investors by allowing them to combine company-specific information with external information, thus allowing for a more accurate assessment of both the risks involved and the potential for future growth. In addition, investors can gain an idea of the success of past operations by comparing them with the performance of similar operations. However, for most diversified MNEs, such external yardsticks are not available. In particular, the provision of disaggregated data may allow investors to compare the success of individual segments with those of other corporations. However, given the very large degree of latitude MNEs have in deciding what constitutes a reportable segment, such an advantage of comparability may be more apparent than real. This is the case especially when comparing profit measures: there is often discretion not only in the choice of segments but also in the methods used for common cost allocations and transfer pricing.

Other users may have a direct relationship, not with the MNE as a whole, but with part of it. Disaggregated data regarding the performance of that segment of the company is then relevant to employees, creditors, and host governments. All these groups are likely to be interested in not only the MNE as a whole, but also that sector of the company that most affects themselves. They will often require information that is even more disaggregated than that currently provided. For example, employees are likely to want information at the plant level, host governments at the individual country level, and creditors at the level of the individual subsidiary or legal entity. However, segmentally disaggregated information will go some way toward meeting these information needs. This is especially important for those groups such as employees and developing-country host governments that often lack the power to demand specific information relevant to themselves.

But are the benefits of segment reporting likely to exceed the costs? Is regulation of the reporting process necessary? If so, what form should it take? How should segments be identified? What should be the content of segment reports? How should the items disclosed be measured and presented? First, let's consider the arguments for and against segment reporting and the research findings available so far.

THE BENEFITS OF SEGMENT REPORTING

The possible benefits of segment data have been examined using a variety of research techniques. Many of the earliest attempts simply asked users whether they required such information. Although this approach might have provided some valuable insights, it also suffered from several major problems or limitations. Particularly important are the problems of ignorance and "gaming." If information is not currently provided or is provided by only a few companies, people may inaccurately assess either the value they would derive from such information or the problems and limitations inherent in its use. *Gaming* can occur if the users of financial statements perceive the information contained in them to be costless or a free good; if this is the case, it is in their best interests to overstate the value of any information to persuade companies to provide it. Because of these problems, more direct tests of usefulness are necessary. Such tests are of two types: (1) predictive ability (forecasting) tests and (2) stock market reaction tests (i.e., how the market views the information disclosed).

Predictive ability tests compare the accuracy of forecasts of future sales or earnings based on consolidated data to that of forecasts based on disaggregated data. Because future earnings are one of the main variables investors are interested in, it is assumed that useful information is any information that helps to predict earnings. However, such an approach implicitly assumes that at least some shareholders not only are capable of using but also will use the information provided in this way. Whether or not this is true is unclear, and thus the implications drawn from these indirect tests of usefulness must be considered with some caution. The alternative approach—stock market reaction testing—appears to have somewhat greater validity. The idea is that if information has an effect on the stock market, that information must have been used, and so the usefulness of the data is tested directly. If the information has no effect, it is either irrelevant or has already been obtained from other sources, so there is no need for disclosure.

Research studies concerned with the prediction of earnings have all concluded that forecasts are more accurate if they are based on line-of-business (LOB) segmental data rather than consolidated earnings. Studies using U.S. data have also found that forecasts based on segment earnings are more accurate than forecasts based on segmental turnover. However, this finding has not been supported by U.K. data. In addition, there is some evidence that the relative accuracy of segment-based forecasts may depend on the size of the corporation, with such disclosures being more useful for small corporations.

Few prediction studies have been done relating to geographical segment disclosures, but research by Roberts (1989), using U.K. data, and Balakrishnan, Harris, and Sen (1990), using U.S. data, found similar results to those involving LOB disclosures (i.e., segment-based forecasts outperformed consolidated-based forecasts). More recently, a study by Behn, Nichols, and Street (2002) using U.S. data following the adoption of SFAS 131 in 1997 confirms the predictive ability of geographical segment data and, in particular, the usefulness of defining geographic segments by individual country.

With respect to stock market studies, there is evidence that disclosure of both LOB and geographical segment data results in a decrease in market assessments of risk of the disclosing corporation (i.e., a decrease in variability of stock [share] prices relative to the overall market). However, some of this evidence is inconclusive, with conflicting studies suggesting that such a relationship does not hold. Accounting-based risk measures formed from both geographical disclosures and LOB asset data appear to be correlated to market risk measures. However, LOB disclosures do not appear to have affected the average risk-equalized market returns of the disclosing corporations, although there is some evidence that they have resulted in a decrease in the variability of such returns. With regard to geographical disclosures, research using both U.S. and U.K. data has shown a significant relationship between such disclosures and market risk assessments.

THE COSTS OF SEGMENT REPORTING

Several arguments against segment reporting disclosures have been proposed; some apply to all corporations, others only in certain situations. It has been argued that the cost of compiling, processing, and disseminating such information will exceed the benefits. However, no evidence is available regarding either the costs of disclosure or any precise quantification of the benefits. At any rate, the excessive cost argument has questionable validity in most cases. MNEs need disaggregated information for internal planning and control purposes and so produce some such information already. Even if the information used internally is not in a form suitable for external reporting, it seems unlikely, given the extensive use of computerized information systems, that the generation of such information will be particularly expensive. This is especially true when one realizes just how much discretion companies have in deciding what constitutes a reportable segment. This means that, to a large extent, segments can be identified in such a way as to suit the already existing internal information systems.

Another, and potentially more serious, cost is that of disseminating information that is likely to benefit existing or potential competitors. This argument of competitive disadvantage is often used by MNEs to press for less restrictive information disclosure requirements. Although this may apply at the corporation level, especially if the same requirements do not apply to corporations of other nationalities, it may not be a problem at the level of the entire economy. If such information aids competition and investor evaluation, it might be considered an advantage rather than a cost to society. Whether this is so will depend on attitudes regarding the desirability of aiding competition and will tend to be largely case-specific, depending on the characteristics of the industries and corporations involved. It does not appear, however, that such information may be advantageous when seen in the wider societal perspective.

Another argument against the competitive disadvantage rationale for nondisclosure is that such disclosures are only an attempt, and not a very successful one, to tip the balance back in favor of corporations operating in a single industry or country. The point is that such corporations disclose far more information about their single segment than do any multisegment MNEs.

The major argument against segment information is that in some cases it may be inappropriate and therefore potentially misleading. The disclosure of segment information implicitly assumes that the segments reported are relatively autonomous and independent of each other. This means that the figures reported for any one segment can be assessed independently of a consideration of the performance of the rest of the company. If, instead, the company is highly integrated, not only are relatively large transfers between the segments likely, but the segment results cannot be understood or considered in isolation from the rest of the company. At the extreme, if the company is highly integrated, any disaggregated results are arbitrary enough to be meaningless. Unfortunately, little evidence is available regarding either the extent to which most companies are integrated or what level of interdependence between parts of the company would invalidate segment information. Thus, although this appears to be a significant problem for some companies, it is difficult to gauge its incidence in practice.

INTERNATIONAL FINANCIAL REPORTING STANDARDS

The IASB (formerly IASC) issued IAS 14 in 1981, which fairly closely followed the requirements in the United States at that time. Thus, it required (for both LOB and geographical segments) information on sales, with internal and external revenues shown separately; operating results and identifiable assets, in either absolute or relative terms; and a reconciliation statement to the consolidated accounts. IAS 14 applied to all listed companies that provided consolidated statements. However, in practice, compliance by non-U.S. MNEs was often only partial. In 1997, following a review, a revised IAS 14 "Segment Reporting" was issued which limits the scope of managerial discretion in segment identification. This approach looks to a company's organization structure and internal reporting system as the basis for identifying segments as this should normally provide the best evidence of an enterprise's predominant source of risks and returns. This will determine whether the "primary" segment reporting format will be business segments or geographical segments, with a higher level of disclosure relative to the secondary reporting format. If risks and returns are strongly affected by both and this is reflected in a "matrix" approach to management, then business segments should be used as the primary segment reporting format. The standard, however, does not prohibit a "matrix" presentation with full segment disclosures on each basis. If neither approach is reflected in the internal organizational and management structure, then either business segments or geographical segments should be chosen as the primary format. Reportable segments are those where the majority of revenue is earned from external customers and where segment revenue is 10 percent or more of total revenue.

The disclosure requirement for primary segments (see Exhibit 9.1) comprises revenues (external and intersegment shown separately), operating result (before interest and taxes), carrying amount of segment liabilities, cost incurred to acquire property, plant, equipment, and intangibles, depreciation and amortization, significant noncash expenses, and share of profit or loss of associates or joint ventures. The secondary segment information required comprises revenues (external and intersegment shown separately) carrying amount of segment assets, and cost incurred to acquire property, plant, equipment, and intangibles. There was a loss of information about profits for secondary segments in contrast to the original IAS 14 which required the same information for both business and geographical segments.

REGULATIONS AROUND THE WORLD

U.S. Requirements

To date, the United States has the most extensive accounting requirements in the world. The SEC has required LOB segment disclosures since 1969, but in 1976 the FASB introduced more comprehensive requirements in SFAS 14, *Financial Reporting for Segments of a Business Enterprise*. This regulation required, for both LOB and geographical segments, the disclosure of revenues from unaffiliated customers, intragroup transfers, operating profit or loss of net income, or other profitability measures, and identifiable assets. In addition, for industry segments, companies were required to disclose depreciation, capital expenditure, and equity in the net income and assets of associates. Unfortunately, these requirements did not provide a clear definition of identifiable segments. For example, SFAS 14 stated:

> Foreign geographical areas are individual countries or groups of countries as may be determined to be appropriate in an enterprise's particular circumstances. Factors to be considered include proximity, economic affinity, similarities in business environments and the nature, scale and degree of interrelationship of the enterprise's operations in the various countries (Para. 34).

Only very general guidance was provided for determining what constitutes an identifiable LOB segment:

> No single set of characteristics is universally applicable in determining the industry segments of all enterprises, nor is any single characteristic determinative in all cases. Consequently, determination of an enterprise's industry segments must depend to a considerable extent on the judgment of the management of the enterprise (Para. 12).

Once the segments had been identified, however, clear guidance was given as to what constituted a reportable segment. For geographical segments, these would be reported if segment sales accounted for at least 10 percent of total sales or if identifiable assets accounted for at least 10 percent of total identifiable assets. Similarly,

Exhibit 9.1 Schedule A—Information About Business Segments (All amounts million)

	Paper Products		Office Products		Publishing		Other Operations		Eliminations		Consolidated	
	20×2	20×1	20×2	20×1	20×2	20×1	20×2	20×1	20×2	20×1	20×2	20×1
Revenue												
External sales	55	50	20	17	19	16	7	7				
Inter-segment sales	15	10	10	14	2	4	2	2	(29)	(30)		
Total revenue	70	60	30	31	21	20	9	9	(29)	(30)	101	90
Result												
Segment result	20	17	9	7	2	1	0	0	(1)	(1)	30	24
Unallocated corporate expenses											(7)	(9)
Operating profit											23	15
Interest expense											(4)	(4)
Interest income											2	3
Share of net profits of associates	6	5					2	2			8	7
Income taxes											(7)	(4)
Profit from ordinary activities											22	17
Extraordinary loss: uninsured earthquake damage to factory		(3)										(3)
Net profit											22	14
Other Information												
Segment assets	54	50	34	30	10	10	10	9			108	99
Investment in equity method associates	20	16					12	10			32	26
Unallocated corporate assets											35	30
consolidated total assets											175	155
Segment liabilities	25	15	8	11	8	8	1	1			42	35
Unallocated corporate liabilities											40	55
Consolidated total liabilities											82	90
Capital expenditure	12	10	3	5	5	5	4	3				
Depreciation	9	7	9	7	5	3	3	4				
Non-cash expenses other than depreciation	8	2	7	3	2	2	2	1				

Source: IASB. IAS14 *Segment Reporting* (revised 1997).

LOB segments would be separately disclosed if either of these requirements were met or if segment profits or losses accounted for at least 10 percent of the profits or losses of all segments that incurred a profit or loss, respectively.

Following a review of SFAS 14, the FASB (working jointly with the Canadian Accounting Standards Board) issued a new standard SFAS 131 in 1997, which limits managerial discretion in segment identification by requiring segments to be consistent with a company's organization structure and internal reporting systems. The new standard SFAS 131 requires disclosures for each reportable segment similar to IAS 14. Reportable segments may be based on lines of business, geographic location, or a combination of both. Additional information is required about the geographic areas of operations if the reportable segment disclosures do not provide this. This second tier of reporting is referred to as enterprisewide disclosures and requires disclosure for: (1) the country of domicile, (2) any individually material country, and (3) all foreign countries in the aggregate. Thus, aggregate information by continent or geographic area groupings as often provided hitherto is no longer permitted. However, while revenue and asset disclosures are required at this level, profits disclosures are not, thus resulting in a loss of information compared to SFAS 14 similar to the IASC's original IAS 14 (Nichols, Street, and Gray, 2000).

SFAS 131 is very similar to the IASB's revised IAS 14 (1997), and now the IASB and FASB are working to even more closely align IAS 14 with SFAS 131 in the context of their global convergence project.

U.K. Requirements

In the United Kingdom, segment disclosure requirements were first introduced by the London Stock Exchange in 1965 and were subsequently incorporated in the 1967 Companies Act with respect to LOB disclosures of sales and profits.

Following the European Union (EU) Fourth and Seventh Directives, the Companies Acts of 1981 and 1989 (now incorporated in the 1985 Companies Act, as amended) required the disclosure of geographical segment turnover, together with LOB disclosure of both sales and profit before tax. The LOB profits disclosure requirement was subsequently repealed in 1996. Geographical profits disclosures were not required, although they were specified as a required disclosure, albeit with some flexibility, by the London Stock Exchange. The Companies Act also states that if any market or class of business is immaterial (a term not defined), it may be combined with another. Even more discretion is given to companies in the additional statement that "if disclosure is seriously prejudicial to the interest of the company that information need not be disclosed" (Schedule 4, para. 55[5]), it being sufficient instead to state that such disclosures have not been made. The only guidance the Companies Act provides regarding segment identification is the statement, "the directors of the company should have regard to the manner in which the company's activities are organized" (para. 55[3]).

The most important new requirement was that such information should be provided in the notes to the accounts, thus falling within the scope of the audit. However, the Companies Act still fails to tackle the more serious problem of segment identification: there are not definitions of what "material" is or what a reportable segment is; consequently, either lack of disclosure or misleading disclosures is possible. Emmanuel and Gray (1977) have shown that leaving this to the discretion of management has led to inadequate or inconsistent disclosures by many large U.K. corporations. Even if such discretion does not encourage deliberate manipulation, "no amount of sophisticated data can remedy the damage caused by segments wrongly identified in the first place."

More recently (1990), an accounting standard SSAP 25, *Segmental Reporting,* was issued by the Accounting Standards Committee. This extended existing legal and stock exchange requirements by requiring the disclosure of segment net assets for both LOB and geographical segments. In addition, geographical segmentation of sales was required both by source—that is, location of production or service facilities—and destination. Geographical segmental profits disclosures were also required, as well as LOB profits disclosures. These changes brought the scope of U.K. regulation to a level similar to that of the United States, if not in the same amount of detail.

Requirements in Other Countries

Many other countries also require segment information; notably, Australia and Canada have extensive requirements comparable to those in the United Kingdom and the United States. In the EU countries, the EU Fourth (1978) and Seventh (1983) Directives have set a minimum requirement of disclosure (i.e., sales by line of business and geographical area). While the United Kingdom goes well beyond this, most European countries have adopted a more secretive approach, though in practice many MNEs go beyond the minimum (e.g., Philips in the Netherlands [see Exhibit 9.2]).

In Japan, segment reporting requirements were only introduced in 1990 and were initially limited to sales, profits, and assets disclosures by line of business but are now broadly consistent with International Accounting Standards (IAS). Although many other countries have aligned themselves with international standards, others have no segment disclosure requirements as yet.

SEGMENT REPORTING PROBLEMS

Segment information now must be audited in many countries, which presents a problem regarding the verifiability of the information. Particular problems involve common cost allocations, intragroup transfers, and transfer pricing. Although these problems mean that the information may not be as verifiable as other items of financial information, a trade-off between verifiability and relevance is required.

A major problem facing the auditor is segment identification. In the absence of clear guidelines, the task of the auditor in assessing whether the segments disclosed are reasonable is extremely difficult. As we noted earlier, U.K. company law leaves segment identification to the discretion of the directors of each corporation on the grounds that what is relevant and reportable will depend on the unique characteristics of each company. In contrast, the FASB in the United States now requires segments to be identified consistent with the way in which management organizes the enterprise for the purpose of making operating decisions and assessing performance.

Exhibit 9.2   Philips

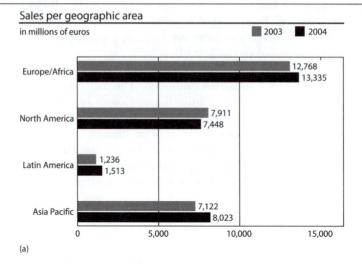

Sales per geographic area

in millions of euros   ■ 2003   ■ 2004

(a)

Income (loss) from operations per geographic area

in millions of euros

	2002	2003	2004
Europe/Africa	888	916	1,225
North America	(521)	(411)	78
Europe/Africa	23	(27)	52
Europe/Africa	30	10	252
Total	420	488	1,607

(b)

Philips is committed to China

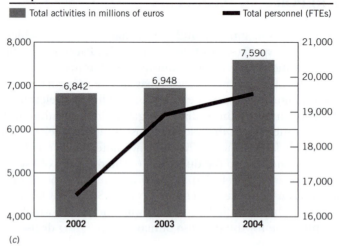

■ Total activities in millions of euros   ▬ Total personnel (FTEs)

(c)

Nominal and comparable sales growth
2004 vs 2003

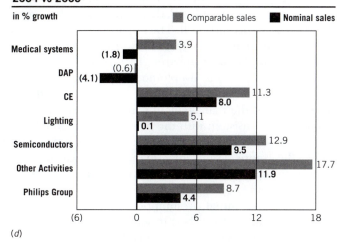

in % growth   ■ Comparable sales   ■ Nominal sales

(d)

Income (loss) from operations per sector

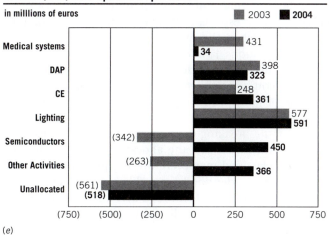

in milllions of euros   ■ 2003 ■ 2004

(e)

In practice, there are differing approaches to geographical segment identification in various countries, but U.K. MNEs, for example, often aggregate sales and
profits by continent. However, there have also been cases of multicontinental aggregation, referring, for example, to Europe, the Middle East, and Africa as one segment. Such an approach is unlikely to be informative given the different economic
and political environments and risk factors involved. In contrast, MNEs in some
continental European countries (e.g., Aga in Sweden) voluntarily disclose additional segmental data, at least with respect to sales and employees, on a much more
disaggregated geographical basis.

The general lack of guidance regarding segment identification implies that
the advantage of comparability between corporations has been sacrificed in favor
of relevance and the opportunity to provide more useful information specific to
each corporation. However, it also means that corporations are often able to

manipulate disclosures to present the best possible picture of their operations and thus manage external perceptions of corporate success. For example, they can hide the poor performance of one area of their operations by aggregating it with another that has done particularly well. The apparent lack of consistency of disclosures in practice suggests that the comparability of information has been sacrificed for an advantage that may be more apparent than real.

It is difficult to know how to overcome the problems of segment identification. Segmentation along organizational lines is desirable in that it provides the important advantage that the management's internal accounting and control system will presumably be consistent with the firm's organizational structure and will make the provision of segmental information to external users a relatively easy and inexpensive task. But, more significantly, management will be disclosing its own view of segments with significant differences in risk and return. If the management accounting reports "are the best that management can produce to guide their own decisions, then there is an initial presumption that the same statements, or less detailed versions of them, are likely best to serve the investor in making his investment and dis-investment decisions" (Solomons, 1968).

Of course, management may be misguided or inefficient, and the organization of the firm therefore may not be an accurate indicator of significant risk and return differences. This is especially likely when the firm is going through a rapid development phase or when the management has not responded adequately to changing business conditions. In addition, diverse activities may be combined organizationally through historical accident or the influence of powerful personalities. On the other hand, combinations may be deliberate because of common demand elasticities, the use of joint production facilities, or interdependence of product. Hence, there may be sound managerial reasons behind a particular organizational structure. Moreover, the breaking down of organizational units into smaller or different components will necessitate the allocation of common costs. Information from segments thus classified may therefore be questionable at least in terms of profits, and the segments identified are unlikely to reflect the company's actual diversification strategy, which is information that would appear to be useful in evaluating and predicting managerial performance.

The Dual-Yardstick Proposal

In support of an organizational approach, similar to that now required by the IASB and in the United States, Emmanuel and Gray (1978) suggested requiring disclosures on an industry (LOB) and geographical basis, which would be at the same time consistent with the MNE's organizational structure. This would provide a discipline on the disclosures supplied, enhance the potential for verification, and ensure an insight into managerial strategy. If the industry/geographical groupings identified internally were then related to an external standard industrial classification (i.e., a dual yardstick), this would not only improve communication but would also be an invaluable aid to protection insofar as segmental data from the firm could then be compared with aggregate, external industrywide, or geographical data.

Emmanuel and Gray suggested a decision criterion to the effect that an organizational unit is a segment for reporting purposes if *all* of the following apply:

1. More than 50 percent of its physical sales volume is sold externally.

2. Revenue and profitability information is accumulated regularly for this unit.

3. Responsibility for the unit's operating performance resides with the immediate manager of the unit.

Effectively, the conditions of a profit center are applied to the organizational units of the corporation. Because of the size of the corporation, different organizational units must be recognized, but this should not be taken to mean that each is run as a separate business activity. The extent of the coordination of the activities can be roughly gauged by the degree of internal versus external trade. Let's consider the application of the proposal to an organization structure such as that of MNE XY in Figure 9.1.

At the first organizational level, assume that the identified units are not consistent with the government's Standard Industrial Classification (SIC) at the desired level of disaggregation. At the next tier, assume that there is partial consistency. With respect to the paper and packaging division, if less than 50 percent of the sales volume of the paper and board department is sold internally and the units are treated as profit centers for internal purposes, then two reportable segments can be identified. For the engineering division, a further tier of the organization structure must be uncovered. The electronics and telephone units are consistent with the SIC at the desired level of disaggregation, and if the three conditions for a profit center are satisfied, two further reportable segments are discovered. On the mechanical engineering side, however, the corporation's organization is inconsistent with the SIC, where pumps, valves, and compressors are presumed to constitute a single heading. The corporation now has a choice regarding the identification of reportable segments given that the subunits conform to the definition of a profit center. The corporation's executives can decide whether the gains from disclosing information for pumps, valves, and compressors separately will outweigh any possible competitive disadvantages. Should separate disclosure not take place, the results of a reportable segment called "Mechanical engineering: Pumps, values, and

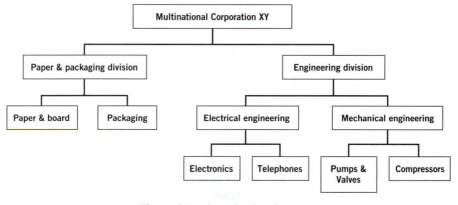

Figure 9.1   Organization Structure

Source: C. R. Emmanuel and S. J. Gray, "Segmental Disclosures by Multibusiness, Multinational Companies: A Proposal," *Accounting and Business Research* (Summer 1978): 175.

compressors" would be disclosed. For MNE XY, given the assumptions about the individual unit's degree of dependence on internal trade, five segments can thus be identified and reported on.

Along with the dual yardstick for identifying segments is the desirability of a requirement for *all* corporations to provide information about managerial responsibilities, organization structure (preferably in the form of a chart showing both the business and geographical elements), and volume of internal transactions. This seems feasible, judging by the best examples of current practice, and would also facilitate auditor verification of the quality of segmental disclosures. Such additional information may also be significant as an indicator of corporate strategy.

The proposal, therefore, attempts to identify reportable segments by combining management's method of operating a corporation's diverse activities with a standard industrial classification. The rigid use of the SIC to identify reportable segments is avoided by initially focusing on the corporation's organization structure, and hence a balance is struck between the use of managerial discretion and a potentially inflexible classification system. The reportable segments identified under the proposal are significant for external users because of the identification process. Successive tiers of the organization structure are uncovered only when disclosure is not consistent with the SIC. The process of disaggregation starts at the top and proceeds downward. It is also unlikely that the proposed process of disaggregation will stop short of identifying segments that have a material effect on the enterprise's operating results. Furthermore, the absence of a quantitative significance criterion reduces the scope for manipulation inasmuch as modifications of the organization structure will carry serious implications for internal control and behavior. The proposal therefore appears to satisfy criteria relating to the identification of realistic, material segments.

In addition to the business activities thus far considered, an international analysis, both by location and markets, also requires consideration. Emmanuel and Gray suggest that the primary yardstick should be the organization structure, identified in the same way as outlined earlier, but that disclosure should be made consistent with the geographical areas considered significant by management, consistent with its risk-return perceptions. In this respect a clear-cut disclosure by continent or country should be made, depending on the organization of the corporation concerned and the emphasis of its activities. Mixing up geographical locations with the markets served from such locations obviously should be avoided.

Emmanuel and Gray acknowledge that this approach to identifying reportable geographical segments is not entirely satisfactory because of the discretion given to management. However, the use of significance criteria or other arbitrary rules is unlikely to be of universal application and thus could result in the dissemination of misleading information.

Considerations of integration on an international scale also must be accounted for so that if external sales—in terms of physical volume—for any international segment corresponding to a specific organizational unit are less than 50 percent, the separate disclosure of that segment can be omitted. A more complex situation arises when more than one organizational unit appears within an identified geographical segment. When the external sales of each unit are less than 50 percent, only the total geographical segment need be disclosed. This indicates that the proposal, with regard to a LOB analysis, can be applied primarily to the organization structure if that structure initially identifies business activities, or it can be applied secondarily to the case where the organization structure initially shows geographical locations. Hence, an international analysis also should be disclosed regardless of whether the organizational structure is business dominated or is some mixture or a combination of both. A crucial distinction concerns the disclosure of home country performance from foreign performance in that this will assist the monitoring of national performance. In exceptional cases, the 50 percent rule would have to be relaxed so that home country performance could be distinguished from other geographical reportable segments.

An application of geographical disclosure relating to location can be illustrated with reference to the business-dominated organization structure of MNE XY (see Figure 9.2).

It is first necessary to establish whether geographical segments exist relating to the business segments already identified from the organization structure. If less than 50 percent of the sales volume of the German or French locations of the paper and board department is sold internally and the units are treated as profit centers for internal purposes, then three reportable geographical segments can be identified. A similar identification procedure can be adopted in the case of packaging; electronics and telephones; and pumps, valves, and compressors. If, for example, in the case of telephones the Canadian unit were selling internally more than 50 percent of its volume to the U.S. unit, then a choice would have to be made whether to aggregate Canada with the United States into a segment entitled North America or to disclose the Canadian unit separately with other similar units as "nonsegmented operations." The appropriate choice seems to depend on the nature of the firms' other activities in the United States, and because there is a separate elec-

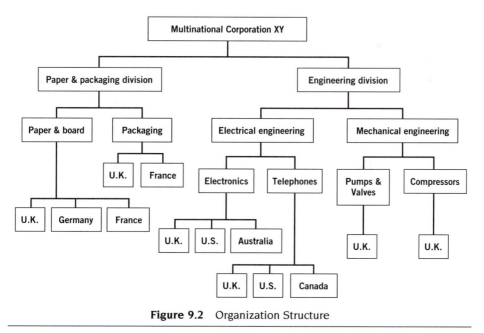

Figure 9.2   Organization Structure

Source: C. R. Emmanuel and S. J. Gray, "Segmental Disclosures by Multibusiness, Multinational Companies: A Proposal," *Accounting and Business Research* (Summer 1978): 176.

Exhibit 9.3 BOC Group

I. Segmental information
a) Turnover (including share of joint ventures and associates)

| | Continuing Operations | | | | | | |
	Process Gas Solutions £ million	Industrial and Special Products £ million	BOC Edwards £ million	Afrox hospitals £ million	Gist £ million	Total Group by Origin £ million	Total Group by Destination £ million
2004							
Europe	**292.8**	**449.1**	**189.1**	–	**239.2**	**1,224.6**	**1,162.7**
Americas	**523.4**	**422.6**	**272.3**	–		**1,218.3**	**1,171.6**
Africa	**36.1**	**230.8**	–	**432.1**	–	**699.0**	**699.4**
Asia/Pacific	**422.9**	**679.8**	**354.7**	–	–	**1,457.4**	**1,565.6**
Turnover	**1,275.2**	**1,782.3**	**816.5**	**432.1**	**293.2**	**4,599.3**	**4,599.3**
2003							
Europe	278.3	430.0	154.3	–	291.8	1,154.4	1,137.4
Americas	517.5	461.7	259.6	–	–	1,238.8	1,191.5
Africa	30.8	201.3	–	353.4	–	585.5	588.0
Asia/Pacific	416.1	658.2	270.2	–	–	1,344.5	1,406.3
Turnover	1,242.7	1,751.2	684.1	353.4	291.8	4,323.2	4,323.2
2002							
Europe	257.1	399.3	150.0	–	263.2	1,069.6	1,055.3
Americas	528.1	464.8	298.9	–	–	1,291.8	1,240.1
Africa	23.6	158.4	–	259.0	–	441.0	443.3
Asia/Pacific	391.8	582.8	293.3	–	1.6	1,215.5	1,279.2
Turnover	1,200.6	1,605.3	688.2	259.0	264.8	4,017.9	4,017.9

Inter segment turnover is not material.
b) Business analysis

| | Continuing Operations | | | | | | |
	Process Gas Solutions £ million	Industrial and Special Products £ million	BOC Edwards £ million	Afrox Hospitals £ million	Gist £ million	Corporate £ million	Total Group £ million
2004							
Total operating profit before exceptional items[1]	190.3	269.5	47.8	59.8	25.1	(15.6)	576.9
Operating exceptional items[1]	(0.8)	(15.6)	(1.0)	–	–	–	(17.4)

	Continuing Operations						
	Process Gas Solutions £ million	Industrial and Special Products £ million	BOC Edwards £ million	Afrox Hospitals £ million	Gist £ million	Corporate £ million	Total Group £ million
Operating profit	**189.5**	**253.9**	**46.8**	**59.8**	**25.1**	**(15.6)**	**559.5**
Loss on disposal of business	–	**(79.5)**	–	–	–	–	**(79.5)**
Profit on disposal of fixed assets	**4.9**	–	–	–	–	–	**4.9**
Capital employed[2]	**1,625.2**	**943.9**	**548.1**	**162.5**	**6.9**	**(66.2)**	**3,220.4**
Capital expenditure[3]	**100.1**	**99.4**	**30.1**	**17.5**	**9.0**	–	**256.1**
Depreciation and amortisation[3]	**156.0**	**101.5**	**40.1**	**12.3**	**12.9**	**1.2**	**324.0**
2003 (restated)							
Total operating profit before exceptional items[1]	184.0	242.7	18.5	46.1	29.2	(14.9)	505.6
Operating exceptional items[1]	(6.9)	(4.5)	(10.6)	–	–	(45.0)	(67.0)
Operating profit	177.1	238.2	7.9	46.1	29.2	(59.9)	438.6
Capital employed[2]	1,822.9	1,158.1	596.1	167.2	0.8	(88.0)	3,657.1
Capital expenditure[3]	93.1	105.2	37.6	17.8	22.3	5.2	281.2
Depreciation and amortisation[3]	165.8	101.2	39.1	9.8	15.8	1.7	333.4
2002 (restated)							
Total operating profit before exceptional items[1]	185.2	248.0	26.1	29.7	25.5	(14.4)	500.1
Operating exceptional items[1]	(24.0)	(18.7)	(27.5)	–	–	(4.3)	(74.5)
Operating profit	161.2	229.3	(1.4)	29.7	25.5	(18.7)	425.6
(Loss)/profit on termination/ disposal of businesses[1]	(21.3)	–	1.1	–	–	–	(20.2)
Capital employed[2]	1,831.3	1,058.1	595.3	105.0	22.8	(61.9)	3,550.6
Capital expenditure[3]	157.3	123.6	42.0	9.2	19.0	3.2	354.3
Depreciation and amortisation[3]	167.7	96.8	41.1	7.2	16.1	2.0	330.9

(continues)

Exhibit 9.3   *(Continued)*

c) Regional analysis

	Europe £ million	Americas £ million	Africa £ million	Asia/Pacific £ million	Total Group £ million
2004					
Total operating profit before exceptional items[1]	155.4	77.4	108.9	235.2	576.9
Operating exceptional items[1]	–	(14.8)	–	(2.6)	(17.4)
Operating profit	155.4	62.6	108.9	232.6	559.5
Loss on disposal of business	–	(79.5)	–	–	(79.5)
Profit on disposal of fixed assets	4.9	–	–	–	4.9
Capital employed[2]	796.6	992.9	335.4	1,095.5	3,220.4
Capital expenditure[3]	72.3	71.8	44.2	67.8	256.1
2003 (restated)					
Total operating profit before exceptional items[1]	144.3	91.8	85.0	184.5	505.6
Operating exceptional items[1]	(7.3)	(49.1)	–	(10.6)	(67.0)
Operating profit	137.0	42.7	85.0	173.9	438.6
Capital employed[2]	866.2	1,225.0	321.5	1,244.4	3,657.1
Capital expenditure[3]	1 027	79.1	36.7	627	281.2
2002 (restated)					
Total operating profit before exceptional items[1]	155.2	121.3	56.7	166.9	500.1
Operating exceptional items[1]	(38.4)	(8.1)	(0.4)	(27.6)	(74.5)
Operating profit	116.8	113.2	56.3	139.3	425.6
(Loss)/profit on termination /disposal of businesses[1]	(1.5)	(18.7)	–	–	(20.2)
Capital employed[2]	907.4	1,241.3	221.2	1,180.7	3,550.6
Capital expenditure[3]	121.4	134.7	25.6	72.6	354.3

1. Including share of joint ventures and associates.
2. Capital employed comprises the capital and reserves of the Group, its long-term liabilities and all current borrowings net of cash and deposits.
3. Subsidiary undertakings only.
4. Net interest and net borrowings are managed centrally and are not directly attributable to individual business segments or regions.

tronics operation, it could be more informative to keep U.S. activities as a separate disclosure.

    Clearly, the auditor's task is an important one in this context, just as in the case of a LOB analysis. He or she is responsible for judging the meaningfulness of the segmental disclosures in the light of the company's international activities, risk factors involved, and the organization of responsibilities to match such activities. It should be emphasized, however, that the examples given serve only to illustrate this proposal. In practice, a complex variety of organization all structures are likely to be found, which will challenge judgment and ingenuity to a greater degree than exhibited before.

Matrix Presentation

From our earlier discussion of regulation, it is evident that in many countries, corporations are required to disclose both LOB and geographical segmental data. However, most corporations provide such information separately rather than in a matrix form of presentation that gives information on the interrelationship of the two types of segments (see, for example, BOC of the United Kingdom in Exhibit 9.3). The general lack of a matrix presentation presents another problem to the users of segment information. Both risk and expected return are dependent on the extent to which specific industry activities are committed to specific countries. A matrix presentation would mean that a more accurate assessment of business prospects is possible. This is because the effect of changes in political, economic, or social conditions in any country will depend on the specific lines of business carried on by the corporation in the country concerned.

SUMMARY

1. The growth of large diversified MNEs presents problems for both MNEs and the users of accounts, especially in terms of assessing a corporation's future cash flows and the risk of uncertainty associated with those future cash flows. Segment reporting (i.e., the disclosure of disaggregated data) is likely to be somewhat effective in meeting the information needs of investors and other users.

2. Results of studies of predictive ability have shown that both LOB and geographical segmental data are more useful than consolidated data for the prediction of earnings.

3. Stock market research relating to risk management suggests that disclosure of LOB and geographical segment data results in a decrease in a company's riskiness as perceived by investors.

4. Although regulation is growing internationally, with important new developments by the IASB and in the United States, the major problem of segment identification is still prevalent. The continuing scope for managerial discretion provides substantial potential for the dissemination of misleading information.

5. Potential constraints on the disclosure of segment data reporting include the costs of compiling, processing, and disseminating information and, more significantly, the costs of competitive disadvantage. The major argument against such disclosure is that in some cases, where the company is highly integrated, it may be inappropriate and therefore potentially misleading.

6. While companies often use the competitive disadvantage argument to counter attempts at further regulation or to justify nondisclosures, there may be wider investment and social benefits from segment reporting.

7. There is scope for introducing segment disclosure guidelines that encourage disclosers and yet do more to control their quality so that they are truly informative.

8. The application of a "dual yardstick" based on internal organizational criteria and an external scheme of industrial/geographical classification seems desirable and is supported by recent developments by the IASB and in the United States.

9.   At the same time, revised IASB and U.S. regulations have resulted in the loss of some geographical information (i.e., profits data).

10.   A matrix analysis of LOB and geographical segment disclosures is likely to provide more insight into risk-return relationships and future prospects than single-dimension disclosures.

Discussion Questions

1.   How is segment information likely to help investors in MNEs?

2.   Discuss the likely benefits of segment reporting, with particular reference to the results of predictive ability and stock market research.

3.   Identify the likely costs of segment reporting.

4.   Under what circumstances could segment reporting be misleading?

5.   The IASBs IAS 14 (revised) does not require profits disclosures for secondary segments. What are the likely reasons for this? Do you agree with this omission from IAS 14?

6.   To what extent has SFAS 131 in the United States overcome the limitations of SFAS 14?

7.   How do segment reporting requirements vary in the European Union? How, and for what reasons, does the United Kingdom differ from other EU countries?

8.   Discuss the problem of segment identification, making reference to the strengths and limitations of current regulation and practice.

9.   Explain the reasons behind using organizational structure as a basis for segment identification.

10.   Discuss the advantages and disadvantages of Emmanuel and Gray's "dual yardstick" proposal.

11.   To what extent are MNE concerns that segment reporting will give rise to competitive disadvantage likely to be justified? Discuss specific situations and items of information.

12.   If the risks of operating in a foreign country (e.g., Mexico) are high, should MNEs be required to disclose information about the operations and assets involved even if they comprise a relatively minor part of the total, for example, 5 percent?

13.   Is it possible to rely on international capital market pressures to stimulate the disclosure of useful segment information by MNEs, or is more focused and detailed regulation necessary?

14.   What are the advantages, from an investor perspective, of a "matrix" approach to segment reporting?

15.   What are the disadvantages, from a management perspective, of "matrix" reporting?

Exercises

Compare the 2004 segment disclosures of Altria (www.altria.com) and Reynolds American (www.reynoldsamerican.com) for exercises 1–5.

1.   What do the segment disclosures reveal about the companies' strategic emphases?

2.   How do the companies' domestic tobacco segments compare?

3.   What do the disclosures have in common? How are they different?

4.   How much of the difference can be attributed to Altria's international status?

5.   Which company would you rather have invested in before reading the segment disclosure? Does reading the segment disclosure of both companies influence your investment inclinations?

Compare and contrast Altria's 2004 segment disclosure with the 2004 segment disclosure of British American Tobacco (www.bat.com). Use the information to do exercises 6–7.

6.   How different are the segment disclosure requirements for the two countries? What information does each company provide beyond the requirements?

7.   Do the segment disclosures help in comparing the performance of the two companies? Which segments of Altria relate to British American Tobacco segments?

Look at the segment disclosures in BOC's 2004 annual report (www.boc.com) for exercises 8–12.

8.   What generated the increase in turnover (sales revenue) during 2004?

9.   Who will likely use the geographically segmented data? Who will likely use the LOB segmented data?

10. If you could buy one LOB or region of the company, which one would you choose? Why? What concerns, if any, do you have about the segmented data misleading you in your decision?

11. What application does exercise 10 have for creditors?

12. How might competitors use the segmented data to their advantage?

13. Based on the organizational chart provided in Figure 9.2, create a possible segmentation of the company by LOB segments. Create a possible segmentation of the company by geographical segments.

14. CurAll Corp. sells bandages of various types to both medical institutions and to retail stores. For internal reporting purposes, the company is divided into two profit centers: retail sales and medical institution sales. The medical institution division makes 40 percent of its sales to the retail division, which uses the larger bandages in prepackaged first-aid kits. The retail division makes 20 percent of its sales to the medical institution division. Assume that both of the profit centers are consistent with the SIC. According to the dual-yardstick proposal, how could the LOB segments be divided for external reporting purposes?

15. CurAll Corp (see exercise 13) has operations in the United States, Canada, and Mexico. The U.S. operations are concerned mostly with corporate affairs, although there is a production plant in Tennessee. Mexico houses two large production plants that handle the majority of the retail product manufacturing and a portion of the medical institution production. Canada has a small plant dedicated to retail products. In addition, each country has its own marketing division, and Mexico sells the majority of its products to the United States and Canada marketing divisions for sale in the United States and Canada. Divide the company into geographical segments according to the dual-yardstick model.

Case: BMW
Case: Nestlé

These cases can be found on the following website: www.wiley.com/college/radebaugh

Selected References

Ajinkya, B.B. 1980. "An Empirical Evaluation of Line of Business Reporting." *Journal of Accounting Research* (Autumn): 343–361.

Balakrishnan, R., T. S. Harris, and P. K. Sen. 1990. "The Predictive Ability of Geographic Segment Disclosures." *Journal of Accounting Research* (Autumn): 305–325.

Behn, B. K., N. B. Nichols, and D. L. Street. 2002. "The Predictive Ability of Geographic Segment Disclosures by U.S. Companies: SFAS No.131 vs SFAS No. 14." *Journal of international Accounting Research* 1: 31–44.

Collins, D. W., and R. Simonds. 1979. "SEC Line of Business Disclosure and Market Risk Adjustments." *Journal of Accounting Research* (Autumn): 352–381.

Edwards, P., and R. A. Smith. 1996. "Competitive Disadvantage and Voluntary Disclosures: The Case of Segmental Reporting." *British Accounting Review* 28(2): 155–172.

Emmanuel, C. R., and S. J. Gray. 1977. "Segmental Disclosures and the Segment Identification Problem." *Accounting and Business Research* (Winter): 37–50.

Emmanuel, C. R., and S. J. Gray. 1978. "Segmental Disclosure by Multibusiness Multinational Companies: A Proposal." *Accounting and Business Research* (Summer): 21–32.

Emmanuel, C. R., and R. Pick. 1980. "The Predictive Ability of U.K. Segment Reports." *Journal of Business Finance and Accounting* (Summer): 201–218.

Financial Accounting Standards Board. 1997. *SFAS 131: Financial Reporting for Segments of a Business Enterprise*. Stamford, CT: FASB.

Gray, S. J., and L. H. Radebaugh. 1984. "International Segment Disclosures by U.S. and U.K. Multinational Enterprises: A Descriptive Study." *Journal of Accounting Research* (Spring): 351–360.

Gray, S. J., and C. B. Roberts. 1988. "Voluntary Information Disclosures and the British Multinationals." In *International Pressures for Accounting Change,* edited by A. G. Hopwood. Englewood Cliffs, NJ: Prentice-Hall.

Herrmann, D. 1996. "The Predictive Ability of Geographic Segment Information at the Country, Continent and Consolidated Level." *Journal of International Financial Management and Accounting* 7(1): 50–73.

Institute of Chartered Accountants in England and Wales. 1990. SSAP 25, *Segmental Reporting.* London: ICAEW.

Meek, G. K., and S. J. Gray. 1989. "Globalization of Stock Markets and Foreign Listing Requirements: Voluntary Disclosures by Continental European Companies Listed on the London Stock Exchange." *Journal of International Business Studies* (Summer): 315–336.

Mohr, R. M. 1983. "The Segment Reporting Issue: A Review of Empirical Research." *Journal of Accounting Research* (Spring): 39–72.

Nichols, N., D. L. Street and S. J. Gray. 2000. "Geographical Segment Disclosures in the United States: Reporting Practices Enter a New Era." *Journal of International Accounting, Auditing and Taxation* 9(1): 59–82.

Ozu, C., and S. J. Gray, 2001. "The Development of Segment Reporting in Japan: Achieving International Harmonization through a Process of National Consensus." *Advances in International Accounting* 14: 1–13.

Prodhan, B. K. 1986. "Geographical Segment Disclosures and Multinational Risk Profile." *Journal of Business Finance and Accounting* (Spring): 15–37.

Prodhan, B. K., and M. C. Harris. 1989. "Systematic Risk and the Discretionary Disclosure of Geographical Segments: An Empirical Investigation of U.S. Multinationals." *Journal of Business Finance and Accounting* (Autumn): 467–478.

Radebaugh, Lee H. 1987. *International Aspects of Segment Disclosures: A Conceptual Approach.* Research Monograph No. 2. Glasgow: University of Glasgow.

Roberts, C. B. 1989. "Forecasting Earnings Using Geographical Segment Data: Some U.K. Evidence." *Journal of International Financial Management and Accounting* (Winter): 130–151.

Senteney, D. L., and M. S. Bazaz. 1992. "The Impact of SFAS 14 Geographic Segment Disclosures on the Information Content of US-Based MNE's Earnings Release." *International Journal of Accounting* (3): 267–279.

Solomons, David. 1968. "Accounting Problems and Some Proposed Solutions." In *Public Reporting by Conglomerates,* edited by A. Rappaport, P. A. Firmin, and S. A. Zeff. Englewood Cliffs, NJ: Prentice-Hall.

Street, D. L., N. Nichols, and S. J. Gray. 2000. "Segment Disclosures under SFAS 131: Has Business Segment Reporting Improved?" *Accounting Horizons* 14(3) (September): 259–285.

Thomas, W. B. 2000. "The Value-Relevance of Geographic Segment Earnings Disclosures under SFAS 14." *Journal of International Financial Management & Accounting* 11(3): 133–155.

United Nations. 1988. *Conclusions on Accounting and Reporting by Transnational Corporations.* New York: revised 1994.

CHAPTER TEN

ACCOUNTING FOR FOREIGN CURRENCY

Chapter Objectives

- Identify the different ways that companies can account for transactions denominated in a foreign currency
- Differentiate between the process of foreign currency conversion and translation
- Compare the different foreign currency translation methodologies: the temporal method and the current rate or closing method
- Present the translation methodologies required by the International Accounting Standards Board (IASB) and the Financial Accounting Standards Board (FASB)
- Illustrate how companies account for foreign exchange

INTRODUCTION

In this chapter and in Chapter 13, we will address the issues raised below in the Strategic Decision Point. How does currency affect your financial performance, and how do you report this to the public? Even companies without foreign operations may have to deal with foreign exchange issues. If you import goods and services from abroad and have to pay in the currency of the exporter, you will either carry a liability denominated in the foreign currency on your books or have to convert your currency into the foreign currency to take title of the goods. If you export to another country and denominate the sale in the foreign currency, you will have to carry the receivable on your books in the foreign currency until you take receipt in the foreign currency and convert into your currency.

Companies with operations in a foreign country, such as Honda with U.S. operations, keep books and records in the currency of the host country. However,

---

Strategic Decision Point

In a press release in January 2005, Honda Motor Company announced that a stronger yen hurt its earnings for the October–December 2004 quarter. There was no information in the release about how are strong yen hurt earnings, but there are two main possibilities. The first is that the strong yen hurt Honda's ability to export autos to the United States. However, the more likely reason is that earnings generated in U.S. dollars by Honda's U.S. operations were worth fewer yen as a result of the strengthening yen/weakening dollar. This had nothing to do with the number of units sold or the dollar profitability of U.S. operations but had everything to do with the fact that Honda had to translate its U.S. operations into yen for consolidation with yen results. The real strategic issue is what can Honda do to keep foreign exchange from having an impact on earnings? A related issue is how can Honda report the impact of changing currency values to its shareholders in earnings announcements and financial statements so that they understand the true impact of currency values on earnings?

---

they are obligated to translate their financial statements from the foreign currency to the home country currency in order to issue consolidated financial statements of their operations worldwide.

BASICS IN FOREIGN EXCHANGE

Foreign exchange can be traded "over-the-counter" (OTC), on an exchange, or over the Internet. The OTC market is composed of commercial banks, such as Bank of America, and investment banks, such as Merrill Lynch. Each OTC trader has a trading room with individuals who specialize in specific currencies. The securities exchanges where foreign currencies are traded include the Philadelphia Stock Exchange, the London International Financial Futures Exchange, and the Chicago Mercantile Exchange, where certain types of foreign exchange instruments, such as futures and options are traded.

The traditional foreign exchange instruments that comprise the bulk of foreign exchange trading are the spot, outright forward, and FX swap markets. Spot transactions involve the exchange of currency within two business days of the date on which the two foreign exchange traders agree to the transaction. The rate at which the transaction is settled is the spot rate. Outright forward transactions involve the exchange of currency three or more days after the date on which the traders agree to the transaction. It is the single purchase or sale of a currency for future delivery. The rate at which the transaction is settled is the forward rate and is a contract rate between the two parties. The forward transaction will be settled at the forward rate no matter what the actual spot rate is at the time of settlement. In a FX swap, one currency is exchanged for another on one date and then swapped (or exchanged) back at a future date. Most often, the first leg of an FX swap is a spot transaction, with the second leg of the swap a future transaction. For example, assume that Toyota (Japan) receives a dividend in U.S. dollars from its subsidiary in the United States but has no use for dollars for 30 days. Toyota could enter into an FX swap with a Japanese bank where it sells the dollars for yen in the spot market and agrees to buy the dollars with yen in 30 days at the forward rate.

In addition to the traditional foreign exchange instruments, there are other instruments, such as futures and options. Futures are traded on an exchange, whereas options can be traded OTC or on a securities exchange, such as the Philadelphia Stock Exchange. A futures contract is an agreement between two parties to buy or sell a particular currency at a particular price on a particular future date as specified in a standardized contract to all participants in that currency futures exchange. Options are the right but not the obligation to trade foreign currency in the future. All of these instruments not considered spot foreign exchange are also known as derivatives. These instruments will be covered in Chapter 13, whereas we will focus more on spot exchange rates in this chapter.

Spot Market

Most foreign currency transactions take place with the foreign traders of banks. Therefore, rates are quoted from the trader's perspective. Ordinarily, the trader will offer two quotes—the bid and the offer price of a foreign currency. For example, the quote for British pounds sterling may appear as follows:

$$\$1.9072/82$$

which means that the trader will buy pounds for $1.9072 (bid) and sell pounds for $1.9082 (offer or ask). The difference between the two quotes is the profit margin for the trader. Quotes are often given in the press as the mid-rate for the currency. For the British pound, the mid-rate would be $1.9077.

Exchange rate quotes can be obtained from a number of sources, such as the *Wall Street Journal* (United States) and the *Financial Times* (United Kingdom) and from one of several online services, such as CNN (http://money.cnn.com/markets/currencies/), Yahoo! (http://finance.yahoo.com/currency?u), and the electronic versions of major newspapers, such as those mentioned above. In addition to getting quotes on the Internet, you can also trade on the Internet through banking and nonbanking institutions. For example, FXCM (Foreign Exchange Capital Markets) is a part of the Refco Group and is the largest nonbank firm in the world that deals in spot foreign exchange transactions. You can set up an account on-line and trade foreign exchange through them. Exhibit 10.1 provides the March 3, 2005, rates published in the *Wall Street Journal*. Two different rates are quoted for each day. The first two columns contain a direct quote (also referred to as U.S. $ Equivalents), which is the amount of local currency equivalent (in this case U.S. dollars) to one unit of the foreign currency. The second two columns contain an indirect quote (also referred to as Currency per U.S. Dollar), which is the amount of foreign currency required for one unit of the local currency. For example, in Exhibit 10.1 the exchange rate for U.S. dollars and Brazilian reals is as follows:

$$\$.3735 \text{ per real (direct) or}$$
$$2.6774 \text{ reals (or reais in Portuguese) per U.S. dollar (indirect)}$$

Exhibit 10.1   Exchange Rates

Exchange Rates				March 3, 2005

The foreign exchange mid-range rates below apply to trading among banks in amounts of $1 million and more, as quoted at 4 p.m. Eastern time by Reuters and other sources. Retail transactions provide fewer units of foreign currency per dollar.

Country	U.S. $ EQUIVALENT		CURRENCY PER U.S. $	
	Thu	Wed	Thu	Wed
Argentina (Peso)-y	.3388	.3383	2.9516	2.9560
Australia (Dollar)	.7830	.7836	1.2771	1.2762
Bahrain (Dinar)	2.6525	2.6524	.3770	.3770
Brazil (Real)	.3735	.3791	2.6774	2.6378
Canada (Dollar)	.8037	.8068	1.2442	1.2395
1-month forward	.8037	.8069	1.2442	1.2393
3-months forward	.8043	.8074	1.2433	1.2385
6-months forward	.8057	.8088	1.2412	1.2364
Chile (Peso)	.001690	.001699	591.72	588.58
China (Renminbi)	.1208	.1208	8.2765	8.2765
Colombia (Peso)	.0004267	.0004295	2343.57	2328.29
Czech Rep. (Koruna)	.04432	.04431	22.563	22.568
Commercial rate				
Denmark (Krone)	.1761	.1765	5.6786	5.6657
Ecuador (US Dollar)	1.0000	1.0000	1.0000	1.0000
Egypt (Pound)-y	.1722	.1722	5.8089	5.8062
Hong Kong (Dollar)	.1282	.1282	7.8003	7.8003
Hungary (Forint)	.005406	.005421	184.98	184.47
India (Rupee)	.02290	.02290	43.668	43.668
Indonesia (Rupiah)	.0001076	.0001078	9294	9276
Israel (Shekel)	.2304	.2307	4.3403	4.3346
Japan (Yen)	.009498	.009554	105.29	104.67
1-month forward	.009521	.009576	105.03	104.13
3-months forward	.009569	.009627	104.50	103.87
6-months forward	.009651	.009709	103.62	103.00
Jordan (Dinar)	1.4114	1.4104	.7085	.7090
Kuwait (Dinar)	3.4247	3.4245	.2920	.2920
Lebanon (Pound)	.0006605	.0006605	1514.00	1514.00
Malaysia (Ringgit)-b	.2632	.2632	3.7994	3.7994
Malta (Lira)	3.0431	3.0491	.3286	.3280
Mexico (Peso) Floating rate	.0899	.0902	11.1185	11.0852
New Zealand (Dollar)	.7272	.7268	1.3751	1.3759
Norway (Krone)	.1595	.1600	6.2696	6.2500
Pakistan (Rupee)	.01685	.01685	59.347	59.347
Peru (new Sol)	.3066	.3065	3.2616	3.2626
Philippines (Peso)	.01822	.01827	54.885	54.735
Poland (Zloty)	.3333	.3334	3.0003	2.9994
Russia (Ruble)-a	.03606	.03605	27.732	27.739
Saudi Arabia (Riyal)	.2667	.2666	3.7495	3.7509
Singapore (Dollar)	.6140	.6152	16.287	1.6255
Slovak Rep. (Koruna)	.03462	.03470	28.885	28.818
South Africa (Rand)	.1676	.1694	5.9661	5.9032
South Korea (Won)	.0009935	.0009926	1006.54	1007.46

(continues)

Exhibit 10.1   (*Continued*)

Country	U.S. $ EQUIVALENT		CURRENCY PER U.S. $	
	Thus	Wed	Thu	Wed
Sweden (Krona)	.1450	.1448	6.8966	6.9061
Switzerland (Franc)	.8470	.8520	1.1806	1.1737
1-month forward	.8485	.8534	1.1786	1.1718
3-months forward	.8517	.8568	1.1741	1.1671
6-months forward	.8573	.8623	1.1665	1.1597
Taiwan (Dollar)	.03254	.03252	30.731	30.750
Thailand (Baht)	.02600	.02608	38.462	38.344
Turkey (New Lira)-d	.7800	.7785	1.2820	1.2645
U.K. (Pound)	1.9077	1.9135	.5242	.5226
1-month forward	1.9044	1.9101	.5251	.5235
3-months forward	1.8983	1.9038	.5268	.5253
6-months forward	1.8904	1.8959	.5290	.5275
United Arab (Dirham)	.2723	.2723	3.6724	3.6724
Uruguay (Peso)				
Financial	.03900	.03910	25.641	25.575
Venezuela (Bolivar)	.000466	.000521	2145.92	1919.39
SDR	1.5248	1.5238	.6558	.6563
Euro	1.3112	1.3138	.7627	.7613

Special Drawing Rights (SDR) are based on exchange rates for the U.S., British, and Japanese currencies. Source: International Monetary Fund.

a-Russlan Central Bank rate. b-Government rate. d-Rebased as of Jan. 1, 2005. y-Floating rate.

Source: Wall Street Journal, March 4, 2005, p. B6.

FOREIGN CURRENCY TRANSCTIONS

Conceptual Issues

Foreign currency transactions are transactions denominated in a currency other than the reporting currency of the firm. The reporting currency is the currency in which the firm's financial statements are issued. For example, a sale by a U.S. firm to a Canadian firm for which payment is to be received in Canadian dollars is considered to be a foreign currency transaction for the U.S. firm. If the payment is to be received in U.S. dollars, the transaction would not be a foreign currency transaction for the U.S. firm, even though the buyer is not a U.S. firm. Foreign currency transactions may involve the buying and selling of goods and services, the borrowing or lending of funds, or the receipt or payment of dividends, royalties, interest payments, or other financial transactions.

No accounting problem arises as long as the transactions are denominated in the firm's domestic currency. If the transaction is settled immediately, the purchase or sale is recorded at the spot rate, and the amount of cash paid or received is also recorded at the spot rate. However, when a transaction is denominated in a foreign currency and payment is settled at a subsequent balance sheet date, the firm needs to resolve four accounting problems:

- The initial recording of the transaction
- The recording of foreign currency balances at subsequent balance sheet dates
- The treatment of any foreign exchange gains and losses
- The recording of the settlement of foreign currency receivables and payables when they come due

Any foreign currency transaction has two components: the monetary component and the nonmonetary component. The monetary component is the cash received/paid or the accounts receivable/payable. An example of the nonmonetary component is the equipment or inventory purchased or sold.

There are many different combinations involved in the solution of these four problems, but the one adopted in IAS 21 by the IASB and SFAS 52 by FASB is the two transactions perspective where foreign exchange gains and losses are recognized in income at each balance sheet date.

Using the purchase of equipment as an example, we see that the two standards require that the equipment and accounts payable amounts be recorded at the spot rate on the transaction date. The philosophy is that the transaction is divided into two parts: (1) the purchase of the equipment and (2) the decision to finance through an accounts payable rather than by paying cash immediately. At subsequent balance sheet dates, the equipment remains at its historical cost, but the accounts payable value changes to reflect the new spot rate. Any difference between the previous and new spot rate is a gain or loss recognized in the current accounting period. The assumption under this approach is that the gain or loss should be reflected in the period in which the exchange rate change occurs rather than be deferred to future periods. Also, a change in the liability value should be reflected as a financing decision, much like interest expense, rather than affect the value of the equipment.

Evolution of IAS 21 and Accounting for Foreign Currency Transactions

The first time the IASC (now the IASB) dealt with foreign exchange issues was in International Accounting Standard 21 (IAS 21), *Accounting for the Effects of Changes in Foreign Exchange Rates,* which was issued in March 1983. IAS 21 provided more options for accounting for foreign currency transactions than did comparable U.S. standards. However, IAS 21 was revised in 1993 as part of the IASC's Comparability of Financial Statements project and is effective for financial statements covering periods beginning on or after January 1, 1995. It was revised again in 2003 with an effective date of January 1, 2005. As noted above, IAS 21 requires transactions to be initially recorded at the spot rate on the date of the transaction. At subsequent balance sheet dates,

- Monetary items should be recorded at the closing rate (the spot rate on the balance sheet date, known as the "current rate" in U.S. terminology).
- Nonmonetary items carried at historical cost should be recorded at the historical exchange rate (the spot rate in effect when the transaction was initially recorded).

• Nonmonetary items carried at fair value should be recorded at the rate in effect when the fair values were determined.

Initially, IAS 21 allowed the following alternative treatment for foreign exchange gains and losses, primarily to satisfy the concerns of developing countries with weak currencies during a time when currencies were fixed instead of floating.

> Exchange differences may result from a severe devaluation or depreciation of a currency against which there is no practical means of hedging and that affects liabilities which cannot be settled and which arise directly on the recent acquisition of an asset invoiced in a foreign currency. Such exchange differences should be included in the carrying amount of the related asset, provided that the adjusted carrying amount does not exceed the lower of the replacement cost and the amount recoverable from the sale or use of the asset.

However, this approach, which was a major departure from standards in the United States and the United Kingdom, was eliminated in the 2003 revision of IAS 21, making the IAS 21 and SFAS 52 treatments the same. This is a good example of how the convergence process brought the IASB and FASB standards to the same conclusion.

Illustration: Accounting for Sales and Purchases Denominated in a Foreign Currency

The following entries illustrate the method required by the IASB and FASB. Assume that a U.S. firm imports equipment from Germany on March 1 for €200,000 when the exchange rate is $1.3112 per euro. Payment in euro does not have to be made until April 30. Assume that on March 31, the exchange rate is $1.3500 and on April 30 is $1.3300. Also, assume that the firm's books are closed at the end of the calendar quarter.

March 1	Purchases	262,240	
	Accounts payable		262,240
	€200,000 × 1.3112		
March 31	Foreign exchange loss	7,760	
	Accounts payable		7,760
	200,000 (1.3112 − 1.3500)		
April 30	Accounts payable	270,000	
	Foreign exchange gain		4,000
	Cash (200,000 × 1.3300)		266,000

Using the same information provided previously but assuming a sale instead of a purchase, we would have the journal entries as follows according to FASB Statement No. 52 and IAS 21:

March 1	Accounts receivable	262,240	
	Sales revenues		262,240
March 31	Accounts receivable	7,760	
	Foreign exchange gain		7,760
April 30	Cash	266,000	
	Foreign exchange loss	4,000	
	Accounts receivable		270,000

Illustration: Accounting for Debt Incurred in a Foreign Currency

Due to interest rate availability or other factors, a firm may incur debt in a foreign currency with an obligation to repay principal and interest in the foreign currency. The general rules applied above apply here as well: the debt is initially recorded in dollars (assume a U.S.-based company for purposes of illustration) at the spot rate. At subsequent balance sheet dates, the debt must be restated in dollars at the new exchange rate, and any resulting foreign exchange gain or loss must be recorded in the income statement immediately. The challenge becomes the payment of interest expense, which we will assume is paid every six months for the sake of illustration. Since interest expense accrues over a period of time but is paid on a specific date, a foreign exchange gain or loss could arise from the difference between the exchange rate on the payment date and the average exchange rate over the period during which interest accrues. The following entries illustrate how to account for principal and interest.

On January 1, assume that a U.S. firm borrows 2 million Swiss francs (CHF) for five years at 3 percent interest paid semiannually in Swiss francs. The principal does not have to be repaid until the end of the loan. Assume also that the loan is adjusted for any exchange rate change every six months. Assume the following exchange rates for the first year:

January 1	$.8064
June 30	$.7901
December 31	$.8839

The average exchange rate for the first six months was $.79825 and for the second six months it was $.8370. The Swiss franc rose sharply at the end of the year. With this information, the journal entries for the first six months would be as follows:

January 1	Cash	1,612,800	
	Notes payable		1,612,800
June 30	Notes Payable	32,600	
	Foreign Exchange Gain		32,600
	(CHF.7901−.8064) × CHF 2million		
	Interest expense	23,948	
	Foreign exchange gain		245
	Cash		23,703
	CHF2,000,000 × (.03/2) = 30,000 × .79825 = $23,948		
	CHF30,000 × .7901 = $23,703		
December 31	Foreign exchange loss	187,600	
	Notes payable		187,600
	(.8839-.7901) × CHF2million		
December 31	Interest expense	25,110	
	Foreign exchange loss	1,407	
	Cash		26,517
	CHF30,000 × .8370 = $25,110		
	CHF30,000 × .8839 = $26,517		

Notice that the average exchange rate is used to compute the interest expense and that the foreign exchange gain or loss is the difference between the interest expense and the cash actually paid in interest at the spot rate on the date of the payment.

TRANSLATION OF FOREIGN CURRENCY FINANCIAL STATEMENTS

As noted in the Strategic Point in the opening of the chapter, Honda was facing earnings pressure because it had to translate the financial statements of its U.S. operations into yen for consolidation purposes during a time when the yen was rising against the dollar. To understand the issues behind translation, it is important to understand terminology. Several terms important to the discussion of translation are functional currency, reporting currency, foreign currency, local currency, exchange difference, and foreign operation. The **functional currency** is the currency of the primary economic environment in which the company operates. The **reporting currency** (called the presentation currency in IAS 21) is the currency in which the parent company prepares its financial statements. The **foreign currency** is any currency other than the functional currency of a company. The **local currency** is the currency of a particular country being referred to. The functional currency could be either the reporting currency or a foreign currency. The **exchange difference** is the difference resulting from translating a given number of units of one currency into another currency at different exchange rates. A **foreign operation** is a subsidiary, associate, joint venture, or branch whose activities are based in a country other than that of the reporting enterprise.

To illustrate these terms, let's assume that a U.S.-based MNE has an operating subsidiary in France that does some importing from the United Kingdom. The functional currency of the subsidiary would be the euro, assuming that the company is relatively autonomous from the parent company and that most of its cash flows are in euros. The local currency of that subsidiary would also be the euro, the British pound would be a foreign currency to the French subsidiary, and the U.S. dollar would be the reporting currency of the consolidated enterprise. Both the euro and the pound would be foreign currencies to the parent company in the United States. If the French operation were an extension of the parent company and relatively dependent on the parent company for inventory, cash flows, and so on, the functional currency might be considered the reporting currency (the U.S. dollar).

Because the French subsidiary imports merchandise from the United Kingdom, it may have accounts payable that are denominated in pounds. This implies that the amount of the liability is actually fixed in pounds because that is the currency in which the liability must be settled. For financial statement purposes, however, the pound liability must be measured in euros or it could not be included with the euro liabilities on the balance sheet. A euro liability would be both measured and denominated in euros. The process of translation involves restating an account from one country to another. If the exchange rate used to translate the account from one currency to another were the rate in effect when the original transaction took place (such as the acquisition of property, plant, and equipment), that rate would be called the historical exchange rate. If the exchange rate used were the one in effect at the balance sheet date, it would be considered the current or closing rate.

As we will point out in this chapter, the translation of financial statements involves dealing with two key issues: the exchange rates at which various accounts are translated from one currency into another (translation methods) and the subsequent treatment of gains and losses. First, we will discuss the major translation methodologies that have been used historically, including the two most widely used methodologies today—the current rate and temporal methods. Next, we will describe the process required for use by the International Accounting Standards Board and the U.S. Financial Accounting Standards Board. With those standards as a base, we will illustrate the translation process and finally show how other countries translate financial statements.

TRANSLATION METHODOLOGIES: AN OVERVIEW

In the process of translation, all foreign currency balance sheet and income statement accounts are restated in terms of the reporting currency by multiplying the foreign currency amount by the appropriate exchange rate. The four major methods that have been used historically in the translation process are the current/noncurrent, the monetary/nonmonetary, the temporal, and the current rate methods.

Current/Noncurrent Method

Under the current/noncurrent method, as shown in Exhibit 10.2, current assets and liabilities are translated at current exchange rates, and noncurrent assets and liabilities and stockholders' equity are translated at historical exchange rates. This method was generally accepted in the United States from the early 1930s until FASB Statement No. 8 was issued in October 1975.

The current/noncurrent method is based on the assumption that accounts should be grouped according to maturity. Anything due to mature in one year or less or within the normal business cycle should be translated at the current rate, whereas everything else should be carried at the rate in effect when the translation was originally recorded.

Monetary/Nonmonetary Method

The attitude of the U.S. accounting profession toward translation began to change in the 1950s when it was suggested that accounts be translated according to their

Exhibit 10.2   Exchange Rates Used to Translate Selected Assets and Liabilities

	Current Noncurrent	Monetary Nonmonetary	Current Rate	Temporal
Cash, current receivables, and payables	C[a]	C	C	C
Inventory	C	H	C	C or H
Fixed assets	H[b]	H	C	H
Long-term receivables and payables	H	C	C	C

[a] C = current exchange rate.
[b] H = historical exchange rate.

nature rather than their date of maturity. Under that approach, accounts were considered as either monetary or nonmonetary rather than current or noncurrent. Monetary assets and liabilities were translated at the current rate, and nonmonetary assets and liabilities and stockholders' equity were translated at historical rates. This approach was a radical departure from the current/noncurrent method in the areas of inventory, long-term receivables, and long-term payables.

The philosophy behind this approach is that monetary or financial assets and liabilities have similar attributes in that their value represents a fixed amount of money whose reporting currency equivalent changes each time the exchange rate changes. Monetary accounts should therefore be translated at the current exchange rate. In the current/noncurrent method, some current assets are monetary (such as cash) and some are nonmonetary (such as inventory carried at cost), and yet all are translated at the current exchange rate. The proponents of the monetary/nonmonetary method consider it more meaningful to translate assets and liabilities on the basis of attributes instead of time.

Temporal Method

The temporal method was originally proposed in Accounting Research Study 12 by the AICPA and formally required in Statement No. 8. According to the temporal method, cash, receivables, and payables (both current and noncurrent) are translated at the current rate. Other assets and liabilities may be translated at current or historical rates, depending on their characteristics. Assets and liabilities carried at past exchange prices are translated at historical rates. For example, a fixed asset carried at the foreign currency price at which it was purchased would be translated into the reporting currency at the exchange rate in effect when the asset was purchased. Assets and liabilities carried at current purchase or sales exchange prices or future exchange prices would be translated at current rates. For example, inventory carried at market would be translated at the current rather than the historical rate. Under historical cost accounting, the temporal method provides essentially the same results as the monetary/nonmonetary method.

The attractiveness of the temporal approach lies in its flexibility. If a country were to change from historical cost accounting to current value accounting, the temporal method would automatically translate all assets and liabilities at current rates. The theoretical attractiveness of this approach is that the branches and subsidiaries of a parent company would be translated into the parent currency in such a way that the parent currency would be the single unit of measure.

Current Rate Method

The current rate method (or closing rate) is the easiest to apply because it requires that all assets and liabilities be translated at the current exchange rate. Only net worth would be translated at the historical rate. This approach is easier to use than the others because a company would not have to keep track of various historical exchange rates. The current rate approach results in translated statements that retain the same ratios and relationships that exist in the local currency. For example, the ratio of net income to sales in local currency is rarely the same in dollars under other translation approaches because a variety of current, historical, and average exchange rates is used to translate the income statement. Because all accounts would be translated at a single exchange rate under the current rate method, the ratio of net income to sales would remain the same in the reporting currency as in the foreign currency.

INTERNATIONAL ACCOUNTING STANDARDS

The International Accounting Standards Committee (now the International Accounting Standards Board) issued IAS 21, "Accounting for the Effects of Changes in Foreign Exchange Rates" in July 1983 with an effective date of January 1, 1985. It was later revised in 1993 as part of the comparability of financial statements project, with an effective date of January 1, 1995. It was revised again in 2003 as part of the convergence project with an effective date of January 1, 2005. IAS 21 was originally issued just after FASB Statement No. 52 (December 1981), so it was able to take advantage of the FASB deliberations in developing a standard. In addition, it was issued about the same time as the relevant Canadian and British standards, and IASC's interaction with the British, Canadian, and American standard-setters, as well as those from other parts of the world, resulted in a standard that would be widely accepted.

IAS 21 contains provisions for both transactions and translation of financial statements. In the case of translating foreign currency financial statements, the closing rate and temporal methods are used, depending on the operating characteristics of the foreign operations. If the foreign operations are integral to the operations of the reporting enterprise, the temporal method is used to translate financial statements into the reporting currency, and any exchange gains and losses are taken to income. When the foreign operation is considered to be a foreign entity, meaning that the activities of the operation are not an integral part of those of the reporting enterprise, the financial statements are translated into the reporting currency using the closing rate method, and any exchange differences are taken to equity until disposal of the net investment. Assets and liabilities are translated at the closing rate, and income and expenses are translated at the rate in effect on the date of the transactions (or an average rate). In the case of hyperinflationary economies, income and expense items are translated at the closing rate instead of an average rate. The financial statements of a foreign entity in a hyperinflationary economy must be adjusted for price-level changes according to IAS 29 and then translated into the reporting currency at the closing rate.

HISTORICAL DEVELOPMENT IN THE UNITED STATES

In the late 1960s and early 1970s, the U.S. dollar came under severe pressure from other currencies, and in 1971 it was devalued approximately 10 percent against its official gold value. During that time, the Accounting Principles Board (APB) was studying the translation issue, and in 1972, Accounting Research Study 12, which recommended the adoption of the temporal method of translation, was issued.

However, the APB was being phased out and the FASB was being organized, so nothing was done with ARS 12.

In December 1973, FASB issued Statement No. 1, *Disclosure of Foreign Currency Translation Information,* to stave off pressure while it deliberated on the more substantive issues of how to translate foreign currency financial statements. It is important to note that the dollar had been devalued again in early 1973 and had finally been cut loose to float freely in the spring of 1973. Thus, the translation issue became much more critical than it had been when the dollar was fixed against most major currencies. In addition, the dollar was essentially floating down in value against most of the major currencies of the industrial world.

On February 21, 1974, the board issued a Discussion Memorandum on translation that addressed a number of important issues. After public hearings were held, the issues in the Discussion Memorandum were consolidated, and an exposure draft was issued. After hearing responses to the exposure draft, the board issued Statement No. 8 in October 1975.

FASB Statement No. 8

According to Statement No. 8, the objective of translation was as follows: "For the purpose of preparing an enterprise's financial statements, the objective of translation is to measure and express (a) in dollars and (b) in conformity with U.S. generally accepted accounting principles (GAAP) the assets, liabilities, revenues, or expenses that are measured or denominated in foreign currency."

The temporal method of translation has already been described briefly, but there are some important things about the temporal principle and Statement No. 8 that have not been addressed. In the income statement, for example, most revenues and expenses are translated at the average exchange rate during the year. In practice, the income statement is translated monthly, and the cumulative balance from prior months is added to the current month's balance to get the cumulative totals for the year. Accounts such as cost of sales and depreciation expense are translated at the exchange rate in effect when the assets were originally purchased.

Another important feature is that Statement No. 8 required that gains and losses from foreign currency transactions and the translation of foreign currency financial statements had to be taken directly to the income statement. That meant that translated earnings were fluctuating depending on what was happening to the exchange rate, independent of the operations of the firm. This area became a source of real contention in the corporate world and was one of the major factors that led to the downfall of Statement No. 8.

In addition, many firms complained about carrying inventory at historical rates in dollars for two reasons. The first reason was simply cost-benefit. The feeling was that if inventory were turning over relatively rapidly and approximating current rates, then it would be a lot easier to compute inventory values if the current rate could be used instead of having to keep track of the old historical exchange rates. The other reason had to do with timing. Managers complained that because inventory was being translated at the historical rate, it was possible for an exchange rate change in one quarter to impact earnings in a subsequent quarter when inventory flowed through the cost of goods sold. They felt that this was distorting the operating performance of each quarter. Thus, a number of critics of Statement No. 8 felt that the statement would be improved if inventory could be carried at current rather than historical exchange rates.

A final major criticism related to the disposition of the gain or loss on long-term debt. Statement No. 8 required that firms translate long-term debt at current rates, a practice already followed by nearly half the U.S. multinationals prior to 1975. Because most of the foreign currency long-term debt in the 1970s was in currencies that were strengthening vis-à-vis the U.S. dollar, U.S. firms were recognizing sizable losses. Many firms felt that because the foreign currency debt was generally being liquidated by foreign currency earnings, there was really no dollar exposure. They also argued that the fixed assets purchased by the debt were a natural hedge or protection against loss since they were constantly generating earnings. Thus, they felt that they should have been able to write off the losses over the life of the assets or treat the losses as an adjustment to interest expense.

Movement to Statement No. 52

As a result of these and other criticisms, the board decided in May 1978 to invite comments on Statements 1 through 12. Of the 200 letters received by the board, most addressed the issues in Statement No. 8. In January 1979, the board decided to add a project to reconsider all or parts of Statement No. 8 to its agenda. In February 1979, a task force containing representatives of the IASC as well as the professional standard-setting bodies in the United Kingdom and Canada was appointed to advise the board.

In August 1980, an exposure draft was issued after 18 public board meetings and 4 public task force meetings. In December 1980, a public hearing was held on the exposure draft, which attracted 360 letters and 47 presentations. In an unprecedented move, the board issued a revised exposure draft on June 30, 1981. This was followed by more public meetings and 260 letters of comment. Finally, in December 1981, Statement No. 52, Foreign Currency Translation, was issued.

FASB Statement No. 52

The development of Statement No. 52 was not an easy matter. There were no clear-cut solutions to the problems raised in Statement No. 8, and the suggestions for change ranged from minor alterations of the statement to a major rethinking of the entire translation process. In the final analysis, the latter approach prevailed, but the vote for both exposure drafts and the final standard was four to three. The minority view held very strongly to Statement No. 8 and could not accept the changes inherent in Statement 52.

One of the major differences in the statements is that Statement No. 52 adopted new objectives of translation. The stated objectives are as follows:

1. Provide information that is generally compatible with the expected economic effects of a rate change on an enterprise's cash flows and equity.

2. Reflect in consolidated statements the financial results and relationships of the individual consolidated entities as measured in their functional currencies in conformity with U.S. GAAP.

Selection of the Functional Currency

The term *functional currency* was used for the first time in the translation literature in conjunction with Statement No. 52. Although we have already defined and illustrated what functional currency means, we need to refine our definition a little more. Exhibit 10.3 contains some information provided in Statement No. 52 on how a company can choose the functional currency.

Conceptually, it is possible for a foreign entity to have more than one functional currency. For example, the entity could sell and distribute products manufactured by the parent company so the functional currency might be that of the parent. However, it might also be manufacturing and selling products locally, so the functional currency for those functions would be the local currency. In practice, the board expected that firms would pick only one functional currency for each operation abroad. Once the functional currency of the operation has been selected, it is possible to begin the translation process. It is important to remember that the functional currency is selected on the basis of operating criteria established by management. If the firm wishes to change the functional currency, it can do so only because the operating criteria used in the initial selection have changed. This is designed so that companies will not change functional currencies capriciously to take advantage of the differences in the financial statements that result from the different translation methods.

The Translation Process

The board defines the translation process in Statement No. 52 as the process of expressing in the reporting currency of the enterprise those amounts that are denominated or measured in a different currency. In the examples given in the balance of this chapter, the reporting currency is defined as the U.S. dollar.

The actual translation process depends on which currency the books and records of the foreign entity are kept in and on how the parent defines the functional currency of the foreign entity. Once those decisions have taken place, the translation process involves either the current rate method or the temporal method.

In a more precise discussion of the translation process, the board refers to the process of "translation" and "restatement." To understand the differences in these terms, refer to the conditions set forth in Figure 10.1. Note that the books and records of the foreign entity can be kept in either the foreign currency or the reporting currency of the parent company. If the books and records are kept in the reporting currency and the functional currency is defined as the reporting currency, no translation process is necessary.

If the books and records of the foreign entity are kept in the foreign currency, the translation process depends on the definition of the functional currency. If the functional currency is the foreign currency, the financial statements are translated into the parent currency using the current rate method.

As Figure 10.1 shows, one exception to the functional currency rule is when the foreign entity is located in a highly inflationary economy. Highly inflationary economies, according to Statement No. 52, are those that have a cumulative infla-

Exhibit 10.3   Factors Influencing the Determination of the Functional Currency

a.   Cash Flow Indicators

1. *Foreign Currency*—Cash flows related to the foreign entity's individual assets and liabilities are primarily in the foreign currency and do not directly impact the parent company's cash flows.

2. *Parent's Currency*—Cash flows related to the foreign entity's individual assets and liabilities directly impact the parent's cash flows on a current basis and are readily available for remittance to the parent company.

b.   Sales Price Indicators

1. *Foreign Currency*—Sales prices for the foreign entity's products are not primarily responsive on a short-term basis to changes in exchange rates but are determined more by local competition or local government regulation.

2. *Parent's Currency*—Sales prices for the foreign entity's products are primarily responsive on a short-term basis to changes in exchange rates; for example, sales prices are determined more by worldwide competition or by international prices.

c.   Sales Market Indicators

1. *Foreign Currency*—There is an active local sales market for the foreign entity's products, although there also might be significant amounts of exports.

2. *Parent's Currency*—The sales market is mostly in the parent's country or sales contracts are denominated in the parent's currency.

d.   Expense Indicators

1. *Foreign Currency*—Labor, materials, and other costs for the foreign entity's products or services are primarily local costs, even though there might also be imports from other countries.

2. *Parent's Currency*—labor, materials, and other costs for the foreign entity's products or services, on a continuing basis, are primarily costs for components obtained from the country in which the parent company is located.

e.   Financing Indicators

1. *Foreign Currency*—Financing is primarily denominated in foreign currency, and funds generated by the foreign entity's operations are sufficient to service existing and normally expected debt obligations.

2. *Parent's Currency*—Financing is primarily from the parent or other dollar-denominated obligations, or funds generated by the foreign entity's operations are not sufficient to service existing and normally expected debt obligations without the infusion of additional funds from the parent company. Infusion of additional funds from the

(continues)

Exhibit 10.3   (*Continued*)

parent company for expansion is not a factor, provided funds generated by the foreign entity's expanded operations are expected to be sufficient to service that additional financing.

f.   Intercompany Transactions and Arrangements Indicators

1. *Foreign Currency*—There is a low volume of intercompany transactions, and there is not an extensive interrelationship between the operations of the foreign entity and the parent company. However, the foreign entity's operations may rely on the parent's or affiliate's competitive advantages, such as patents and trademarks .

2. *Parent's Currency*—There is a high volume of intercompany transactions, and there is an extensive interrelationship between the operations of the foreign entity and the parent company. Additionally, the parent's currency generally would be the functional currency if the foreign entity is a device or shell corporation for holding investments, obligations, intangible assets, and the like, that could readily be carried on the parent's or affiliate's books.

Source: Financial Accounting Standard Board, *Statement of Financial Accounting Standards No. 52, Foreign Currency Translation* (Stamford, CT: FASB, December 1981), pp. 26–27.

tion rate of approximately 100 percent over a 3-year period. This is equivalent to an average rate of 26 percent compounded annually. For reasons discussed later in this chapter, the temporal method must be used.

As another, though rare, possibility, the books and records are kept in the foreign currency, but the functional currency is a third currency. In that situation, the

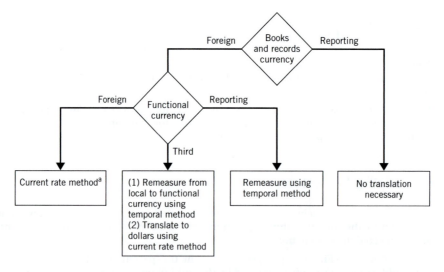

Figure 10.1   Translation or Remeasurement of Foreign Currency Financial Statements into the Reporting Currency

[a] In the case of a highly inflationary economy, the local currency may be the functional currency from an operating standpoint, but the dollar is considered the functional currency from a translation standpoint.

financial statements need to be remeasured from the foreign currency to the functional currency using the temporal method and then translated into the reporting currency using the current rate method. The rationale behind the concept of remeasurement is to produce the same results as if the transactions had actually taken place in the functional currency. Thus, nonmonetary assets are restated in the functional currency at the exchange rate in effect when the assets were acquired in the foreign currency.

As a final possibility, the books and records are kept in the foreign currency, but the functional currency is defined as the reporting currency. In that situation, the foreign currency financial statements are remeasured into the reporting currency using the temporal method.

The important thing to note from this discussion is that IAS 21 and Statement No. 52 use both the current rate method and the temporal method of translating and remeasuring financial statements from a foreign currency to U.S. dollars. The key is to know in which currency the books and records are kept and how the functional currency of the foreign entity is defined. Thus, Statement No. 52 has not necessarily simplified the translation process, and we cannot forget all the problems that occurred with Statement No. 8. Also, it is incorrect to refer to Statement No. 52 as the current rate method since it encompasses both methods.

The Translation Process Illustrated

Earlier in this chapter, we mentioned that the translation process has to deal with two issues: which exchange rate (current or historical) must be used to translate each individual account in the financial statements and how the resulting translation gain or loss is to be recognized in the statements.

Exhibit 10.4 contains the relevant exchange rates and basic assumptions that are needed to translate the financial statements in Exhibits 10.5 and 10.6. Note that

Exhibit 10.4 Relevant Exchange Rates

Exchange Rates	($ per £)
Rate in effect when capital stock was issued; the long-term notes payable was incurred and fixed assets were acquired	1.85
December 31, 2003	1.48
Average for 2004	1.53
December 31, 2004	1.56
Rate for December 31, 2003 inventory	1.50
Rate for December 31, 2004 inventory	1.45
Dividend rate June 30, 2004	1.55
Assume that taxes were paid evenly throughout the year	

Retained Earnings	Dollar Value
Retained Earnings 12/31/03 (current rate method)	$11,560
Retained Earnings 12/31/03 (temporal method)	$12,360

Exhibit 10.5   Pounds Sterling Balance Sheet (in thousands)

Grover Mfg. Plc

	December 31	
	2004	2003
Assets		
Current assets		
Cash and receivables	4,000	3,000
Inventory	4,500	3,000
Total	8,500	6,000
Fixed assets		
Land	3,000	3,000
Building (cost £10,000)	7,000	8,000
Equipment (cost £10,000)	4,000	6,000
Total	14,000	17,000
Total Assets	22,500	23,000
Liabilities and Stockholders' Equity		
Current liabilities	5,500	6,000
Long-term liabilities		
Notes payable	3,000	5,000
Deferred income taxes	2,500	2,000
	5,500	7,000
Stockholders' Equity		
Capital stock	5,000	5,000
Retained earnings	6,500	5,000
	11,500	10,000
Total Liabilities and Stockholders' Equity	22,500	23,000

two different retained earnings figures are given for the current rate and temporal methods. We will explain this later in the chapter. Also, note that even though taxes were paid evenly throughout the year, dividends were paid only on June 30.

The Temporal Method

Remember that the temporal method is used to remeasure financial statements from a foreign currency to the functional currency. Assume that Grover Manufacturing Plc is the British subsidiary of a U.S. firm and that the functional currency is defined as the U.S. dollar rather than the British pound. Use of the temporal method requires that we do the following:

Exhibit 10.6   Pounds Sterling Statement of Income and Retained Earnings

Grover Mfg. Plc
Statement of Income and Retained Earnings for the Year Ended
December 31, 2004 (pounds in thousands)

Sales		18,000
Expenses:		
Cost of goods sold	9,000	
Depreciation	3,000	
Other expenses	2,100	14,100
Income before Taxes		3,900
Income Taxes		1,900
Net Income		2,000
Retained Earnings, December 31, 2003		5,000
		7,000
Dividends		500
Retained Earnings, December 31, 2004		6,500

1. Remeasure cash, receivables, and liabilities at the current balance sheet rate.

2. Remeasure inventory (which is carried at historical cost in this case), fixed assets, and capital stock at the appropriate historical exchange rates.

3. Remeasure most revenues and expenses at the average rate for the year; cost of sales and depreciation expense are translated at the appropriate historical exchange rates.

4. Take all remeasurement gains or losses directly to the income statement.

To accomplish these purposes, it is easier to remeasure the balance sheet before the income statement. Notice that in Exhibit 10.7 there is no exchange rate associated with retained earnings. This is because the December 31, 2004, retained earnings amount is the difference between total assets and liabilities less the other stockholders' equity accounts (in this case, just capital stock). Thus, the retained earnings balance must be $12,255 at the end of the year.

The remeasured statement of income and retained earnings is found in Exhibit 10.8. Notice that in the income statement cost of goods sold and depreciation expense are not remeasured at the same exchange rate as are other revenues and expenses. In the case of cost of goods sold, different rates are used for beginning inventory, purchases, and ending inventory. Depreciation expense is translated at the historical rate in effect when assets were purchased.

Notice in the income statement that there is a translation loss of $1,160. That figure is derived by working backward. We know from the balance sheet in Exhibit 10.8 that the ending retained earnings balance must be $12,255. Because we remeasured the dividend amount and were provided the beginning retained earnings (RE) balance, we can derive the net income figure for the year (ending RE + dividends–beginning RE = NI). All the other accounts were remeasured, so the translation

Exhibit 10.7 Remeasured Balance Sheet: Temporal Method

Grover Mfg. Plc
Translated Balance Sheet (Temporal Method) December 31, 2004 (in thousands)

	Pounds	Exchange Rate	Dollars
Assets			
Cash and receivables	4,000	1.56	6,240
Inventory	4,500	1.45	6,525
Land	3,000	1.85	5,550
Building—net	7,000	1.85	12,950
Equipment—net	4,000	1.85	7,400
	22,500		38,665
Liabilities and Stockholders' Equity			
Current liabilities	5,500	1.56	8,580
Notes payable	3,000	1.56	4,680
Deferred taxes	2,500	1.56	3,900
Capital stock	5,000	1.85	9,250
Retained earnings	6,500		12,255
	22,500		38,665

gain is the amount that must be plugged in to arrive at the net income figure. The important thing to note here is that the translation gain is taken directly to the income statement rather than to the balance sheet.

The Current Rate Method

The current rate method is far easier to determine. It is used when the functional currency is defined as the foreign currency and is by far the more widely used translation method. To accomplish the translation process, the following steps must be performed:

1. Total assets and liabilities are translated at the current exchange rate.
2. Stockholders' equity accounts are translated at the appropriate historical exchange rates.
3. All revenue and expense items are translated at the average exchange rate for the period.
4. Dividends are translated at the exchange rate in effect when they were issued.
5. Translation gains and losses are taken to a special accumulated translation adjustment account in stockholders' equity.

In the current rate method, it is better to translate the income statement before translating the balance sheet because the translation gain or loss becomes a balance sheet plug figure rather than an income statement plug figure as in the temporal method. Notice that in Exhibit 10.9 all income statement accounts are trans-

Exhibit 10.8   Remeasured Statement of Income and Retained Earnings:
Temporal Method

Grover Mfg. Plc
Translated Statement of Income and Retained Earnings (Temporal Method) for the Year
Ended December 31, 2004 (in thousands)

	Pounds	Exchange Rate	Dollars
Sales	18,000	1.53	27,540
Expenses:			
Cost of goods sold	9,000	*a*	14,040
Depreciation	3,000	1.85	5,550
Other expenses	2,100	1.53	3,213
Translation loss (gain)			1,160
	14,100		23,963
Income before Taxes	3,900		3,577
Income Taxes	1,900	1.53	2,907
Net Income	2,000		670
Retained Earnings (12/31/03)	5,000		12,360
	7,000		13,030
Dividends	500	1.55	(775)
Retained Earnings (12/31/04)	6,500		12,255
Beginning inventory	3,000	1.50	4,500
Purchases	10,500	1.53	16,065
Goods available for sale	13,500		20,565
Ending inventory	4,500	1.45	6,525
	9,000		14,040

a Cost of goods sold.

lated at the average exchange rate for the period. The beginning retained earnings balance was provided in Exhibit 10.4, and dividends are translated at the exchange rate in effect when they were paid. Thus, the ending retained earnings balance is derived from the other figures rather than plugged in from the balance sheet.

In Exhibit 10.10, all assets and liabilities are translated at the current exchange rate. Capital stock is translated at the exchange rate in effect when it was issued, and retained earnings are picked up from Exhibit 10.9. All that is left is the accumulated translation adjustment, which is a $5,155 loss that makes the balance sheet balance. It is important to note that the translation adjustment is taken to stockholders' equity rather than to the income statement, as was the case under the temporal method.

Foreign Currency Transactions

Earlier in the chapter, we learned that gains and losses from foreign currency transactions are taken to the income statement. For example, assume that the British subsidiary suffers a foreign exchange loss of £10,000 from an import denominated in deutsche marks. The loss would be translated into dollars at the 2004 average

Exhibit 10.9   Translated Statement of Income and Retained Earnings: Current Rate Method

Grover Mfg. Plc

Translated Statement of Income and Retained Earnings (Current Rate Method) for the Year Ended December 31, 2004 (in thousands)

	Pounds	Exchange Rate	Dollars
Sales	18,000	1.53	27,540
Expenses:			
Cost of sales	9,000	1.53	13,770
Depreciation	3,000	1.53	4,590
Other expenses	2,100	1.53	3,213
	14,100		21,573
Income before taxes	3,900		5,967
Income taxes	1,900	1.53	2,907
Net income	2,000		3,060
Retained earnings (12/31/03)	5,000		11,560
	7,000		14,620
Dividends	500	1.55	775
Retained earnings (12/31/04)	6,500		13,845

Exhibit 10.10   Translated Balance Sheet: Current Rate Method

Grover Mfg. Plc

Translated Balance Sheet Current Rate Method December 31, 2004 (in thousands)

	Pounds	Exchange Rate	Dollars
Assets			
Cash and receivables	4,000	1.56	6,240
Inventory	4,500	1.56	7,020
Land	3,000	1.56	4,680
Buildings—net	7,000	1.56	10,920
Equipment—net	4,000	1.56	6,240
Total	22,500		35,100
Liabilities and Stockholders' Equity			
Current liabilities	5,500	1.56	8,580
Notes payable	3,000	1.56	4,680
Deferred taxes	2,500	1.56	3,900
Capital stock	5,000	1.85	9,250
Retained earnings	6,500		13,845
Accumulated translation adjustment	____		(5,155)
Total	22,500		35,100

exchange rate of $1.53, and the $15,300 loss would probably show up on the income statement under "other income/other expense." Gains and losses on foreign currency debt are often shown as an adjustment of interest expense. This is true for both the temporal and current rate methods of translation.

Intercompany Transactions

Various types of intercompany transactions occur between a parent and subsidiary. Some are considered long term, such as when a parent company loans money to a subsidiary but does not expect to have the loan repaid. Others are short term, such as when a parent lends money to a subsidiary and expects the loan to be repaid. In addition, intercompany profits can arise when the parent sells goods or services to a subsidiary, and a portion of these profits can be related to exchange rate changes.

Long-Term Investment   An intercompany transaction that is of a long-term investment nature is one where settlement is not planned or anticipated in the foreseeable future. For example, assume that the parent company lends $500,000 to its British subsidiary on January 1, when the exchange rate was $1.7845. The British subsidiary would carry the loan on its books at £280,190. At the end of the year when the exchange rate is $1.6889, the loan would be worth £296,051, giving rise to a foreign exchange loss of £15,861. If the loan is expected to be paid back, the loss would be recognized in the income statement of the British subsidiary and translated into dollars at the average exchange rate for the year for consolidation purposes. However, if the loan is considered long term in nature, the exchange loss will be taken to the separate component of stockholders' equity if the financial statements are translated by the current rate method and to the income statement if remeasured by the temporal method.

Elimination of Intercompany Profits   Intercompany profits, such as those arising from a sale from a parent to subsidiary, must be eliminated upon consolidation, combination, or the equity method, and such profits are based on the exchange rates at the dates of the sales or transfers. For example, assume that a U.S. parent company sells $100,000 in software to its British subsidiary on October 1 when the exchange rate is $1.8119 and the year-end rate balance sheet rate is $1.6889. The determination of intercompany profits is found in Exhibit 10.11. Notice that the inventory is carried on the subsidiary books at £55,191. When the exchange rate changes to $1.6889 at the end of the year, the dollar equivalent of the inventory using the current rate method becomes $153,590. However, the parent company profit of $25,000 must be eliminated from the inventory upon consolidation, so the inventory is carried at $128,690 instead of $75,000, which was the value of the inventory when the sale was made. Under the temporal method, the inventory is carried at historical cost, so the inventory is the same at the balance sheet date as it was at the transfer date.

Statement of Cash Flows

The guidelines for preparing the statement of cash flows for an MNE can be found in FASB Statement No. 95 and are basically the same as those found in Interna-

Exhibit 10.11   Elimination of Intercompany Profits

	Transfer	Rate	Balance Sheet	Rate
	$1.8119/£		$1.6889/£	
	Local Currency	U.S. Dollars	Local Currency	U.S. Dollars
Inventory Transfer Price	55,191	100,000	55,191	153,690
Parent cost		75,000		75,000
Parent Profit Component		25,000		25,000
Inventory after profit elimination		75,000		128,690

tional Accounting Standard 7. IAS 7 is one of the few standards that the SEC will allow foreign firms to use when registering in the United States rather than having to reconcile to U.S. GAAP. A cash flow statement should report flows of cash and cash equivalents classified by operating activities, investing activities, and financing activities. Cash equivalents are short-term investments that are purchased and sold as part of the firm's cash management activities, rather than as part of its operating, investing, and financing activities. Using the example of our U.S. parent and British subsidiary, the following steps must be followed in preparing a statement of cash flows.

- The British subsidiary first prepares its own statement of cash flows in British pounds.
- Next, the cash flows are translated into dollars using the actual exchange rate in effect when the cash flows took place or the average exchange rate for the year.
- Finally, the translated cash flows are consolidated with the parent company's cash flow statement.

Net income is the beginning point for a cash flow statement, and the consolidated income statement may carry unrealized foreign exchange gains and losses, such as those that arise from carrying a foreign currency receivable or payable. Because these gains and losses are not cash flows, they must be excluded from cash flows from operating activities. One approach would be to disclose these gains and losses as a reconciling item between net income and net cash flow from operating activities. In addition, exchange rate changes can affect foreign currency cash balances during a period. The resulting gain or loss must be reported as a separate item on the reconciliation of the change in cash and cash equivalents during the period.

Rather than disclose the effect of exchange rate changes as an adjustment to operating income, it is more common to show it as a separate component of cash flows for the period. For example, DaimlerChrysler, which was formed by the merger of DaimlerBenz, a German company, and Chrysler, a U.S. company, prepares its consolidated financial statements according to U.S. GAAP and uses the euro as the currency of its financial statements, although it also provides financial information in U.S. dollars. In its consolidated cash flow statement, it discloses the effect of foreign exchange rate changes on cash and cash equivalents maturing within three months as a separate item after cash provided by operating, investing, and financing activities.

Disclosure of the Impact of IAS 21

IAS 21 requires that the following information be disclosed:

1. The amount of exchange differences included in the net profit or loss for the period.
2. Net exchange differences classified as equity as a separate component of equity; and a reconciliation of the amount of such exchange differences at the beginning and end of the period.
3. When the reporting currency is different from the currency of the country in which the enterprise is domiciled, the reason for using a different currency. The reason for any change in the reporting currency should also be disclosed.
4. A change in the functional currency of either the reporting entity or a significant foreign operation and the reason therefore.

IAS 21 also makes provisions for convenience translations. This occurs when an entity simply translates all financial statements into another currency at the closing rate so that readers can see the information in their own currency. The financial information resulting from a convenience translation would not conform with IAS 21, so the firm needs to provide the following information:

1. Clearly identify the supplementary information to distinguish it from the information that complies with IFRS.
2. Disclose the currency in which the supplementary information is displayed.
3. Disclose the entity's functional currency and the method of translation used to determine the supplementary information.

Disclosure of the Impact of Statement No. 52

Statement No. 52 is very specific about what needs to be disclosed:

1. The aggregate transaction gain or loss included in income.
2. An analysis of the changes during the period of the separate component of stockholders' equity, including at least the following:
    a. Beginning and ending amount of cumulative translation adjustments.
    b. Aggregate adjustment for the period resulting from translation adjustments and gains and losses from certain hedges and intercompany balances.

   c. Amount of income taxes for the period allocated to the translation adjustments.

   d. Amounts transferred from cumulative translation adjustments and included in determining net income for the period as a result of the sale or complete or substantially complete liquidation of an investment in a foreign entity.

That information can be provided in a separate financial statement, in notes to the financial statements, or as a part of a statement of changes in equity. There does not seem to be any uniform or suggested method for determining where or in which format the information is to be displayed.

Firms usually disclose their translation policies in the footnotes, as noted below in the case of DaimlerChrysler, which is a part of Footnote 1, Summary of Significant Accounting Policies, 2004 Annual Report:

> The assets and liabilities of foreign operations where the functional currency is not the euro are generally translated into euro using period-end exchange rates. The resulting translation adjustments are recorded as a component of accumulated other comprehensive loss. The statements of income (loss) and the statements of cash flows are translated using average exchange rates during the respective periods. The assets and liabilities of foreign operations in highly inflationary economies are translated into euro on the basis of period-end rates for monetary assets and liabilities and at historical rates for non-monetary items, with resulting translation gains and losses recognized in earnings. Further, for foreign operations in such economies, depreciation and gains and losses from the disposal of non-monetary assets are determined using historical rates.

Note that DaimlerChrysler basically uses the current rate method for all operations except for highly inflationary economies (only one economy in 2004). In those cases, it uses the temporal method, whereas IAS 21 requires that financial statements be adjusted to current values and translated at the closing rate.

As noted, DaimlerChrysler uses the current rate method for its operations in all countries except those that are highly inflationary. In addition, Daimler-Chrysler provides separate information on the cumulative translation adjustment in the consolidated statements of changes in stockholders' equity, as shown in Exhibit 10.12.

One difficulty associated with this disclosure process is that the focus is on the measurable transactions and translation gains and losses. It is important for management to spend some time in the annual report explaining the rest of the impact of the translation of financial statements on the operations of the firm. In early 2004, for example, the U.S. dollar was rising against the euro but not against the Japanese yen. That strength turned to weakness in mid-2004, but the dollar again began to rise rather sharply in early 2005 before falling again. During these times of dollar strength, at the same time that many foreign economies were relatively weak as compared with the U.S. economy, many U.S. firms were experiencing a translated dollar profit squeeze. This can be illustrated by the following example:

	Income FC	Exchange Rate	Dollars
First Quarter 2004	FC100,000	$1.00	$100,000
First Quarter 2005	FC110,000	$0.25	$27,500

Exhibit 10.12 Consolidated Statements of Changes in Stockholders' Equity, DaimlerChrysler

(In millions of €)	Capital Stock	Additional Paid-in Capital	Retained Earnings	Accumulated other comprehensive income (loss)				Treasure Stock	Total
				Cumulative Translation Adjustment	Available-for-sale Securities	Derivative Financial Instruments	Minimum Pension Liability		
Balance at January 1, 2001	2,609	7,299	29,461	3,285	198	(408)	(22)	–	42,422
Net loss	–	–	(662)	–	–	–	–	–	(662)
Other comprehensive income (loss)	–	–	–	565	(137)	71	(884)	–	(385)
Total comprehensive loss									(1,047)
Stock based compensation	–	20	–	–	–	–	–	–	20
Purchase of capital stock	–	–	–	–	–	–	–	(66)	(66)
Re-issuance of treasury stock	–	–	–	–	–	–	–	66	66
Dividends	–	–	(2,358)	–	–	–	–	–	(2,358)
Balance at December 31, 2001	2,609	7,319	26,441	3,850	61	(337)	(906)	–	39,037
Net Income	–	–	4,718	–	–	–	–	–	4,718
Other comprehensive income (loss)	–	–	–	(3,238)	(135)	1,402	(6,301)	–	(8,272)
Total comprehensive loss									(3,554)
Stock based compensation	–	57	–	–	–	–	–	–	57
Issuance of shares upon conversion of notes	24	482	–	–	–	–	–	–	506
Purchase of capital stock	–	–	–	–	–	–	–	(49)	(49)
Re-Issuance of treasury stock	–	–	–	–	–	–	–	49	49
Dividends	–	–	(1,003)	–	–	–	–	–	(1,003)
Other	–	(39)	–	–	–	–	–	–	(39)
Balance at December 31, 2002	2,633	7,819	30,156	612	(74)	1,065	(7,207)	–	35,004
Net income	–	–	448	–	–	–	–	–	448
Other comprehensive income (loss)	–	–	–	(1,561)	407	1,162	444	–	452
Total comprehensive income									900
Stock based compensation	–	95	–	–	–	–	–	–	95
Issuance of shares upon conversion of notes	–	1	–	–	–	–	–	–	1
Purchase of capital stock	–	–	–	–	–	–	–	(28)	(28)
Re-issuance of treasury stock	–	–	–	–	–	–	–	28	28
Dividends	–	–	(1,519)	–	–	–	–	–	(1,519)
Balance at December 31, 2003	2,633	7,915	29,085	(949)	333	2,227	(6,763)	–	34,481

Income rose in foreign currency from 100,000 to 110,000 over the year, an increase of only 10 percent, due primarily to a weak economy. However, the dollar equivalent fell from $100,000 to $27,500, a drop of 72.5 percent. Even though the economy was growing, the currency was falling at a faster rate, so the dollar equivalent of earnings also fell. It is important to report this type of situation to shareholders so they can better understand the reported results.

CONVERGENCE

As part of the move to create a set of standards acceptable for adoption in the EU in 2005, IASB examined IAS 21 and looked for ways to resolve some of the differences in the standard with international standards. In the early years when Statement No. 8 and IAS 21 were first issued, there were several differences in the two standards as well as differences with standards in the United Kingdom and Canada. However, the convergence process has eliminated the substantive differences among the standards. IAS 21 as revised in 2003 is an excellent example of how the process of convergence has resulted in a standard that is universally acceptable.

SUMMARY

1. Foreign exchange can be traded through commercial and investment banks (over the counter or OTC) on exchanges such as the Philadelphia Stock Exchange or on the Internet. The largest volume of transactions takes place in the OTC market.

2. Spot trades take place within two business days, and forward trades take place anytime after two business days.

3. Foreign currency transactions are transactions whose terms are denominated in a currency other than the entity's reporting currency.

4. For foreign currency transactions, the IASC and FASB require that the original transaction be translated into dollars at the exchange rate in effect on that date. Amounts receivable or payable in a foreign currency are translated at the current exchange rate at subsequent balance sheet dates. Foreign exchange gains and losses are taken to the income statement immediately.

5. Companies translate foreign currency financial statements into the parent currency to assist the readers of financial statements and to enable management to compare results across different countries.

6. The functional currency is the currency of the primary economic environment in which the company operates.

7. The translation methodologies used in the past are the current/noncurrent method, the monetary/nonmonetary method, the temporal method, and the current rate or closing rate method.

8. The temporal method translates monetary assets and liabilities at the current rate and other accounts at current or historical exchange rate, depending on their characteristics. Assets and liabilities carried at past exchange prices (such as fixed assets carried at historical cost) are translated at the historical exchange rate. Assets and liabilities carried at current cost are translated using the current exchange rate.

9.   The current rate method translates assets and liabilities at the current rate and shareholders' equity at historical rates. Income statement items are translated at the average exchange rate.

10.   Under the temporal method, translation gains and losses go to income; under the current rate method, they go to shareholders' equity.

11.   IAS 21 and FASB Statement No. 52 require financial statements to be translated using either the temporal or the current rate methods.

12.   Under the temporal method translation gains and losses are recognized in the current period's income. Under the current rate method, they are taken to equity.

13.   Foreign exchange gains and losses are reported in the statement of cash flows as a reconciling item between net income and net cash flow from operating activities or as a separate component of cash flows for the period.

14.   In their annual reports, companies typically disclose the translation method they use and the amount of the translation gain or loss for the period and the impact of foreign exchange on operations.

Discussion Questions

1.   Some might argue that Statement No. 52 is an international standard because the FASB received a great deal of input from the IASC and from other countries while it was developing the standard. What are the strengths and weaknesses of this type of international collaboration? Does it weaken the current IASB's position as an international standard-setter if it allows the United States or any other country to set a standard before it does?

2.   Why do you think most U.S. companies use the current rate method as allowed under Statement No. 52 when the only method allowed prior to that was the temporal method or some variation of that method?

3.   Imperial Chemical Industries PLC (ICI) is a British chemical company that lists ADRs on the New York Stock Exchange. In its annual report, ICI identifies its policies for dealing with foreign exchange as follows:

> Profit and loss accounts in foreign currencies are translated into sterling at average rates for the relevant accounting periods. Assets and liabilities are translated at exchange rates ruling at the date of the Group balance sheet. Exchange differences on short-term foreign currency borrowings and deposits are included with net interest payable. Exchange differences on all other balances, except relevant foreign currency loans, are taken to trading profit. In the Group accounts, exchange differences arising on consolidation of the net investments in overseas subsidiary undertakings and associates are taken to reserves, as are differences arising on equity investments denominated in foreign currencies in the Company accounts. Differences on relevant foreign currency loans are taken to reserves and offset against the differences on net investments in both Group and Company accounts.

Which translation methodology does ICI use? Do their policies seem consistent with what is required by FASB's Statement No. 52?

Toward the end of their annual report, they also include reconciliation information consistent with Form 20-F that is required by the SEC. In that section, ICI notes that under U.K. GAAP, foreign currency differences arising on foreign currency loans are taken to reserves and offset against differences arising on net investments (if they act as a hedge) and that U.S. GAAP is more restrictive. In what way is it more restrictive?

4. XYZ Company, a manufacturer of computer peripheries, assembles a particular product line at a wholly owned facility in Singapore. The product is designed at XYZ's headquarters in the United States, but the different components used in the assembly process are manufactured throughout Asia and shipped to Singapore for final assembly. Some of the components are manufactured in multiple locations, so the customer can actually designate where XYZ should source the components. The final product is assembled in Singapore and then shipped via Emery Freight to customers throughout Asia. XYZ Singapore does not buy any components from the United States, but it invoices all of the components purchased from Asian suppliers in U.S. dollars. In addition, it sells the product to Asian customers in U.S. dollars. However, all of its expenses in Singapore are paid in Singapore dollars. Most of the key marketing decisions are made by the U.S. marketing staff, although the Singapore staff acts as a liaison with Emery Freight personnel and deals with the local workers, most of whom come from Sri Lanka on short-term work visas.

    XYZ prefers to translate the results of its Singapore subsidiary into dollars using the current rate method. What is the advantage to XYZ of using the current rate method? As its auditor, what do you think of its decision? If its decision is wrong and it should be using the temporal method, is it possible for XYZ to change?

5. When it comes to translating the financial statements of entities in highly inflationary countries, which of the following approaches makes more sense and why?

    a. Remeasure using the temporal method, even though the functional currency is the local currency for operation purposes.

    b. Restate for inflation and translate using the current rate method.

6. Why do currency differences affect foreign exchange reporting?

7. What difference has the introduction of a comprehensive income statement made to U.S. accounting for foreign exchange?

8. Choose a country and prepare a report on the quarterly exchange rates for the currency of that country against the U.S. dollar over the past four quarters. Assuming that a U.S. company has a subsidiary in that country and that the foreign entity is relatively independent from the parent company, how would you anticipate that the exchange rates would impact the results of operations when translated into dollars?

9. Why do you think it has been so difficult for accounting regulators to deal with accounting for foreign exchange over the last 25 years?

10. Under the original IAS 20 rules, companies were permitted to adjust the value of fixed assets purchased abroad and payable in the foreign currency for foreign exchange losses resulting from a devaluation of the currency of the country of the purchaser. Why do you think the IASC permitted that approach, and why do you think its successor, the IASB, eliminated that option?

Information for questions 11–15:

In its annual report, the Swedish company, Volvo, discloses the following information about its policy for dealing with foreign currencies:

In preparing the consolidated financial statements, all items in the income statements of foreign subsidiaries and joint ventures (except subsidiaries in highly inflationary economies) are translated to Swedish kronor at the average exchange rates during the year (average rate). All balance sheet items except net income are translated at exchange rates at the respective year-ends (year-end rate). The differences in consolidated shareholders' equity arising as a result of variations between year-end exchange rates are charged or credited directly to shareholders' equity and classified as restricted or unrestricted reserves. Movements in exchange rates change the book value of foreign associated companies. This difference affects restricted reserves directly. … Financial statements of subsidiaries operating in highly inflationary economies are translated to Swedish kronor using the monetary method. Monetary items in the balance sheet are translated at year-end rates and nonmonetary balance sheet items and corresponding income statement items are translated at rates in effect at the time of acquisition (historical rates). Other income statement items are translated at average rates. Translation differences are credited to, or charged against, income in the year in which they arise.

11. What is the translation methodology that Volvo uses? Is it consistent with IAS 21?

12. Is Volvo's approach to accounting for highly inflationary economies more similar to the IAS 21 or FASB Statement No. 52 approach? Explain.

13. Look up the exchange rate for the Swedish kronor and Japanese yen for 2004. Assume that Volvo exports automobiles to Japan and invoices the sales in Japanese yen. From January 1, 2004 to December 31, 2004, did the Swedish kronor strengthen or weaken against the yen? Would Volvo have recognized foreign exchange gains or losses on exports, and where would they show up in the financial statements?

14. Assume that Volvo had an operating subsidiary in Japan during that period. Would it have picked up translation gains or losses during 2004? Where would these gains or losses show up on the financial statements?

15. Assume that Volvo has to adopt IAS 21 as part of the EU's move to implement IFRS by the IASB. Will Volvo have to make any changes in its approach to accounting for foreign currencies? What will it have to do differently?

Exercises

1. **Exchange Rate Relationships.** Below are the exchange rates between the U.S. dollar and five different currencies. The rates are quoted in terms of the number of units of the foreign currency to the dollar.

	December 31, 2003	December 31, 2004
Euro	.79670	.73310
British pound	.56250	.51920
Swiss franc	1.2423	1.1318
Chinese yuan	8.2867	8.2865
Brazilian real	2.9030	2.66150

a. Against which currencies did the U.S. dollar weaken in 2004? strengthen?

b. What is the exchange rate of each currency on December 31, 2004 in terms of dollars per unit of the foreign currency?

c.   Which currency changed the most against the dollar in 2004? the least?

2.   **Exchange Rate Relationships.** Below are the exchange rates between the U.S. dollar and five different currencies. The rates are quoted in terms of the number of dollars per unit of the foreign currency.

	December 31, 2003	December 31, 2004
Mexican peso	.089110	.0896540
Argentine peso	.34410	.33660
Thai baht	.02526	.025680
S. Korean won	.00083720	.00097510
Indian rupee	.0220	.022890

a.   Against which currencies did the U.S. dollar weaken in 2004? strengthen?

b.   What is the exchange rate of each currency on December 31, 2004 in terms of units of foreign currency per dollar?

c.   Which currency changed the most against the dollar in 2004? the least?

3.   Assume the following spot exchange rates between the U.S. dollar and the British pound sterling:

March 1	$1.8685
March 31	$1.8258
April 30	$1.7740

On March 1, XYZ, a U.S. company, sells goods to a British importer for £1,000,000. Payment is to be received on April 30, and XYZ adjusts its financial statements quarterly. What are the journal entries for XYZ on March 1, March 31, and April 30? Was the dollar strengthening or weakening over the period of the contract?

4.   Assume the following spot exchange rates between the U.S. dollar and the British pound sterling:

March 1	$1.8685
March 31	$1.8258
April 30	$1.7740

On March 1, XYZ, a U.S. company, sells goods to a British importer for $1,868,500 at the spot rate and denominates the sale in dollars. Payment is to be received on April 30, and XYZ adjusts its financial statements quarterly. What are the journal entries on March 1, March 31, and April 30? Was the dollar strengthening or weakening over the period of the contract?

5.   Assume the following spot exchange rates between the U.S. dollar and the British pound sterling:

March 1	$1.8685
March 31	$1.8258
April 30	$1.7740

On March 1, XYZ, a U.S. company, buys goods from a British exporter for £1,000,000. Payment is to be made on April 30, and XYZ adjusts its financial statements quarterly. What are the journal entries on March 1, March 31, and April 30? Was the dollar strengthening or weakening over the period of the contract?

6. Assume the following spot exchange rates between the U.S. dollar and the Japanese yen:

March 1	¥107.40
March 31	¥105.64
April 30	¥109.82

    On March 1, XYZ, a U.S. company, sells goods to a Japanese importer for ¥10 million. Payment is to be received on April 30, and XYZ adjusts its financial statements quarterly. What are the journal entries for XYZ on March 1, March 31, and April 30? Was the dollar strengthening or weakening over the period of the contract?

7. Assume the following spot exchange rates between the U.S. dollar and the Japanese yen:

March 1	¥107.40
March 31	¥105.64
April 30	¥109.82

    On March 1, XYZ, a U.S. company, buys goods from a Japanese importer for ¥10 million. Payment is to be made on April 30, and XYZ adjusts its financial statements quarterly. What are the journal entries for XYZ on March 1, March 31, and April 30? Was the dollar strengthening or weakening over the period of the contract?

8. On January 1, XYZ, a U.S. firm, borrows €1,000,000 from a German bank for five years at 6 percent interest paid semiannually in euro. The principal does not have to be paid until the end of the loan. The principal is adjusted for any exchange rate changes every six months. Assume the following exchange rates for the first year of the loan:

January 1	$1.2575
June 30	$1.2082
December 3!	$1.3640

    Assume that the average exchange rate for each six-month period is the simple average for that period. What are the journal entries for January 1, June 30, and December 31? Was the dollar strengthening or weakening over the period of the contract?

9. Rouse Company, a developer of major shopping centers, built two shopping centers in Canada and financed more than 90 percent of the cost with a loan from Canadian lenders. The loan would be paid off with rental income from the shopping centers with no recourse to Rouse Company.

    a. Assume that Rouse treated the U.S. dollar as the functional currency for translation purposes and that the Canadian dollar was weakening against the U.S. dollar. What do you think would have been the impact of that situation on the income statement?

    b. Rouse argued to the FASB that its operations in Canada constituted a natural hedge and that it should not have to reflect any translation gains or losses in income. What do you think they meant by a "natural hedge," and what is your opinion about their contention?

    c. How would your answer in question "a" differ if Rouse treated the Canadian dollar rather than the U.S. dollar as the functional currency?

    d. Given the assumptions in the case, which currency should be the functional currency?

    The following is an example of a U.S. company with a U.K. subsidiary Use the information to answer questions 10–13:

	Fourth Quarter 2003			Fourth Quarter 2004		
	Pound Sterling	U.S. Dollar Equivalent per Pound	U.S. Dollars	Pound Sterling	U.S. Dollar Equivalent per Pound	U.S. Dollars
Net sales	£5,020	1.723	$8,649	£5,390	1.863	$10,042
Cost of sales	3,320	1.67	5,544	3,465	1.798	6,230
Gross profit	1,700		3,105	1,925		3,812
Operating expenses	1,170	1.723	2,016	1,315	1.863	2,450
Pretax results	530		1,089	610		1,362
Income taxes	310	1.723	534	315	1.863	587
Net earnings	**£220**		**$555**	**£295**		**$775**

10. Was the U.S. dollar strengthening or weakening against the pound from the third quarter of 2003 to the fourth quarter of 2003? From the third quarter of 2004 to the fourth quarter of 2004?

11. Was the temporal method or the current rate method used to translate this income statement?

12. Analyze the effect of translation on reported sales and earnings from one year to the next and compare the dollar and pound changes.

13. If the income statements had been translated at the average exchange rate, what would have been the impact on your answer for question c?

14. RadCo International is a U.S. firm with a wholly owned subsidiary in France. The basic assumptions involved in the French subsidiary and its interaction with the parent company are as follows:

Relevant Exchange Rates (U.S.$/euro)

December 31, 2003	$1.2557
December 31, 2004	$1.3644
Historical Rate	$1.0000
Average during 2004	$1.3101
Average during fourth quarter, 2003	$1.2112
Average during fourth quarter, 2004	$1.3041

Balance Sheet (in € in thousands)

	12/31/03	12/31/04
Cash	1,000	2,000
Accounts receivable	3,900	4,725
Inventories	3,600	4,700
Fixed assets	27,500	27,500
Accumulated depreciation	(2,750)	(5,500)
Total	**33,250**	**33,425**
Accounts payable	6,500	6,000
Long-term debt	12,500	10,800
Capital stock	6,200	6,200
Retained earnings	8,050	10,425
Total	**33,250**	**33,425**

Income Statement (in €, thousands)	
Sales	31,500
Expenses	
Cost of goods sold	(18,000)
Depreciation	(2,750)
Other	(4,500)
Taxes	(1,500)
Net income	4,750
Dividends	2,375

a. The functional currency of the subsidiary is the euro, and the financial statements have been recast in U.S. GAAP to assist in the translation process.

b. Capital stock was issued and fixed assets were acquired when the exchange rate was €1.05 per dollar; dividends are paid at a rate of $1.3644 per euro.

c. Inventories were all acquired in the previous quarter.

d. Purchases, sales, and other expenses occurred evenly throughout the year.

e. There is a zero beginning balance in the accumulated translation adjustment account.

f. Inflation in France has been in the single digits in recent years.

Exercise: Translate the financial statements into U.S. dollars.

15. RadCo International is a U.S. firm with a wholly owned subsidiary in Mexico that uses the dollar as its functional currency. The relevant facts in the case are as follows:

Relevant Exchange Rates (Pesos/U.S.$)	
Historical Rate	5.0000
December 31, 2003	8.5000
December 31, 2004	9.4900
Average during 2004	9.0000
Average fourth quarter 2003	8.4500
Average fourth quarter 2004	9.2000

Balance Sheet (in Mexican pesos in thousands)		
	12/31/03	12/31/04
Cash	20,000	14,000
Accounts receivable	40,000	110,000
Inventories	40,000	30,000
Fixed assets	100,000	100,000
Accumulated depreciation	(20,000)	(30,000)
Total	**180,000**	**224,000**
Accounts payable	30,000	50,000
Long-term debt (U.S.$120,000)	1,020	1,139
Long-term peso debt	44,000	44,000
Capital stock	60,000	60,000
Retained earnings	44,980	68,861
Total	**180,000**	**224,000**

Income Statement
(in Mexican pesos in thousands)

Sales	230,000
Expenses	
Cost of goods sold	(110,000)
Depreciation	(10,000)
Other	(80,000)
Taxes	(6,000)
Foreign exchange loss	(119)
Net income	32,881
Beginning inventory	40,000
Purchases	100,000
	140,000
Ending inventory	30,000
Cost of goods sold	110,000

a. Most of the transactions take place in Mexican pesos, although the subsidiary borrowed money in U.S. dollars. The financial statements have been recast into U.S. GAAP to facilitate the translation process.

b. Capital stock was issued, fixed assets were acquired, and long-term dollar debt was incurred when the exchange rate was 5.0000 pesos per dollar.

c. Inventories are acquired during the previous quarter.

d. Purchases, sales, and other expenses occurred evenly throughout the year.

e. Fixed assets are being depreciated on a straight-line basis over 10 years.

Exercise: Translate the peso financial statements into dollars.

Case: Kamikaze Enterprises
Case: Coca-Cola

These cases can be found on the following website: www.wiley.com/college/radebaugh

Selected References

Accounting Standards Committee. 1983. "Foreign Currency Translation." *Statement of Standard Accounting Practice No. 20,* London, U.K.: ASC.

Aiken, M., and D. Ardern. 2003. "Choice of Translation Methods in Financial Disclosure: A Test of Compliance with Environmental Hypotheses." *British Accounting Review* 35(4): 327–349.

Ayres, F. L., and J. L. Rodgers. 1994. "Further Evidence on the Impact of SFAS 52 on Analysts' Earnings Forecasts." *Journal of International Financial Management and Accounting* Vol. 5, Iss. 2 (June): 120–141.

Bartov, Eli. 1997. "Foreign Currency Exposure of Multinational Firms: Accounting Measures and Market Valuation." *Contemporary Accounting Research* 14(4): 623–652.

Bartov, Eli, and Gordon M. Bodnar. 1995. "Foreign Currency Translation Reporting and the Exchange-rade Exposure Effect." *Journal of International Financial Management & Accounting* 6(2): 93–114.

Choi, Frederick D. S., and Ronald R. Gunn. 1997. 'Hyperinflation Reporting and Performance Assessment." *Journal of Financial Statement Analysis* 2(4): 30–38.

Cooper, Kerry, Donald R. Fraser, and Malcolm R. Richards. 1978. "The Impact of SFAS 8 on Financial Management Practices." *Financial Executive* 46(6): 26–40.

Demirag, I. S. 1987. "A Review of the Objectives of Foreign Currency Translation." *International Journal of Accounting* (Spring): 69–85.

Financial Accounting Standards Board. 1975. "Accounting for the Translation of Foreign Currency Transactions and Foreign Currency Financial Statements." *Statement of Financial Accounting Standards No. 8*. Stamford, CT (October).

Financial Accounting Standards Board. 1981. "Foreign Currency Translation." *Statement of Financial Accounting Standards No. 52*. Stamford, CT (December).

Houston, C. O. 1989. "Foreign Currency Translation Research: A Review and Synthesis." *Journal of Accounting Literature* 8: 25–48.

Hughes, John, Jing Liu, and Mingshan Zhang. 2004. "Valuation and Accounting for Inflation and Foreign Exchange." *Journal of Accounting Research* 42(4): 731–754.

International Accounting Standards Board. 2003. "IAS 21—The Effects of Changes in Foreign Exchange Rates." *International Financial Reporting Standards* (London: IASB), pp. 21–1 to 21–27.

International Accounting Standards Board. 2003. "IAS 29—Financial Reporting in Hyperinflationary Economies." *International Financial Reporting Standards* (London: IASB), pp. 29–1 to 29–11.

Lorensen, Leonard. 1972. *Accounting Research Study No. 12*. "Reporting Foreign Operations of U.S. Companies in U.S. Dollars." New York: AICPA.

Pourciau, Susan, and Thomas F. Schaefer. 1995. "The Nature of the Market's Response to the Earnings Effect of Voluntary Changes in Accounting for Foreign Operations." *Journal of Accounting, Auditing & Finance* 10(1): 51–70.

Rotenberg, W. 1998. "Harmonization of Foreign Currency Translation Practices: Canadian Treatment of Long Term Monetary Items." *The International Journal of Accounting* 33(4): 429.

Soo, B. S., and L. Gilbert Soo. 1994. "Accounting for the Multinational Firm: Is the Translation Process Valued by the Stock Market?" *Accounting Review* 69(4): 617–637.

CHAPTER ELEVEN

INTERNATIONAL ACCOUNTING FOR PRICE CHANGES

Chapter Objectives

- Identify the major ways that companies and their financial statements are impacted by inflation
- Compare general purchasing power and current value approaches to inflation accounting
- Review the requirements of the International Accounting Standards Board (IASB) on accounting for price changes and inflation
- Examine inflation accounting developments in the United Kingdom, United States, and continental Europe
- Examine inflation accounting developments in South America
- Evaluate the evolution of current value accounting in the Netherlands
- Consider prospects for the development of accounting practices that more clearly reflect the impact of price changes and inflation

INTRODUCTION

Inflation has been a persistent worldwide phenomenon that has had a devastating impact on the economies of many countries over the years. Argentina, Brazil, Israel, Mexico, and Russia have been among the worst sufferers of hyperinflationary conditions. Annual rates of inflation in these countries have often exceeded 100 percent and have been as high as 2,000 percent in Brazil and Russia. Even in

---

Strategic Decision Point

Inflation has been brought under control in many developed countries, but hyperinflation continues to impact some emerging economies and remains a global threat. At the same time, prices continue to fluctuate in many industries, including very importantly the petroleum industry. BP (www.bp.com) is a company that has recognized the limitations of historical cost accounting and has taken the initiative to calculate profits using more up-to-date replacement costs as a way of reporting trading results on a more relevant basis. As pressures to provide more transparent and reliable information increase, it seems likely that more companies will follow BP's lead.

---

the major industrialized countries, inflation reached double figures in the mid-1970s, and in the United Kingdom it went up to a high of 25 percent. Not surprisingly, there has been increasing concern in the countries most affected to adopt "inflation accounting" systems which will remedy the defects of conventional historical cost accounting and reveal the impact of price changes and inflation on earnings and assets.

In this chapter, we analyze alternative approaches to accounting for price changes and inflation internationally and review international harmonization initiatives.

IMPACT OF INFLATION ON THE CORPORATION

The effect of inflation on the financial position and performance of a corporation can result in inefficient operating decisions by managers who do not understand its impact. In terms of financial position, financial assets such as cash lose value during inflation because their purchasing power diminishes. For example, if a business holds financial assets such as cash during a period when inflation rises by 10 percent, that cash has 10 percent less purchasing power at the end of the period than at the beginning. Conversely, holding financial liabilities is beneficial because the business will pay its obligations in the future with cash that has lost some of its purchasing power. The caveat here is that financial liabilities, such as short- and long-term bank loans, often carry very high interest rates in inflationary economies.

The effect of inflation on nonmonetary assets is reflected in both the income statement and the balance sheet. During a period of rising prices, current sales revenues are matched against inventory that may have been purchased several months earlier and against depreciation computed on the historical cost of property, plant, and equipment that may have been purchased several years ago, despite the fact that replacing inventory and fixed assets has become more expensive.

These income statement and balance sheet effects could lead the corporation into liquidity problems as the cash generated from revenues is consumed by the ever-increasing replacement cost of assets. The overstatement of income that results from matching old costs with new revenues could lead to demands from shareholders for increased dividends and from employees for higher wages, even though the corporation is watching its cash dwindle.

Much has been said in recent years about how conventional accounting misrepresents a corporation's real financial position. The concern is that analysts and investors cannot make informed financial decisions without understanding the impact of inflation. Accordingly, the type of accounting measurement system used as well as its interpretation is an essential issue to all user groups. The measurement of income is also relevant to a wide range of concerns including share prices, business stability, wages, job security, and economic growth. In the context of the MNE, these concerns are heightened with different traditions of accounting measurement.

While there may be some recognition of the necessity to introduce a system of accounting for price changes or inflation accounting, except in countries such as Germany where it is considered likely to institutionalize inflation, the term *inflation accounting* covers a variety of possible methods. The major alternative approaches are "general purchasing power accounting" and "current value accounting."

ACCOUNTING MEASUREMENT ALTERNATIVES

General purchasing power accounting includes all systems designed to maintain the real purchasing power of capital or shareholders' equity in the corporation by accounting for changes in the *general level of prices* (i.e., the general purchasing power of money). This is the strict meaning of the term *inflation,* though the term *inflation accounting* is generally used in a very broad sense. Variations on the term *general purchasing power accounting* include constant dollar accounting or general price level accounting in the United States and current purchasing power accounting (CPP) in the United Kingdom.

Current value accounting, on the other hand, includes all systems designed to account for current values or changes in specific prices. These include current cost accounting and replacement value accounting systems, which aim to maintain the physical capital, productive capacity, or operating assets of the corporation; and current exit (or selling) price accounting, which aims to maintain shareholders' equity but in terms of the selling prices of the corporation's net assets. Although a wide range of alternatives is proposed within each of these broad classifications—together with "real value" systems, which combine elements of both—the use of inflation accounting systems in practice is not well developed.

In essence, therefore, there are two philosophies about how to account for inflation. General purchasing power accounting is concerned that the value of money has gone down or up, whereas current value accounting is concerned that the cost of specific assets has gone up or down. It is possible to apply these approaches to all items in the financial statements that can be adjusted or to only some of the items in the financial statements that can be used separately or in conjunction with each other. Whatever the approach, it is necessary to identify which accounts are to be adjusted, what is to be the basis for the adjustment (such as an index), and where the adjustment is to be reflected in the financial statements.

General Purchasing Power Accounting

The general philosophy supporting general purchasing power accounting is to report assets, liabilities, revenues, and expenses in units of the same purchasing power. The approach here is that the monetary unit of measure should be uniform while retaining the basis of measurement used in the financial statements (e.g., historical cost).

In most countries, financial statements are prepared on a historical cost-nominal currency basis. This means that the statements are not adjusted for changes in the general price level. Under GPP accounting, the nonfinancial items in the financial statements (inventory, plant, and equipment) are restated to reflect a common purchasing power, usually at the ending balance sheet. For example, assume that a firm purchased a machine on January, 1, 2005, for $10,000 and that the general price level, as measured by the consumer price index, increased by 15 percent during the year. On December 31, the machine would appear on the balance sheet at $11,500 ($10,000 + [$10,000 × 0.15]) from which depreciation would be deducted, adjusted in GPP terms, to be charged against income. This implies that it would take $11,500 of end-of-year purchasing power to buy what $10,000 bought on January 1. For the year-end financial statements, the financial assets and liabilities (cash, receivables, payables) would not be adjusted because they are already stated in terms of December 31 purchasing power, but all other assets (including inventory), liabilities, revenues, and expenses (including depreciation would be adjusted. When the 2004 and 2005 financial statements are compared, however, all the items in the 2000 accounts—including the financial assets and liabilities—would be restated to December 31, 2005, purchasing power to ensure comparisons with the 2005 financial statements.

It has been suggested that GPP accounting should be applied to financial assets and liabilities as well. Cash, for example, loses purchasing power during an inflationary period because it cannot purchase as much at the end of the period as it did at the beginning. Debtors benefit during inflation, however, because they can pay their debts at the end of the period with cash whose purchasing power has fallen. Therefore, a firm that has increased its net financial asset position during an inflationary period suffers a loss in purchasing power, whereas a firm that has increased its net financial liability position enjoys a gain in purchasing power. The GPP accounts would reflect this loss or gain in a separate monetary items adjustment.

A further issue concerns the nature of the index to be used to make the GPP adjustments. As we noted earlier, the consumer price index is the one most widely used around the world to measure inflation. It measures the changes in prices for a wide range of consumer goods and services that are purchased for final consumption. However, because the index is consumer-oriented, it may not necessarily reflect the change in prices that directly affect a given corporation.

Current Value Accounting

As we have already noted, *current value accounting* is concerned with the rise or fall in the cost or value of specific assets, not with the overall loss of purchasing power of a currency. Under this concept, income is not considered to be earned until the corporation has maintained its capital in current value terms. Under current value accounting, a new basis for valuing assets replaces the traditional historical cost approach.

There are two major approaches to current value accounting: current cost (or replacement cost) and current exit price (selling price or net realizable value). *Cur-*

rent cost accounting, the most widely accepted method, is used for more classes of nonmonetary assets. Under this approach, assets are valued at what it would cost to replace them. However, whether the value should reflect the same asset being replaced or a similar asset performing the same function with a newer technology has been the subject of considerable discussion. *Current exit price accounting*, on the other hand, values assets, especially finished goods inventory, at what they could be sold for, less cost to complete and sell the items. In Dutch *exit value theory*, a further distinction is made between liquidation, value, and the going-concern concept. Under the *going-concern concept*, the asset is valued at the estimated sales price on normal completion of production.

Current value accounting results in holding gains and losses when nonmonetary assets are revalued. This is the gain or loss during the period the asset is held by the corporation. The gains and losses involved can either be taken into the income statement or reflected on the balance sheet as a capital adjustment account. A further issue concerns the determination of current values. For inventory, suppliers' lists are most commonly used because they reflect the most current prices for the items. Fixed assets are more complex. Property and plant are usually revealed according to a specific index, such as a construction cost index. Equipment may be revalued on the basis of a supplier list or engineering estimates—especially for machinery that is custom designed and built. Appraisal values are also a possibility for fixed assets. Current value accounting is obviously more complex to administer because it requires a mixture of actual prices, estimates, appraisal values, and indices for homogeneous groups of assets.

To see the impact that the use of current value accounting can have on income, assume that a corporation had sales revenues of $1,000,000, current cost of goods sold of $900,000, and historical cost of goods sold of $700,000. Under current cost accounting, operating gross profit (i.e., the difference between sales revenues and current cost of goods sold) would be $100,000. Under historical cost accounting, gross profit would be $300,000 (i.e., the difference between sales revenues and historical cost of goods sold). However, some of the historical cost profit was derived from holding inventory during a period when its specific price was increasing. Thus, the difference between the current cost of goods sold and the historical cost of goods ($900,000 – $700,000 = $200,000) can be considered a realized holding gain. It is realized because the assets were actually sold during the period.

Current Value: GPP Accounting

Although we have discussed GPP and current value accounting separately, many accountants and economists believe that the two should be combined in a *real value accounting system*. Assume, for example, that an asset was acquired at the beginning of the year for $150,000 and that at the end of the year the current value of the assets was $190,000, but the asset measured in end-of-year GPP terms was $165,000. The total holding gain of the asset would be:

$$\begin{array}{r} \$\ 190,000 \\ \underline{\$ -150,000} \\ \underline{\$\ 40,000} \end{array}$$

However, the "real" holding gain (the gain net of the impact of inflation) would be only $25,000:

$$
\begin{aligned}
&\$\ 190{,}000 \\
&\underline{-65{,}000} \\
&\underline{\$\ \ \ 25{,}000}
\end{aligned}
$$

It is important to note that changes in the general level of prices (i.e., inflation) will tend to differ from changes in specific prices (current values) relevant to the corporation. Indeed, even zero inflation may be the outcome of a number of specific price changes, which, on average, show that no inflation has occurred. The impact that matters, from the corporation's perspective, is the net impact of prices directly affecting the corporation relative to the average level of prices affecting the GPP of money.

INTERNATIONAL FINANCIAL REPORTING STANDARDS

The first reaction of the IASC (now IASB) to inflation accounting came in 1977 in IAS 6, *Accounting Responses to Changing Prices*. At that point, however, there was no definitive standard in either the United States or the United Kingdom, and there was substantial uncertainty as to how the inflation accounting issue would be resolved in those two countries.

IAS 6 was very brief because the IASC attempted to set standards that are essentially a narrowing of available options and had to rely on a consensus of its member organizations. In 1977, inflation accounting was a hot topic, but no clear-cut consensus had emerged. Therefore, the IASC decided to do the next best thing—require disclosure of the methods being used.

A more definitive inflation standard did not emerge until 1981 with the issuance of IAS 15, *Information Reflecting the Effects of Changing Prices,* which replaced IAS 6. By that time, the FASB had issued SFAS 33, *Financial Reporting and Changing Prices,* in September 1979, and the Accounting Standards Committee (ASC) in the United Kingdom had issued SSAP 16, *Current Cost Accounting,* in April 1980. With the influence and support of those two countries, the IASC was ready to issue a more definitive standard.

Rather than require one specific way to account for inflation, the IASC recognized that a difference of opinion still existed as to how inflation should be accounted for in the financial statements. As IAS 15 pointed out:

> There is not yet an international consensus on the subject. Consequently, the International Accounting Standards Committee believes that further experimentation is necessary before consideration can be given to requiring enterprises to prepare primary financial statements using a comprehensive and uniform system for reflecting changing prices. Meanwhile, evolution of the subject would be assisted if enterprises that present primary financial statements on the historical cost basis also provide supplementary information reflecting the effects of price changes. (para. 18).

The standard discussed the merits of each of the two major philosophical approaches to accounting for inflation, the GPP approach and the current cost approach, but it did not attempt to take a stand. The following major types of information which reflect the effects of changing prices were recommended for disclosure by IAS 15.

1. The amounts of the adjustment to or the adjusted amount of depreciation of property, plant, and equipment.

2. The amount of the adjustment to or the adjusted amount of cost of sales.

3. The adjustments relating to monetary items, the effect of borrowing, or equity interests when such adjustments have been taken into account in determining income under the accounting method adopted.

4. The overall effect on results (income) of the adjustments as well as any other items reflecting the effects of changing prices that are reported under the accounting method adopted.

5. When a current cost method is adopted, the current cost of property, plant and equipment, and inventories.

6. The method adopted to compute the information called for in the preceding items, including the nature of any indices used.

Although the IASC encouraged corporations to disclose the information described in these six items, they decided that such disclosures were not necessary to conform with international accounting standards because "the international consensus … that was anticipated when IAS 15 was issued has not been reached."

IAS 15 was important, however, because it recognized the need for information to be disclosed about the impact of price changes and inflation and gave some specific guidelines that companies can follow to improve the quality of disclosure. The fact that the underlying information from country to country may differ, of course, is a problem, but the accounting profession clearly cannot agree on a universal solution. This is not surprising given the lack of evidence to support one system over another. Indeed, the available evidence concerning, for example, the utility of current cost accounting is not encouraging. However, more disclosures would assist financial statement users worldwide.

IAS 15 was supplemented in 1989 by IAS 29 on financial reporting in hyperinflationary economies, which requires restatements for GPP changes in hyperinflationary economies, that is, generally where there is 100 percent inflation over three years, regardless of whether the financial statements of the enterprise concerned are based on a historical cost or current value approach. In December 2003, IAS 15 was withdrawn by the IASB, leaving the focus of any inflation adjustments and disclosures very much restricted to hyperinflationary economies.

IAS 16, on property, plant, and equipment, was revised in 1998 and is also relevant in that a current value accounting approach is permitted specifically as an alternative to historical cost. The basis to be used is "fair value," which is usually market value for existing use in the case of land and buildings and depreciated replacement cost for plant and equipment. Regular revaluations are required so that book values do not differ materially from fair values at the balance sheet date.

COMPARATIVE NATIONAL REGULATION AND PRACTICE

The practice of inflation accounting varies throughout the world and to a considerable extent is a function of the rate and impact of inflation. Substantial experience of inflation accounting has been gained following the hyperinflation experienced in South America, most notably in Argentina, Brazil, and Chile. The hyperinflationary conditions experienced by South American countries would appear to explain their relatively rapid adoption of the inflation accounting system compared to other countries.

Inflation Accounting in the United Kingdom, United States, and Continental Europe

In the United Kingdom, the accounting profession introduced SSAP 16 in 1980 after long debate, which required current cost accounting financial statements either as supplementary statements or as the main accounts, with the proviso that historical cost accounts must also be provided. However, SSAP 16 was officially withdrawn in 1988 following declining inflation levels and criticism from business. Currently, only a few companies provide voluntary current cost disclosures. At the same time, many companies make periodic revaluations of their land and buildings to market values (approximating exit or selling prices).

In the United States, regulation was first introduced with a legal requirement imposed by the SEC in 1976 (Accounting Series Release 190) to disclose replacement cost information relating to depreciation, cost of sales, fixed assets, and inventory. Subsequently, in 1979, the FASB issued Statement of Financial Accounting Standards No. 33, requiring supplementary disclosures on both a GPP and a current cost basis. However, by 1986, with SFAS 82 and SFAS 89, SFAS 33 was no longer mandatory after a cost-benefit analysis of its requirements and a decline in the rate of inflation rendered it obsolete.

Both GPP and current cost disclosures were required by SFAS 33. In addition to adjusted income disclosures, the current costs of inventory, plant, and equipment were required to be disclosed along with increases or decreases in current costs adjusted for GPP changes (i.e., net of inflation). A further required item of disclosure was the purchasing power gain or loss on net monetary items. The noteworthy feature of this standard was its experimental nature; it made available an array of information prepared using different inflation accounting systems. An example of the required disclosures is provided by Nabisco Brands in its 1983 annual report (see Exhibit 11.1).

In contrast, the current cost accounting system in the United Kingdom provided for four adjustments—depreciation, cost of sales, monetary working capital, and gearing. The gearing adjustment, which abated the other operating adjustments by the proportion of debt financing, was a matter of some controversy in that it incorporated an element of the GPP approach by recognizing that a gain was to be derived from holding net monetary liabilities in a period of inflation.

In Australia, Canada, and New Zealand, developments were much more tentative than in the United Kingdom and the United States. The accounting profes-

Exhibit 11.1   Nabisco Brands: Adjustments for Changing Prices

Consolidated Statement of Income Adjusted for the Effects of Changing Prices
Year Ended December 31, 1983

(In Millions, Except per Share Data)	Historical Basis	Adjusted for Changes in Specific Prices (Current Cost)
Net sales	$5,985.2	$5,985.2
Cost of sales	3,650.8	3,669.1
Depreciation expense	131.1	206.7
Other expenses	1,560.4	1,560.4
Interest expense	76.8	76.8
Provision for income taxes	243.5	243.5
Net income	$322.6	$228.7
Net income per common share	$4.86	$3.45
Gain from decline in purchasing power of net monetary liabilities		$34.4
Increase in specific prices of inventories and property, plant, and equipment held during the year[a]		$34.2
Less effect of increase in general price level		(113.1)
Excess of increase in general price level over changes in specific prices		$(78.9)
Foreign currency translation adjustment		$(107.9)

[a] At December 13, 1983, the current cost of inventory was $759.6 million and the current cost of property, plant, and equipment, net of accumulated depreciation was $2231.2 million.

Five-Year Comparison of Selected Supplementary Financial Data Adjusted for the Effects of Changing Prices

(Dollars in Millions, Except per Share Data)	1983	1982	1981	1980	1979
Net Sales—Total					
Historical cost	$5,985.2	$5,871.1	$5,819.2	$5,587.2	$4,975.3
Constant dollar	5,985.2	6,060.1	6,377.1	6,755.5	6,829.2
Net Sales—Ongoing Businesses					
Historical cost	$5,985.2	$5,463.4	$5,049.7	$4,848.8	$4,349.7
Constant dollar	5,985.2	5,639.3	5,533.8	5,862.8	5,970.6
Net Income					
Historical cost	$322.6	$314.7	$266.3	$234.8	$186.5
Current cost	228.7	254.0	157.0	114.8	100.0

(Dollars in Millions, Except per Share Data)	1983	1982	1981	1980	1979
Net Income per Common Share					
Historical cost	$4.86	$4.83	$4.21	$3.73	$2.97
Current cost	3.45	3.90	2.48	1.82	1.59
Net Assets at Year-End					
Historical cost	$1,710.8	$1,835.9	$1,522.8	$1,344.1	$1,200.3
Current cost	2,386.4	2,639.2	2,579.5	2,472.6	2,483.5
Excess of Increase in General Price Level over Changes in Specific Prices	$(78.9)	$(196.6)	$(43.9)	$(110.4)	$(96.5)
Gain on Net Monetary Liabilities	$34.4	$41.1	$88.7	$115.6	$134.5
Cash Dividends Declared per Common Share					
Historical cost	$2.28	$2.05	$1.77	$1.60	$1.45
Constant dollar	2.28	2.12	1.94	1.93	1.99
Market Price per Common Share at Year End					
Historical cost	$41.00	$36.75	$31.00		
Constant dollar	40.31	37.51	32.86		
Average Consumer Price Index (1967 = 100)	298.4	289.1	272.3	246.8	217.4

Source: Nabisco, 1983 Annual Report.

sions in those countries issued recommendations based essentially on the current cost accounting system required in the United States but with some local variations, especially with regard to the treatment of monetary items.

In continental Europe, there has been much less enthusiasm for introducing inflation accounting despite official recommendations on the subject—for example, in France and Germany. In some countries, there have nevertheless been instances in which periodic revaluations were required or permitted, for example, in France in the late 1970s when revaluations using government indices were required for all long-term or fixed assets. However, these revaluations did not have an impact on earnings for tax purposes, as any additional depreciation was canceled out by a credit transfer from the revaluation reserves. Although the Netherlands is renowned for the development of replacement value accounting, there is no compulsion to use the system, or even professional standards on the subject. In Sweden, there are no requirements on inflation accounting, but some notable voluntary disclosures have been made, for example, by Astra (see Exhibit 11.2), which

Exhibit 11.2   Astra (Sweden): Impact of Inflation

It is difficult, both theoretically and practically, to calculate the impact of inflation on an international group that is affected by changes in exchange rates, when inflation rates vary sharply between countries in which the subsidiaries are located. However, each year since 1975, Astra has chosen to present an approximate calculation of the effect of inflation on group earnings. Since 1981, the calculations have generally follow, a draft recommendation in favor of current cost accounting issued by the Swedish Institute of Authorized Public Accountants (FAR). This means, among other things, that all costs of a sold product are restated to reflect the cost situation at the time of sale: the costs of goods, as well as depreciation, are expressed in current costs. In addition, increases in value of inventories and fixed assets—whether realized or not—shall be shown in the year's earnings. In the adjoining calculation, the simplified assumption has been made that the increases in value conform to the Swedish rate of inflation, which means that any real change in value has not been taken into account. The company's monetary working capital has been affected by inflation during the year. The change in purchasing power of the monetary working capital has been calculated on the basis of the change in the consumer price index during the year in Sweden. In the same way, the effect of inflation on financial receivables and liabilities has reduced the interest income and interest expense shown. Similarly, the change in purchasing power has been calculated on the deferred tax liability.

	Conventional Accounting	Current Cost Accounting	Amounts in SEK m. Difference
Operating income	23,755	23,755	—
Operating expenses	(16,393)	(16,485)	(92)[1]
Operating earnings	7,362	7,270	(92)
Depreciation	(862)	(1,060)	(198)
Operating earnings after depreciation	6,500	6,210	(290)
Nonoperating income	1,393	996	(397)[2]
Nonoperating expenses	(125)	(57)	68[3]
Minority interest	50	50	—
Pretax earnings	7,818	7,199	(619)
Taxes	(1,726)	(1,726)	—
Change in purchasing power of deferred tax liability	—	57	57
Net earnings	6,092	5,530	(562)
Earnings per share, SEK	9.92	9.01	(0.91)

[1] Change in purchasing power of noninterest-bearing operating receivables and liabilities, SEK 47 m, and change in price of goods sold, calculated in local currency and translated at year-end exchange rates, SEK (139) m.

[2] Change in purchasing power of nonoperating receivables.

[3] Change in purchasing power of nonoperating liabilities.

Ten-Year Summary

The table shows that inflation did not have any appreciable effect on Astra's conventionally adjusted net earnings. Real earnings averaged about three-quarters of conventionally adjusted earnings and had an insignificantly lower rate of growth.

In real terms, Astra's net earnings increased annually at an average rate of 35 percent during the period 1984–1993.

Exhibit 11.2 (*Continued*)

Value at Each Year's Prices	1984	1985	1986	1987	1988	1989	1990	1991	1992	1993
CONVENTIONAL ACCOUNTING										
Net earnings, SEK m	383	554	597	635	747	991	1,432	2,182	3,527	**6,092**
Earnings per share, SEK	0.62	0.90	0.97	1.03	1.21	1.62	2.38	3.60	5.76	**9.92**
CURRENT COST ACCOUNTING										
Net earnings, SEK m	299	425	468	480	570	752	977	1,745	3,246	**5,530**
Earnings per share, SEK	0.49	0.69	0.76	0.78	0.93	1.22	1.59	2.83	5.27	**9.01**

Value at 1993 Prices	1984	1985	1986	1987	1988	1989	1990	1991	1992	1993
CONVENTIONAL ACCOUNTING										
Net earnings, SEK m	639	860	888	905	1,008	1,262	1,640	2,312	3,668	**6,092**
Earnings per share, SEK	1.04	1.40	1.44	1.47	1.64	2.05	2.73	3.81	5.99	**9.92**
CURRENT COST ACCOUNTING										
Net earnings, SEK m	499	661	698	684	769	957	1,119	1,849	3,376	**5,530**
Earnings per share, SEK	0.81	1.07	1.13	1.11	1.25	1.55	1.88	3.06	5.51	**9.01**

Source: Astra, 1993 Annual Report.

regularly disclosed current cost accounting data until its merger with Zeneca (U.K.). Similarly, Switzerland has no requirements but some interesting cases of current value accounting in practice (e.g., Nestlé uses current replacement costs for tangible fixed assets in its main accounts).

Taken overall, regulatory developments worldwide have been few and relatively recent. The major alternative inflation accounting systems of GPP accounting and current value accounting have both been in evidence, although current cost accounting, for a time, was the more popular system in a number of Anglo-American countries before losing favor altogether as inflation levels fell and the costs of compliance exceeded benefits. Voluntary current cost disclosures are still encouraged, but there appears to be little regard for their current usefulness among corporations and financial analysis.

Inflation Accounting in South America

With hyperinflation rampant in recent years in a number of South American countries, notably Brazil and Argentina, it is not surprising that there have been pressures to adopt inflation accounting systems.

In Brazil, inflation accounting adjustments were used as early as the 1950s, but a new company law in 1976 required a general indexation approach to restate historical costs in terms of current purchasing power as of the date of the financial statements. The index used was defined by law as the index recognized by the government for the purpose of adjusting its own debt. All corporations were required to restate their balance sheets with respect to property, plant, and equipment and related depreciation, investments, and deferred costs and shareholders' equity. The net effect of these adjustments was included in income for the year. However, with dramatically reduced levels of inflation, these requirements were withdrawn as of January 1996.

In Argentina, inflation accounting systems were introduced primarily through the initiative and involvement of the accounting profession. In 1972, a statement was issued recommending the publication of supplementary GPP financial statements. While compliance was initially modest, it increased in the 1980s to the extent that most major companies produced inflation-adjusted accounts. However, in 1995, the GPP adjustment requirements were removed following a period of low inflation.

Current Value Accounting in the Netherlands

In the Netherlands, the Dutch have been aware of current value accounting for a long time. The extensive training of accountants in business economics has resulted in an accounting philosophy that is concerned with current values and costs and with sound business-economic principles and practices. While there are no set requirements for the use of current value accounting, as either primary or supplementary information, there is some support for its use, though it is dwindling. While some firms use current cost statements as their primary statements, it is more common to see partial current costs statements or historical cost statements with supplementary disclosures.

If there are no requirements for current cost or GPP accounting, why focus on the Netherlands? The first reason involves the theories of Professor Theodore Limperg, who is often called the father of replacement value theory because of his pioneering work in the Netherlands in the 1920s and 1930s. He focused on the strong relationship between economics and accounting and believed that income should not be earned without maintaining the source of income of the business from a going-concern or continuity standpoint. Therefore, income is a function of revenues and replacement values rather than historical costs. In addition, Limperg maintained that current value information should be used by all decision makers—management as well as shareholders.

The second reason for looking at the Netherlands is to learn from the experience of the large Dutch multinational Philips, which was a pioneer preparer of current value financial statements. In fact, Philips first used this approach in 1936 for internal cost accounting purposes and introduced it in 1952 into its primary accounts for financial reporting purposes. But in 1992 the company decided to revert to historical cost accounting on the grounds that it would improve communications to shareholders, simplify accounting systems and procedures considerably, and be more in line with international accounting practices (see Exhibit 11.3).

Nevertheless, Philips is an interesting and valuable example of the application of current value accounting in practice. In its current value financial statements, Philips used current replacement values together with a gearing adjustment to reflect the extent to which there were benefits accruing from financing assets from loan rather than equity capital. Under its current value accounting system, both the balance sheet and income statement were adjusted; in certain instances the lower business value (or net realizable value) was taken as the current value. For inventory, standard costs were determined at the start of each year. As prices changed during the year, an index was developed by the purchasing department for homogeneous groups of assets and applied to the standard cost to yield the current value. The indices were prepared quarterly or bimonthly in situations in which inflation was more extreme.

Current values were determined by the purchasing department for fixed assets (either individually or in homogeneous groups), by the engineering department for specifically designed pieces of equipment, and by the building design and plant engineering department for buildings. As in the case of inventory, indices were often used to update current values of homogeneous groups of assets. The increase (or decrease) in value of inventory and fixed assets due to specific price changes was credited (debited) to a revaluation surplus account in the balance sheet rather than to the income statement. The effect of current value changes showed up in the income statement as a higher or lower cost of goods sold (as a result of increases or decreases in inventory prices) and higher or lower depreciation expense.

However, as Brink (1992) has shown, Philips tended for some years to apply replacement value accounting in a way that was far from conservative and designed to enhance profits. The treatment of inventory value reductions and the gearing adjustment in hyperinflationary countries, for example, was especially controversial, quite apart from accounting policies relating to foreign currencies, goodwill, and intangibles in general. Against this background, Philip's surprise loss in 1990 of 4.24 billion guilders would seem to have led to some serious questioning of the

Exhibit 11.3 Philips (Netherlands): Accounting Policies

Changes in the Preparation of the 1992 Annual Report

In the 1991 annual report reference was made to a reappraisal of our policies and procedures within the framework of Operation Centurion. This reappraisal included close scrutiny of our accounting policies and our financial reporting in order to:

- improve communication with the shareholders;
- considerably simplify our accounting systems and procedures;
- be more in line with current international accounting practices.

In view of the above, it has been resolved with effect from January 1, 1992:

1. to replace current cost accounting with historical cost accounting;
2. to replace the local currencies in highly inflationary countries with a functional currency, generally the U.S. dollar;
3. to capitalize the amounts of goodwill arising from acquisitions made as from January 1, 1992, and to amortize these amounts over a period not exceeding 40 years. In previous years goodwill was charged directly to stockholders' equity;
4. to capitalize certain software development costs when it is determined that the resulting software products will be marketable over an extended period. The amortization period will depend on the nature of the product involved but in no event will exceed three years. For reasons of prudence no expenditures were capitalized in 1992.

Additionally, it has been resolved to apply the American standard (FAS 106) with regard to postretirement health care benefit plans. This means that in accordance with this standard a provision covering such costs will be created over a 20-year period, beginning January 1, 1993, for the United States and January 1, 1995, for all other countries.

To simplify the accounting procedures, costs of basic research and general and administrative expenses in the corporate centers and the national organizations are no longer allocated to the specific product sectors.

With regard to the transition from current cost to historical cost accounting and the use of the U.S. dollar as functional currency in highly inflationary countries, the 1991 information has been restated for purposes of comparability. The effects of the change in accounting for goodwill and changes in consolidation are reflected in the notes to the 1992 financial statements. Income from operations per product sector for 1991 has been adjusted in line with the change in allocation of general costs.

Source: Philips, 1992 Annual Report.

usefulness of the current replacement value accounting system and to its eventual demise.

PROBLEMS AND PROSPECTS

The existence of significant levels of inflation and price volatility in many countries suggests that the need for and use of inflation accounting systems is likely to remain the subject of some controversy in the foreseeable future.

Although GPP accounting has been in use in some hyperinflationary South American countries, no examples of current cost accounting standards or regulations in the United Kingdom and the United States at the national level survived the demise of the inflation accounting experiments of the mid-1980s. Nevertheless, some European companies are making voluntary current value disclosures.

Controversy, however, still surrounds many aspects of current cost accounting, particularly with respect to the gearing adjustment and the treatment of gains and losses on monetary items. Other problems include the use of indices, particularly with respect to foreign subsidiaries, and the verification of current costs of corporations in industries experiencing rapid technological change.

Given the recent interest in current or fair value accounting, it is hoped that there will be some further experimentation with various types of price change accounting systems. There may also be a growing appreciation of the circumstances under which alternative approaches may or may not be feasible or useful in measuring profits and assets. The usefulness of exit or selling prices in the context of changing prices, particularly with regard to the value or property and investments, may also be better appreciated. There also seem to be opportunities for using other relevant sources of information such as cash flows.

SUMMARY

1.   Inflation is a worldwide phenomenon with varying impact in different countries. In recent years, countries such as Argentina, Brazil, Chile, Israel, Mexico, and Russia have been among the worst sufferers of hyperinflationary conditions.

2.   Under inflationary conditions, where prices are continually changing, traditional historical cost accounting becomes defective and misleading as a basis for decision making.

3.   The major alternative approaches to accounting for price changes and inflation are GPP accounting and current value accounting.

4.   GPP accounting includes all systems designed to maintain the current (constant) purchasing power of the corporation's equity.

5.   Current value accounting, on the other hand, includes all systems designed to account for changes in specific prices such as current cost (or replacement value) accounting and current exit (or selling) price accounting.

6.   Real value accounting systems, which combine elements of both of the major approaches involved, are also available.

7.   The early international standards adopted a disclosure approach whereby companies were encouraged to experiment, provided the accounting methods used and amounts involved were disclosed in sufficient details to inform users. More recently, the IASB has required that inflation adjustments be made only in the context of hyperinflationary economies.

8.   At the national level, experience with inflation accounting systems is varied, with the hyperinflationary countries of South America using GPP accounting while the Anglo-American countries, with more moderate rates of inflation, experiment with current cost accounting. Significantly, as the rate of inflation has declined in the Anglo-American countries, so has the support for current cost accounting.

9.   Interesting cases of voluntary disclosures by MNEs can be found in a number of countries, notably the Netherlands, Sweden, Switzerland, and the United Kingdom.

10.   Given the continuing presence of inflation, albeit at varying rates around the world, and the daily reality of changing prices it is likely that the subject of price change accounting will continue to be important and controversial. Further experimentation seems desirable given the lack of knowledge about the usefulness of the various alternatives.

Discussion Questions

1.   How do price changes and inflation affect the financial position and performance of a corporation?

2.   What operational problems does inflation create for management?

3.   Explain and critically comment on the philosophy underlying general purchasing power accounting.

4.   Explain and critically comment on the philosophy underlying current value accounting.

5.   Explain and critically comment on the philosophy underlying current value-general purchasing power (real value) accounting.

6.   To what extent has the IASC/IASB contributed to a solution to the problems of accounting for changing prices?

7.   Explain the nature of the current cost accounting experiments in the United Kingdom and the United States. Why did these experiments come to nothing?

8.   Explain how Philips (the Netherlands) determined current costs for its financial reports. What were the reasons given for reverting to historical cost in 1992? Was this decision justifiable in your opinion?

9.   Under what circumstances are corporations likely to voluntarily disclose the impact of price changes and inflation?

10.   To what extent is a disclosure approach to inflation accounting likely to overcome problems of comparability internationally?

11.   Inflation in Russia and China has been relatively high in recent years, and yet no inflation accounting systems have been introduced. Should inflation accounting be required, and, if so, which approach would you recommend be used?

12.   In Germany, there has been resistance to any form of inflation accounting and a concern to maintain a strictly historical cost approach. Why is this, and can such an approach be justified on theoretical grounds?

13.   Search the Internet to discover some company examples of current value accounting in practice.

14.   Search the Internet to discover a country where some form of inflation accounting has been practiced in the past and explain the approach used.

15.   Do you think International Financial Reporting Standards should be introduced to require a more current or "fair value" approach to the measurement of assets and liabilities?

Exercises

Exercises 1–8
Company ABZ invested $200,000 cash in new equipment at the beginning of 2005. The equipment was depreciated evenly over 10 years with an expected salvage value of $10,000.

In 2008, inflation hit the economy hard, raising the CPI from 200 to 245. It is estimated that it would cost $400,000 to replace the machine.

1. According to the GPP theory, how should the company represent the equipment on its balance sheet at the end of 2008? How much depreciation expense will ABZ recognize in 2009 for the equipment? What are the corresponding journal entries for the change in value?

2. According to current cost accounting, how should the company represent the equipment on its balance sheet at the end of 2008? How much depreciation expense will ABZ recognize in 2009 for the equipment? What are the corresponding journal entries for the change in value?

3. According to current exit price accounting, how should the company represent the equipment on its balance sheet at the end of 2008? How much depreciation expense will ABZ recognize in 2009 for the equipment?

4. According to the real value accounting system, how should the company represent the equipment on its balance sheet at the end of 2008? How much depreciation expense will ABZ recognize in 2009 for the equipment?

5. How is the company's financial position different if the equipment is purchased with debt instead of cash?

6. Now assume that ABZ is a subsidiary of ZBA, which is based in Brazil. If Brazil has inflation of 15 percent in 2005 and 25 percent in 2006–2008, how much would the book value of the equipment be in reals? What if Brazil had inflation of 35 percent in 2006–2008?

7. If the company sells the equipment at the beginning of 2009 for $325,000, how much gain or loss is recognized under each of the three accounting treatments?

8. If ABZ does sell the equipment for $325,000, what are the potential benefits and dangers in the current high-inflation economy?

Exercises 8–9

You are the controller of a medium-sized, publicly held phone company. The year has not been good, and inflation has hit the telecommunications industry. The industry saw an average price increase of 10 percent, while the rest of the economy had inflation of 3 percent. OnCall, the company you work for, is confident that the rest of the economy will catch up to the inflation of the telecommunications industry within the next two years.

9. How should inflation impact the balance sheet and income statement of OnCall in the current year?

10. Assuming that in two years the rest of the economy does catch up to the price level in the telecommunications industry, how should OnCall's balance sheet and income statement look at that point in time with regard to inflationary accounting?

11. Under IAS 29, how much would a gallon of gasoline have to cost before the U.S. dollar were considered hyperinflationary? Assume that the price of gas is representative of the rest of the economy and a gallon of gas costs $2.00.

Exercises 12–15

White Light Electric, Inc. sells light fixtures in the United States. In 2010 the company began operations, with total equity investments of $50 million (all cash). White Light used the money to purchase and outfit a manufacturing plant for $30 million. The plant, comprising 80 percent of the purchase price (the balance was for the land), is to be amortized straight-line over 25 years with no expected salvage value. The plant revenues (and thus the total company revenues) in 2010 were $70 million, with 7 percent gross profit and $1.9 million in SG&A. By the end of 2010, the CPI had risen from 210 to 350.

12. Prepare a basic balance sheet and income statement for White Light Inc. for 2010 under the general purchasing power accounting approach.

13. Prepare a basic balance sheet and income statement for White Light Inc. for 2010 under the current cost accounting approach.

14. Compare the two sets of financials using rate-of-return ratios.

15. Has White Light increased its net financial position or its net financial liability position? Is that good or bad?

Case: BP
Case: Fosters Brewing Group

These cases can be found on the following website: www.wiley.com/college/radebaugh

Selected References

Brink, H. L. 1992. "A History of Philips Accounting Policies on the Basis of its Annual Reports." *European Accounting Review* (December): 255–275.

Choi, F. D. S. 1987. "Resolving the Inflation/Currency Translation Dilemma." *Management International Review* 27(2): 26–34.

Choi, F. D. S., and R. R. Gunn. 1997. "Hyperinflation Reporting and Performance Assessment." *Journal of Financial Statement Analysis* (Summer): 30–38.

Goudeket, A. 1966. "An Application of Replacement Value Theory." *Journal of Accounting* (July): 37–47.

International Accounting Standards Committee. 1981. International Accounting Standard 15, *Information Reflecting the Effects of Changing Prices*. London IASC (November; reformatted 1994).

International Accounting Standards Committee. 1989. IAS 29, *Financial Reporting in Hyperinflationary Economies* (reformatted 1994).

International Accounting Standards Committee. Revised 1998. IAS 16, *Property, Plant and Equipment*. London: IASC.

Kirkman, P. 1985. *Inflation Accounting in Major English-Speaking Countries*. Englewood Cliffs, NJ: Prentice-Hall.

Lee, T. A. 1985. *Income and Value Measurement*. 3d ed. New York: Van Nostrand Reinhold.

Mey, A. 1966. "Theodore Limperg and His Theory of Values and Costs." *Abacus* (September): 3–23.

Muis, Jules S. 1975. "Current Value Accounting in the Netherlands: Fact or Fiction." *Accountant* (November): 98–104.

Mumford, M. 1979. "The End of a Familiar Inflation Accounting Cycle." *Accounting and Business Research* (Spring).

Schmidt, F. 1930. "The Impact of Replacement Value." *Accounting Review* (September): 235–242.

Sweeney, H. W. 1927. "Effect on Inflation on German Accounting." *Journal of Accountancy* (March): 180–191.

Van Offeren, D. H. 1990. "Accounting for Changing Prices in Dutch Annual Reports." *Advances in International Accounting* 3: 87–106.

Whittington, Geoffrey. 1983. *Inflation Accounting*. New York: Cambridge University Press.

Whittington, Geoffrey. 1984. "The European Contribution to Inflation Accounting." In *Congress Proceedings,* European Accounting Association, Sixth Annual Congress 1983, University of Glasgow, Scotland.

Zeff, S. A., and H. Z. Ovando. 1975. "Inflation Accounting and the Development of Accounting Principles in Chile." *Accountant's Magazine* (June).

CHAPTER TWELVE

CORPORATE GOVERNANCE AND CONTROL OF GLOBAL OPERATIONS

Chapter Objectives

- Describe different strategies multinational enterprises (MNEs) can pursue
- Provide a brief explanation of different structures an MNE adopts as it modifies its strategy in response to increased globalization
- Understand the need for effective corporate governance and provide a model for understanding the various cultural, legal, and market factors that determine the cross-national diversity of governance structures
- Gain an understanding of the challenges faced by MNEs in maintaining effective internal controls
- Learn about the transfer of information in MNEs and the strategic role played by information technology
- Understand how firm strategy and structure affect the accounting function

INTRODUCTION

Decisions about which businesses to be in, where to locate operations, and how to be competitive are all part of a firm's strategy. Strategy is also the firm's response to changes in the global business environment or its attempts to predict, preempt, and exploit future environmental changes for its own benefit.

Strategic Decision Point

IKEA, the Swedish company, is the first truly global home furnishings retailer. Founded by Ingvar Kamprad in the mid-1940s to compete against traditional stores that sold expensive furniture, IKEA's strategy is very simple: offer the broadest range of furniture at the lowest price possible. IKEA drove down costs by establishing partnerships with suppliers, using cheaper materials, distributing furniture in knock-down kits, and adding the customer to the supply chain by having them pick up the kits, take them home, and assemble the furniture. To maintain a consistent company philosophy, Kamprad published a book outlining the IKEA philosophy that all store employees were required to read and internalize. Most store managers are Swedes who are ingrained with the Kamprad philosophy, even in the IKEA stores in China which boast Mandarin-speaking Swedish managers. Although products are standardized, IKEA has to offer some local products that meet local tastes. But IKEA has clearly succeeded worldwide by having a standardized look and feel, whether in Sweden, Switzerland, the United States, or China. It is a global company with a very centralized, global strategy.

In this chapter we outline how strategic change is reflected in changes to the firm's organizational structure, corporate governance, and control system. The accounting and information systems of a firm, in turn, are presented as an integral part of the firm's control system. These systems are also affected by changes in the firm's organizational structure and will change as strategy and structure change.

GLOBAL STRATEGIC ISSUES

Globalization refers to the deepening relationships and broadening interdependence among people from different countries. From a corporate perspective, globalizing a company involves increasing business activities worldwide. However, the nature of the global strategy varies from company to company. A company must decide to what extent decision making should be held in a few key centers (centralized) or distributed to a large number of business units. The problem with centralization versus decentralization is that the very terms connote a mutually exclusive situation—decision making must be either centralized or decentralized. However, the global environment is too complex for such a simple dichotomy. Companies can be described as either **multidomestic** (also referred to as multilocal) or global in their approach to world markets. With the multidomestic approach, individual subsidiaries are allowed to compete independently in different domestic markets, and with the **global** approach, the entire worldwide system of product and market position is pitted against the competition. For example, Philips, the Dutch consumer electronics MNE, was organized prior to World War II. With the outbreak of the war, the different national organizations were cut off from the home office, and they developed into very strong national organizations, which resulted in a multidomestic approach to growth. On the other hand, Matsushita, the Japanese consumer electronics company, maintained very strong control over its international operations, so that the national organizations had very little independence from the home office.

Hout, Porter, and Rudden (1982) suggest that companies that are more likely to adopt a multidomestic strategy are those that have products that differ greatly from country market to country market. Such companies also have high transportation costs or their industries lack sufficient scale economies to give the global competitors a significant competitive edge. Economies of scale may be too modest; R&D may be closely tied to a specific market; transportation costs and government barriers to trade may be too high; and distribution systems may be too fragmented and too hard to penetrate. A global strategy is more likely when significant benefits gained from worldwide volume—in terms of either reduced unit costs or superior reputation or service—are greater than the additional costs of serving that volume. These volume advantages may come from larger production plants or runs, more efficient logistics networks, higher volume distribution networks, or high levels of investment in R&D. The relationship between multidomestic/global dichotomy and centralization/decentralization is that as a company becomes more global, the emphasis shifts toward greater centralization. As countries increase in importance, they must be brought within the global manager's reach. However, this is not a given: compare the fairly centralized U.S. firm Procter and Gamble and the much more decentralized Anglo-Dutch firm Unilever in the case at the end of the chapter.

The term *global* can mean different things. Hamel and Prahalad (1992) differentiate between global competition, global businesses, and global companies. Global competition occurs when companies cross-subsidize national market share battles in pursuit of global brand and distribution positions. Rather than focus strictly on the home national market, global competition requires firms to attack competition in markets worldwide, including the home market of the foreign competitor. An example would be the U.S. auto industry, which, when placed under threat in the 1980s, had to react by going global. Similar battles have been fought in the airline industry.

Global businesses are those in which the minimum volume required for cost efficiency is not available in the company's home market, forcing those companies to pursue markets overseas, possibly supplying the market from domestic production. A good example is the steel industry or the international textiles industry. When China joined the World Trade Organization (WTO), access to the U.S. and European markets in textiles and apparels was governed by the Multifibre Agreement, a system of national quotas that limited access to the markets but at least guaranteed that countries with quotas would be able to sell to the United States and Europe. However, the WTO got the members to agree to replace the quotas with tariffs beginning in 2005, and the Chinese began to invest in state-of-the art textile and apparel manufacturing facilities to take advantage of the new environment. The cost effectiveness of their factories depended on their ability to penetrate the markets of the industrial countries and take away market share from other developing countries. Another example is the aircraft industry where Boeing and Airbus spread their very high R&D costs across global markets to achieve break-even and above volumes. Since the 1990s one has seen a decline in the number of producers of large commercial aircraft, and an increase in cross-industry mergers as the cost and risk of designing a single new aircraft became higher and higher.

Global companies have distribution systems in key markets that enable cross-subsidization, international retaliation, and world-scale volume. Again the key players in the airline industry such as British Airways, KLM, and American come to mind. More recently, one may need to go beyond the concept of companies to strategic alliances such as Star Alliance where 15 member carriers from different countries (Air Canada, Air New Zealand, ANA, Asiana Airlines, Austrian, bmi, LOT Polish Airlines, Lufthansa, Scandinavian Airlines, Singapore Airlines, Spanair, Thai, United, U.S. Airways, and Varig) have distribution systems in key markets that enable cross-subsidization, international retaliation, and world-scale volume.

Bartlett and Ghoshal (1989) identify three global imperatives that influence organizational structure, the degree of centralization of decision making, and the organizational culture of the firm:

1. **Forces for global integration: the need for efficiency.** Companies need to achieve economies of scale in such areas as product lines, parts design, and manufacturing operations. These economies are driven by cost factors as well as by the more harmonized tastes and preferences of consumers.

2. **Forces for local differentiation: the need for responsiveness.** Government interference and different market structures and consumer preferences require closer attention to local differences.

3. **Forces for worldwide innovation: the need for learning.** This imperative involves developing and diffusing worldwide innovations and linking and leveraging knowledge.

The problem for firms is that they need to deal with all three imperatives rather than focus on just one. For example, it is possible for a company to have to focus on integrating some areas while still needing to be responsive to different markets in different countries.

Bartlett and Ghoshal believe that firms need to move to a **transnational** strategy rather than a multidomestic or global strategy to deal most effectively with the three imperatives just described. In this approach, corporate assets are dispersed, interdependent, and specialized. This contrasts with multidomestic companies, which are decentralized and independent, or global companies, which are highly centralized and globally scaled.

As firms make the transition from domestic to international, they first begin with a core strategy which is often developed in the home country and which is the basis of the sustainable strategic advantage of the firm (Yip, 2003). That is the path that IKEA chose as noted in the beginning of the chapter. Then the firm internationalizes by moving to different countries as noted in Figure 12.1. If the different national units remain relatively independent and autonomous of the home office, the firm pursues a multidomestic strategy. However, the next step involves a global strategy (see Figure 12.1). If the flow of communication and control is primarily from the home office to the different national units, the company pursues a relatively centralized global strategy. However, if the firm follows a transnational strategy, it develops a higher level of communication and coordination across the national companies.

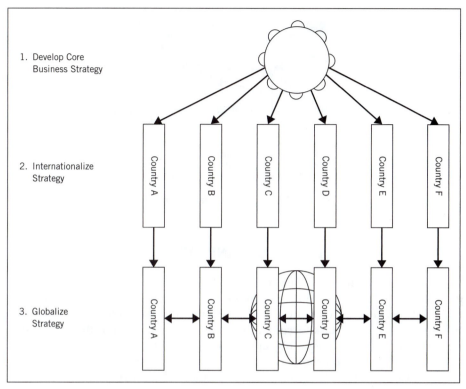

Figure 12.1   Components of a Total Global Strategy

Source: Yip (2003), p. 4.

In terms of the role of overseas operations, national units make differentiated contributions to integrated worldwide operations in what is termed a *transnational organizational structure* (see Figure 12.2). In other words, each national unit plays a different role, and these roles vary from country to country. One overseas operation may be a manufacturing facility, whereas another might define its role by the need to service its local market. On the other hand, multidomestic firms exploit local opportunities, whereas global firms simply implement parent company strategies. Knowledge is developed jointly in a transnational firm and is shared worldwide. This contrasts with multidomestic firms, which develop and retain knowledge in each local unit, or global firms, which develop and retain knowledge at the center. A good example of this is the strategy that Toyota is pursuing in Europe. As the European Union (EU) eliminated import quotas for autos in 2005, the Asian auto companies raced to establish a strategy for deeper penetration of the European market. Toyota decided to partner with the French company PSA Peugeot Citroën to manufacture small cars in the Czech Republic, one of the newest members of the EU, to supply the European market. The manufacturing facility was actually designed and built in Japan by Toyota's suppliers and tested in a virtual factory (Edmondson, 2005). The new plant in the Czech Republic will be run by Japanese and French managers and monitored by engineers from Toyota's factories in Japan.

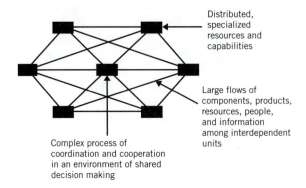

Distributed, specialized resources and capabilities

Large flows of components, products, resources, people, and information among interdependent units

Complex process of coordination and cooperation in an environment of shared decision making

Figure 12.2   Transnational Organization

INFORMAL AND SUBTLE MECHANISMS

Before examining the role of organizational structure as a follow-up to strategy, it is important to understand informal and subtle mechanisms of control, such as lateral relations, informal communication, and organizational culture. *Lateral relations* refers to the variety of task forces and meetings held throughout the formal structure to accomplish corporate objectives. An example is having product managers and geographic area coordinators get together to discuss strategy. The global brand manager for Unilever's Dove soap heads up a global team responsible for coordinating and expanding the Dove brand around the world. This is especially significant for companies that enter into strategic alliances with each other, such as Star Alliance in the airline industry.

Informal communication involves the network of personal contacts that one develops over time in the organization. We even saw examples of this in the relief efforts after the tsunami destruction in South Asia in 2004–2005. Suren Sornalingam, a logistics manager for Nike in Europe and an ethnic Tamil, decided to join the efforts of the Tamils Rehabilitation Organization (TRO) in providing relief to Tamils in northern and northeastern Sri Lanka. The TRO was able to maintain contact over the years with ethnic Tamils around the world and utilize their skills in the relief efforts (Hookway and Solomon, 2005).

Organizational culture is the outcome of the process of socializing individuals within a firm and across national boundaries, which allows things to be done by different people in similar or consistent ways. As noted in the IKEA example at the beginning of the chapter, the founder of IKEA established a philosophy that he tried to instill in all workers around the world. Specially trained "IKEA ambassadors" were assigned to key positions in all units to spread the company's philosophy and values by educating their subordinates and by acting as role models (Bartlett, 1990). The informal and subtle mechanisms may be the keys to managing global companies in the future.

ORGANIZATIONAL STRUCTURE

The managerial challenge of the twenty-first century is to coordinate the growing network of interdependent international activities. There are two major classifications of mechanisms for coordinating activities in MNEs: (1) structural and formal mechanisms, and (2) informal and subtle mechanisms.

In practice, control is shifting from the formal to the more informal ways of coordinating activities. To understand the transition from structural to informal and subtle control mechanisms, it is important to better understand the structural issues. As a domestic firm evolves into an MNE, numerous pressures, both internal and external, put strains on the firm's organizational structure. Some responsibilities are shifted, new ones are created, and occasionally, existing ones are eliminated. As responsibilities change, so do the reporting and communication flows. Furthermore, the degree of control, both exercised and exercisable, changes over time as the firm grows in size, geographic spread, and product lines, and as changes occur in countries' sociopolitical and socioeconomic environments. New opportunities arise, as do new threats, and thus a firm's organization is constantly evolving. Failure to properly adjust the organizational structure to the changing environments may result in internal conflict and poor performance. Internal conflict and poor performance also create pressure for organizational change.

Domestic Structure

Consider the typical evolution of a multinational firm from its beginning as a purely domestic firm. The first evolutionary stage involves export activities in the form of occasional, unsolicited orders from foreign buyers. Typically, no one in the purely domestic company has much, if any, knowledge about these matters. External experts, such as export management companies and freight forwarders, are used to develop an export strategy.

As exports grow in volume, the use of external experts can become increasingly expensive, and the firm may, and typically does, decide to internalize the export activities by hiring new personnel for what becomes an export department, thereby also gaining greater control over its export activities. As Figure 12.3 shows, the export group is typically a subgroup of the firm's marketing division, with only advisory or clerical capacity and no authority to commit resources.

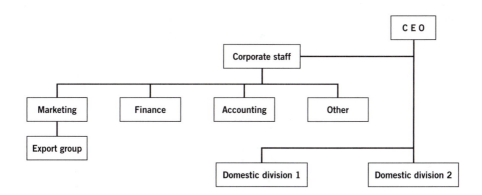

Figure 12.3 Domestic Organization with Initial Export Group

As foreign market opportunities and sales increase, this export group grows commensurately in size and sophistication. Foreign sales representatives may be added, leading ultimately to the establishment of foreign sales offices to better identify new customers and better serve all customers. By this stage, several internal strains have occurred. The first strain concerns responsibility for exports. Does the export group only advise domestic divisions, or is it empowered to make commitments? In the advisory situations, the export group feels constrained and seeks greater authority. In the commitment situation, domestic divisions feel a loss of power. In addition, there are strains related to internal pricing and profit allocations. The export group wants low transfer prices from the domestic division so it can obtain larger profits on its export sales, whereas the domestic division seeks higher transfer prices on goods it sells to the export group so that it can capture more of the profit. Furthermore, the export group may need to rely on the product and technical expertise of the larger domestic divisions, which, if obtained, puts pressure on the domestic staff and also leads them to request greater compensation.

International Division Structure

At a later stage, it often becomes advisable to establish foreign production facilities. For example, it may become cheaper to produce abroad, or foreign governments may restrict imports or raise tariffs. Once foreign production is established, whether by a licensing agreement, a joint venture, or a wholly owned subsidiary, some existing organizational pressures abate while others arise. Specifically, many of the previous disputes over production allocation, scheduling, product adaptations, and transfer pricing diminish because previous export markets are now served by foreign rather than domestic production. New problems of responsibility and control arise. Someone or some group must take responsibility for the growing foreign operations, and control becomes more difficult because changes occur in at least two operating environments (domestic and foreign). Typically, because of the growing diversity of international operations, an international division replaces the old export division (see Figure 12.4). Furthermore, because foreign activities are still a rather insignificant percentage of total corporate sales, substantial autonomy is given to the new division. As foreign operations expand further, however, the international division itself must exercise tighter control over its numerous operations and activities. To do so, it adds staff and, therefore, complexity. It also begins to fight harder for more corporate resources, which puts it into conflict with domes-

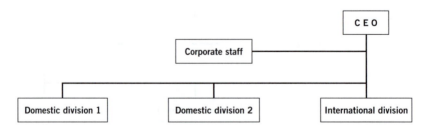

Figure 12.4   International Division

tic divisions that also want greater resources. In essence, the firm can become split into two rival factions, and suboptimization can result.

Global Structure

To minimize conflicts and potential suboptimization, the firm typically undergoes a major reorganization, adopting a global product structure or global geographic structure (see Figures 12.5 and 12.6). In the global product structure, previous distinctions between domestic and international divisions are eliminated, and product division managers are given responsibility and control over the worldwide production and sale of their products. In the global geographic structure, existing domestic and international operations become part of one of several geographic divisions. Firms typically select one of these structures based on a number of criteria related to their products and markets. For example, companies with narrow, relatively simple, and stable product lines often choose the global geographic structure, particularly when their products require many local adaptations or expert knowledge of local consumption practices, government policies, and so on. In short, a geographic structure works best when country or regional expertise is more important than product knowledge and expertise.

Conversely, when the product line is wide or when the products are complex and subject to rapid technological change (i.e., product knowledge and expertise are more important), the global product structure is often chosen. Unilever has been moving in that direction as it has tried to move from a very decentralized company to one in which certain product lines, such as Dove soap and a new line of Dove products in hair care, deodorants, and skin care now have global oversight and a global brand manager who is responsible for standardizing packaging, formulation, and advertising (Ball, 2005). Global product structures are also more likely to emerge when there is a greater need for production and logistical coordination, as in vertically integrated firms or firms pursuing international production rationalization. The Procter and Gamble case at the end of the chapter presents an opportunity for you to analyze a recent restructuring decision, its source, and implications.

Yet, as was the case with organizational changes, some former problems and pressures abate while others arise. In the global product structure, old battles

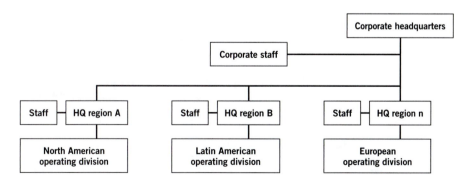

Figure 12.5   Global Geographically Oriented Organization

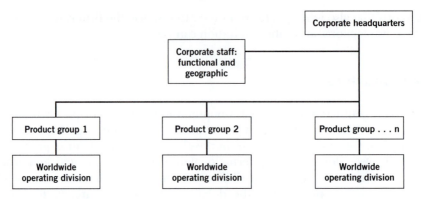

Figure 12.6   Global Product-Oriented Organization

between domestic and foreign divisions are reduced, but battles between product divisions are accentuated. As product lines gain worldwide market share, there is a need to develop regional expertise for the product lines. In the geographic structure, new battles emerge between geographic divisions as they fight for the latest in product developments and for resources for expansion.

To better coordinate and control global operations, still another organizational structure emerged—that of the global grid/matrix structure (see Figure 12.7). In this three-dimensional structure, product divisions, geographic areas, and functional areas share power and responsibilities. For example, a proposed expansion of sales of industrial equipment in the Far East involved an MNE's industrial equipment group, its Far East regional group, and finance and marketing groups at headquarters. Through such a combination, the company management hoped

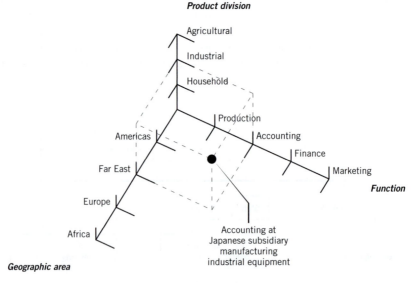

Figure 12.7   Global Grid Organization

there would be better coordination of global activities by taking a more holistic and less suboptimal approach.

However, the matrix has not turned out to be the solution to organization dilemmas. As Bartlett and Ghoshal (1989) note, there are numerous shortcomings to the matrix:

> In practice, however, the matrix proved all but unmanageable, especially in an international context. Dual reporting led to conflict and confusion; the proliferation of channels created informational logjams as a proliferation of committees and reports bogged down the organization; and overlapping responsibilities produced turf battles and a loss of accountability. Separated by barriers of distance, language, time, and culture, managers found it virtually impossible to clarify the confusion and resolve the conflicts.

The solution to the organizational dilemma is more complex than organizational structure; it involves the attitude toward the role between the parent company and the different affiliates worldwide (the centralization/decentralization dilemma) as well as the frame of mind of top management (the informal and subtle mechanisms). These organizational issues strongly influence the managerial accounting system of the firm, from the nature of the information system and the establishment of accounting policies, to the internal controls established to ensure compliance and the evaluation of the performance of foreign operations and their managers.

CORPORATE GOVERNANCE

In very simple terms, all business activities consist of a set of resources and people who put forth effort to make those resources as profitable as possible. Most of the time the people financing the resources, typically shareholders, are not the same as those who manage them. Shareholders want to ensure that management will act in their best interest as they manage the firm's resources.

Corporate governance is about "the determination of the broad uses to which organizational resources will be deployed and the resolution of conflicts among the myriad participants in organizations" (Daily et al., 2003). Corporate governance has become a prominent issue in recent years. The corporate scandals created by Enron, WorldCom, Parmalat, and many other firms have caused the public to wonder if their money is safe in the hands of self-interested managers. Those who have investigated the scandals commonly suggest that better corporate governance can go a long way toward keeping management in check and increasing investor confidence.

Large corporations now have entire websites dedicated to "corporate governance and responsibility." These websites provide plenty of information on how the board of directors is structured and how top management is compensated, and they normally contain statements on ethics and responsibility. The concept of *board oversight* has become a hot management topic—focusing on the role of the board of directors as a check and balance on management. Large institutional investors are focusing on *shareholder activism*—the practice of being actively involved in influencing management's decisions in strategic areas and management compensation.

Thus, understanding corporate governance is important to understanding today's business environment.

Internal Governance Mechanisms

People and organizations invest in business ventures to maximize their own wealth. They do this by putting money into the hands of managers who are expected to provide a return on their investment. Because they do not control the daily operations of the business, providers of capital set up corporate governance mechanisms to insure that management acts in the best interest of the owners. Those mechanisms that are controlled directly by the owners of the firm are called *internal governance mechanisms* (see Figure 12.8). Internal governance mechanisms include the *board of directors* and the *ownership structure* (Denis & McConnell, 2003).

Most corporations have a board of directors, whose job is to represent the interests of owners (typically shareholders). The board hires, controls, and fires management, and determines management's compensation. It is also ultimately responsible for the internal controls of the firm. Typically, a board is composed of several committees, each reflecting its responsibilities. For example, IBM's board of directors has three committees: the Audit Committee, the Executive Compensation and Management Resources Committee, and the Directors and Corporate Governance Committee. Most large MNEs have boards with similar committees.

Board members are appointed by the owners of the firm. Boards of directors are normally composed of members of management and outside members who do not participate in the daily operations of the firm. Best practices in governance suggest that boards should have a large proportion of outside, independent board members. At the same time, they propose that the CEO and the chairman of the board should be separate individuals. This helps insure that the board is independent and willing to contradict management if they act against shareholder interests.

The ownership structure is a strategic decision that determines how capital will be infused into the firm and how wealth will be distributed among the various parties. For example, in the United States and the United Kingdom publicly traded companies sell shares of stock to many individual shareholders around the world. These owners do not know each other, so ownership is said to be *dispersed*. In other

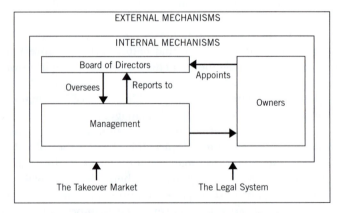

Figure 12.8   Corporate Governance Mechanims

countries, banks or wealthy families tend to own the controlling interest of firms. This is called *concentrated ownership*. Other countries have a large number of *state-owned enterprises,* such as China. A trend in the United States in the last few decades has been the increase of *institutional shareholders*. These are large funds or companies that own significant portions of a firm and exercise a controlling interest. No matter what the ownership structure of a firm is, it will have important strategic and financial implications.

A challenge comes when firms from one ownership system and governance structure invests in a country with a different system of ownership and corporate governance. Chinese firms have been investing in South America to get access to raw materials and markets, but they are finding some challenges in their expansion. Chinese managers are accused of separating their Chinese workers from local workers and of not working effectively with local suppliers and businesses. Because they do not have to worry about unions and shareholders in China, they are having difficulty coping with a very different labor and ownership environment in their foreign operations (Millman and Wonacott, 2005).

External Governance Mechanisms

The governance mechanisms that are not directly controlled by the current owners of the firm are called *external governance mechanisms* (see Exhibit 12.8). These include the *takeover market* and the *legal system*.

When a firm is performing poorly, it can be purchased by new owners who believe they can somehow better manage the firm and make it more profitable. This is an external control mechanism called the *takeover market*. In countries with highly developed securities markets, such as the United States and United Kingdom, the takeover market is very active because anyone with sufficient money can purchase a majority of the shares of a company and take over its operations. This ability to externally take over a firm helps ensure that resources are used in the most efficient way possible in the market. In markets with less developed securities markets, such as in most of the emerging markets, taking over a firm requires more direct negotiation with current management.

Recent studies have shown that different legal systems act as important external controls on firms. For example, some common law systems such as these in the United States and the United Kingdom offer very good protection to small, individual shareholders. On the other hand, code law systems such as those in Germany and France offer better protection to large institutional shareholders. Other legal systems offer almost no protection to either type of owner. The implication is that the legal system can favor the infusion of capital into firms by protecting certain types of shareholders, or it can adversely affect the infusion of capital by offering very little protection to potential investors.

The combination of internal and external governance mechanisms in place in any given firm determines the governance structure of the firm. As our understanding of different mechanisms grows, several important questions arise. Is there an ideal governance structure that all firms should have? How do cultural and political differences affect governance structures? How should large MNEs structure their governance relationships?

INTERNATIONAL IMPORTANCE OF GOVERNANCE

Several events have converged to give corporate governance a prominent role in today's business world. The increase in investment opportunities through the growth of securities markets in countries outside of the United States and the United Kingdom requires listed firms to become more transparent in their business and reporting practices. The demand for information is growing from the increased numbers of potential investors. The corporate meltdowns of the past 15 years have shattered investor confidence worldwide. In the early 1990s, several European companies failed due to fraud and other preventable conditions. In 1997, the Asian stock markets crashed as a manifestation of the speculative spirit among companies in several emerging Asian markets. Most recently, we have seen the collapse of giants like Enron and WorldCom and the scandals created by frauds at Parmalat, Xerox, Shell, Ahold, and others.

These events have triggered the creation of Codes of Best Practice in corporate governance all over the world. The first major document aimed at improving governance practices was issued in the United States in January 1978 was entitled *The Role and Composition of the Board of Directors of the Large Publicly Owned Corporation.* The report explained the director's main duties as: (1) overseeing the management and board selection and succession; (2) reviewing the company's financial performance and allocating its funds; (3) overseeing corporate social responsibility; and (4) ensuring compliance with the law (Charkham, 1995). In 1989, the Hong Kong Stock Exchange issued its first code, followed by Ireland in 1991. However, codes of best practice did not become prominent until corporate scandals made the need for them apparent.

In 1992, as a response to the fall of some large corporations, the United Kingdom appointed a committee to issue recommendations to improve governance practices. The result was *The Financial Aspects of Corporate Governance,* commonly known as the Cadbury Report, in honor of the person who chaired the investigation. The Report is a comprehensive survey on boards of directors, covering board composition, director's training and compensation, auditing and internal controls, and shareholder rights and responsibilities. One of its sections, entitled "The Code of Best Practice," provides recommendations regarding boards of directors. The most prominent suggestions include:

- Having a specific number of outside, independent directors who are not immersed in the daily operations of the business.
- Creating specific committees to carry out the main functions of the board, including the audit committee, the remuneration (compensation) committee, and the nominations committee.
- Appointing different individuals to the roles of chairman of the board and CEO.

Although the Cadbury Report was written as a set of recommendations, the London Stock Exchange requires all listed companies to comply with the Code of Best Practice. If a company is not compliant, it must explain the reasons for its deficiency.

The issuance of the Cadbury Report coincided with the globalization of business and became the trigger for many other countries and organizations to issue their own codes. These Codes of Best Practice are now found in countries all over Europe, Asia, and Latin America. Most major stock exchanges require listed companies to comply with a Code of Best Practice. Companies themselves are taking the initiative to provide information regarding their governance practices on their websites and annual reports.

There is still debate over whether these codes should be enforced by law or followed on a volunteer basis. As already mentioned, stock exchanges already require listed companies to comply with one code or another. Some argue that this may be enough to increase investor confidence. However, if codes are not enforced by law, investors may feel that they have no legal protection against those companies that fail to comply with the code.

Another issue regarding the use of Codes of Best Practice is how to measure compliance with the code. How do companies know if they have effective governance practices in place? A creative solution originated in Germany. In 2000, the German Society of Financial Analysts created the *Scorecard for German Corporate Governance* (see Exhibit 12.1 for a few items in each category of the Scorecard). The scorecard is a set of yes/no questions firms can answer based on the German Code of Best Practice. The scorecard gives firms a score ranging between 0 and 100 based on compliance in seven areas of governance: corporate governance commitment, shareholders and the general meeting, cooperation between management board and supervisory board, management board, supervisory board, transparency, and reporting and audit of the annual financial statements. The Scorecard reflects the German legalistic approach to business.

Not only has the German Scorecard become a useful measurement tool in its own country, but it has become the basis of similar evaluation approaches worldwide, especially in emerging countries lacking formal governance practices (Strenger, 2004). The scorecard is now formally used in the Philippines and Indonesia. A similar kind of scorecard was developed to evaluate 72 companies in Latin America. In Europe, the scorecard approach is used as a consulting tool to evaluate firms.

As corporate governance continues to increase in prominence, we should ask ourselves if effective governance practices are the solution to corporate fraud. The answer is no. Firms must do a lot more than implement a Code of Best Practice to gain investors' confidence. The introduction to the Cadbury Report puts it best:

> Had a Code such as ours been in existence in the past, we believe that a number of the recent examples of unexpected company failures and cases of fraud would have received attention earlier. It must, however, be recognised that no system of control can eliminate the risk of fraud without so shackling companies as to impede their ability to compete in the market place.

STUDIES ON INTERNATIONAL CORPORATE GOVERNANCE PRACTICES

Most studies on corporate governance have been conducted on U.S. firms. However, there is a growing body of research on international corporate governance. This section outlines the main findings of these studies as reported by Denis and McConnell (2003).

Exhibit 12.1 Exerpts from a Scorecard for German Corporate Governance

---

I. Corporate Governance-Commitment (10%)

!	I.1	Does the company have its own specific corporate governance principles based on the German Corporate Governance Code?
!	I.2	Are these principles based on the Code easily available to all stakeholders (e.g. via Internet) in an up-to-date version?
!	I.3	Do these company principles include an explicit commitment to adapt them to best practice developments of corporate governance?

II. Shareholders and the General Meeting (12%)

!	II.1	Are the agenda of the General Meeting, any opposing shareholder proposals, management comments thereto and the voting results made available to all shareholders on the Internet in a timely manner? **(2.3.1,** *2.3.2)*
!	II.2	Can voting rights be exercised (at least via proxies) using the Internet? **(2.3.3,** *2.3.4)*
!	II.3	Can shareholders follow General Meetings also via the Internet? *(2.3.4)*

III. Cooperation between Management Board and Supervisory Board (15%)

!	III.1	Is there a written understanding between the Management and Supervisory Boards with regard to regular, timely, and comprehensive information by the Management Board? **(3.4)**
!	III.2	Do terms of reference exist for the Supervisory Board detailing its rights and duties, stipulating inter alia the transactions requiring approval and the information duties of the Management Board? **(3.3, 5.1.3.)**
!	III.3	Do the representatives of the shareholders and of the employees of codetermined Supervisory Boards meet separately to prepare the Supervisory Board Meetings? *(3.6)*

IV. Management Board (10%)

!	IV.1	Does the Management Board issue business principles, company policy guidelines and terms of reference, which regulate inter alia co-operation within the Management Board? **(4.2.1)**
!	IV.2	Are the fixed and variable compensation elements of the Management Board published separately and by individual? **(4.2.4)**
!	IV.3	Is the variable compensation of the Management Board linked to the relative value creation (e.g. relative performance, economic profit)? **(4.2.3 p.2)**

V. Supervisory Board (15%)

!	V.1	Do defined criteria exist to ensure the qualification of Supervisory Board members (e.g. professional qualification and experience, sufficient time, international experience)? **(5.4.1)**
!	V.2	Are there no more than two former members of the Management Board on the Supervisory Board and do Supervisory Board members refrain from directorships or advisory tasks for important competitors of the company? **(5.4.2)**
!	V.3	Do re-appointments of Management Board members take place at the earliest one year before the end of the original appointment period and with due consideration of age limits? **(5.1.2)**

VI. Transparency (20%)

!	VI.1	Are all investors (not only shareholders according to § 53a AktG - German Securities Act) and financial analysts informed equally ('Fair Disclosure') via the Internet and also in English? **(6.3, 6.4, 6.8)**
!	VI.2	Are regular capital market conferences (like analyst meetings) held?
!	VI.3	Is there a detailed analysis of deviations from major previously published performance and strategy targets?

VII. Reporting and Audit of the Annual Financial Statements (18%)

!	VII.1	Are the Reports prepared according to IAS / US-GAAP **(7.1.1),** and are International Standards on Auditing (ISA) or the US Generally Accepted Auditing Standards (US-GAAS) applied complementary to the IDW (German Institute of Auditors) Standards on Auditing?
!	VII.2	Is sufficient independence an important criterion for the selection of the auditors? **(7.2.1)**
!	VII.3	Does the Supervisory Board set an appropriate level for the auditing fee?

Source: C. Strenger. 2004. "The Corporate Governance Scorecard: A Tool for the Implementation of Corporate Governance," *Corporate Governance: An International Review* 12(1): 11–15.

Board of Directors

As stated previously, the purpose of the board of directors in the United States is to protect shareholder interests. This responsibility is prescribed by law. Boards are composed of a mix of inside and outside directors, and there is a growing tendency to separate the roles of CEO and chairman of the board.

Most European states do not have laws prescribing the role or makeup of boards of directors. Therefore, boards in Europe do not always have the primary goal of protecting shareholders. Although most boards are unitary, some European countries like Austria and Germany have two-tiered boards, generally consisting of a managing board, composed of executives of the firm, and a supervisory board. In Germany, representation of employees on the supervisory board, termed co-determination, is mandatory.

In recent years, several European nations have issued Codes of Best Practice in corporate governance, beginning with the United Kingdom in 1992 with the issuance of the Cadbury Report, as mentioned on p. 316.

In Japan, firms are more likely to appoint outside directors following periods of poor financial performance. Such appointments tend to improve stock returns, operating performance, and sales growth. However, it is very common for firms in distress to turn to their banks to provide management supervision and control. Banks perform the role of outside corporate governance.

In Russia, most firms are majority owned by insiders and employees, and boards are solidly controlled by insiders. Most managers indicate resistance to outsiders on the board. Those board members that are outsiders are typically holders of large blocks of stocks. A government decree urging that boards be composed of no more than one-third insiders has been ignored by all but a very few small Russian companies. The Russian oil giant, Yukos, was touted in 2001 as a company ready to adhere to world corporate governance standards. However, the CEO of Yukos was jailed for corporate tax evasion, and Yukos was broken up by the Russian government. Good corporate governance is still a challenge in Russia.

Several studies have tried to associate the structure of the board of directors with firm profitability, market value, or other measures of success. The board characteristics that have been most extensively studied are the relative proportion of outside directors and the size of the board.

For U.S. firms, these studies have shown that higher proportions of outside directors are associated not with superior firm performance, but with better decisions concerning such issues as acquisitions, executive compensation, and CEO turnover. At the same time, board size is negatively related to both general firm performance and the quality of decision making. In other words, boards that are too large (more than 10 to 12 members) tend to make worse decisions than smaller boards. Finally, poor firm performance, CEO turnover, and changes in ownership structure are often associated with changes in the membership of the board.

The growing body of research on international firms has also shown a lack of association between the proportion of outside directors and firm performance. However, results do suggest that top management turnover is associated with more outside board members. This means that independent directors are more willing to contradict management's decisions and even fire management if necessary.

Executive Compensation

From a governance perspective, an executive compensation package is deemed effective if it aligns top executives' interests with those of their shareholders. A guaranteed salary, for example, provides little incentive for an executive to maximize firm value for the shareholders because the executive will get the salary no matter how the firm performs. On the other hand, performance-based compensation such as stock grants and stock options provide very strong incentives to maximize firm value; as firm value increases, so does the executive's compensation. United States studies have shown that the sensitivity of pay to performance has increased over time. Most of this sensitivity comes through executive ownership of common stock and of options on common stock. Stock options are the fastest growing component of CEO compensation in the United States. Overall, the evidence on international executive compensation is very small. However, studies in Japan and Spain show that performance-based compensation is increasing in those countries, although not at the pace it has increased in the United States.

Ownership Structure

The first studies in ownership structure of firms focused on four countries: the United States, the United Kingdom, Germany, and Japan. It was found that in the United States and the U.K., firm ownership tends to be *dispersed* among a large amount of unrelated shareholders who buy and sell shares in open markets. These are called *market-centered economies*. On the other hand, German and Japanese ownership of firms tends to be *concentrated* among majority owners such as banks or other large financial institutions. These are called *bank-centered economies*.

As further studies began to look beyond these four countries, it was found that concentrated ownership structures were the most common form of ownership outside of the United States and the United Kingdom. For example, firms in continental Europe are mostly family owned and controlled. In Israel, banks and institutional investors are the most common majority shareholders. In China, ownership is split relatively equally between the government, institutions, and domestic individuals. It is hard to know if this concentrated ownership is due to a lack of highly developed stock markets, or if the lack of highly developed stock markets is an outgrowth of this preference for concentrated ownership.

Studies have shown that outside of the United States, concentrated ownership is positively associated with firm performance. For example, a study of East Asian companies found that strong government ownership was positively associated with performance while corporate ownership negatively affected performance. In several other countries, it was shown that bank ownership is associated with positive firm performance.

Another worldwide trend in recent years has been to sell traditionally state-owned enterprises to private investors. This dramatic shift in ownership structure is known as *privatization*. Several studies have shown that after privatization, firms significantly increase their profitability. Other reported effects include cost savings, more efficiency, better employment conditions, and increased dividends. The results are very similar for developed and emerging markets.

The External Control Market

When a firm is performing poorly owing to bad management or underutilization of assets, the external market may act as a control mechanism. A *hostile takeover* occurs when a firm is purchased without soliciting bids. The United States has the most active takeover market, in which unsolicited tender offers are regularly made for existing firms, For example, the proposed merger between Canadian brewer Molson and United States brewer Coors ran into problems because some of Molson's shareholders felt that the merger of equals was actually a takeover by Coors. Even though Molson had a larger market capitalization, higher profitability, and a stronger domestic base, the headquarters of the new company was expected to move to Coors' headquarters with two Coors executives as the head of the new venture. The United Kingdom also has an active takeover market. However, the rest of the world does not show a significant takeover activity, so the external market has not been shown to be a common governance control tool.

The Legal System

As mentioned previously, most firms outside the United States and the United Kingdom tend to have a concentrated ownership structure. La Porta et al. (1998) explain that this preference for concentrated ownership can be explained by a country's legal system. Generally speaking, countries have either a common law legal system, such as the United States and the United Kingdom, or a civil law system, such as Germany and France. In a study of 49 countries, La Porta et al. found that common law countries provide the strongest degree of protection for shareholders, whereas the laws of civil law countries provide the least amount of protection to shareholders.

Furthermore, they found that countries offering the strongest investor protection tend to have firms with a more dispersed ownership structure, whereas countries offering weak investor protection tend to have firms with a more concentrated ownership structure. For example, in the United States, the three largest equity holders of the 10 largest domestic firms own 20 percent of the firm. For the 49 countries studied by La Porta et al., the ownership concentration of the three largest shareholders was 45 percent. Denis and McConnell (2003, p. 21) explain that "concentrated ownership may be a reasonable response to a lack of investor protection. If the law does not protect the owners from the controllers, the owners will seek to be controllers."

Convergence of Governance Practices

Most of the research on corporate governance has focused on which governance structure or system is "the best." Trends in recent years have shown that firms worldwide are converging toward fairly similar systems. United States firms are showing increased amounts of concentrated ownership through institutional shareholders, whereas German firms are moving their two-tier boards to unitary boards. It is generally accepted that having an important proportion of outside directors helps keep management in check. Codes of Best Practice, such as the Cadbury Report, all agree on some fundamental points. Proponents of improved governance practices agree that governments should provide strong protection to shareholders to fuel investment.

Will we see a complete convergence and agreement in governance practices and systems worldwide? Or will national and cultural differences continue to prevail? The question is not easy to answer. Apparently, some of the "best practices" seem to work everywhere. However, it seems unreasonable to expect complete agreement on how to best structure the ownership-management relationship and ignore regional differences in culture, legal systems, economic systems, and market maturity. In the following section we present some evidence on how these factors determine the corporate governance structure of firms.

CROSS NATIONAL DIFFERENCES IN CORPORATE GOVERNANCE

Aguilera and Jackson (2003) explain why different countries choose different configurations for their corporate governance structures. They see corporate governance as the interplay between three key groups—capital (shareholders), management, and labor (employees). Traditional corporate governance theory focused only on the interaction between shareholders and management, so the addition of labor as a key player in the governance literature is a new concept as presented by Aguilera and Jackson in Figure 12.9.

Figure 12.9 also shows the different factors within each player's domain that influence how that player relates to the firm and thus affects the corporate governance structure. Each of those factors will take on a different dimension in different countries based on the culture, legal system, and maturity of the market.

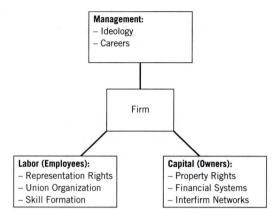

Figure 12.9   Institutional Domains Shaping Corporate Governance

Source: Adapted from Aguilera & Jackson (2003).

Capital

Capital refers to the shareholders or owners of the company. Three factors determine how shareholders exercise control to the firm: the property rights granted by the legal system, the characteristics of the financial system, and the existence of interfirm networks. Aguilera and Jackson suggest that shareholders exercise control in two different ways: *commitment* or *liquidity.* Commitment refers to holding shares in the company for a long period of time, expecting long-term profits and growth. Liquidity refers to the active buying and selling of shares, searching for short-term profits as share prices fluctuate.

Property Rights   In countries with property rights predominantly favoring large shareholders (such as banks or large corporate investors), owners tend to pursue strategic interests toward the firm and exercise control via commitment. For example, Japan's property rights favor banks and other large shareholders and virtually leave small shareholders unprotected. In such countries, shareholders exercise control of firms by holding stocks for longer periods of time (commitment) and for purposes other than making a short-term profit. Japanese networks, called Keiretsu, extensively use long-term, stable cross-shareholding among firms in the network. Examples of Keiretsu are Mitsubishi, Mitsui, and Sumitomo.

On the other hand, U.S. laws tend to favor small, minority shareholders. These types of capital providers exercise power through liquidity by quickly buying and selling shares to make a profit as opposed to holding stocks for the long term.

Financial System   In countries with predominantly bank-based financial systems, capital providers tend to exercise control over the firm via debt and commitment. Germany, for example, tends to have a stronger bank-based system. Investors typically put money in banks, which in turn finance firms via debt. On the other hand, in countries with predominantly market-based financial systems, capital tends to exercise control over the firm via equity and liquidity. In the United States, the equity market is more open to individuals investing directly in firms, so control is exercised through the buying and selling of stocks.

Interfirm Networks   The term *interfirm network* refers to cross ownership between governments, management, banks, and other firms, such as in Japan and Europe. In countries such as these, with a high degree of multiplexity in interfirm networks, capital tends to pursue strategic interests toward the firm and exercise control via commitment. Other countries such as the United Kingdom, with lower degrees of multiplexity in interfirm networks, capital tends to pursue financial interests toward the firm and exercise control via liquidity.

Labor

Employee relationships with the firm determine the type of control employees can exercise. As Figure 12.9 shows, the degree of influence exercised by employees on the firm depends on three factors: representation rights, union organization, and skill formation. Two terms are important in order to understand Aguilera and Jackson's propositions: *external control* and *internal participation,* which they explain as follows:

> External control refers to situations where decision making remains the prerogative of management. Here employees seek to control firms' decisions externally, with the threat of collective action (e.g., strikes) … Employee representation is "independent" of management and preserved in strict separation from cooperative institutions that engage labor in firms' decision making. Alternatively, employees might participate in firms' decisions through internal channels of decision making to codetermine management actions. Participation does not end managerial authority but aims at democratizing decisions (Agulera and Jackson, 2003, p. 455).

Representation Rights   In countries with predominantly strong representation rights, labor tends to pursue strategies of internal participation. In European countries where employees have more power through unions, such as Germany, employees show internal participation. This means being involved more directly in management decision making. In countries with predominantly weak representation rights, such as China and many countries in Southeast Asia, labor tends to pursue strategies of external control. Because U.S. employees have less power than European employees, they don't show as much internal participation. Thus, they resort to external control by going on strikes and like action.

Union Organization   In countries with predominantly class-based and craft-based unionism, labor tends to pursue strategies of external control. Class and craft-based unions are just what the name says: unions of people in similar classes or crafts (e.g., automakers or farm workers). These types of unions do not identify themselves with a specific firm because their class or craft is not firm specific, so they exercise external control and show less internal participation, as in the United States. In countries with predominantly enterprise-based forms of unionism, labor tends to pursue strategies of internal participation. Japan, for example, has many enterprise based unions, which are very firm specific. Employees of these firms feel a long-term commitment to the firm and value job security highly, so they seek internal participation in management decisions.

Skills Formation   In countries with predominantly market- and state-based skill formation institutions, labor tends to acquire portable skills and to pursue strategies of external control. The United States has employees trained in more general skills, which are more portable, so employees do not feel a long-term commitment to a specific firm. This leads to external rather than internal participation. In countries with predominantly firm-based skill formation institutions, like Japan, labor tends to acquire firm-specific skills and to pursue strategies of internal participation.

Management

Management will relate to the firm based on managerial ideology and career formation.

Ideology   In countries where managerial ideologies legitimize generalist knowledge and/or hierarchical decision making, management tends to have greater autonomy in relation to the firm and a financial orientation. United States and French managers are trained in general skills, with an emphasis on finance. Decisions in these countries are hierarchical (top down) rather than "democratic." Managers in this type of context will be more autonomous and focused on financial performance. In countries where managerial ideologies legitimate scientific specializations and/or consensual decision making, management tends to have greater commitment to the firm and a functional orientation. For example, in Germany, managers are specialized in technical areas and are taught to use consensual decision making.

Career Formation   In countries with predominantly closed managerial labor markets, management tends to have greater commitment to the firm and a functional orientation. Closed managerial labor markets are those in which companies promote heavily from within, like Japan. Managers have vast experience in one firm and are very specialized in one or many areas, or functionally oriented. In countries with predominantly open managerial labor markets, management tends to have greater autonomy in relation to the firm and a financial orientation. The U.S. job market is less stable, or open, where managers are brought in from other firms. Thus, managers are less tied to one specific firm and seek to enhance their reputation and personal value by maximizing the share value of the firm they manage.

Aguilera and Jackson provide an interesting framework to help us understand why firms are structured in certain ways in different regions of the world. Understanding these factors is important for MNEs making strategic decisions about where to set up operations and how to structure foreign operations based on the labor market, managerial styles and preferences, and the financial and legal systems of their target countries.

INTERNAL CONTROLS

With the rise of fraudulent financial reporting and other corporate scandals, internal controls have become a key responsibility of the board of directors. One of the main purposes of good governance practices is to ensure that strong internal controls are maintained over the assets of the firm. Most boards of directors have an Audit Committee, which manages the internal and external audit, including the monitoring of internal controls.

In 1985, the Committee of Sponsoring Organization of the Treadway Commission, known as COSO, was formed to improve the quality of financial reporting through business ethics, effective internal controls, and corporate governance. The COSO framework on internal controls, widely accepted as the authoritative source on controls, defines internal control as follows:

> Internal control is broadly defined as a process, effected by an entity's board of directors, management and other personnel, designed to provide reasonable assurance regarding the achievement of objectives in the following categories:

- Effectiveness and efficiency of operations.
- Reliability of financial reporting.
- Compliance with applicable laws and regulations.

Furthermore, the COSO framework identifies five different components of an internal control system:

1. **Control Environment:** The control environment sets the tone of an organization, influencing the control consciousness of its people. It is the foundation for all other components of internal control, providing discipline and structure. Control environment factors include the integrity, ethical values, and competence of the entity's people; management's philosophy and operating style; the way management assigns authority and responsibility, and organizes and develops its people; and the attention and direction provided by the board of directors.

2. **Risk Assessment:** Every entity faces a variety of risks from external and internal sources that must be assessed. A precondition to risk assessment is establishment of objectives, linked at different levels and internally consistent. Risk assessment is the identification and analysis of relevant risks to achievement of the objectives, forming a basis for determining how the risks should be managed. Because economic, industry, regulatory and operating conditions will continue to change, mechanisms are needed to identify and deal with the special risks associated with change.

3. **Control Activities:** Control activities are the policies and procedures that help ensure management directives are carried out. They help ensure that necessary actions are taken to address risks to achievement of the entity's objectives. Control activities occur throughout the organization, at all levels and in all functions. They include a range of activities as diverse as approvals, authorizations, verifications, reconciliations, reviews of operating performance, security of assets and segregation of duties.

4. **Information and Communication:** Pertinent information must be identified, captured and communicated in a form and timeframe that enable people to carry out their responsibilities. Information systems produce reports, containing operational, financial and compliance-related information, that make it possible to run

and control the business. They deal not only with internally generated data, but also information about external events, activities, and conditions necessary to informed business decision making and external reporting. Effective communication also must occur in a broader sense, flowing down, across and up the organization. All personnel must receive a clear message from top management that control responsibilities must be taken seriously. They must understand their own role in the internal control system, as well as how individual activities relate to the work of others. They must have a means of communicating significant information upstream. There also needs to be effective communication with external parties, such as customers, suppliers, regulators, and shareholders.

5. **Monitoring:** Internal control systems need to be monitored—a process that assesses the quality of the system's performance over time. This is accomplished through ongoing monitoring activities, separate evaluations or a combination of the two. Ongoing monitoring occurs in the course of operations. It includes regular management and supervisory activities, and other actions personnel take in performing their duties. The scope and frequency of separate evaluations will depend primarily on an assessment of risks and the effectiveness of ongoing monitoring procedures. Internal control deficiencies should be reported upstream, with serious matters reported to top management and the board. (COSO Executive Summary)

These components of internal controls apply to local as well as multinational entities. However, MNEs face added challenges due to their size and the complexity of operating in different environments. Establishing a well-understood control environment becomes difficult when integrating different philosophies, operating styles, and ethical values among several cultures. The risk assessment activities are more complex because MNEs face not only the home country's risks, but the risks of multiple markets combined. Finally, establishing adequate control activities, providing clear and constant information and communication, and constantly monitoring very large and geographically dispersed firms are more difficult than doing these functions for a local firm. One of the solutions to the informational needs of maintaining an effective internal control system is information technology (IT). The last section of this chapter discusses some of the IT tools that help MNEs succeed in their control responsibilities.

The Sarbanes-Oxley Act of 2002

The corporate scandals of Enron and WorldCom in the United States, as well as frauds such as Parmalat, Ahold, and Shell in Europe, have made it evident that firms can do better at monitoring their internal controls. As a reaction to these events, the U.S. government issued the Sarbanes-Oxley Act on July 30, 2002.

This new law establishes very strict reporting requirements for public firms in the United States, as well as for foreign firms listed on U.S. stock exchanges. Section 404 of the Act establishes that it is management's responsibility to maintain an adequate internal control structure over procedures for financial reporting. The Act requires management to issue a yearly report with an assessment of the effectiveness of internal controls. This report is to be issued along with the annual report and must be independently assessed by the firm's auditor. The requirement became effective on November 15, 2004 for U.S. firms. Foreign firms listed in U.S. exchanges must be compliant by July 15, 2005.

Although this mandate seems simple on the surface, it has very broad implications. In order to assess the effectiveness of its internal controls, firms have poured millions of dollars into documenting and improving internal controls on any activity affecting the financial reporting process, from issuing checks on a day-to-day basis to approving new investments with long-term effects. A study by Ernst & Young showed that large American firms would spend more than 100,000 man-hours to comply with Section 404. Some critics of Section 404 observe that the onerous requirements of the Act are drawing foreign direct investment from the United States. The New York Stock Exchange (NYSE) has seen a significant slow-down in foreign listings since Sarbanes-Oxley, from 50 to 60 a year before the Act was passed to 16 in 2003. For example, Air China listed with the London Stock Exchange in late 2004 instead of the NYSE to avoid having to comply with all the requirements of the Act (*The Economist,* 2004).

On the other hand, some argue that the increased transparency provided by complying with the Act is an advantage to firms. As financial reporting becomes more transparent, investors will have more confidence and require lower rates of return from those firms who comply with Sarbanes-Oxley. It is expected that compliant companies will be seen as "best practice" firms. Although the Act may deter foreign investment from smaller firms, large new listings on American exchanges have not declined. Despite the Air China case, the largest Chinese new listings in foreign markets in 2004 occurred in the NYSE.

Another interesting dimension of Section 404 is that it applies to all operations of U.S.-based MNEs. Thus, if the MNE has operations in China, Japan, and Korea, it must document the internal controls in all three of those countries, not just in the United States. This is a challenge for firms operating in countries where controls have traditionally been more lax.

THE ROLE OF INFORMATION TECHNOLOGY IN MNEs

Tremendous advances have been made in computer and network technology in the last decade. Probably the most visible change in the transfer of information has been the dissemination of the Internet. MNEs now can be constantly in touch with subsidiaries and customers in any part of the world with the click of a button. These factors have converged to give the information technology (IT) function a key strategic role in firms. An effective information system is a source of competitive advantage. For example, Wal-Mart and its suppliers share a database that gives real-time information on stocking levels, sales, and costs on any store in any part of the globe. IT can also make the accounting and internal control functions more efficient.

As an MNE becomes larger and enters more countries, it faces the challenge of compatibility of information from various divisions. During the late 1980s and early 1990s, most companies had separate information systems for each functional area and division. A large MNE such as Shell or IBM, with all of its divisions and functions, had literally thousands of independent systems with different sets of data, reports, and supporting personnel. A step forward in the late 1990s was the proliferation of Enterprise Resource Planning (ERP) software. The purpose of ERP is to integrate all departments and functions under one computer system. In other words, all companywide data is stored in one place and can be extracted and manipulated in any way to fit the needs of the different functions and departments of a firm.

Firms that implement ERP systems receive the following benefits: integration of financial information, integration of customer order information, standardization and increased speed in the manufacturing process, reduction in inventories, and standardization of HR information (Koch, 1999). These are tremendous advantages, to say the least. At the same time, the implementation of such a large-scale system presents challenges to large companies such as MNEs. Some of the most common problems encountered in installing ERP systems are the costs of training, integration and testing, customization, data conversion, and consulting fees. In addition, MNEs must consider the added challenges of playing in the global market.

Theories and Realities of Global Information Processing

Egelhoff (1991) identifies four dimensions or types of information processing that are relevant for MNEs:

1. *Routine:* Inputs are frequent and homogeneous. It is appropriate to have rules and programs, standard operating procedures, and so on.
2. *Nonroutine:* This type of information is relatively unique and infrequent.
3. *Sequential:* Information flows in a predetermined direction across parties to an information-processing event.
4. *Reciprocal:* Information flows back and forth between parties in a kind of give-and-take manner not previously determined.

In general, accounting information for MNEs tends to be relatively routine and sequential. It tends to be electronically integrated at the parent company level, and it must have extensive reach within the IT platform (i.e., the technology of computers, software telecommunications, and office technology, including the telephone, fax, e-mail, and so on). Reach refers to the number of locations that the IT platform can link together. Obviously, reach is much more difficult in the international arena. The key is to determine how to share information across organizational lines internationally.

MNEs pull together operations in different countries through mergers, acquisitions, and strategic alliances, for example, and it is not uncommon for the various companies to use different software and hardware, resulting in what is known as a heterogeneous network. This makes the standardization of the IT platform a nightmare. Unilever, for example, tried to standardize its back-office operations, such as billing systems, car leasing, and travel services, but it ran into difficulty with different country managers. Italian managers refused to meet with the team that was trying to bring together these different operations worldwide, so the team could not include Italy in its efforts. However, a new category of software designed to solve this problem, *middleware,* mediates between the different kinds of hardware and software found on large networks and gives a network the appearance of harmony, even though the individual components change and expand over time. Even with the new software, the cultural issues involving management from different countries need to be solved.

MNEs and Transborder Data Flows

The free flow of information across national borders is vital to the successful operation of an MNE's management information system (MIS) and, by extension, the operation of the MNE itself. Furthermore, the management of this information flow is as important as the management of company assets and production. The ability of an MNE's computers to communicate with each other in a transnational network allows information to be stored, processed, retrieved, and used in decision making with great efficiency, and it facilitates communications, planning, strategy formulation, and control. However, many countries have enacted legislation that affects transborder (transnational) data flows. For these and a number of other reason MNEs in the future will be confronted with increased risks related to transborder flows.

Foremost among the many concerns of nation-states over transborder data flows (TBF) are privacy, economics, and national security. *Privacy concerns* deal with employee information such as religious and political affiliations, family background, race, sex, and employment history. *Economic concerns* center on industrial espionage involving corporate data piracy and the impact of TBF on local data processing industries and MNEs' decision-making processes. By restricting TBF, some governments have sought to force MNEs to use local processing industries and thereby increase their size and sophistication. Others have hoped that by restricting TBF, more autonomy in decision making will be given to subsidiaries because headquarters will have less information with which to base decisions for subsidiaries. These economic concerns are also related to *national security concerns.* Countries seek limitations on TBF to protect against political espionage and theft of industrial properties and designs and other economic data that could weaken their security. Satellite communication nets pose a major control problem in this respect.

Governments also affect the flow of information through the infrastructure of the Information Superhighway. It makes no sense for companies to invest millions of dollars to establish an internal network that combines data, video, and voice communications when the system grinds to a halt outside the building. Local telephone lines are the primary carriers of information. The transmission speed on these lines often causes data flow to slow dramatically—from 10 million bits per second within the building, to only 56,000 bits per second outside the building. Governments can respond to this challenge by investing huge amounts in building the infrastructure or in deregulating the communication sector so that competition will bring in investment and drive service and drive down costs. However, the deregulation game is not an easy one in that governments worry about the public policy ramifications of any decision. The use of fiber optics is improving the flow of data worldwide, and some countries are investing tremendous resources in fiber optics.

Management Information Systems and the Strategy of the Firm: Some Final Thoughts

Drawing on the work of Bartlett and Ghoshal (1989), we pointed out earlier that in approaching the global market, firms can adopt a transnational or decentralized (multidomestic) approach. Firms that take more of a multidomestic approach do not tend to integrate their IT platforms to the same extent as firms that have a more global orientation. MNEs that follow the Bartlett and Ghoshal transnational model tend to be more interactive. This implies a flow of information that is more reciprocal than sequential, a situation especially common in the budgeting process.

Another alternative is to view this interaction between administrative units of the company using the approach of Gupta and Govindarajan (1991), which is illustrated in Figure 12.10. As this figure shows, knowledge flows can be grouped along two different dimensions: the outflow of knowledge from the subsidiary to the rest of the corporation and the inflow of knowledge from the rest of the corporation to the subsidiary. These flows of knowledge result in four generic subsidiary roles: global innovator, integrated player, implementer, and local innovator.

As a *global innovator,* the subsidiary provides knowledge for other units. Information flows would be sequential, according to the Egelhoff model, but the information would flow from, rather than to, the subsidiary.

As an *integrated player,* the subsidiary creates knowledge that is shared with other units in the company, but it also receives knowledge. Information flows would be reciprocal rather than sequential. This clearly fits the transnational model.

As an *implementer,* the subsidiary does not generate much knowledge for the rest of the units, but it receives knowledge from other units, principally from the parent company. This is the more traditional global MNE, where power and knowledge are centralized.

As a *local innovator,* the subsidiary innovates locally, but its innovations are of little value to the rest of the firm. This would be more like a multidomestic firm where local differences overwhelm common knowledge. Thus, the information flows are kept to a minimum.

Prior studies in marketing, finance, and manufacturing have shown that several factors contribute to the autonomy given to foreign subsidiaries. Among the

Figure 12.10   Variations in Subsidiary Strategic Contexts: A Knowledge Flows-Based Framework

most prominent factors contributing to the subsidiary's autonomy in those functional areas are the following:

- Number of broad product lines the company offers for sale in the subsidiary's country
- The extent to which the subsidiary modifies products of the parent
- Percentage of local managers on the subsidiary's board of directors
- Subsidiary's sales expressed as a percent of parent's overall sales
- Number of employees in the subsidiary
- Percentage change in the number of products offered for sale by the subsidiary over the last five years
- Extent to which the competitive climate of the subsidiary has changed over the past three years
- Number of years since the subsidiary was founded or acquired

Studies of these factors show that they are positively correlated with the subsidiary's autonomy. Mirchandani and Lederer (2004) studied how these very same factors affect the information systems autonomy given to roughly 100 U.S. subsidiaries of foreign MNEs based on these same factors. Surprisingly, they found that none of these factors increases the systems autonomy given to the subsidiaries by the parent company. Mirchandani and Lederer's findings suggest that the information systems function is treated differently in MNEs than in more traditional functions such as marketing, finance, and manufacturing. Perhaps parent companies give their subsidiaries less autonomy in the systems area to ensure that the transfer of information throughout the MNE is done through compatible systems. Perhaps headquarters is hesitant to provide too much autonomy in the design and implementation of information systems for security reasons. In fact, security of data has been repeatedly stated as one of the main concerns of managers when it comes to the transfer of information.

FIRM STRATEGY, STRUCTURE, AND THE ACCOUNTING FUNCTION

Centralization, Strategy, and the Accounting Function

As discussed earlier in the chapter, accounting and control derive their value from what they can provide to the firm's strategy and are affected by the structure of the firm. For example, the degree of centralization may also affect the nature of the accounting and control function. At its simplest level, some types of accounting/record keeping may be fairly easily centralized. Thus many U.S. firms use a central location to process all basic data; for example, several large insurance companies in the United States use facilities in Bangalore, India, to process the myriad of accounting associated with policy accounting.

An argument can be made, however, for the decentralization of control. For example, multidomestic firms face local differences in environmental constraints, which can be cultural, legal, political, and economic. These differences require that they adapt to the way business is done, which is different from the parent country. Sharp and Salter (1997) argue that even the fundamental beliefs about behavior on which control systems are based in the United States and Canada are not valid in Asia. Bartlett and Ghoshal's (1989) transnational organizational philosophy also would influence the accounting function. To be globally competitive and flexible in the multinational arena, management needs to legitimize diverse perspectives and capabilities and develop multiple and flexible coordination processes. Thus, it would appear that the MNE needs an information system that provides a significant flow of information from parent to affiliate, from affiliate to parent, and between affiliates. Such a system is very different from either a highly decentralized or a highly centralized operation.

A strong case is made to disaggregate financial accounting since reporting standards vary considerably from country to country. Sometimes governments control the way the books and records of the firm are kept, thus leading to the decentralization of the accounting function to the local country. On the other hand, it may be important to centralize the accounting function because of the *parent firm*'s need to consolidate its worldwide operations according to the GAAP of the *parent company's* country. Local differences may cause a different set of books to be kept, but the parent company will probably still require that a set of books be kept according to parent company GAAP. Coca-Cola, for example, uses policy manuals to extend a more centralized philosophy to the accounting function. Management developed a comprehensive, easy-to-reference accounting manual to help maintain strong financial controls over operations. A universal chart of accounts was established so that each account in the balance sheet and income statement would be consistent worldwide. Based on the chart of accounts, definitions of each account were written and policies and procedures governing the use of each account and the flow of information into the financial statements were developed. A separate section was written about translating financial statements from local currencies into U.S. dollars.

The Use of Informal Controls

As noted earlier, the matrix organizational structure was developed to deal with the global complexities involved in product lines and geographic areas. However, it was also noted that the matrix often did not work for a variety of reasons. As one manager pointed out, the challenge is not so much to build a matrix structure as it is to create a matrix in the minds of managers. The key is to develop a corporate culture that allows the firm to be competitive globally following three key methods used by successful managers to develop a global orientation.

1. Develop and communicate a clear and consistent corporate vision.
2. Manage human resource tools effectively to broaden individual perspectives and develop identification with corporate goals.
3. Integrate individual thinking and activities into the broad corporate agenda by means of a process called co-option—that is, pulling people out of their narrow and isolated areas of responsibility and helping them to develop a broader, more global perspective.

These rules are as true in accounting as they are in marketing or any other function. Accountants need to understand the information requirements of the MNE in order to avoid the narrow parent company perspective that is so common in globally centralized firms. Several years ago, the authors met with financial managers of a few British subsidiaries of U.S. MNEs, who described their frustration with home office accounting personnel. Because of a lack of international experience and expertise, home office personnel had a difficult time relating to the specific problems of the British subsidiaries. This was especially true of any issue related to foreign exchange.

Bartlett and Ghoshal (1989) point out the following with respect to managers (which can be generalized to accountants): "One pervasive problem in companies whose leaders lack this ability [to pull individual managers together] or fail to exercise it, is getting managers to see how their specific responsibilities relate to the broad corporate vision." To involve accountants in this global vision, it is important to recruit, select, and train accountants for the global environment. This entails understanding local accounting issues as well as the global demands of the MNE. In addition, accountants must understand the global vision of the firm. It is not enough to be technically competent; the accountant also must understand the global imperatives of the firm and the ways he or she can contribute to these imperatives through a good information system.

SUMMARY

1.   MNEs typically adopt a multidomestic, global, or transnational strategy to face the opportunities and challenges of globalization.

2.   Informal and subtle mechanisms are becoming increasingly more important means of managing MNEs.

3.   A firm's structure reflects its strategy. As a firm goes from purely domestic to truly global, it progressively moves from a domestic structure to an international division structure and finally to a truly global structure.

4.   Corporate governance exists to determine the relationships between the various stakeholders in a firm, how resources will be allocated, and how conflicts among the stakeholders will be resolved.

5.   Internal governance mechanisms include the board of directors and the ownership structure of the firm. External mechanisms include the takeover market and the legal system in which the firm operates.

6.   The board of directors plays a key role in monitoring management performance and representing the interests of shareholders.

7.   Globalization along with the failure of large corporations has triggered the creation of Codes of Best Practice in governance in all major markets worldwide.

8.   Research on governance practices worldwide has provided an understanding of how boards of directors, ownership structures, takeover markets, and legal systems across various nations should combine to create effective governance structures in MNEs.

9.   The interplay of employees, managers, and shareholders faced with different cultural, legal, and financial systems helps us understand why different governance practices prevail in different countries.

10.   Internal control is one of the key responsibilities of the board of directors and management. Internal control is a process designed to achieve the companies' objectives in three key areas: effectiveness and efficiency of operations, reliability of financial reporting, and compliance with applicable laws and regulations.

11.   The organizational complexity of MNEs makes the internal control function challenging. MNEs must adequately address the five control components suggested by COSO.

12.   The Sarbanes-Oxley Act of 2002 has far-reaching effects on the internal controls of MNEs.

13.   Information technology is a key aspect of maintaining a sound internal control and accounting system. ERP and the Internet are effective tools for transmitting information in MNEs.

14.   The transfer of information in MNEs should reflect the firm's corporate strategy.

15.   The strategy and structure of MNEs affect the accounting function by determining the level of aggregation of financial reporting and by demanding accountants to develop expertise in international accounting.

Discussion Questions

1.   Under what conditions should an MNE adopt a multidomestic strategy? How about a global strategy or a transnational strategy?

2.   The implication from the discussion in this chapter is that as a company becomes more global, it concentrates more on the informal and subtle mechanisms for controlling global operations than it does the structural and formal mechanisms. Why is this so? Do you think structural and formal mechanisms are becoming obsolete? Discuss your reasons.

3.   Explain how lateral relations, informal communications, and organizational culture act as informal control mechanisms.

4.   This chapter presents the typical evolution of a firm from its purely domestic beginnings to an international status—from domestic to international division to global. How might the accounting function be affected through each one of these three steps?

5.   Most Codes of Best Practice in corporate governance agree on the importance of having a certain number of outside, independent directors in the board of directors. However, research has found no relationship between outside directors and firm profitability. Does this mean that having outside directors is unnecessary? Besides profitability, what are the advantages of outside directors?

6.   The Cadbury Report on corporate governance contains the following statement:

> Had a Code such as ours been in existence in the past, we believe that a number of the recent examples of unexpected company failures and cases of fraud would have received attention earlier. It must, however, be recognised that no system of control can eliminate the risk of fraud without so shackling companies as to impede their ability to compete in the market place.

Do you agree with this statement? If good governance won't completely prevent fraudulent behavior, what will?

7. Codes of Best Practice in governance have surfaced worldwide in great degree as a response to fraud and corporate failures. Although compliance with some Codes of Best Practice is required by some stock exchanges, they remain mostly as guiding principles to improve governance practices. On the other hand, the Sarbanes-Oxley Act of 2002 is a U.S. law that imposes criminal penalties for non-compliance. Which of these approaches is more effective? Can you think of a third approach to improving governance practices?

8. Some argue that the requirements of Sarbanes-Oxley's Section 404 regarding internal controls are too strict and will negatively affect foreign direct investment in the United States. Others argue that complying with Section 404 and listing in the U.S. stock markets is advantageous to foreign firms by setting them apart as "best practice" companies. Which argument do you support? Justify your answer.

9. Shleifer and Vishny (1997) define corporate governance as follows: "Corporate governance deals with the ways in which suppliers of finance to corporations assure themselves of getting a return on their investment." Using the concepts you learned from this chapter, explain this definition in your own words.

10. Do you think there's one best way of structuring governance mechanisms, or can there be more than one effective way of organizing them? Justify your answer.

11. Think of the legal system in your own country. Does it tend to protect large or small shareholders (owners) of companies? How does the legal system affect the ownership structure of companies in your country?

12. Recall Aguilera and Jackson's model on the cross-national differences in corporate governance. How well does this model predict the governance mechanisms for a typical company in your own country? What area of governance does the model predict best (capital, labor, or management)? Is there anything that the model has left out?

13. The COSO framework on internal controls identifies five components of an internal control system: control environment, risk assessment, control activities, information and communication, and monitoring. What challenges do MNEs face in trying to establish each of these components?

14. List the different way in which information technology can help MNEs in the internal control and accounting functions.

15. In a market that is becoming more and more global, what skills do accountants need to develop?

Exercises

1. In October 2004, General Motors announced a change in its practices regarding new model development. The following excerpt from *The Wall Street Journal* explains the change:

   General Motors Corp. is the biggest car company in the world. The company was created, as its name suggests, by bringing together many smaller motor-car makers in the early decades of the 20th century. ... In the U.S., Cadillac, Chevrolet, Buick and Oldsmobile all functioned as separate entities with their own manufacturing plants. That philosophy applied overseas as well. GM bought Britain's Vauxhall Motors in 1925, Germany's Adam Opel in 1929, and Australia's Holden in 1931. Each of these and many other overseas units had their own manufacturing and product-development divisions. ... In the mid-1980s, as pressure rose from Japanese rivals in the mass market and German makers in luxury cars, [the formula stopped working]. Now GM has [centralized the design and production of new models]. ... By tapping engineers in far-flung units [such as India, South Korea, and China] who previously would have worked only on local models, GM is hoping to speed up development of U.S. models without spending more. [One executive] stresses that GM's goal isn't to offer cars that look the same in every market: "We want to have all of these variations, but we want these variations to be plug-and-play." GM's struggle to find the balance between local autonomy and central control is a familiar one for global corporations. Mr. Wagoner [CEO] says he wants GM to be the winner in what he calls "a race to the middle" in the centralization vs. decentralization debate." (New Driver: Reversing 80 Years of History, GM Is Reining in Global Fiefs, *Wall Street Journal*, October 6, 2004)

    a.   What was GM's traditional global strategy? What is its new strategy?

    b.   What were the advantages of the old strategy? What are the advantages of the new strategy? Which one do you think is best for an auto manufacturer?

    c.   Recall the discussion on forces for global, forces for local differentiation, and forces for worldwide innovation. How have these forces affected GM's strategy and structure?

    d.   What type of information transfer does the new structure foster: routine, nonroutine, sequential, or reciprocal?

2.   Hoeschst is a German chemical company operating in different product lines and different geographic areas. Its major business areas are chemicals (23 percent of sales), fibers (15 percent), polymers (17 percent), health (24 percent), engineering and technology (15 percent), and agriculture (6 percent). Across these product lines, Hoeschst produces products as diverse as phosphorus and phosphates used in detergents, textile dyes, polyester auto tire cords, cellulose acetate fibers for cigarette filters, polyvinyl chloride (PVC), automotive paints, pharmaceuticals, cosmetics, offset printing plates, engineering ceramics, herbicides, and animal vaccines. Most of Hoeschst's product lines face significant global competition. On the geographic side, Hoeschst sells products in the European Union (51 percent of total sales); other European countries (7 percent); North America (21 percent); Latin America (7 percent); and Africa, Asia, and Australasia (14 percent).

    a.   What type of an organizational structure makes the most sense for Hoeschst?

    b.   What would be some of the major international accounting problems Hoeschst might face?

    c.   Given its size and geographical dispersion, what information transfer challenges might Hoeschst face? How can IT ease those challenges?

3.   Procter & Gamble (P&G) is a well-known MNE based in the United States. At the end of this chapter is a case on P&G's restructuring efforts. To prepare for the issues discussed in the case, go to www.pg.com and answer the following questions.

    a.   Read about P&G's product lines and geographical operations. What kind of organizational structure would you guess the company has currently?

    b.   In the section on corporate governance and responsibility, learn about the board of directors. What percentage of outside directors does P&G have? Are the roles of chairman and CEO split? What are the different committees on the board of directors?

    c.   What challenges would P&G face in designing an effective management control system?

    d.   Learn about the audit committee of the board of directors. Who heads the audit committee, and what is his background? How important is the internal audit function at P&G?

4. Varig is an airline company based in Brazil. The company is 55.67 percent owned by FRB-Par Investimentos, a local holding company. The rest of Varig's shares are owned as follows: Brazilian Government (30.68 percent); Interunion Capitalização, a private firm (7.4 percent); Instituto Aerus de Seguridade Social, a pension fund (5.19 percent); Estado do Rio Grande do Sul, a state in southern Brazil (0.44 percent); Varig's Employees (0.29 percent); Foreigners (0.34 percent). Varig lists its shares on several Brazilian stock exchanges.

    a. Based on Varig's ownership structure, what can you predict about the property rights, financial system, and the prevalence of interfirm networks in Brazil?

    b. Based on your predictions, how do capital holders exercise control over Varig? (*Hint:* Review this chapter's discussion on the cross-national diversity of corporate governance.)

5. Now that you have considered Varig's ownership structure, consider Bayer, the German pharmaceutical firm. Bayer's ownership structure is as follows: Banks and insurance companies (55 percent), individuals (24 percent), investment funds (12 percent), trade and industry (3 percent), others (6 percent).

    a. What differences do you notice between Bayer's and Varig's ownership structures?

    b. What does Bayer's structure tell you about the property rights, financial system, and prevalence of interfirm networks in Germany?

6. As mentioned in the text, informal controls are becoming a key aspect of managing an organization. One of those controls is organizational culture. IKEA, the Swedish giant, has managed to become the world's largest furniture retailer with more than 200 stores in more than 20 countries. Despite its international growth, IKEA has kept its strong Scandinavian roots and philosophy in all its locations. To learn more about the company's culture, do the following activities:

    a. Visit www.ikea.com and learn more about what the firm calls "the IKEA concept." What is the IKEA concept? How does this concept translate into IKEAs products and stores?

    b. Now go to www.ikea.com/corporate/work, where you will find a link to IKEA's culture and values. How does the firm's culture reflect the IKEA concept? How does the culture as an informal control allow different people to do things in a consistent manner?

7. Companies worldwide are coming to realize that good governance structures and policies alone are not sufficient to gain the public's trust. Firms must convince potential investors that management is ethical, competent, and trustworthy. Thus, many firms have established written codes of ethics. One of those companies is Shell, the giant Dutch oil company. Go to www.shell.com and find Shell's code of ethics. Answer the following questions:

    a. What are the key requirements of the code?

    b. To whom does the code apply?

    c. Who is responsible for enforcing the code?

    d. At the end of this chapter you will find a case on *The Royal Dutch/Shell Scandal.* What aspect of the code did management fail to follow?

8. In the United States, public companies are required to file a Proxy Statement, which includes a report on executive compensation. This report contains the compensation structure of top management and the directors. Find and compare the reports on executive compensation for IBM and Intel, two U.S. MNEs in the same industry.

    a. What percentage of each CEO's compensation is made of salary, bonus, stock options, and stock grants?

    b. In your opinion, which firm's compensation structure best aligns top management's interests with those of the shareholders?

9. DaimlerChrysler is a well-known German-American MNE that produces automobiles such as Mercedes, Chrysler, and Jeep. Pretend DaimlerChrysler has hired you to evaluate its compliance with the German Code of Best Practice. Use the *Scorecard for German Corporate Governance* questions presented in this chapter (Exhibit 12.1) to perform your evaluation. Visit the "investor relations" section of www.daimlerchrysler.com to gather the necessary information. Once you have answered all the questions in the scorecard, write a one-page memo to the chairman of DaimlerChrysler's board of directors outlining the strengths and weaknesses in the firm's compliance with the German code.

10. Most Codes of Best Practice on corporate governance are available to the general public. Go to an Internet search engine and find the Code of Best Practice for your country. If your country doesn't have one, choose a country of your interest and look up its Code of Best Practice.

    a. What does the code suggest on the role and composition of the board of directors?

    b. Does the code suggest any specific committees for the board of directors?

    c. Does it require that the roles of chairman of the board and CEO be separate?

    d. What other areas of governance does the code cover?

11. Choose one company from two or more different regions in the world, preferably in the same industry. Learn about the ownership structure and the board of directors of your chosen companies, and then compare your findings across companies.

    a. What similarities and differences do you notice?

    b. What do your findings suggest about the differences in the legal, financial, and cultural aspects of the regions in which these firms operate?

    c. Do your findings support the research findings on international corporate governance presented in this chapter?

12. At the end of this chapter you will find a case on *The Royal Dutch/Shell Scandal*. Interestingly, Shell was on the 2004 CalPERS Focus List. After you have read the case, download the recommendations for improvement for Shell made by CalPERS from the 2004 Focus List.

    a. What problems does CalPERS identify in Shell's governance and business practices?

    b. What recommendations for improvement does CalPERS make?

    c. If you were a Shell shareholder, would you make any additional recommendations?

13. When it comes to shareholder activism as a means of corporate control, CalPERS is one of the most active institutional shareholders in monitoring management performance and financial performance. CalPERS is the largest public pension plan in the United States and the third largest in the world. It serves more than 1,050,000 state, local government and school district employees. The fund's activism is well known and has caused large companies to amend their governance practices. Visit www.calpers.com and find the "Shareowner Action" section. Answer the following questions:

    a. What policies does CalPERS have with regards to executive compensation?

    b. The CalPERS Focus List contains a set of companies in the CalPERS fund that, in the fund's opinion, need to make improvements in their governance and business practices. What companies are on the most recent Focus List? Choose a company from the list. What does CalPERS want that company to modify?

c. CalPERS also has a Monitoring List to recognize firms that have made improvement to their governance practices "without undue publicity from being named to the Focus List." What companies are on the most recent Monitoring List? Choose a company from the list and learn about the improvements it made.

d. Why does CalPERS have the power to make companies change? Do individual investors have the same power?

14. Effective November 15, 2004, management of public companies in the United States was required by the Sarbanes-Oxley Act to report on the effectiveness of internal controls. In addition, auditors must provide an independent assessment of management's report. Find the annual report for a public U.S. firm issued after the effective date and read the reports of management and the independent auditors.

15. United Airlines entered into a strategic alliance with Thai Airways to develop and market airline services.

a. Would you characterize this strategic alliance as a global innovator, an integrated player, a local innovator, or an implementer from the standpoint of United? What is your logic for your choice?

b. What are some of the problems that United might face in establishing appropriate informal and subtle control mechanisms for the strategic alliance?

Case: P&G and Unilever—Restructuring for Growth
Case: The Royal Dutch/Shell Scandal

These cases can be found on the following website: www.wiley.com/college/radebaugh

Selected References

Aguilera, R. V., and A. Cuervo-Cazurra. 2004. "Codes of Good Governance Worldwide: What Is the Trigger?" *Organization Studies* 25(3): 417–446.

Aguilera, R. V., and G. Jackson. 2003. "The Cross National Diversity of Corporate Governance: Dimensions and Determinants." *Academy of Management Review* 29(3): 447–465.

Ball, Deborah. 2005. "Despite Revamp, Unwieldly Unilever Falls Behind Rivals." *Wall Street Journal,* January 3, pp. A1, A5.

Bartlett, C. A., and A. Ghoshal. 1989. *Managing Across Borders.* Boston: Harvard Business School Press.

Bartlett, Christopher. 1990. "Ingvar Kamprad and IKEA." *Harvard Business School Case* 9-390-132, revised July 22, 1996.

Cadbury Commission. 1992. *The Financial Aspects of Corporate Governance,* London: Gee & Co. Ltd.: London, Burgess Science Press. Available from http://www.kaew.co.uk/viewer/index.cfm.

Charkham, J. P. 1995. "Keeping Good Company: A Study of Corporate Governance in Five Countries." New York: Oxford University Press.

Committee of Sponsoring Organizations of the Treadway Commission (COSO). 2004. *Internal Control—Integrated Framework.* New York: AICPA, 1992.

Daily, C. M., C. R. Dalton, and A. A. Cannella. 2003. "Corporate Governance: Decades of Dialogue and Data." *Academy of Management Review* 28(3): 371–382.

Daniels, John D., Lee H. Radebaugh, and Daniel L. Sullivan. 2002. *Globalization and Business.* Upper Saddle River, NJ: Pearson Prentice-Hall.

Demirag, I. S., and J. F. Solomon. 2003. "Developments in International Corporate Governance and the Impact of Recent Events." *Corporate Governance: An International Review* 11(1): 1–7.

Denis, D. K., and J. J. McConnell. 2003. "International Corporate Governance." *Journal of Financial and Quantitative Analysis* 38(1): 1–36.

The Economist, 2004. "404 Tonnes of Paper." December, p. 142.

Edmondson, Gail. 2005. "Revved Up for Battle." *Business Week,* January 10, p. 52.

Egelhoff, W. G. 1991. "Information-Processing Theory and the Multinational Enterprise." *Journal of International Business Studies* 22: 341–388.

Gupta, A. K., and V. Govindarajan. 1991. "Knowledge Flows and the Structure of Control within Multinational Corporations." *Academy of Management Review* 16(4): 768–792.

Hamel, G., and C. J. Prahalad. 1992. "Do You Really Have a Global Strategy?" In *Transnational Management,* edited by C. Bartlett and S. Ghoshal. Homewood, IL: Richard D. Irwin.

Hookway, James, and Jay Solomon. 2005. "In Sri Lanka, Aid to Tamils Deepens Political Tensions." *Wall Street Journal,* January 11, p. A1.

Hout, T., M. E. Porter, and E. Rudden. 1982. "How Global Companies Win Out." *Harvard Business Review* (September–October). Vol. 60, Iss. 5, p. 98–109.

Khanna, T., and G. P. Krishna. 2004. "Globalization and Convergence in Corporate Governance: Evidence from Infosys and the Indian Software Industry." *Journal of International Business Studies* 35(6): 484–507.

Koch, D. S. 1999. "The ABC's of ERP." www.CIO.com (December).

La Porta, R., F. Lopez-de-Silanes, A. Shleifer, and R. W. Vishny, 1998. Law of Finance. *Journal of Political Economy* 106: 1113–1155.

Millman, Joel, and Peter Wonacott. 2005. "For China, a Cautionary Tale." *Wall Street Journal,* January 11, p. A18.

Mirchandani, D. A., and A. L. Lederer. 2004. "IS Planning Autonomy in US Subsidiaries of Multinational Firms." *Information and Management* 41: 1021–1036.

Nohria, N., and S. Ghoshal. 1997. *The Differentiated Network: Organizing Multinational Corporations for Value Creation.* San Francisco: Jossey-Bass.

Sarbanes-Oxley Act of 2002, U.S. Public Law 107–204 (U.S. Congress).

Sharp, D. and S. Salter. 1997. "Project Escalation and Sunk Costs: A Test of the International Generalizability of Agency and Prospective Theories," *Journal of International Business Studies,* 28(1): 101–121.

Shleifer, A. and R. Vishny. 1997. "A Survey of Corporate Governance, *Journal of Finance.* 52: 737–783.

Strenger, C. 2004. "The Corporate Governance Scorecard: A Tool for the Implementation of Corporate Governance." *Corporate Governance: An International Review* 12(1): 11–15.

Yip, George S. 2003. *Total Global Strategy II.* Upper Saddle River, NJ: Pearson Prentice-Hall.

CHAPTER THIRTEEN

MANAGING FOREIGN EXCHANGE EXPOSURE

Chapter Objectives

- Examine exchange rates, including foreign exchange derivatives, and the nature of the foreign exchange market

- Discuss the nature of the international monetary system and the determination of exchange rates.

- Identify the different types of foreign exchange exposure.

- Illustrate different hedging strategies, both financial and operating.

- Show how the International Accounting Standards Board (IASB) and Financial Accounting Standards Board (FASB) account for hedges.

- Present a foreign exchange risk management strategy

INTRODUCTION

In Chapter 10, we discussed the basics of foreign exchange and introduced the concept of a spot exchange rate and how it is used to translate foreign currency transactions and foreign currency financial statements from one currency to another. In this chapter, we will expand our discussion of foreign exchange and examine how companies define and measure foreign exchange exposure and adopt different strategies to eliminate or minimize foreign exchange risk. It is interesting to note in the fourth-quarter earnings announcement below by Nokia that the impact of currency on earnings was important enough to warrant a discussion. That impact and subsequent company strategies are the subjects for discussion in this chapter.

342

Strategic Decision Point

Nokia, the Finnish cell phone giant, started off 2004 weakly, but it rebounded by the end of the year. Although Nokia is by far the biggest mobile phone manufacturer in the world, it has strong competition from Motorola, Siemens, LG, Sony Ericsson, and Samsung. The challenge is that Nokia is based in the euro zone, as are Siemens and Ericsson, where the strong euro makes exports relatively expensive. In addition, Nokia's U.S.-based earnings are relatively smaller when translated into euros during a period when the euro is strong. In its 2004 fourth-quarter earnings report, Nokia stated that sales rose 3 percent to €9.06 billion, despite the adverse impact of currency exchange rates. Is the adverse impact due to Nokia's exports, its U.S. operations, or both? What can Nokia do to minimize the impact of currency on earnings?

FOREIGN EXCHANGE

Basic Exchange Rates

In Chapter 10, we noted that foreign exchange can either be traded over-the-counter (OTC) or on an exchange. In addition, we defined spot transactions as those that involve the exchange of currency the second day after the date on which the two foreign exchange traders agree to the transaction. The rate at which the transaction is settled is the spot rate. We also defined forward transactions as those that involve the exchange of currency three or more days after the date on which the traders agree to the transaction. An outright forward is the single purchase or sale of a currency for future delivery. The rate at which the transaction is settled is the forward rate and is a contract rate between the two parties. The forward transaction will be settled at the forward rate no matter what the actual spot rate is at the time of settlement. Before going into other derivatives—foreign currency instruments other than spot transactions—let's discuss forward contacts in more detail.

Outright Forward Market

A forward contract is a contract between a foreign currency trader and client for the future sale or purchase of foreign currency. The forward contract is a derivative because its future value is based on the current spot exchange rate. During a period of foreign exchange stability, there may be relatively little difference between the current spot and forward rate. In Exhibit 13.1, for example, forward rates are quoted for several currencies. The spot and 90-day forward rates quoted for pounds in the *Wall Street Journal* are as follows:

Exhibit 13.1   Exchange Rates

Exchange Rates   March 3, 2005

The foreign exchange mid-range rates below apply to trading among banks in amounts of $1 million and more, as quoted at 4 p.m. Eastern time by Reuters and other sources. Retail transactions provide fewer units of foreign currency per dollar.

Country	U.S. $ EQUIVALENT		CURRENCY PER U.S. $	
	Thu	Wed	Thu	Wed
Argentina (Peso)-y	.3388	.3383	2.9516	2.9560
Australia (Dollar)	.7830	.7836	1.2774	1.2762
Bahrain (Dinar)	2.6525	2.6524	.3770	.3770
Brazil (Real)	.3735	.3791	2.6771	2.6378
Canada (Dollar)	.8037	.8068	1.2442	1.2395
1-month forward	.8037	.8069	1.2442	1.2393
3-months forward	.8043	.8074	1.2433	1.2385
6-months forward	.8057	.8088	1.2412	1.2364
Chile (Peso)	.001690	.001699	591.72	588.58
China (Renminbi)	.1208	.1208	8.2765	8.2765
Colombia (Peso)	.0004267	.0004295	2343.57	2328.29
Czech, Rep. (Koruna)	.04432	.04431	22.563	22.568
Commercial rate				
Denmark (Krone)	.1761	.1765	5.6786	5.6657
Ecuador (US Dollar)	1.0000	1.0000	1.0000	1.0000
Egypt (Pound)-y	.1722	.1722	5.8089	5.8062
Hong Kong (Dollar)	.1282	.1282	7.8003	7.8003
Hungary (Forint)	.005406	.005421	184.98	184.47
India (Rupee)	.02290	.02290	43.668	43.668
Indonesia (Rupiah)	.0001076	.0001078	9294	9276
Israel (Shekel)	.2304	.2307	4.3403	4.3346
Japan (Yen)	.009498	.009554	105.29	104.67
1-month forward	.009521	.009576	105.03	104.43
3-months forward	.009569	.009627	104.50	103.87
6-months forward	.009651	.009709	103.62	103.00
Jordan (Dinar)	1.4114	1.4104	.7085	.7090
Kuwait (Dinar)	3.4247	3.4245	.2920	.2920
Lebanon (Pound)	.0006605	.0006605	1514.00	1514.00
Malaysia (Ringgit)-b	.2632	.2632	3.7994	3.7994
Malta (Lira)	3.0431	3.0491	.3286	.3280
Mexico (Peso) Floating rate	.0899	.0902	11.1185	11.0852
New Zealand (Dollar)	.7272	.7268	1.3751	1.3759
Norway (Krone)	.1595	.1600	6.2696	6.2500
Pakistan (Rupee)	.01685	.01685	59.347	59.347
Peru (new Sol)	.3066	.3065	3.2616	3.2626
Philippines (Peso)	.01822	.01827	54.885	54.735
Poland (Zloty)	.3333	.3334	3.0003	2.9994
Russia (Ruble)-a	.03606	.03605	27.732	27.739
Saudi Arabia (Riyal)	.2667	.2666	3.7495	3.7509
Singapore (Dollar)	.6140	.6152	16.287	1.6255
Slovak Rep. (Koruna)	.03462	.03470	28.885	28.818
South Africa (Rand)	.1676	.1694	5.9666	5.9032
South Korea (Won)	.0009935	.0009926	1006.54	1007.46

Country	U.S. $ EQUIVALENT		CURRENCY PER U.S. $	
	Thu	Wed	Thu	Wed
Sweden (Krona)	.1450	.1448	6.8966	6.9061
Switzerland (Franc)	.8470	.8520	1.1806	1.1737
1-month forward	.8485	.8534	1.1786	1.1718
3-months forward	.8517	.8568	1.1741	1.1671
6-months forward	.8573	.8623	1.1665	1.1597
Taiwan (Dollar)	.03254	.03252	30.731	30.750
Thailand (Baht)	.02600	.02608	38.462	38.344
Turkey (New Lira)-d	.7800	.7785	1.2820	1.2845
U.K. (Pound)	1.9077	1.9135	.5242	.5226
1-month forward	1.9044	1.9101	.5251	.5235
3-months forward	1.8983	1.9038	.5268	.5253
6-months forward	1.8904	1.8959	.5290	.5275
United Arab (Dirham)	.2723	.2723	3.6724	3.6724
Uruguay (Peso)				
Financial	.03900	.03910	25.641	25.575
Venezuela (Bolivar)	.000466	.000521	2145.92	1919.39
SDR	1.5248	1.5238	.6558	.6563
Euro	1.3112	1.3136	.7627	.7613

Special Drawing Rights (SDR) are based on exchange rates for the U.S., British, and Japanese currencies. Source: International Monetary Fund.

a-Russlan Central Bank rate. b-Government rate. d-Rebased as of Jan. 1, 2005. y-Floating rate.

Source: Wall Street Journal, March 4, 2005, p. B6.

	British Pounds
90-day forward	$1.8983
Spot	1.9077
Points	− 94

The spread in pounds is -.0094, or 94 points. Because the forward rate is less than the spot rate, the pound is selling at a discount of 94 points. If the forward rate had been greater than the spot rate, the pound would have been selling at a premium in the forward market.

The premium or discount is normally quoted at the number of points above or below the spot rate, but it could also be expressed in annualized percentage terms. The formula used to determine the percentage is as follows:

$$\text{Premium (discount)} = \frac{F_o - S_o}{S_o} \times \frac{12}{N} \times 100$$

where Fo is the forward rate on the day that the contract is entered into, So is the spot rate on that day, N is the number of months forward, and 100 is used to convert the decimal to percentage amounts (i.e., $0.05 \times 100 = 5\%$).

Using the British pound example,

$$\text{Premium} = \frac{1.8983 - 1.9077}{1.9077} \times \frac{12}{3} \times 100 = -1.97\%$$

which means that the pound sterling is selling at a 1.97 percent discount below the dollar spot rate.

Swaps

One of the fastest growing and most popular derivatives of foreign exchange is the swap. A swap is a simultaneous spot and forward transaction. For example, assume that a U.S. company has just received a dividend from a French subsidiary, but it has no use for the euros for 30 days. It could take the euros and deposit them in a French bank for 30 days to earn interest, or it could enter into a swap transaction. In a swap, the U.S. company would take the euros to its bank and convert them into U.S. dollars to use for 30 days in the United States. At the same time, it would enter into a forward contract with the bank to deliver dollars in 30 days in exchange for euros at the forward exchange rate.

A variation on the spot/forward swap is a foreign currency swap that is entered into because of interest rate differentials. To illustrate this type of swap, suppose that a Japanese company would like to borrow floating-rate (a floating-rate note, or FRN) U.S. dollars to finance a foreign investment in the United States, but the company is not very well known outside Japan. Also, suppose that a U.S. company would like to borrow fixed-rate Japanese yen to fund an investment in Japan but is also not well known in Japan. A financial intermediary, such as an investment bank, could put the two companies together through a currency swap. The Japanese company issues a fixed-rate yen bond, turns the yen proceeds over to the U.S. company, and agrees to pay the U.S. company its dollar coupon on principal obligations on a U.S. dollar FRN that the U.S. company would issue. In addition, the U.S. company would turn the proceeds of the dollar FRN over to the Japanese company. At the end of the swap agreement, the Japanese company would return the dollars to the U.S. company, and the U.S. company would return the yen to the Japanese company. The swap exchange rate is the rate at which the two companies agree to exchange yen for dollars.

Futures

A foreign currency future resembles a forward contract insofar as it specifies an exchange rate sometime in advance of the actual exchange of currency. However, a futures contract is traded on an exchange, not over the counter with a commercial or investment bank. A forward contract is tailored to the amount and time frame that the company needs, whereas a futures contract is for a specific amount and specific maturity date. The futures contract is less valuable to a company than a forward contract. However, it may be useful to speculators and small companies that do not have a good enough relationship with a bank to enter into a forward contact or that need a contract for an amount that is too small for the forward market.

The Philadelphia Board of Trade offers currency futures contracts in the Australian dollar, British pound, Canadian dollar, euro, Japanese yen, and Swiss franc. Contract sizes vary per currency. For example, one futures contact in British pounds is £62,500, whereas a contract in Euros is €125,000, or $32,763 and $95,338, respectively, at the spot rates in Exhibit 13.1. Contract months for futures contracts are March, June, September, and December. The last day of trading is the Friday before the third Wednesday of the month, and contracts must be settled in U.S. dollars. As you can see, futures contracts are far less flexible than forward contracts, but they are one example of an exchange-traded instrument.

Options

Another derivative is an option, which is the right but not the obligation to trade foreign currency at a given exchange rate on or before a given date in the future. Options can be traded on an exchange, such as the Philadelphia Stock Exchange, or with a financial intermediary, such as an investment banker like Goldman Sachs.

There are two parties to an option, the writer of the option and the holder of the option. The writer of the option sells the option, and the holder of the option buys the option from the writer. The holder has the power to exercise or execute the option, that is, to elect to make the exchange made possible by the option. The holder of the option must pay an up-front fee (premium) to the writer of option, but it is the holder, not the writer, that determines whether or not the option will be exercised.

An option can be either a put option or a call option. A put option gives the holder the right to sell foreign currency to the writer of the option, and a call option gives the holder the right to buy foreign currency from the writer of the option.

The cost of the option is composed of a premium and a brokerage fee. The premium must be paid by the holder to the writer of the option as soon as the option is entered into, and no refund of the premium is given to the holder if the option is not exercised. The premium is like an insurance premium—you pay it whether you collect or not. If the option is written on an exchange, such as the Philadelphia Stock Exchange, a fee must be paid to the stockbroker at the time the option is entered into and must also be paid if the option is exercised.

To illustrate the cost of an option, assume that a U.S. company enters into a put option on June 1 on the Philadelphia Stock Exchange to sell Japanese yen (¥) for dollars on September 30. Assume that the yen is trading at $0.009251 per yen on June 1 or 108.10 per dollar, and that the size of the options contract is ¥6,250,000 or $57,819 at the spot rate on June 1. Also, assume that the strike price, the price at which the option will be settled, is 93 or $0.0093 per yen (¥107.53 per dollar) and that the premium is $0.000179 per yen.

In addition to the premium, there is also a brokerage fee for entering into an exchange-traded contract. If the holder exercises the option, there is another brokerage fee charged at the exercise date. Although there is no set brokerage fee, we assume for our example that the cost is $25 per contract. If we need to sell ¥100 million, we need to buy 16 contracts of ¥6,250,000 each (¥100 million/6,250,000 = 16). For a strike price of 93, each contract would cost

$$¥6,250,000 \times \$0.000179 = \$1,118.75$$

Brokerage cost   =   25.00

Total $1,143.75

For 16 contracts, the total cost is $1,143.75 \times 16 = $18,300$. This means that if we want to hold a put contract to sell ¥100 million at a strike price of 93, it will cost $18,300. If we decide to exercise the option, it will cost an additional $400 ($16 \times 25), and we will receive $930,000 for our ¥100 million. By the expiration date in September, we need to decide whether or not to exercise the option. If the spot rate on the expiration date is equal to the strike price ($0.0093), the option is considered to be "at-the-money," and we do not need to exercise the option. Thus, we will walk away from the premium of $18,300, but we do not have to pay the additional $400. If the spot rate on the expiration date is greater than $0.0093, the yen will be stronger against the dollar than at the strike price, and we will receive more dollars for ¥100 million than if we exercised the option. Therefore, the option is considered "out-of-the-money" because the strike price is unfavorable relative to the market price.

For example, if the spot rate at the exercise date in September were $0.0098, we would not exercise the option, and we would receive the following amount of yen:

$$¥100,000,000 \times $0.0098 = $980,000$$

which is greater than the $930,000 at the strike price. Since the premium and initial brokerage expense are sunk costs, they do not factor into the decision on whether or not to exercise the option.

On the other hand, if the spot rate were less than $0.0093, the yen would be weaker against the dollar than at the strike price, and we would receive fewer dollars from the yen than if we exercised the option. Therefore, the option is considered to be "in-the-money" because the strike price is favorable relative to the market price, and we would exercise the option.

Therefore, the option sets a lower limit on what will be received for the ¥100 million. If the spot rate at the end of September were $0.0090, we would exercise the option and incur another brokerage cost, and we would receive the following for the yen:

$$
\begin{aligned}
¥100,000,000 \times $0.0093 \quad &= $930,000 \\
\text{Brokerage cost to exercise} = \quad &\underline{\quad - 400} \\
\text{Total proceeds} \quad &= $929,600
\end{aligned}
$$

Of course, we also paid a premium of $18,300, so our net proceeds would be $911,300. Without the option, we would have received $900,000, which is still less than the net proceeds above. The weaker the yen becomes against the dollar, the better the option looks. Thus, the option ensures that the least we will ever receive for the yen is $911,300 ($929,600 less the initial brokerage cost and premium of $18,300), an effective exchange rate of $0.009113 (¥109.7 per dollar).

Options can be traded on an exchange as well at OTC, whereas a futures contract is only traded on an exchange. Exhibit 13.2 illustrates some of the differences between an exchange-traded instrument and one traded OTC. Although the OTC market offers flexibility, there are many advantages to exchange-traded instruments as well, especially in transparency and audit trail.

Foreign Exchange Markets

Foreign exchange is traded 24 hours a day around the world by a variety of institutions. According to a Central Bank survey of foreign exchange market activity by

Exhibit 13.2   Comparison of OTC and Exchange Market Features

	UCOM[a]	OTC[b]
Contract Specifications	Standardized & Customized	Customized
Regulation	Securities and Exchange Commission (SEC)	Self-regulated
Type of Market	Open outcry, auction market	Dealer market
Counterparty to Every Transaction	'AAA'-rated Options Clearing Corporation (OCC)	Bank on the Contra-side
Transparency/Visible Prices	Yes	No
Margin Required for Short Positions	Yes	No[c]
Orders Anonymously Represented in the Market	Yes	No
Required to Mark Positions Daily	Yes	No[c]
Audit Trail	Complete sequential and second-by-second audit trail of each transaction	No
Participants	Public customers, as well as corporate and institutional users	Corporate and institutional users

[a] United Currency Options Market

[b] Over the counter

[c] Not a requirement, but available.

Source: Philadelphia Stock Exchange, http://www.phlx.com/products/currency/guide/guide3.htmlc/omp. Accessed March 26, 2005.

the Bank for International Settlements in Basel, Switzerland, global net turnover of foreign exchange is estimated to be $1.9 trillion per business day.

Foreign exchange is traded among banks in the interbank market, through foreign exchange brokers, through securities brokers on different securities exchanges, and over the counter by nonbank financial institutions, such as investment banks. The interbank market is the most important market in trading foreign exchange. In the 2004 BIS Survey, 53 percent of the traditional foreign exchange transactions (spot, forward, and swap) market activity were with reporting dealers, 33 percent with other financial institutions, and only 14 percent with nonfinancial customers.

In addition to dealing directly with each other, banks also deal indirectly with each other through specialists called foreign exchange brokers. For example, if a bank were holding British pounds (a long position in pounds) and they wanted to sell the pounds, they could contact a broker who would find a bank willing to buy the pounds. Traders execute about 40 to 50 percent of their trades with other banks through computers, another 10 percent through telephones, and the remaining 30 to 40 percent through brokers. The most significant change in trading activity is the movement to more computer-based trades as banks begin to link together to facilitate trading.

Outside of bank trades, foreign exchange is also traded through specialized markets such as the International Monetary Market of the Chicago Mercantile

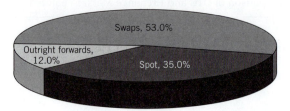

Figure 13.1 Reported Traditional Foreign Exchange Market Turnover, 2004

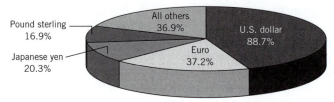

Figure 13.2 Currency Distribution of Reported Foreign Exchange Market Turnover, 2004

Exchange, the London International Financial Futures Exchange, and the Philadelphia Stock Exchange. The listed exchanges tend to specialize in derivatives such as futures and options, and one must deal through a securities broker to effect the trades. The brokers make deals on the exchange floor rather than over the telephone. In contrast, the over-the-counter market involves investment banks such as Goldman Sachs and Bankers Trust and is a rapidly growing source of derivatives for the corporate customer.

In traditional foreign exchange transactions, the most widely traded instrument are swaps, followed by spot transactions and outright forwards, as noted in Figure 13.1. The BIS survey separates other derivatives into another data set that examines foreign exchange instruments (swaps, options, and other instruments) and interest rate instruments. However, their survey only covers OTC instruments and not exchange-traded instruments.

The most widely traded currency in the world is the U.S. dollar, which figures on one side of 88.7 percent of net reported turnover (each currency trade involves two currencies). This means that nearly every foreign exchange trade involves the U.S. dollar on one side of the transaction. Figure 13.2 shows that the four major trading currencies are the U.S. dollar, the euro, the yen, and the pound sterling. The six largest trading pairs involve the U.S. dollar, with the U.S. dollar/euro representing 28 percent of all currency trades, based on 100 percent rather than 200 percent in the turnover figures illustrated in Exhibit 13.2.

The International Monetary System

Although foreign currencies are traded quite freely, there is a form of supranational influence that tries to encourage a certain amount of order. The International Monetary Fund (IMF) was created in 1944 with the primary objective of promoting exchange stability. At that time, the currencies of 133 member countries were assigned a fixed exchange rate or par value based on gold and the U.S. dollar; gold was worth $35 an ounce, and currencies were quoted on that basis. Currencies were allowed to float freely in a band of 1 percent on either side of par value. However, stability did not last forever. Countries like Brazil were constantly devaluing their currency—permanently decreasing the par value in terms of gold and the dollar. Others were experiencing periodic changes, such as the British pound in 1967. But the major trading currencies were still adhering fairly well to par values. In December 1971, after significant pressure against the U.S. dollar, the IMF allowed the U.S. dollar to formally devalue and also allowed currencies to float $2\frac{1}{4}$ percent on either side of par value without a formal devaluation or revaluation.

Continued pressure on the dollar in early 1973 forced a devaluation, and subsequent instability finally forced the major trading countries of the world to break loose from the fixed rate system and adopt one with greater flexibility.

Exchange Rate Arrangements   As part of the move to greater flexibility, the IMF permitted countries to select and maintain an exchange arrangement of their choice, as long as they properly communicated their arrangement to the fund. Each year, the fund receives information from the member countries and classifies each country into one of several categories, which may or may not be the same as the officially announced regime for a country. In several of the categories, countries lock the value of their currency onto another currency and allow the currency to vary by plus or minus 1 percent against that value. Several currencies in Latin America, such as Ecuador and formerly Argentina, dollarized their currencies by locking them onto the dollar. Similarly, several countries in Africa locked their currencies onto the French franc. Fifty-three countries peg their currencies to something else, such as a currency or a basket of currencies, and the peg is either fairly rigid or it is allowed to crawl or change in value.

Another large group of countries adopts a free float or a managed float. In both cases, market forces basically set the value of the currency. In the case of the managed float, the government intervenes to influence the value of the currency, but in the context of market forces.

The important thing from the standpoint of foreign exchange risk management is to determine the currency regime of the country of the home office of a company as well as the regimes of countries where the company has operations. For example, in 2004, the dollar was falling against the euro, the British pound, and the yen, whereas it was relatively stable against the Chinese yuan and many currencies of Southeast Asia. Thus, U.S. trade with and operations of U.S. companies in Europe were affected very differently by exchange rate movements than were U.S. trade with and U.S. operations in Asia, especially China.

The Determination of Exchange Rates

A variety of political and economic factors affect exchange rates and their relative values; among the most important factors are the following:

- purchasing power parity or inflation differentials
- relative interest rates
- the forward exchange rate

Purchasing power parity (PPP) refers to relative prices in one country versus those of another. According to PPP, a change in relative inflation must result in a change in exchange rates in order to keep the prices of goods in two countries fairly similar. In essence, the exchange rate should make the cost of a product the same in one country as it is in another, taking into consideration transportation costs. However, PPP is more useful as a long-run indicator of exchange rate differences than it is a short-term predictor of exchange rates. Country A with a higher rate of inflation should have a weakening currency, or consumers in Country B would never buy products from Country A. Conversely, countries with relatively low rates of inflation should have a stronger currency.

Interest rates in two countries are related to each other through inflation and exchange rate differences. According to the Fisher Effect, the nominal interest rate equals the real rate of interest worldwide plus the expected inflation rate. If the nominal interest rate in Country A is lower than that in Country B, Country A's inflation is expected to be lower. Taking that one step further, one sees that the country with the higher nominal interest rate should have a higher rate of inflation, so its currency would be expected to weaken in the future against the low-interest-rate (and therefore low-inflation) country. This is known as the International Fisher Effect. However, this gets complicated in practice in that there is no universal understanding about what the real rate of interest should be worldwide. As a result, interest rate differentials also involve investors' perceptions of potential returns.

Earlier in the chapter, we discussed the forward rate and computed the difference between the forward and spot rates. However, why is the forward rate sometimes at a premium and sometimes at a discount? The answer is that the forward rate differs from the spot rate by a percentage equal to the interest rate differential. Combining our two earlier theories, we observe that the forward rate differs from the spot rate by a percentage equal to the projected exchange rate. As illustrated in Figure 13.3, the actual future spot rate should be fairly close to the forward rate, but it does not have to be the same. However, the forward rate is an unbiased predictor of the future spot rate, which means that it is neither systematically above nor below the actual future spot rate. Chances are that the forward rate will be a good predictor of the future.

Although these are the major long-term reasons for exchange rate differentials, a number of political and economic issues can have a short-run influence on currency values. In 2002 during the presidential elections in Brazil, the Brazilian real fell against the U.S. dollar because of concerns over the election of a leftist president in Brazil. However, the president turned out to be a fiscal conservative, which resulted in the markets calming down and the real strengthening against the dollar. In March 2005, the U.S. dollar rose against the euro because the U.S. Fed announced that it was going to continue raising interest rates due to inflationary expectations. Even though inflation should result in a weakening of a currency, in this case, inflation resulted in a strengthening of the dollar. That is because dollar-denominated assets will yield a higher return with higher interest rates, and the narrowing of interest rate differentials with the euro was helping to lift the value of the dollar.

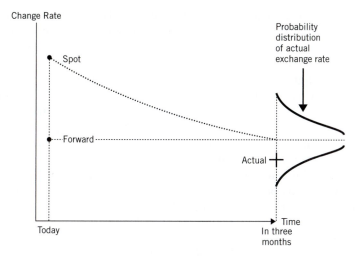

Figure 13.3   The Unbiased Forward Rate Theory. This theory says, in effect, that the forward rate follows a random walk; this implies that the spot rate follows a random walk with drift.

Source: Dufey, Gunter and Ian H. Giddy. 2003. "Management of Corporate Foreign Exchange Risk," in *International Finance and Accounting Handbook,* 3rd Edition, Frederich D.S. Choi, editor (New York: John Wiley & Sons), p. 6.21.

TYPES OF HEDGING EXPOSURE

There are three major types of foreign exchange exposure: transaction exposure, translation or accounting exposure, and economic exposure.

Transaction Exposure

When a company engages in foreign currency transactions, such as buying or selling real property, paying or issuing dividends, or entering into and paying back debt, a foreign exchange risk is incurred because the company has accounts receivable or payable that must eventually be settled. In Chapter 10, we discussed how to account for these transactions. If a U.S. exporter were to receive payment in U.S. dollars from a British importer, there would be no immediate impact on the exporter if the dollar/pound exchange rate were to change. However, the British importer would have a cash flow gain or loss from the change in exchange rates because its accounts payable would change in value as the exchange rate changes.

Translation or Accounting Exposure

Whereas a transaction exposure involves a pending exchange of cash and potential exchange rate risk, an accounting exposure arises when a company translates its financial statements from one currency to another for consolidation purposes. For example, Dell has a subsidiary in Brazil that keeps its books and records in Brazilian reais. The degree of exposure depends on how Dell translates the financial statements of its subsidiary into U.S. dollars. If it uses the current rate method of translation, then all accounts except owners' equity change in value as the exchange rate changes. Even the income statement is affected by exchange rate changes, because it is translated at the average exchange rate for the period. If Dell uses the temporal method of translation, then only the monetary accounts are translated into dollars at the current rate method and thus exposed to exchange gains and losses. The income statement is treated the same as under the current method from the standpoint of translation.

Exhibit 13.3 illustrates the concept of exposure from the point of view of an exposed asset or liability position. An exposed asset position is one where the assets translated at the current rate exceed the liabilities translated at the current rate. An exposed liability position is just the opposite. In the case of a U.S. company investing in Japan, an exposed asset position in a strong Japanese yen results in a translation gain because the dollar value of the yen assets rises as the yen appreciates against the dollar. An exposed liability position results in a translation loss because the value of the yen liabilities rises as the yen appreciates. If the yen were weakening against the dollar, the exposed asset and liability positions would result in a loss and a gain, respectively.

The current rate method is likely to have an exposed asset position because all assets are translated at the current rate. The size of the exposed position depends on what percentage of the assets is financed by debt. The temporal method is likely to have an exposed liability position because the only exposed assets are cash, receivables, and inventory carried at market values. If the firm uses very little debt to finance assets, it might have a small exposed liability position or be relatively balanced in its exposure.

Translated income is very much like an asset position, so firms are positively exposed with income earned in a strong currency country. However, income earned in a weak currency country will be reduced by the weak exchange rate.

As a result, the exposure impact on income is more consistent with the current rate method. Under the current rate method, an investment in a strong currency country will result in a translation gain that is taken to equity, as noted in Chapter 10. At the same time, translated income will get an extra kick from the strong currency. This is also consistent with dividend flows. Dividend flows from a strong currency country will benefit from the rising exchange rate. Dividend flows from a weak currency country will lose value due to the weakening exchange rate.

The results under the temporal method will be mixed, however. If the firm has an exposed liability position in a strong currency country, the translation of the financial statements will result in a translation loss that will be taken to the income

Exhibit 13.3   Exposure

	Strong Foreign Currency	Weak Foreign Currency
Net Asset Position	Gain	Loss
Net Liability Position	Loss	Gain

statement. However, the income statement itself will be positively benefited by the strong currency. Thus, the impact on income will be mixed and volatile, depending on the degree of movement of the exchange rate.

Economic Exposure

Economic exposure, also known as operating exposure, is the potential for change in expected cash flows. It arises from the pricing of products, the sourcing and cost of inputs, and the location of investments. Pricing strategies have both an immediate and a long-term impact on cash flows. For example, if a U.S. company sells products to a British importer in U.S. dollars, it would seem that the foreign exchange risk would be all on the shoulders of the British importer. However, if the dollar strengthens against the pound, the British importer will face a serious problem.

Assume that the exporter sells products for $500 per unit at an exchange rate of $1.90 per pound for a cost to the importer of £263. At a 10 percent markup, the importer would sell the product for £289.30 per unit. If the dollar were to strengthen to $1.85 per pound, the exporter has two choices. He can continue to sell the merchandise at the same price, or he could lower the price. The first choice is to continue to sell the merchandise to the importer at $500, which would now cost the importer £270. At the higher price, the importer might lose market share if consumers are not willing to pay the higher price. At a 10 percent markup, the product would now cost £297 per unit, or £19.13 higher than before the exchange rate change. Instead of raising the price, the importer could absorb the cost increase in its profit margin and continue to sell the product for £289.3. However, its profit would only be £19.30 (289.3 − 270) instead of £26.30 (289.3 − 263). Another possibility would be for the exporter to lower its price in dollars to $487 so that it would still cost the importer £263 to import the product. If the exporter can't afford to reduce its price and take a smaller margin, or if the importer can't afford to raise its prices or take a smaller profit margin, the importer may have to look for a new supplier.

During 2004 when the dollar was falling against the euro, Superior Products Inc., a U.S.-based company, found that prices for valves it was sourcing from Germany were continuing to rise. As a result, Superior's management decided to begin producing the valves itself and selling them to U.S. customers. When the Germans realized what was happening, they lowered their prices, but it was too late (Aeppel, 2005).

The first exposure we discussed was transactions exposure, which involves sales that have already been made. However, companies also have future transactions that might be part of a long-term sales or purchasing agreement or that are anticipated to happen because of past sales patterns. These kinds of future events are more economic exposure than transactions exposure because of the different ways to account for and hedge them.

Economic exposure has strategic implications since the currency of a country could impact the competitiveness of the country as a production location. Bison Gear & Engineering Corp., a small U.S. manufacturer, used to have assembly and warehouse facilities in the Netherlands during a time when the dollar was strong against the euro. However, when the dollar began to fall, Bison management decided to close down the facility and ship the equipment back to the United States where it could manufacture in a cheaper U.S. environment for sale back into Europe (Aeppel, 2005). That may or may not have been the correct solution, especially since Bison was trying to decide in 2005 whether or not to reopen a European operation due to rising demand in Europe. But this is an example of economic exposure.

HEDGING STRATEGIES

When a company is faced with foreign exchange risk, it has to decide what to do. One strategy is to do nothing and just let earnings rise and fall as the exchange rate changes. Duffey (2003) identifies six reasons why management may take a "do-nothing" approach.

1. Managers do not take time to understand the issue. They consider risk-aversion tools as speculation and do not want to bother with them.

2. Managers claim that exposure cannot be measured, which is true, especially for economic exposure.

3. They say that the firm is hedged through the hedging of transactions, without understanding the broader economic exposure.

4. They say that the firm does not have any exchange risk because it does all of its transactions in the reporting currency. Again, it ignores economic risk.

5. They argue that doing business is risky and that the firm gets rewarded for bearing risks, both business and financial.

6. The balance sheet is hedged on an accounting basis, especially when the functional currency is the reporting currency.

However, most companies use financial or operating strategies to hedge foreign currency risk.

Financial Strategies

One way to hedge exposure is to use the derivative financial instruments described above: foreign exchange forwards, currency futures, and currency options. In addition, a company can enter into foreign currency debt, which is both a financial and an operational strategy. In terms of foreign currency transactions, a company would enter into a derivative hedge to offset the actual or anticipated cash flow. For example, if a company sells products to foreign customers, denominates the sale in foreign currency, and extends credit to the purchaser, it is exposed to a foreign exchange gain or loss if the exchange rate changes. Thus, the foreign currency receivable needs to be offset by a foreign currency payable. One way would be to enter into a forward contract, futures contract, or option to deliver foreign currency at the same time the company was expected to collect foreign currency from the foreign customer. That way a gain on the foreign currency receivable would be offset by a loss in the foreign currency payable, thus netting the gain and loss. The actual amount that the company would receive depends on the cash set by the derivative contract. The opposite would be true of a purchase denominated in a foreign currency. Because the company has a payable denominated in foreign currency, it would have to enter into a derivative contract to receive an equal amount of foreign currency in order to offset the payable. Thus, losses or gains on one would be offset by gains or losses on the other.

In addition to derivative contracts, a company could use foreign currency debt as a hedge. For example, assume that Apex Inc., a U.S.-based company, sells merchandise to Products plc, a British customer, and has to denominate the sale in British pounds. Payment will be received in 30 days. Apex could borrow British pounds in London, convert them into dollars, and deposit them in an interest-bearing account in the United States or in the Eurodollar market in London. At the end of 30 days, Apex will receive the British pounds from Products plc and use the proceeds to pay off the loan. The total amount received from the sale will be the amount of the principal at the beginning of the transaction plus the interest earned on the deposit. Apex management could compare the proceeds of the loan with the proceeds from a forward contract or other derivative instrument to see which would offer the greatest yield. Of course, the foreign currency loan, forward contract, and futures contract are easy to compare up front. However, it is more difficult to compare those instruments with an option because the option guarantees the lowest amount possible that Apex could receive, while allowing Apex to generate even greater earnings if the future spot rate of the pound strengthens significantly against the dollar.

Companies also use derivatives to hedge income statement or balance sheet exposure. Most companies provide future estimates of earnings for analysts, so it is in their best interest to eliminate as much risk in this forecast as possible. In addition, the monetary assets and liabilities of foreign operations are also subject to gains or losses from exchange rate changes. Thus, companies can enter into options or forward contracts to hedge those positions. Net income is similar to an asset for hedging purposes, so management could enter into a forward contract or option to sell foreign currency to offset the estimated amount of foreign earnings. Similarly, a company with a net monetary asset position, which is the case with companies that translate foreign currency financial statements by the current rate method, will pursue the same strategy as covering net income. If the company has a net liability position, it would enter into contracts to buy, rather than sell, foreign currency.

Operating Strategies

Operating hedges are more complicated and costly than financial hedges and usually involve betting on the exposure of the entire firm rather than just specific financial transactions. When Toyota first began to service the U.S. market, it did so through exports to the United States. However, as the Japanese yen began to rise against the dollar, Toyota was forced to invest in the U.S. market to insulate itself from the strong yen and weak dollar. Concerned about possible trade barriers, it made the strategic decision to invest a large amount of money in the U.S. market to offset political and economic barriers that were expected to last a long time.

As another example, the U.S. furniture industry has long had a reputation for good quality and reasonable prices. But Chinese manufacturers of furniture invested large amounts of money in state-of-the-art machinery and, coupled with cheap labor, established a strong manufacturing capability. They were also aided by a currency that was locked on to the dollar, even though most experts agreed that the Chinese yuan was significantly undervalued. That made Chinese goods even cheaper. As a result, many U.S. furniture companies began to import kits from China, which were cheaper than making furniture themselves, especially in office furniture, dining room sets, and bedroom sets. Strategically, they were forced to react to a unique exchange rate environment that forced them to focus on assembly of Chinese kits instead of investing in new equipment and manufacturing the furniture themselves.

In addition to manufacturing and sourcing decisions, companies can balance costs with revenues. For example, if a company generates its revenues in euros but incurs its costs in dollars, it may need to figure out how to generate revenues in dollars to hedge its dollar costs or incur euro costs to hedge its euro revenues. This could involve changing production locations or sourcing decisions. For example, a company that sells to European customers might consider manufacturing in Europe so that it generates expenses in euros that it can offset with euro revenues. Or the company might consider incurring costs in euros, either in the form of components or other things that the company buys, so that it can use its euro revenues to pay its euro costs.

Foreign Exchange Risk Management Strategies

Now that we have looked at different types of exposures, how do companies actually formulate a good strategy? There are four basic steps to protect a company from exchange rate exposure:

- Define and measure exposure.
- Organize and implement a reporting system that monitors exposure and exchange rate movements.
- Adopt a policy assigning responsibility for minimizing—or hedging—exposure.
- Formulate strategies for hedging exposure.

Define and Measure Exposure   Earlier in the chapter, we discussed the three major types of exposure: transaction, translation, and economic. It is important for a company's information system to differentiate among the three different exposures, because each may require a different hedging response, and the way to account for the hedging instruments depends on the type of exposure, as we will see in the next system.

Organize and Implement a Reporting System   Next, the company must establish a reporting system that monitors both exposure and exchange rate movements. Since exposure varies with time, the reporting system must not only identify the exposure at a given point in time, but it must also forecast exposure into the future in order to establish a good hedging strategy. This requires a lot of input from local operations whose management is in a better position to forecast exposure levels. Management should set up a uniform reporting system for all of its subsidiaries. The report must identify the exposed accounts that the company wants to monitor, the amount of exposure by currency of each account, and the different time periods being considered. This information must be transmitted from each subsidiary or country operation to headquarters to determine the overall level of exposure of the company. For example, a subsidiary in France could have a net exposed asset position, whereas a subsidiary in Germany could have a net exposed liability position. With this information, the parent company can decide if it wants to hedge the exposure in each individual country or if it wants to offset the exposed positions in France and Germany and just hedge the difference.

In addition to monitoring the exposed position, it is important to monitor exchange rate movements. Companies can develop an in-house capability to track exchange rate movements by using their own economists, or they can outsource this function by utilizing one or more commercial banks. Dell gets exchange rate forecasts from several banks and then develops its own consensus forecast of exchange rates. Another possibility is to use the forward contract rate for different periods in the future to forecast rates. Whichever method is used, the company needs to forecast the direction and magnitude of exchange rate changes to determine how its exposed positions could be affected.

Adopt a Policy Assigning Responsibility   The third step is to determine who is ultimately responsible for protecting the company from exchange rate movements. In part, this depends on the strategic orientation of the company. Multidomestic companies are more likely to delegate hedging strategies to national organizations, whereas global companies are more likely to centralize hedging strategies. The degree of control maintained at the central level depends on the importance of the foreign subsidiary's operations to total corporate performance and the capabilities at the foreign subsidiary level. Corporate treasury needs to determine overall policy, such as how to define exposure, what types of exposure are to be hedged and at what level, and what types of hedging instruments are acceptable. In addition, corporate treasury can provide consensus forecasts on exchange rate movements to help local management. Local management, however, must develop good capabilities in foreign exchange risk management. Through local banking relationships, local management may also be able to develop good forecasts of exchange rate movements. Local subsidiary management needs to establish and execute strategies that fit within corporate guidelines. The more centralized the strategy, however, the more likely corporate treasury will take responsibility for hedging strategies, thus freeing up local management to focus on operations.

Formulate Hedging Strategies   Once the decision is made as to which level in the organization will set policy, the next step is to formulate and execute a strategy. As noted above, that involves deciding which exposures will be hedged and which hedging techniques will be used. The choice of exposures to be hedged depends on the risk aversion of the company and management's confidence level in their ability to predict exposures accurately. One could argue that hedging a transactions exposure is obvious. Hedging will eliminate speculative gains, but it will also avoid losses and will give the company sure knowledge of what it will receive, especially in the case of forward contracts. Options will eliminate the downside risk but allow the possibility of upside gain if corporate treasury decides to not exercise the contract.

One example of foreign exchange risk management strategies is Dell, the large U.S.-based computer company. Dell is very aggressive in using forwards and options to hedge all foreign exchange exposure. Many companies will only hedge cash flow exposure, but Dell hedges everything. Because revenues are so difficult to forecast, Dell's Brazilian operations hedge about 80 percent of forecasted revenues. However, the local team has become very adept at forecasting revenues and executing a strategy in order to reach its target. Corporate treasury monitors currency movements worldwide and provides support to foreign subsidiary treasury personnel in terms of currency forecasts and hedging strategies. Within the broad framework provided by corporate treasury, local treasury establishes a specific strategy and then works with corporate treasury to execute the strategy. This is a good example of close interaction between corporate and local treasury in designing and implementing hedging strategies.

ACCOUNTING FOR FOREIGN CURRENCY DERIVATIVES

As noted above, managers can use derivatives to hedge or protect against foreign exchange risk. Regardless of which derivative a manager decides to use, the key is to cover the risk of the underlying transaction.

Hedging Strategies and Accounting for Derivatives

Firms can use a variety of derivative financial instruments to hedge an exposure, and there are unique ways to account for them depending on the nature of the derivative and what it is used for. Accounting for the hedging of receivables and payables denominated in a foreign currency is relatively straightforward. However, international business is more complicated, and so is the accounting for derivatives used to hedge international business activity. A company can enter into a firm commitment to purchase or sell inventory or capital equipment at some point in the future. Some companies do a significant amount of business abroad and are able to forecast their future sales, even though no firm commitment to sell has taken place. They may prefer to hedge a certain percentage of their estimated future sales. Also, many companies bid in foreign currency on large projects and may want to enter into a hedge to protect the bid in case it is awarded to them. In this case, an option is widely used because the bid is uncertain and the option need not be exercised.

Hedging Standards

Several key standards deal with accounting for derivatives. In December 1998, the International Accounting Standards Board issued IAS 39: Financial Instruments: Recognition and Measurement. After a few revisions, the effective date for the standard was moved to January 1, 2001. However, the standard has undergone additional revisions since then and is still a source of contention between the Board and certain European countries, notably France. IAS 39 (Revised 2004) took effect on January 1, 2005 as part of the convergence project. Accounting for derivatives related to foreign exchange is a part of IAS 39 rather than IAS 21, "The Effects of Changes in Foreign Exchange Rates."

Accounting for derivatives in the United States is found in FASB Statement No. 133, "Accounting for Derivative Instruments and Hedging Activities," which was issued in June 1998. However, its implementation date was delayed to fiscal years beginning after June 15, 2000. SFAS No. 133 adopts the treatment for hedging foreign currency transactions that was delineated in SFAS No. 52, "Foreign Currency Translation." For example, if a company purchases inventory abroad and is extended credit in the foreign currency, it is exposed to a foreign exchange gain or loss between the transaction date and the settlement date. If it enters into a derivative transaction to hedge its exposure, the accounting treatment is covered in the same way as required by SFAS No. 52, which we will illustrate below. Accounting for all other derivatives is also covered by SFAS No. 133. Accounting for derivatives by the IASB and FASB is very similar.

A derivative is a financial instrument or other contract with all three of the following characteristics:

1. It has one or more **underlyings** and one or more **notional amounts** or payment provisions, or both. Those terms determine the amount of the settlement or settlements, and, in some cases, whether or not a settlement is required.

2. It requires no initial net investment or an initial net investment that is smaller than would be required for other types of contracts that would be expected to have a similar response to changes in market factors.

3. Its terms require or permit net settlement, it can be readily net by a means outside the contract, or it provides for delivery of an asset that puts the recipient in a position not substantially different from net settlement. (*Statement of Financial Accounting Standards* No. 133, par. 6).

For purposes of this discussion, the underlying is foreign exchange, although the underlying for other derivatives could be something else, such as an interest rate or commodity like gold or silver. The notional amount is the number of units of foreign currency that will be traded. For example, if a U.S. firm owes a Japanese supplier ¥100,000,000 and enters into a forward contract to hedge the liability, the underlying for the forward contract would be Japanese yen and the notional amount would be ¥100,000,000.

SFAS 133 deals with a variety of derivative financial instruments, not just derivatives whose underlying is foreign exchange. Basically, both IAS 39 and Statement 133 require that all entities recognize derivatives as assets or liabilities in the statement of financial position and that they subsequently measure them at fair values. Changes in fair value from one period to the next are recorded in the comprehensive income statement.

Derivative instruments can be designated as a fair value hedge, a cash flow hedge, or a foreign currency hedge.

- Fair value hedge—a hedge of the exposure to changes in the fair value of a recognized asset or liability, or of an unrecognized firm commitment, that is attributable to a particular risk. Gains and losses are recognized in current income along with the gains and losses on the hedged item. An example would be the above example of a U.S. company that buys from a Japanese supplier and hedges the payable in yen.

- Cash flow hedge—a hedge of the exposure to variability in the cash flows of (1) a recognized asset or liability or of (2) a forecasted transaction that is attributable to a particular risk. The gain or loss is initially reported as a component of other comprehensive income (outside earnings) and subsequently reclassified into earnings when the forecasted transaction affects earnings. An example would be when a company enters into forward contracts or options to hedge future sales which are not firm commitments.

- Foreign currency hedge—a hedge of the foreign currency exposure of (1) an unrecognized firm commitment, (2) an available-for-sale security, (3) a forecasted transaction, or (4) a net investment in a foreign operation. Numbers 1 and 2 are treated as fair value hedges, and 3 is treated as a cash flow hedge. For number 4, the gain or loss is reported in other comprehensive income as part of the cumulative translation adjustment.

The importance of qualifying for hedge accounting provisions according to SFAS No. 133 is that the statement provides for a symmetrical matching of timing the recognition of the gain or loss of the derivative with the gain or loss on the underlying transaction. In the case of the yen liability above, a rise in the value of the yen would cause the dollar equivalent of the yen liability to rise, resulting in a foreign exchange loss. However, if the firm enters into a forward contract to receive yen from the bank, a rise in the yen receivable would result in a foreign exchange gain, offsetting the loss on the liability. That is the symmetrical nature of hedge accounting.

Illustration: A Forward Contract to Hedge a Foreign Currency Transaction

Prior to the issuance of Statement No. 133, Statement No. 52 contained provisions for accounting for the hedge of a foreign currency denominated asset or liability. Statement No. 133 basically retains the provisions of Statement No. 52, which says that derivative hedging instruments, such as a forward contract, are measured at fair value, with changes in fair value recognized in current earnings. Those changes would basically offset the foreign exchange gains or losses from the underlying assets or liabilities.

Assume the following information for Redex Imports, a U.S. company purchasing inventory from a British supplier on May 1 and incurring a liability of £50,000 that must be paid on July 30. The actual flow of goods and money is illustrated in Figure 13.4.

$1.8500	spot rate on May 1
$1.8700	forward rate quoted on May 1 for delivery on July 30
$1.8800	spot rate on June 30

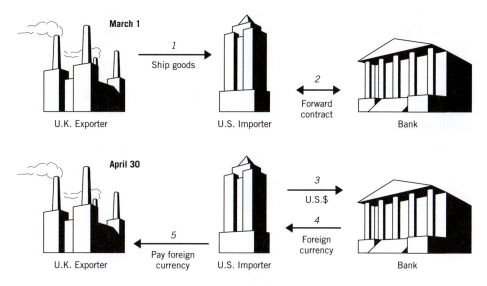

Figure 13.4   The Use of a Forward Contract to Hedge a Transaction

$1.8900	forward rate quoted on June 30 for delivery on July 30
$1.9000	spot rate on July 30

May 1	Purchases	92,500	
	Accounts payable		92,500
	to record the purchase at the spot rate		
	of $1.8500		

A memorandum entry is made to record Redex's commitment to deliver dollars to the bank and receive £50,000 at the forward rate of $1.8700. No entry is made because there was no investment made in the forward contract. It is an executory contract that will be settled in the future. However, the forward contract will have a market value that must be recorded if the forward rate changes at future balance sheet dates. Thus, we have to keep track of the value of the contract on June 30, which is the end of the calendar quarter. If Redex could have paid immediately for the purchase, it would have paid $92,500. Since it does not have the cash yet, it accepts the credit terms of the supplier but incurs foreign exchange risk. However, the forward contract guarantees that will pay $93,500 in 90 days, so it has eliminated the foreign exchange risk.

June 30	Foreign exchange loss	1,500	
	Accounts payable		1,500
	£50,000 × (1.8800–1.8500)		

Because the British pound strengthened against the dollar from May 1 to June 30, the liability is worth more, which results in a loss.

	Forward contract	1,000	
	Foreign exchange gain		1,000
	£50,000 × (1.8900–1.8700)		

On June 30, Redex holds a forward contract to deliver dollars for British pounds worth \$93,500 (\$1.8700 × £50,000). On June 30, a similar contract for delivery on June 30 would cost \$94,500 (1.8900 × £50,000), so Redex must recognize the positive value of its contract on the balance sheet. The gain on the forward contract is recognized in earnings.

On July 30, Redex delivers dollars to the bank (settling its forward contract obligation), receives foreign exchange, and delivers the foreign exchange to the British exporter to settle the liability.

July 30	Accounts payable	94,000	
	Loss	1,000	
	Cash		95,000

The cash value represents £50,000 at the spot rate of \$1.9000.

	Forward Contract	500	
	Gain		500
	£50,000 × (1.9000 – 1.8900)		

This marks up the value of the contract since the last balance sheet date.

| | Cash | 1,500 | |
| | Forward contract | | 1,500 |

This records the net settlement of the forward contract with the bank. To summarize the key parts of the transaction, Redex Imports received inventory valued at \$92,500 and paid a total of \$93,500 in cash, which is a foreign exchange loss of \$1,000. However, if Redex had not entered into the forward contract, it would have paid \$95,000. So the cost of \$1,000, which is the premium at which the pound was selling in the forward market, is simply a cost of doing business.

One complicating factor with the new derivatives standard is that forward contracts represent future obligations, whereas the amount of the forward contract recognized on the balance sheet (\$1,000 in the June 30 entry above) is undiscounted. Since the cash flows on the contract will not be recognized until a future period (July 30 in this case), the market value should be adjusted for the time value of money. Assume that Redex's marginal cost of borrowing is 6 percent per annum. The discounted present value of the forward contract for one month (June 30–July 30) is determined as follows:

$$\$1.8900 - 1.8700 = 0.02 \times 50,000 = \$1,000/(1 + 0.06/12) = \$995$$

Illustration: A Forward Contract to Hedge a Firm Commitment

The new rules to account for a forward contract to hedge a firm commitment are significantly more complex than those under the old GAAP rules. However, the end result is basically the same. The forward contract sets the value of the cash that the firm will pay, no matter what happens to the future spot rate. An example of a firm commitment would be where Redex Imports, a U.S. company, enters into a commitment to purchase capital equipment for £1,000,000 from a British manufacturer with delivery to take place on April 30 and payment to be made on May 31. Figure 13.5 illustrates the different parts of the transaction. Due to instability in foreign exchange markets, Redex is exposed to a possible foreign exchange loss. As a result,

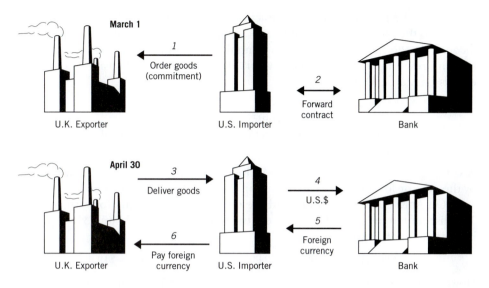

Figure 13.5   The Use of a Forward Contract to Hedge a Commitment

it enters into a forward contract with the foreign exchange trader at a bank to hedge the commitment. The contract hedges both the commitment period and the period until the payment is made. Because the forward contract is a hedge of the fair value of an accounts payable with the British manufacturer, it is treated in the same way as a fair value hedge. As such, the contract is recognized as an asset and marked to market. Changes in value are taken to the income statement. Changes in the value of the firm commitment are also taken to the income statement, so the changes in the forward contract and the changes in the firm commitment should effectively offset each other, which is the objective of the hedge.

Assume that the relevant spot exchange rates are as follows:

$1.4900	March 1
$1.5200	March 31
$1.5500	April 30
$1.5950	May 31

Assume also that the relevant forward exchange rates for June 30 delivery are as follows:

$1.5700	March 1
$1.5850	March 31
$1.5900	April 30

No entry is made on March 1, because there is a fixed future commitment rather than an actual contract. However, on March 31, the forward contract must be marked to market, and the resulting gain or loss taken to income. Assume that Redex's marginal cost of borrowing is 6 percent per annum. The discounted present value of the forward contract for two months (March 31–May 31) is determined as follows:

$$1.5850 - 1.5700 = .015 \times 1,000,000 = \$15,000/(1 + .06/6) = \$14,851$$

Thus, the fair value of the contract would show up as $14,851 on the balance sheet, and the same amount would be recognized as a gain in other comprehensive income. At the same time, the firm commitment would fall by a corresponding amount, resulting in a loss being recognized in other comprehensive income. The entries on March 31 are:

Forward Contract	14,851	
Gain on forward contract		14,851
Loss on firm commitment	14,851	
Firm commitment		14,851

According to SFAS No. 133, the gain or loss on the forward contract can be offset by the gain or loss on the hedged item, in this case the firm commitment.

On April 30, we need to record the change in value of the forward contract. The discounted present value of the contract for one month (March 31 – April 30) is computed as follows:

$$\$1.5900 - 1.5700 = .02 \times 1,000,000 = \$20,000/(1+.06/12) = \$19,900.$$

However, the contract has increased in value by only $5,049 since the last balance sheet date ($19,900 – $14,851).

The journal entries on April 30 are

Forward Contract	5,049	
Gain on forward contract		5,049
Loss on firm commitment	5,049	
Firm commitment		5,049
Equipment	1,530,100	
Purchase commitment	19,900	
Accounts payable		1,550,000

Since Redex takes title to the equipment on April 30, it must recognize the accounts payable at the spot rate and close out the purchase commitment account. The value of the equipment is a plug figure—the difference between the value at the spot rate on April 30 and the present value of the change in the purchase commitment. The accounts payable will be settled on May 31.

On May 31, the forward contract will be settled and payment will be made to the exporter, so the new value of the contract is the same as the spot rate on May 31. The value of the forward contract on May 31 is computed as follows:

$$\$1.5950 - \$1.5700 = .025 \times 1,000,000 = \$25,000$$

Since the contract value on April 30 was $19,900, the change in value is $5,100. The final journal entries on May 31 are:

Forward contract	5,100	
Gain on forward contract		5,100
Foreign exchange loss	45,000	
Accounts payable		45,000
Accounts payable	1,595,000	
Forward contract		25,000
Cash		1,570,000

The bottom line is that Redex Imports has to pay $1,570,000, the amount set by the forward contract entered into on March 1. No matter what happens to the future spot rate or the market value of the forward contract at successive balance sheet dates, the amount set by the contract still determines what the importer must pay.

Illustration: A Forward Contract to Hedge a Foreign Currency Forecasted Sale

One benefit of Statement 133 is that it allows hedge accounting for a foreign currency forecasted sale or purchase. Many companies doing business abroad have developed enough experience to have a good idea what their export sales volume will be during a given time period. They have not sold anything yet or even entered into a firm commitment to sell, but they still have a good idea how much they will sell. Rather than wait for the sale to take place to enter into a hedge, they can enter into one at any time and still be able to use hedge accounting.

Assume that XYZ company assesses its exposed position periodically and determines monthly hedging strategies for the coming quarter. On March 1, XYZ estimates that it will sell £1,000,000 of inventory to British customers effective April 30. At that time, XYZ enters into a forward contract to hedge the British pounds receivable. The relevant exchange rates are:

Date	Spot Exchange Rate ($/£)	Forward Exchange Rate for Settlement on April 30
March 1	$1.4772	$1.4900
March 31	$1.4950	$1.5050
Date of sale	$1.5100	$1.5100

Based on these exchange rates, the forward contract needs to be updated to fair market value with gains and losses going into income. Also, it is important to note that the contracts need to be adjusted at an appropriate discount rate, which we assume to be 6 percent for this example. The nominal value of the adjustment is the difference between the original forward rate quoted on March 1 and the rate quoted on March 31 and the difference between the March 31 forward rate and the actual spot rate on the date of sale.

Date	Nominal Value	Fair Value	Gain or Loss for the Period
March 1	0	0	0
March 31	($15,000)	($14,925)	($14,925)
April 30	($20,000)	($20,000)	($ 5,075)

The fair value adjustment on March 31 is computed as follows:

$$15,000/[1+(.06/12)] = 14,925$$

The adjustment is negative, because the original contract will yield $1,490,000 on the sale, whereas the exporter could have earned more cash on the contract at the new forward rate at the end of the quarter. Thus, the old contract is not worth as much as a new contract would have been.

Given the previous information, the journal entries for the hedge and forecasted sales are as follows:

March 1	No entry		
March 31	Other comprehensive income	14,925	
	Forward contract		14,925
April 30	Other comprehensive income	5,075	
	Forward contract		5,075
	Foreign currency	1,510,000	
	Sales		1,510,000
	To record the sale to the importer and receipt of British pounds at the spot rate on April 30.		
	Forward contract	20,000	
	Cash	1,490,000	
	Foreign currency		1,510,000
	To record the delivery of foreign currency to the bank at the April 30 spot rate, the closing out of the forward contract, and the receipt of dollars at the forward rate.		
	Sales	20,000	
	Other comprehensive income		20,000
	To transfer the loss on the forward contract from comprehensive income to earnings through sales revenues at the time of sale.		

The entries on April 30 were given to show the actual flow of cash and subsequent adjustments. What hedge accounting does is allow the firm to record sales revenues at the same rate as the cash received—the forward rate on the contract entered into on March 1. Granted, XYZ would have been better off not entering into the forward contract because it would have received $1,510,000 on April 30 at the spot rate. But on March 1, there was no guarantee that the pound would strengthen against the dollar, generating higher dollar receivables. That is the chance you take with a forward contract.

Illustration: An Option Contract to Hedge a Foreign Currency Forecasted Sale

Instead of using a forward contract, XYZ could use a put option to hedge the receivable from forecasted sales in British pounds. Assume that XYZ enters into a put option for £1,000,000 on March 1 at a strike price of $1.4900 and a premium of $20,000. The sale is expected to take place on June 30, the same time that the option contract expires. On March 1, the following entry is made:

Foreign-currency options	$20,000	
Cash		$20,000

to reflect the payment of the premium to the writer of the contract. This will be written off as a loss on hedging activities over the life of the option.

The option will also be adjusted to its fair value, and the adjustment will go to comprehensive income. When the sale is finally recorded, these adjustments will be taken from other comprehensive income and used to adjust the amount of sales.

The bottom line is that sales revenues and cash received will be at least the strike price, or $1,490,000. If the pound strengthens against the dollar, the option will not be exercised, and XYZ will convert the pounds into dollars at the spot rate. It will still incur the cost of the premium, but it will receive more dollars as the pound strengthens.

USE OF DERIVATIVES TO HEDGE A NET INVESTMENT

Statement 133 allows hedge accounting for the hedge of a net investment. Gains and losses on a derivative used to hedge a net investment are taken to a separate component of shareholder's equity rather than taken directly to income. That assumes, of course, that the derivative is designated and is effective as a hedge of the net investment. Since the derivative used to hedge the net investment is marked to fair value at the end of each accounting period, the gain or loss may be included in the cumulative translation adjustment to the extent that the changes represent an effective economic hedge of the net investment.

DISCLOSURE OF DERIVATIVE FINANCIAL INSTRUMENTS

In recent years there has been a lot of publicity about losses due to derivatives, and disclosure has been inaccurate due to the off-balance-sheet nature of the instruments. Most experts agree that derivatives, including foreign currency derivatives, are subject to several kinds of risk:

- Market risk—the risk of loss due to unexpected changes in interest and exchange rates
- Credit risk—the potential loss from counterparty nonperformance
- Liquidity risk—related to market liquidity of instruments held and, therefore, closely related to market risk
- Operating risk—linked to inadequate controls that ensure following a properly defined corporate policy

The key is to determine how best to disclose the extent of the risk to users. As a result of IAS 39 and FASB Statement 133, companies are improving and standardizing their disclosures on financial instruments. Companies using derivatives are required to provide both qualitative and quantitative information about the derivatives. In particular, companies must disclose their objectives for holding derivative financial instruments, the context needed to understand these objectives, and strategies for achieving the objectives. Separate information should be provided to fair value, cash flow, and foreign currency hedges. In addition to the qualitative information, companies are also required to provide quantitative information, such as the beginning and ending balances of derivatives recorded in comprehensive income as well as changes to those balances in each year reported (see *SFAS 133*, paragraph 43 and *IAS 39*, paragraphs 166–170 for more information).

DaimlerChrysler, the German auto manufacturer, prepares its financial statements according to U.S. GAAP and thus adopts *SFAS No. 133*. For most of its for-

Exhibit 13.4   DaimlerChrysler's Derivative Instruments and Hedging Activities

DaimlerChrysler uses derivative financial instruments such as forward contracts, swaps, options, futures, swaptions, forward rate agreements, caps and floors for hedging purposes. The accounting of derivative instruments is based upon the provisions of SFAS 133, "Accounting for Derivative Instruments and Hedging Activities", as amended. On the date a derivative contract is entered into, DaimlerChrysler designates the derivative as either a hedge of the fair value of a recognized asset or liability or of an unrecognized firm commitment (fair value hedge), a hedge of a forecasted transaction or the variability of cash flows to be received or paid related to a recognized asset or liability (cash flow hedge), or a hedge of a net investment in a foreign operation. DaimlerChrysler recognizes all derivative instruments as assets or liabilities on the balance sheet and measures them at fair value, regardless of the purpose or intent for holding them. Changes in the fair value of derivative instruments are recognized periodically either in earnings or stockholders' equity, as a component of accumulated other comprehensive loss, depending on whether the derivative is designed as a hedge of changes in fair value or cash flows. For derivatives designated as fair value hedges, changes in fair value of the hedged item and the derivative are recognized currently in earnings. For derivatives designated as cash flow hedges, fair value changes of the effective portion of the hedging instrument are recognized in accumulated other comprehensive loss on the balance sheet, net of applicable taxes, until the hedged item is recognized in earnings. The ineffective portions of the fair value changes are recognized in earnings immediately. Derivatives not meeting the criteria for hedge accounting are marked to market and impact earnings. SFAS 133 also requires that certain derivative instruments embedded in host contracts be accounted for separately as derivatives.

Source: DaimlerChrysler's Annual Report 2004, p. 113.

Exhibit 13.5   DaimlerChrysler's Foreign Currency Risk Management

As a consequence of the global nature of DaimlerChrysler's businesses, its operations and its reported financial results and cash flows are exposed to the risks associated with fluctuations in the exchange rates of the U.S. dollar, the euro and other world currencies. The Group's businesses are exposed to transaction risk whenever revenues of a business are denominated in a currency other than the currency in which the business incurs the costs relating to those revenues. This risk exposure primarily affects the Mercedes Car Group segment. The Mercedes Car Group segment generates its revenues mainly in the currencies of the countries in which cars are sold, but it incurs manufacturing costs primarily in euros. The Commercial Vehicles segment is subject to transaction risk, to a lesser extent, because of its global production network. At Chrysler Group revenues and costs are principally generated in U.S. dollars, resulting in a relatively low transaction risk for this segment. The Other Activities segment was exposed to a low transaction risk resulting primarily from the U.S. dollar exposure of the aircraft engine business, which DaimlerChrysler conducts through MTU Aero Engines. Effective December 31, 2003 DaimlerChrysler sold all its equity interests in MTU Aero Engines.

In order to mitigate the impact of currency exchange rate fluctuations, DaimlerChrysler continually assesses its exposure to currency risks and hedges a portion of those risks through the use of derivative financial instruments. Responsibility for managing DaimlerChrysler's currency exposures and use of currency derivatives is centralized within the Group's Currency Committee. Until the disposition of MTU Aero Engines, effective December 31, 2003, the Currency Committee consisted of two separate subgroups, one for the Group's vehicle businesses and one for MTU Aero Engines. Each subgroup consisted of members of senior management from each of the respective businesses as well as from Corporate Treasury and Risk Controlling. Since January 1, 2004, the Currency Committee consists exclusively of those members who previously formed the subgroup responsible for the vehicle business. Corporate Treasury implements decisions concerning foreign currency hedging taken by the Currency Committee. Risk Controlling regularly informs the Board of Management of the actions of Corporate Treasury based on the decisions of the Currency Committee.

Source: DaimlerChrysler's Annual Report 2004, p. 157.

Exhibit 13.6   DaimlerChrysler's Fair Value of Financial Instruments

	At December 31, 2004		At December 31, 2003	
	Carrying Amount	Fair Value	Carrying Amount	Fair Value
(In millions of euro)				
Financial instruments (other than derivative instruments):				
Assets				
Financial Assets	1,610	1,610	1,631	1,631
Receivables from financial services	56,785	57,558	52,638	53,919
Securities	3,884	3,884	3,268	3,268
Cash and cash equivalents	7,771	7,771	11,017	11,017
Liabilities:		–		–
Financial liabilities	76,620	78,594	75,690	75,690
Derivative instruments:				
Assets:				
Currency contracts	1,287	1,287	2,380	2,380
Interest rate contracts	2,667	2,667	3,695	3,695
Liabilities:				
Currency contracts	152	152	267	267
Interest rate contracts	196	196	163	163

Source: DaimlerChrysler's Annual Report 2004, p. 156.

eign subsidiaries, DaimlerChrysler uses the current rate method of translating for-eign currency financial statements into euros, the parent currency. In its 2004 annual report, it provides a great deal of information about its hedging activities from both a qualitative and quantitative perspective. Exhibit 13.4 is a section from DaimlerChrysler's 2004 Annual Report that describes its derivative instruments and hedging activities. Exhibit 13.5 provides more specific information about the com-pany's foreign currency risk management activities from note 33. Exhibit 13.6 illus-trates the carrying amounts and fair values of their group financial instruments.

The fair value of a financial instrument is the price at which one party would assume the rights and/or duties of another party. Fair values of financial instru-ments have been determined with reference to available market information at the balance sheet date and the valuation methodologies discussed below. Considering the variability of their value-determining factors, the fair values presented therein are only an indication of the amounts that the Group could realize under current market conditions.

SUMMARY

1.   A derivative is a contract, the value of which changes in accordance with the price movements in a related or underlying commodity, such as foreign exchange. The most important foreign currency derivatives are forwards, swaps, futures, and options.

2. A forward contract is a contract between a foreign currency trader and client for the future sale or purchase of foreign currency. A swap is a simultaneous spot and forward transaction. A foreign currency futures contract is an exchange-traded derivative that specifies a future exchange rate. An option is the right, but not obligation, to trade foreign currency in the future at an agreed-upon rate.

3. The daily foreign exchange market activity is approximately $1.9 trillion. The most important markets in foreign exchange are London, New York, and Tokyo, and the most widely traded currencies are the U.S. dollar, the euro, the Japanese yen, the British pound, and the Swiss franc.

4. The International Monetary Fund (IMF) was organized in 1944 to promote exchange stability. The IMF classifies exchange rate regimes as follows: currencies that are pegged to a currency or composite of currencies, currencies whose exchange rates have displayed limited flexibility compared with either a currency or group of currencies, and countries whose exchange rates are more flexible.

5. Purchasing power parity relates relative inflation to a currency's value. A country experiencing relatively high inflation should be expected to have a relatively weak currency in the future.

6. Countries with a relatively high interest rate generally have higher inflation and should have a currency that falls in value in the future, all things being equal.

7. Companies must establish policies to hedge transaction exposure, translation exposure, and economic exposure.

8. Companies may use financial strategies or operating strategies to hedge exposure.

9. A good foreign exchange risk management strategy should define and measure exposure, organize and implement a reporting system that monitors exposure and exchange rate movements, adopt a policy for assigning responsibility for hedging exposure, and formulate a hedging strategy.

10. Two key standards that deal with accounting for derivatives are IAS 39: Financial Instruments: Recognition and Measurement, and FASB Statement No. 133: Accounting for Certain Derivative Instruments and Certain Hedging Activities.

11. Derivatives have an underlying and a notional value. For purposes of this chapter, the underlying is foreign currency, and the notional value is the number of units of the foreign currency.

12. Derivatives can be designated as a fair value hedge, a cash flow hedge, or a foreign currency hedge.

13. According to IAS 39 and FASB Statement 133, companies generally disclose the types of financial instruments they use, their notional principal amounts, and their fair values. In addition, they may disclose other information, such as carrying values and maturities of the derivatives and qualitative information about their hedging strategies.

Discussion Questions

1. What are the major differences between a forward contract and a futures contract and between a forward contract and an options contract?

2. Assume that a U.S. company enters into a call option to buy Japanese yen for dollars to pay a Japanese supplier. The strike price is ¥110 per dollar. If the spot rate on the transaction date is ¥105 yen, is the contract in the money, out of the money, or at the money? Should the company exercise the option or let it lapse and convert at the spot rate?

3. Assume that a U.S. company enters into a call option to buy Japanese yen for dollars to pay a Japanese supplier. The strike price is ¥110 per dollar. If the spot rate on the transaction date is ¥110 yen, is the contract in the money, out of the money, or at the money? Should the company exercise the option or let it lapse and convert at the spot rate?

4. Assume that a U.S. company enters into a call option to buy Japanese yen for dollars to pay a Japanese supplier. The strike price is ¥110 per dollar. If the spot rate on the transaction date is ¥115 yen, is the contract in the money, out of the money, or at the money? Should the company exercise the option or let it lapse and convert at the spot rate?

5. Assume that a U.S. company enters into a put option to sell British pounds that it will receive from a British importer. The strike price is $1.9500 pounds per dollar. If the spot rate on the transaction date is $1.9800, should the company exercise the option or let it lapse and convert at the spot rate?

6. Pick a currency and see if you can find out which exchange rate arrangement it uses. Check the website of the International Monetary Fund for details.

7. If the rate of inflation in Ecuador is 25 percent per annum and the rate of inflation in Brazil is 12 percent per annum, which country should have the higher interest rate? Why? Which country should have the stronger currency? Why?

8. Define the following three exposures: transaction, translation, economic.

9. If a U.S. company uses the current rate method to translate the financial statements of foreign subsidiary A into dollars and the currency of country A is strengthening against the dollar, would you expect the U.S. company to recognize translation gains or losses? Where would these gains or losses show up on the financial statements?

10. If a U.S. company uses the current rate method to translate the financial statements of foreign subsidiary A into dollars and the currency of country A is weakening against the dollar, would you expect the U.S. company to recognize translation gains or losses? Where would these gains or losses show up on the financial statements?

11. What are the major reasons why some companies do not hedge foreign exchange risk?

12. If they do hedge their foreign exchange risk, what strategy do they need to consider?

13. Assume that a U.S. exporter sells merchandise to a German importer with payment to be received in 30 days. Describe how the exporter can use foreign currency debt to hedge the exposure. Then explain how they can use a forward contract. How would you compare the cost between the two hedging possibilities?

14. What is the difference between an underlying and a notional amount for a derivative?

15. If a firm enters into a forward contract to hedge a purchase denominated in a foreign currency, is the hedge a fair value hedge or a cash flow hedge? Would any gains or losses on the contract be included in current income or comprehensive income?

Exercises

1. Nissan announced that it was closing some factories in Japan and shifting production to the United States to shelter itself from foreign exchange risks that it faces when exporting cars to the United States. Describe the risk that Nissan is concerned about. Describe the pros and cons of using forward contracts to hedge Nissan sales to the United States and whether or not they are a better solution than moving production to the United States.

2. Pick a foreign currency of your choice and graph the value of the currency against the U.S. dollar over the past 12 months. Based on what has happened to the exchange rate, describe the financial challenges facing an exporter from that country or an exporter to that country.

3. In the chapter, we discussed how companies can use derivative financial instruments to hedge against a potential loss on a foreign currency receivable or payable. If there are possible losses from denominating receivables and payables in a foreign currency, why don't firms insist that receivables and payables always be in their own currency instead of a foreign currency?

4. Siemens is a German company that generates its revenues in energy, industry, information and communications, and health care. It has operations all over the world. In the notes to its financial statements, Siemens states:

   > Due to the weakness of the German mark relative to the British pound, the U.S. dollar and several Asian currencies, total assets increased DM2.7 billion upon translation of foreign currency accounts. As a result, the negative translation adjustment in shareholders' equity was substantially reduced. Net sales decreased DM1.5 billion, due to the opposite impact of annual average exchange rates on the related statement of income accounts.

   Explain what this means in terms of exposure and the impact of exchange rates on reported results.

5. On January 1, XYZ, a U.S. company, purchased inventory from a Japanese supplier for ¥100,000,000, with payment to be made on February 28. At the same time, it decided to enter into a forward contract to hedge the yen liability. Assume the following exchange rates relative to the transaction:

¥110 per $	January 1 spot rate
¥108	forward rate quoted on January 1 for delivery on February 28
¥109	spot rate on January 31
¥109	forward rate quoted on January 31 for delivery on February 28
¥112	spot rate on February 28

   How many dollars would XYZ have to pay the Japanese supplier, and what would be the dollar value of the purchase?

6. On January 1, XYZ, a U.S. company, sold inventory to a Japanese supplier for ¥100,000,000, with payment to be received on February 28. At the same time, it decided to enter into a forward contract to hedge the yen receivable. Assume the following exchange rates relative to the transaction:

¥108 per $	January 1 spot rate
¥110	forward rate quoted on January 1 for delivery on February 28
¥108.5	spot rate on January 31
¥109	forward rate quoted on January 31 for delivery on February 28
¥112	spot rate on February 28

How many dollars would XYZ receive after converting the proceeds from the Japanese customer, and what would be the dollar value of the purchase?

7. On March 1, QRS, a U.S. company, purchased inventory from a German supplier for €100,000. At the same time, QRS entered into a forward contract to hedge the euro liability which must be settled on May 31. Assume the following exchange rates:

€0.7705	March 1 spot rate
€0.7600	forward rate quoted on March 1 for delivery on May 31
€0.7700	spot rate on March 31
€0.7620	forward rate quoted on March 31 for delivery on May 31
€0.7600	spot rate on May 31

a. Assuming that no forward contract is entered into and that the books are closed at the end of the quarter, what would be the journal entries for the exporter on March 1, March 31, and May 31?

b. Assuming that a forward contract is entered into and that the discount rate is 6 percent, what would be the journal entries on March 1, March 31, and May 31?

8. On January 1, XYZ, a U.S. exporter, sold merchandise to a German supplier for €100,000. At the same time, it decided to enter into a forward contract to hedge the euro receivable. Assume the following exchange rates relative to the transaction.

$1.3000/euro	January 1 spot rate
$1.2800	forward rate quoted on Jan 1 for delivery on Feb 28
$1.3500	spot rate on January 31
$1.3300	forward rate quoted on January 31 for delivery on Feb. 28
$1.3100	spot rate on February 28

a. How many dollars would XYZ receive from the sale, and what would be the dollar value of the sale?

b. Assuming that no forward contract is entered into and that the books are closed at the end of the each month, what would be the journal entries for the exporter on January 1, January 31, and February 28?

c. Assuming that a forward contract is entered into and that the discount rate is 6 percent, what would be the journal entries on January 1, January 31, and February 28?

9. On January 1, ABC, an Australian exporter sold wool to a British importer for £500,000 at an exchange rate of £2.4405 per Australian dollar. At the same time, they entered into a forward contract to hedge the receivable. Assume the following exchange rates relative to the transaction.

£2.4405	January 1 spot rate
£2.5000	forward rate quoted on Jan 1 for Feb 28 delivery
£2.4800	spot rate on January 31
£2.4900	forward rate quoted on Jan 31 for Feb 28 delivery
£2.4950	spot rate on February 28

a. How many A$ would the exporter receive from the sale, and what would be the dollar value of the sale?

b. Assuming that no forward contract is entered into and that the books are closed at the end of each month, what would be the journal entries for the exporter on January 1, January 31, and February 28?

c. Assuming that a forward contract is entered into and that the discount rate is 6 percent, what would be the journal entries on January 1, January 31, and February 28?

10. On January 1, ABC, an Australian exporter entered into a firm commitment to sell wool to a British importer for £500,000. Delivery will be made on February 28, and payment will be made on March 30. At the same time, they entered into a forward contract to hedge the receivable. Assume the following exchange rates relative to the transaction and that the books are closed at the end of each month.

£2.4405	January 1 spot rate
£2.5000	forward rate quoted on Jan 1 for March 30 delivery
£2.4600	spot rate on January 31
£2.4900	forward rate quoted on Jan 31 for March 30 delivery
£2.4750	spot rate on February 28
£2.4800	forward rate quoted on February 28 for March 30 delivery
£2.4950	spot rate on March 30

a. How many A$ would the exporter receive from the sale, and what would be the dollar value of the sale?

b. Assuming that no forward contract is entered into and that the books are closed at the end of each month, what would be the journal entries for the exporter on January 1, January 31, February 28, and March 30?

c. Assuming that a forward contract is entered into and that the discount rate is 6 percent, what would be the journal entries on January 1, January 31, February 28, and March 30?

11. On January 1, ABC, an Australian importer entered into a firm commitment to buy cloth from a British exporter for £500,000. Delivery will be made on February 28, and payment will be made on March 30. At the same time, the importer entered into a forward contract to hedge the liability. Assume the following British £ exchange rates relative to the transaction and that the books are closed at the end of each month.

£2.4405	January 1 spot rate
£2.5000	forward rate quoted on Jan 1 for March 30 delivery
£2.4600	spot rate on January 31
£2.4900	forward rate quoted on Jan 31 for March 30 delivery
£2.4750	spot rate on February 28
£2.4800	forward rate quoted on February 28 for March 30 delivery
£2.4950	spot rate on March 30

a. How many A\$ would the importer pay, and what would be the dollar value of the purchase?

b. Assuming that no forward contract is entered into and that the books are closed at the end of each month, what would be the journal entries for the exporter on January 1, January 31, February 28, and March 30?

c. Assuming that a forward contract is entered into and that the discount rate is 6 percent, what would be the journal entries on January 1, January 31, February 28, and March 30?

d. Would the importer have been better off not entering into the contract? Explain.

12. DEF Inc., a U.S. exporter, has been selling merchandise to its Japanese importer for over 10 years. It has a good idea how much merchandise it will deliver each month, even though it has not yet booked the sales. On March 1, the president of DEF Inc. asked the CFO to provide an estimate of sales revenues for April in dollar terms, even though DEF Inc. invoices the sales in yen to cater to the customer. The CFO's estimate is that they will sell ¥1,000,000 in April and will book the sale at the end of the month. After researching exchange rates, the CFO found the following:

Date	Spot Exchange Rate	Forward Rate for April 30 Delivery
March 1	¥105	¥103
March 31	¥104	¥102.5
April 30	¥101	¥101

a. What are the nominal values, fair values, and period gains or losses for March 1, March 31, and April 30? Assume a discount rate of 6 percent.

b. What are the journal entries on March 1, March 31, and April 11?

c. Would the exporter have been better off not entering into the forward contract? Explain.

13. DEF Inc., a U.S. importer, has been buying merchandise from its British importer for over 10 years. It has a good idea how much merchandise it will purchase each month, even though it has not yet booked the purchases. On March 1, the president of DEF Inc. asked the CFO to provide an estimate of purchases for April in dollar terms, even though DEF Inc. has to pay in British pounds. The CFO's estimate is that they will buy £100,000 in April and will book the purchases at the end of the month. After researching exchange rates, the CFO found the following:

Date	Spot Exchange Rate	Forward Rate for April 30 Delivery
March 1	£1.7000	£1.7800
March 31	£1.7500	£1.7900
April 30	£1.8000	£1.8000

a. What are the nominal values, fair values, and period gains or losses for March 1, March 31, and April 30? Assume a discount rate of 6 percent.

b. What are the journal entries on March 1, March 31, and April 11?

c. Would DEF Inc. have been better off not entering into the forward contract? Explain.

14. Assume that Apex Inc., a U.S.-based company, sells merchandise to Products plc, a British customer, and has to denominate the sale in British pounds with payment to be received in 90 days. Apex will receive £500,000 from the importer. In order to hedge

the receivable, Apex decides to borrow British pounds for 90 days at 12 percent and deposit the pounds in an interest-bearing account.

a.   How much will Apex have to borrow to cover its receivable?

b.   If Apex deposits the money in an interest-bearing account yielding 8 percent, what will be the cash received from the sale, assuming no tax effect? The spot rate at the beginning of the transaction is $1.8500 per pound, and the rate 90 days later is $1.8000.

15.   Assume that Apex Inc., a U.S.-based company, sells merchandise to Quigley Inc., an Australian importer, and has to denominate the sale in Australian dollars with payment to be received in 90 days. Apex will receive A$500,000 from Quigley. In order to hedge the receivable, Apex decides to borrow Australian dollars for 90 days at 10 percent and deposit the Australian dollars in an interest bearing account.

a.   How much will Apex have to borrow to cover its receivable?

b.   If Apex deposits the money in an interest-bearing accounting yielding 8 percent, what will be the cash received from the sale, assuming no tax effect? The spot rate at the beginning of the transaction is A$1.2907 per U.S. dollar, and the rate 90 days later is $1.3500.

Case: Nokia's Foreign Exchange Exposure
Case: RadCo International

These cases can be found on the following website: www.wiley.com/college/radebaugh

References

Aeppel, Timothy. 2005. "Weak Dollar Lifts Sales for U.S. Manufacturers." *Wall Street Journal,* January 20, p. B1.

Bank for International Settlements. 2004. *Central Bank Survey of Foreign Exchange and Derivatives Market Activity.* BIS: Basel, Switzerland (May).

Bartov, E. 1997. "Foreign Currency Exposure of Multinational Firms: Accounting Measures and Market Valuation." *Contemporary Accounting Research* 14(4) (Winter): 623–652.

Bartov, E., and G. M. Bodnar. 1995. "Foreign Currency Translation Reporting and the Exchange-Rate Exposure Effect." *Journal of International Financial Management & Accounting* 6(2) (Summer): 93–114.

Beaver, W. H., and M. A. Wolfson. 1992. "Foreign Currency Translation and Changing Prices in Perfect and Complete Markets." *Journal of Accounting Research* (Autumn): 528–550.

Choi, F. D. S., and R. R. Gunn. 1997. "Hyperinflation Reporting and Performance Assessment." *Journal of Financial Statement Analysis* 2(4) (Summer): 30–38.

Christie, Eilidh, and Andrew Marshall. 2001. "The Impact of the Introduction of the Euro on Foreign Exchange Risk Management in UK Multinational Companies. *European Financial Management* 7(3): 419–434.

Cowell, Alan. 2004. "Nokia Falters, and the Finns Take Stock." *The New York Times,* September 4, Internet version.

Dhanani, Alpa, and Roger Groves. 2001. "The Management of Strategic Exchange Risk: Evidence from Corporate Practices." *Accounting and Business Research* 31(4): 275–290.

Duffey, G., and I. H. Giddy. 1995. "Uses and Abuses of Currency Options." *Journal of Applied Corporate Finance* 8(3): 49–57.

Duffey, G., and I. H. Giddy. 2003. "Management of Corporate Foreign Exchange Risk," in *International Finance and Accounting Handbook* by Frederick D. S. Choi, ed. NY: John Wiley and Sons.

Eiteman, D. K., A. I. Stonehill, and M. H. Moffett. 1998. *Multinational Business Finance.* Reading, MA: Addison-Wesley.

Financial Accounting Standards Board. 1998. *Accounting for Derivative Instruments and Hedging Activities.*

Hagelin, Niclas, and Bengt Pramborg. 2004. "Hedging Foreign Exchange Exposure: Risk Reduction from Transaction and Translation Hedging." *Journal of International Financial Management and Accounting* 15(1): 1–20.

Hughes, John, Jing Liu, and Mingshan Zhang. 2004. "Valuation and Accounting for Inflation and Foreign Exchange." *Journal of Accounting Research* 42(4): 731–754.

International Accounting Standards Board. 2005. *Financial Instruments: Recognition and Measurement.*

Janowski, D. 1999. "Global Pricing/Risk Management Techniques." *TMA Journal* 19(5): 20–29.

Lessard, D. R., and J. B. Lightstone. 1986. "Volatile Exchange Rates Can Put Operations at Risk." *Harvard Business Review* (July/August): 107–114.

Logue, D. E., and G. S. Oldfield. 1997. "Managing Foreign Assets When Foreign Exchange Markets Are Efficient." *Financial Management* (Summer): 16–22.

Moffett, M. H., and J. K. Karlsen. 1994. "Managing Foreign Exchange Rate Economic Exposure." *Journal of International Financial Management and Accounting* (June): 157–175.

Nokia Form 20-F 2004.

Perrottet, C. 1998. "Don't Hide From Risk—Manage It." *Journal of International Business Strategy* 19(5): 9–12.

PricewaterhouseCoopers. 1998a. *A Guide to Accounting for Derivative Instruments and Hedging Activities* (July 31): 2.

PricewaterhouseCoopers. 1998b. *The New Standard on Accounting for Derivative Instruments and Hedging Activities.* New York: Pricewaterhouse Coopers.

Pringle, David, and Joon Knapen. 2005. "Nokia Reports 3% Increase in Sales." *Wall Street Journal*, January 28, p. B3.

Reinhardt, Andy and Moon Ihlwan. 2005. "Will Rewiring Nokia Spark Growth?' *Business Week*, February 14, pp. 46–47.

Wallace, J. 1998. "Best Practices in Foreign Exchange Risk Management." *TMA Journal* 18(6): 48–55.

CHAPTER FOURTEEN

INTERNATIONAL BUDGETING AND PERFORMANCE EVALUATION

Chapter Objectives

- Identify the major stages in the strategic control process
- Describe different ways to evaluate the performance of managers and companies in the international context
- Present the results of different studies on performance evaluation by U.S. and non-U.S. firms
- Discuss how foreign currencies impact the budgeting and performance evaluation process
- Review the problems involved with setting intracorporate transfer prices
- Examine the major issues and trends in performance evaluation, including the use of Economic Value Added (EVA) and the Balanced Scorecard

INTRODUCTION

In this chapter we look at some of the special problems faced by management in controlling the multinational enterprise. As with control in a domestic environment, control in the global environment begins with a strategic objective and includes all elements of planning and monitoring the success of a global strategy to meet those objectives. The focus of the planning process is to give strategic direction to the firm and then an operational plan to get the firm to achieve the strategic direction. The role of the management accountant in this planning process is to work with top management to identify the necessary performance criteria and then to monitor achievements against these criteria.

Strategic Decision Point

Nestlé, the largest food and beverage company in the world, is headquartered in tiny Switzerland but has 511 factories in 86 countries. Some of its major challenges are to maintain control of its far-flung operations, evaluate performance of its six main product groups and three major geographic areas, and improve shareholder value. Its major shareholders are Swiss (42 percent), U.S. (22 percent), British (10 percent), French (8 percent), and German (5 percent) citizens. Thus, it has to answer to shareholders in many different countries. Although Nestlé does not disclose its sales in Switzerland, 32.7 percent of its sales are made in Europe. Since it generates its primary financial statements in Swiss francs, it has to deal with the fact that the majority of its revenues occur outside of Switzerland and in many different currencies. Thus, Nestlé is forced to establish budgets in different currencies, evaluate performance based on operating results in those currencies, and explain price, volume, and currency variances to local and top management.

THE STRATEGIC CONTROL PROCESS

In a study of European multinational enterprises (MNEs) by Gupta and Govindarajan (1991), the following stages in a formal strategic control system were identified:

1. Periodic strategy reviews for each business, typically on an annual or less frequent basis.

2. Annual operating plans, which increasingly include nonfinancial measures along with the traditional financial ones.

3. Formal monitoring of strategic results, which may be combined with the budget monitoring process.

4. Personal rewards and central intervention.

Having too rigid a strategic control system can be difficult for a company that is in a rapidly changing industry, but there are some distinct benefits from a formal process:

1. Greater clarity and realism in planning

2. More "stretching" of performance standards

3. More motivation for business unit managers

4. More timely intervention by central management

5. Clearer responsibilities

For such a system to work, it is necessary to select the right strategic objectives based on an analysis of the competition and the strengths of the firm. Then suitable targets need to be set according to the strategy of the firm. Many firms attempt to benchmark their performance based on key competitors, but it is often difficult to get good data on global competitors. The system needs to be tight enough and demanding enough to put pressure on management to perform. It is common to find strategic plans that are too general, so there is a real challenge to take the plans and targets and use them to push management. Finally, it is important not to let the process get so big, complicated, and bureaucratized that it gets in the way of creative thinking and solid performance.

Trying to implement this concept in a global environment is not easy. Different operating environments make it difficult and complicated to establish and implement a strategic control system. Such operating environments include culture; legal systems (which may limit a strategic objective to increase market share or become the market leader); political differences that could influence the role the firm is allowed to play in the country; and economic systems, including inflation and market size and growth.

EMPIRICAL STUDIES OF DIFFERENCES IN MANAGEMENT ACCOUNTING AND CONTROL PRACTICES ACROSS NATIONS

Setting Objectives: A Global Overview

A great deal has been written on strategy for the corporation. As it relates to multi-nationals, the setting of strategic objectives usually requires managers to focus on choosing a suitable numeric target. Objectives can be quantified in terms of a particular budget number or financial ratio and seem to vary considerably from country to country. Possible targets include:

1. return on investment
2. sales
3. cost reduction
4. quality targets
5. market share
6. profitability
7. budget to actual

Each of these has its value. The most appropriate method to be used in a multi-national is, in theory, best defined by the focus of the unit for which the target is being set. Sales or market share is particularly relevant for a unit that has no control over its input costs and whose primary purpose is to sell the goods of some other unit. Profitability, measured as a ratio or some other measure, is most appropriate for a full fledged strategic business unit (i.e., a unit of a group of companies which makes its own business decisions at all levels—for example, a major division or subsidiary). In addition, targets for a unit should be linked not only to its objective, but also to that part of its operations which it controls. This theoretical concern aside, there is considerable evidence that the core objective of the corporation differs from country to country or culture. The studies that follow illustrate this point.

Studies of U.S. Multinationals

In one of the first important studies of the objectives of MNEs, Robbins and Stobaugh (1973) studied nearly 200 U.S.-based MNEs, representing almost all major U.S. industries with investments abroad and ranging in size of annual foreign sales from $20 million upward. With regard to measures of financial performance, the main conclusions from their research were as follows:

1. The many tangible and intangible items that entered into the original investment calculations were rarely taken into account in evaluating the foreign subsidiaries' performance. For example, the value or cost of a parent company's loan guarantee for a subsidiary, cost of safety stocks of inventory for foreign and U.S. operations, or the potential cost of being excluded from a market by a competitor who moves first.

2. Foreign subsidiaries were judged on the same basis as domestic subsidiaries.

3. The most utilized measure of performance for all subsidiaries was return on investment (ROI).

4. Because of the inherent limitation and problems of calculating ROI equitably for all subsidiaries, nearly all the multinationals used some supplementary device to gauge foreign subsidiaries' performance.

5. The most widely used supplementary measure was comparison to budget.

Additional support for the findings of this study continues even though some 25 years have passed since the original study. In a sample of 70 U.S. chemical multinationals (see Morsicato, 1980), it was found that multiple measures were used, including (in descending order of use) profit, ROI, and budgeted versus actuals for profit and sales. Abdallah and Keller (1985) in a survey of 64 U.S. MNEs identified four key factors (see Exhibit 14.1). As with other studies, budgets, profits, and ROI dominate the list.

After the initial studies of U.S. corporate performance objectives, a variety of studies have examined practices in other countries. Some of the countries are quite similar culturally to the United States.

Exhibit 14.1   Evaluating Foreign Subsidiaries and Foreign Subsidiary Managers

	Percent of the Total 64 MNEs	
Financial Measures	Foreign Subsidiary (%)	Foreign Subsidiary Manager (%)
Return-on-investment (ROI)	74	67
Profits	78	66
Budgeted ROI compared to actual ROI	66	64
Budgeted profit compared to actual profit	86	87
Other measures	36	36

Source: W. Abdallah and D. Keller, "Measuring the Multinational's Performance," *Management Accounting* (1985): 28.

Studies of U.K. Multinationals

Appleyard, Strong, and Walton (1990) studied the performance objectives of 11 British MNEs and found that the British companies preferred to use budget/actual comparisons, followed closely by some form of ROI. In the ROI measure, the profit measure used was either profit before interest and tax or profit after interest but before tax, even though tax rates vary significantly from country to country. In addition, they found that British firms tended to use the same ROI measure for foreign subsidiaries that they do for domestic subsidiaries.

Studies of Japanese Multinationals

Studies in countries whose cultures differ significantly from the United States often produce very different results. Shields, Chow, Kato, and Nakagawa (1991) reviewed the objectives used by Japanese and U.S. MNEs as found in the literature of the two countries and identified several important performance objectives used to evaluate divisional managers. As Exhibit 14.2 shows, there are some major differences between the two countries. The Japanese tend to rely on sales as their most important criterion by far, whereas U.S. firms prefer ROI.

Similarly, Bailes and Assada (1991) studied and compared the objectives of 256 Japanese and 80 U.S. MNEs. The respondents were asked to identify the first, second, and third goals for division managers; their answers are summarized in Exhibit 14.3. Bailes and Assada (1991) found that most Japanese firms (86.3 percent) preferred to use sales volume as their overall objective, with net profit after corporate overhead being a poor second (44.7 percent). American companies, by

Exhibit 14.2   Criteria Used for Evaluating Divisional Managers

Sources	Japan A (%)	United States A (%)
Sales	69	19
Sales growth	28	28
Market share	12	19
Asset turnover	7	13
Return-on-sales	30	26
ROI	7	75
Controllable profit	28	49
Residual income	20	13
Profit minus corporate costs	44	38
Manufacturing costs	28	13
Other	8	17

Source: Michael Shields, Chee W. Chow, Yutaka Kato, and Yu Nakagawa, "Management Accounting Practices in the U.S. and Japan: Comparative Survey Findings and Research Implications," *Journal of International Financial Management and Accounting* 3, no. 2 (Spring 1991): 68.

Exhibit 14.3 Top Budget Goals for Division Managers

	Japan (%)	United States (%)
Sales volume	86.3	27.9
Net profit after corporate overhead	44.7	35.0
Controllable profit	28.2	51.8
Profit margin on sales	30.7	30.5
Sales growth	19.4	22.4
Return on investment (ROI)	3.1	68.4
Production cost	40.7	12.4

Source: Jack C. Bailes and Takayuki Assada, "Empirical Differences between Japanese and American Budget and Performance Evaluation Systems," *International Journal of Accounting* 26, no. 2 (1991): 137.

contrast, tend to use ROI most often as the divisional budget goal (68.4 percent) followed by controllable profit (51.8 percent). It is important to note how unimportant ROI appears to be to the Japanese firms. Demirag (1994) found that Japanese companies in the United Kingdom tended to use sales and market share targets over the longer term.

Studies of APEC Multinationals

Looking at East Asia, research by Merchant, Chow, and Wu (1995) found little evidence suggesting a link between national culture and firms' goals in Taiwan. However, the sample consisted of only four firms. Comparing the perspectives of more than 400 managers in Australia, the United States, Singapore, and Hong Kong, Harrison and Harrell (1994) simply concluded that Anglo-American managers prefer shorter term but more quantitative objectives. These studies will be discussed further in the budgeting section.

Taken together, these studies find that the objectives of companies from various nation-states vary considerably. It is interesting to note that the Asian nations, which are less individualistic and by and large more long-term oriented, tend to pick objectives that less directly reflect immediate returns, choosing those objectives that fit a longer-term market dominance profile.

The Budget Process Across Countries: Basics

The budget process involves taking the firm's objectives and setting them out in a series of formal plans, both short and long term. The issues that generally need to be resolved are:

1. Is there a formal budget-setting process?
2. Who participates in the budget process and how?

3. What style of communication (formal versus informal) should be used?

4. How are the budget objectives set?

5. Should the budgeting process be the same for domestic and foreign sub-sidiaries?

Other more general issues of concern are, for example:

6. What time period should be covered (short versus long term)?

7. Should there be a specific monetary objective for the plan, or would a nonquantitative objective be more appropriate?

8. How does volatility in the industry and/or different national environments affect the budget process?

Cross-National Studies of Participation in Budgeting

Much of the Anglo-American practice in budgeting assumes that the budget process is improved through the participation of the persons involved in carrying out the budget. If managers are permitted to participate in setting their own budget targets, they not only feel better about them (satisfaction) but also tend to perform better. This type of behavior was documented in a series of experiments by Brownell (1982), who suggested that for participation to work fully, managers must feel like insiders (i.e., that their participation will actually influence decisions and have some impact on the outcome). This concept of insider/outsider is described as "locus of control."

This concept of the value of participation in budgeting may be uniquely Anglo-American. It implies first that managers at all levels care that their opinions are sought and feel that they can make a contribution without retribution. Frucot and Shearon (1991), for example, conducted a study using Mexican managers to test this proposition.

Studies of Mexican Companies   Given that Mexico is a high power distance/low individualism culture, Frucot and Shearon (1991) anticipated that Mexican managers might not favor participation even given insider status (i.e., they would rather be dictated to).

Frucot and Shearon (1991) tested their hypotheses on a sample of 83 Mexican managers in both indigenous firms and subsidiaries of U.S. multinationals. The results were initially surprising. Overall, the performance of the Mexican managers in indigenous firms was related to participation and locus of control. Therefore, initially it appeared that there was no difference between the behavior of Mexican managers and typical U.S. managers.

Unlike U.S. managers, however, the insider/outsider dimension did not affect the satisfaction levels of Mexican managers (in indigenous firms). The managers of the firms studied initially appeared to be happier and motivated by a higher level of participation regardless of whether they saw themselves as running the show. However, when the sample of Mexican managers was divided by company rank, lower-level managers seemed to prefer a less participative style.

Of greatest concern to MNEs is that Mexican managers of entirely foreign-owned subsidiaries showed almost no desire to participate in the budgeting process.

Unlike their American counterparts, they regarded themselves as powerless and the process as alien. An American or, for that matter, a British firm, would receive a rude shock when it realized that its employees in Mexico had little commitment to the budget process and that they might well tell their managers merely what they expected them to hear.

Studies of APEC Multinationals   A similar series of experiments was conducted, comparing Australia (low power distance/high individualism) and Singapore (high power distance/low individualism). Harrison (1992) anticipated a significant international difference in the ability of budget participation to explain levels of satisfaction among managers. Coming from a relatively authoritarian culture, the Singaporeans were expected to dislike or perhaps feel uncomfortable with budget participation. Harrison hypothesized that Singaporeans would therefore prefer a lower level of participation than their Australian counterparts. In fact, there was no significant relationship between national origin and participation, interaction and satisfaction. Overall, both groups seemed to prefer a participative style of budgeting. Harrison therefore argues that budgetary participation universally enhances job satisfaction regardless of culture. It should be noted that Harrison makes no comments about performance, which after all is the objective of participation. Harrison does not attempt to stratify his sample as Frucot and Shearon (1991) did. We therefore do not know if Asian senior managers take a different perspective from those in the junior ranks, a key concept when one is trying to argue that the power structure affects the desire to participate. Overall, the research to date appears to indicate that some of the Western participative budgetary techniques are transferable, but one must be very careful at what level they are transferred.

Study of a Large Finnish MNE   Hassel and Cunningham (1996) studied the effects of participation in the budgeting process on the performance of the subsidiaries of a large Finnish MNE. They found that the extent to which information is exchanged between headquarters and subsidiary managers had a positive effect on the performance of domestic subsidiaries. However, the exchange of information had no effect on the performance of foreign subsidiaries. Hassel and Cunningham explain the results by suggesting that performance is enhanced at the domestic level because of shared culture, values, and a clear understanding of the economic environment between headquarters and the subsidiary. They suggest that for domestic subsidiaries the major advantage of communication throughout the budgeting process is the exchange of information about markets and technology. These findings are reasonable because headquarters operate in very different environments than their foreign subsidiaries. Therefore, the budgeting process is more than just a performance tool—it becomes a key element in the transfer of knowledge within a geographically and culturally dispersed MNE.

Other Issues in the Budgeting Process

The previous section discussed the role of participation in the budget process. Although this is certainly important, it is only one facet of the process. This section looks at other key variables such as how communication takes place (formal versus informal), the time frame for budgets (long versus short), and the objectives.

Research into the budget process as it unfolds in different countries has focused primarily on differences between Anglo-American and Asian cultural groups. More recently, research in this area, though continuing to focus on Asia, has switched to the ASEAN region in what has colloquially been referred to as the "Five Dragon" or "Mini Dragon" area. This area includes Hong Kong, Singapore, Taiwan, Malaysia, and possibly Thailand and Indonesia. Although this group is not monolithic in cultural structure, it is generally seen as sharing common Confucian values, which include long-term orientation and an unwillingness to "lose face." This Asian culture tends to be collectivist in that citizens of most countries in the group tend to subjugate individual rights to group needs and are moderate to high on the Power Distance scale.

U.S./Japan Comparisons   Some of the implications of these cultural differences appear in studies of the budgeting process which compare Asian and Anglo-American countries. Bailes and Assada (1991) compared the budgetary behavior of 80 U.S. and 256 Japanese listed companies. Their results indicated that more than 90 percent of companies in both countries prepared master budgets. However, they found that the process of arriving at this master budget varied. Among the points that are statistically significant are the following:

1. The average length of time spent preparing annual budgets was nearly 12 days longer for the American companies (69.72 days) than the Japanese companies.

2. As previously discussed, the primary budget objective arising from the Japanese process was increased sales volume or market share. From the U.S. companies, the primary budget objective was, overwhelmingly, ROI.

3. Division managers in American firms are more likely to participate in budget committee discussions and influence the budget committee than are their Japanese counterparts.

4. Japanese companies also tended to follow a bottom-up approach, where all levels participated in the planning, though much of the contribution was informal. Formal meetings tended to be infrequent and while managers' wishes were considered, they were less important in the process than group consensus.

5. Japanese managers are more likely to use budget variances to recognize problems on a timely basis and to use budgets to improve the next period's budget.

6. American managers are more likely to be evaluated by the budgets.

7. The bonus and salary of an American manager are much more likely to be influenced by budget performance than are those of Japanese managers.

These differences are very interesting. American managers tend to be more involved in the budgeting process, are evaluated by budgets, and are rewarded or penalized by budgets. Japanese managers tend to look at budget variances as a way to improve performance. Between the Americans and the Japanese, there is clearly a national difference in budgeting.

Ueno and Sekaran (1992) also compared U.S. and Japanese budgeting practices, framing their discussion more formally within Hofstede's cultural paradigm. Using a sample of controllers and other senior managers at manufacturing companies, they found several culturally predictable phenomena. As found in Bailes and Assada (1991), U.S. managers used more formal meetings, communication, and coordination in budget planning. Put in its cultural context, Ueno and Sekaran interpret this control process as the natural outcropping of individualism. Thus, the process of budgeting becomes one of drawing together the diverse and often conflicting interests that manifest themselves in an individualist society.

Some of the other budgetary trends found in Ueno and Sekaran also appear to have cultural roots. U.S. budget makers tended to create more "slack," which was ascribed to individuals trying to enhance their own power bases and self-esteem. This calculating behavior of creating slack, which in turn created comfortable goals and more easily achievable targets, was linked to the individualism dimension and the individual reward structure of most U.S. companies. Finally, as would be expected from a country high on the Confucian dimension, Japanese managers tended to care less about identifying controllability of items and tended to measure performance over a longer time horizon than U.S. managers. A few of the findings of Ueno and Sekaran (1992) run contrary to the view of Bailes and Assada (1991). Despite having a longer performance reward period, Japanese managers did not have an appreciably longer planning horizon than U.S. managers. One must remember, however, that much long-term planning takes place outside of the formal numeric atmosphere of a budget.

Budgetary and Planning Systems of APEC Multinationals   Harrison, McKinnon, Panchapakesan, and Leung (1994) examine the budgetary and planning systems of Australia and the United States, and then Singapore and Hong Kong. They drew on the national cultural dimensions of power distance, individualism, and Confucian dynamism to predict and explain differences in philosophies and approaches to organizational design, management planning, and control systems in Asian and Anglo-American countries. Data was gathered by survey questionnaires mailed to senior accounting and finance executives in 800 organizations.

The results of Harrison et al. (1994) were largely as predicted and, in general, provide support for the importance of national culture in influencing organizational design and management planning and control systems. In particular, the cultural values of Anglo-American society relative to East Asian society are associated with a greater emphasis on decentralization, and responsibility centers in organizational design and quantitative and analytical techniques in planning and control. By contrast, the cultural values of East Asian society are associated with a greater emphasis on long-term planning and on group-centered decision making.

Interaction of Culture and Geographic Distance   The studies referenced so far focus on cultural differences in budgeting practices. Hassel and Cunningham (2004) studied how the combination of culture and geographic distance, or *psychic distance*, influence the budgeting process. They found that when headquarters use budgets heavily as a control mechanism, subsidiaries that are culturally similar and geographically close to headquarters (low psychic distance) show stronger financial performance than subsidiaries that are culturally different and located far away from headquarters (high psychic distance). These findings suggest that budget controls work most effectively for those subsidiaries that are closer to the parent in psychic distance. However, the results are contrary to the traditional belief that MNEs should use budgets heavily to control far-flung subsidiaries. These findings are important because they suggest that cultural differences and geographical distance require more sophisticated evaluation techniques, some of which are discussed throughout the rest of this chapter.

CHALLENGES OF CONTROL IN THE GLOBAL FIRM

Planning and Budgeting Issues

Multinational corporations contend with an array of external factors, internal considerations, and other forces that influence budget policies, composition, and control. Budgeting in a global business environment calls for an enhanced level of coordination and communication through the company because of the variety of powerful components that affect organizational performance. Although multinationals need to be concerned about cultural differences and their impact on national budgeting practices, there are additional considerations in the budgeting process of these companies. Of particular importance is the impact of foreign exchange differences on cross-border operations.

Indeed, the major international issue surrounding the establishment of a budget for an MNE is to determine the currency in which the budget should be prepared: the local currency or the parent currency. For a Swiss MNE, for example, is it better to evaluate all its foreign operations in terms of the local currency results or the results translated into francs? This choice can be highly significant if major changes occur in the exchange rates. It is possible for a profit in local currency to become a loss in the parent company's currency, and vice versa. If a Swiss company's Mexican subsidiary earned a profit in pesos but a loss when translated into francs, should the subsidiary's performance be evaluated favorably or unfavorably? Most firms resolve this dilemma by considering the main purpose of the foreign operations. If it is to provide a return to parent company shareholders that maximizes their domestic purchasing power, then typically an "after-translation" basis is used. A "before-translation" basis is more likely to be used by a firm that truly considers itself a multinational firm seeking global optimization or one that leaves considerable autonomy to each foreign operation.

The foreign currency issue also raises the issue of controllability. Whether a currency rises or falls in value and by how much is clearly beyond the control of a single MNE or any one of its parts. Therefore, because proper performance evaluation should exclude the impact on results of events over which the unit or person had no control, one can argue that the before-translation basis is better than the after-translation basis. In the case of the Swiss-Mexican situation, if the peso profits become translated into franc losses, the Mexican manager should not be penalized for a result that is out of his or her control. On the other hand, if the Mexican manager is given the authority and responsibility to hedge against potential foreign exchange losses, then he or she could be evaluated in terms of translated profitability.

The value of establishing the budget in the local currency is that management operates in that currency, and the local currency is more indicative of the overall operating environment than the present currency would be. In addition, the exchange rate is something over which local management has no control, so it would be unwise to have a key uncontrollable item as part of the budgeting and evaluation process.

Conversely, it is often difficult for top management in the parent country to understand budgets generated in different currencies. This is especially true for a geographically diverse firm such as Coca-Cola, which might have budgets generated in 100 or more different currencies. Translating the budgets into the parent currency allows top management to consolidate the budgets into a firm-wide view of the coming year. Also, because top management has to report to shareholders in the parent currency, they might want the strategic business unit (SBU) or subsidiary management to think in terms of parent-country profitability as well.

There are three possible approaches to dealing with foreign exchange in the budgeting process as it relates to performance evaluation of managers:

1. Allow operating managers to enter into hedge contracts with corporate treasury so they can "contract away" their exposures, as discussed in Chapter 13.

2. Adjust the actual performance of the unit for variations in the real exchange rate after the end of the period.

3. Adjust performance plans in line with variations in the real exchange rate.

Ways to Bring Foreign Exchange into the Budgeting Process

Lessard and Lorange (1977) identify the different ways that firms can translate the budget from the local currency into the parent currency and then monitor actual performance (see Exhibit 14.4). Three different exchange rates are used in Exhibit 14.4. The first is the actual exchange rate that was in effect when the budget was established, the second is the rate that was projected at the time the budget was established in the local currency, and the third is the actual exchange rate that was in effect when the budgeted period actually takes place. The attractiveness of the first exchange rate is that it is an objective spot rate that actually exists on a given day. It is a reasonable rate to use in a stable environment, but it may be meaningless in an unstable foreign exchange environment. The projected rate is an attempt on the part of management to forecast what it thinks the exchange rate will be for the budgeted time period. For example, management might project in June 2005 that the exchange rate between the U.S. dollar and the British pound will be $1.8600 during December 2005, so that would be the projected exchange rate used in the budgeting process. The actual exchange rate found in cell E-3 is an update of the exchange rate that was in effect when the budget was established. It provides the actual exchange rate in effect when the time period takes place.

Exhibit 14.4   Possible Combinations of Exchange Rates in the Control Process

Rate Used for Relative Determining Budget ╲ Rate Used to Track Performance to Budget	Actual at Time of Budget	Projected at Time of Budget	Actual at End of Period
Actual at time of budget	A-1	A-2	A-3
Projected at time of budget	P-1	P-2	P-3
Actual at end of period (through updating)	E-1	E-2	E-3

Source: Donald R. Lessard and Peter Lorange, "Currency Changes and Management Control: Resolving the Centralization/Decentralization Dilemma," *Accounting Review* 52 (July 1977): 630.

These three exchange rates need to be considered for both the establishment of the budget and the monitoring of performance. In cells A-1, P-2, and E-3, the exchange rate used to establish the budget and monitor performance is the same, so any variances will be due to price and volume, not the exchange rate. The value of P-2 over A-1 and E-3 is that it forces management to think initially of what its performance will be if the forecast is reasonably accurate. A-1 never takes into account what the exchange rate will be, and it does not attempt to reconcile the budget from the original rate with that of the actual rate. Given the instability in exchange rates, however, some would argue that a forecast exchange rate is no more accurate than any other exchange rate. E-3 does take into consideration what performance is at the actual exchange rate, but it does not force management to be forward thinking during the budget process.

A-3 and P-3 result in a variance that is a function of operating results and exchange rate changes. Under A-3, the budget is established at the initial exchange rate, but actual performance is translated at the actual exchange rate. Thus, there is an exchange rate variance that is the difference between the original and the actual rate. P-3 results in a variance that is the difference between what management thought the exchange rate would be and what it actually was at the end of the operating period. If management's forecast was reasonably accurate, P-3 should result in a very small foreign exchange variance. If the exchange rate between the parent and local currency is relatively stable, A-3 should also result in a relatively small foreign exchange variance. However, it is important to realize that the use of A-3 and P-3 means that someone (usually local management) will be held accountable for exchange rate variances.

Demirag and De Fuentes (1999) surveyed U.K.-based MNEs to learn what combination of exchange rates they use to prepare the budget and evaluate foreign subsidiary performance. Their findings are summarized in Exhibit 14.5. Of the 51 MNEs, 10 firms used A-1, 19 used P-2, and none used E-3. Thirty-six firms used the forecast rate for setting the budget and/or monitoring actual results. Exhibit 14.5 shows that most of the MNEs preferred a forecasted rate to prepare the budget and to evaluate subsidiaries, which suggests that managers make an effort to think of what exchange rates will be during the budgeting process. No firms used the actual rate at the end of the budget period to prepare the budget, although this rate was one of the most commonly used for performance evaluation. Five firms used A-3

Exhibit 14.5 Exchange Rates Used by U.K. MNEs

Rate Used to Determine Budget ↓	Rate Used for Realized Performance			
	Actual at Time of Budget	Projected at Time of Budget	Actual at End of Period	Total
Actual at Time of Budget	A-1 10 Firms	A-2 0 Firms	A-3 5 Firms	15 Firms
Projected at Time of Budget	P-1 0 Firms	P-2 19 Firms	P-3 17 Firms	36 Firms
Actual at End of Period	E-1 0 Firms	E-2 0 Firms	E-3 0 Firms	0 Firms
Total	10 Firms	19 Firms	22 Firms	

Source: Adapted from Demirag and De Fuentes, "Exchange Rate Fluctuations and Management Control in UK-Based MNCs: An Examination of the Theory and Practice," *The European Journal of Finance* (1999): 3–28.

and 17 firms used P-3, which produce exchange rate variances. Demirag and De Fuentes (1999) reported that the majority of the time headquarters management was held responsible for exchange rate variances. Interestingly, Demirag and De Fuentes (1999) obtained the same results of an identical study performed over a decade earlier (Demirag, 1986). These findings suggest that in the last decade MNEs have not changed the way they use exchange rates to evaluate foreign subsidiaries and their managers.

A more complex example of a flexible budget that involves foreign exchange is provided in Exhibit 14.6. Assume that this budget is established in British pounds for the British subsidiary of a U.S. firm. The budget is established in pounds, but U.S. management wants the budget and actual performance translated into dollars for evaluative purposes. The local currency budget for March 2005 is established at a sale price of £150 per unit and a variable cost of £100 per unit. The actual selling price is £155 per unit, and the actual variable cost is £110 per unit. The budgeted volume is 6,000 units, and the actual number of units sold is 5,500.

The actual results in local currency are computed using the actual sales volume, actual sales price per unit and variable cost per unit, and actual fixed costs. The flexible budget is computed by using the actual units sold, the budgeted sales price per unit and variable cost per unit, and budgeted fixed costs. The static budget is computed by using the budgeted sales volume, the budgeted sales price per unit and variable cost per unit, and the budgeted fixed costs.

There are three important (hypothetical) exchange rates for this example:

$1.8123   The actual exchange rate on October 1, 2004, when the budget was established

$1.8604   The projected exchange rate for March 2005

$1.8590   The actual average exchange rate for March 2005

Following the budget and actual results in British pounds are the translated versions of the financial statement and variance analysis according to the approaches outlined in Exhibit 14.6: A-1, P-2, E-3, A-3, P-3.

For approaches A-1, P-2, and E-3, there are no exchange rate variances (column 7) because the same exchange rate is used to translate the budget and actual

Exhibit 14.6 The Flexible Budget—A Foreign Currency Analysis

	Budgeted	Actual
Sales Volume	6,000	5,500
Sales Price	150	155
Variable Cost	100	110
Fixed Costs	200,000	200,000

Exchange Rate Information

Actual at Time of Budget	$ 1.8123
Projected at Time of Budget	$ 1.8604
Actual at End of Period	$ 1.8590

Note:
F: Favorable Variance
U: Unfavorable Variance

	(1) Actual Results	(2) Flexible Budget	(3) Static Budget	(4) Flexible Budget Variances (1)–(2)	(5) Sales Volume Variance (2)–(3)	(6) Actual Results at Budget Rate	(7) Exchange Rate Variance (1)–(6)
Budget and Actual in Local Currency							
Units Sold	5,500	5,500	6,000	0	(500)	—	—
Sales Revenues	852,500	825,000	900,000	27,500	(75,000)	—	—
Variable Costs	605,000	550,000	600,000	55,000	(50,000)	—	—
Contribution Margin	247,500	275,000	300,000	(27,500)	(25,000)		
Fixed Costs	200,000	200,000	200,000	0	0		
Operating Income	47,500	75,000	100,000	(27,500) U	(25,000) U		
Budget and Actual Translated into Dollars (A-1)							
Units Sold	5,500	5,500	6,000	0	(500)	—	—
Sales Revenues	1,544,986	1,495,148	1,631,070	49,838	(135,923)	—	—
Variable Costs	1,096,442	996,765	1,087,380	99,677	(90,615)	—	—
Contribution Margin	448,544	498,383	543,690	(49,838)	(45,308)		
Fixed Costs	362,460	362,460	362,460	0	0		
Operating Income	86,084	135,923	181,230	(49,838) U	(45,308) U		

Budget and Actual Translated into Dollars (P-2)

Units Sold	5,500	5,500	6,000	0	(500)	—	—
Sales Revenues	1,585,991	1,534,830	1,674,360	51,161	(139,530)	—	—
Variable Costs	1,125,542	1,023,220	1,116,240	102,322	(93,020)	—	—
Contribution Margin	460,449	511,610	558,120	(51,161)	(46,510)	—	—
Fixed Costs	372,080	372,080	372,080	0	0	—	—
Operating Income	88,369	139,530	186,040	(51,161) U	(46,510) U	—	—

Budget and Actual Translated into Dollars (E-3)

Units Sold	5,500	5,500	6,000	0	(500)	—	—
Sales Revenues	1,584,798	1,533,675	1,673,100	51,123	(139,425)	—	—
Variable Costs	1,124,695	1,022,450	1,115,400	102,245	(92,950)	—	—
Contribution Margin	460,103	511,225	557,700	(51,123)	(46,475)	—	—
Fixed Costs	371,800	371,800	371,800	0	0	—	—
Operating Income	88,303	139,425	185,900	(51,123) U	(46,475) U	—	—

Budget and Actual Translated into Dollars (A-3)

Units Sold	5,500	5,500	6,000	0	(500)	5,500	—
Sales Revenues	1,584,798	1,495,148	1,631,070	89,650	(135,923)	1,544,986	—
Variable Costs	1,124,695	996,765	1,087,380	127,930	(90,615)	1,096,442	—
Contribution Margin	460,103	498,383	543,690	(38,280)	(45,308)	448,544	—
Fixed Costs	371,800	362,460	362,460	9,340	0	362,460	—
Operating Income	88,303	135,923	181,230	(47,620) U	(45,308) U	86,084	—

Budget and Actual Translated into Dollars (P-3)

Units Sold	5,500	5,500	6,000	0	(500)	5,500	0
Sales Revenues	1,584,798	1,534,830	1,674,360	49,968	(139,530)	1,585,991	39,812
Variable Costs	1,124,695	1,023,220	1,116,240	101,475	(93,020)	1,125,542	28,254
Contribution Margin	460,103	511,610	558,120	(51,508)	(46,510)	460,449	11,558
Fixed Costs	371,800	372,080	372,080	(280)	0	372,080	9,340
Operating Income	88,303	139,530	186,040	(51,228) U	(46,510) U	88,369	2,218 F

results. For A-1, the exchange rate is the actual rate at the time the budget is set ($1.8123). For P-2, the exchange rate is the projected rate at the time the budget is set ($1.8604). For E-3, the exchange rate is the actual rate at the end of the period ($1.8590). The only variances are the dollar equivalents of the price and volume variances that occur in the local currency. There are no results in column 6 since the exchange rate used for setting the budget and monitoring results is the same. Thus there is no exchange rate variance in column 7.

Under approach A-3, columns 2-6 are translated at the actual exchange rate in effect on October 1, 2004, when the budget was set. Column 1 is translated at the actual exchange rate for March 2005, so the exchange rate variance is the difference between the actual rate on October 1, 2004, and the actual exchange rate for March 2005. Note that column 6 under A-3 is the same as column 1 under A-1.

Under approach P-3, columns 2 through 6 are translated at the projected exchange rate, and column 1 is translated at the actual average exchange rate for March 2005. The exchange rate variance is the difference between the projected rate made at the time the budget was set and the actual exchange rate. Note that column 6 under P-3 is the same as column 1 under P-2. The exchange rate variance is smaller for P-3 than for A-3, because the projected rate used to translate the budget should more closely approximate the future actual exchange rate, thus resulting in a lower variance. However, that depends on how easy it is to forecast future spot rates and how stable/unstable the currency is.

Budgeting and Currency Practices

What do MNEs actually do? In the Robbins and Stobaugh study (1973), fewer than half the firms surveyed judged subsidiary performance in terms of translated dollar amounts, and only 12 percent used both standards. Morsicato (1980) found that a significant number of firms in her sample used both dollar and local currency budgets compared to actual profits and actual sales.

In his study of British subsidiaries of Japanese firms, Demirag (1994) noted that the "companies indicated that financial statements presented in sterling (local currency) provided them with better understanding of the performance of their companies' operations and their management. … None of the companies translated their profit budgets into yen for performance evaluation purposes … [and] none of the parent companies sent a copy of the translated yen statements." The parent currency financial statements were sent to Japan for translation into yen at a company fixed standard exchange rate. In essence, subsidiary managers were unaware of their performance in parent currency terms, which is different from Demirag's Survey of U.K.-based MNEs mentioned above.

Capital Budgeting

Capital budgeting is the longer-term relation of the operational budgeting discussed previously. However, many of the considerations discussed, particularly as they relate to economic exposure, continue to apply. As in short-term planning or budgeting, long-range planning or capital budgeting must take into consideration anticipated exchange rate movements for discounting cash flows. This becomes part of the risk factor involved in discounting future cash flows, along with any environmental uncertainty. Environmental uncertainty can be mild, such as the risk of unexpected heavier taxation, or severe, such as the risk of expropriation. In general, the risk effect is greater in less developed countries than in wealthier countries, but even in the latter, there are many adverse events that are unpredictable.

Because of the risks inherent in international capital budgeting, MNEs must use sophisticated techniques to forecast cash flows, assess risks, and determine the appropriate discount rate to arrive at the net present value (NPV) of an investment option. Hasan et al. (1997) analyzed the factors that lead foreign subsidiaries of U.S. MNEs to use sophisticated capital budgeting techniques. They found that subsidiaries that were majority owned by the parent company were more likely to use NPV, APV, or IRR to make investment decisions. Subsidiaries that were large, publicly traded, and had been in business for several years tended to use complex methods such as the weighted average cost of capital (WACC) to determine the discount rate.

These findings suggest that MNEs recognize the complexities and risks of investing in foreign markets and require their subsidiaries to adjust for country-specific factors and risks and to use the best tools available to make capital budgeting decisions. At the same time, the use of these techniques presents several issues in evaluating the performance of long-term investments of subsidiaries. For example, should managers in more volatile environments be evaluated in the same way as those in more stable environments for capital budgeting performance? What is the best performance basis in each situation?

Whether or not standardized reporting practices are used in a multinational company, there is a real issue as to whether foreign operations and their managers can be evaluated on a global basis or merely on a national basis. It was noted earlier that comparing ROI is a primary method used to evaluate both individual operations and individual managers on a standardized or global basis. But can effective decisions be arrived at in this manner? Sometimes, when environmental factors are used in long-term strategic decisions, the outcome may appear to be at odds with the quest for strong ROIs on a year-to-year basis. Therefore, capital budgeting may require even more judgment than operational budgeting.

INTRACORPORATE TRANSFER PRICING

One of the additional elements of management of the multinational is intracorporate transfer pricing. This refers to the pricing of goods and services that are transferred (bought and sold) between members of a corporate family—for example, parent to subsidiaries, between subsidiaries, from subsidiaries to parent, and so on. As such, internal transfers include raw materials, semifinished and finished goods, allocation of fixed costs, loans, fees, royalties for use of trademarks, copyrights, and other factors. In theory, such prices should be based on production costs, but in reality often they are not.

MNEs have internal and external motivations to establish transfer prices (Eden, 2001). Internal motivations include maximizing performance, financial efficiencies, and performance incentives for managers of different subsidiaries. External motivations stem from tax laws in the various countries in which the MNE oper-

Exhibit 14.7 Factors Shaping MNE Transfer Pricing Policies

Factors shaping MNE transfer pricing policies	Percent of Respondents Who Identify Factor as:											
	Main Priority			Important But Not Main Priority			Not Very Important			Not Important at All		
	1999		1997	1999		1997	1999		1997	1999		1997
	Parents	Subs		Parents	Subs		Parents	Subs		Parents	Subs	
Internal motivations												
Maximizing operating performance	40	42	45	33	32	29	19	14	22	8	8	4
Financial efficiencies	25	25	24	45	42	48	22	24	48	8	6	6
Performance incentives	12	15	11	27	26	27	39	37	44	22	18	18
External (tax-related) motivations												
Optimizing tax arrangements	23	23	25	45	51	51	25	16	20	7	7	4
Documentation in preparation for transfer pricing audit	35	52	25	38	29	48	20	14	21	7	1	6

Sources: Ernst and Young (1994; 14; 1997; 10).
Eden, Lorraine. "International Taxation, Transfer Pricing, and the Multinational Enterprise", *Oxford Handbook of International Business* (London, UK, 2001), p. 595.

ates. A 1999 Ernst & Young survey of over 500 finance and tax officials for several MNEs revealed their main motivations for establishing transfer prices. Exhibit 14.7 shows the results of the survey compared to a similar survey in 1997. Notice that the 1999 survey breaks down MNEs by parent and subsidiary, while the 1997 survey shows results for the MNE as a whole.

Exhibit 14.7 shows that maximizing operating performance was the main internal reason for establishing transfer prices for 40 percent of parents and 42 percent of subsidiaries in 1999. The next most important internal motivation was obtaining financial efficiencies (25 percent of parents and subsidiaries). The least important internal reason was to establish performance incentives.

The main external motivation was to prepare documentation for a transfer price audit, followed by optimizing tax arrangements. In fact, in 2003, 86 percent of parents and 93 percent of subsidiaries identified transfer pricing as the most important international tax issue they currently face (Ernst & Young 2003).

In practice, internal transfers are often priced at higher than market to lower the income of a subsidiary, which reduces the local tax burden. Conversely, companies may underprice goods sold to foreign affiliates, and the affiliates can then sell them at prices that their local competitors cannot match. If tough antidumping laws exist on final products, a company can underprice components and semifinished products to its affiliates. The affiliates can then assemble or finish the final product at prices that would have been classified as dumping prices had they been imported directly into the country rather than produced domestically.

High transfer prices might be used to circumvent or significantly lessen the impact of national controls. A government prohibition on dividend remittances could restrict a firm's ability to maneuver income out of a country. However, overpricing the goods shipped to a subsidiary in such a country would make it possible for funds to be taken out. High transfer prices are also of considerable value to a firm when it is paid a subsidy or earns a tax credit on the value of goods it exports. The higher the transfer prices on exported goods, the greater the subsidies earned or tax credit received.

High transfer prices on goods shipped to subsidiaries might be desirable when a parent wishes to lower the apparent profitability of its subsidiary. This might be desirable because of the demands of the subsidiary's workers for higher wages or greater participation in company profits; because of political pressures to expropriate high-profit, foreign-owned operations; or because of the possibility that new competitors might be lured into the industry by high profits. There might also be inducements for having high-priced transfers go to the subsidiary when a local partner is involved, the inducement being that the increase in the parent company profits will not have to be split with the local partner. High transfer prices may also be desired when increases from existing price controls in the subsidiary's country are based on product costs (including high transfer prices for purchases).

The pricing decisions just described illustrate the dilemma faced by MNEs between complying with tax laws, which try to maximize revenue collection in each country, and trying to maximize their own profits. This dilemma leads to the possibility of *transfer pricing manipulation*, "the over or under-invoicing of related party transactions in order to avoid government regulations" (Eden, 2001).

In response to transfer pricing manipulation, national tax authorities have adopted the *arm's length standard (ALS)*, which requires transfer prices to be set "as if the transactions had taken place between unrelated parties acting at arm's length in competitive markets" (Eden, Dacin, and Wan, 2001). Although this appears simple, many times there are no competitive markets for the products transferred within MNEs. For example, certain raw materials that are extracted by one division and then sold to another division may not be sold in the open market. In this case, establishing an arm's length price for the raw material is complicated. For this and other reasons, MNEs are increasingly being audited by local governments.

It is clear that the internal motivations for transfer pricing are very different from the external motivations. One possible solution to this discrepancy is to use two sets of prices: one for performance evaluation and motivation purposes (internal), and one to comply with ALS requirements. Baldenius, Melumad, and Reichelstein (2004) report that this practice is becoming more common among MNEs.

The issue of transfer pricing manipulation introduces an ethical dilemma for MNE managers, who must balance their profit-maximizing goals with compliance with laws and regulations. Transfer prices can be used in legal ways to enhance performance and motivate subsidiary managers. At the same time, they can be used illegally. Although some transfer pricing practices are clearly regulated by local laws, others may not be clearly defined. Managers must be careful when dealing with the "gray" areas in transfer pricing. For example, DHL, the U.S.-based air courier business, was fined roughly $60 million in 1998 by U.S. tax authorities for inappropriate transfer pricing of intangible assets (Przysuski et al., 2003).

Transfer pricing will continue to be a complex issue because of the dilemma described above. Eden (2001) points out three trends that will play a major role in transfer pricing in the coming years:

- *Globalization:* As MNEs increase in spread and mobility, transfer prices become more pervasive and complicated to regulate.

- *Regionalization:* As trading agreements such as NAFTA, Mercosur, and the EU become more prevalent, authorities within those jurisdictions must come to agreements on taxing issues so as to minimize cross-national conflicts.

- *The Internet:* The Internet allows trading between geographically dispersed buyers and sellers in an electronic context in which no taxing authority exists. Regulators will have to figure out the new issues brought up by internet transfers.

Matching Price to Market Conditions

The conditions that firms use to establish a particular transfer pricing strategy are summarized in Exhibit 14.8. The maximum advantage would be gained when all these conditions line up on a country basis. For example, the parent operates from a country whose characteristics call for high transfer prices coming in and low transfer prices going out, while the conditions of the subsidiary's country call for the opposite.

Consider the left column of Exhibit 14.8. If the parent sells at low prices to the subsidiary and buys from it at high prices, income is shifted to the subsidiary, less-

Exhibit 14.8   Conditions in Subsidiary's Country Inducing High and Low Transfer Prices on Flows Between Affiliates and Parent

Conditions in Subsidiary's Country Inducing *Low Transfer Prices* on Flows from Parent and *High Transfer Prices* on Flows to Parent	Conditions in Subsidiary's Country Inducing *High Transfer Prices* on Flows from Parent and *Low Transfer Prices* on Flows to Parent
High ad valorem tariffs	Local partners
Corporate income tax rate lower than in parent's country	Pressure from workers to obtain greater share of company profit
Significant competition	Political pressure to nationalize or expropriate high-profit foreign firms
Local loans based on financial appearance of subsidiary	Restrictions on profit or dividend remittances
Export subsidy or tax credit on value of exports	Political instability
Lower inflation rate than in parent's country	Substantial tie-in sales agreements
Restrictions (ceilings) in subsidiary's country on the *value* of products that can be imported	Price of final product controlled by government but based on production cost
	Desire to mask profitability of subsidiary operations to keep competitors out

Source: Jeffrey S. Arpan, *Intracorporate Pricing: Non-American Systems and Views* (New York: Praeger, 1972).

ening the overall tax burden. At the same time, the impact of a high ad valorem tariff in the other country is lessened. In addition, the impact of foreign exchange rationing on imports from the parent and dividend payments to the parent are lessened, the subsidiary's ability to penetrate its local market is enhanced, the parent is less affected by its government's restrictions on capital outflows, and so on.

Under this set of conditions, the subsidiary country gains somewhat more than the parent country: more funds, more taxable income, greater economic growth of the subsidiary, and more export revenues. It loses somewhat in other areas, however, as local competitors may suffer adversely, have lower profits, pay less taxes, and lay off workers if the foreign subsidiary actively pursues a market penetration strategy. The government pays greater subsidies or gives more tax credits because of the subsidiary's artificially high value of exports and, like the government of the other country, its national control is lessened. Unfortunately for firms, conditions seldom line up as nicely from their standpoint as either column of Exhibit 14.8 depicts. It is far more likely that a country will simultaneously experience conditions from both sides of the table. Thus, it is difficult to determine whether the firm will receive a net benefit from high or low transfer prices.

Allocation of Overhead

As with transfer pricing of goods, the allocation of overhead has national and cross-national implications. On the cross-national side, firms must determine what to do with corporate overhead. For example, IBM's world headquarters is located in New

York, but its operations are located worldwide. How does IBM allocate those costs to its operations in different countries, and what are the tax implications of this issue? This becomes a real issue for performance evaluation because the allocation of corporate overhead directly reduces operating profit, which reduces return on invested capital, potentially pushing that return below the company's cost of capital. On the purely national side, companies struggle with the general concept of allocating overhead and the ways that affects product costs.

Cross-Border Allocation of Expenses

If it were not for differences in tax rates worldwide, companies could allocate corporate overhead based on sales revenues in each subsidiary or on some other basis. However, different tax rates complicate the situation. For companies headquartered in high-tax countries, there is an incentive to charge as many expenses as possible against parent company income. However, this practice tends to overstate expenses, understate income, and understate taxes in the parent country.

In the United States, for example, the Internal Revenue Service (IRS) allocates and apportions all of a firm's expenses, losses, and other deductions to specific sources of income (sales, royalties, dividends) and then apportions the expenses between domestic and foreign source income. The IRS provides specific guidelines on how to allocate expenses between domestic and foreign source income.

The problem with using tax law to allocate overhead is that it likely eliminates any possibility for the firm to select an allocation basis that is consistent with its manufacturing strategy. When tax implications are ignored, overhead is allocated differently. The Japanese, for example, have established a direct link between allocating overhead and corporate goals.

As Hiromoto (1988) shows, Japanese managers are less concerned about how allocation techniques measure costs than they are about how the allocation techniques motivate employees to drive down costs. An example involves Hitachi, the Japanese electronics firm. In one highly automated plant, the Hitachi cost accounting system allocates overhead based on direct labor hours, which does not seem to make sense in a highly automated environment. However, Hitachi management is trying to reduce direct labor as a way to reduce cost, so allocating overhead based on direct labor encourages management to automate faster.

Another important aspect of overhead we have learned from the Japanese is that overhead cannot be reduced over the long run by simply cutting costs; the entire manufacturing process needs to be redesigned. Blaxill and Hout (1991) point out that as automation and organizational complexity increase—a real problem for MNEs—so, too, does overhead. However, MNEs find that they have to struggle to pick up or maintain market share against global competitors. In addition, the high-tech companies have to devote more and more of their scarce resources to R&D, so there is pressure on management to react. The reaction usually comes in one of two ways: prices are dropped and costs are cut, or the firm gets out of certain product lines and develops a niche. What we have learned from the Japanese is that companies can lower overhead permanently and remain competitive only if they design controllable and highly integrated manufacturing processes.

PERFORMANCE EVALUATION ISSUES

Budgets, both long and short term, are in essence plans. Transfer prices and target costing can affect prices. In the end these plans must be implemented. With the help of these techniques, whether singly or as a combined plan, managers must perform if the firm is to survive. The performance of those carrying out the plan thus needs to be measured and rewarded. Properly measuring the performance of an individual, a division, or even a company as a whole is never simple or easy. One reason for this is that different bases of measurement result in different measures of performance. Moreover, the individual or unit being evaluated does not control many events affecting performance. Strategic differences in subsidiaries may also result in different performance evaluation measures.

For example, Gupta and Govindarajan (1991) identify several issues surrounding performance evaluation that are complex in the global environment. Subsidiaries can be global innovators, integrated players, implementers, or local innovators, as explained in Chapter 12. Global innovators and integrated players tend to be high transferors of knowledge to other units. Gupta and Govindarajan propose that units that are global innovators and integrated players need performance evaluation systems that are relatively flexible compared with the other two groups. They tend to rely more on behavioral controls (i.e., those involving surveillance of the manager's decisions and actions) and less on output controls (i.e., end results of performance) than do the other two groups. Global innovators also tend to need more autonomy than do implementers, with integrated players and local innovators somewhere in between. In addition, Gupta and Govindarajan propose that global innovators tend to rely more on internal control of their performance than on external control—the control of powerful others, luck, and so on. These major differences in the strategic objectives of subsidiaries can obviously influence performance evaluation dramatically.

A variety of events that affect performance evaluation are out of the control of managers or subsidiaries. First, let us consider the basis of measurement. There are many possible criteria against which to judge performance. Furthermore, no single basis is equally appropriate for all units of an MNE. For example, a production unit is more appropriately evaluated on cost reduction, quality control, meeting shipment targets (dates and quantities), and other measures of efficiency. For a sales subsidiary, however, these measures are less appropriate (if appropriate at all) than such measures as market share, number of new customers, or other measures of effectiveness. Similarly, profitability may be appropriate for a subsidiary that is a true profit center but inappropriate for a subsidiary in a high-tax rate country that, for global tax minimization purposes, is instructed to minimize profits or even maximize losses. These situations suggest the desirability and advisability of using multiple bases for performance measurement—that is, different ones for different kinds of operations in different countries. Yet even multiple measures have their problems. First, it is more difficult to compare the performance of different units measured under different criteria. Second, it is more expensive to set up and operate a multiple-criteria system. Thus, the decision must be based on a cost-benefit analysis. This idea of using different measures for different country environments is consistent with the multidomestic approach to strategy discussed in Chapter 12. However, as Borkowski (1999) points out, if the main goal of a firm is to maximize shareholder wealth, using the same performance criteria allows a firm to keep that main goal in mind and act consistently to achieve it. Borkowski's argument is consistent with the global approach to strategy discussed in Chapter 12.

Complicating matters even more are the interdependencies of an MNE's operations. For example, a multinational automobile company may produce its steel in Japan, have it stamped in the United States, have its tires made in Canada, its axles in Mexico, its engines in Germany, and its radios in Taiwan, all for final assembly in the United States. If any one part of its far-flung operations experiences performance problems, that operation's problems will spread to the other operations. Thus, a dock strike in Germany could affect the performance of the German subsidiary, the U.S. assembly plant, and all sales subsidiaries worldwide. Proper performance evaluation would have to eliminate these uncontrollable impacts for the interdependent subsidiaries as well as for the German subsidiary. Furthermore, if other than arm's length transfer prices were used on any of the intercorporate sales, the reported results would not be within the control of either the selling or buying subsidiary (unless they both agreed to the transfer price), and, in any case, would not reflect real performance.

Properly Relating Evaluation to Performance

One of the more curious aspects of empirical studies discussed earlier in the chapter was the finding that multinationals from Western countries especially rely on ROI as the major or one of the most important measures of performance. Where intercorporate transfers are significant and are not at arm's length prices, the ROI income numerator is highly arbitrary and, in one sense, fictitious. Also, a subsidiary manager whose evaluation is based on ROI may choose to borrow heavily in the local currency. This in turn affects the borrowing capacity of the entire firm and potentially the price of its stock and possibly subjecting the parent's consolidated financial statements to significant foreign currency losses if the borrowings are in hard currencies. Perhaps most important, ROI is not appropriate for some foreign operations, such as subsidiaries producing only for other subsidiaries, sales subsidiaries buying all their products from other subsidiaries, or subsidiaries striving to break into highly competitive, low-margin markets. The problems related to using ROI as a standard measure of performance apply to other measures as well.

The need for standardization brings us back to the one method of performance evaluation that can meet most criteria without undue limitations: the comparison of performance with plan. This method permits each affiliate to be judged on its own, according to the plan it was given, and can be used to compare subsidiary performances. However, it is a reasonable basis of performance measurement only if the original plans were logical and reasonable. Therein lies one danger of the comparison to plan technique. The other danger is that subsidiary managers' inputs to the plan may be tempered by their desire to surpass the plan's expectations. For example, they might deliberately project a bleak picture. However, if the planning and budget process is sufficiently deliberative, participative, iterative, and honest, both of these dangers can be minimized.

ECONOMIC VALUE ADDED

One tool that companies are using to measure performance is economic value added (EVA), something economists call economic profit. Basically, EVA is after-tax operating profit minus the total annual cost of capital. It is a measure of the value added or depleted from shareholder value in one period. A positive EVA requires that a company earn a return on its assets that exceeds the cost of debt and equity, thus adding to shareholder value. EVA is an actual monetary amount of value added, and it measures changes in value for a period. EVA is also used primarily for performance evaluation and compensation rather than for capital budgeting purposes. EVA is calculated as follows:

ROIC *Return on invested capital:* operating profit minus cash taxes paid divided by average invested capital

WACC *Weighted average cost of capital:* (net cost of debt × % debt used) + (net cost of equity × % equity used)

AIC *Average invested capital:* Average stockholders equity + average debt

$$EVA = [ROIC - WACC] \times AIC$$

As an example of EVA, assume the following data:

Total revenues	$6,500 (million)
Total costs	4,000
Total operating expenses	1,800
Cash taxes paid	230
Stockholders' equity (Average)	1,500
Debt (Average)	2,370
After-tax cost of debt	5.5%
% debt used	40%
Cost of equity	15%
% equity used	60%

Operating profit = 6500 − 4000 − 1800 − 230 = 470

$$AIC = 1,500 + 2,370 = 3,870$$
$$ROIC = 470/3870 = 12.1\%$$
$$WACC = (5.5\% \times 0.40) + (15\% \times 0.60) = 11.2\%$$
$$EVA = (12.1\% - 11.2\%) \times 3870 = 34.83$$

Although EVA is not a large number in this example, ROIC is greater than Cost of Capital, so the company is adding to shareholder value. As former Coca-Cola CEO Roberto Goizueta noted, "we raise capital to make concentrate, and sell it at an operating profit. Then we pay the cost of that capital. Shareholders pocket the dif-

Exhibit 14.9   Economic Value-Added (EVA) Statement—Infosys

Economic value-added measures the profitability of a company after taking into account the cost of all capital including equity. It is the post-tax return on capital employed (adjusted for the tax shield on debt) minus the cost of capital employed. It is those companies which earn higher returns than cost of capital that create value. Those companies which earn lower returns than cost of capital are deemed destroyers of shareholder value.

Economic Value-Added Analysis

Year ended March 31,	2004	2003	2002	2001	2000
1. Average capital employed (in Rs. crore)	3,124.82	2,493.40	1,734.97	1,111.47	703.87
2. Average debt/total capital (%)	–	–	–	–	–
3. Beta variant	1.27	1.57	1.41	1.54	1.48
4. Risk-free debt cost (%)	5.20	6.00	7.30	10.30	10.45
5. Market premium	7.00	7.00	7.00	7.00	8.00
6. Cost of equity (%)	14.09	16.99	17.17	21.08	22.29
7. Cost of debt (post tax) (%)	NA	NA	NA	NA	NA
8. Weighted average cost of capital: (WACC) (%)	14.09	16.99	17.17	21.08	22.29
9. PAT as a percentage of average capital employed (%)[a]	39.80	38.29	46.57	56.08	40.63
10. Economic Value-Added (EVA) (Rs. in crore) Operating-profit (PBT excluding extraordinary income)	1,357.46	1,079.28	943.39	696.03	325.65
Less: tax	227.54	201.00	135.43	72.71	39.70
Less: cost of capital	440.29	423.63	297.90	234.30	156.89
Economic value-added	689.63	454.65	510.06	389.02	129.06
11. Enterprise value (Rs. in crore) Market value of equity	32,908.69	26,847.33	24,654.33	26,926.35	59,338.17
Less: Cash and cash equivalents[b]	2,872.77	1,684.30	1,026.96	577.74	508.37
Add: debt	–	–	–	–	–
Enterprise value	30,035.92	25,163.03	23,627.37	26,348.61	58,829.80
12. Ratios EVA as a percentage of average capital employed (%)	22.07	18.23	29.40	35.00	18.34
Enterprise value/average capital employed	9.61	10.09	13.62	23.71	83.58

Notes:

1. The cost of equity is calculated by using the following formula:
   return on risk-free investment + expected risk premium on equity investment adjusted for the variant for Infosys in India.

2. Till last year, the average beta variant for software stocks in the U.S. was used in the above calculation.

3. The figures above are based on consolidated Indian GAAP financial statements.

[a] PAT = Profit After Tax

[b] Includes investment in liquid mutual funds.

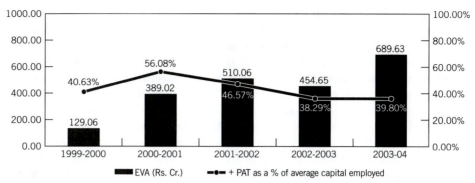

Exhibit 14.9 *(continued)*

ference." Some companies now disclose EVA in their annual reports—an interesting example is given by Infosys Technologies from India (see Exhibit 14.9).

As noted in its statement, Infosys computes EVA on its consolidated financial statements according to Indian GAAP. Since Infosys has operations outside of India, it has to make sure that financial information has first been converted back to Indian GAAP, and then it must translate foreign currency information into Indian rupee. Differences in accounting standards as well as changing currency values can influence the EVA computations. Besides these differences in accounting practices, globalization also affects the inputs required to compute EVA. Managers must consider the risks inherent to international investing to obtain the appropriate costs of debt and equity. For example, the cost of equity must be adjusted for country-specific risks to reflect the true cost of investing in that country. For all these reasons, accurately obtaining the EVA for an MNE requires a clear understanding of the several markets in which the firm operates.

THE BALANCED SCORECARD

The concept of the Balanced Scorecard (BSC) is another approach to performance measurement increasingly being used by companies, especially in the United States and Europe. Approximately 50 percent of Fortune 1,000 companies in North America and about 40 percent in Europe use a version of the BSC, according to a recent survey by Bain & Co. (Gumbus and Lyons, 2002). This approach endeavors to more closely link the strategic and financial perspectives of a business. Developed by Kaplan and Norton (1992), this approach takes a broader view of business performance. The Balanced Scorecard provides a framework to look at the strategies giving rise to value creation from the following perspectives:

1. *Financial*—growth, profitability, and risk from the perspective of shareholders
2. *Customer*—value and differentiation from the customer perspective
3. *Internal business processes*—the priorities for various business processes that create customer and shareholder satisfaction
4. *Learning and growth*—the priorities to create a climate supporting organizational change, innovation, and growth.

Although the focus is still ultimately on financial performance, the balanced score-card approach reveals the drivers of long-term competitive performance. In simple terms, learning and growth help create more efficient business processes, which create value for customers, who reward the firm financially. The challenge is to clearly identify these drivers, to agree on relevant measures, and to implement the new system at all levels of the organization. The significant aspect about this measurement approach, however, is that it also creates a focus for the future because the measures used communicate to managers what is important.

Although a firm's BSC is a proprietary strategic tool and is generally not available to the general public, its principles are evident in the strategic decisions made by MNEs. IKEA, the Swedish firm, is a case in point. With strong roots in the Swedish culture and a centralized operating style, IKEA has grown to become the world's largest furniture retailer. The company uses a global strategy, as discussed in Chapter 12, to spread a simple concept: to offer the broadest range of furniture at the lowest price possible. IKEA's success begins with internal learning and growth

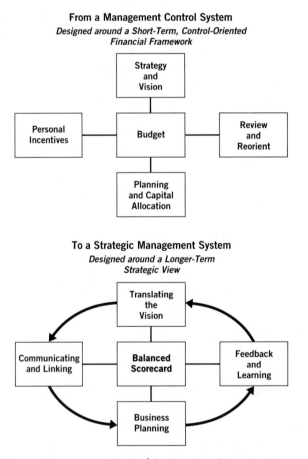

Figure 14.1   From a Management Control System to a Strategic Management System

Source: Kaplan and Norton. 2001. *The Strategy Focused Organization.* Cambridge, MA: Harvard Business School Press.

by insuring that all employees are trained in the cost-saving, hands-on, customer-focused mentality. This enables employees to focus on creating efficient processes that keep costs down. For example, the design team is constantly looking for new materials and suppliers to lower the cost of furniture without sacrificing quality. Since its founding, IKEA identified a customer base that would find value in low-cost, innovative furniture: young couples looking to furnish their first apartment. This strategic cohesiveness has rewarded the company with phenomenal growth. In 2004, IKEA operated 200 stores in 30 countries, with sales of $13.6 billion.

Although the BSC offers the advantages of logically connecting financial performance with its nonfinancial drivers, establishing a coherent scorecard for an MNE has its challenges. For example, as IKEA grows, it faces different customer bases in different countries. IKEA must also ensure that its streamlined product line has appeal in its several markets of operation. The cultural, geographical, and financial complexity of an MNE makes it challenging to establish a set of interrelated, cause-and-effect performance measures. This task appears simpler for MNEs with global strategies like IKEA. However, multidomestic MNEs such as Philips, the Dutch electronics company, have successfully implemented the BSC concept.

Perhaps the Balanced Scorecard helps solve many of the control and evaluation dilemmas presented throughout this chapter. Adequate use of the BSC helps managers avoid using only one measure of performance (such as ROI or sales growth), and forces them to link financial measures with the nonfinancial factors that drive them. In addition, subsidiaries are evaluated based on a coherent set of performance bases instead of just one base that may or may not be directly controlled by that subsidiary. Thus, Kaplan and Norton (2001) have refined the BSC concept into a strategic management system that replaces the traditional focus on the budget as the center for the management process (Figure 14.1).

SUMMARY

1.   The strategic control process for MNEs begins with a clear understanding of the strategy of the firm and its subsidiaries.

2.   The role of the management accountant in the strategic planning process is to identify the criteria for performance and to monitor achievements against these criteria.

3.   Several studies have been conducted on the performance evaluation measures of global companies. They tend to conclude that MNEs use multiple measures to evaluate performance, but budgets and ROI are especially popular forms of evaluation.

4.   Major differences in preferred performance measures exist from one country to another. For example, U.S. managers prefer ROI, whereas Japanese managers prefer sales.

5.   The budgeting process for MNEs is complex and is affected by differences in culture, economic systems, and the role of each subsidiary.

6.   It is important to determine whether performance evaluation measures should be developed in the local currency or the parent currency. The local currency is fairer to the local manager, but the parent currency is important because top management needs to answer to shareholders based on parent currency performance.

7. In establishing the budget and monitoring performance, management can use the exchange rate in effect when the budget was established, a projected exchange rate, or the exchange rate in effect when actual performance has occurred.

8. In using the rates just described, management can use the same rates for the establishment of the budget and for performance evaluation or use different rates for budgeting and evaluation. However, using the same rates for both processes is recommended.

9. Capital budgeting is the long-term aspect of the budgeting process.

10. Highly integrated MNE operations create problems for foreign subsidiaries because of transfer pricing problems.

11. Transfer prices are used by management to reduce taxes and costs, lessen the impact of national laws and tariffs, and motivate managers.

12. Cross-border costing and allocation of overhead are complicated for MNEs because headquarters must consider the laws, taxes, and different purposes of its subsidiaries.

13. MNEs must use the appropriate base of measurement to evaluate the performance of managers and subsidiaries. A good base of measurement is one over which the manager or subsidiary has direct control.

14. Economic Value Added, or EVA, is a financial performance measurement tool that helps companies know if they are covering their cost of capital.

15. The Balanced Scorecard (BSC) approach to performance evaluation was designed to go beyond traditional financial measures. Specifically, the BSC measures performance from four perspectives: financial, customer, internal business process, and learning and growth.

Discussion Questions

1. How can management accounting play a role in the strategic planning process?

2. What are some of the national similarities and differences in performance evaluation techniques?

3. MNEs often transfer their domestic performance evaluation systems into the international environment. Why is that the case? Are there any advantages to this practice? What problems could they encounter by using the same system?

4. Some argue that participation by managers at all levels in the budgeting process helps motivate managers to perform better. Others argue that participation does not necessarily improve performance; instead, its primary benefit is the exchange of information about changes in markets and technology throughout the firm. Which position do you support? Why?

5. Should the local currency or the parent currency be used to establish the budget? Justify your answer.

6. Should the local currency or the parent currency be used for performance evaluation? Justify your answer.

7. Which of the methods for setting the budget and monitoring performance as discussed by Lessard and Lorange eliminate the impact of foreign exchange variances? Which of those approaches would you prefer to use and why?

8. Who should be held responsible for foreign exchange fluctuations? Would your answer be different if an exchange loss occurred even after hedging for exchange risk? Justify your answer.

9. What added challenges do MNEs face in determining the cash flows and discount rates for capital budgeting purposes? (*Hint:* what are the extra risks faced by MNEs overseas?)

10. MNEs use transfer prices to circumvent local laws to obtain a favorable position for the firm. For example, high transfer prices from headquarters to a foreign division may be used to lower the tax burden of the subsidiary. In your opinion, is this ethical? Why or why not?

11. Explain why MNEs don't use the same base to allocate overhead across all subsidiaries.

12. What is the main consideration when choosing a base of measurement to evaluate the performance of a division or manager?

13. Most companies use the same reports to evaluate the performance of the subsidiary and of subsidiary management. Do you agree with this approach? Justify your answer.

14. What does EVA measure? How is it different from ROI? In your own words, explain why a positive EVA increases shareholder value.

15. How can the Balanced Scorecard (BSC) help MNEs establish a set of adequate performance measurement criteria for the entire company, its subsidiaries, and subsidiary managers?

Exercises

1. The following table shows performance measures for a Korean subsidiary of a large Dutch MNE:

Performance Measure	2005			2006		
	Budgeted	Actual	% Difference	Budgeted	Actual	% Difference
Sales Revenue	$ 1,500,000	$ 1,600,000	6.67%	$ 1,700,000	$ 1,650,000	−2.94%
Variable Costs	700,000	750,000	7.14%	800,000	800,000	0.00%
Fixed Costs	500,000	500,000	0.00%	530,000	530,000	0.00%
Income Tax Expense	90,000	175,000	94.44%	185,000	128,000	−30.81%
Net Income	$ 210,000	$ 175,000	−16.67%	$ 185,000	$ 192,000	3.78%
Market Share %	35.00%	39.00%	4.00%	40.00%	41.00%	1.00%
Return on Investment (ROI)	11.00%	10.00%	−9.09%	10.50%	11.50%	9.52%

In addition, you know the following facts:

- The Korean subsidiary receives finished goods from an Indian subsidiary. The transfer price is negotiated between the Korean and Indian subsidiary. The Korean subsidiary sells the goods in its home country and other neighboring countries.

- The budget is prepared by the Dutch parent company based on past performance and corporate earnings targets.

- The budgeted tax rate for 2005 was 30 percent. However, new legislation increased the tax rate to 50 percent for 2005. Thus, the budgeted tax rate for 2006 was 50 percent. The actual tax rate for 2006 was 40 percent.

- The parent company evaluates all subsidiaries based on ROI. ROI is calculated based on the price paid for the subsidiary and yearly net income.

Based on this information, answer the following questions:

a. Do you agree with headquarters' use of ROI to evaluate its Korean subsidiary? Why?

b. If not ROI, which performance base should be used to evaluate the Korean subsidiary? Why?

c. Based on your answer to the previous question, would you give the subsidiary a good or bad evaluation in 2005? How about in 2006?

d. If the Korean subsidiary prepared its own budget, would you use a different base? What if it also manufactured its own finished goods?

2. Consider the different performance evaluation criteria listed in the table in Exercise 1.

a. If the parent company in Exercise 1 were Anglo-American, which would most likely be the preferred measure used to evaluate its Korean subsidiary?

b. What if the parent were based in Japan?

c. What do these preferences reveal about the management style and orientation of these different cultures?

3. Lucas Inc. is the Mexican subsidiary of a U.S.-based multinational. In December 2004, it established the following budget for February 2005:

Number of units sold	23,000
Selling Price per unit	125 pesos
Variable Costs per unit	110 pesos
Fixed Costs	150,000 pesos

At the end of February 2005, Lucas actually sold 24,500 units at the budgeted price but at a variable cost of 112 pesos per unit. Fixed costs were as budgeted. Headquarters uses A-1 to deal with foreign exchange budget planning and performance. The relevant exchange rates for the February 2005 budget are the following:

Exchange rate when budget was established	0.08931 pesos
Projected exchange rate when budget was established	0.09034 pesos
Actual exchange rate at the end of February 2005	0.08971 pesos

a. Translate Lucas's budget into U.S. dollars and determine the sales volume and flexible budget variances. (*Suggestion:* use a spreadsheet to organize the data as in Exhibit 14.6.)

b. Now translate Lucas's budget using P-2 and E-3.

c. Do you agree with headquarters' use of A-1 in the budgeting process? Explain your answer.

4. Use the same information as in Exercise 1, but assume that management uses A-3 to deal with foreign exchange budget planning and performance.

a. Translate Lucas's budget into U.S. dollars and determine the sales volume, flexible budget, and foreign exchange variances.

b. Why does a foreign exchange variance arise when using A-3?

5. Use the same information as in Exercise 1, but assume that management uses P-3 to deal with foreign exchange budget planning and performance.

    a. Translate Lucas's budget into U.S. dollars and determine the sales volume, flexible budget, and foreign exchange variances.

    b. Now that you have used five different rate combinations, which one do you think is most useful in preparing the budget? Which rate is most useful in evaluating the performance of Lucas Inc.? Which combination is the best in your opinion?

6. MultiCorp is a French-based company with operations in China. In determining the budget for 2005, MultiCorp looks at its historical performance in China and notes that for March 2004, its operations were as follows:

Number of units sold	5,000
Direct cost of materials and labor	€400,000
Fixed manufacturing costs	€350,000
Selling price	€100 per unit

In trying to establish the budget in Chinese yuan for March 2005, MultiCorp does not anticipate a change in fixed costs, but its direct cost of materials and labor is expected to rise 10 percent, and its selling price is expected to rise by 15 percent. Sales are expected to increase by 2 percent.

       On October 1, 2004, when the budget is established, the spot rate is €0.09727 per yuan, and the projected average exchange rate for March 2005 is € 0.09558 per yuan. At the end of March 2005, MultiCorp's management looked at actual results and discovered the following: the actual average exchange rate was € 0.09458, the selling price € 112, and the cost per unit of direct materials and labor € 90 per unit. A total of 4,800 units were sold.

    a. Determine the sales volume variances, the flexible budget variances, and the foreign exchange variances in euros for the following budget translation techniques according to the Lessard and Lorange model:

     A-1

     A-3

     P-2

     P-3

     E-3

    [*Suggestion:* use a spreadsheet to organize the data as in Exhibit 14.6.]

7. Use the data and questions in Exercise 5, but modify the following:

Exchange rate when the budget was established	€ 0.09727
Projected exchange rate	€ 0.09448
Actual exchange rate during March 2001	€ 0.09883
Units actually sold	5,200

8. Suppose you are a manager for a large MNE. You have recently been assigned to supervise several foreign subsidiaries in a politically and economically unstable region. One of your responsibilities is to help establish the budget for the subsidiaries and evaluate their performance at the end of the budget period. Budgets are prepared in the local currency of each subsidiary and then translated into the parent currency. Following is the exchange rate history for a particularly unstable country:

Exchange History	
Date	Local to Parent
January 1, 2001	2.1340290
July 1, 2001	0.0003201
January 1, 2002	0.0003401
July 1, 2002	0.0003391
January 1, 2003	1.0032410
July 1, 2003	3.3583000
January 1, 2004	3.3510000
July 1, 2004	0.0007037
January 1, 2005	0.0006841
July 1, 2005	0.0007141

The average exchange rate for the period was 1.09177021, and the high was 3.3672471. After reviewing the trend in the table, you are troubled about which combination of exchange rates to use for preparing the budget and for performance evaluation purposes.

a. Recall the exchange rates from Exhibit 14.4. What combination of rates would you use to prepare the budget and evaluate the subsidiary in question (e.g., A-1, P-2, etc.)? Justify your answer.

b. Using A-1, P-2, or E-3 would be different from A-3 or P-3. Why are they different?

c. How can hedging be a useful alternative in this situation?

9. Assume the same information as in Exercise 6. Besides being involved in the regular budgeting process, you are responsible for making capital budgeting decisions. For example, you make decisions regarding the acquisition of entire companies and large assets in the countries you supervise. To aid you in your decisions, you use NPV, discount rates, and other financial tools. Consider the following questions:

a. When making a capital budgeting decision, how does political and financial risk in unstable regions affect the discount rate used to get the NPV?

b. Suppose a project shows a positive NPV after using the best financial analysis possible. What extra qualitative factors would you consider before making a final decision?

c. Suppose you decide, along with the local managers, to invest in a project that ultimately proves unprofitable due to unexpected conditions in the local economy. Who should be held responsible for the outcome?

10. Uplift International Ltd. is a multinational forklift manufacturer based in the United Kingdom. The forklift engines are designed and manufactured in its Manchester plant and then shipped to a subsidiary in Brazil, where the forklift bodies are made. Recently, Uplift introduced a line of forklifts featuring a new engine, which it had spent several years and millions of dollars developing. To spread out and recapture the R&D costs of the new engine, Uplift increased the transfer price of the engines sold to its Brazilian subsidiary.

The Brazilian government stated that the new transfer price included, in effect, a hidden royalty payment from the subsidiary to the parent. Such payments are illegal by Brazilian law, and hence the new transfer price was unacceptable. In addition, the Brazilian tax authority pointed out that the new transfer price would result in higher expenses and lower taxes for the Brazilian subsidiary. Finally, the government felt that Uplift was not justified in charging its subsidiary for overhead that didn't benefit the subsidiary.

As a result, Uplift lowered its transfer prices on engines shipped to Brazil (eliminating the R&D allocation) to comply with the Brazilian government's ruling. At that point, the British government became upset because it felt that Uplift should have been collecting R&D fees from its subsidiaries (which were obviously benefiting from it). Furthermore, by not collecting R&D fees, Uplift was shifting taxable income out of the United Kingdom and into Brazil. Meanwhile, the Brazilian customs authority became upset because, as a result of the lower transfer prices, it was receiving less duty (tariffs) than before. In sum, Uplift seemed to be in a position in which it could please no one.

    a.   Was Uplift justified in attempting to allocate to its subsidiaries, through increased transfer prices, the development costs of the new engines?

    b.   If a company is justified in allocating overhead, R&D, and other similar expenses to its subsidiaries, what would be the most equitable method of doing so?

    c.   In situations in which some countries will not allow subsidiaries to pay the parents for such allocations, how should a parent handle these "debts"?

    d.   What can Uplift International Ltd. do to resolve the intra-Brazilian government conflict between the tax and customs authorities?

11.   Diverse Corporation is a holding company with varied product lines in different geographic areas. Its major business areas are restaurants (27 percent of sales), food processing (23 percent), dairy products (15 percent), and snack foods (19 percent). All other businesses account for the rest of its sales. On the geographic side, Diverse sells products in Europe (51 percent of sales), North America (21 percent); Latin America (18 percent); and Africa, Asia, and Australasia (10 percent). Because the nature of its businesses requires a profound understanding of local tastes and preferences, Diverse has adopted a multidomestic strategy, as described in Chapter 12.

       Simple Corporation operates fast-food franchises in all major cities across the world. Simple's world-famous meals are sold in North America (33 percent of sales), Asia (21 percent), Europe (20 percent), Latin America (15 percent), and other parts of the world (11 percent). While local tastes require some minor adaptations to its menu, Simple has been very successful with a core of similar products that have a broad appeal among children and teenagers in most countries. Thus, Simple has adopted a global strategy, as described in Chapter 12.

    a.   Assume you are a regional manager responsible for several subsidiaries of Diverse Corporation. Should you use the same or different evaluation criteria for each subsidiary? How about for the managers of each subsidiary?

    b.   How would your answer be different for Simple Corporation?

    c.   How do the different strategies affect the performance evaluation decisions of Diverse and Simple?

12.   Use the following selected financial data to calculate EVA for KZH Enterprises for 2006:

	31-Dec-2005	31-Dec-2006
Sales Revenue	$11,000,000	$11,500,000
Cost of Good Sold	7,000,000	7,800,000
Other Expenses	1,100,000	1,250,000
Cash Taxes Paid	760,000	800,000
Stockholder's Equity	3,000,000	3,500,000
Total Liabilities	5,500,000	6,000,000
Cost of Debt (After Tax)	6.00%	6.00%
Cost of Equity	11.00%	12.00%

a.   Explain in your own words what the 2006 EVA for KZH means.

b.   What would a negative EVA mean?

13.   The EVA Statement for InfoSys Technologies in Exhibit 14.8 contains the following explanation:

> Economic value-added measures the profitability of a company after taking into account the cost of all capital including equity. It is the post-tax return on capital employed minus the cost of capital employed. It is those companies which earn higher returns than cost of capital that create value. Those companies which earn lower returns than cost of capital are deemed destroyers of shareholder value.

a.   Explain why "companies which earn higher returns than cost of capital create value."

b.   Why does a return lower than the cost of capital destroy shareholder value?

c.   Computing EVA requires accurate estimates of the cost of debt and cost of equity. What should MNEs consider when computing cost of debt and equity for their foreign subsidiaries?

14.   Royal Philips Electronics of the Netherlands is Europe's biggest electronics company and one of the largest in the world. With sales of € 30.3 billion in 2004, Philips operates in over 60 countries and employs over 160,000 people. The company is a market leader in medical products, color television sets, electric shavers, lighting, and silicon system solutions. Around the turn of the century, Philips began a program named *Business Excellence through Speed and Teamwork* (BEST) to achieve world-class excellence in every aspect of the business. One of the main tools used to drive change and communicate the new strategy was the Balanced Scorecard (BSC).

The initiative to use the BSC was a top-down directive from the Board of Management to all divisions worldwide. Philip's BSC was organized along four "critical success factors" (CSF): Competence (knowledge, technology, leadership, and teamwork), Processes (drivers for performance), Customers (value propositions), and Financial (value, growth, and productivity). Each CSF is connected to the others: as competence increases, processes are improved, which leads to providing value to customers, which makes the company financially stronger. First, top-level goals were set for each CSF. Then managers at each subsequent level of the organization set goals for each CSF based on the top-level goals. Each goal had to be accompanied by a measurable objective and logically connected to goals of upper and lower level divisions. Thus, goals at all levels of the BSC were aligned with each other. As an example, a division might set goals based on the four CSFs as follows:

- *Financial:* Economic profit realized, income from operations, working capital, etc.
- *Customers:* Rank in customer survey market share, repeat order rate complaints, etc.
- *Processes:* Percentage reduction in process cycle time, capacity utilization, etc.
- *Competence:* Leadership competence, training days per employee, etc.

According to a manager in charge of the BSC, "In this process, employees have analyzed what makes the business successful and gained a greater understanding of the business enterprise." In addition, the BSC acted as a tool to facilitate communication, sharing of best practices, and overall cultural change. Overall, satisfaction with the BSC at Philips has been high.

a.   What are the advantages of the BSC goal-setting process over the traditional budgeting process? What are the disadvantages of the BSC over the traditional budgeting process?

    b.   How can the BSC be useful in solving the problem of choosing the "right" performance base to evaluate managers and subsidiaries?

    c.   How did the BSC help Philips integrate its geographically dispersed employees, divisions, and product lines?

    d.   Notice that the ultimate focus of the BSC is still on financial performance. What is the purpose of the other three focus areas (customer, process, learning and growth)?

15.   Read the *Niessen Apparel* case on our website. After reviewing the situation, Chuck Niessen hires you as a consultant to create a new control and evaluation system for Niessen. During your initial meetings with Chuck, he expressed interest in creating a Balanced Scorecard for Niessen Apparel. Since he has very little knowledge about the BSC, he has asked you to prepare a brief memo containing the following information:

    a.   A concise explanation of the BSC and its basic components.

    b.   A list of areas in which the BSC can be useful to Niessen Apparel. Chuck is especially interested in how the BSC can help him evaluate and control foreign subsidiaries like the Peruvian assembly plant.

    c.   An example of a possible BSC for Niessen Apparel at the corporate level and at the subsidiary level.

Case: Niessen Apparel
Case: Global Telecom

These cases can be found on the following website: www.wiley.com/college/radebaugh

Selected References

Abdallah, W., and D. Keller. 1985. "Measuring the Multinational's Performance." *Management Accounting* 67(4): 26–30.

Appleyard, A., N. Strong, and P. Walton. 1990. "Budgetary Control of Foreign Subsidiaries." *Management Accounting* (U.K.) (September): 44–45.

Arpan, J. 1972. *Intracorporate Pricing: Non-American Systems and Views.* New York: Praeger.

Bailes, J., and T. Assada. 1991. "Empirical Differences between Japanese and American Budget and Performance Evaluation Systems." *International Journal of Accounting* 26(2): 131–142.

Baldenius, T., N. D. Melumad, and S. Reichelstein. 2004. "Integrating Managerial and Tax Objectives in Transfer Pricing." *The Accounting Review* 79(3): 591–615.

Blaxill, M., and T. Hout. 1991. "The Fallacy of the Overhead Quick Fix." *Harvard Business Review* 69(4): 93–101.

Borkowski, S. C. 1999. "International Managerial Performance Evaluation: A Five Country Comparison." *Journal of International Business Studies* 30(3): 533–555.

Brownell, P. 1982. "A Field Study Examination of Budgetary Participation and Locus of Control." *The Accounting Review* 57(4): 66–77.

Chow, C. W., M. D. Shields, and A. Wu. 1999. "The Importance of National Culture in the Design of and Preference for Management Controls for Multinational Operations." *Accounting, Organizations, and Society* 24(5/6) (July/August): 441–461.

Demirag, I. S. 1994. "Management Control Systems and Performance Evaluations in Japanese Companies: A British Perspective." *Management Accounting* (U.K.) 72(7): 18–20, 45.

Demirag, I. S., and C. De Fuentes. 1999. "Exchange Rate Fluctuations and Management Control in UK-based MNCs: An Examination of the Theory and Practice." *European Journal of Finance* 5(1): 3–29.

Demirag, I., and A. Tylecote. 1996. "Short-term Performance Pressures on British and Scandinavian Firms: Case Studies." *European Management Journal* 14(2): 201–206.

Eden, L. 2001. "International Taxation, Transfer Pricing and the Multinational Enterprise." In *The Oxford Handbook of International Business,* edited by Alan Rugman and Thomas Brewer. London: Oxford University Press.

Eden, L., M. T. Dacin, and W. P. Wan. 2001. "Standards across Borders: Crossborder Diffusion of the Arm's Length Standard in North America." *Accounting, Organizations and Society* 26(1): 1–23.

Eiteman, D. K. 1997. "Foreign Investment Analysis." In *International Accounting and Finance Handbook,* 2nd ed., edited by F. D. S. Choi. New York: John Wiley.

Ernst & Young. 2003. *Transfer Pricing 2003 Global Survey.* Washington, DC: Ernst & Young International.

Frucot, V., and W. Shearon. 1991. "Budgetary Participation, Locus of control, and Mexican Managerial Performance and Job Satisfaction." *Accounting Review* 66(1): 80–99.

Gumbus, A., and B. Lyons. 2002. "The Balanced Scorecard at Philips Electronics." *Strategic Finance* 84(5): 45–50.

Gupta, A., and V. Govindarajan. 1991. "Knowledge Flows and the Structure of Control Within Multinational Corporations." *Academy of Management Review* 32(2): 768–792.

Harrison, G. 1992. "The Cross-Cultural Generalizability of the Relation between Participation, Budget Emphasis and Job Related Attitudes." *Accounting Organizations and Society* 17(1): 1–15.

Harrison, P., and A. Harrell. 1994. "An Incentive to Shirk, Privately Held Information and Managers' Project Evaluation Decisions." *Accounting, Organizations and Society* 19(7): 569–577.

Harrison, G., J. L. McKinnon, S. Panchapakesan, and M. Leung. 1994. "The Influence of Culture on Organizational Design and Planning and Control in Australia and the United States Compared with, Singapore and Hong Kong." *Journal of International Financial Management & Accounting* 3: 242–261.

Hasan, I., L. P., Shao, and A. T. Shao. 1997. "Determinants of Capital Budgeting Strategies: An Econometric Analysis of US Multinational Subsidiaries." *Multinational Business Review* 5(1): 68–77.

Hassel, L. G. 1991. "Performance Evaluation in a Multinational Environment." *Journal of International Financial Management and Accounting* 3(1): 17–38.

Hassel, L. G. and G. M. Cunningham. 1996. "Budget Effectiveness in Multinational Corporations: An Empirical Test of the Use of Budget Controls Moderated by Two Dimensions of Budgetary Participation under High and Low Environmental Dynamism." *Management International Review* 36(3):245–267.

Hassel, L. G., and G. M. Cunningham. 2004. "Psychic Distance and Budget Control of Foreign Subsidiaries." *Journal of International Accounting Research* 3(2): 79–94.

Hiromoto, T. 1988. "Another Hidden Edge – Japanese Management Accounting," *Harvard Business Review* (July/August): 22–26.

Ito, K., and K. R. Macharzina. 2000. "Strategic Planning Systems." In *International Accounting and Finance Handbook,* 2nd ed., edited by F. D. S. Choi. New York: John Wiley.

Kaplan, R. 1983. "Measuring Manufacturing Performance: A New Challenge for Managerial Accounting Research." *Accounting Review* 58(4): 687.

Kaplan, R., and D. Norton. 1992. "The Balanced Scorecard—Measures that Drive Performance." *Harvard Business Review* (January–February): 71–79.

Kaplan, R. S., and D. P. Norton. 2001. *The Strategy-Focused Organization.* Cambridge, MA: Harvard Business School Press.

Lessard, D. 1996. "International Financial Markets and the Firm." *The Journal of Finance* 51(2): 765–767.

Lessard, D., and P. Lorange. 1977. "Currency Changes and Management Control: Resolving the Centralization/Decentralization Dilemma." *Accounting Review,* p. 628–637.

Lessard, D., and S. Zaheer. 1996. "Breaking the Silos: Distributed Knowledge and Strategic Responses to Volatile Exchange Rates." *Strategic Management Journal* 17(7): p. 513–533.

Merchant, K. A., C. W. Chow, and A. Wu. 1995. "Measurement, Evaluation, and Reward of Profit Center Managers: A Cross-Cultural Field Study." *Accounting, Organizations, and Society* 20(7/8): 619–638.

Morsicato, H. 1980. *Currency Translation and Performance Evaluation in Multinationals.* Ann Arbor, MI: UMI Research Press.

Przysuski, M., H. Swaneveld, V. Nagarajan, and S. Lalapet. 2003. "Important Transfer-Pricing Lessons for Multinationals," *Canadian Tax Journal* 51(2): 950.

Robbins, S., and R. Stobaugh. 1973. "The Bent Measuring Stick for Foreign Subsidiaries." *Harvard Business Review* 51: 80–88.

Shields, M., C. Chow, Y. Kato, and Y. Nakagawa. 1991. "Management Accounting Practices in the U.S. and Japan: Comparative Survey Findings and Research Implications." *Journal of International Financial Management and Accounting* 3(1): 61–77.

Ueno, S., and U. Sekaran. 1992. "The Influence of Culture on Budget Control Practices in the USA and Japan: An Empirical Study." *Journal of International Business Studies* 23(4): 659–674.

Wijewardena, H., and A. De Zoysa. 1999. "A Comparative Analysis of Management Accounting Practices in Australia and Japan: An Empirical Investigation." *International Journal of Accounting* 34(1): 49–70.

CHAPTER FIFTEEN

INTERNATIONAL AUDITING ISSUES

Chapter Objectives

- Discuss important factors influencing the quality of the accounting and auditing profession
- Discuss the nature of global audit services and examine the challenges of auditing across borders
- Describe the structure of the audit industry and the strategies of the global public accounting firms in servicing clients worldwide
- Provide a comparative international analysis of audit standards
- Explain the role of the International Federation of Accountants (IFAC) in harmonizing auditing standards worldwide

INTRODUCTION

Auditors are increasingly practicing internationally, both as individuals and as firms. The main impetus behind this movement has been the globalization of business, which has accelerated especially in recent years. As enterprises became multinational, they asked that their financial advisers be equally multinational. As a result, professional accountants have organized themselves into global organizations, providing a wide range of services throughout the world. This chapter examines the role of the external auditors in their interaction with the multinational enterprise (MNE). It also examines the largest auditing firms in their role as global service corporations and some of the unique problems they experience.

The external auditor is an independent professional who works closely with clients to provide global value-added services such as tax advice, training, review of financial control systems and, in more remote locations, basic accounting services. Given that audit firms often have offices and correspondents in a larger number of

---

Strategic Decision Point

Faced with declining profits in 2004, the Swedish company, Electrolux, the world's largest producer of powered appliances, announced that it would no longer list its shares as ADRs on NASDAQ in order to cut costs and because trading volumes were so low. Electrolux's auditor is PricewaterhouseCoopers, which was hired in 2002, the year that Sarbanes-Oxley (SOX) was enacted in the United States. PwC performs its audit in accordance with the Swedish Companies Act and Swedish auditing standards. For statements filed in the United States, it also audits in accordance with U.S. generally accepted auditing standards. For countries outside of Sweden and the United States, PwC uses legal audit guidelines from the respective countries and audit guidelines adopted by the International Federation of Accountants. The cost of the global audit is significant, and SOX has been a problem for all firms, especially foreign firms from countries with different legal requirements and governance practices. Although Electrolux was moving to comply with SOX guidelines, the cost of implementation was apparently too steep to deal with, even though it did not specifically mention SOX as a reason for de-listing. Most experts agree that the cost of compliance with SOX will far exceed the cost of the annual audit. Is this a cost issue for just one firm, or will other foreign firms be forced to de-list in the face of high compliance costs in the U.S. market? What does this mean to companies trying to raise capital abroad, to U.S. stock markets trying to attract foreign firms, and to auditors trying to generate more business while at the same time comply with U.S. auditing requirements?

---

countries than any single multinational firm, external auditors have also become repositories of information about operating conditions for firms wishing to move into a location.

THE ACCOUNTING AND AUDITING PROFESSION

According to Messier et al. (2006), "auditing is a systematic process of objectively obtaining and evaluating evidence regarding assertions about economic actions and events to ascertain the degree of correspondence between those assertions and established criteria and communicating the results to interested users." Based on this definition, successful auditing has three important requirements: an objective (independent), competent person; quantifiable (and verifiable) information; and established criteria (or auditing standards).

Just as these issues must be addressed in the domestic setting, they must also be addressed in the international setting. There are differences worldwide in the way one becomes an auditor, the form and content of the financial statements, and auditing standards. In addition to the difficulty of solving these problems in a national setting, there is also the problem of crossing national boundaries. For example, is it possible for the auditor of the German company BMW to rely on the opinion of a U.S. auditor for a subsidiary of BMW in the United States, given that GAAP are different in the United States, that the qualifications of a U.S. auditor are different from those of a German auditor, and that the auditing standards in the United States are different from those in Germany? As noted above, PwC audits Electrolux worldwide, but is PwC the same in every country?

The quality of the auditing profession in each country is a function of several factors, such as the reputation of the accounting and auditing profession, the quality of the educational system, and the certification process. Reputation is important because it determines whether or not the profession is able to attract competent people.

Educational systems vary with respect to the specific training they provide potential candidates for the accounting profession. In some countries, such as the United States, a high value is placed on the university experience of students, and firms that recruit at the universities are familiar with the backgrounds students will have when they graduate. In other countries, especially developing countries, accounting education may not be that important or even available. Accounting is often viewed as a discipline within economics, and little attention is paid to accounting education. That type of educational system might not prepare students for careers in accounting in quite the same way as would be expected in an industrialized country. The educational system might also be influenced by the role an accountant is expected to play. In Germany, for example, tax accounting is emphasized.

Finally, the licensing process is carried out by the private sector in some countries and the public sector in others. In the United States, each state is empowered to certify a candidate, and the states vary in terms of educational and experience requirements. However, the National Uniform CPA exam is prepared by the Board of Examiners of the American Institute of CPAs (AICPA), a private-sector organization. Certification in the United Kingdom is also a private-sector process. In Germany and France, however, the government is much more involved in the certification process. In Germany, the government certifies a candidate only after following a series of steps, including a government-regulated admission and examination procedure.

The certification or licensing process is also a function of several other factors, such as the identity of the candidate, educational requirements, experience requirements, and examination. An additional aspect of certification is the issue of reciprocity, or the ability of a certified accountant in one country to practice in another. This will be discussed in more detail later.

GLOBAL AUDIT SERVICES AND THE INTERNATIONAL AUDITING CHALLENGE

Although each firm differs, the services provided by the global audit firm include:

1. Audit/Attestation and Assurance Services
2. Tax Advisory and Compliance Service
3. Consulting/Management Advisory Services

The services described in Exhibit 15.1 provide a broad taxonomy that applies equally well to domestic and global firms. What is different about the global cor-

Exhibit 15.1   Attestation, Assurance, Consulting/Tax

	Attestation	Assurance	Consulting/Tax
Result	Written conclusion about the reliability of the written assertions of another party	Better information for decision-makers Recommendations might be a by-product	Recommendations based on the objectives of the engagement Tax documents for the government Tax advice
Objective	Reliable information	Better decision making	Better outcomes
Independence	Required by standards	Included in definition	Not required
Substance of Auditor Output	Conformity with established or stated criteria	Assurance about reliability or relevance of information. Criteria might be established, stated, or unstated	Recommendations; not measured against formal criteria
Form of Auditor Output	Written	Some form of communication	Written or oral

poration is the complexity of these functions and the number of potential audit locations. Procter and Gamble operates in 140 countries each with its own unique reporting rules, currency, and taxes. Their auditors have to review their operations in each of these countries, plus file a tax return in many of them. They also have to prepare a consolidated return in P&G's home base in the United States.

Although audit responsibilities are similar for international and domestic operations, conventional wisdom suggests the existence of some unique challenges in the foreign environment, such as local accounting practices, foreign currency, local legal and business practices, language and customs, and distance. Although most large companies attempt to standardize their accounting practice worldwide, it does not happen everywhere. Local records may be kept according to local accounting procedures, which makes it difficult to use a standardized audit package. Also, the infrequency of audits (because of distance) may mean that there is insufficient accounting data to provide a clear audit trail.

In a survey of the then "Big Six" audit firms, MNE audit experts rated the following risks as most influential in determining the scope of a multinational audit (Hermanson, 1993):

1. Significant or unusual transactions at a subsidiary
2. Size of a subsidiary (in terms of revenue, net income, or assets)
3. Large changes in a subsidiary's net income
4. Audit committee expectations
5. Competence of subsidiaries' accounting personnel

Interestingly, the results of the survey suggest that auditors of MNEs are mainly concerned with the same risks of a domestic audit. None of the risks listed above are unique to MNEs. This lack of additional risks in MNE auditing is confirmed by Hermanson and Carcello, (1996), who find no important differences in the incidence of "audit failures" (issuing a clean audit report prior to a client's bankruptcy) between MNE audits and domestic audits. Although these results imply that in general the same risk factors exist for domestic and MNE audits, further research on the risks of MNE audits is needed to come to a firmer conclusion. For example, a joint report by the U.K. partnerships of the Big Four firms concluded that litigation risks of auditing MNEs are higher than usual (The Banker, 2004).

Even if risks for domestic and international audits are similar, the execution of international audits is more complex due to several factors, which are discussed next.

AUDIT CHALLENGES: LOCAL BUSINESS PRACTICES AND CUSTOMS

Audit and assurance procedures employed by audit firms are designed to confirm past transactions, assess the quality of the control system, and determine future areas of risk. Local business practices and customs can create challenges in simply confirming what has happened, as well as in assessing future risks. Examples of such challenges include:

1. *Predominance of cash.* Although paying expenses by cash, rather than check, is common practice in many countries (particularly emerging market economies), it makes record keeping of expenses and revenue control difficult. Japan provides a good example of some of the challenges that arise in cash management. It isused to be very common for the Japanese to use cash instead of checks for some transactions. To send cash in the mail, they used money envelopes carried in special pouches by the mail carrier. Larger businesses used checks, but banks often provided only computerized lists of transactions rather than canceled checks. This made it difficult to check the signature and authorization of actual checks during the audit. Because of the interlocking nature of the banks, many payments were made by bank transfers directly from one bank account to another. The only verification of the transfers was a computer printout. Some firms used a variety of transfers to keep the government from verifying earnings for a tax base.

2. *Inability to confirm accounts receivable.* In most cases, the confirmation letter itself must be translated into another language. Relying on the customer to return the confirmation is another challenge because foreign customers lack experience with confirmations. It may not be customary for local auditors to send confirmations for accounts receivable or even to confirm year-end bank balances. The mail service may also be inefficient and unreliable, and it may take weeks before the customer receives the confirmation letter, if the customer receives it at all. In emerging markets where qualified staff are rare, audit confirmations are often seen as an intrusion and are responded to with caution. This is particularly true in some countries where auditors must by practice or law report to the government without necessarily telling their client.

AUDIT CHALLENGES: CURRENCY, LANGUAGE, AND LAW

Foreign Currency   Foreign currency restrictions and transfer requirements should be known for each country in which the auditor works. In addition, the auditor must be aware of corporate procedures for translating financial statements and recording foreign currency transactions so that reports sent to the parent in its own currency are prepared properly. Management must determine which translation methodology is to be used, and the auditor needs to determine if the choice is based on the right criteria, using the appropriate accounting standard.

Language and Culture   Ignorance of the local language can be a fatal handicap when the auditor deals with bilingual personnel. Having to rely on a translator may mean that the auditor is not getting the full story. In many countries, the financial statements must be kept in the local language and currency, so knowledge of that language is essential. Sometimes, knowing the language can be useful for getting information in touchy situations. For example, two auditors of the Brazilian subsidiary of a large multinational energy company noticed that a purchasing agent was driving a relatively expensive car. Because the two auditors spoke the local language, they were able to go to the man's home and interview his father. They found out from the proud father that his son was so important he received a 5 percent commission on everything he bought for the company. Needless to say, the purchasing agent did not last long in his position.

Interaction of Home Country and Local Law   Home countries occasionally have laws that extend to subsidiaries of their domestic companies that operate abroad. These laws may contradict or conflict with laws in the host country. Examples include boycotts on doing business with certain countries or anti-boycott legislation where the auditor must certify that no country is being discriminated against. Other examples include human rights or other social disclosure. Perhaps one of the most intrusive of such extraterritorial laws is the U.S. Foreign Corrupt Practices Act, which not only forbids most forms of bribes but also specifies what minimum accounting controls must be in place. The passage of Sarbanes-Oxley in 2002 introduced a significant complicating factor for foreign companies operating in the United States as well as U.S. companies operating abroad, especially for Section 404 which introduced annual certification of internal controls over financial reporting by the company's CEO and its external auditors. Although the SEC delayed implementation of Section 404 for foreign registrants until 2006, it is obvious that national laws in the United States will have a big impact on internal control and external auditing for foreign as well as U.S. companies.

AUDIT CHALLENGES: DISTANCE AND ORGANIZATION FOR PROVIDING AUDIT SERVICES

The auditor of a large multinational corporation has a very difficult time organizing the firm's services properly. For example, Coca-Cola, the American beverages company based in Atlanta, Georgia, has operations all over the world. Its auditor, Ernst & Young, also has an office in Atlanta, which is responsible for the audit. One of the partners in the Atlanta office is assigned as the partner in charge of the worldwide audit. That partner must decide on the scope of the audit, taking into consideration such factors as:

1. The countries where Coca-Cola has subsidiaries
2. The materiality of each subsidiary vis-à-vis the corporation as a whole
3. The existence of a branch, subsidiary, or correspondent of the auditor in the country or city of each major subsidiary; and so on

A major challenge of auditing outside the home base is distance. Far-flung operations are not audited as frequently or as thoroughly as the domestic operations, making the foreign audit even more difficult. It is often impossible to conduct pre-audit and post-audit visits, so most communication has to be by telephone, e-mail, fax, or mail. The earlier example on confirming accounts receivable illustrates the difficulty of distance. When post-audit problems arise, it may be impossible to get an answer quickly or to communicate adequately.

Given the need to cover clients in widely dispersed areas, how do public accounting firms service their multinational clients? The simplest way is for a professional to travel from the home office to service a client abroad. This would be sufficient as long as the foreign sector was a small part of the client's overall operations. However, this approach is unsatisfactory in the long run because of the complexity of the international audit and tax environments and the increasing internationalization of most of the firm's larger clients.

Beyond the traveling auditor approach, the firm must make increasing commitment to physical or legal presence overseas. The lowest level of commitment uses a variety of relationships with host-country correspondent firms. These can range from very weak to very strong.

At one end of the scale, the local correspondent may be a representative who performs services for more than one accounting firm. A very loose operating relationship may exist. At the other end of the scale, a very strong correspondent relationship may exist in which the local firm performs services exclusively for one foreign public accounting firm. Whether an auditing firm expands abroad through strong or weak correspondent relationships, the partners in other countries remain separate, autonomous organizations. Unlike a corporation, which retains equity control over its far-flung operations, these partnerships are built on mutual benefit and service. There are situations in which an auditing firm in one country owns operations in other countries, but those are the exception rather than the rule.

A stronger presence abroad is to be part of a global alliance of firms that share technology, clients, and sometimes staff. These alliances may be separate legal entities that use the parent firm's name or a derivative thereof. The partnership in individual countries retains its separate identity, but a more cohesive cooperative effort exists among the firms through the international partnership. With one exception all the global audit firms operated in this manner until the mid-1990s and still do so in many countries. Ernst & Young, for example, used to be known as Ernst & Young in the United States, Canada, and other large English-speaking countries, Ernst & Young—Henry Martin, Lisdero y Asociados in Argentina, and Ernst & Young—Punongbayan & Araullo in the Philippines. This arrangement allowed for local knowledge plus global clients, but without the tight control of a single firm.

The strongest presence for any global firm would be a single entity with common equity holdings. This can be achieved by expanding outward through branches of the original firm or by the merging of previously independent entities. Home office personnel often fill the important positions in foreign branches until domestic personnel can be trained to take over. In some cases, local firms are acquired; in others, new firms are established. The branch concept, coupled with strong central management, provides for tighter control over services.

AUDIT CHALLENGES: AUDIT IMPEDIMENTS FROM INTERNATIONAL DIVERSITY, AVAILABILITY, AND TRAINING OF AUDITORS

If the audit firm should choose to open a branch rather than rely on correspondents, it faces the challenge of getting satisfactory staff on the ground. These challenges include problems of reciprocity for its expatriate staff being transferred in, lack of local audit staff, and a variety of training models for preparing staff for the audit function. We now examine the profession and the firms that it serves.

The Supply of Auditors   The number of accountants also depends on barriers to entry to the profession, such as strict educational and testing requirements. In Exhibit 15.2 we compare the number of accountants in a country by computing a ratio of the number of accountants in the country to the population, that is, the accountants per capita. It is interesting to note that emerging market countries such as Mexico have a small number of accountants per capita compared with the high-income countries. Also, countries with a tradition of standards designed to service the government (code law countries) have a relatively smaller number of accountants. For example, the United Kingdom, with close to 22 million fewer people than Germany, has six times Germany's number of accountants.

International Differences in Training of Practicing Auditors   Not only do numbers of accountants vary between countries but also the training of potential audit professionals can vary considerably. In some countries, such as the United States, a high value is placed on the university education of students, and firms that recruit at universities are familiar with the background of students when they graduate. The educational system might also be influenced by the role an accountant is expected to play (e.g., managerial accountant, tax accountant). Like many of the learned professions, preparation to become a practicing accountant includes the timeless elements of formal education, experience, and examination.

There are essentially three different models of accounting education leading to certification:

1. The apprenticeship approach, patterned after the British experience, which does not require specific university training in accounting

2. The university-based model for certification, similar to the approaches used in the United States and Germany

3. The dual-track model, found in the Netherlands and France, which permits either approach.

Exhibit 15.2   Accountants per Capita

Country	Accountants per Thousand	Certified or Chartered Accountants	Population (2004)
Canada	2.13	69,157	32,507,874
Australia	2.02	40,159	19,913,144
United Kingdom	1.63	98,283	60,270,708
United States	1.49	437,333	293,027,571
Netherlands	0.83	13,513	16,318,199
South Africa	0.51	21,856	42,718,530
Denmark	0.42	2,248	5,413,392
Germany	0.20	16,129	82,424,609
Korea	0.15	7,169	48,598,175
Malaysa	0.13	3,009	23,522,482
Japan	0.11	14,235	127,333,002
India	0.10	110,256	1,065,070,607
Bulgaria	0.08	570	7,517,973
Mexico	0.06	6,186	104,959,594
China	0.05	61,255	1,298,847,624

Source: IFAC.org and CIA World Factbook 2004
Accountants per thousand reflect the number of members of the different associations that are members of IFAC and may not represent all accountants in a country.

Each model has its strength, but auditors may be unfamiliar with the competence level of staff in all countries. In the apprenticeship model, even after several years of study, staff with significant experience may not yet be qualified, in a professional sense. One may often get staff that is relatively junior for many years. In the university model, staff may be qualified and yet not as fully experienced as one would like. One solution for the global firm is to concentrate on developing a stronger human capital base through common global training and internship or foreign residency programs. It is common to find accountants in various stages of their careers, usually from the manager level up, working in foreign offices to learn the challenges of audits in those countries and to train local accountants in the ways of the international firm. When these accountants return to their home countries, they can more effectively perform local subsidiary audits that comply with the requirements in countries where the client's parent company is located. This in turn allows the engagement partner for the parent to express an opinion.

Reciprocity (a mutual recognition of the ability to practice)   As we saw earlier, the number of accountants available in any particular country varies significantly. It would therefore seem natural that if international business activity grows in a country with relatively few accountants, auditors would move from relative surplus countries such as the United States and the United Kingdom to countries in need. Even between surplus countries, it would often seem to be a reasonable conclusion that such intracountry flows would speed up the global audit process. However, as the International Federation of Accountants noted in a 1995 Statement of Policy:

> National professional institutes and national regulatory authorities have been reluctant to accept the professional qualifications of foreign accountants for regulated services. Conditions of residence, citizenship, special educational criteria and examinations have been set, conditions which are, in many cases, impossible to meet. Moreover, some of these criteria do not pertain to the professional qualifications. Given the international scope of the accountancy profession, professionally qualified accountants, both as individuals and firms, are increasingly seeking to be recognized in foreign countries, and often see these barriers as unreasonable.
>
> The demand for recognition of foreign accountancy qualifications has been given special impetus by the successful completion of the Uruguay Round of trade negotiations, and the General Agreement on Trade in Services (GATS). The GATS addresses regulatory obstacles to international trade and foreign investment in service industries, including the cross-border practice of accountancy and other professions. It sets out a series of rules to discipline government intervention in the marketplace, to ensure that foreign or internationally-affiliated service providers, firms and professionals enjoy the same privileges as their domestic counterparts or competitors with respect to government regulation and to remove discriminatory obstacles to market entry and practice by persons from other countries. Signatories to the GATS and its provisions bind their national and sub-national regulatory authorities. (Recognition of Professional Accountancy Qualifications Statement of Policy of Council par 3–4)

Thus, the multilateral agreement, the General Agreement on Trade in Services (GATS), which is a part of the World Trade Organization (WTO), addresses these problems of qualifying to practice in other countries in two ways. First, it requires countries to administer their licensing rules in a reasonable, objective, and impartial manner and forbids using them as disguised barriers to trade. Countries are also required to establish specific procedures for verifying the competence and credentials of professionals from other countries. Second, it encourages countries to recognize other countries' qualifications, either autonomously or through mutual recognition agreements.

Reciprocity has varied in practice over time. At one time, British accountants could and did have a valid global certificate to practice. This changed most dramatically in the United States but also in Canada and Australia in the 1970s. Fairly open reciprocity in the United States disappeared with a 1977 court decision. In the 1990s, regional economic integration began a return to reciprocity. The free trade agreement signed between the United States and Canada in 1989 initiated a closer degree of economic cooperation between the two largest trading partners in the world, and it also created closer cooperation in accounting. On September 1, 1991, a memorandum of understanding entitled "Principles for Reciprocity" was signed between the AICPA, the NASBA, and the Canadian Institute of Chartered Accountants (CICA). According to the agreement, a professionally qualified accountant in one country could ask for the other country's qualification, subject to taking an exam on the local tax and legal framework. This special exam eliminated the need for Canadian accountants, for example, to take the Uniform CPA exam. This short-form exam has been extended to members of the Institute of Chartered Accountants of Australia who similarly take the short-form IQEX exam. IQEX is an acronym for the International Uniform Certified Public Accountant Qualification

Examination. The Examination is one of the requirements used to assess the professional competence of Australian and Canadian Chartered Accountants who wish to obtain the CPA certificate.

In a similar regional reciprocity situation, the European Union (EU) issued a series of directives that must be incorporated into national law in each country. The Eighth Directive, as adopted by the Council of Ministers of the European Union in 1984, deals with the qualifications of statutory auditors. Within the EU auditors from one country are allowed to practice in another member country if two conditions are met. The conditions are:

1. The auditor must have obtained qualifications that are deemed to be equivalent to the reviewing authorities in the host country.

2. The auditor must demonstrate that they understand the laws and requirements for conducting statutory audits in the host country.

The rules for reciprocity are relatively flexible in several other countries. In the Netherlands, for example, the Ministry of Economic Affairs may issue a license to a foreign accountant on the grounds of proof of suitable qualifications obtained abroad and satisfactory moral standing. The French recognize foreign diplomas from countries that grant reciprocal treatment once the candidate has passed an oral examination administered by the Ministry of Education covering French law, tax and accounting, and ethics. However, the Germans and British are as strict as the United States in not granting reciprocity easily.

Since the early 1990s, there were discussions between the United States and the EU about granting reciprocity, but the parties disagreed on many issues. After the corporate meltdowns of the early 2000s in the United States the establishment of the PCAOB (Public Company Accounting Oversight Board) as a tough overseer of audit firms accentuated the differences between the parties even more. The PCAOB demanded the creation of a similar organization in Europe to oversee the audit profession. Initially, the EU complained that the PCAOB's standards were too tough on auditors. However, the accounting scandals of Ahold NV of the Netherlands and of Parmalat SpA of Italy helped convince the EU of the need for tougher oversight. In early 2004, the European Commission issued a legislative proposal that mirrors much of Sarbanes-Oxley. After much negotiation, the parties agreed on standards requiring regular rotation of auditors, independent audit committees at every company, and registration and regular inspection by the new U.S. watchdog.

The completion of the agreement depends on the EU's enactment of a proposal obliging members to establish national audit watchdogs. Each EU country and the European Parliament still must approve the proposal. It then needs to be implemented by each EU member, a process that will take two to four years (Miller, 2004). As of the writing of this chapter, the proposal still had not been approved.

GLOBAL ACCOUNTING FIRMS

Structure of the Audit Industry

As in business, generally there are large and small audit firms. In the United States alone, there are more than 45,000 CPA firms. However, the audit profession is characterized by a few very large public accounting firms that conduct the audits of most of the world's largest corporations. These firms, known as the "Big Four," are: Deloitte, Ernst & Young, PricewaterhouseCoopers, and KPMG. In fact, the Big Four audit 97 percent of all public companies in the United States with sales over $250 million, more than 80 percent of public companies in Japan, two-thirds of those in Canada, all of Britain's 100-biggest public companies, and they hold over 70 percent of the European market by revenue (Economist, 2004). Exhibit 15.3 identifies the top international firms in 2003 by worldwide revenues

A major development since the early 1980s with respect to the competitive position of the major public accounting firms is merger activity. Until a few years ago, the audit market was dominated by the "Big Eight," then the "Big Six," and today by the "Big Four" just mentioned. In 1989, in rapid succession, Deloitte Haskins & Sells and Touche Ross announced they would merge into a new U.S. firm, Deloitte & Touche (DT), and Ernst & Whinney and Arthur Young announced the formation of a new U.S. firm, Ernst & Young (EY). Although discussions took place between Arthur Andersen (AA) and Price Waterhouse, a merger did not result. It is very difficult for such large firms to mesh together, especially where there are significant differences in organizational culture. In 1998, Price Waterhouse successfully merged with Coopers and Lybrand to form PricewaterhouseCoopers (PwC). Attempts to merge Ernst & Young and KPMG were stymied by regulators.

In recent years, the corporate scandals of Enron, WorldCom, and other large firms have produced dramatic changes in the accounting profession. Although most of these changes occurred in the United States, they have had the most impact on the large international accounting firms. The fall of Arthur Andersen, one of the most prominent public accounting firms in the world, was the first of such changes. Andersen's license was revoked by U.S. regulators in 2002 after the firm was indicted for obstruction of justice in the investigation of the Enron scandal. The indictment harmed the firm's reputation so much that clients and the public lost confidence in Andersen's integrity, and the firm disintegrated soon after. That same year, the Sarbanes-Oxley Act was enacted in the United States. The Act established the Public

Exhibit 15.3   Top International Accounting Firms by Revenue (2003)

Firm	Sales ($ bn)	% Increase	Employees
Deloitte & Touche	15.10	21	119,770
PricewaterhouseCoopers	14.70	7	122,820
Ernst & Young	13.10	30	102,968
KPMG	12.20	13	98,900
BDO International	2.70	11	23,226
RSM International	2.10	14	20,436
Grant Thornton International	2.00	N/A	N/A
Moores Rowland International	1.80	14	20,852
Horwath International	1.60	1	18,454
Baker Tilly International	1.50	10	17,029

Source: International Accounting Bulletin

Company Accounting Oversight Board (PCAOB) to regulate the accounting profession and monitor the work of public accounting firms. In addition, the Act prohibits accounting firms from providing several nonaudit services to audit clients, including bookkeeping, financial information systems design and implementation, internal audit outsourcing, and legal and expert services (such as consulting) unrelated to audit services (Sarbanes-Oxley Act, 2002). Although tax services are not explicitly prohibited, in practice public companies are hiring different companies to provide audit and tax services. What is not clear is whether firms are keeping their auditors and hiring a new firm to do the tax work, if they are keeping their original firm to do the tax work but hiring a different auditor, or if they are trying to keep using the same firm to do both work. It remains to be seen how this problem will be resolved and is a good area of future research.

The events of 2002 have had a major impact on the international auditing profession. The combination of stronger oversight, prohibition of nonaudit services, and the fall of Andersen have increased risks for the large international firms. In addition, large public MNEs now have few firms to choose from with the necessary expertise to provide audit, tax, and consulting services. For example, in January 2005, Best Buy, the large electronics superstore, dismissed Ernst & Young as its auditor due to conflicts of interest (Taub, 2005). This left Best Buy with only three large international accounting firms to choose from who were capable of performing its yearly audit. Once Best Buy chose a new auditor, it was left with only two firms to choose from to provide all nonaudit services.

Finally, in June 2002 the PCAOB released Audit Standard 2, which requires management of all public firms listed in U.S. stock exchanges, including foreign MNEs, to provide a statement certifying the effectiveness of its internal controls. Auditors are required to certify management's assessment on a yearly basis. This requirement has increased the workload of international firms tremendously. Given the shortage of qualified personnel, firms have had to drop several clients to comply with the new audit requirement of the PCAOB. As noted above, the SEC announced in March 2005 that it would delay Sarbanes-Oxley for foreign companies, recognizing the difficulty of compliance.

As can be seen, the events of the recent years have far-reaching effects on the audit industry. Firms auditing large MNEs must be careful to maintain their reputations while trying to remain profitable.

Another trend for public accounting firms is to organize around industry. For example, KPMG is organized around four industry-specific lines of business: consumer and industrial businesses; financial services; health care and public sector; and information, communications, and entertainment. Industry-focus teams are established for assurance and tax services. The result is more of a matrix form of organization, with the industry as the primary focus and functional organizations as a secondary focus. This model of organizational structure is similar to the Global Product Organization discussed in Chapter 12.

Besides audit services, international firms offer a wide variety of services, including tax and consulting. As a result of the Sarbanes-Oxley prohibition to provide audit and nonaudit services to the same public client, some of the firms have sold off some of their nonaudit practices. For example, PricewaterhouseCoopers sold its consulting practice to IBM in 2002 (Grant and Bennett, 2002). With respect to its tax services, some of the firms have begun transferring some routine tax services to developing markets in order to cut costs. For example, Ernst & Young is sending some simple tax-return processing work to India (Wessel, 2004), whereas other firms have resisted outsourcing or are considering a strategic response to their competitors.

From a manager's point of view, both the strategy and structure of audit firms indicate that they have in many ways achieved high levels of success. On the one hand, they provide value to their clients and yet unlike many other service agencies, they do this through a structure and strategy that are suitable to their role as global corporations and from which they no doubt learn how to serve their clients more effectively. All of this has been achieved in an industry that is nationally regulated and where the supply of skills in no way matches the pattern of global growth.

Strategies of the Global Audit Firm

As a global firm and a global service provider, public accounting firms have traditionally expanded abroad to better service their clients and to provide a line of defense against other global accounting firms that might be tempted to encroach on their client base. Companies that have switched from small or medium-sized auditors to more international auditors often give the following reasons for the switch:

1. The need to reflect the increasing size of our overseas business.
2. The need to have one firm auditing all companies within the group.

A good example of global strategy was the battle over the expanding Varity audit. In 1990, KPMG took over the audit engagement of Varity Corporation, which had three business groups: Massey-Ferguson, a tractor manufacturer; Perkins, a diesel engine manufacturer; and Kelsey-Hayes, a wheel and brake components manufacturer. When Varity acquired Kelsey-Hayes in 1989, it decided to submit its audit work to open bid, and KPMG won out over Deloitte & Touche, Ernst & Young, and Price Waterhouse. As KPMG developed its bid, the partner chosen to coordinate the engagement visited 30 Varity locations throughout the world and prepared a bid based on KPMG's strength worldwide. The partner felt that his global experience, especially his work with British clients, given Varity's significant British operations, was a key factor in the decision.

One of the major reasons for the mergers discussed above is the increasing globalization of business. Large audit firms have increasingly become multinational firms with strong global focus and control rather than a loose alliance of related service providers. This has been especially true in Europe, where the implementation of the Fourth Directive has required more firms to be audited than had been the case previously. Furthermore, the European Union's expansion and elimination of most of the remaining barriers to free trade and investment by the end of 1992 caused these firms to look more closely at their ability to service clients outside their home markets.

Mergers between audit firms allow them to gain stronger market share in emerging markets where they previously had a small presence. Suk-yee Lee (2005) reports on the effects of 1990 mergers of Ernst & Whinney and Arthur Young, and Deloitte Haskins & Sells and Touche Ross in Korea. Suk-Yee Lee finds that after the mergers, these firms increased their market shares in Korea significantly, to a level comparable to the more established firms. In addition, this increased market power allowed them to charge higher prices for their services because of their increased credibility and international presence.

Many other national markets opened up to mergers, acquisitions, and new foreign investment in the early and mid-1990s. In 1991, for example, India decided to open up its market and allow foreign firms to have a majority equity position in Indian companies, something that had been restricted in the past. Regional trade agreements have also resulted in an opening of markets to audit and tax services. For example, the 1993 NAFTA treaty and its predecessor, the U.S./Canada free trade agreement, also opened up markets in North America. It was clear at that point that the auditors had to follow the lead of their clients to provide adequate service. Given that most of the large corporations in the world are in the United States, Canada, Europe, and Asia, the auditing firms began to look at ways to strengthen their presence in each of those major markets.

The liberalization of the Greek audit market provides an instructive example of how large international audit firms can add value to clients in emerging markets. Until 1992, the Greek audit industry had been centrally regulated by state-controlled Body of Sworn-in Accountants, which appointed auditors for those companies subject to a statutory audit. When liberalization came, the large international firms entered the market. Citron and Manalis (2001) found that the Greek companies most likely to hire an international audit firm after deregulation were those seeking international financing or with large foreign shareholding, those listed in public stock exchanges, those in the finance sector, and those large in size. These findings suggest that companies in emerging markets hire large international audit firms because they add credibility to the financial statements, allowing these companies to obtain international financing and to list in foreign exchange markets. Because of their size and combined expertise, international audit firms are able to respond to the needs of an increasingly global business environment.

AUDIT STANDARDS

The growth of national and international capital markets has turned the spotlight on the auditor as an important credibility link between the corporation and investor-creditor. Outsiders are interested in an objective, independent view of the financial statements of a firm. National corporations—especially in countries where the auditing profession has not achieved an international reputation—are turning increasingly to global accounting firms to certify their financial statements and thereby attract international investors. The use of international auditors emphasizes that auditing standards and practices, like accounting standards and practices, vary considerably from country to country. The major factors we will discuss here are sources of audit guidelines and audit requirements, differences in audit standards, and audit opinions.

The development of auditing standards in a given country is a complex dynamic of cultural, legal-political, and economic variables, so one would not expect total uniformity. Auditing standards come from the public (government) sector, the private sector, or a combination of the two. In many countries, the government often takes the lead by incorporating audit requirements and, to a lesser extent, standards, into law. Traditionally, this thrust was most common in developing countries where the accounting profession was not well organized or sufficiently strong. One major exception among the in industrialized countries was

Germany, which is legalistic and prescriptive and whose auditing profession has historically been established and regulated by law. The German case is interesting because the accounting profession there makes recommendations on audit standards that are then incorporated into law by the government.

In the United States, for many years the AICPA, a private organization, was responsible for setting audit standards. However, the massive corporate frauds of the past few years caused the auditing profession to come under fire, with a loss of confidence in the auditors' work. As mentioned earlier, Congress passed the Sarbanes-Oxley Act, which created the PCAOB. The PCAOB was charged with responsibility for setting and enforcing audit standards for audits of public companies listed in U.S. stock exchanges. This event marked the end of a long tradition of self-regulation by the audit profession. The PCAOB responds directly to the SEC, a government entity, so audit standards now are in effect set by the public sector. The United Kingdom and Canada still maintain private bodies to set audit standards.

There are wide differences in the requirements for audits worldwide. Here, however, we are specifically discussing compliance audits rather than operational or other kinds of audits. A compliance audit is one that is undertaken to determine if the auditee is following procedures or guidelines established by a higher authority. In the United States, annual independent audits are required of firms traded on a national exchange as well as firms with more than 500 shareholders and assets of more than $5 million. However, most other large companies have audits, and many banks and regulatory agencies require them. In Canada, public corporations, private corporations meeting certain tests of size, municipalities, universities, hospitals, and most nonprofit organizations are required to be audited. In the United Kingdom, all limited companies must be audited.

The Fourth Directive of the EU, which we discussed earlier in the context of accounting standards, is also a source of auditing requirements. Although the Fourth Directive does not deal with audit standards and practices or the qualifications of auditors—which is left up to the Eighth Directive—it does require that firms that fall under the guidelines of the Fourth Directive be audited. That is an important legal consideration, because most countries in the EU have incorporated the Fourth Directive into their national law. Basically, the Fourth Directive requires the publication and audit of public companies. However, it allows countries to exempt small and, in some cases, medium-sized companies from the audit requirement. Because of the long tradition of auditing financial statements in the United Kingdom, small companies there are still required to be audited. Germany, however, has decided to exempt small companies from the audit requirement.

Just because a large number of countries require an audit does not mean that all audits are done the same way. Financial statements come from the firms' books and records, which reflect the underlying transactions the firm engages in. The term *audit* could mean that the financial statements accurately reflect the books and records of the firm. The audit would entail tracing the data from the books and records to the financial statements, a relatively simple process. The auditor would rely primarily on the honesty of management and would not be as concerned as his or her counterpart in the United States or United Kingdom with confirming inventory taking or bank balances.

A more extensive audit would determine whether the books and records accurately reflect the original transactions. This would involve a more extensive investigation of the internal control system to make sure that corporate procedures for recording transactions are clearly established, communicated, and followed. It would also involve more extensive tests of original transactions and tracing their eventual flow through the records to the financial statements.

There are many reasons why audit standards vary from country to country. In the United States and the United Kingdom, there are broadly based capital markets and a highly qualified accounting profession. The capital markets require that financial statements be independently verified, and the profession has developed and refined audit standards over time. The air of skepticism has encouraged fairly rigid tests. It will be interesting to see how differences between the standards of these two traditionally similar countries evolve now that the U.S. audit profession is becoming government regulated.

Culture often plays a part as well. In Japan, bank deposits and loans payable are obtained from the company rather than by independent confirmation, because the latter would show too much distrust in company personnel, which could mean a loss of face.

A comparative international analysis of audit standards with respect to the audit function, ethical standards and enforcement, and audit reports is shown for a selection of countries in Exhibit 15.4.

International Harmonization of Audit Standards

Although multinationals, audit firms, and governments attempt to standardize their practices and permit the cross-national transfer of audit services, obstacles to auditing will still exist. Much as the IASC, now IASB, is attempting to harmonize financial reporting practices, IFAC is attempting to harmonize audit standards and audit professions globally (see Exhibit 15.5).

IFAC grew out of the International Coordination Committee for the Accounting Profession (ICCAP), which was organized in 1972 at the International Congress of Accountants in Sydney, Australia. The purpose of establishing the ICCAP was to lay the groundwork for more formal organizations to help achieve the goals of accounting harmonization. This was accomplished with the establishment of the International Accounting Standards Committee (IASC), now IASB, in 1973 and the IFAC in Munich at the 1977 international congress. IFAC's membership comprises representatives of 163 national professional accountancy bodies from 113 countries, representing more than 2.5 million accountants employed in public practice, industry and commerce, government, and academe.

To accomplish its objectives, IFAC's boards and committees set standards in the following areas:

- International standards on auditing, assurance engagements, and related services
- International Standards on Quality Control
- International Code of Ethics
- International Education Standards
- International Public Sector Accounting Standards

Exhibit 15.4   Comparative International Audit Standards

PANEL A

THE AUDIT FUNCTION

	Required to Be Audited	Election of Auditor	Objective or Purpose of Audit	Sources of Auditing Standards
North and South America				
Argentina	An independent audit is required by Argentinean legal control authorities like Inspeccion General de Justicia, Taxes Departments, Central Bank, etc.	Appointed by the board of directors or by the shareholders at the annual meeting for the period subject to review, so as to increase the reliability of accounting information	To issue a technical opinion as to whether the statement presents fairly the entity's financial position and results for the period subject to review, according to Professional Accounting Standards so as to increase the reliability of accounting information.	Professional Auditing Standards are issued by the professional organizations. The Argentinean GAAS are similar to U.S. GAAS.
Mexico	Every company registered with the Comision Nacional de Falores (National Securities Commission), all companies filing a consolidated tax return and for tax purposes all companies with income of Pesos 2,412,000 or more than 300 employees in the previous fiscal year.	Generally appointed by the general manager, the board of directors, or the shareholders.	The objective of an audit is to express an opinion regarding the company's financial statements. The purpose of an audit of a small company would include providing financing, tax and social security services and meeting the requirements of the National Securities Commission. The general law of commercial companies requires all corporations to appoint at least one statutory auditor or (comisario), who is required to submit an annual report to the shareholders on accounting and administrative matters	Set forth in technical bulletins issued by the Comision de Normas y Procediniemto de Auditoria of the Mexican Institute of Public Accountants, and summarized and classified in the publication *Auditing Standards and Procedures*, issued by the Mexican Institute of Public Accountants.

(continues)

Exhibit 15.4 *(Continued)*

PANEL A

THE AUDIT FUNCTION

	Required to Be Audited	Election of Auditor	Objective or Purpose of Audit	Sources of Auditing Standards
United States	Companies traded on a national stock exchange, companies that have over 500 shareholders and assets of over $5 million (amounts vary depending on applicable state laws), and certain types of financial service industries (if required to file with the Securities and Exchange Commission or regulated or funded by federal agencies).	Recommendation by the audit committee or board of directors and approved by the shareholders.	The expression of an opinion on the fairness with which the financial statements presents fairly, in all material respects, financial position, results of operations, and its cash flows in conformity with generally accepted accounting principles.	Statements on Auditing standards are issued by the Auditing Standards Board, the senior technical body of the AICPA designated to issue pronouncements on auditing matters.
Europe The Netherlands	All public companies, private companies, cooperative societies, and mutual guarantee associations if they meet at least two of the following criteria; assets exceed 7.5 million guilders; net turnover exceeds 15 million guilders; average number of employees exceeds 49. All insurance companies and institutions registered under Dutch Credit System Supervision Act and investment companies under Dutch	Appointed by shareholders at the annual meeting or by the supervisory board of the board of directors.	To ensure that balance sheets and accompanying notes present a true and fair view of the financial position; and that profit and loss statements and notes give a true and fair view of the results of operations of a company for the fiscal year under review.	NIVRA has adopted International Standards on Auditing issued by IFAC. They have been translated to the Dutch with specific modifications as necessary.

United Kingdom	Investment Companies Supervision Act.

All limited companies above a specified size limit. Small companies may request audit; separate requirements exist for charities; other bodies/interested parties may request "audit" service for a wide range of enterprises. | Appointed/reappointed annually by shareholders' majority vote at annual general meeting; in exceptional circumstances casual vacancies may be appointed by Secretary of State for Trade and Industry | An independent examination and opinion, for shareholders, on whether the financial statements give a true and fair view of the state of the company's affairs as at the balance sheet date and of the profit and loss for the year then ended and have been properly prepared in accordance with the Companies Act 1985. | The Auditing Practices Board (APB) established in 1991 by the Consultative Committee of Accountancy Bodies (CCAB) comprising the six principal accountancy bodies in the UK and Republic of Ireland |
| Italy | In Italy there are two bodies charged with auditing: The Board of Statutory Auditors (*Collegio Sindacale*) and the Auditing Firm. The first is composed of three to five members and it is compulsory for all companies in the legal form of Stock Company and for Limited Liability Companies that have a capital above 200 million liras. However, a board is required also if, in two consecutive financial years, the company exceeds two of the following limits: (a) assets—4.70 million liras, (b) earnings from sales and provisions of services—9.500 million liras; average staff employed during the financial years—50 units. | Proposed by the board of directors and elected by the general meeting of shareholders. | To ensure that the financial statements taken as a whole give a true and fair view of the financial position and results in compliance with the civil code. | Auditing standards are issued by the Dottori Commercialisti and the Ragionieri Collegialisti; and approved by the National Association of Auditors' Firms (ASSIREVI) and by CONSOB. Similar to International Standards on auditing. |

(continues)

Exhibit 15.4 (Continued)

PANEL A

THE AUDIT FUNCTION

	Required to Be Audited	Election of Auditor	Objective or Purpose of Audit	Sources of Auditing Standards
	The Auditing Firm is compulsory for listed companies and other entities that operate in particular economic sectors. A recent decree specifies the regulation concerning appointments for the Board of Statutory Auditors and for Audit firms in listed companies. Particularly: Auditing firms are in charge of the independent audit of financial statements (and some additional financial information); Statutory Auditors have to control the behavior of directors and the internal control systems of the company.			
France	The following are required to be audited: public limited companies, some limited companies, and some nonprofit organizations (associations, football leagues, political parties, etc.)	Elected or reelected by the shareholders for a six-year term.	To certify that all reports and financial statements conform to existing rules and regulations and give a fair and true view.	Companies Act of 1966 and standards published by the Compagnie Nationale des Commissaires aux Comptes, (CNCC). These standards are in accordance with IFAC's standards (IAPC)

Germany	Public companies (including cooperatives), and stock corporations, insurance companies, banks, and government-directed enterprises, audits provided by disclosure law, special audits of relations with affected companies, Small companies are exempted.	Elected by shareholders at annual meeting in case of statutory audit.	To determine that financial statements comply with the company's status under legal regulations (German Law) and give a true and fair view.	Commercial laws and jurisdiction are the primary basis, but the Institute of Wirtschaftsprüfers issues professional standards and guideliness.
Sweden	Any company with limited liability status. This includes limited liability companies, branches of foreign companies, cooperative units, and banks	The Companies Act requires appointment of at least one auditor by the shareholders.	To satisfy requirements of the Companies Act and to determine if a company's accounts are fairly presented.	The Companies Act states that the audit should be carried out in accordance with generally accepted auditing standards. SBPA recommendations and sections of the Companies Act are the main sources of the auditing standards. These standards are much less detailed than U.S. standards and professionals rely on judgment when applying specific standards
Asia and Pacific				
Australia	All public and "large" entities have to be audited. A company is "large" if it has two of the following three attributes: consolidated gross revenue of \$10 million; consolidated gross assets of \$5 million; 50 or more employees.	Board of directors with shareholders' approval; client's management; or Auditor General; and at the choice of the body to be audited.	Corporation Law requires that accounts show a true and fair view and comply with the Accounting Standards and the Corporation Regulations; accounts should be presented fairly and be in accordance with the trust deed.	Auditing shandards (AUS) and guidelines (AUG) approved by the ICAA and ASCPA

(continues)

Exhibit 15.4 (*Continued*)

PANEL A

THE AUDIT FUNCTION

	Required to Be Audited	Election of Auditor	Objective or Purpose of Audit	Sources of Auditing Standards
Japan	Corporations with more than 500 million yen in capital stock or more than 20 billion in liability stocks; public stock and debentures exceeding 500 million yen; stocks registered for the stock exchange or over the counter; plans to list on the exchange; and labor unions and educational institutions receiving a subsidy from governmental bodies; corporations applying for financing from the Small Business Investment Development Corporation.	Under the commercial Law Code, the auditor and auditing officer are appointed at the stockholders' general meeting. Under the Securities and Exchange Act, the auditor (CPA or corporate) is appointed by the board of directors.	The commercial Law Code does not specify the purposes of an audit; the Securities and Exchange Act specifies that it is to protect indirectly public interests and investors, to confirm that the financial statements fairly and appropriately show the financial position and results, and that they are prepared in conformity with accounting principles.	No Commercial Law Code; the Auditing Standards require: (1) experience, ability, independence; (2) a fair, impartial attitude; (3) due care; (4) refusal to use or reveal confidential information; (5) sufficient evidence for a reasonable basis for an opinion; (6) planning, execution; and (7) audit procedure, timely and extent of tests based on internal controls, materiality and audit risk.
Hong Kong	All companies incorporated and registered under the companies Ordinance except certain private companies.	Appointed by the shareholders at the annual meeting.	Show a true and fair view at the balance sheet date and of profit and loss for the financial year and compliance with the Companies Ordinance, certain private companies must show a true and correct view.	Statements of Auditing-Standards of the HKSA regulations of the Companies Ordinance.
Singapore	All incorporated companies, both public and private.	Appointed by the shareholders at the annual meeting.	To determine whether accounts give a true and fair view of the company's affairs in accordance with provisions of the Companies Act.	Statements of Auditing Guidelines and Practices of the Institute of Certified Public Accountants of Singapore. Closely follow international standards.

PANEL B

ETHICAL STANDARDS AND ENFORCEMENT

	Ethical Standards	Enforcement	Legal Liability	Responsibility for Detection of Fraud
North and South America				
Argentina	Argentinean Code of Ethics issued by the FACPCE, which aims to safeguard the public against careless or unscrupulous professionals.	A disciplinary court elected by the direct vote of all registered professionals.	Failure by an auditor to perform his or her duties, with regard to the examination of financial statements, may lead to monetary, criminal, professional, or other consequences applicable under the regulations of the control authorities involved. Due to negligence by the auditor, in the event of deception or fraud, the auditor may be responsible for paying damages to the client or another party.	An auditor may be held criminally responsible, not necessarily for the perpetration of crimes, but rather for complicity or concealment, such as providing false or misleading examinations of financial statements.
Mexico	The Mexican Institute of Public Accountants has issued a code of ethics to guide its members in moral conduct and to declare its intentions to serve society with trust, diligence, and self-respect.	The Mexican Institute Public . Accountants	The auditor may be sued if the audit is not conducted according to the standards and procedures issued by the Mexican Institue of Public Accountants and a third party is affected.	A statutory auditor is responsible for the vigilance of the company and the administration.
United States	The bylaws of the AICPA require that members adhere to the Rules of Code of Professional Conduct. These Principles of the Code of Professional Conduct of the AICPA express the profession's recognition of its responsibilities to the public, to clients, and to colleagues.	The Council of the AICPA is authorized to designate bodies to promulgate technical standards under the Rules, and the bylaws require adherence to those Rules and Standards Compliance with the code or Professional Conduct depends primarily on members' understanding and voluntary actions, secondarily on reinforcement by peers and on	The auditor may be held legally and professionally liable when he or she fails to apply due professional care in the application of the required auditing standards.	The auditor should assess the risk that fraud may cause the financial statements to contain a material misstatement. Based on that assessment, the auditor should design the audit to provide reasonable assurance of detecting errors and irregularities, due to fraud that are material tot he

(continues)

Exhibit 15.4 (Continued)

PANEL B

ETHICAL STANDARDS AND ENFORCEMENT

	Ethical Standards	Enforcement	Legal Liability	Responsibility for Detection of Fraud
	They guide members in the performance of their professional responsibilities and express the basic tenets of ethical and professional conduct.	public opinion, and, ultimately, on disciplinary proceedings, when necessary, against members who fail to comply with the rules.		financial statements.
Europe The Netherlands	The Rules of Conduct for accountants (GBA) prohibit discrediting the profession, the use of information for one's own gain. They require preserving records of evidence and keeping information about a client confidential. Key issues addressed are impartiality, confidentiality quality of work, and independence.	Complaints received by the Disciplinary Board and the Board of Appeal.	Criminal and civil liability for criminal offense (fines to imprisonment), for negligence, acts discrediting the profession; the latter part is enforced by the Disciplines Board, not by the law; for violating professional rules (resulting in written warning, written reprehension, suspension (maximum 6 months), and expulsion).	In principle, management bears responsibility for the financial statements; however, auditors can also be taken to court if they fail to detect errors. Auditors are not responsible for irregularities (intentional distortions of financial statements) if they have performed their audit with due and professional care. Material fraud that is detected, but not redressed, must be reported to the authorities.
United Kingdom	Each RSB has an ethical guide; all stress integrity, objectivity, independence, professional competence and due care, professional behavior, and confidentiality.	Each RSB must have rules for enforcing compliance with SASs; penalties may include withdrawal of registration so that person becomes ineligible to perform company audits. Monitoring is carried out, for example, by the Joint Monitoring Unit of the ICAEW/ICAS.	Rule of "joint and several" liability means that auditors may carry the full cost of negligence even where this is partly the fault of directors; liability to third party exists at common law where loss is clearly attributable to reliance on a report prepared negligently and the party preparing the report knew (or should have known) it would be relied upon.	Required to plan audit so as to obtain sufficient evidence to give reasonable assurance that the financial statements are free from material misstatement, whether caused by fraud or other irregularity or error.

Country				
Italy	The rules of association of the Ordine Nazionale del Dottori Commercialisti and of the Collegio Nazionale dei Ragionieri include specific ethics requirements relating to independence and competence. Auditing Standard No. 1 of the Consiglio Nazionale del Dottori Commercialisti specifies the following requirements for the auditor: Competence as a condition for acceptance of the auditor's work, exercise of due professional care in the conduct of the audit, integrity, and independence.	Ethical standards are enforced by the professional associations.	The auditor is legally and professionally liable only when he or she fails to apply, or incorrectly applies, the required auditing standards.	No specific requirements. According to the ISA, the auditor is not responsible for failure to detect fraud or illegal acts if the auditing procedures appropriate in the circumstances have been competently performed.
France	Set both by law and the Code of Professional Ethics adopted by the Compagnie Nationale, including rules on independence, incompatible functions, advertising, use of title or firm name, relationships with colleagues, connection between predecessor and successor.	Penalties are set by law, and in several cases by the Compagnie Nationale des Commissaires aux Comptes, which may take disciplinary action.	Violation of laws that regulate the profession are subject to Penal Code. Requirements are stated by law. Auditors are required to carry liability insurance.	No responsibility, but liable to client and third parties for fraud and negligence; must report known illegal acts by client to government authorities and/or public prosecutor.
Germany	A code of ethics covers legally required audits. Detailed guidelines issued by the Institute of CPAs, and by the Chamber of Auditors include independence, professional care,	A self-regulated body can warn, reprimand, fine, or expel an auditor who is guilty of not performing duties in accordance with professional law and standards.	Unlimited liability to clients and third parties for false statements or other intentional violations. Liability is limited in case of negligence. Breach of confidentiality is a criminal offence.	Expected to conduct the examination in an impartial and conscientious manner. Liable if failure to discover fraud results from negligence.

(continues)

Exhibit 15.4 *(Continued)*

PANEL B

ETHICAL STANDARDS AND ENFORCEMENT

	Ethical Standards	Enforcement	Legal Liability	Responsibility for Detection of Fraud
	partial responsibility, discretion, impartiality, professional conduct, and elimination of incompatible duties.			
Sweden	The FAR has developed rules of professional ethics similar to those followed by U.S. CPAs.	Sanctions may be imposed by the Supervisory Board by Public Accountants.	The auditor can be held liable for client damages that were intentional or caused by carelessness.	The auditor is responsible for fraud only if the failure to detect it was intentional or caused by carelessness.
Asia and Pacific				
Australia	Code of Professional Conduct (CPC) of the ICAA and ASCPA	Disciplinary committees in the . profession	The ethical standards per se do not give rise to legal liability. However, under the Corporation Law, criminal sanctions may be invoked against dishonest auditors, and de-registration may be a remedy against inappropriate conduct. Civil remedies for auditors' negligence are also available.	The auditor has no responsibility for reporting on control structures, other than reporting significant problems in the management letter to the Board or Audit Committee on a timely basis. Specific requirements to see and detect fraud do not at present exist.
Japan	The CPA law and the JICPA code prohibit the impairment of trust and require independenc, secrecy and restrictions of advertising. Punishment may be administered for false and unreasonable attestation	Under CPA Law, the Minister of Finance is empowered to investigate violations and to assess penalties, including warning, suspension, or withdrawal from registration. The CPA has the right to vindicate himself or herself. The JICPA Punishment Committee also enforces ethical standards. The president of the JICPA determines penalties according to the views of the committee and the board.	Under the Securities and Exchange Act, if investors lose because of material errors in audited financial statements, the auditor or firm must compensate for an error unless they can prove lack of intention and the use of due care. Under the Commercial Law Code, the auditor must compensate client for breach of contract and for materiality false items in an audit report if the auditor cannot prove due care.	The auditor must use due care to detect causes of material difference in financial statements. The auditor must report actions that contradict the directors' duties to the statutory auditors of the client.

Hong Kong	The Hong Kong Society of Accountants has issued statements of professional ethics originally based on those issued by the Institute of Chartered Accountants in the United Kingdom, but in some cases updated based on AICPA's professional conduct.	The Hong Kong Society acts as the disciplinary body.	Criminal liability for auditors who willfully make untrue statements in the prospectus or who induce another person by fraudulent or reckless misrepresentation to invest money. The auditor is liable for damages to the client and in some cases to third parties for negligence resulting in financial loss. Negligence may also be treated as a criminal offense.	The auditor is not expected to search for fraud but must be aware of the possibility of it and investigate fully if there are grounds for suspicion.
Singapore	The rules of the Accountants Act call for integrity and confidentiality, and prohibit incompatible functions, advertising, encroachment on the business of others, certification of estimates, acceptance of benefits from service for clients without consent, and acts discreditable to the profession. The standards on independence parallel those set by the United Kingdom.	The Disciplinary Committee of the ICPAS and PAB may censor, expel, or suspend a member. It may also issue fines of up to $5,000 and the costs of an investigation.	There is liability for damages to the client and in some cases third parties for negligence in performing an audit, and criminal liability for willfully making untrue statements in a prospectus. Negligence may also bring criminal liability.	The auditor is expected to seek reasonable assurance that material fraud has not occurred; if material fraud has taken place, the auditor must ensure that the error is corrected or that its effect is indicated in the financial information. The Companies Act also requires reporting of fraud under certain circumstances to the Ministry of Finance.

PANEL C

AUDIT REPORTS

Reporting Requirement

North and South America

Argentina   Standard audit report formats have been issued by the Buenos Aires CPCE. Although not mandatory, they are generally used. The FACPCE sets the minimum data that must be included in an audit report. The important elements are:

1. The name of the reports audited and the related periods and the name of the companies.

2. The conduct of the audit in accordance with auditing standards.

3. The auditing standards.

(continues)

447

Exhibit 15.4 (*Continued*)

AUDIT REPORTS

PANEL C	Reporting Requirement
	4. The opinion as to fairness of statements.
	5. Statements presented in accordance with professional accounting standards.
	6. The name of those requiring audit or services.
Mexico	In all cases in which the name of the public accountant is associated with financial statements or information, he or she should express in a clear and unmistakable manner
	1. The nature of his or her relation with such information.
	2. His or her opinion on the same.
	3. The important limitations, when applicable, that were imposed on the examination, the qualifications derived from them, the important reasons why an adverse opinion is expressed, or the reasons why a professional opinion cannot be expressed after an examination is performed in accordance with auditing standards.
	The auditor, when rendering his or her opinion on financial statements, should observe that
	1. They were prepared in accordance with generally accepted accounting principles.
	2. Such principles were applied on a consistent basis.
	3. The information presented therein and in the related notes is adequate and sufficient for its reasonable interpretation.
USA	In a standard three-paragraph report, the auditor first identifies the company and financial statements being audited and states the responsibilities of management and the auditor. Second, the auditor must indicate the scope of the examination and whether or not the audit complies with generally accepted auditing standards and that this is a sufficient basis for an opinion. Third, he or she must state whether the financial statements are presented fairly in accordance with GAAP. The auditor must express an opinion on the financial statements as a whole or assert that an opinion cannot be expressed.
Europe	
The Netherlands	The wording is not specified by law. According to ISA 700 "The Auditors' Report on Financial Statements" which has been adopted by NIVRA, the auditors' report includes among others both scope and opinion paragraphs. In the scope paragraph reference is made to the ISAs. In the opinion paragraph the auditor clearly states as to whether the financial statements give a true and fair view in accordance with the financial reporting framework and, where appropriate, whether the financial statements comply with statutory requirements.

United Kingdom The auditor's report sets out respective responsibilities of directors and auditor's scope of audit; basis of opinion and statement of opinion. By statute it must cover the balance sheet, profit and loss account and related notes; by auditing standards it extends to other financial statements prescribed by accounting standards, such as the cash flow statement. The opinion is stated on whether the financial statements give a true and fair view and comply with statutory requirements. The scope section explains that auditors read other information contained in the audit report, including the corporate governance statement, and consider the implications for their report if they become aware of inconsistencies. The scope section also explains the auditor's responsibilities in relation to the directors' report, the accounting records, information and explanations required, and rules regarding the disclosure of directors' remuneration.

Italy The auditor's report consists of four main paragraphs. The first identifies the financial statements and defines the responsibilities of both the Directors and the Auditors. The second (or scope) paragraph includes the source of accounting standards used, the parts of the director's report necessary for a clear understanding of the responsibility. The third paragraph identifies any material departure or deviation from generally accepted accounting standards. The fourth paragraph is the opinion paragraph. A fifth paragraph might be present for emphasis on significant matters.

France The auditor must certify the financial statements or qualify the report following a standard format based on International Auditing Standard. A second report is required, detailing agreements entered into between the company and legally defined related parties. There is also a standard format for this second report.

Germany According to the German Commercial Code the auditor's report to the corporation must contain a description of the process and the result of the audit, including management's report, an estimation of future development, a statement of compliance with legal regulation, and a statement explaining the company's risk management system.

The auditor must also provide a summary that covers the content, type, and volume of the audit; an evaluation of the audit result; and statements as to whether or not the financial statements and management's report present a true and fair view.

Sweden Chapter 10 of the Companies Act states that the auditor's report should include statements about

1. The preparation of the annual report in accordance with the Act.

2. The adoption of the balance sheet and income statement.

3. The proposal included in the administration report for disposition of the unappropriated earnings or deficit.

4. The discharge from the liability of members of the board of directors and the managing director.

(continues)

449

Exhibit 15.4 *(Continued)*

PANEL C

AUDIT REPORTS

	Reporting Requirement
Asia and Pacific	
Australia	The standards report has the following format:
	We have audited the accounts of X Limited on pages _____ to _____, and the Statement by Directors in accordance with Australian Auditing Standards" (scope paragraph).
	In our opinion the accounts of X Limited are properly drawn up in accordance with the provisions of the Companies (XXX) Code and so as to give a true and fair view of:
	(i) The state of affairs of the company at — 19— and the profit of the company for the year ended on that date; (ii) the other matters required by Section 269 of the Code to be dealt with in the accounts; and are in accordance with applicable approved accounting standards and Australian Accounting Standards (opinion paragraph).
Japan	The auditor's report must outline the scope of the audit performed and state in opinion on the financial statements, expressing whether the statements fairly present the financial position, results of operations and cash flows. It must also state matters that are also reported in the financial statements but that the auditor wants to call attention to.
Hong Kong	The auditor's report must state whether the balance sheet and profit-and-loss account have been prepared properly in accordance with the Companies Ordinance and whether they give a true and fair view of the state of affairs at the year's end and of the profit or loss for the year. The report must also express an opinion as to whether proper books of account have been kept, whether proper returns have been received from the branches, and whether the accounts agree with the books and returns. The report should be modified if the auditor has not received all required information and if disclosures about officers' and directors remunerations are inadequate.
Singapore	The auditor's report must state whether the accounts and, when relevant, consolidated accounts give a true and fair view. The report must also express an opinion as to whether the accounting and other records, including the registers, have been kept properly for a fair presentation and for compliance with stipulations on disclosure in the Companies Act. Reference is made to statements of auditing standards in a similar format to International Auditing Standards.

Source: Adapted from Belverd E. Needles, Jr. (2000), "Taxonomy of Auditing Standards" in Choi, F.D.S. (ed.), *International Accounting and Finance Handbook.* (New York: John Wiley & Sons), 2nd edition, Chapter 5.

Exhibit 15.5   International Federation of Accountants (IFAC)

International Federation of Accountants

Organization Overview

IFAC is an organization of national professional accountancy organizations that repreent accountants employed in public practice, business and industry, the public sector, and education, as well as some specialized groups that interface frequently with the profession. Currently, it has 153 member bodies in 113 countries, representing 2 million accountants. IFAC's structure and operations provide for representation of its diverse member organizations.

Objective

IFAC strives to develop the profession and harmonize its standards worldwide to enable accountants to provide services of consistently high quality in the public interest. IFAC will fulfill this objective within the framework of its new Constitution.

Primary Activities

IFAC's leadership, its committees and task forces work with member bodies to achieve this objective by:

- **Serving as international advocates**. IFAC develops and promotes high quality technical, professional and ethical publications and guidance for use by accountants employed in every sector.

- **Acting as agents for change**. IFAC provides leadership on emerging issues, the impetus for the liberalization of accountancy services, and a universal voice for the world's accountants on issues of public and professional concern. Much of this is accomplished through outreach to numerous organizations that rely on or have an interest in the activities of the international accountancy profession.

- **Facilitating the development of a harmonized worldwide accountancy profession**. IFAC fosters the advancement of strong national professional accountancy organizations. It works closely with regional accountancy organizations and outside agencies to accomplish this.

Source: www.ifac.org

In addition, IFAC has been heavily involved in addressing issues related to small and medium-sized companies in the developing countries. One of its committees is a developing nations permanent task force.

In regard to auditing, the International Auditing and Assurance Standards Board (IAASB) develops International Standards on Auditing (ISAs) and International Standards on Review Engagements, which deal with the audit and review of historical financial statements, and International Standards on Assurance Engagements, which deal with assurance engagements other than the audit or review of historical financial information. The IAASB also develops related practice statements. These standards and statements serve as the benchmark for high-quality auditing and assurance standards and statements worldwide (IAASB Handbook, 2005).

There are a number of major benefits of developing and enforcing internationally acceptable auditing standards:

1. The existence of a set of ISAs, which are known to be enforced, will give readers of audit reports produced in other countries justifiable confidence in the auditor's opinion. By thus lending credibility to the work of the foreign auditor they enable that auditor to lend credibility to the financial statements upon which he or she is reporting.

2. ISAs will reinforce the benefits that are already flowing from the existence of international accounting standards by providing readers with greater assurance that the accounting standards are being adhered to.

3. Adding strength to ISAs will assist readers in making international financial comparisons.

4. ISAs will provide further incentives to improve and extend the set of standards.

5. The existence of ISAs will aid in the flow of investment capital, especially to developing economies.

6. The development of an international set of standards will make it easier for developing countries to produce domestic auditing standards.

7. Effective and credible auditing is necessary in all instances where there is a separation between management (which produces financial reports) and outsiders (who use the reports). The need is all the greater in the case of MNEs because management is separated from the outsiders by greater differences in culture, political and economic systems, geographical boundaries, and the like. Thus, ISAs are, in this respect, even more important than national ones.

Following criticism of its global effectiveness in enforcing audit standards, IFAC agreed to a restructuring plan in May 2000 where, as part of the restructuring, IFAC and the large international accounting firms have undertaken a major new initiative. This was designed to raise standards of financial reporting and auditing globally in an effort to protect the interests of cross-border investors and promote international flows of capital. A key aspect of this effort was is the establishment of a new IFAC-sponsored grouping of accounting firms, known as the Forum of Firms, that works closely with IFAC in developing and encouraging implementation of international accounting and auditing standards.

The Forum of Firms is open to participation by any firm with offices in more than one jurisdiction or that has, or intends to have, transnational clients and is willing to comply with rigorous quality obligations that include:

- Institution of policies and practices in compliance with ISAs and the IFAC Code of Ethics
- Maintenance of appropriate internal control procedures including intrafirm practice review
- Agreement to implement training on international accounting and auditing standards including the Code of Ethics
- Agreement to subject assurance work to periodic external quality assurance
- Agreement to support the development of the professional bodies and implementation of international standards of accounting and auditing in developing countries

It would seem that the most important of these obligations is the agreement to subject all the firm's offices in all jurisdictions to independent quality assurance reviews. Although peer review on a national basis has taken place in several countries such as the United States and Canada, this will represent the first effort to implement global peer review and look at each of the large firms as one entity throughout the world. Membership in the forum is conditional on compliance with these reviews. The Forum of Firms is primarily funded by participating firms that will also contribute additional resources to strengthen IFAC's audit standards and monitoring work. The Forum works alongside the new International Forum on Accountancy Development (IFAD), spearheaded by IFAC, to improve the quality of global accounting and auditing. In addition, an independent Public Oversight Board will see to it that the activities of IFAC and its Forum of Firms are in the public interest.

IFAD was established following the Asian financial crisis in heeding a 1997 call from James Wolfensohn then president of the World Bank. The accounting profession was criticized for not doing enough to enhance the accounting capabilities of developing and emerging nations. Following discussions between the World Bank and IFAC, it was agreed to form IFAD, representing an alliance of accountancy groups and firms across the world. IFAD is intended to be a means by which regulators, international financial institutions, investors, and representatives of the accountancy and auditing profession come together to ensure that economic downturns such as the Asian financial crisis are not repeated (see Exhibit 15.6).

IFAD has been undertaking country-by-country reviews of accounting standards, ethics and disciplinary procedures, corporate governance, banking, and company law. IFAD has benchmarked information collected through these individual country reviews against international standards and will finance consultants to visit countries to help close the gaps wherever these may be identified. IFAD is firmly committed to encouraging conformity and consistency of national accounting standards with IAS.

The key to global acceptance and enforcement of International Accounting Standards depends very much on the successful implementation of IFAC's and IFAD's new initiatives. In particular, IFAD needs to promote education addressing IAS, ISA, and IFAC's Code of Ethics on a global basis. IFAC's Forum of Firms also

Exhibit 15.6 International Forum on Accountancy Development

Objectives of IFAD

1. Promote understanding by national governments of the value of transparent financial reporting, in accordance with sound corporate governance

2. Assist in defining expectations as to how the accountancy profession (in both the public and private sectors) should carry out its responsibilities to support the public interest

3. Encourage governments to focus more directly on the needs of developing countries and economies in transition

4. Help harness funds and expertise to build accounting and auditing capacity in developing countries

5. Contribute to a common strategy and framework of reference for accountancy development

6. Promote cooperation between governments, the accountancy and other professions, the international financial institutions, regulators, standard setters, capital providers and issuers

IFAD has provided a mechanism through which those with an interest in raising reporting and auditing practices can communicate and can develop the partnerships necessary to promote change in an effective and efficient manner.

Source: www.ifad.net

needs to insist on the comparable implementation of accounting and auditing standards on a global basis. Despite the difficulty of setting and enforcing a uniform set of standards worldwide, the IFAC has made significant strides toward harmonization. The European Commission has stated that it intends to adopt ISAs for all audits in Europe effective January 2007. South Africa adopted the entire set of ISAs effective January 2005. The standard-setting bodies of Canada, Australia, and New Zealand are working with the IAASB on many harmonization efforts. Other countries such as Singapore, Hong Kong, Russia, and Argentina have adopted ISAs as well (Sylph, 2005).

Given the United States' dominance in the audit industry, and considering that the "Big Four" are all based in that country, getting the PCAOB to collaborate in the harmonization process will prove crucial to the success of IFAC's initiatives. The recent establishment of the PCAOB in the United States may slow down the harmonization process in that country because the new standard-setting body is focusing its efforts on regulating the U.S. market and regaining investor confidence in the profession (Giles, Venuti, and Jones, 2004). Despite the task faced by the PCAOB in its own country, the chief accountant of the SEC, the body that oversees the PCAOB, said:

> I support convergence between U.S. and international accounting standards. Having a common accounting language that's usable around the globe would be a dream come true. For U.S. investors to be able to understand one set of international standards rather than those of 50 different countries will be a tremendous improvement. I also [want] to be clear that we're looking for the best accounting standards globally, not the lowest common denominator. I'm very

supportive of the way in which the IASB has conducted its affairs, and the European community ought to be commended for moving in the direction of international accounting standards in such a short period of time. (*Journal of Accountancy*, p. 70, 2005)

Only time will tell if the efforts of IFAD and IFAC can overcome national, cultural, and other barriers and achieve global acceptance and enforcement of IAS and International Standards of Auditing (ISA) in countries around the world. In the meantime, IFAC's Forum of Firms should take the lead by upgrading their quality standards to a consistent worldwide level and ensure compliance with IAS and ISA as well as IFAC's Code of Ethics throughout their global networks.

SUMMARY

1. Successful auditing requires an objective (independent), competent person; quantifiable (and verifiable) information; and established criteria (or auditing standards).

2. The quality of the auditing profession is a function of several factors, such as the reputation of the accounting and auditing profession, the quality of the educational system, and the certification process. The certification or licensing process for an auditor differs by country and is a function of several factors, such as the identity of the candidate, educational requirements, experience requirements, and examination.

3. Although auditing an MNE does not significantly increase engagement risk for an accounting firm, several factors make the execution of an international audit more complex than a domestic audit.

4. Auditing in the international context is a challenging task because of the differences in local business practices and customs; currency, language and law; distance and organizational issues; and the availability of suitable personnel.

5. Auditors can service their global clients by sending auditors from the home office to foreign locations; by establishing correspondent relationships with foreign auditing firms; or by investing in a foreign auditing practice through a branch office, a joint venture with a local auditing firm, or a wholly owned company.

6. Reciprocity, or the ability of a certified accountant in one country to practice in another, continues to be a challenging issue worldwide. The General Agreement on Trade in Services (GATS) was established to help address this issue.

7. The international audit industry is characterized by concentration by a few large firms. The Big Four, the world's largest accounting firms, are responsible for auditing most of the largest MNEs.

8. The fall of Arthur Andersen and the Sarbanes-Oxley Act of 2002 have significantly affected the accounting profession worldwide by reducing the supply of international auditing firms worldwide and limiting the scope of service each firm can provide to any single client.

9. A major development in the global strategies of the world's largest auditing firms in recent years has been the merger of firms such as Deloitte

Haskins & Sells with Touche Ross, Arthur Young with Ernst & Whinney, and Price Waterhouse with Coopers and Lybrand to form larger auditing firms that are better able to audit global corporations.

10. The mergers just mentioned have allowed the large firms to meet the growing international needs of MNEs. In addition, international auditing firms provide value to companies in emerging markets by facilitating the process of obtaining financing from more developed countries.

11. National audit standards differ from country to country for a variety of reasons including the stage of development of capital markets, the maturity of the accounting profession, and the cultural environment.

12. The establishment of the PCAOB in the United States ended a long tradition of self-regulation by the auditing profession in that country. The PCAOB has a strong influence on the Big Four accounting firms.

13. The International Federation of Accountants (IFAC) is attempting to harmonize auditing standards and practices so that financial statement users worldwide can be confident of the accuracy and reliability of the underlying financial statements.

14. The harmonization of international auditing standards has many benefits, all of which help increase confidence of investors in the reliability of financial statements.

15. Many countries have begun adopting ISAs, including the European Union, which will adopt ISAs beginning in January 2007. However, much work still needs to be done to achieve the goal of complete harmonization in auditing standards.

Discussion Questions

1. The auditor certification process varies considerably by country. Some countries require a university degree coupled with a formal examination to obtain a license, while others have less stringent requirements. Do you think a formalized certification process is necessary? Why?

2. If you were a certified accountant in your home country and wanted to practice as an auditor in another country, it is unlikely that you would be allowed to practice right away. Why do these barriers to entry exist? What strategies could you pursue to service your clients in markets where you are not allowed to practice?

3. Although conventional wisdom suggests that auditing an MNE is riskier than auditing a domestic company, the text cites a study which concludes that MNE audits do not present additional risks. Do you agree with the study's findings? Justify your answer.

4. The text cites a study which concludes that auditing an MNE is no riskier than auditing a domestic company. Does this mean that auditing an MNE requires the same capabilities as auditing a domestic company? What are some of the challenges global auditing firms face in trying to service their clients?

5. If you were the engagement partner responsible for the audit of an MNE, what challenges would you face in coordinating the audit work? What strategies would you apply to facilitate the work?

6. Why are the audits of most of the largest global companies done by the Big Four accounting firms? How do these large firms provide value to their customers?

7. Recall Exhibit 15.3, which shows the worldwide revenues of the largest audit firms. Critics of the audit profession point out that the concentration of audit services among the Big Four can lead to a reduction in audit quality owing to lack of competition. Why would this be a cause for concern? How can this issue be reversed?

8. It was mentioned in the chapter that KPMG has reorganized itself around four industry-specific lines of business: consumer and industrial businesses; financial services; health care and public sector; and information, communications, and entertainment with industry-focus teams for assurance and tax services. Why do you think KPMG moved to this type of organizational structure rather than remain organized by service (assurance and tax? Which of the global strategies mentioned in Chapter 12 most closely resembles this reorganization?

9. The corporate scandals of recent years have shaken the auditing industry. Explain the effects that the fall of Arthur Andersen and the passage of the Sarbanes-Oxley Act of 2002 have had on the profession so far.

10. The Sarbanes-Oxley Act prohibits accounting firms from providing many nonaudit services to its audit clients. Why was this rule created? Do you agree with it? Why?

11. You have the opportunity to work on an internship in a foreign country for an audit firm with an office in that country. What would be the advantages and challenges of such an experience? What would you do to prepare for that experience?

12. In some countries, such as Canada, auditing standards are developed and enforced by private organizations, and the profession is pretty much self-regulated. In other countries, the government is responsible for setting and enforcing auditing standards. In your opinion, which approach is better? Justify your answer.

13. IFAC is attempting to harmonize auditing standards and practices. What are the benefits of having a set of generally accepted international standards? What challenges does the IFAC face in conducting such an effort?

14. Even if full harmonization of auditing standards is achieved, the question remains as to how they will be enforced worldwide. In your opinion, how can the enforcement problem be solved?

15. What are the prospects of IFAC achieving its goal of worldwide reliability of financial statements? What roles do the Forum of Firms and IFAD play in the harmonization effort?

Exercises

1. The certification process for auditors varies significantly by country. Learn about the certification requirements in your own country and answer the following questions:

   a. What is the name of the organization responsible for certifying auditors? Is it a government agency or a private agency?

   b. What steps must a person follow to become a certified auditor in your country? Are there minimum education requirements? Is a formal exam required to become certified?

   c. In your opinion, do these requirements help ensure that auditors are competent? What, if anything, would you improve about the certification process?

2. As was mentioned in the chapter, reciprocity is the ability of an accountant to practice in a different country. For this to be possible, the foreign country must recognize the qualifications of the accountant. The General Agreement on Trade in Services (GATS), sponsored by the WTO, was established in 1995 to promote the cross-border transfer of services, including accounting. Go to www.wto.org and find the section on services. Answer the following questions.

    a. What is the main purpose of GATS?

    b. What are the basic obligations for members of GATS?

    c. Find the section on "accountancy services." From time to time, committees from different countries post proposals on how to foster reciprocity in accounting services. Find a recent proposal and read it. What does the proposal suggest? Do you think the ideas in the proposal are beneficial for the profession worldwide?

3. The following article reports on one of the many challenges faced by auditors in serving MNEs:

    > Worried about partner defections, Big Five accounting and consulting firm KPMG International said it will spend $100 million to more fully tie together its world-wide computer systems. Dubbed "KWORLD," KPMG's attempt to develop a new, global "digital nervous system" marks the first time the firm has devoted such a large amount of money to a computer overhaul. Currently, KPMG's computers aren't fully integrated world-wide. KPMG typically spends $50 million a year on upgrading its computers. Last month, top partners at KPMG Canada threatened to defect to Arthur Andersen, citing as one of their reasons the difficulty in serving multinational clients due to KPMG's unintegrated systems. KPMG hopes a more integrated system will calm some nerves. KPMG's new system, which the firm will begin rolling out next month will come with a new global online-messaging and "knowledge sharing" platform in which partners can access corporate client information from anywhere in the world, says Michael J. Turillo, KPMG's international chief knowledge officer." ("KPMG to Fully Integrate Its Global Computer System," *Wall Street Journal* (Eastern edition), New York, May 27, 1999. p. 1)

    a. What difficulties might KPMG's partners have had in serving multinational clients without an integrated system?

    b. How can information technology (IT) help solve some of the coordination and communication issues of auditing an MNE?

    c. IT can only go so far to solve the international auditor's communications issues. How do culture, language, and differences in local audit practices affect the effectiveness of communications in an international audit engagement?

4. As mentioned in the text, as of the writing of this chapter an agreement between the United States and the European Union on auditor reciprocity and regulation was pending approval by members of the EU and by the European Parliament. Visit www.europa.eu.int to learn more about the proposal its progress in the approval process.

5. Although the Sarbanes-Oxley Act (SOX) is a U.S. law, Section 404 of SOX requires the auditors of publicly listed companies in the United States, including foreign firms, to audit the internal controls of the company and issue an opinion on the effectiveness of controls in addition to the traditional opinion of the financial statements. Suppose you are the engagement partner for the audit of Morgan Inc., a U.S.-based MNE with a subsidiary in Argentina. In the past, you have relied on the work of local auditors for the Argentine subsidiary. This year you are unsure about how much to rely on the work of local auditors to comply with Section 404. After all, Argentina is not subject to SOX and auditors there have little experience auditing internal controls in such a rigorous man-

ner. You are also concerned that management of the Argentine subsidiary is unaware of SOX and its requirements under Section 404. Based on this scenario, answer the following questions:

   a.   Should you rely on the work of the local auditors to comply with Section 404? Justify your answer.

   b.   How can you make up for the lack of training of the local auditors?

   c.   How would you coordinate the internal controls audit in the Argentine subsidiary?

6. The following report was published on December 18, 2004:

> On December 15th [2004] Air China joined the growing ranks of Chinese companies listed on western stock exchanges. Unlike several other big Chinese firms, the national airline chose to land at the London Stock Exchange rather than in New York. One reason is thought to be that listing in America has become increasingly burdensome since Congress passed the Sarbanes-Oxley act in 2002. ... Several European firms have said that they would consider delisting from American exchanges, given the cost of compliance with the law. The most onerous part of the act is Section 404, [which] requires ... public companies (and their external auditors) to appraise the internal controls over financial transactions and to report any weaknesses ... The number of controls that big companies must test and document can run into the tens of thousands, down to limiting who can sign company checks. Not surprisingly, this is expensive. Sarbanes-Oxley (mostly Section 404) cost General Electric about $30m in extra payments to its auditor in 2003. J.P. Morgan Chase says that it has 130 employees working full-time on compliance with the rule. And according to a study by Ernst & Young, an audit firm, half of America's large public companies estimated that they would devote more than 100,000 man-hours to compliance with Section 404 in its first year. The load should ease thereafter ... Some audit firms are so overloaded that they have been dumping less profitable clients, usually smaller companies.
>
> Foreign firms ... listed on an American exchange must comply with Section 404. ... Several might consider delisting—but they cannot deregister from the SEC if they have more than 300 American investors. All this may be harming American exchanges' ability to compete with European rivals for new listings. ... Of course, against the expense and lost business must be weighed the benefits of better auditing and more trustworthy accounts. "There is something to be said for listing on the exchange with the highest standards," says Christian Brakman of the NYSE. The NYSE thinks that European corporate governance regulation is already tightening too, thus reducing the competitive gap. For listed companies, there may be no escaping the paperwork." ("404 Tonnes of Paper," *The Economist*, 373, no. 8406: 142)

   a.   What challenges does Section 404 present to the auditors of foreign MNEs wishing to list in U.S. exchanges?

   b.   Training staff on how to audit internal controls has been a major expense for audit firms. How can international audit firms train staff located in countries not subject to the Sarbanes-Oxley Act?

   c.   Despite the challenges you just listed, do you see any opportunities for auditors in helping MNEs comply with Section 404?

7. The fall of Arthur Andersen in 2002, one of the world's most renowned professional services firms, rocked the auditing industry. The story of Andersen's demise is important in understanding the current situation of the audit profession. Find the article *"Sad Account: Andersen's Fall From Grace Is a Tale of Greed and Miscues—Pushed to Boost Rev-*

enue, Auditors Acted as Sellers, Warred With Consultants—'Three Pebbles and a Boulder'" by Ken Brown and Ianthe Jeanne Dugan in the *Wall Street Journal* (Eastern edition) dated June 7, 2002. After reading it, answer the following questions:

    a. Summarize the events that led to Andersen's indictment. In your opinion, what caused the fall of Arthur Andersen?

    b. In 1913, founder Arthur Andersen said, "We want to measure our contribution more by the quality of the service rendered than by whether we are making a good living out of it." How did Andersen go from its founder's mentality to being guilty of fraud?

    c. How has the disappearance of Andersen affected the international audit industry?

8. PricewaterhouseCoopers (PwC) is one of the "Big Four" audit firms. Visit www.pwc.com to learn more about this firm.

    a. Where does the firm have offices? What are the benefits of having a presence in so many locations? What are the challenges of providing accounting services in such a dispersed set of locations?

    b. What industries does PwC cover?

    c. Learn about one important issue faced by the audit profession today. What is the issue? How is it affecting the profession? [*Hint:* look for a section on current events or a press release link.]

    d. Find PwC's most recent Annual Review. What does the review contain? Choose an area that interests you and learn more about it.

    e. If available, find the PwC website for your own country and learn about the firm's activities there.

9. The following announcement was published in March 2001:

> Ernst & Young Inc. (EY) has announced that it is merging its China division with leading mainland China accounting firm Da Hua. The merger will create the firm Ernst & Young Da Hua, and is driven by the need of EY to enhance its domestic presence in mainland China. Da Hua will benefit from the international exposure and the technical backup and resources associated with big five firms. Da Hua is rated as the number one audit firm on mainland China by the Chinese Securities Regulatory Commission (CSRC), in terms of the number of listed companies it audits and the asset base of listed client companies. The new union will be a fully-fledged merger according to EY, with seven senior managers of Da Hua joining as partners of the new firm. Anthony T Y Wu, chairman of Ernst & Young Inc.'s operations in China, will serve as chairman of the new firm. Wu predicted that the removal of the quota of CSRC on listings would lead to "an explosion" in the number of companies seeking a listing on the mainland China and Hong Kong, China bourses. ("E&Y Announces Merger in China," *Accountancy,* 127, no. 1291 (2001): 10.

    a. How did the merger benefit both Ernst & Young and Da Hua?

    b. What kind of clients do you predict Ernst & Young Da Hua will attract? How will those clients benefit from having an internationally known auditor?

    c. What challenges do you predict these two firms will have in trying to integrate their practices and personnel?

10. Learn more about the audit function, ethical standards, and audit reports of your own country.

    a. Is there an organization responsible for setting audit standards? Is it a private or a government organization? Describe the process by which audit standards are created.

    b. Does the profession have a written code of ethics? If so, describe the independence requirement for auditors in your country.

    c. Who is required to be audited by law? What does the audit report for these companies contain?

11. Use the information in Exhibit 15.4 to compare the audit function, ethical standards and enforcement, and audit reports of three countries from different continents. Develop a matrix that includes countries down one side and the three dimensions just described across the top so you can compare and contrast the different countries. Answer the following questions:

    a. Which of the three countries has the most stringent requirements? Which one has the least stringent requirements?

    b. Do you see a correlation between the economic development of a country and the sophistication of its auditing profession? If so, explain your findings.

    c. Why is a strong, trustworthy auditing profession in a country necessary to foster investment?

12. The establishment of the PCAOB in the United States as the standard-setting body for the audit profession marked the end of a long tradition of self-regulation by auditors in that country. Visit www.pcaobus.org and download the most recent annual report.

    a. What is the mission of the PCAOB?

    b. Read the registration requirements for auditors in the United States. As of the writing of this book, the PCAOB required any foreign auditors that prepare or furnish an audit report with respect to any U.S. company to register with the PCAOB and be subject to a review every three years. Do you agree with the PCAOB's policy on foreign auditors?

    c. What type of firms does the PCAOB inspect annually?

    d. When was the first auditing standard set by the PCAOB? What is the main requirement in Standard No. 1?

13. The International Federation of Accountants' (IFAC) strategic plan for 2005–2008, found on www.ifac.org, provides an excellent discussion of the environmental factors influencing the accounting and audit professions worldwide. Understanding these factors will help you have a better understanding of the opportunities and challenges faced by the auditing industry. Read Section 4 of IFAC's strategic plan and answer the following questions:

    a. What are the three global environmental factors affecting the audit profession?

    b. What factors are affecting the accounting profession in general?

    c. What factors are specifically affecting the audit profession?

    d. How do all these factors affect IFAC's mission to harmonize audit standards and unify the audit profession worldwide?

14. In Exercise 10 you read Section 4 of IFAC's strategic plan for 2005–2008. Sections 5 and 6 of the plan outline the organization's objectives and priorities for the upcoming years. Read these two sections and answer the following questions:

    a. What are IFAC's main objectives?

    b. Do you agree with IFAC's mission? What are the benefits of having a set of worldwide auditing standards?

    c.   Do you think it is possible to harmonize auditing standards worldwide? Justify your answer.

15.   The International Auditing and Assurance Standards Board (IAASB) is the arm of the IFAC specifically charged with setting ISA's. Find one of the IAASB's current projects by going to www.ifac.org/IAASB.

    a.   What is the standard about?

    b.   How long has the IAASB been working on this project?

    c.   When is the new standard expected to be approved?

    d.   Find an explanation of the process followed by the IAASB in writing an ISA. Describe the process in one paragraph.

Case: Lucas International: Coordinating an International Audit
Case: Xerox Corporation

These cases can be found on the following website: www.wiley.com/college/radebaugh

Selected References

AAA. 1973. A Statement of Basic Auditing Concepts. Committee on Basic Auditing Concepts (Studies in Accounting Research No. 6). Sarasota, FL: American Accounting Association.

The Banker. 2004. "Big four are playing with fire in auditing multinationals, says PwC." *The Banker* 154(939): 8.

Barrett, M., D. Cooper, and K. Jamal. 2005. "Globalization and the Coordinating of Work in Multinational Audits." *Accounting, Organizations & Society* 30(1): 1–25.

Carmichael, D. R. 1985. "International Harmonization of Auditing Standards." In *Comparative International Auditing Standards,* edited by Belverd E. Needles, Jr., pp. 165–182.

CICA/AICPA. 1999. Continuous Auditing. Research Report commissioned jointly by the Canadian Institute of Chartered Accountants and the American Institute of Certified Public Accountants. Toronto, Ontario: CICA.

Citron, D. B., and G. Manalis. 2001. "The International Firms as New Entrants to the Statutory Audit Market: An Empirical Analysis of Auditor Selection in Greece, 1993 to 1997." *European Accounting Review* 10(3): 439–460.

Economist. 2004. "Called to Account." *The Economist* 373(8402): 71–74.

Giles, J. P., E. K. Venuti, and R. C. Jones. 2004. "The PCAOB and Convergence of the Global Auditing and Accounting Profession." *The CPA Journal* 75(3): 36–40.

Hermanson, D., 1993. "Multinational External Audit Planning." *International Journal of Accounting* 28(3): 206–215.

Hermanson, D., and J. Carcello. 1996. "An Analysis of Multinational 'Audit Failures'." *International Journal of Accounting* 31(3): 281–282.

"In the Public Interest." 2005. *Journal of Accountancy,* 1/05, 199, 1; p. 63 (actual quote on p. 70)

IFAC Handbook of International Auditing, Assurance, and Ethics Pronouncements. 2005. International Federation of Accountants.

International Federation of Accountants. www.ifac.org.

International Forum on Accountancy Development. www.ifad.net.

Ivancevich, S. H., and A. Zardkoohi. 2000. "An Exploratory Analysis of the 1989 Accounting Firm Megamergers." *Accounting Horizons* 14(4): 389–402.

Klaassen, J., and J. Buisman. 1995. "International Auditing." In C. Nobes, and R. Parker, *Comparative International Accounting.* Hertfordshire, U.K.: Prentice-Hall, pp. 440–465.

Messier, William F., Jr., S. M. Glowen, and D. F. Prowitt. 2006. *Auditing Assurance Services: A Systematic Approach,* 4th ed. New York: McGraw-Hill, p. 2.

Miller, John W. 2004. "U.S. and EU Reconcile Audit Issues; Two Sides Bridge Divide over Regulation of Firms with Plan for Watchdogs." *Wall Street Journal* (Eastern edition), March 26, p. B.2.

Needles, B. E., Jr., ed. 1985. *Comparative International Auditing Standards.* Sarasota, FL: American Accounting Association.

Needles, B. E., Jr., 2000. "Taxonomy of Auditing Standards." In *International Accounting and Finance Handbook,* edited by F. D. S. Choi. New York: John Wiley, Chapter 5.

Needles, B., Jr., T. McDermott, and R. Temkin. 1991. "Taxonomy of Auditing Standards," in Handbook of International Accounting, Chapter 6, edited by F. D. S. Choi. New York: John Wiley.

Needles, B. E., Jr., S. Ramamoorti, and S. W. Shelton. 2000. "The Role of International Auditing in the Improvement of International Financial Reporting." In *International Accounting and Finance Handbook,* edited by F. D. S. Choi. New York: John Wiley.

Nicolaisen D. T. 2005. "In the Public Interest." *Journal of Accountancy* 199(1): 63–69.

North American Trade Pacts and CA Free Trade Given Recognition Bonus. 1992. *World Accounting Report.* (April): 2, 6.

PAR. 1998. "U. N. Criticizes CPAs for Role in Asian Crisis." *Public Accounting Report* (November 15): 4.

Pomeranz, F. 1986. "Auditing International Operations." In Cashin's *Handbook for Auditors,* 2nd ed., edited by J. A. Cashin, P. D. Neuwirth, and J. F. Levy. Englewood Cliffs, NJ: Prentice-Hall, pp. 23–1–23–17.

Roussey, R. S. 1999. "International Accounting and Auditing Standards in Practice." Presentation at the 34th International Accounting Conference sponsored by the Center for International Education and Research in Accounting (CIERA), University of Illinois at Urbana-Champaign (April 22–24).

Smith, A. 1995. "The United States-Canada Bilateral Agreement on Reciprocity from an U.S. Perspective." *IFAC Newsletter* 19(1): 1–3.

Stamp, E., and M. Moonitz. 1979. *International Auditing Standards.* Englewood Cliffs, NJ: Prentice-Hall.

Street, D. L., and S. J. Gray. 2001. "Observance of International Accounting Standards: Factors Explaining Noncompliance." The Association of Chartered Certified Accountants, 2001.

Street, D. L., S. J. Gray, and S. M. Bryant. 1999. "Acceptance and Observance of International Accounting Standards: An Empirical Study of Companies Claiming to Comply with IASs." *The International Journal of Accounting* 34(1): 11–48.

Suk-Yee Lee, D. 2005. "The Impact of the Big 8 Mergers on Market Power: Evidence from the Hong Kong Market." *Journal of International Financial Management & Accounting* 16(1): 69–97.

Sylph, James M. 2005. "Global Convergence—Near or Far?" In Auditing Section 2005 Mid-Year Conference, American Accounting Association, New Orleans, January 14. Available on http://www.ifac.org/Library.

Taub, Stephen. 2005. "Best Buy Parts w/E&Y," *CFO.com.* Jan 05, 2005.

Tie, R. 2000. "IFAC, Firms to Apply International Standards Consistently." *Journal of Accountancy* 189(4): 20–21.

Turner, L. 1998. Remarks by Lynn Turner, Chief Accountant, United States Securities and Exchange Commission, at the Twenty-Sixth Annual National Conference on Current SEC Developments.

Walker, Norman R. 1997. "Managing the Audit Relationship in an International Context." In *Handbook of International Accounting,* Chapter 6, edited by F. D. S. Choi. New York: John Wiley, pp. 21.1–21.26.

Wessel, David. 2004. "The Future of Jobs: New Ones Arise, Wage Gap Widens." Wall Street Journal, Apr. 2, 2004. Available on www.wsjclassroomedition.com/outsourcing/out_barbell.htm.

CHAPTER SIXTEEN

INTERNATIONAL TAXATION ISSUES

Chapter Objectives

- Identify the major factors that influence the different tax systems used worldwide

- Discuss the role that the tax credit and tax treaties play in avoiding double taxation when firms earn income in different countries

- Explain how income from controlled foreign corporations may be taxed differently than income from noncontrolled foreign corporations

- Compare the tax treatment and book treatment of foreign exchange gains and losses due to foreign currency transactions and the translation of foreign currency financial statements

- Discuss the tax dimensions of intracorporate transfer pricing

- Illustrate how international tax planning can influence cash flows

INTRODUCTION

The game between tax authority and corporation or individual is an ancient one played with all the gusto of any natural rivalry. As the tax authority sets up a new defense to plug the gaps, the corporation adjusts its strategy and tries to open up a new hole or take advantage of existing ones. For the multinational enterprises (MNE), every taxing authority around the world has its own set of defenses that must be adjusted to.

The challenge is significant, and home office tax accountants must work with specialists in tax law from each country in which the firm operates as well as with technical advisers in exchange controls and cash flow possibilities. This chapter

Strategic Decision Point

Motorola, one of the world's largest mobile-phone companies, has operations that span across the world. As such, it has control over transfer prices between its operations in different countries. In August of 2004, Motorola announced that the Internal Revenue Service (IRS) was seeking an extra $500M in taxes from the company. The IRS claims that Motorola set transfer prices in order to avoid paying U.S. taxes. They claim Motorola should have had an additional $1.4 billion in U.S. income during the period. As such, the IRS might force Motorola to make adjustments that would shift profit from other countries to the United States.

Transfer pricing is a major international tax issue as more and more companies become multinational enterprises. Because many companies use transfer prices to transfer profits from high-tax countries to low-tax countries, the IRS and other international organizations are working to help improve and better regulate this issue.

considers the philosophy of tax systems and taxation, especially as that philosophy relates to foreign source income and taxes related to revenues and earnings from international operations.

Although tax systems vary around the world, it is commonly accepted that each country has the right to tax income earned inside its borders. That is where the similarity stops. Opinions diverge as to the classes of revenue considered taxable, how expenses are determined, and what kinds of taxes should be used (such as direct or indirect). Moreover, there are differences in adherence to tax laws based on cultural differences and attitudes toward enforcement.

DIRECT TAXES

Corporate Income Tax

The two approaches to taxing corporate income are the classic and the integrated systems. The classic system used in the United States, Belgium, the Netherlands, and Luxembourg, for example, taxes income when it is received by each taxable entity. Thus, the earnings of a corporation are taxed twice—when the corporation earns them and when they are received as dividends by shareholders. The United States, however, has decreased the double-taxation burden by lowering the dividend tax rate so that it is taxed at a preferential rate.

The integrated system tries to take taxation of both the corporation and the shareholder into consideration in order to eliminate double taxation. In most cases, there is only partial rather than full integration, so double taxation is not completely eliminated. There are two ways to integrate a system:

1. Through a split rate as in Germany, in which the normal tax rate for most companies is 45 percent; the rate is reduced, however, to 30 percent for profits that are distributed.

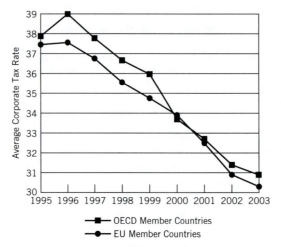

Figure 16.1 OECD and EU Average Corporate Tax Rates—1995–2003

2. The second and dominant approach to integration is imputation, which involves taxing earnings at the same rate whether remitted as a dividend or not, but allowing a partial or full tax credit for the shareholders. This is the approach followed by most of the remaining countries in the European Union (EU), as well as such non-EU countries as Canada, Australia, New Zealand, and Japan—but with different results. Most of the European countries using the integrated approach have adopted a system of giving partial credits to shareholders on tax paid by the corporation when income is distributed to the shareholder. This is the approach followed in the United Kingdom where the corporate tax rate is a flat 31 percent. When shareholders are taxed on their dividends, a portion of the corporate income tax paid by the corporation is imputed to the shareholders so the income is not double taxed. Other countries, like Italy and France, have a full imputation system in which shareholders get a tax credit that eliminates their tax burden.

It is interesting to note that in general, corporate tax rates have been coming down in recent years, notably in the OECD and EU (see Figure 16.1).

What Income Is Taxable?

Even without leaving home, a corporation may begin to interact with the nuances of different tax systems: income derived from the export of goods and services as well as from a foreign branch or foreign corporation. Worldwide foreign source income from the export of goods and services is taxable when earned. Tax incentives, such as the Foreign Sales Corporation in the United States, may be used to encourage exports, however. These incentives have the effect of taxing foreign source income differently from domestic income.

Taxing the earnings of foreign branches and foreign corporations is more complex. Two different approaches to the taxation of foreign source income are the territorial approach and the worldwide approach. The territorial approach as used in Hong Kong, for example, asserts that only income earned in Hong Kong should be taxed there; foreign source income should be taxed in the country where it is generated, not in Hong Kong.

The worldwide approach, as used in the United States, taxes both domestic and foreign source income. This may lead to double taxation because that income may be taxed in two different countries. The two major ways to minimize double taxation where foreign source income is taxed is through the tax credit (allowing the company a direct credit against domestic taxes for the foreign income taxes already paid) and tax treaties. In addition, some countries that use the worldwide approach do not tax earnings of foreign subsidiaries until the parent receives a dividend. This is known as the deferral of taxation of foreign source income.

Within a given country, the tax authorities normally tax income on earnings of all corporations, even when foreign investors own them. For example, the German subsidiary of General Motors is taxed like all corporations in Germany. The domestic branch of a foreign corporation is normally taxed at the same rate as domestic corporations.

Determination of Expenses

Another factor that causes differences in the amount of taxes paid is the way countries treat certain expenses for tax purposes. Expenses are usually a matter of timing. If R&D expenses are capitalized, for example, their impact on taxable income will be spread over the period in which they are written off. If they are treated as expenses in the period in which they are incurred, the impact will be immediate.

Opinions also differ from country to country as to the useful life of an asset. If one government allows a company to write off an asset in 5 years, whereas in another country the same asset has a taxable useful life of 10 years, the tax burdens in the two countries will be quite different. In addition, there may be a big difference between a country's statutory and effective tax rate. A high statutory tax rate with a liberal determination of expenses may result in a relatively low taxable income and thus low effective tax rate, and this is the rate that is of concern to the investor. For example, when the United States passed the Tax Reform Act (TRA) of 1986, the U.S. government lowered tax rates, but it broadened the base of taxable income so that it would continue to collect roughly the same amount of revenue. Thus, the effective tax rate did not change as much as did the statutory tax rate. This same effect spread throughout most of the other OECD countries during the late 1980s where rates were reduced and the tax base broadened. A few exceptions are France, Germany, and Italy, where tax rates were reduced but the base was not broadened.

Withholding Tax

The income earned by the foreign subsidiary or affiliate of a multinational is taxable in the foreign country, and the tax is levied against the foreign corporation, not against the parent. However, the actual cash returns to the parent in the form of dividends, royalties (payments made by the foreign corporation to the parent for the use of patents, trademarks, processes, and so on), and interest on intracompany debt are taxable to the parent. Normally, a country levies a withholding tax on payments to the nonresident investor. This tax varies in size from country to country and depends on whether the country has a tax treaty with other countries.

INDIRECT TAXES

Value-Added or Goods and Services Taxes

In some countries, such as the United States, the individual direct income tax is the most important source of revenue for the government. In other countries, like France, indirect taxes are very important. Examples of indirect taxes are consumption taxes (such as the sales tax in the United States), the VAT (Value-Added Tax), excise taxes, estate and gift taxes, employment taxes, and different kinds of user fees.

Value-Added Tax   In Europe, the VAT, sometimes referred to as the TVA, is a source of considerable government income and is also the major source of revenue for funding the operations of the EU. The basic concept behind the VAT is that a tax is applied at each stage of the production process for the value added by the firm to goods purchased from the outside, which have been subject to the VAT. The tax is charged by businesses on the value of their sales, but the tax burden eventually falls on the consumer because a company that pays VAT on its own expenses can reclaim the tax that was already paid. The major method for computing the VAT and the one required in the EU is the subtractive method. Exhibit 16.1 demonstrates how to compute the VAT in the United Kingdom where the VAT rate is 17.5 percent. The VAT differs from a sales tax in that the entire sales tax appears at the retail level rather than at each stage of the process. In addition, the VAT is not listed separately to the consumer. For example, the consumer would not pay

Exhibit 16.1   The Value-Added Tax

Calculation	Manufacturer	Wholesaler	Retailer	Consumer
Net cost of goods	£0.00	£10.00	£14.00	£23.50
Markup		£4.00	£6.00	
Net selling price	£10.00	£14.00	£20.00	
VAT chargeable (17.5% × Net selling price)	£1.75	£2.45	£3.50	
Gross selling price	£11.75	£16.45	£23.50	
Accounting for VAT				
Due to Customs and Excise	£1.75	£2.45	£3.50	
Recoverable from Customs and Excise	£0.00	£1.75	£2.45	
Net VAT Paid	£1.75	£0.70	£1.05	

the retailer £23.50 plus a VAT of £4.11. The £23.50 that the consumer pays the retailer includes the VAT.

THE AVOIDANCE OF DOUBLE TAXATION OF FOREIGN SOURCE INCOME

Credits and Deductions

The foreign branches and subsidiaries of MNEs are subject to a variety of taxes, both direct and indirect, in the countries where they operate. The problem is that the income earned in the foreign country may be subject to income taxes twice: when the earnings are realized in the foreign location and when they are realized in the parent country. In the United States, for example, income from foreign corporations is usually taxed when a dividend is remitted to the parent company. The company may choose to treat the taxes paid as a credit that can be applied against their tax liability, or it can deduct the tax from income to reduce taxable income.

The simple illustration in Exhibit 16.2 demonstrates the difference in U.S. tax liability that arises from double taxation, a tax deduction, and a tax credit. In the double taxation column, the foreign source income is taxed at 30 percent in the foreign country and at 35 percent in the United States (using the U.S. federal rate). Thus, the total tax paid is $65, the net income after all taxes is only $35, and the effective tax rate is 65 percent. In the deduction column, the U.S. tax rate of 35 percent is levied on the income that results from deducting the foreign income tax from the gross income of the foreign corporation. Thus, the U.S. tax is only $24.50, the total tax paid is $54.50, and the net income after tax in both countries is $45.50, definitely better than in the double taxation situation. Notice that under the tax credit column, U.S. income tax of $5.00 is assessed against the foreign source income because the tax rate in the foreign country (30 percent) is lower than it is in the United States (35 percent). In U.S. tax law, an excess credit (if the foreign tax rate exceeds the U.S. tax rate) can be carried back and applied against foreign source income of prior years or carried forward to be applied against foreign source income in future years.

Exhibit 16.2 Treatment of Foreign Corporate Income Tax

	Double Taxation	Deduction	Credit
Income earned by the foreign corporation	$100.00	$100.00	$100.00
Foreign tax at 30% on $100	30.00	30.00	30.00
Net income after tax	$70.00	$70.00	$70.00
U.S. tax at 35% on $100	35.00		
U.S. tax at 35% on $70		$24.50	
U.S. tax at 35% on $100 less foreign tax at 30% on $100			5.00
Net income after taxes in U.S.	$35.00	$45.50	$65.00
Effective tax rate	65%	54.5%	35%

A key point to grasp is that a tax must be considered an income tax to be creditable; the VAT described earlier would be eligible for deduction but not for the credit. In determining the tax credit in the United States, for example, the predominant nature of the foreign tax must be that of an income tax as defined in the United States. Thus, a tax might be considered an income tax in one country but still not be eligible for the credit if that tax is deemed something else from the perspective of the IRS in the United States.

In the United States, the tax credit is available only for taxes on income paid directly by the U.S. corporation (e.g., the withholding tax on dividends) or deemed to have been paid by it. The deemed direct tax is the corporate income tax actually paid by the foreign corporation to the foreign government and deemed to have been paid by the U.S. parent.

Tax Treaties

As we have noted, with the spread of business worldwide, income earned in one country may be subject to taxation in other countries. Philosophical differences about how income should be taxed have given rise to treaties between countries to minimize the effect of double taxation on the taxpayer, protect each country's right to collect taxes, and provide ways to resolve jurisdictional issues. In the area of double taxation, treaties can specify that certain classes of income would not be subject to tax, can reduce the rate on income and/or withholding taxes, and can specifically deal with the issue of tax credits. Although the latter point could be considered a duplication of the Internal Revenue Code, its specification in a tax treaty would simply strengthen the tax credit concept. It could also deal with specific types of taxes that could be considered creditable, and so on. Among other things, tax treaties tend to reduce or eliminate the taxes on dividends, interest, and royalty payments.

A pattern of tax treaties was developed by the OECD in 1963 and subsequently amended and reissued. That pattern, initially resisted by the U.S. government, was accepted in principle in the model tax treaty approved by the United States in 1977. The treaty contains 29 articles dealing with such issues as the taxes covered, the persons and organizations covered, relief from double taxation, the exchange of information between competent authorities of contracting nations, and the conditions under which a treaty may be terminated. The model treaty also deals with issues such as who is allowed to tax income, how income is to be characterized, how expenses are to be allocated, what rights exist to certain types of deductions, and how rates of tax on foreign investors can be reduced.

Sometimes treaties are comprehensive; other times they amend existing treaties or deal with specific issues. In 1994, for example, the United States and Canada signed an agreement resulting in significant reductions in tax rates on cross-border payments of dividends, interest, and royalties (revised in 2002). The rate on direct investment dividends would be reduced from 10 percent to 5 percent; the rate on interest would fall from 15 percent to 10 percent; and the rate on most royalties would drop from 10 percent to zero.

U.S. TAXATION OF FOREIGN SOURCE INCOME

The Tax Haven Concept

A tax haven is a phenomenon that has emerged from the philosophy that foreign source income should not be taxed at all or should be taxed only when declared a dividend. A tax haven may be defined as a place where foreigners may receive income or own assets without paying high rates of tax upon them. Tax havens offer a variety of benefits, including low taxes or no taxes on certain classes of income. Because of these benefits, thousands of so-called mailbox companies have sprung up in such exotic places as Liechtenstein, Vanuatu (formerly New Hebrides), and the Netherlands Antilles.

Some examples of types of tax haven countries are as follows:

1. Countries with no income taxes, such as the Bahamas, Bermuda, and the Cayman Islands.

2. Countries with taxes at low rates, such as the British Virgin Islands.

3. Countries that tax income from domestic sources but exempt income from foreign sources, such as Hong Kong, Liberia, and Panama.

4. Countries that allow special privileges; generally their suitability as tax havens is limited.

To take advantage of a tax haven, a corporation would ordinarily set up a subsidiary in the tax haven country through which different forms of income would pass. The goal is to shift income from high tax to tax haven countries. This is normally accomplished by using the tax haven subsidiary as an intermediary. For example, a British manufacturer could sell goods directly to a dealer in Germany and concentrate the profits in Britain. It could equally well sell the goods to a tax haven subsidiary at cost and then sell the goods to the German dealer at a profit, thus concentrating the profits in the tax haven corporation. Income shifting is generally accomplished through transfer pricing, which will be discussed later in the chapter.

Many countries are naturally concerned about minimizing the opportunities for using tax havens where they are likely to be disadvantaged. The OECD, for example, plans to impose sanctions on countries offering "harmful" tax competition (see Exhibit 16.3).

The Controlled Foreign Corporation

As we noted earlier, a U.S. corporation may choose to produce and sell in the foreign country through a branch of the parent or through a foreign corporation in which the parent has an equity interest. The tax implications of these situations are interesting. The income or loss of a foreign branch must be combined with parent income for tax as well as book purposes in the period in which the income or loss occurs. In the case of a foreign corporation, however, a U.S. parent does not declare income from a foreign corporation for tax purposes until it actually receives a dividend. This is the principle of deferral—the income is deferred from U.S. taxation

Exhibit 16.3 Article from *The Economist*, January 29, 2000

As globalization ebbed and flowed, the taxman's share of economic output went relentlessly up, despite warnings from politicians that globalization would make it harder for government to collect taxes and thus to provide public services. But now a new factor has entered the equation: the Internet. It epitomizes borderlessness, and the irrelevance of being in a particular physical location. By being everywhere and nowhere at once, it seems certain to speed up globalization. And in doing so, according to the Organization for Economic Cooperation and Development, it might damage tax systems so badly that it could "lead to governments being unable to meet the legitimate demands of their citizens for public services."

Shopping Around

The Internet has dawned just as tax collectors are getting worried about another aspect of globalization: tax competition. Both the European Union and the OECD have declared war on "harmful" low-tax policies used by some countries to attract international businesses and capital. The OECD says that tax competition is often a "beggar-thy-neighbor policy" which is already reducing government tax revenues, and will start to be reflected in the data during the next couple of years. The Internet has the potential to increase tax competition, not least by making it much easier for multinationals to shift their activities to low-tax regimes, such as Caribbean tax havens, that are physically a long way from their customers, but virtually are only a mouse-click away. Many more companies may be able to emulate Rupert Murdoch's News Corporation, which has earned profits of £1.4 billion ($2.3 billion) in Britain since 1987 but paid no corporation tax there.

Source: The Economist, January 29, 2000.

until it is received as a dividend. As mentioned earlier, the deferral principle is a basic tenet of the taxation of foreign source income.

The deferral principle works most of the time, but an exception is made for a certain class of income (i.e., Subpart F income) of a certain type of corporation (i.e., a controlled foreign corporation). In general, Subpart F income is not deferred but must be declared by the U.S. parent corporation as soon as it is earned by the foreign corporation. However, we first must define a controlled foreign corporation (CFC). A CFC is a foreign corporation in which "U.S. shareholders" hold more than 50 percent of the voting stock. A U.S. shareholder, for tax purposes, is a person or enterprise that holds at least 10 percent of the voting stock of the foreign corporation.

Subpart F Income

Why does it make a difference for tax purposes whether a foreign corporation is a CFC? As Figure 16.2 shows, if the foreign corporation is not a CFC, its income is automatically deferred until remitted as a dividend to the shareholders. If the foreign corporation is a CFC, the deferral principle may not apply to certain kinds of income. To understand this, it is necessary to go back in history a few years. As mentioned earlier, sometimes U.S. corporations do business in tax haven countries and therefore benefit from low or nonexistent income taxes. If a tax haven corporation was actively involved in the production and sale of goods and services, there was no problem. However, the U.S. government noticed that many companies were setting

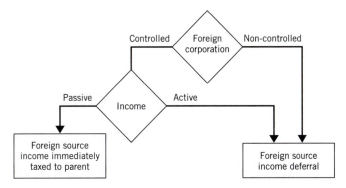

Figure 15.2   U.S. Taxation of Income from Foreign Branches and Corporations

up tax haven corporations just to avoid paying U.S. tax. Therefore, the Revenue Act of 1962 minimized the tax avoidance practices of multinationals. The Act allowed a U.S. corporation to apply the deferral principle to its portion of income derived from the active conduct of a trade or business of a CFC, but it could not defer its portion of passive income, referred to as Subpart F income in the Internal Revenue Code.

Subpart F income is divided into eight groups: (1) insurance of U.S. risks, (2) foreign-based company personal holding company income, (3) foreign-based company sales income, (4) foreign-based company services income, (5) foreign-based company shipping income, (6) foreign-based company oil-related income, (7) boycott-related income, and (8) foreign bribes.

Insurance of U.S. Risks   The first category of Subpart F income, insurance of U.S. risks, arose because many U.S. corporations were setting up a foreign insurance subsidiary in a tax haven country and paying insurance premiums to the subsidiary on U.S. and foreign risks. The parent could deduct the premiums as expenses, and the subsidiary was paying little or no tax on the premium income. After the Revenue Act of 1962, the income from the premiums is taxable to the parent when earned by the CFC.

Foreign-based Company Personal Holding Company Income   Foreign-based company personal holding company income includes dividends, interest, royalties, and similar income that arises from holding rights rather than from actually producing or selling goods and services. However, the income must be derived from sources outside the country where the CFC is organized. For example, if Multicorp established a holding company in Switzerland that owned Multicorp's subsidiaries in France and Spain, the dividends received by the holding company would be considered Subpart F income to Multicorp.

Foreign-based Company Sales Income   Foreign-based company sales income arises from the sale or purchase of goods produced and consumed outside the country where the CFC is incorporated. For example, a U.S. company could sell merchandise to an unaffiliated buyer in France but have the paperwork go through a tax haven CFC in Switzerland. On paper, the U.S. company would sell to the Swiss Company (probably a wholly owned subsidiary), which would sell to the French company. Prices would be set to concentrate profits in the Swiss company. However, that income would be considered Subpart F income under the 1962 law and would have to be declared by the U.S. company. It should also be noted that the income is considered Subpart F income as long as the CFC in Switzerland is not actively involved in selling and servicing the product with its own staff. If that were to happen, the income would be active rather than passive (see Figure 16.2).

Foreign-based Company Services Income   Foreign-based company services income arises from contracts utilizing technical, managerial, engineering, or other skills. For example, a U.S. hotel management firm could enter into a contract to manage a hotel for an investor in the Middle East and have the management fee billed to a tax haven subsidiary in Switzerland. That fee would be considered Subpart F income to the U.S. firm.

Foreign-based Company Shipping Income   Foreign-based company shipping income arises from using aircraft or ships for transportation outside the country where the CFC is incorporated.

Foreign-based Oil-Related Company Income   Foreign-based oil-related income arises from large oil or natural gas producers in a country outside the country where the CFC is incorporated.

Boycott-related Income and Foreign Bribes   The inclusion of bribes and boycotts as Subpart F income resulted from the TRA of 1976. To penalize companies that supported the Arab boycott of Israel, Congress decided to classify income from operations resulting from countries involved in certain international boycotts as Subpart F income. In addition, the income from those operations does not enjoy the full benefit of the tax credit.

Bribes paid to foreign government officials as explained in the Foreign Corrupt Practices Act (FCPA) of 1976 are considered a new class of Subpart F income, even though the bribes are not really a form of income to the parent and the bribes are not deductible expenses. These two twists of the law have nothing to do with tax avoidance like the other dimensions of Subpart F income; they were included simply to punish offenders of other laws.

In summary, Subpart F income has several implications. For foreign corporations that are not CFCs, income is not taxable to the U.S. shareholder (the parent corporation) until a dividend is declared. For CFCs active income is also deferred, but passive or Subpart F income must be recognized by the parent when earned, regardless of when a dividend is declared. The only major exception to the rule is that if the foreign-based company income of a CFC is less than 5 percent of gross income of $1 million, none of it is treated as Subpart F income. If the foreign-based company income exceeds 70 percent of gross income, all the company's income is treated as Subpart F income.

The United States, like most industrialized countries, uses the worldwide approach, which means that the IRS taxes U.S. residents on their worldwide income.

However, the situation just described, of CFCs and Subpart F income, is a uniquely American philosophy. The industrialized countries that tax worldwide income generally tax the income only if a dividend is declared to the parent company.

TAX EFFECTS OF FOREIGN EXCHANGE GAINS AND LOSSES

In Chapters 10 and 11, we discussed the accounting requirements in FASB Statement No. 52 for translating foreign currency transactions and foreign currency financial statements into the parent currency (hereafter referred to as dollars). We noted that FASB prefers to recognize the impact of an exchange rate change when the event takes place rather than defer that impact into the future. Therefore, transaction gains and losses are recognized in income when the rate changes, not when the transaction is finally settled. In the case of financial statements, gains and losses that arise under the current rate method are taken directly to a separate component of stockbrokers' equity, whereas gains and losses that arise under the temporal method are taken directly to income.

The treatment of these gains and losses for tax purposes is not consistent with the requirements of Statement No. 52. Generally, gains and losses from foreign currency transactions are treated as ordinary income on loss and are recognized only when realized; gains or losses cannot be recognized while foreign currency balances are being held.

Foreign Currency Transactions

The IRS treats foreign currency transactions from the two-transactions perspective just as Statement No. 52 does. However, it does not recognize gains and losses until the financial obligation has actually been settled. Assume that a U.S. importer purchases a piece of equipment on credit from a German supplier for 1 million Euro on December 1 when the rate is $0.64/€. On December 31, the rate moves to $0.65, and on January 31 when the supplier is paid by the importer, the rate is $0.67. For financial reporting and tax purposes, the original transaction would be recorded at $640,000. On December 31, the firm would recognize a loss of $10,000 (1,000,000 € [0.65–0.64]) for financial statement purposes to reflect the higher value of the liability, and on January 31 it would recognize a loss of $20,000 (1,000,000 € [0.67–0.65]) to reflect the increase in value of the liability.

For tax purposes, however, the firm would wait until January 31 when it settles the financial obligation to determine the gain or loss. In this case, it would recognize a loss of $30,000 (1,000,000 € [0.67–0.64]) to reflect the difference between the amount at which the liability is initially recorded and the amount at which it is settled.

Branch Earnings

U.S. tax law has introduced the concept of a qualified business unit (QBU), which is a trade or business for which separate books are kept. For tax purposes, the earn-

Exhibit 16.4   Determination of Taxable Income on a Foreign Branch

Branch profits before tax		FC 130,000
Tax[a]		<u>30,000</u>
Branch profits after tax		FC 100,000
12/31 distribution		FC 50,000
Average exchange rate		$0.55 per FC
12/31 exchange rate		$0.58 per FC
Branch profits included in U.S. taxable income:		
Branch profits after tax @ $0.55		$55,000
Branch tax @ $0.58		17,400
Distribution @ $0.58	$29,000	
Distribution @ $0.55	<u>27,500</u>	
Foreign exchange gain		<u>1,500</u>
		$73,900
Tax credit:		
FC 30,000 @ $0.58 = $17,400		

Note: FC = foreign currency.
[a] Assume taxes are paid at the end of the year.

ings of a QBU can be divided into two parts: earnings that have been distributed back to the home office and earnings that are retained in the foreign location. In the case of a branch, both types are taxable to the home office. The amount of earnings distributed to the home office is translated at the exchange rate in effect on the date of the transfer, and branch profits are translated at the average exchange rate.

This translation approach is called the profit-and-loss approach by the IRS, which requires that the profit-and-loss statement of the branch be translated into dollars at the average exchange rate for the year. A difference between the average exchange rate and the exchange rate when the distribution is made can give rise to a gain or loss, as illustrated in Exhibit 16.4. Because branch tax was paid at the end of the year instead of evenly throughout the year, it must be translated at the year-end rate instead of at the average rate. The foreign exchange gain is the amount of the distribution times the difference between the average rate (at which branch profits are already translated) and the exchange rate when the distribution is made. Thus, the total amount of branch profits included in parent income includes the foreign exchange gain. The tax credit is computed by translating the actual branch profits tax at the exchange rate in effect when the taxes were paid.

Taxable Earnings from Foreign Corporations

Earlier in this chapter when we discussed the recognition of earnings from a foreign corporation and the related tax credits, we assumed that the amounts were translated into dollars. Now we need to show how dividends and tax credits are

Exhibit 16.5   Determination of Taxable Income on the Tax Credit on Earnings from a Foreign Subsidiary

Earnings before foreign tax	£500,000
Foreign income tax paid	165,000
Earnings after foreign tax	£335,000

Dividends paid: £100,000 @ $1.55 = $155,000
£100,000 @ $1.50 = $150,000

Tax credit:

£200,000/335,000 × £165,000 = £98,507

£98,507 × $1.54 = $151,701

Grossed-up dividend: $155,000 + $150,000 + $151,701 = $456,701

Dividends/Profits × Foreign taxes paid = Tax credit

translated into dollars for tax purposes. The recognition of earnings of a foreign corporation depends on whether the corporation is a CFC. When the foreign corporation is not a CFC, income is not recognized by the U.S. parent until a dividend is distributed. In such a case, the tax credit formula, as we discussed earlier, is as shown in Exhibit 16.5.

Assume that a British corporation earns £500,000, pays corporate income tax of £165,000 evenly throughout the year, and declares two dividends to the U.S. investor of £100,000 each (on June 30 when the exchange rate was $1.55 and on December 31 when it was $1.50). The average rate for the year was $1.54. In this case, the taxable income and tax credit would be computed as shown in Exhibit 16.5. The dividends are translated at the rate in effect when they are paid, and income taxes, for purposes of computing the deemed direct tax, are translated at the rate when they were paid. Because the foreign subsidiary is not taxed until a dividend is declared, the parent company does not have to translate the financial statements into dollars for tax purposes.

Controlled Foreign Corporation

As we discussed earlier, a CFC has two types of income: non-Subpart F income and Subpart F income. The non-Subpart F income is not taxed to the parent company until a dividend has been distributed, so the same rules as described earlier apply for the non-CFC situation. In the case of Subpart F income, the IRS assumes that a constructive dividend has been declared at the end of the year, so it is necessary to translate the financial statements of the firm into dollars. The profit-and-loss statement is translated into dollars at the average exchange rate for the year, as for branch earnings.

TAX INCENTIVES

For the purposes of this chapter, tax incentives are of two major types: incentives by countries to attract foreign investors and incentives by countries to encourage exports of goods and services.

Tax incentives to invest usually involve tax holidays of one form or another. The Brazilian government provides a 10-year tax holiday for companies that invest in the impoverished Northeast and Amazon regions of the country. Mexico does not offer a tax holiday for foreign investors, but it does provide tax credits for companies that invest in counties located outside the metropolitan areas, such as in Baja and along the border with the United States.

Another popular form of incentive involves exports. In the EU, many export products are zero-rated, which means that exports are not assessed the VAT. This allows firms to offer their products at a lower price than they otherwise could. Both Japan and Mexico also have an internal VAT but do not apply the VAT against exports.

Within the United States and United Kingdom, many local authorities can and do offer reductions in or the elimination of local property taxes. U.S. cities and states can often be persuaded to waive state and city income taxes for a major investment.

Foreign Sales Corporation

The Foreign Sales Corporation Act of 1984 was signed into law on July 18, 1984, as a part of the TRA of 1984, and the new law was designed to replace the Domestic International Sales Corporation (DISC) legislation that had been in existence in the United States since 1972.

The DISC was established in the 1970s to encourage exports by U.S. firms. Although it was not a taxable entity, its income was taxed to its shareholders (generally the MNE that established the DISC) at a reduced tax rate. However, the DISC was just a paper shell rather than an operating company, so it violated subsidy rules established by the General Agreement on Tariffs and Trade (GATT), now known as the World Trade Organization (WTO). The Foreign Sales Corporation (FSC) was established in response to the criticism from GATT members.

In 1999, the European Union (EU) challenged the FSC at the World Trade Organization (WTO) as a violation of the Subsidies and Countervailing Measures (SCM) portion of the Uruguay Round Code. The WTO did not rule on the EU claim that FSC violates the SCM because exports are taxed more favorably than production for the home U.S. market. However, the WTO did rule that the FSC is not a permissible application of the territorial approach—that is, the exemption approach—to avoiding taxation of foreign source income because the FSC invokes the territorial principle for only the export segment of foreign source income. As a result of this violation and other questions raised, FSCs were phased out by 2001.

TAX DIMENSIONS OF EXPATRIATES

Most countries tax the earnings of their residents. However, the United States goes further than many industrialized countries by taxing the worldwide income of its citizens. A survey by Business International revealed that of eight major Western countries, the United States is the only one that taxes its expatriates on worldwide income. The United States does, however, provide some relief for citizens who have been residents outside the United States for an uninterrupted period that includes an entire taxable year. Specifically, U.S. citizens can take the Foreign Earned Income Exclusion if their tax home is in a foreign country, they have foreign income, and they are bonafide citizens of another country for an uninterrupted period that includes an entire tax year or are present in another country for at least 330 days during any 12 consecutive months.

INTRACORPORATE TRANSFER PRICING

Internal pricing, also known as intracorporate transfer pricing or just transfer pricing, refers to the pricing of goods and services that are transferred (bought and sold) between members of a corporate family—for example, parent to subsidiaries, between subsidiaries, from subsidiaries to parent, and so on. As such, internal transfers include raw materials, semifinished and finished goods, allocation of fixed costs, loans, fees, royalties for use of trademarks, copyrights, and other factors. In theory, such prices should be based on production costs, but in reality they often are not. As discussed in Chapter 15, transfer pricing is also a management control tool, and tax minimization may clash with the objective of motivating management to enhance profitability.

Transfer Pricing and Tax Havens

Companies can use transfer pricing to shift their profits to tax havens to lessen their tax burden. For example, a company may set its transfer price lower than normal to a tax haven subsidiary. When that subsidiary subsequently sells the product, the profits remain mostly with them and are thus taxed at a lower rate. Creative transfer pricing can also be used in acquisitions, research and development activities, and restructuring to minimize taxes.

Although industrial countries such as the United States have been concerned about the transfer pricing policies of their own domestic firms, they are now becoming concerned about the transfer pricing policies of foreign investors. In 1992, there was significant discussion in the United States over possible transfer pricing violations by Japanese auto firms. The concern was that the Japanese were under-invoicing the import of parts and components used in U.S. assembly operations, thus minimizing customs duties and giving the firms a competitive advantage over U.S. manufacturers. Exhibit 16.6 shows the results of a survey by Tang (1992) of factors influencing the transfer pricing decisions of Fortune 500 companies in 1977 and 1990. The consistently most important factors besides corporate profitability were differential tax rates, restrictions on repatriation of profits or dividends, and the competitive position of foreign subsidiaries.

Tax Considerations in Transfer Pricing Decisions

In an article entitled "The Corporate Shell Game," *Newsweek* magazine gave an overly simplistic, hypothetical example of a U.S. company that manufactured goods

Exhibit 16.6 Importance of Environmental Variable Influencing International Transfer Pricing Behavior

Ranking of Average Importance Score		Variables	Average Importance Score	
1990	1977		1990	1977
1	1	Overall profit to the company	4.04	3.94
2	4	Differentials in income tax rates and income tax legislation among countries	3.45	3.06
3	2	Restrictions imposed by foreign countries on repatriation of profits or dividends	3.32	3.24
4	3	The competitive position of subsidiaries in foreign countries	3.31	3.16
5	6	Rate of customs duties and customs legislation where the company has operations	3.04	2.99
6,7,8	8	Restrictions imposed by foreign countries on the amount of royalty or management fees that can be charged against foreign subsidiaries	2.90	2.85
6,7,8	11	Maintaining good relationships with host governments	2.90	2.75
6,7,8	9	The need to maintain adequate cash flows in foreign subsidiaries	2.90	2.83
9	7	Import restrictions imposed by foreign countries	2.71	2.89
10	5	Performance evaluation of foreign subsidiaries	2.69	3.01
11	16	The need of subsidiaries in foreign countries to seek local funds	2.61	2.40
12	12	Devaluation and revaluation in countries where the company has operations	2.44	2.71
13,14	15	Antidumping legislation of foreign countries	2.38	2.45
13,14	20	Antitrust legislation of foreign countries	2.38	2.14
15	17	The interests of local partners in foreign subsidiaries	2.36	2.30
16	10	Rules and requirements of financial reporting for subsidiaries in foreign countries	2.34	2.78
17	14	Volume of interdivisional transfers	2.31	2.53
18	13	Rates of inflation in foreign countries	2.24	2.57
19	19	Risk of expropriation in foreign countries where the company has operations	2.01	2.23
20	18	U.S. government requirements on direct foreign investments	1.94	2.27

Source: R. Y. W. Tang, "Transfer Pricing in the 1990s," *Management Accounting* (February 1992).

through its German subsidiary and sold them to its Irish subsidiary, which in turn sold the goods back to the U.S. parent company. The goods were manufactured at a cost of $80 by the German subsidiary and sold for the same amount to the Irish subsidiary. Even though the tax rate in Germany is 45 percent, there is no tax on the transaction. The Irish subsidiary then sells the goods to the U.S. parent for $150, earning a profit of $70. Because the tax rate in Ireland is only 4 percent for that transaction, the Irish subsidiary pays only $2.80 in tax. The U.S. parent then sells the goods for $150, earning no profit and paying no tax, even though the U.S. tax rate is 35 percent. Thus, the U.S. company ends up paying only $2.80 in income taxes, and this amount is paid in Ireland.

Naturally, transfer pricing has caught the attention of tax authorities world-wide, especially with the increase in MNEs. This attention has triggered a variety of new laws and penalties of which MNEs need to be aware. According to Ernst & Young's Transfer Pricing 2003 Global Survey, 86 percent of MNE parent company respondents and 93 percent of subsidiary respondents identified transfer pricing as their most important international tax matter. Audits by tax authorities are becoming more of a rule rather than an exception. The survey also indicated that if a company is subject to an adjustment as a result of an examination, their chances of being threatened with a penalty are 1 in 3 and the chances of paying one are 1 in 7. These rates are also expected to increase. In addition, the survey revealed that 40 percent of reported adjustments resulted in double taxation. It is essential that MNEs reevaluate their transfer pricing policies upon a merger or acquisition. The sale of tangible goods remains the most audited transaction among MNEs, although the percentage is decreasing while the percentage of audits relating to services and intangibles is increasing.

U.S. Rules   In the United States, Section 482 of the Internal Revenue Code governs transfer pricing rules. The Code section permits the IRS to distribute, apportion, or allocate gross income, deductions, credits, or allowances between related enterprises if it feels that tax evasion is taking place. The IRS requires that all transfers among related enterprises take place at "arm's length" prices, which are defined as the prices that would be obtained between unrelated entities. A controlled transaction meets the arm's length standard if the results of the transaction are consistent with the results that would have been realized if uncontrolled taxpayers had engaged in the same transaction under the same circumstances (arm's length result). As a result, the IRS is concerned about monitoring transfers in the following five areas: loans and advances, performance of services, use of tangible property, use of intangible property, and sale of tangible property.

Methods for Determining Arm's Length Prices   In making the allocations, the key for the IRS is to try to establish what an arm's length price should be. For the sale of tangible property, that price can be determined in one of six ways as the comparable uncontrollable price method, the resale price method, the comparable profits method, the cost-plus method, the profits split method, and other methods. The first method uses the concept of a market price to determine the transfer price. Of course, an external market for the same or very similar product must exist for this method to be used. The IRS also allows for differences resulting from reductions in variable expenses (such as selling expenses).

If it is impossible to use the comparable uncontrollable price method, the firm must then use the resale price method. Assume that the manufacturer in the United States sells a product to an independent distributor in Hong Kong, which sells the product directly to any other firm. The IRS would then take the price established by the distributor to outside customers and back out any costs to completion plus a normal profit margin to determine the transfer price from the manufacturer to the distributor.

The cost-plus method involves the costs of manufacturing the product plus a normal profit margin from the sales of similar products. Obviously, it is difficult to justify costs and normal profit margins. The other three methods are less common and are used as a last resort.

TAX PLANNING IN THE INTERNATIONAL ENVIRONMENT

As we have seen, the tax dimensions of international operations are very complex. The tax environment is unique in each national setting, and the advice of competent local staff who understand the tax situation is essential. In spite of the individual nature of each country, we can nevertheless use some general concepts as tax planning guides.

Choice of Methods of Servicing Foreign Markets

There are a variety of ways in which a firm can choose to service its foreign markets: exports of goods and services and technology, branch operations, and foreign subsidiaries.

Exports When exporting goods and services, a firm must decide whether to service the products from the parent country or from a foreign location. A U.S. firm needs to consider the benefits of operating through a sales office abroad. When the firm decides to license technology abroad, it must be aware of the withholding taxes and relevant tax treaties.

Foreign Branches Operating abroad through a branch has several distinct benefits. Because branch profits and losses are not subject to deferral, it is often beneficial to open a branch when first operating abroad since the initial years are normally loss years. The home office could use branch losses to offset home office income for tax purposes. Branch remittances are usually not subject to withholding taxes as are dividends from subsidiaries. For example, in Belgium there is a withholding tax on branch remittances, but a tax treaty with the United States eliminates that tax. Natural resource companies like to operate through branches abroad because the IRS allows branches to use the depletion allowance and other tax benefits relating to natural resources. These benefits come back directly to the parent company.

Foreign Subsidiaries A major tax benefit of operating abroad through a subsidiary is that its income is usually sheltered from taxation in the home country until a dividend is remitted. In the United States, that is true for all subsidiary income except the passive income of a CFC. This underscores the importance of making sure the operations of a CFC in a tax haven country are legitimate so the firm does not have to worry about the Subpart F provisions. The major problem with operating through a subsidiary is that any losses sustained cannot be recognized by the parent company. Thus, the subsidiary form of organization is much more valuable after the start-up years, when the operations become profitable.

Location of Foreign Operations   The location of foreign operations is influenced by three major tax factors: tax incentives, tax rates, and tax treaties. The importance of tax incentives was emphasized in the Brazilian and Mexican examples in the tax incentives section of this chapter. The existence of tax incentives can materially reduce the cash outflow required for an investment project, which will increase the net present value of the project. That tax effect could change the timing of an investment decision.

Because the determination of revenues and expenses for tax purposes is a function of tax law in most countries, it is important to be intimately familiar with local tax laws. Because this is almost impossible for someone in corporate headquarters, it is necessary to have competent tax and legal help in each local country.

Tax treaties have a critical impact on the cash flows related to withholding taxes on dividends, interest, and royalties. Strict attention to tax treaties can help investors choose the location of their legal operations wisely (which may or may not be the same as the location of their managerial operations). For example, the withholding tax between the United States and the United Kingdom is 15 percent according to a bilateral treaty, whereas both countries have a 5 percent withholding agreement with the Netherlands. A U.S. company would be better off establishing a holding company in the Netherlands to receive dividends from its British operations, subject to a 5 percent withholding tax. The Dutch holding company could then remit a dividend to the U.S. parent subject to a 5 percent withholding tax, which would be better than the 15 percent withholding tax between the United States and the United Kingdom. This is just one example of the ways tax treaties can be used to improve the cash flows of foreign investors.

Transfer Pricing

As we discussed earlier, transfer pricing is a method of equalizing taxes globally. This ability is limited by the increasing vigilance of tax authorities, particularly those of the United States, but possibilities exist. Care needs to be taken (as with other strategic issues) that in the final decision tax considerations do not crowd out important management control and other essential issues.

SUMMARY

1.   The territorial approach to taxing income asserts that foreign source income should be taxed where earned and not mixed with domestic source income. The worldwide philosophy treats all income as taxable to the parent. This leads to double taxation, which can be minimized by the tax credit and tax treaties.

2.   Under the deferral concept, earnings of foreign subsidiaries are not taxed until remitted as a dividend. Tax laws in different countries often allow an accelerated recovery of the cost of assets in order to encourage economic growth.

3. The classic system of corporate income taxation taxes income when it is received by each taxable entity, which leads to double taxation. The integrated system of taxation tries to eliminate double taxation through a combination of a split-rate system and tax credits.

4. Countries often collect a withholding tax on dividends, interest, and royalties paid to foreign investors. These levies can be reduced through tax treaties. The value-added tax (VAT) is an indirect tax that is an important source of revenue in many countries, especially in Europe. It is applied at each stage of the production process for the value added by the firm to goods purchased from the outside.

5. The IRS allows U.S. companies a credit against their U.S. tax liability for income taxes paid to a foreign government. A company can choose to treat those taxes, along with all other direct and indirect taxes that they might incur, as a deduction to arrive at taxable income.

6. Tax treaties can specify that certain classes of income would not be subject to tax, reduce the rate on income and/or withholding taxes, and specifically deal with the issue of tax credits. A tax haven is a country that has no income tax, taxes income at low rates, or exempts from taxation income from foreign sources. For tax purposes, foreign exchange gains and losses on foreign currency transactions are not recognized until the financial obligation has been settled.

7. In the United States, a controlled foreign corporation (CFC) is any foreign corporation that is majority-owned by U.S. shareholders. Income from a non-CFC is not taxed until a dividend is sent to the U.S. investor. Active income from a CFC also qualifies for the deferral privilege and is not taxed until remitted as a dividend. Passive income (Subpart F income) is income not derived from the active conduct of a trade or business. It is taxable to the parent when earned and the deferral principle does not apply.

8. Branch remittances are translated at the exchange rate in effect when the remittance is sent to the home office. Remaining branch earnings are translated using the profit-and-loss method, where they are translated at the average exchange rate for the year. Dividends from subsidiaries are translated into dollars at the exchange rate in effect on the date that the dividend is paid. The different elements in the tax credit are also translated at that same exchange rate.

9. The Foreign Sales Corporation (FSC) provides tax advantages to exporters, but it requires exporters to set up a sales office abroad. Some countries provide tax holidays, such as the forgiveness of income taxes for a period, to attract foreign investors.

10. International tax planning requires that a firm take taxes into consideration when determining the type of operation to be followed in servicing international markets (exporting, licensing, branches, or subsidiaries) and the location of the operation (by considering tax incentives, tax rates, and tax treaties).

Discussion Questions

1. A company has subsidiaries in host countries A and B. Country A has a statutory corporate tax rate of 30 percent, whereas Country B's is 40 percent. What are some specific reasons that Country B's effective tax rate might actually be more favorable to the firm?

2. Assume that a U.S. company wishing to shelter its foreign source income from U.S. taxes uses the Netherlands Antilles. Using a review of the literature outside the text, answer the following questions:

   a. Why is the Netherlands Antilles such a good tax haven country?

   b. What problems does the Netherlands Antilles face as a tax haven country?

   c. What impact could the United States' repeal of the 30 percent withholding tax on interest from securities have on use of the Netherlands Antilles as a tax haven country?

3. How does the existence of classic and integrated corporate tax systems affect the financing decisions of multinational corporations?

4. Discuss the differences between a sales tax and a VAT tax. Why might some countries use the VAT tax as their major source of income over the income tax?

5. How are tax treaties used to help mitigate the issues of international taxation?

6. What is Subpart F income, and how is it accounted for? What are the reasons behind this treatment?

7. Discuss the differences between FASB Statement No. 52's treatment of foreign currency transactions and the tax treatment of foreign currency transactions. What is the reasoning behind the different treatment?

8. What is the role of the Foreign Sales Corporation (FSC)? Why did the European Union challenge the FSC with the World Trade Organization?

9. Discuss the U.S. regulation to tax its citizens on worldwide income. Is this policy justified or is it overboard?

10. How do companies use transfer pricing to minimize their tax burden?

11. Why and how do tax authorities get involved in the transfer pricing situation?

12. According to the survey by Tang mentioned in this chapter, what are the most important factors companies consider in establishing transfer prices? What might cause this survey to provide less than accurate reasons for actual practices?

13. The North American Free Trade Agreement (NAFTA) includes the United States, Canada, and Mexico, with the possibility that other Latin American countries might be added as new members. What are some of the questions that must be addressed if their tax systems are to be harmonized? What stands in the way of harmonization?

14. Discuss the pros and cons of the different ways to service foreign markets: exports, branch operations, and foreign subsidiaries.

15. You have just been hired by a small start-up company that is expanding quickly overseas. What tax advice would you give it as it explores different ways to penetrate foreign markets?

Exercises

Exercises 1–4 refer to the following information. Assume a VAT situation where the tax rate is 15 percent, with export sales exempt. The manufacturer does not purchase inputs on which VAT has been paid, and its net selling price to the wholesaler before VAT is £250. The wholesaler adds value of £300, and the retailer adds value of £500 to the consumer.

1. What are the gross and net selling prices at the manufacturer, wholesaler, and retailer levels?

2. How much in VAT is paid to the tax authorities at each level?

3. What is the final amount that the domestic consumer pays, and how much of that is VAT?

4. Would your answer to 3 be the same if the retailer were to export the goods instead of selling them to a domestic consumer?

5. ABC Company has income from the following countries:

Country	Type of Operation	Gross Earnings	Income Tax Rate
United States	Parent	500,000	40%
X	Branch	(10,000)	25%
Y	Distribution	120,000	5%
Z	100%-owned	400,000	45%

ABC's subsidiary in Z declares a 40 percent dividend; Z's withholding tax on dividends is 5 percent. Both the branch and the distribution facility, which is wholly owned, retain all earnings. The distribution earnings are considered to be foreign-based company sales income. What is ABC's final U.S. tax liability?

6. Puerto International has a branch in Mexico that manufactures a garage door alarm for people with mountain bike racks that fit on the top of their cars. The subsidiary earned $800,000 in 2000 before tax, with Mexican corporate tax rates at 40 percent. Taxes were paid evenly throughout the year. How much income did Puerto have to include in its U.S. taxable income in 2000, and what was the tax credit?

Exercises 7 and 8 refer to the following: In 2000 San Fernando Drilling shipped 300 diamond drill bits to its subsidiary in Ecuador. The drill bits were shipped at San Fernando's cost of $1 million each to avoid Ecuador's duty of 20 percent. In 2000 Ecuador's income tax on foreign subsidiaries was 35 percent, and the U.S. corporate tax rate was 35 percent. In 2001, Ecuador proposed to raise the corporate tax rate to 45 percent, eliminate duties, and impose a 10 percent VAT. The U.S. rate would remain the same.

7. What action (if any) should San Fernando take on its export pricing?

8. What possible U.S. government action may result from your decision in 7?

9. As a U.S. congressman from South Carolina, you are considering proposing a bill to eliminate a state income tax of 7 percent and a sales tax of 5 percent and replace it with a value-added tax of 10 percent. Discuss the pros and cons of such an action. You should note that a typical South Carolina family spends about 80 percent of its taxable income on goods and services that would be covered by this tax.

Exercises 10–12 refer to the following Belgian Coordination Center.

When the United States Tax Reform Act (TRA) of 1986 was enacted, the basic corporate tax rate in the United States dropped from 46 to 34 percent. At that time, corporate tax rates in Europe ranged from 35 to 56 percent. Since then, corporate tax rates in some European countries have fallen, but they are generally higher than in the United States.

To attract significant high-level foreign investment, Belgium enacted several favorable tax provisions in the late 1980s. Belgium is an interesting country. With 10 million people, it is only the eighth largest country in the European Union. However, it is the sixth largest in per capita GNP, second in population density (and eleventh in the world), and first in the European Union in urbanization. In 1988, 66 percent of Belgium's GNP was in services, 32 percent in manufacturing, and only 2 percent in agriculture.

One important tax attraction is the possibility of establishing a coordination center. A coordination center can be established for one or more of the following activities: development and centralization of advertising; supply and gathering of information; insurance and reinsurance; R&D; relations with national and international authorities; financial; accounting and administrative services; currency hedging; and other related activities. Most coordination centers are financial and accounting in nature.

The activities of the center are free from Belgian exchange controls and are virtually tax free. Taxes are based on a small percentage (usually 8 percent) of expenses, except for salary costs and finance charges. Any dividends paid by the center to its parent company are exempt from paying withholding tax. A coordination center can hold title to assets that it can lease to other members of the corporate group both inside and outside Belgium. The center can also be used to finance operations in other countries. For example, a member of the corporate group in Germany could borrow money from the coordination center and pay all interest to the center.

10. How does the establishment of the coordination center impact the tax liability of companies that lease assets from the center and companies that finance asset acquisitions through the center?

11. What would be the impact on the tax liability of the parent company of the activities listed in question 10?

12. Other than the issues identified in question 11, what are some other reasons why a U.S. company might want to establish a coordination center in Belgium? What must it do to gain the maximum tax benefits from operating in Belgium?

13. What tax issues might an U.S. expatriate have when working in Belgium?

Exercises 14 and 15 refer to the following information. Multinatl Inc. has a manufacturing facility in Zolondia which incurs costs of $1,000,000 for goods it sells to its retail outlet in Aborla. The retailer resells these goods to consumers for $2,000,000. Operating expenses in Zolondia and Aborla are $100,000 and $150,000, respectively. Zolondia and Aborla levy a corporate income tax of 30 percent on taxable income in their jurisdictions.

14. If Multinatl Inc. raises its transfer price from $1,300,000 to $1,600,000 for these goods going from Zolondia to Aborla, what effect would this have on total consolidated taxes?

15. If the tax rate were different in each country: Zolondia tax rate = 20 percent and Aborla tax rate = 40 percent, what would be the tax effects of the transfer pricing action?

Case: Transfer Pricing
Case: Midwest Uniforms

These cases can be found on the following website: www.wiley.com/college/radebaugh

Selected References

Arpan, J. 1972. *Intracorporate Pricing: Non-American Systems and Views*. New York: Praeger.
Avi-Yonah, R. 1995. "The Rise and Fall of Arm's Length: A Study in the Evolution of U.S. International Taxation." *Virginia Tax Review* 15(1): 89–159.

Baker, A., M. Carsley, and R. O'Connor. 1997. "Two Approaches—One Result," *International Tax Review.* Transfer Pricing Issue. p. 107–113.

Bodner, P. 1997. "International Taxation." In *International Accounting and Finance Handbook,* 2nd ed., edited by F. D. S. Choi. New York: John Wiley, pp. 39:1–21.

Borkowski, S. C. 1997. "Factors Affecting Transfer Pricing and Income Shifting: Between Canadian and U.S. Transnational Corporations." *International Journal of Accounting* 32(4): 391–415.

Borstell, T. 1997. "Introduction to Transfer Pricing." *International Tax Review* (April).

Bovenberg, A. L., S. Crossen, F. Vanistendael, and J. Westerburgen. 1992. *Harmonization of Company Taxation in the European Community: Some Comments on the Ruding Committee Report.* The Netherlands: Kluwer.

Burns, J. 1980. "Transfer Pricing Decisions in U.S. Multinational Corporations." *Journal of International Business Studies* (Fall): 23–39.

Cavusgil, S. 1996. "Transfer Pricing for Global Markets." *Journal of World Business* 31(4): 66–78.

Commerce Clearing House. 1999. *Standard Federal Tax Reports.* Chicago: CCH.

Eberhartinger, E. L. E. 1999. "The Impact of Tax Rules on Financial Reporting in Germany, France, and the U.K." *International Journal of Accounting* 34(1): 93–119.

Ernst & Young. 2003. *Transfer Pricing 2003 Survey.* New York.

Hufbauer, G. C. 2002. The FSC Case: Background and Implications. Institute for International Economics. http://www.iie.com/publications/papers/hufbauer0102.htm.

James, S. R., and C. W. Nobes. 1999. *The Economics of Taxation.* Englewood Cliffs, NJ: Prentice-Hall. http://www.irs.gov.

Klassen, K., M. Lang, and M. Wolfson. 1993. "Geographic Income Shifting by Multinational Corporations in Response to Tax Rate Changes." *Journal of Accounting Research* 31 (Supplement): 141–173.

KPMG Global Tax Services. www.tax.kpmg.net.

Lamb, M. 1995. "When Is a Group a Group? Convergence of Concepts of 'Group' in European Union Corporation Tax." *European Accounting Review* 4(1): 33–78.

Lamb, M., C. W. Nobes, and A. D. Roberts. 1998. "International Variations in the Connections Between Tax and Financial Reporting." *Accounting and Business Research* 28(3): 173–188.

Marty, L. "The Corporate Shell Game," *Newsweek* Vol. 117, Issue 15, (April 15, 1991), p. 48.

Nobes, C. W. 1980. "Imputation Systems of Corporation Tax in the EEC." *Accounting and Business Research* 10(38): 221–231.

O'Connor, W. 1997. "International Transfer Pricing." In *International Accounting and Finance Handbook,* 2nd ed., edited by F. D. S. Choi. New York: John Wiley, pp. 1–38.

Picciotto, S. 1992. *International Business Taxation.* London: Weidenfeld and Nicolson.

Plasschaert, S. 1994. "The Multiple Motivations for Transfer Pricing Modulations in Multinational Enterprises and Governmental Counter-Measures: An Attempt at Clarification." *Management International Review* 34: 36–50.

Ruchelman, S. C., L. Schneidman, and F. B. Voght. 1998. "The Good, The Bad, and The Ugly: Recent Cases Addressing International Tax Transactions." *International Tax Journal* 24(2): 1–35.

Tang, R. Y. W. 1992. "Transfer Pricing in the 1990s." *Management Accounting* 73(8): 22–26.

Tate, C. 1998. "Transfer Pricing: The New Tax Minefield." *Australian CPA* 68 (6): 46–47.

Turner, R. 1998. "Proceed with Caution." *CA Magazine* 131(6): 33–34.

Yancey, W. F., and K. S. Cravens. 1998. "A Framework for International Tax Planning for Managers." *Journal of International Accounting Auditing and Taxation* 7(2): 251–272.

Name and Company Index

SUBJECT INDEX